UNDER THE GENERAL EDITORSHIP OF
MARSHALL D. KETCHUM
UNIVERSITY OF CHICAGO
HOUGHTON MIFFLIN ADVISER IN FINANCE

MONEY AND

ECONOMIC ACTIVITY

READINGS IN MONEY AND BANKING

THIRD EDITION

Edited **by LAWRENCE S. RITTER**

Chairman, Department of Finance

Graduate School of Business Administration

New York University

HOUGHTON MIFFLIN COMPANY • BOSTON

New York · Atlanta · Geneva, ILL. · Dallas · Palo Alto

GENERAL EDITOR'S INTRODUCTION

Professor Ritter, in the first paragraph of his Preface, refers to the difficulty that instructors in money and banking courses may have in keeping interest in the subject at a high level and thus successfully "competing for student interest with the always beckoning nonacademic lures of campus life." These "non-academic lures" do indeed exist and they represent formidable competition. But, since the instructor in money and banking also competes with other instructors for the student's time, he must be concerned with whether the student is allocating a "fair" portion of his time to money and banking. The student may divide his time between curricular and "other" activities on bases other than his enchantment with his academic program. But his allocation of curricular time is at least partly a function of his "interest" in the course, and this in turn results from how meaningful and relevant the course content is made to appear.

Thus the instructor in money and banking, in competing with his colleagues for the student's time, faces the problem of how he may best motivate the students before him. For many courses, including money and banking, the use of books of readings is an admirable method for motivation, and banking is one of this group of courses. A book of readings is designed to supplement the basic textbook in the course. In what sense does it supplement? Textbooks in money and banking are dissimilar in many respects, but they all discuss the controversial issues (and few subjects have more such issues than money and banking). They cite, and perhaps quote briefly, what others have said, pro or con of the issues, and they present the author's tentative conclusions. This textbook format in the presentation of matters of controversy provides the link between the text and a book of readings. When the textbook author considers the guidelines of monetary policy, he may refer to Henry Simons and his "Rules versus Authorities in Monetary Policy," but in the textbook there is space for no more than the bare outline of Simons' program. If the textbook author has done his job well, he has referred to Simons in such a manner as to arouse the student's interest in learning more about him. This interest will be fleeting if the student finds that he must go to the library and find the February, 1936, issue of the *Journal of Political Economy*. But interest in what Simons has to say will lead to knowledge of what he has to say if the student can reach to the back of his desk and have immediately available a book containing Simons' article.

The first two editions of this book, published in 1952 and 1961, have enabled tens of thousands of students to read many of the most stimulating documents and articles in professional journals, and these editions have saved these students thousands of man-hours they would otherwise have spent in searching for these materials in libraries. The availability of this rich periodical literature in money and banking in a book of readings has certainly assisted students to achieve an optimal mix of time allocation.

A book of readings can be successful only if it contains at least some articles that most teachers of the subject consider important and provocative. Professor Ritter made a wise choice of materials in the first two editions of his book. The principal evidence of this is the extraordinarily wide use that has been made of these editions since 1952. I am confident that this book, the third edition, will be as enthusiastically received as the first two.

A brief statement of Professor Ritter's academic attainments will be sufficient to indicate his scholarship, his acquaintance with the literature of money and banking, and his competence to select articles which, singly and as an organized group, will enhance students' knowledge and understanding. He received his formal education at Indiana University and the University of Wisconsin. He has served on the faculties of Michigan State University and Yale University, and has also filled a number of non-academic posts, among them chief of the Domestic Research Division of the Federal Reserve Bank of New York and economist for the Commission on Money and Credit. He has written widely in the professional journals, and in addition has been editor of the *Journal of Finance* since 1964. He is currently professor of finance and chairman of the Department of Finance at the Graduate School of Business Administration of New York University.

The basic organization of the second edition is retained in this third edition. Ritter has followed closely the organization of the leading textbooks in arranging the parts of his book. Instructors will note the similarities: introduction, the structure of commercial banking; central banking; monetary policy; fiscal policy and debt management; and, finally, the world economy. The principal changes are in the contents of the separate parts. In Part 1, Introduction to a Monetary Economy, a new chapter has been added, Money, Debt, and Financial Markets, with articles dealing with the saving-investment process and the market for loanable funds, and with the structure of the flow-of-funds accounts. Part 2 has three chapters as formerly, but the contents are focused more sharply on the sources of bank funds, the uses of bank funds, and competition in the financial markets. In Part 3, The Instruments of Central Banking, there are, first, a chapter dealing with the monetary and fiscal problems growing out of World War II, and then three chapters organized around the principal "instruments," open market operations, the discount rate, and reserve requirements. In line with recent emphasis upon matters of policy, the number of articles in Part 4, The Theory and Practice of Monetary Policy, has been extended from 13 to 15, and Part 5, Fiscal Policy and Debt Management, now contains 10 articles as compared with four in the second edition. And finally, increased recognition of the significance of the interrelations of national economies has led to the inclusion of six articles in Part 6, The World Economy, as against two in the previous edition.

This third edition, then, will serve thousands more of instructors and students in their task of learning how our financial system operates, and will, further, attract the attention of many of the thousands of former students who learned from previous editions of this book and who have now moved on into occupations where knowledge of this subject is so necessary to their effective functioning within our economy and our society.

University of Chicago   Marshall Ketchum

PREFACE

Money and banking, by almost any criterion, should be an exciting subject. Students enrolling in it usually do so with an air of anticipation. Not only does it appear to be important, but even intriguing. It might seem, therefore, that instructors of undergraduate money and banking courses would have little difficulty in competing for student interest with the always beckoning non-academic lures of campus life.

Unfortunately, initial student interest all too often seems to vanish by the end of the first month of classes. Although involved in a study which should prove fascinating, enthusiasm frequently wanes and is replaced by a mixture of boredom and confusion. Students often work diligently, yet feel unrewarded; too frequently they find the course a jumble of dry and unrelated facts and eventually leave it with a number of undigested "T" accounts and no coherent pattern.

This third edition of *Money and Economic Activity*, like its predecessors, has been compiled to help make courses in money and banking and related subjects come alive as an important, exciting, and meaningful part of the world about them. To these ends, the selections have been chosen with three main criteria in mind: their readability for the undergraduate student, their relevance to actual and prospective developments, and the presentation of contrasting viewpoints on vital and controversial issues of public policy.

Almost every chapter begins with a selection which provides a broad over-view of the topic at hand. In this way the student can become generally oriented before proceeding to articles which explore particular facets at more advanced levels. Chapter One and the introductions to the selections provide further cohesion by relating the selections to each other and to the central theme — the impact of money and the financial system on economic activity. In these ways I have tried to provide a perspective which will, I hope, increase understanding by keeping an over-all pattern in front of the student from beginning to end. (At the same time, of course, the volume retains the two great advantages of a book of readings: diversity and flexibility. The student has a convenient opportunity to encounter a variety of points of view from authoritative sources. And, since to a large extent the articles are self-contained, the instructor can easily vary the arrangement to suit specific course needs.)

As in the two previous editions, I have again reproduced most of the selections in their entirety rather than reprinting brief excerpts from a larger number of sources. A few editorial abridgements have been made here and there, primarily to enhance student readability, but for the most part they consist of removing some charts and tables and many footnotes. The body of the text has been retained intact in almost all cases in order to retain fully the style, the flavor, and the argument of the original.

It is customary for authors to justify a textbook revision, setting forth in some detail the reasons that impelled them to tamper with what presumably was the final word only a few short years ago. In this case, however, no reader could have read through the previous editions of this book (1952 and 1961) and emerged believing he had a firm grasp of the "final word." What he should have obtained was a better understanding of contemporary monetary and financial problems and future developments, an appreciation of the value of facts and objective analysis of them, and a respect for viewpoints other than his own. Perhaps, also, the attainment of these goals might leave an imprint which will have some carry-over into problems and issues of the contemporary world other than in the area of money and banking. In any event, the rapid pace of developments in financial theory and practice since 1961 has required a corresponding reorientation of this volume. Indeed, 31 out of the 64 selections in this edition are new. I hope, however, that they are not ephemeral.

New York University   Lawrence S. Ritter

CONTENTS

PART 1
INTRODUCTION TO A MONETARY ECONOMY

CHAPTER ONE
MONEY IN THE UNITED STATES TODAY

CHAPTER TWO
MONEY AND GOLD

CHAPTER THREE

MONEY, DEBT, AND FINANCIAL MARKETS

8 The Saving-Investment Process and the Market for Loanable Funds — *John G. Gurley*   **50**

9 The Structure of the Flow-of-Funds Accounts — *Lawrence S. Ritter*   **55**

PART 2

COMMERCIAL BANKING

CHAPTER FOUR

SOURCES OF BANK FUNDS: COMPETITION FOR SAVINGS

10 Sources of Commercial Bank Funds: An Example of "Creative Response" — *Federal Reserve Bank of Cleveland*   **65**

11 Implications of the Big Trend in Banking — *E. Sherman Adams*   **71**

12 Compensating Balance Requirements: The Results of a Survey — *Nevins D. Baxter and Harold T. Shapiro*   **82**

13 A Run on the Banks — *Marriner S. Eccles*   **92**

CHAPTER FIVE

USES OF BANK FUNDS: LOANS AND INVESTMENTS

14 Continuous Borrowing through "Short-Term" Bank Loans — *Federal Reserve Bank of Cleveland*   **98**

15 How High Can the Loan-Deposit Ratio Go? — *David P. Eastburn*   **104**

16 The Prime Rate — *Albert M. Wojnilower and Richard E. Speagle*   **109**

17 First Steps in Banking — *Punch*   **119**

CHAPTER SIX
COMPETITION IN FINANCIAL MARKETS

PART 3

THE INSTRUMENTS OF CENTRAL BANKING

CHAPTER SEVEN
WAR FINANCE AND ITS AFTERMATH

CHAPTER EIGHT
OPEN MARKET OPERATIONS

CHAPTER NINE
THE DISCOUNT RATE AND DISCOUNT POLICY

CHAPTER TEN
RESERVE REQUIREMENTS

PART 4
THE THEORY AND PRACTICE OF MONETARY POLICY

CHAPTER ELEVEN
HOW EFFECTIVE IS MONETARY POLICY?

CHAPTER TWELVE

COST-PUSH INFLATION AND THE DILEMMA OF MONETARY-FISCAL POLICY

CHAPTER THIRTEEN

THE ADMINISTRATION OF MONETARY POLICY

PART 5

FISCAL POLICY AND DEBT MANAGEMENT

CHAPTER FOURTEEN

FISCAL POLICY

CHAPTER FIFTEEN
DEBT MANAGEMENT

PART 6

THE WORLD ECONOMY

CHAPTER SIXTEEN
INTERNATIONAL FINANCE

PART 1

INTRODUCTION TO A MONETARY ECONOMY

CHAPTER ONE

MONEY IN THE UNITED STATES TODAY

1

MONEY, INCOME, AND ECONOMIC ACTIVITY

Lawrence S. Ritter

INFLATION AND DEPRESSION

To the college student of today inflation must seem as usual and normal a state of affairs as did depression to the student of the 1930's. The last few decades have seen a persistent upward pressure on prices just as the 1930's saw an equally persistent hangover of unemployment and bankruptcy. It is often difficult to say which of these two conditions is the greater evil; certainly we would be better off without large doses of either.

The post-World War II inflation in the United States, for example, has been a cause of much concern. Consumer goods prices have practically doubled since the end of World War II, and there are widespread expectations that rising prices are likely to continue into the indefinite future, thus lowering the living standards of all those with fixed or relatively fixed money incomes. The more firmly and widely held is the idea that prices are likely to rise in the future, the more businessmen, workers, and investors are apt to take measures to protect themselves from the effects of such price rises.

But individual or group efforts to escape the impact of inflation, as opposed to Governmental measures to stop the inflation itself, are likely to result only in more inflation. Individuals or groups invariably react to paying higher prices by raising their own prices in retaliation. The end result is more inflation rather than less.

By comparison with other inflations, recent price rises in the United States hardly indicate the proportions which that state of affairs is capable of achieving once it really takes hold: in Germany at the end of 1923 it took 1,200,400,000,000 paper marks to buy what only 35 marks could purchase just two years earlier, and in Hungary it took 1.4 nonillion pengoes to buy in 1946 what only 1 pengo could obtain in 1938. (One nonillion equals 1,000,000,000,-000,000,000,000,000,000.) Consider the plight of the older person living on fixed retirement or insurance payments, or the creditor who loaned money before the inflation and is repaid under such circumstances.

Depression also results in suffering and deprivation. In 1932 over 12 million workers were involuntarily unemployed in the United States alone; almost one out of every four breadwinners was unable to find a job. Even such figures give no idea of the human cost involved — the fruitless all-day searches for jobs when there are no jobs, the deterioration through idleness of skills laboriously acquired, the panic that takes hold and the homes that are broken when the inflow of income ceases and past savings begin to vanish, the humiliation and loss of self-confidence of the receiver of charity. There were still over nine million unemployed in 1939; evidently only war brought us out of the depression — and into inflation. No one is left unscathed by such upheavals.

Our primary purpose is to obtain some understanding of the monetary framework that envelops our economy. To the extent that we understand what money is and what its effects are we may develop at least more informed viewpoints regarding matters that affect the course of our own destiny. In order to approach the monetary system with this perspective it is first necessary to lay the foundations by becoming familiar with some basic analytical tools; to this end it is useful to examine more closely the economic system and the role of money in the economic processes.

THE CIRCULAR FLOW OF SPENDING AND INCOME

Let us first take a bird's-eye view of the economy as a whole, for that purpose dividing all society into two separate and distinct groups: *households* and *business firms*. This is a very simplified picture, even excluding the government. For the time being we can consider the government as one of the business firms.

The main function of households is *consumption*, the deriving of sustenance and enjoyment from goods and services, with the aim of directly satisfying human wants. The main function of business firms is quite different: *production*, the combining of the factors of production into a salable product, with the aim of maximizing profits. The same individuals in society are usually members of both groups; that is, the same worker, or businessman, plays a dual role in economic life. In his capacity as a worker, or businessman, he produces goods and services in order to receive money income. As householder, he helps consume the products of industry, attempting to satisfy seemingly insatiable human wants. But even though both groups, workers and householders, are composed in large part of the same people, analytically their functions and aims are separate and distinct.

The essence of economic activity is revealed in the *inner circle* of Figure I. Start at the bottom and move along the inner circle to the right; householders, or individuals, supply productive services to business firms in the form of land, labor, capital, and enterprise. These factors of production are then combined in the business firm to produce products which,

when completed, are sold by the firms to the households. The process is circular; the members of a society combine to produce the things that they themselves need and will consume. The complete inner circle thus represents a flow of "real" services of productive agents to the firms, and the "real" goods and services which are forthcoming from their efforts. These products return to the same productive agents and their families, who purchase them in their capacity as consumers.

Although the inner circle represents the basic circular flow within society, it is by itself a misleading representation of the means whereby that process is carried on. For individuals do not work for payment in kind. Factory workers do not supply their eight hours of labor per day in order to receive, at the end of the week, a quantity of the finished product which they helped to produce. Instead, they work for money. And with this money income they then buy, through money expenditure, the output of the firms. Money thus functions as *a means of payment* or *a medium of exchange*, the intermediary through which exchanges of commodities and services are effected in our society.

The *outer* circle thus represents the so-called monetary veil which in a sense partially conceals the real processes which are the heart of economic life. Taken together, both circles describe, although inadequately, the over-all picture of economic activity as we know it. Householders supply productive services (land, labor, capital, and enterprise) to the firms, for which they receive a corresponding flow of money income payments (rent, wages, interest,

FIGURE I

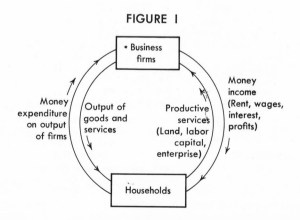

and profits) from the firms. This is represented on the right-hand side of Figure I. With this money income consumers may, through monetary expenditure, purchase the output of finished goods and services produced by the firms. The money income is thereby transformed into real income, as represented by the left-hand side of Figure I.

SAVING AND INVESTMENT

As it stands, however, Figure I is incomplete in two major respects. For it implies, first, that all the money income received by consumers is re-spent by them to purchase the products of industry. In addition, it also implies that business firms produce only consumer goods; that is, consumers are represented as purchasing the total output of the firms. Neither implication is an accurate representation of reality.

Instead of spending all of their income, most individuals attempt to do some saving, that is, to refrain from spending everything on consumer goods currently, perhaps in order to have a reserve available for future needs. Saving is shown on the lower part of Figure II, with householders spending only part of their income on consumer goods; the rest is now channeled into saving. Note the definition of saving as merely income available for disposal which is not spent on consumer goods; saving equals disposable income minus consumption expenditure. Notice particularly that saving does *not* mean hoarding. Hoarding, as the

term is commonly used, refers to a particular way of disposing of saved funds, as stuffing them in a strong box or merely holding them idle. But our definition of saving is not concerned with what happens to the funds after they are withheld from consumption. Saving is defined as merely income available for expenditure which is *not* spent on *consumer* goods. The saved funds might (or might not) be hoarded or put in the bank or spent on investment goods. Or they might be used to buy stocks or bonds or used to repay some old debts. In *any* case, since this income is not spent on consumer goods, it is saving, by definition. It is easy to become confused if this is not constantly kept in mind. Taken by itself, then, saving is an act of *not* spending, while consumption is a positive act of expenditure. Thus, to the extent to which such saving occurs, the flow of spending by householders to purchase the consumer goods output of industry will be that much decreased.

Figure I must also be amended in another respect. It implies that firms produce only goods bought by consumers, for householders are represented as the only purchasers of the products of the firms, and this would indicate that business firms produce only consumer goods. In addition, however, many firms are engaged in the manufacture of capital or investment goods, such as machine tools, office buildings, and carbon paper, goods purchased for use in production, or for re-sale if purchased by a wholesaler or retailer, rather than for the direct satisfaction of human wants. This output is not purchased by consumers to satisfy wants directly, but by other business firms for use in the productive process. These firms are introduced in the upper part of Figure II. They hire productive agents and disburse money income to them, just as do the firms selling consumer goods, but their products go to and are paid for by other firms rather than going to and being paid for by householders. The expenditure by business firms on currently produced real output[1] is termed investment expenditure,

FIGURE II

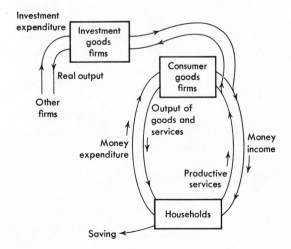

---

[1] "Currently produced" output, because we are interested in total production and employment for society as a whole during a particular current period of time. The purchase of already existing assets — as old houses or used cars — does not give rise to employment or in-

just as the expenditure by householders is termed consumer spending. Note the definitions of consumer expenditure and investment expenditure which are used: consumer expenditure is spending by consumers to purchase currently produced real goods and services to be used to satisfy human wants directly; investment expenditure is spending by business firms to purchase currently produced real goods to be used in the process of producing goods for sale.

An example might clarify the meaning of the definitions. Consumption expenditure is spending on currently produced consumer goods by householders; saving is income available which is *not* spent on consumer goods; investment is spending on currently produced real capital goods by business firms. If an individual receives $100 in income for a week's work and spends $80 of it purchasing consumer goods, consumption expenditure obviously equals $80. How much saving has occurred? Automatically we can say that $20 has been saved, for saving is merely income available which is *not* spent on consumer goods. Disposable income minus consumer expenditure equals saving, or $20 in this case. If, now, the individual with whom we are concerned puts the saved $20 in the bank, has he invested it? Has $20 of investment taken place? Or what if he buys a government bond? Or some General Motors stock? In each case the answer is *no*. Investment is *expenditure on capital goods by business firms*. In no one of the cited cases has this occurred. It is still merely savings, with the funds transferred either to a bank, to the government, or to the seller of the stock. In the general usage of the man in the street the term investment would be applied to each of these cases. In economics, however, this general or business usage of the term is replaced by the

specific definition mentioned above. If the bank lends $20 to a business firm, investment still has not occurred. Only if the business firm spends the funds purchasing currently produced real capital goods do we finally have $20 of investment expenditure to match the $20 of saving.

Saving and investment are usually performed by different people and for different reasons. Investment expenditure is undertaken by business firms; saving is done mainly by householders. Investment is undertaken mainly to make profit; saving is undertaken largely to provide for future contingencies. In some cases the two are joined in one act, as when a farmer refrains from consuming all his available income (saves) so that he may purchase a new tractor (investment). But these situations are quantitatively of minor importance, and therefore the distinction between the two should constantly be kept in mind.

Let us return to our two categories of spending — consumption and investment expenditure. All expenditure on current final output can be divided into these two categories, consumer spending and investment spending. Together they comprise total expenditure on currently produced output. To the extent to which investment expenditure occurs, it should be clear that the flow of total spending to purchase the products of firms will be that much greater than it would be if that investment expenditure were not present, assuming consumption spending to be given. It has previously been shown that the act of saving, in itself, diminishes the flow of total spending on the products of firms; it is now seen that the act of investment, in itself, increases that flow. It can thus be concluded that the flow of total spending will be increased, decreased, or remain constant, if the flow of investment is more than, less than, or equal to the flow of saving. As we will see later, *financial institutions* play a crucial role in channeling savings into the hands of those who need funds for investment.

SOME FUNDAMENTAL IDENTITIES

(1) It is not difficult for the economist to measure the left-hand outer circles, representing total spending on currently produced fin-

---

crease the total wealth of society *as a whole*, but merely transfers already existing wealth about within society. "Real" output, because we exclude purely financial transactions, i.e., trading in paper claims, such as stocks or bonds, also on the ground that they are merely transfers within society and do not increase the *real* wealth of society in the aggregate. Nor do such financial transactions generate employment except perhaps indirectly. Building a factory represents real investment; buying an old one or a share of stock does not.

ished products of firms: by adding up the various money amounts spent, a sum total may be computed. But a conceptual difficulty arises in the measurement of the left-hand inner circles, representing the "real" output of finished goods for which the money is spent. Some firms produce guns, some bread, some radios. The economist uses *money value* as the common denominator.

We have seen previously that one function performed by money is that of serving as a generally accepted means of payment, a medium of exchange. In addition money also serves as a common denominator of values, a standard for evaluations. Relative values and debts are expressed in terms of money; just as the yard is the unit of measurement for distance and the pound for weight, the dollar is the unit of measurement for values. This function is usually expressed by saying that money is the *unit of account* (or *standard of value*) used by society. The "real" flow is thus reckoned in monetary terms, just as is the expenditure to purchase it.

The result is a fundamental identity: since the money value of an object is by definition merely what it will bring in exchange, the sum of money expended in the purchase of an article and the money value of that article must be one and the same amount. If an article is sold for $100, its value is $100. If it is sold for $200, that must be its value. The money value, being the sum of money a thing can command in exchange, must be equal to the sum of money that is spent in obtaining it. Similarly, *the total money expenditure to purchase current finished output must be equal to the total money value of the current final output produced.*[2]

If in all of society only ten automobiles are produced in a period of time, and they sell for $2,000 each, what can we say about the total

spending during that period and the value of the output produced? Both must equal $20,000, neither more nor less. The total spending on final output in a period and the value of that output must be equal because, as with two sides of a coin, they are but two ways of viewing the same thing! They cannot differ because if more is spent in purchasing the output, its value is, *ipso facto*, that much higher; and its money value is not higher, as far as the economist is concerned, unless it can bring more money in exchange. Nor is the value of output lower unless that output commands less money in exchange, in which case *both* money expenditure to purchase it and the money value of the output are correspondingly decreased.

To go a step further: As before, we may again divide total spending into its two component parts: consumption (C) and investment expenditure (I). Thus consumption plus investment expenditure must be equal to the total value of output produced. But the value of that output can also be divided into its components; the money value of any group of items is necessarily a matter of the physical number of commodities (T) multiplied by their average price (P). Thus the value of ten automobiles priced at $2,000 each is $20,000; the value of one loaf of bread priced at 25 cents is 25 cents; the value of two radios priced at $30 each is $60. (Just as the total value of output produced may be said to be equal to the physical number of final items currently produced (T) multiplied by the average price per unit (P), similarly we are all aware of the fact that we can reckon the total number of miles driven by a car as equal to the number of hours driven multiplied by the average speed per hour.) Breaking both total spending and total value of output produced in a period into their component parts yields the formulation C + I = PT.

(2) Let us look at the same subject from a slightly different angle. Although nothing new will be examined, it is often useful to view the same process from several different perspectives. So far we have looked upon total spending as consisting of two types of spending, consumption and investment expenditure. But total spending could also be looked upon as

[2] It would seem, at first glance, as though it could only be said that the total value of money expenditure to purchase current finished output equals the total value of the current final output sold. However, by definition, a consumer good is not produced until it is sold to a consumer; if a product is not yet sold to a consumer it is considered an investment good, for it will be carried in the inventory of some firm and all firm inventories are considered investment goods.

consisting of the quantity of money in existence (M) multiplied by the average number of times each unit of money is spent on final products in a period of time. If this average rate of turnover on current final output of each unit of money, known as income velocity (V), is multiplied by M, the result is the perhaps already familiar *equation of exchange*, MV = PT.[3] Again this is but a different formulation of the same truism previously presented as C + I = PT: total spending on output and the value of that output are equal. At times, however, one formulation may be more fruitful, and at times the other.

Some economists in the past, following some form of the MV = PT formulation, have asserted that changes in the supply of money invariably alter the price level, that price changes are due to and are in proportion to changes in the quantity of money. Following this view, if the quantity of money rises ten per cent, prices will rise ten per cent; if the quantity of money falls ten per cent, prices will fall ten per cent. But this view, the strict *quantity of money theory* of the price level, is hardly tenable. In the first place, a change in the quantity of money may be offset by opposing changes in velocity. But even if velocity does not change, so that an increase in the quantity of money does result in greater total expenditure, either the MV = PT or the C + I = PT formulation clearly shows that if total spending increases *either* prices or the number of items produced may rise. And if total spending decreases, *either* prices or physical production may fall. There is, therefore, no necessary proportional relationship between changes in the supply of money and changes in the general level of prices, for, even if velocity is assumed to remain constant, output rather than prices may respond to a change in spending.

Depression or recession is a situation in which spending falls and the result is in good

part a reduction of physical production rather than of prices. Of course, prices as a rule do fall in many areas; but the significant aspect is the reduction in physical output that accompanies the decreased spending. Reduced production generally means fewer men employed, since increases or decreases in the volume of physical production are, in the short run at least, usually accompanied by the hiring or firing of the labor force. Thus, by depression or recession is generally meant a situation of high unemployment.

Inflation, on the other hand, is generally defined in relation to prices rather than physical production or employment. If total expenditure rises, the value of output produced must also rise with it. This means that either prices or physical production, or both, must rise. In cases where there currently exists a large reservoir of unemployment, this rise in the value of output is most likely to be accomplished through increased physical output rather than price rises, thus decreasing the level of unemployment. But less desirable results occur if total spending increases when the economy is already producing at close to capacity, when unemployment is already small and full employment is near; in such cases it is difficult to increase real output and it is more likely that prices will rise rather than physical production (and employment) to equate the value of output with the higher total of expenditure. Inflation, which might be roughly defined as a state of rising prices, is thus usually a hazard of periods of high employment, to be feared most at times when the curse of unemployment is just beginning to be satisfactorily removed.

(3) Another identity, revolving about the concept of income, is also worth noting. Again we are merely shifting our perspective, viewing the same process from still another angle. *By money income received during a period of time is meant payment for productive activity currently rendered.* This total amount can be subdivided into the four commonly used categories: wages, rent, interest, and profit. Wages, rent, and interest are costs to the businessman; profits are the difference between his money receipts and those costs.

[3] This formulation of the equation of exchange is slightly different from the traditional usage in that traditionally the *total number of transactions* and their average price level are the subjects of interest rather than, as here, only *current final products* and their price level. The formulation in the text is thus often termed the income form of the equation of exchange.

Costs (that is, wages, rent, and interest) plus profit must then equal the total money receipts. But the money receipts for final products sold during any one period of time must be equal to the money spent in buying them, for the sum total received by sellers and the sum total spent by buyers cannot differ. They are the same thing, at one time viewed from the sellers' side, and at another time from the buyers' side. *Money income received in any one period (wages, rent, interest, and profit) is therefore equal to total spending on final output in that period* (C + I), which is itself, as we have seen, equal to the value of output produced in that period (PT). *Thus for any one period of time money income must equal the value of output produced.*

Money income earned during a period is therefore equal to the value of output, which in turn must be equal to the total expenditure upon that output. We have all been aware of the fact that income is the *source* of most expenditure — in other words, that it is difficult to spend unless one receives the income with which to do so. In addition, while it is not so readily recognized, income is also the *result* of expenditure. Spending on new consumption and investment goods gives rise to earned income of an equal dollar amount. Increases in total spending must, then, raise money income and the value of output. If physical production (T) increases, rather than prices (P), the increase in money income is also an increase in real income; if only prices rise, higher money incomes are no more valuable in real terms, for it will take that much more money to purchase the same goods and services.

Building upon these relationships, it is now possible to modify Figures I and II in such

a way as to show more than merely the direction of monetary and real flows. By making use of the identities reviewed in this section we can also show the quantitative size of income and output. Thus Figure III differs from its predecessors in that we now have, instead of plane circular arrows, one huge circular *pipe*, the size of which indicates the quantitative magnitude of the flow. In addition, only the upper half of the circular flow is shown.

Start at the left-hand side of Figure III. In any one period of time, the sum of consumption and investment expenditure together make up total current spending upon the output of business firms. This may be any amount, of course, but visualize the width of the total spending pipe in Figure III as measuring that amount, whatever it may be. The width of the same pipe then also measures the value of output produced in that period, for, as we have seen, the value of output received by purchasers (PT) must be equal to the total sum of money spent in purchasing it. Similarly, the income earned from productive activity must be represented by a pipe of equal width, for the value of output and income earned are two sides of the same coin.

Figure III thus portrays in skeletal form the interrelated basic flows that constitute the economic processes. Moving over to the right-hand side of the diagram, we realize that the income earned from productive activity flows to the householders and that part of this income is re-spent on consumer goods. The rest is, by definition, saved (and therefore withdrawn from the spending stream). Assuming investment expenditure by business firms (an injection into the spending stream) equal to the amount saved, the result is a repetition of the same dollar volume of total spending, value

FIGURE III

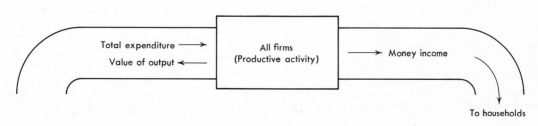

of output, and income. The size of the pipe thus remains unchanged as the process is repeated.

Spending, income, and employment are constantly fluctuating, of course, rather than remaining constant over time. This can easily be portrayed by Figure III. Since the dollar amount of spending and income is represented by the width of the pipe, if we assume that the total spending pictured above in Figure III is that which will result in full employment, it is only necessary to visualize depression as a narrower (smaller) money flow and inflation as a wider (larger) stream. All three quantities, however — total spending, the value of output, and income earned — must always be equal in dollar magnitude at any one moment of time, as we have seen. It is possible for them to change, to get larger or smaller, for the pipe to get wider or narrower, but it must be kept in mind that a change in one necessitates a change in all. Increased spending means an increased value of output and higher income; decreased spending means a decreased value of output and lower income. The entire pipe, in other words, may get wider or narrower as economic activity quickens or slackens, but at any one moment of time it is still true that total spending must be equal to the value of output and to the sum total of income earned.

CHANGES IN THE FLOW OF SPENDING AND INCOME

It is possible to integrate further the material discussed above and at the same time investigate more closely the process of *changes* in the level of spending and income — the fluctuations we call depression and inflation — without introducing any essentially new ideas beyond those already mentioned. The present section should thus serve both as a review and a further elaboration.

If we are to speak of changes in the level of economic activity we must refer to changes over a span of time. The explicit introduction of time periods into the analysis is therefore of great value in clarifying the significance of key relationships. *By a period let us mean a length of time in which money income can be earned, but the earned funds not re-spent.*

The funds earned in any one period of time become disposable (that is, available for spending) in the next period. The period might be conceived of as a week; payment for the week's work is received at the end of the week and is not allowed to be spent until the following week. With this simple technique we can now (Figure IV) illustrate three possibilities with regard to the level of income: it can (1) remain constant, (2) fall, or (3) rise.

In Period 1 assume that total spending equals 100 dollars. Therefore income earned and the value of output for Period 1 must also equal 100 dollars. This earned income for Period 1 now automatically becomes the *disposable* income, the income available for spending, in the succeeding Period 2. In effect, we are now ready to investigate the disposal of the earned 100-dollar income possessed by the householders.

(1) In Period 2a, 100 dollars of income — the earned income of the previous period — is available for disposal. Let us assume that 80 dollars is spent on consumer goods. Then, by definition, 20 dollars is saved, for saving is disposable income minus consumption expen-

FIGURE IV

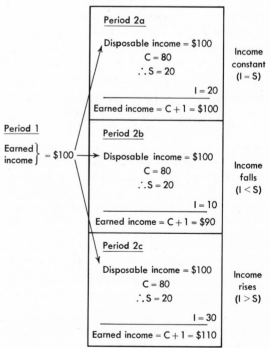

diture. Total spending, however, includes investment expenditure as well as consumer expenditure; it is equal to the sum of the two. Recall that saving and investment are distinctly different acts, largely performed by different groups and for different reasons. There is no automatic mechanism equating the two in the sense the terms have been used herein. *If* we assume that investment expenditure by business firms is 20 dollars, then total spending in Period 2a amounts to 100 dollars. As a result, the value of output and the income earned in Period 2a remain constant, as compared to the previous period, at 100 dollars. We may conclude that money income will remain constant when investment in a period *is equal to* saving out of the disposable income of that period.[4]

(2) Rather than Period 2a, let us now assume an alternative Period 2b following Period 1, with Period 2b differing from Period 2a only in our assumption regarding investment. Again 100 dollars of disposable income is available, the earned income of Period 1. Again let us assume that 80 dollars is spent on consumer goods, which means that saving of 20 dollars takes place. Now, however, we assume that investment expenditure by business firms totals but 10 dollars, resulting in total expenditure in Period 2b equal to but 90 dollars (C + I). As a result, the value of output and income earned in Period 2b must fall to 90 dollars, a decrease from the 100-dollar income level of the previous period. We may conclude that money income will fall when investment in a period *is less than* saving out of the disposable income of that period.

(3) As a last alternative, let Period 2c follow Period 1. Again assume 80 dollars spent on consumer goods, resulting in the saving of 20

[4] The fact that money income will remain constant when saving equals investment means only that income has reached a state of equilibrium and will not tend to change. The saving-investment equalty has no ethical connotations and is not necessarily a desirable state of affairs, for the level of income maintained may well be one at which there is severe unemployment. Assuming that our aim is to achieve full employment with stable prices, the desirability of maintaining income constant (or of having it rise or fall) would depend upon whether that level of income were one of full employment, under-employment depression, or hyper-employment inflation.

dollars. However, now assume investment expenditure equal to 30 dollars for this case. Then total spending in Period 2c amounts to 110 dollars; the value of output and earned income must rise correspondingly, an increase over the 100-dollar income level of Period 1. We may conclude that money income will rise when investment in a period *is greater than* saving out of the disposable income of that period.[5]

We could proceed beyond the diagram and note that the disposable income of the period following Period 2c would then be 110 dollars. Since the amount of consumer spending depends to a great extent upon disposal income, this period which follows Period 2c might well see a rise in consumer spending above 80 dollars due to the rise in disposable income from 100 to 110 dollars. As a result, assuming investment expenditure remains at 30 dollars, earned income will tend to rise further, continuing to do so until the volume of saving forthcoming is sufficient to match the now increased level of investment. Income might thus *eventually*, over many periods, rise by

[5] Some students, who have studied an analysis involving saving and investment elsewhere, may be bothered because they have perhaps previously learned that saving and investment *must always be equal,* and this seems difficult to reconcile with the above. The difference is due entirely to different definitions of saving. Here we have defined saving in a period as equal to the *disposable* income of the period minus consumption expenditure in that period. But those who see saving and investment as always equal define saving in a period as equal to the *earned* income of the period minus consumption expenditure in that period. With the latter definition, saving and investment *must* always be equal because they are *defined* in such a way as to make them equal — saving in a period is defined as the earned income of that period minus consumption, and since consumption plus investment make up the earned income of the period, investment must also equal that earned income minus consumption. With such a definition the reader will note that Period 2b yields saving of 10 dollars and Period 2c yields saving equal to 30 dollars, both equal to the volume of investment in the period. While such a definitional equality between saving and investment may be useful for some purposes, it is of little aid and is frequently responsible for much confusion insofar as an understanding of the casual forces making for changes in national income is concerned. Therefore we prefer to define saving in relation to the *disposable* income of the period in which the saving takes place, thus allowing saving and investment to differ and permitting income changes to be explained as a resultant of that difference.

much more than the original Period 2c excess of investment over saving. This idea has been labeled the *multiplier principle*, since the eventual rise in income might well be a multiple of the original excess of investment over saving that started the snowball-like process under way. Notice that the crux of the multiplier principle lies in the assumption that investment will remain at its new level sufficiently long for the process to work itself out and in the assumed dependence of consumption upon income; the specific size of the multiplier in any particular case will depend upon the extent to which consumption changes following a change in income.[6]

THE IMPORTANCE OF MONEY AND THE FINANCIAL SYSTEM

Since the economic processes are carried on through the medium of money, it is well to take more explicit account of the importance of that element in the foregoing process. We have seen that when saving out of the disposable income of a period is greater than the amount that can profitably be spent on investment goods, income will contract. The drain of savings is greater than the inflow of investment. As a result the new money income created is less than that of the previous period. The question of where the excess money goes to is often bothersome to many. If money income in Period 2 is less than that of Period 1, what happened to the difference? One hundred dollars of disposable income is available at the beginning of a period, and 80 dollars is spent on consumer goods. Then 20 dollars must be saved; but if investment is only 10 dollars, what has happened to the other 10 dollars? The answer is that either of two things may have occurred: (1) money may have been

destroyed, that is, the actual supply of money may have been reduced, or (2) there may have occurred an increased amount of hoarding of existing money, an increase in holdings of idle cash. In terms of our former equation, the decrease in income (= PT) must mean a reduction in M, the destruction of part of the money supply, or a decrease in V, a slower rate of turnover of the same amount of money. In either case, this means decreased spending.

Such an increase in cash hoards illustrates a third function of money. We have already seen that in modern society money functions as a medium of exchange and as a standard of value. Since it is recognized as a generally acceptable means of payment, money acquires a uniqueness of its own as a thing of value which it is desirable to possess. Money is readily salable, it gives its holder a wide range of choice over other objects, and it is stable in value in dollar terms. Money is thus the most liquid of all assets; the holder of money is the bearer of options which can be exercised at a moment's notice with no loss in dollar value. The term "liquid assets" is used in direct opposition to the more common term "frozen assets," that is, assets which are not readily salable, which are not stable in sale value in terms of dollars upon short notice, and which cannot be "liquidated" (or sold) without severe loss.

Due to these advantages of holding wealth in the form of more liquid rather than less liquid assets, a consideration which may exist for a variety of reasons and vary in intensity from time to time, much wealth is held in the form of money rather than other things, for money satisfies most completely the preference for liquidity. Money thus also functions as a *store of value*. In a sense this function is the exact opposite of the medium of exchange (or means of payment) function. The former is a matter of *holding* money, the latter a matter of *spending* it. To the extent that a given quantity of money serves more fully as a store of value, it will be held longer and spent less. An increase in liquidity preference is thus closely akin to an increase in hoarding or a decrease in V, with each unit of money held longer and spent less rapidly than heretofore.

We have also seen that when saving out of

[6] Similar statements can be made regarding the sequel to Period 2b. The disposable income of the period following Period 2b would be 90 dollars. As a result of this fall in disposable income from 100 to 90 dollars, consumer spending might well fall below 80 dollars in that period following Period 2b. Thus, assuming investment expenditure remains at 10 dollars, earned income would tend to fall further, continuing to do so until the volume of saving forthcoming is no greater than the now diminished level of investment. Income might thus, over many periods, fall by much more than the original Period 2b deficiency of investment as compared to saving.

the disposable income of a period is less than investment expenditure in that period, income will expand. The drain of savings is less than the inflow of investment. As a result, the new earned money income of the period is greater than that of the previous period. Similar to the question of where the excess money goes to, in the case of contraction, is that of where the money comes from when investment is greater than saving. One hundred dollars of disposable income is available at the beginning of a period, and 80 dollars is spent on consumer goods. Then 20 dollars remains as savings; but if 30 dollars is spent on investment goods, where does the extra 10 dollars come from? Again the answer is that either of two things may have occurred: (1) money may have been newly created, that is, the actual supply of money may have been increased, or (2) cash hoards previously existing, accumulated from funds earned many periods back, may be released and put into the spending stream. In terms of our former equation, the increase in income ($= PT$) must mean an increase in M, the creation of new money, or an increase in V, a more rapid rate of turnover of the same quantity of money. In either case, there is increased spending.

The relation between saving and investment is thus a most important factor to consider in any investigation of the causal mainsprings that lie behind depression and inflation. Closely related is the possibility of money creation and destruction as well as changes in the desire to hold money in idle hoards rather than use it currently as a means of payment. In all these processes the crucial role of the commercial banks will shortly become apparent. For not only do they aid in channeling saved funds into the hands of those who are thus enabled to make investment expenditures, but they also, remarkably enough, as the following selection demonstrates, are capable of creating and destroying money itself.

Finally, financial institutions other than commercial banks — such as insurance companies and savings and loan associations — are also crucially important in the saving-investment process. While they do not create or destroy money, they do play an active role in channeling saving into the hands of would-be investment spenders. In thus acting as "financial intermediaries" between savers and investors, they are a crucial link in the income generation process. We shall examine their role more closely in Chapter Three.

2

MONEY, THE COMMERCIAL BANKS, AND THE FEDERAL RESERVE*

Lorie Tarshis†

By far the most important part of our money supply is in the form of demand deposits (or check-book money) rather than currency (or pocket-book money). At the start of 1966 there was only about $35 billion of coin and currency in this country as compared with about $135 billion of check-book money. The banking system is the source as well as the habitat of this predominant form of money. In the first part of this selection

* From Lorie Tarshis, *Modern Economics: An Introduction* (Boston: Houghton Mifflin Company, 1967).

Reprinted by the courtesy of the publisher and the author.
† Stanford University.

Professor Tarshis clearly explains the power of the commercial banks to create money, carefully distinguishing between the individual bank and the banking system as a whole. The second part of the selection deals with the Federal Reserve Banks and their relation to the commercial banks. Although a more thorough description of the functions and activities of the Federal Reserve is postponed until later (see especially Part 3), it is useful to obtain first a survey view of the entire monetary and banking framework before proceeding to closer examination of any part.

The selection below approaches the subject by using balance sheet changes as the illustrative device. It is most important that the student gain complete mastery of this technique as a tool of analysis, for it is by far the most useful method through which to gain an adequate understanding of the financial system. Money and banking is a fairly complex subject, and it is often extremely difficult to understand clearly the effects of particular transactions unless the resulting balance sheet changes are traced through. In addition, most of the succeeding selections in this volume, even though they may not contain balance sheets, assume a familiarity with this method of analysis on the part of the reader and use appropriate terminology. Thus they will be much more intelligible to those who have first thoroughly mastered the technique as introduced below.

I. MONEY AND THE COMMERCIAL BANKS

KINDS OF MONEY

First we shall describe precisely what money is. This might seem unnecessary until you examine carefully the contents of your own wallet — even when they are "thin," their variety may be surprising. First look at the coins — the nickels, dimes, pennies, and quarters. Notice that there is no statement on them that the money is "backed" and there is no "promise to pay." Yet these coins buy things just as readily as any other kind of money.

How much of this kind of money exists? If we had added together the value of all of the coins in all of our pockets, in penny banks, in sugar jars, and in the tills of business firms, it would have amounted to a little over $3½ billion in early 1965. This, of course, is more than enough for one pocket but it is a relatively insignificant sum in comparison with the amounts of other types of money.

Now let us examine the bills, which range in face value from one dollar to ten thousand dollars. They are of two main types; silver certificates and Federal Reserve Notes. (There are certain other types of bills also but their circulation is very restricted.) Measured by the amount in circulation, Federal Reserve Notes are much the most important kind of paper money. Those in pockets, jars, and tills (that

is, in circulation generally) at the beginning of 1965 had a face value of almost $34 billion. Notes of this kind are issued by the Federal Reserve Banks on conditions to be described later. The face of such a bill bears the legend: "This note is legal tender for all debts, public and private, and is redeemable in lawful money at the United States Treasury, or at any Federal Reserve Bank." In addition, the note states that "The United States of America will pay to the bearer on demand five dollars" (or the face value of the bill). These legends most certainly raise questions. For example, what is lawful money? How will the United States pay to the bearer the five dollars which he may demand? With another five-dollar bill?

Silver certificates, of which there were about $0.9 billion worth in circulation in early 1965, bear a somewhat less ambiguous set of statements: "This certificate is legal tender for all debts, public and private" and "This certifies that there is on deposit in the Treasury of the United States of America five dollars" (or the face value of the bill) "in silver payable to the bearer on demand." Silver certificates used to be more common. For example, in the early 1960's and the 1950's there were about $2 billion worth but they are now being replaced by Federal Reserve Notes.

The face value of all bills and coins in circulation came to about $38¾ billion in the early months of 1965. In other words, we possessed about $38¾ billion worth of paper money and coins at that date or about $190 worth for every person. This figure is very much higher than it was at the end of 1938, when it stood at about $7 billion, or $50 a person, but on a per capita basis it is no different from the 1946 figure.

As consumers, we do much of our trading with money of these kinds — coins and bills. But we should not be misled into supposing that most transactions are financed in this way. When a manufacturing concern buys raw materials, when an investment bank sells securities, or when the government pays for the construction of a large dam, payment is not effected by the transfer of bills. Instead, *a check* is drawn by the purchaser in favor of the seller. In terms of volume, the kind of money which is thereby transferred is much more important than the kind transferred in the form of currency. For example, in April 1965, in comparison with the $38¾ billion in currency outstanding, there was in existence about $125 billion in what we may for the moment call check-money. And not only is the amount of check-money far in excess of the amount of currency but check-money, because it circulates much more rapidly than currency, supports an even larger percentage of all transactions than we might suppose from simply comparing amounts.

DEMAND DEPOSITS

Since the volume of check-money is so much greater than that of all other kinds of money combined, we must devote special attention to it. When someone writes a check, he instructs his bank to transfer a part of his demand deposit or checking account to another person. The check is an order to transfer funds from a demand deposit. Check-money is nothing more than a *demand deposit* (or a checking account) in a commercial bank. But while we have called demand deposits a form of money, they are not always quite the same as currency money. A seller would rarely question a purchase financed by either a bill or a coin. An order to transfer a bank deposit is, however, less readily acceptable. When an ordinary individual writes a check, it is usually necessary

for him to identify himself before it is accepted. Still, it is easy to overemphasize this difference. While it is sometimes an awkward difference for those of us who carry on only a small amount of our business by check, it would be equally awkward, or perhaps more awkward, if we tried to pay for a one-dollar purchase with a hundred-dollar bill. And a firm which habitually finances most of its business by writing checks has no difficulty whatsoever in paying by check. No one would question a check drawn by General Motors. The acceptability of an order to transfer demand deposits by a reputable business firm is virtually as good as the acceptability of Federal Reserve Notes.

There are other kinds of wealth, even financial wealth, which are unacceptable under most circumstances for ordinary transactions and for that reason are not treated as money — since, by "money," we mean that which is *generally acceptable as a means of payment*. Government bonds or a personal savings account cannot be directly used to finance the purchase of, let us say, an automobile. Time deposits (savings accounts), unlike demand deposits, cannot be transferred by check. Hence, if one wants to "spend" a time deposit, he must first withdraw it from the bank in the form of currency. Then he can spend the currency. Since savings deposits are not readily transferable and sellers are unwilling to accept them in payment, they are not usually counted as a form of money.

We *could* include savings deposits as money for some purposes; for that matter, we could include government bonds. But the usual definition of money draws the boundary between demand deposits and savings deposits since only the former is generally acceptable as a means of payment. The line is not inflexible. In the immediate postwar period in Europe, American cigarettes were at least as acceptable as any other type of asset and frequently they were more acceptable than French francs, Italian lire, or German marks. Thus we might logically have included cigarettes as a part of the money supply of those countries; and if Italians had been unwilling to accept lire, we should have had to exclude lire in computing the amount of "money" in Italy. In normal circumstances, however, we include only currency and demand deposits in the money supply.

RESERVES AGAINST DEMAND DEPOSITS

A demand deposit in a bank is, of course, an *asset* or an item of wealth for the depositor. From the point of view of the bank, however, the deposit is a *liability* or debt because the bank must pay it and, what is worse from the bank's standpoint, it must pay it *on demand*. And unlike the promise to pay on the Federal Reserve Note, which does not specify the form in which payment is to be made, a demand deposit obligates the bank to make payment either by giving currency to the depositor or by transferring the deposit to another person — as the depositor chooses.

Now imagine yourself in the bank's position with a large debt outstanding which you might have to pay at any time. Surely prudence would dictate that you should have some means of payment on hand; some immediately available assets which your creditors would accept as payment. Long experience would give some information as to the amount of such assets. Let us suppose you had a number of creditors; at any time, some would be increasing their claims while others would be seeking payment. Thus the chances are that your "quick" assets could be well below the level of your liabilities, without exposing you to any difficulty.

A bank is in very much the same kind of situation. Since it may at any time have to meet the claims of its creditors or depositors, it must be careful to have enough suitable assets on hand. But the bank knows, again on the basis of long experience, that its reserves of such assets can be much below its liabilities. Only when there is "a run on the bank" do most of its depositors demand payment; otherwise they draw out only a small part of the total in any one day. To make matters even more convenient for the bank, as some depositors are making their withdrawals, others are adding to their accounts. Thus a bank with deposit liabilities of $100,000,000 may have to meet daily claims of only $150,000 — and while some of its depositors are demanding currency or writing checks on their accounts, others are

depositing currency and checks drawn on other accounts. Consequently, the reserves which a prudent bank keeps against its demand deposits are normally much lower than the deposits themselves. The law requires reserves that are only a small fraction of the bank's deposits but even that fraction is normally above the level which would be dictated by prudence alone.

In this country the bulk of the banking business is carried on by commercial banks which are members of the Federal Reserve System. Member banks, as these are called, must keep reserves which are at least as much as a certain percentage of their demand deposit liabilities, the exact figure depending upon the rules established by the Board of Governors of the Federal Reserve System. In August 1965 the specified ratios were 16½ per cent for larger "reserve city" banks and 12 per cent for all others.[1] Thus a bank in New York City or Chicago had to have reserves of suitable assets equal to at least 16½ per cent of its deposit liabilities due on demand. These figures can be changed by the Board without getting the approval of Congress, so long as the change keeps the required ratio between 10 per cent and 22 per cent for banks in the larger cities and between 7 per cent and 14 per cent for the rest.

Now since these reserves presumably have to be kept in order to meet possible withdrawals of demand deposits, we would expect them all to be held in the form of currency. However, although a bank by law can hold its reserves in the form of currency if it wishes to do so, in fact most banks do not do this. Strange though it may seem, the typical bank holds most of its reserves as deposits which it maintains in a Federal Reserve Bank, for reasons which will become clear later.

THE FEDERAL RESERVE BANKS — PRELIMINARY

What are these Federal Reserve Banks? Essentially, they are banks *for* banks; they perform almost the same functions for a commercial bank that a commercial bank performs for the individual depositor. There are twelve of them in the country, situated in large centers of population — New York, Boston, Philadel-

---

[1] The percentages given here are minimum values. The bank may hold reserves in excess of these figures.

phia, Chicago, San Francisco, and so on. Every commercial bank which is a member of the Federal Reserve System is affiliated with one of them. The Federal Reserve Banks themselves have little direct contact with the public. Most of their business is carried on with commercial banks or with the government rather than with ordinary business firms. Although they are technically owned by the commercial banks, they are public institutions and play an important part in controlling the activities of commercial banks.

By using facilities provided by the Federal Reserve Banks, the banking system can quickly transfer deposits between two individuals who have accounts in different banks and in different places. If someone with an account in the Wells Fargo Bank in San Francisco draws a check for $1,000 in favor of someone with an account in a bank in Los Angeles, the latter may either deposit the check in his bank or cash it and take currency. If he deposits it, the Los Angeles bank has the check for $1,000 and it owes $1,000 more to its depositor. It sends the check for collection to the Federal Reserve Bank of San Francisco, which is the appropriate Federal Reserve Bank for all of California as well as for several neighboring states. The Federal Reserve Bank, upon receiving it, reduces the Wells Fargo Bank's deposit with the Reserve Bank by $1,000 and increases that of the Los Angeles bank by the same amount. Finally, the Wells Fargo Bank reduces the account on which the check was drawn by $1,000. To summarize: when a check is written on bank A and given to someone with an account in bank B, changes are made in four accounts. The account of the payor decreases; that of the payee rises; bank A's deposit account in the Federal Reserve Bank declines; and bank B's increases. The transfer of funds by check between individuals with accounts in different banks thus causes a transfer of the deposits kept by commercial banks in the Federal Reserve Banks. But remember: these deposits of commercial banks in the Federal Reserve Banks are the legal reserves of the commercial banks against their deposit liabilities.

Thus, when a person writes a check on his account and gives it to another person with an account in a different bank, the *reserves* of one bank are reduced, while the reserves of the other are increased.

A commercial bank uses its deposits in a Federal Reserve Bank in the same way that an individual uses his deposit in a commercial bank. One bank can transfer funds to another by having the Reserve Bank reduce its account and increase that of the other. Conversely, it can have the Reserve Bank collect for it from another bank by adding the amount to its reserve deposit and subtracting that amount from the reserve deposit of the paying bank. Also, just as you may go to your bank and draw out currency, having your deposit fall as a result, so a commercial bank may draw currency against its deposits in the Federal Reserve Bank.

THE ACTIVITIES OF A COMMERCIAL BANK

With this sketch of the organization of the banking system, we can begin our analysis of how the bank, by trading IOU's, manages to create demand deposits. As a first step, we shall have to examine the operations of commercial banks.[2] We may do this best by following the activities of one of them, paying careful attention to the effects of its action upon its assets and its liabilities. We shall summarize these effects by drawing up a simple balance sheet, or statement of assets and liabilities, after analyzing each operation.

To begin with, let us suppose that a number of citizens of a certain town decide to organize a bank. They have a certain amount of cash in their possession with which to begin — let us say $5,000,000. After they have gone through the legal formalities, their bank is chartered and becomes, we shall suppose, a member of the Federal Reserve System. At this stage Balance Sheet 1 shows assets of $5,000,000

BALANCE SHEET 1			
Assets		*Liabilities and Capital*	
Cash	$5,000,000	Capital Stock	$5,000,000

in cash and liabilities (or, properly, "capital") consisting of the rights which the owners of the

[2] A commercial bank is any bank which accepts demand deposits (checking accounts).

bank could exercise if it were to be liquidated (the value of these rights is called capital stock) of $5,000,000.

Almost everything the bank does will have an effect upon two or more items in the balance sheet. *In order to facilitate comparison, the items that are changed by the step under discussion will be marked with an asterisk.*

The bank now acquires buildings and equipment with which to carry on its business. If $500,000 is paid for this property Balance Sheet 2 then looks like this:

BALANCE SHEET 2

Assets		Liabilities and Capital	
Cash	$4,500,000*	Capital Stock	$5,000,000
Property	500,000*		

The bank is now open for business. Let us say that it decides, for a beginning, to rid itself of some of its holdings of cash, partly to make its premises less attractive to young men who think they have found a new way to quick riches and partly because it wants to earn something. To realize these two aims, it buys $4,000,000 of government bonds and it sends $400,000 to the Federal Reserve Bank to be entered in its deposit account with "the Fed." After this operation, its Balance Sheet looks like this:

BALANCE SHEET 3

Assets		Liabilities and Capital	
Cash	$ 100,000*	Capital Stock	$5,000,000
Government Bonds	4,000,000*		
Property	500,000		
Deposits in Federal Reserve Banks	400,000*		
	$5,000,000		$5,000,000

Next, suppose that the bank's first depositor comes in with a check for $100,000 which he wants credited to his new account. His check we assume, has been written by someone with an account at a different bank. Our bank "collects" the check through "the Fed." We then have:

BALANCE SHEET 4

Assets		Liabilities and Capital	
Cash	$ 100,000	Demand Deposits	$ 100,000*
Government Bonds	4,000,000	Capital Stock	5,000,000
Property	500,000		
Deposits in FRB	500,000*		
	$5,100,000		$5,100,000

We shall assume for convenience that the legal reserves against deposit liabilities must be held in the form of deposits in the Federal Reserve Bank, and that vault cash does not count. Second, we shall assume that the *reserve requirement* has been set at 20 per cent.

Now, suppose that the bank's one depositor writes a check in favor of someone who decides to start a deposit account in this bank. There will now be two depositors but the total amount of deposit liabilities will remain unchanged; and so will all the other entries.

Next, suppose that the bank's depositors pay bills with checks drawn on their accounts to the amount of $50,000; all these checks are deposited in other banks. Its accounts will show:

BALANCE SHEET 5

Assets		Liabilities and Capital	
Cash	$ 100,000	Demand Deposits	$ 50,000*
Government Bonds	4,000,000	Capital Stock	5,000,000
Property	500,000		
Deposits in FRB	450,000*		
	$5,050,000		$5,050,000

Now, let one of its depositors withdraw $30,000 in cash and suppose that the bank in order to keep its vault cash at the $100,000 level, asks "the Fed" to send it as much in currency, charging its account in "the Fed." The *net* result of these two operations will be:

BALANCE SHEET 6

Assets		Liabilities and Capital	
Cash	$ 100,000	Demand Deposits	$ 20,000*
Government Bonds	4,000,000	Capital Stock	5,000,000
Property	500,000		
Deposits in FRB	420,000*		
	$5,020,000		$5,020,000

It should be noticed at this point that the bank's reserves — its deposits in the Federal Reserve Bank — fall when the bank asks for cash or when one of its depositors writes a check payable to someone with an account in a different bank. Similarly, its reserves are raised when it deposits cash in the Federal Reserve Bank or when one of its depositors receives a check drawn on a different bank and deposits it to his own account. There are still other ways, as we shall see, by which the bank's reserves may be affected, but for the present it is essential to mark only these.

Banks earn most of their profits either by receiving interest payments on government bonds or on other securities that they hold or by lending to private borrowers. The more securities the bank holds and the greater the amount it lends, the more it receives as interest. Hence a bank is generally anxious to increase its holdings of securities and to lend more — provided that it feels sure of being repaid. What then sets the limit on the amount it can lend or the amount of securities it can purchase? In order to answer this, we shall first have to see what happens when it lends — or, in other words, when it trades its IOU for one from the borrower.

CREDIT EXPANSION: THE INDIVIDUAL BANK

When a bank lends, the borrower does not ordinarily stuff his pockets with hundred-dollar bills, thank the manager, and leave. Instead, the bank, after accepting the borrower's note, which promises repayment at a certain date, gives him, not currency, but the right to write checks on, or otherwise make use of, a deposit equal to the amount of the loan minus the charge for interest. In other words, the lending bank creates a demand deposit in favor of the borrower.

Does this not mean that a bank can lend without limit since, after all, it takes only a very small amount of work by a bookkeeper to set up an account for the borrower? Unfortunately not, for there *is* a limit, or rather there are *two limits*. The obvious one is that as the bank lends more and more, its demand deposits increase. Then, since it is required by law to hold reserves equal to at least a certain percentage of its deposits, the amount of its reserves will ultimately set a limit on the amount it may lend. When its deposit liabilities are a mere $20,000, as they were in our last balance sheet, it needs deposits in the Federal Reserve Bank of at least $4,000, assuming the reserve ratio required is 20 per cent. Of course, since its reserves are now $420,000, this limit is far, far away; but it could be reached if the bank were to lend enough. However there is another limit on lending which operates much more quickly and this we must examine carefully.

When a bank lends, it adds the amount of the loan to its demand-deposit liabilities since the borrower is allowed to draw on his account to that amount (minus interest which is paid in advance). But surely if he borrows, he will want to make full use of this privilege because he must pay interest on the amount of his loans. Normally, he will spend the borrowed funds by writing checks, most of which are likely to go to people with accounts in *other* banks. Now we have already seen (Balance Sheet 5) that when a depositor writes a check on his account in favor of an individual whose account is in a different bank, the amount of the check is transferred through the Federal Reserve Bank and the reserves of the bank on which the check is drawn are reduced, while those of the receiving bank are increased. When the borrower writes checks on his newly created account, *the lending bank's reserves fall*, unless by a lucky chance the checks are given to firms or persons who keep their deposits in the lending bank. Thus, if a bank lends, say, $100,000, it is likely to lose reserves of about the same amount.

The effect on the bank's reserves will be much the same if the lender withdraws currency instead of writing checks. If he draws out a large amount in cash, the bank may have to call on the Federal Reserve Bank to replenish its stock of currency (see Balance Sheet 6). When a bank lends, it must therefore be prepared to have its reserves fall by the full amount of the loan. This sets a much more immediate limit to its lending powers than the rise in its demand-deposit liabilities. Let us see why.

Suppose that a businessman with an excellent credit standing comes to the bank and asks to borrow $420,000. The manager naturally appreciates the importance of getting this business; a good borrower is so much gold to the bank and to turn him down when the bank needs customers would probably damage the bank's earning ability for the future. So the manager agrees to make the loan and advises the bookkeeper to set up a checking account for the borrower.[3] After this operation, the accounts would be:

BALANCE SHEET 7(a)

Assets		Liabilities and Capital	
Cash	$ 100,000	Demand Deposits	$ 440,000*
Government		Capital Stock	5,000,000
Bonds	4,000,000		
Loans Due	420,000*		
Property	500,000		
Deposits in			
FRB	420,000		
	$5,440,000		$5,440,000

So far the bank's reserves would be more than adequate since it would need only $88,000 (= 20% of $440,000) in reserves and it has $420,000. But if the borrower were to write checks for the whole amount of his loan, as he might be expected to do, and if these checks were deposited for collection in other banks, our accounts would change alarmingly:

BALANCE SHEET 7(b)

Assets		Liabilities and Capital	
Cash	$ 100,000	Demand Deposits	$ 20,000*
Government		Capital Stock	5,000,000
Bonds	4,000,000		
Loans Due	420,000		
Property	500,000		
Deposits in			
FRB	0*		
	$5,020,000		$5,020,000

The bank's reserves would be deficient by $4,000, since it has none and it is required by law to have reserves of at least 20 per cent of $20,000. Thus, unless it could do something to increase its reserves, it could *not* safely lend as much as $420,000.

[3] To avoid problems of arithmetic, assume that the borrower pays the interest due when the loan is repaid.

How much, then, could it agree to lend without having to expose itself to such a situation?[4]

Going back to Balance Sheet 6 will provide a clue. From that we can determine that the bank had *excess* reserves of $416,000 (= $420,000 of available reserves minus the $4,000 required against its deposit liabilities). Let us say then that the businessman sought to borrow *$416,000* which is the amount by which its actual reserves exceed required reserves. The accounts would then show, assuming such a loan:

BALANCE SHEET 8(a)

Assets		Liabilities and Capital	
Cash	$ 100,000	Demand Deposits	$ 436,000*
Government		Capital Stock	5,000,000
Bonds	4,000,000		
Loans Due	416,000*		
Property	500,000		
Deposits in			
FRB	420,000		
	$5,436,000		$5,436,000

So far the bank's reserve position is of course more than comfortable. But the businessman, we can imagine, did not borrow in order to be able to show a large bank account. He borrowed to pay bills to his suppliers and others. So we suppose that he writes checks for the full amount of his loan and that they are all in favor of firms which keep their accounts elsewhere. Once the checks have been deposited and cleared, the account will show:

BALANCE SHEET 8(b)

Assets		Liabilities and Capital	
Cash	$ 100,000	Demand Deposits	$ 20,000*
Government		Capital Stock	5,000,000
Bonds	4,000,000		
Loans Due	416,000		
Property	500,000		
Deposits in			
FRB	4,000*		
	$5,020,000		$5,020,000

---

[4] Obviously, it is not a really bad situation because the bank could readily sell some of its bonds for cash and deposit the proceeds in "the Fed." But we are interested here in determining what its safe lending limit would be, assuming it does not want to do anything to correct a deficiency in its reserves. This is especially important because while *one* bank can perhaps increase its reserves, the same opportunity may not be available to *all* banks taken together. We shall see why later.

And the bank's reserves will be at the legal minimum. Hence we may conclude that although a bank cannot safely lend an amount greater than its excess reserves, it can lend up to that amount without threatening its ability to meet its reserve requirements.

CREDIT EXPANSION: THE BANKING SYSTEM

When a bank lends, it has to face the loss of its reserves; that fact, as we have seen, restricts its lending ability. But — and this point is of critical importance for an understanding of the banking *system* — whatever the lending bank *loses* in reserves *is gained by other banks.* When, as in our last balance sheet, its reserves decline by $416,000, those of other banks *increase* by a like amount. And when its lending ability is exhausted, as it is if its situation continues as in Balance Sheet 8(b), the lending ability of the other banks, which now have larger reserves, is increased — though not by quite so much.

How does it work? Let us suppose that another bank has made loans of $40,000 and the whole sum is transferred to our bank. We assume that the other bank was able to lend because it had excess reserves but the transfer of the $40,000 reduced its reserves, just as a similar transfer did for our bank. And now let us see what happens to our bank's accounts after the $40,000 has been collected:

BALANCE SHEET 9

Assets		Liabilities and Capital	
Cash	$ 100,000	Demand Deposits	$ 60,000*
Government		Capital Stock	5,000,000
Bonds	4,000,000		
Loans Due	416,000		
Property	500,000		
Deposits in			
FRB	44,000*		
	$5,060,000		$5,060,000

It has gained $40,000 in reserves. However, its *excess* reserves have not increased by the full amount because its deposit liabilities have also increased by $40,000. It now needs reserves of $12,000 and since its reserves are $44,000, its excess reserves are $32,000. It may therefore lend an additional $32,000.

The picture we have then is that a bank can lend up to the amount of its excess reserves. When it does so, at least some of the excess is transferred to other banks which can then expand their loans. However, even though their reserves rise by the same amount as that by which the reserves of the lending bank decline, the other banks are unable to expand their loans by this full sum because, when their reserves rise, so do their demand-deposit liabilities.

Still, it is clear that the banking system, as distinguished from a single bank, can expand loans by much more than the amount of total excess reserves. By how much may all the banks, taken together, expand their loans when they have excess reserves? To illustrate, let us suppose that banks have excess reserves of $1 million, that — to simplify the analysis — all banks are required to keep reserves of at least 20 per cent against their deposit liabilities, and that the public does not want to increase its holdings of cash. At the first stage, the banks which hold the excess reserves may lend $1 million.[5] Then, when these new borrowers write checks on their newly created deposits, the lending banks may expect to lose to other banks reserves equal to approximately $1 million. As the other banks find their reserves increased by $1 million, they find their demand deposits also increased by the same sum. Hence their *excess* reserves now come to only $800,000. The banks that made the loans — compare Balance Sheet 8(b) — will no longer have any excess reserves if the full amount of their loans is transferred to other banks. But the *other* banks will now have excess reserves of $800,000.

To put it differently, *total* reserves of the entire banking system are not affected on account of the loans but they are redistributed. However, demand deposits are now $1 million higher than formerly and, against this amount, $200,000 additional reserves must be kept. The

---

[5] After they do so, their demand deposits rise by $1 million so that they need $200,000 more reserves than before (20 per cent of $1 million). But this is not troublesome since, so long as the demand deposits are there, they have plenty of excess reserves to cover them. It is when the borrowers write checks on these new demand deposits and the checks on the lending banks are collected in favor of other banks that trouble may arise. Only then are the reserves of the lending banks reduced.

upshot is that while total reserves are the same, *excess* reserves fall from $1 million to $800,000 and they are held by different banks.

Successive stages in this process are easy to follow. The banks which now hold excess reserves of $800,000 can lend up to that amount so that their demand deposits increase by just as much. As checks are written on these new deposits, they are shifted to different banks and the lending banks find themselves with no excess reserves left. Other banks, however, now have new deposits of $800,000 and new reserves of $800,000 or *excess* reserves of $640,000. (Required reserves have risen by $160,000.) Hence loans can again be increased, this time by $640,000. Demand deposits rise by this amount and $128,000 more reserves are required against them. Excess reserves now fall to $512,000; and the process can go on still further. It will be seen that if the banking system possesses excess reserves of $1 million initially, it may lend originally $1 million and then $800,000 + $640,000 + $512,000 + $409,600, and so on, with each term equal to 80 per cent of the one preceding. The sum of all these terms is $5 million. Thus, if the required reserve ratio is 20 per cent, the banking system may expand loans (or more accurately, demand deposits) by five times the amount of its original excess reserves.[6]

We may conclude that, although no *single bank* can safely increase its loans by any more than its excess reserves — compare Balance Sheets 7(a) and 8(a) — the *banking system* as a whole can expand loans by a multiple of its excess reserves. As one bank lends, it, in a sense, *exports* excess reserves to other banks which in their turn become enabled to lend more. As they do so, they export reserves to still other banks. However, as banks lend more and more, demand-deposit liabilities grow and conse-

quently the amount of excess reserves falls, *even though the total reserves of the banking system do not change*. This, of course, eventually sets a limit upon further expansion.

If some banks with excess reserves refuse to expand their loans, they will not lose their reserves to other banks. Furthermore, other banks which do lend more are likely to lose some of their reserves to the non-lending banks so that the transferred reserves become, as it were, sterile. If sterile reserves grow in amount, the reserves available to the *lending banks* decline and their power to expand loans is checked more quickly. It follows that the banking system can expand loans to the full amount set out above only if *all* banks are willing to lend up to the full amount that their reserve position permits. With some unwilling to do this, the whole banking system is less able to expand loans.

BANK PURCHASES OF SECURITIES

A bank may also trade its own IOU for another by purchasing securities and giving their sellers checking accounts. If our bank, in the situation indicated in Balance Sheet 9, wanted to buy government bonds, it could pay for them by opening an account in favor of the sellers. If it bought $30,000 worth of government bonds, its position would be:

BALANCE SHEET 10

Assets		Liabilities and Capital	
Cash	$ 100,000	Demand Deposits	$ 90,000*
Government Bonds	4,030,000*	Capital Stock	5,000,000
Loans Due	416,000		
Property	500,000		
Deposits in FRB	44,000		
	$5,090,000		$5,090,000

The purchase of securities (not financed by cash) thus affects the accounts in the same way loans do, and the very factors that limit the bank's ability to lend also limit its ability to buy securities. Since, with increased deposit liabilities, it must face the likelihood of losing reserves, it cannot safely buy securities amounting to more than excess reserves. But since anything it loses from its own reserves goes to other banks, they in their turn are put in a stronger position to make loans or buy securities.

---

[6] The reader may be interested to develop the general rule. It is this: If the required reserve ratio is R and excess reserves are E, the banking system may expand its loans by E/R. In the case discussed above, the ratio was .2; the excess reserves were $1 million; hence the total possible expansion in loans was $1 million/0.2, or $5 million. In brief, the banking system as a whole can expand loans by a multiple of the original amount of its excess reserves and that multiple is the reciprocal of the required reserve ratio. (The reciprocal of 20 per cent — or one-fifth — is five, and five times $1 million equals $5 million.)

CREDIT CONTRACTION

When the banking system has excess reserves of a certain amount, banks can lend[7] much more than this amount. And when they lend, they create demand deposits — which, as we saw, are money. Hence, if banks generally come into possession of increased reserves, their ability to create money is enhanced. On the other hand, if their reserves decline, they are less able to create money. Indeed, they may be compelled to destroy it, for, just as making loans creates demand deposits, so the repayment of loans destroys demand deposits.

A borrower normally pays back a loan by a check drawn on his own account and the payment of this check *reduces* the bank's demand deposits by the amount repaid. Suppose a borrower repays a $30,000 loan. Since demand deposits are reduced, money has been detroyed:

BALANCE SHEET 11

Assets		Liabilities and Capital	
Cash	$ 100,000	Demand Deposits	$ 60,000*
Government		Capital Stock	5,000,000
Bonds	4,030,000		
Loans Due	386,000*		
Property	500,000		
Deposits in			
FRB	44,000		
	$5,060,000		$5,060,000

If our bank suffers a large loss in reserves, it will be compelled to call in loans and sell securities or, if loans are maturing, it will have to refuse to renew them. Let us suppose, for instance, that a depositor wrote a check for $42,000 on his account and paid it to someone who kept his account in a different bank:

BALANCE SHEET 12

Assets		Liabilities and Capital	
Cash	$ 100,000	Demand Deposits	$ 18,000*
Government		Capital Stock	5,000,000
Bonds	4,030,000		
Loans Due	386,000		
Property	500,000		
Deposits in			
FRB	2,000*		
	$5,018,000		$5,018,000

[7] This term will henceforth include the purchase of securities.

Since the bank's reserves are now inadequate, it must either acquire more reserves or reduce its demand deposits. We shall discuss in the next section how it may add to its reserves. For the moment, let us suppose that it does not take such a step but instead undertakes to reduce its demand deposits. Its present reserves are adequate to support only $10,000 in demand deposits, so it has to adopt measures to bring its demand deposits down by at least $8,000. It may do this by reducing either its loans or its security holdings by that amount. Quite probably it will do a little of both. If it allows loans of $4,000 to mature and sells $4,000 worth of securities to *its own* depositors:

BALANCE SHEET 13(a)

Assets		Liabilities and Capital	
Cash	$ 100,000	Demand Deposits	$ 10,000*
Government		Capital Stock	5,000,000
Bonds	4,026,000*		
Loans Due	382,000*		
Property	500,000		
Deposits in			
FRB	2,000		
	$5,010,000		$5,010,000

If instead it had sold $4,000 worth of securities to those who had accounts in other banks and had let $4,000 of loans mature, the end result would have been:

BALANCE SHEET 13(b)

Assets		Liabilities and Capital	
Cash	$ 100,000	Demand Deposits	$ 14,000*
Government		Capital Stock	5,000,000
Bonds	4,026,000*		
Loans Due	382,000*		
Property	500,000		
Deposits in			
FRB	6,000*		
	$5,014,000		$5,014,000

Here, though the selling bank gains reserves, it does so at the expense of other banks, for the buyers pay by checks against their accounts and the funds are transferred by the Federal Reserve Bank.

When reserves are inadequate, banks must reduce their demand-deposit liabilities. The required reduction will normally be a multiple of the amount by which the reserves are deficient. The analysis proceeds along the lines followed in determining the ability of the banking system to increase its total lending when it has excess reserves. But there is a difference: while banks are *enabled* to lend more freely when they hold excess reserves, they are *required* to reduce their demand deposits when they have inadequate reserves.

How the amount of their reserves is determined will be discussed in the next section.

SUMMARY

Demand deposits make up most of the money of the economy, and almost all the economy's business is carried on by the transfer of this kind of money. Banks create demand deposits when they lend or buy securities and destroy such deposits when their loans are repaid or when they sell securities. When they hold reserves that exceed the amounts required by law, they are able to lend more freely or to buy more securities. Because their interest return is likely to be greater if they expand their loans and security holdings, they are under inducement to do so. But a *single bank* cannot safely lend an amount greater than its excess reserves, though it can lend up to that amount without threatening its ability to meet its reserve requirements. It cannot lend more because it is likely to lose reserves equal to the full amount of its additional loan. Although any bank, considered individually, may not safely expand its loans and "investments" by an amount greater than its excess reserves, the *banking system* may do so by several times the amount of its excess reserves. Hence, if banks acquire additional excess reserves, they are able to increase the amount of money by several times as much as the additional excess reserves. When a single bank in a system lends, it has to face the loss of its reserves. But what it loses in reserves is gained by other banks. And when its lending ability is exhausted, the lending ability of other banks, now with larger reserves, is increased. The banking system can thus expand demand deposits by a multiple of its excess reserves, the particular multiple being the reciprocal of the reserve ratio.

When reserves are inadequate, banks have to reduce their demand deposits. To do so they are *compelled* to reduce loans or investments.

The process works the same way in contraction as it does in expansion. Although no one bank need reduce its demand deposits by more than the deficiency in its reserves, the banking system as a whole must reduce total loans and investments by several times the amount of the deficiency in reserves. Indeed, if reserves were just adequate to start with and were then reduced, the banks would be *compelled* to destroy money amounting to perhaps four or five times the amount of the deficiency in reserves. Again, the exact multiple is the reciprocal of the reserve ratio.

Power over reserves — or, more accurately, over excess reserves — thus gives conditional power over the amount of money. If the Federal Reserve Banks can reduce excess reserves — and, as we shall see, they can — they are able to *force* the commercial banks to reduce the amount of money in existence. If they can increase the reserves, they give an *incentive* to member banks to increase the amount of money.

II. THE FEDERAL RESERVE SYSTEM

The Federal Reserve System is responsible for the monetary health of the economy. It is able to discharge that responsibility because it can exercise some authority over the lending operations of member commercial banks. The latter are required by law to have reserves against their deposit liabilities, which they hold primarily in the form of deposits in the Federal Reserve Banks. It is our objective in the present section to examine in some detail the nature of the Federal Reserve System's control and the methods of exercising it.

METHODS OF CONTROL

The Federal Reserve Banks' control stems from their power to alter the excess reserves of member banks. Commercial banks *may* lend[8] more freely when their excess reserves are raised but they *must* reduce their loans when their reserves become deficient. If the Board of Governors of the Federal Reserve System

---

[8] References to commercial bank lending include both lending in the ordinary sense and the buying of securities.

decides that the amount of money should be increased, it can raise the excess reserves of the member banks so that the latter are able to lend more freely. If the Board of Governors wants to reduce the amount of money, it can drive member banks' reserves below the legal minimum and thereby compel them to call in loans. Power to alter the excess reserves of the member banks thus means power to influence the amount of money, no matter how the member banks feel about it. If the Federal Reserve System wants excess reserves to decline, the commercial banks can do nothing to prevent it; if it wants them to increase, the commercial banks find themselves willy-nilly with increased excess reserves. The Federal Reserve System can alter the size of member bank excess reserves in either of two ways: by changing the ratio of reserves that are required against a given volume of demand deposits, or by changing the actual volume of reserves which member banks hold.

Let us illustrate the first of these procedures. In January 1965 the member banks of the Federal Reserve System had demand-deposit liabilities of about $117.50 billion, against which they had to keep reserves of about 14.7 per cent. They also had time-deposit (savings account) liabilities of about $106.40 billion, against which they were required to hold reserves of only 4 per cent. Thus total reserves required were approximately $21.53 billion, while they actually had on hand reserves of $21.86 billion and hence excess reserves of approximately $0.33 billion. Their reserve position may be presented as follows:

Selected Items: All Member Banks, January 1965 *(in billions of dollars)*		
Deposits in Federal Reserve Banks $21.86[9]	Demand Deposits Time Deposits	$117.50 $106.40

Within limits, the Board of Governors of the Federal Reserve System may change the

[9] Actually, about $3 billion of the $21.86 billion were held in the form of vault cash rather than deposits in the Federal Reserve. However, for purposes of simplicity we will assume that all reserves are held in the form of deposits at the Federal Reserve.

reserve ratios required. What would have happened if the Board had wanted to induce the member banks to lend more freely and therefore had reduced the reserves required to, let us say, an average of 10 per cent for demand deposits and 3 per cent for time deposits? The member banks would have been required to hold reserves of $14.94 billion against their deposits — the sum of 10 per cent of $117.50 billion and 3 per cent of $106.40 billion. Their excess reserves would then have risen from $0.33 billion to $6.92 billion. But even with so great an expansion in excess reserves they would not necessarily have expanded loans. Such an increase in reserves would only have increased their *ability* to do so, not necessarily their *willingness*.

If, in contrast, the Federal Reserve System had wished to force the member banks to reduce the volume of outstanding loans, it could have raised reserve requirements. If the requirements had been raised to 18 per cent for demand deposits and 6 per cent for time deposits, member banks would then have had to maintain reserves of about $27.53 billion. Since they had only $21.86 billion on deposit with the Federal Reserve Banks, they would have had a deficiency of $5.67 billion in their reserves and therefore would have been forced to reduce their demand-deposit liabilities. This they could have done, as we have seen, by allowing loans to mature without renewal and by selling securities.

The Federal Reserve System has used this method of control rather sparingly, feeling perhaps that it is too powerful and blunt an instrument to use for short-run adjustments in bank-lending policies.

The Federal Reserve System may also take action to bring about a change in the actual amount of reserves which member banks possess. As we saw, member banks were required in January 1965 to hold reserves of $21.53 billion against their deposit liabilities but actually had $21.86 billion. If the Federal Reserve System had been able to increase these reserves to $23 billion, member banks would have held excess reserves of $1.47 billion, instead of the $0.33 billion they had, and this growth in their excess reserves might have induced some of them to lend more freely. Or if, to consider the opposite situation, the Federal Reserve System had taken steps to reduce the reserves of the member banks by $2 billion to a total of $19.86 billion, their reserves would have been deficient by $1.67 billion and the banks would have been compelled to reduce their demand deposits. It is clear that the Federal Reserve System can affect member bank lending operations by changing the actual volume of reserves, as well as by changing the required reserve ratios. We shall now consider the two methods by which the Federal Reserve System can alter the actual volume of reserves of the member banks.

OPEN-MARKET OPERATIONS

First let us analyze "open-market operations." A commercial bank pays for the securities it purchases by opening a deposit in the name of the seller.[10] When a Federal Reserve Bank buys securities, it does the same thing — it pays for them by a check drawn on itself. If it buys the securities *directly from member banks*, their reserve deposits are increased, for they have the sums they receive added to their deposits in the Federal Reserve Bank. If the checks are for $1 billion, member bank deposits in the Federal Reserve Bank increase by a like amount. We can see this more clearly by setting up a simple balance sheet for all member banks which will present the situation both before and after the purchase. (Once again, in order to facilitate comparison, the items that are changed by the step under discussion will be

BALANCE SHEET 1

All Member Banks —
Before Federal Reserve Bank
Purchase of Securities
(in billions of dollars)

Loans and Investments	$79	Demand Deposits	$100
Deposits in FRB[11]	21		

[10] It comes to the same thing if the commercial bank pays for them by means of a check drawn against itself. The seller gets the check, deposits it in his bank and total deposits rise.

[11] There are other assets such as bank furniture and equipment which need not be set out in this balance sheet or in those that follow.

marked with an asterisk.) Let us assume that member banks have a reserve requirement of 20 per cent.

After the Federal Reserve Bank has purchased $1 billion worth of securities from the member banks, their combined accounts are as follows:

BALANCE SHEET 2

All Member Banks —
After Federal Reserve Bank
Purchase of Securities
(in billions of dollars)

Loans and Investments	$78*	Demand Deposits	$100
Deposits in FRB	22*		

Since their demand-deposits liabilities are not changed, member banks do not *require* additional reserves and yet their reserves have actually gone up by $1 billion. Hence, if they had $1 billion in excess reserves before, they would now hold $2 billion in excess reserves.

If the Federal Reserve Bank buys securities *from the public*, rather than from the banks, the excess reserves of member banks will be affected in the same way, but to a somewhat lesser extent. Suppose as before that the Federal Reserve Bank purchases $1 billion worth of securities on the open market, this time from the non-bank public, and pays for them by check. Private individuals and firms receive checks totaling $1 billion drawn on the Federal Reserve Bank. As the checks are deposited in commercial banks, the deposit liabilities of these banks increase by $1 billion. They in turn send the checks to the Federal Reserve Bank, which pays by raising member bank deposits in the Federal Reserve Bank by $1 billion. The resulting Balance Sheet 3 for the member banks is shown below:[12]

BALANCE SHEET 3

All Member Banks —
After Federal Reserve Bank
Purchase From Public
(in billions of dollars)

Loans and Investments	$79	Demand Deposits	$101*
Deposits in FRB	22*		

[12] Balance Sheet 1 illustrates the original situation.

If the reserve requirement is 20 per cent and member banks had excess reserves of $1 billion before the purchase, they now have excess reserves of $1.8 billion.

Whether the Federal Reserve System buys directly from the member banks or from the public, the actual reserves of member banks rise by the full amount of purchase. If the securities are bought from member banks, the deposit liabilities of these banks are unaffected, whereas if they are bought from the public, member bank deposit liabilities also grow by the same amount as their reserves. This means that even though the actual reserves of the member banks rise by the same amount in both instances, their *excess* reserves increase by *less* in the latter case than in the former, for notwithstanding the increase in reserves, member banks are required to hold higher reserves against their now increased deposit liabilities.

When the Federal Reserve System *sells* securities, the reserves of member banks decline and excess reserves are lowered. If it sells to member banks, the buyers pay from their deposits in the Reserve Banks and their excess reserves fall by the full amount of the transaction. If the Federal Reserve System sells directly to the public, the buyers normally pay by checks drawn on commercial banks. When these checks are collected, the deposit liabilities of the member banks are reduced and their reserves fall by the same amount. Their *excess* reserves do not fall by quite so much as the transaction, however, since their deposit liabilities are now reduced as well.

The effectiveness of this measure for reducing member bank reserves is limited when the Federal Reserve Banks hold only a small sum in government securities. In December 1939, for example, member banks had excess reserves of $5.2 billion. But at that date the Federal Reserve Banks held only $2.5 billion worth of government securities. It is obvious that, even if they had sold all their securities, excess reserves would have remained very high.

When the Federal Reserve Banks buy or sell securities or, to give the process its technical name, engage in open-market operations, they do so on their own initiative. Their motive is to raise or lower the reserves of member banks and in that way to influence the member banks toward an easier or tighter lending policy. This in turn results in the creation, or destruction, of money. And it must be emphasized that the commercial banks are unable to do anything to offset these measures. If the Federal Reserve System wants to reduce the reserves of the member banks, it can do so by selling securities.

And while any single member bank may succeed in avoiding a reduction in its reserves by selling securities to other banks, or to individuals who have accounts in other banks, if it does so the reserves of the other banks will fall even more than they would have otherwise. Total member bank reserves will change inescapably by the value of the securities bought or sold by the Federal Reserve Banks. Furthermore, by raising the price at which it will buy, the Federal Reserve System can always find someone willing to sell securities to it and similarly, by lowering the price at which it will sell, it can always find someone to buy securities from it. Since it is not in business to make a profit, the Federal Reserve System is free to change its buying and selling prices as it wishes.

Hence open-market operations are one means, and generally an effective means, by which the Federal Reserve System can control the size of member bank reserves. Of all of its instruments, it is the one most frequently used, being employed almost continuously to make day-to-day adjustments in member bank reserve positions in accordance with the Federal Reserve System's judgment of whether bank lending should be encouraged or discouraged.

FEDERAL RESERVE REDISCOUNTING

The Federal Reserve Banks may also exercise control by varying the terms on which member banks can rediscount and borrow. When a commercial bank lends, it receives from the borrower a note which bears his promise to repay at a designated date in the future a larger sum than he actually receives. He may, for example, have to agree to repay the bank $100,000 in a year in order to get $94,000 today. Such a note is said to be *discounted* by the bank at 6 per cent. The note is, of course regarded by the bank as an asset, like such other promises to pay as government bonds or industrial securities. If the bank holds the note for one year, it can demand $100,000 from the lender. Obviously, it is not a piece of paper one would throw away.

The bank may also use the note to build up its reserves. It can take it to a Federal Reserve Bank and ask to have it *rediscounted*. When this is done, the Federal Reserve Bank takes over the note and gives the member bank $100,000 minus the amount of the rediscount. If the note still has six months to run and if the Federal Reserve Bank's rediscount rate is 4 per cent, the member bank receives $98,000. Since it undertook to have the note rediscounted in order to build up its reserves, it will take payment by having that sum added to its deposit in the Federal Reserve Bank. On its balance sheet there will be a reduction in its loans and an increase in its deposits with the Federal Reserve Bank. Obviously its reserve position has become stronger.

When notes are rediscounted, the initiative comes from the member banks. Nevertheless, the Federal Reserve Banks exercise definite control over rediscounting, essentially by controlling the rediscount rate. The higher the rate, the smaller the amount given to member banks for a rediscounted note. For instance, if the rate had not been 4 per cent in the example above but 6 per cent, the member bank would have received only $97,000, instead of $98,000. When the rate is high, then, member banks are discouraged from rediscounting. Hence, by manipulating the rediscount rate, the Federal Reserve System is able to encourage or discourage the use of this method of raising reserves. In addition, if a particular bank rediscounts too frequently, the Federal Reserve Bank may also remind it that rediscounting is a "privilege" and not a "right."

Member banks want to rediscount only when they seek higher reserves; otherwise they have no reason for doing so. When they have excess reserves, they are not tempted to rediscount, no matter how low is the rediscount rate. Control over the rediscount rate, therefore, can serve no purpose unless member banks chronically need larger reserves. During the 1920's, when commercial banks habitually rediscounted notes with the Federal Reserve Banks, changes in the rediscount rate had important effects on

the size of member bank reserves. During the 1930's and much of the 1940's, when member banks generally had substantial excess reserves, rediscounting was rarely used so that changes in the rediscount rate were of minor importance. In the past two decades rediscounting has again become an important source of member bank reserves and the rediscount rate has regained a prominent position in the operations of the Federal Reserve System.

Finally, the commercial banks in recent years have made greater use than formerly of the willingness of the Federal Reserve System to lend to them directly on their own notes instead of on customers' notes. In this kind of operation, a commercial bank's liabilities are increased because it now owes the amount of its notes directly; but its assets, in the form of loans due, are not reduced. As with rediscounting, it gets the proceeds in the form of an increase in its reserves or, in other words, of its deposits with the Federal Reserve Banks. Also as with "rediscounting," the initiative for this kind of action comes from the commercial banks.

A good deal of attention is given by some economists to the "free reserve position" of the commercial banks. It is measured by the difference between their excess reserves and the amount of their borrowings from the Federal Reserve System — whether direct or in the form of rediscounted paper. When it becomes negative it means that commercial banks' excess reserves are less than their debt to the Federal Reserve System and this is taken generally to signify that the commercial banks are under pressure to reduce their own loans to the public, even though they have "excess reserves."

In summary: The Federal Reserve Banks can control member bank excess reserves, and hence their lending policy, by varying the reserve ratios required, by buying or selling securities, and by changing the rediscount rate. These methods are sometimes ineffective, as when member banks are not rediscounting or when the Reserve Banks hold only a small amount of government securities. Moreover, as we shall see, the Reserve Banks are not able to employ without limit these methods to build up member bank reserves because of the restrictions set on their own activities by the Federal Reserve Act.

We turn now to the rules by which the Reserve Banks are governed.

THE FEDERAL RESERVE BANKS

Just as member banks have to keep reserves against their demand- and time-deposit liabilities, so the Federal Reserve Banks have to keep reserves against certain of their liabilities. The chief of these liabilities has already been referred to: the deposits which constitute the reserves of the member banks. As your deposit in the bank is a liability from the bank's point of view, so your bank's deposit in the Federal Reserve Bank is a liability from the point of view of the Federal Reserve System. Until 1965 the Federal Reserve Banks had to keep reserves against the deposits of their member banks of at least 25 per cent; that rule has since been amended and no reserves are now required.

The other important "liability" of the Federal Reserve Banks, in terms of the amount outstanding, is the Federal Reserve Notes in circulation. We have already seen that these notes, which are issued by the Federal Reserve Banks, promise that a note "is redeemable in lawful money at the United States Treasury, or at any Federal Reserve Bank." That statement marks them as a liability of the Federal Reserve Banks, although it is not one which should worry the "Fed" very seriously. Nevertheless, the law requires reserves of at least 25 per cent against the amount of Federal Reserve Notes outstanding. (Many economists wonder what the purpose of this rule really is. It has no effect on the value of money; it is unlikely to influence policy — unless management is very foolish. In short, it appears to be nothing but an expensive form of "window dressing.")

The reserves which the Federal Reserve Banks have to keep must be in the form of gold, or rather of gold certificates, which are essentially warehouse receipts for the gold.[13]

[13] The law also specifies that the Federal Reserve System must hold additional assets as reserves against the Federal Reserve Notes outstanding, these being sufficient to total 100 per cent when combined with the gold certificates; the additional reserves must be in the form of government securities or rediscounted paper. Thus the total of the government securities, eligible paper, and gold certificates held as reserves against the Federal Reserve Notes is 100 per cent, with at least 25 per cent of the total in the form of gold certificates.

(The gold itself is owned by the U.S. Treasury, which issues a gold certificate to the Federal Reserve System, dollar for dollar against the gold it owns.) These reserve requirements impose limits on the actions of the Federal Reserve System, although not very rigid ones, since the Board of Governors of the Federal Reserve System may suspend the reserve requirements in emergencies and Congress can always change the law.

We can see the function of the reserve requirements most clearly by analyzing the items in the balance sheet of the Federal Reserve Banks.

BALANCE SHEET 4

All Federal Reserve Banks: End of May 1965
(in billions of dollars)

Assets		Liabilities	
Gold Certificates	$14.0	Federal Reserve	
U.S. Government		Notes Outstanding	$34.4
Securities	38.3	Deposits	17.5

At the end of May 1965 the Federal Reserve Banks had to have reserves in the form of gold certificates of at least $8.6 billion against the Federal Reserve Notes outstanding. Since actually they had $14.0 billion in gold certificates, they had excess reserves of about $5.4 billion.[14]

FEDERAL RESERVE NOTES

When commercial banks need more currency, they get it by calling on the Federal Reserve Banks — that is, by drawing cash against their accounts with the Federal Reserve Banks, just as you or I might draw cash out of our own accounts. Where then does a Federal Reserve Bank get the currency? It prints it.[15] When it transfers the notes to the member

[14] In 1944 and earlier, reserve requirements for the Federal Reserve Banks were much higher: *40 per cent* in the form of gold certificates against Federal Reserve Notes and *35 per cent* against member bank deposits in the Federal Reserve Banks. If these rates had been effective in May 1965, the Reserve Banks would have had to reduce member bank reserves or Federal Reserve Notes in circulation *or have had to have the law changed.* The reader should apply these ratios to the data for May 1965 given in Balance Sheet 4.

[15] More accurately, it is printed, by the Bureau of Engraving and Printing of the United States Treasury, for the Federal Reserve Banks.

banks, its liabilities, in the form of Federal Reserve Notes outstanding, are increased, for these notes in the hands of the public represent "claims" that can be made against it.

When commercial banks have on hand more currency than they need, they send some back to the Federal Reserve Banks and their accounts in the Federal Reserve Banks rise. From the point of view of the latter, such an increase means increased deposit liabilities to the member banks. Total liabilities, however, remain the same. The Federal Reserve Notes are liabilities (IOUs) of the Federal Reserve Banks and assets (cash) to anyone else who holds them. But these notes, in the possession of the Federal Reserve Banks, are regarded as so much paper.[16] If they are not crumpled and worn, they are stored against the day when member banks may want them again. Otherwise they are destroyed. But when they come back to a Federal Reserve Bank, the reduction in its liability for Federal Reserve Notes outstanding offsets the increased liability created by the increase in member bank deposits.

Let us now trace the effects of a rise in the circulation of Federal Reserve Notes on the balance sheets of both the member banks and the Federal Reserve Banks. The commercial banks know that, with the approach of Christmas, currency withdrawals will be large. Let us say that they expect net withdrawals of $1 billion in the four weeks proir to Christmas. How will these withdrawals affect the balance sheet of the member banks and of the Federal Reserve Banks? Suppose that initially their accounts are as follows:

BALANCE SHEET 5(a)

All Member Banks, November 1
(in billions of dollars)

Assets		Liabilities	
Cash	$ 0.5	Demand Deposits	100.0
Deposits in FRB	16.0		

BALANCE SHEET 5(b)

Federal Reserve Banks, November 1
(in billions of dollars)

Assets		Liabilities	
Gold Certificates	$14.0	Federal Reserve Notes Outstanding	36.0
		Member Bank Deposit	16.0

In anticipation of withdrawals during November, the commercial banks request $1 billion in currency and, as they acquire it, the two Balance Sheets 5(a) and (b) just given will alter thus:

BALANCE SHEET 6(a)

All Member Banks, November 30
(in billions of dollars)

Assets		Liabilities	
Cash	$ 1.5*	Demand Deposits	$100.0
Deposits in FRB	15.0*		

BALANCE SHEET 6(b)

Federal Reserve Banks, November 30
(in billions of dollars)

Assets		Liabilities	
Gold Certificates	$14.0	Federal Reserve Notes Outstanding	$37.0*
		Member Bank Deposit	15.0*

Then, when the public withdraws the $1 billion of currency from the commercial banks, the accounts of these banks are again changed:

BALANCE SHEET 7

All Member Banks, December 20
(in billions of dollars)

Assets		Liabilities	
Cash	$ 0.5*	Demand Deposits	$99.0*
Deposits in FRB	15.0		

The balance sheet of the Federal Reserve Banks will not be altered by these last withdrawals. The public now holds more currency but its demand deposits have fallen by the same amount. The member banks have smaller reserves but their deposit liabilities are likewise lower. The Federal Reserve Bank has exchanged one kind of liability, deposits of member banks, for another, Federal Reserve Notes.

After Christmas the whole process is reversed. The public no longer wants to hold so much cash. Merchants normally decide at this time to deposit some of their surplus currency and the commercial banks, since they do not need it all in their tills, send it back to the Federal Reserve Banks. Consequently, both balance sheets are altered, at each step, in the opposite direction to that indicated above.

THE FLOW OF GOLD

The banking system is affected when gold enters or leaves the country or when gold, newly mined in this country, is sold to the government. When a Federal Reserve Bank — or, in the final analysis, the Treasury of the United States — acquires gold, member bank deposits and reserves are increased. And whether the gold comes from abroad or from domestic mines, the effects on the banking system are essentially the same. Let us suppose that a United States commercial bank acquires a claim in a foreign country through an American exporter who, having sold goods abroad, has been paid by a check drawn on a foreign bank. If he then deposits the check in his own bank, the bank has a claim on a foreign bank which might be met by the payment of gold. At the same time, of course, member bank deposit liabilities are raised. When the gold comes in, the commercial bank sends it to a Federal Reserve Bank and is paid by an increase in its deposits in the Federal Reserve Bank. The Reserve Bank then sends the gold to the United States Treasury, which takes title to it, and in exchange the Treasury gives gold certificates to the Federal Reserve System. These gold certificates are, by law, as we have seen, the reserves of the Federal Reserve Banks. Thus the import of gold creates a chain of effects: Deposit liabilities of member banks are increased and the banks acquire claims to be met in gold; member bank reserves are increased by the amount of gold imported and hence the deposit liabilities of the Federal Reserve Bank are increased by this amount; and finally, the reserves of the Federal Reserve Bank rise. When gold

leaves the country, which has been by far the more common situation over the 1950's and the first half of the 1960's, the effects are just the opposite: The reserves of both the Federal Reserve Banks and the member banks fall.

Thus, between 1952 and 1965, about $9 billion of gold was sent out of the United States to other countries. We will examine the causes and consequences of this gold outflow later. For the moment, it is sufficient to point out that it has led to a $9 billion decline in the reserves of the Federal Reserve Banks and would have led to a similar decline in member bank reserves and deposits if offsetting actions — mainly in the form of open-market operations and changes in reserve requirements — had not been taken by the Federal Reserve System.

It is advisable at this point to review the effects of the banking system's various activities on the items that enter into the balance sheets of both member banks and Federal Reserve Banks. When the Federal Reserve Banks buy securities from the public, member bank deposit liabilities and member bank reserves increase by the amount of the purchase. Similarly, the security holdings of the Reserve Banks and their deposit liabilities go up. When the public increases its holdings of Federal Reserve Notes, deposit liabilities of the member banks and their reserves both fall. Moreover, the deposit liabilities of the Federal Reserve Banks decline, while Federal Reserve Notes outstanding, which are liabilities of the Reserve Banks, increase. Finally, when gold flows into the country, member bank reserves and deposit liabilities increase; the Federal Reserve Banks gain gold certificates and their deposit liabilities also rise. Naturally, when the Federal Reserve Banks sell securities, or reduce Federal Reserve Notes outstanding, or when we lose gold, the effects are just the opposite.

SUMMARY

We should now have a clear picture of the operations of the Federal Reserve System. It can affect the willingness of member banks to lend and invest by changing the actual amount of member bank reserves — by open-market operations or altering the rediscount rate — or by changing the required reserve ratios which member banks must meet.

While the Federal Reserve System's control over the member banks is not absolute, it can, if it pursues its policies vigorously enough, usually force the reserves of the member banks down far enough to compel them to reduce their lending. On the other hand, the Federal Reserve System is not as powerful in stimulating an expansion in lending. The most it can do is give the member banks a larger volume of excess reserves. But while this *permits* mem-

ber banks to lend more freely, it does not *compel* them to do so. They must first find satisfactory borrowers who want to borrow.

The Federal Reserve System is more likely to be successful, then, in checking an increase in bank lending when the demand for loans is strong than in stimulating an increase when the demand for loans is weak. The monetary system seems to be well provided with efficient brakes, but its accelerator is rather uncertain.[17]

[17] Whether the brakes are actually as efficient as they seem to be will be examined further in Part 4.

3

A DOLLAR IS A DOLLAR IS A DOLLAR*

An Exchange of Letters

A monetary system, and especially ours, is not a structure which would appeal to the logician or engineer seeking to find the reason for and purpose of each part. Rather, it is a product of historical circumstance, each event leaving its vestigial remnant in some form or other. The concept of "lawful money" as used today is such a product, cluttering our monetary system to give evidence of the heritage of the past and defying reason in terms of present-day needs. As such it now serves mainly as a source of embarrassment to the Treasury and the butt of such humor as Money and Banking teachers may possess, as is illustrated by the selection below.

The following beguiling exchange of letters took place between the United States Treasury and a curious citizen of Cleveland.

December 9, 1947

Honorable John W. Snyder
Secretary of the Treasury
Washington, D.C.

Dear Sir:

I am sending you herewith via Registered Mail one ten-dollar Federal Reserve note. On this note is inscribed the following:

"*This note is legal tender for all debts,*

* From *American Affairs*, Vol. X, No. 2 (April, 1948). Reprinted by the courtesy of the publisher.

public and private, and is redeemable in lawful money at the United States Treasury or at any Federal Reserve Bank."

In accordance with this statement, will you send to me $10.00 in lawful money.

Very truly yours,
A. F. DAVIS

Encl.
Registered Mail
Return Receipt Requested

* * *

TREASURY DEPARTMENT
FISCAL SERVICE
WASHINGTON 25

Office of
Treasury of The United States
In replying please quote JLS:mw

December 11, 1947

Mr. A. F. Davis
12818 Colt Road
Cleveland 1, Ohio

Dear Mr. Davis:

Receipt is acknowledged of your letter of December 9th with enclosure of one ten dollar ($10.) Federal Reserve Note.

In compliance with your request two five-dollar United States notes are transmitted herewith.

Very truly yours,
(s) M. E. SLINDEE
Acting Treasurer

Enclosures.

* * *

December 23, 1947

Mr. M. E. Slindee
Acting Treasurer
Treasury Department
Fiscal Service
Washington 25, D.C.

Dear Sir:

Receipt is hereby acknowledged of two $5.00 United States notes, which we interpret from your letter to be considered as lawful money. Are we to infer from this that the Federal Reserve notes are not lawful money?

I am enclosing one of the $5.00 notes which you sent to me. I note that it states on the face,

"The United States of America will pay to the bearer on demand five dollars."

I am hereby demanding five dollars.

Very truly yours,
A. F. DAVIS

A.F.Davis:NW
Enclosure
Registered Mail
Return Receipt Requested

* * *

TREASURY DEPARTMENT
FISCAL SERVICE
WASHINGTON 25

Office of Treasurer of
the United States

December 29, 1947

In Replying Please Quote JLS:mw

Mr. A. F. Davis
12818 Colt Road
Cleveland 1, Ohio

Dear Mr. Davis:

Receipt is acknowledged of your letter of December 23rd, transmitting one $5. United States Note with a demand for payment of five dollars.

You are advised that the term "lawful money" has not been defined in federal legislation. It first came into use prior to 1933 when some United States currency was not legal tender but could be held by national banking associations as lawful money reserves. Since the act of May 12, 1933, as amended by the Joint Resolution of June 5, 1933, makes all coins and currency of the United States legal tender and the Joint Resolution of August 27, 1935, provides for the exchange of United States coin or currency for other types of such coin or currency, the term "lawful currency" no longer has such special significance.

The $5. United States note received with your letter of December 23rd is returned herewith.

Very truly yours,
(s) M. E. SLINDEE
Acting Treasurer

Enclosure.

Editorial Postscript: In 1964 the inscriptions "Will pay to the bearer on demand" and "Is redeemable in lawful money" were dropped because, according to Deputy Treasurer W. T. Howell, "they have not had a significant meaning for many years." They were deleted, Mr. Howell said, "in order to avoid a complete absurdity."

4

THE GIRO, THE COMPUTER, AND CHECKLESS BANKING*

Federal Reserve Bank of Richmond

Our present check payment system is not the only system capable of doing the job. Indeed, it may not even be the most efficient system currently in existence. What our payments arrangements may look like in the computerized world of the year 2000 is described below.

A speedy and efficient payments system is essential to the functioning of a modern economy. In the United States and England, as in most of the Anglo-American world, most payments are made in currency and coin or by checks drawn on commercial banks. While this system has functioned remarkably well over the years, the growing volume of payments promises to create serious problems in the transportation and processing of checks. The cost to the public of operating the check clearing and collection system is estimated at about $3.3 billion annually, and this cost is almost certain to increase as the volume of payments increases. Moreover, while the check payments system is quite accurate, the growing cost and sometimes considerable delays in collecting checks impairs the usefulness of checkbook money as a medium of exchange.

Some informed observers predict drastic changes in the payments system of the United States in the coming years. These changes would almost eliminate checks and greatly reduce the use of currency. In the payments system envisaged, the average United States citizen may pay his monthly bills to the doctor, the utility company, the mortgage company, and others, not by mailing checks to each of them but by instructing (perhaps by telephone) the bank holding his deposit account to transfer specified amounts from his account

* From *Monthly Review*, Federal Reserve Bank of Richmond (April, 1966). Reprinted by the courtesy of the Federal Reserve Bank of Richmond.

to the accounts of designated payees. He may receive his salary payment in the form of a notice from his bank that the amount has been added to his account. When his wife goes shopping, she may make payment by using a special telephone arrangement to instruct a bank's computer to transfer the appropriate amount from the family bank account to that of the store.

These and even more dramatic changes in the payments system may result from combining modern electronic data processing techniques with the so-called "giro transfer" system which has been used in some continental European countries for years but which has been largely untried in the United States. The giro system has characteristics that make it particularly suitable for the use of computers, although it does not require their use. In fact, the European systems operated effectively for many years without computers. A brief description of the giro transfer system may indicate some of the possibilities inherent in it.

NATURE OF GIRO TRANSFER SYSTEMS

The giro system possesses a number of fundamental characteristics in common with the check payments system. Basically it involves deposit balances held by individuals and businesses with some institution and systematic arrangements for the transfer of these balances from payer to payee. It differs from the checking system chiefly in the manner of effecting these transfers. Under the familiar checking system, the payer delivers to the payee a written order, i.e., a check, directing the institution holding his account to pay a certain sum of money at sight. The check may pass through numerous hands, and through two or more banks and/or a clearing house, before it is presented to the drawee bank. In the typical giro transaction, the payer delivers to the drawee institution an order directing it to transfer a specified sum from his account to that of the payee and to advise the payee of the transfer. Thus giro transfers are more direct and involve both less time and less paper handling than ordinary check transfers.

Giro transfers are simplest when both the payer and the payee have accounts at the same institution. They can be made to work with comparable efficiency, however, where the payer and the payee use different institutions. Numerous institutions, for example, may be members of a common giro system which incorporates arrangements for automatic transfers between member institutions as well as for transfers between the customers of these institutions. Such arrangements exist today in some European countries. It is reasonably clear that existing facilities for clearing checks between banks in this country could easily be converted into an effective giro system embracing most, or even all, banks.

As they stand today, the giro systems abroad center around a variety of institutions. Some are operated by the postal service, some by central banks, and some by commercial banks. Others center around facilities provided by savings banks, by municipalities or by credit cooperatives. In some European countries, as many as four or five separate giro systems operate side by side.

The postal giro is perhaps the most important of the giro systems found in the continental European countries. In many of these countries, commercial banks cater primarily to business and industrial accounts and do not, as a rule, offer the special individual checking account services so common in the United States. The postal services of these countries, with their numerous offices, quite naturally became involved in transfers between individuals, and the postal giro was largely an outgrowth of these circumstances. Postal giros offer nation-

wide coverage, but it should be noted in this connection that equally extensive coverage is possible, and in some countries already exists, under giros operated by systems of private commercial banks.

Foreign giro systems provide an efficient, convenient, and inexpensive payments system not only for individuals but for many businesses as well. This method of payment is particularly attractive to insurance companies, public utilities, mail order houses, and other businesses regularly receiving large numbers of remittances. These organizations are saved much of the work and expense of handling and banking large quantities of checks and currency, and they may well receive credit for funds sooner than if checks were used. For those who must make regular remittances, such as mortgage payments or insurance premiums, it is frequently possible to arrange for automatic transfer of specified amounts at regular intervals.

INTEROFFICE TRANSFERS

Giro systems usually have numerous offices scattered over wide geographical areas. This is particularly true of the postal systems as shown in the diagram on this page. Accordingly, regional offices are usually maintained for centralized record keeping and for making

Interoffice Transfer in the Japanese Postal Giro System

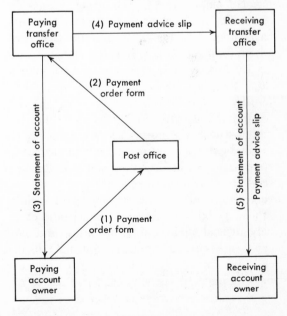

interoffice transfers. The accompanying diagram, based on the Japanese postal transfer system, shows how funds may be quickly transferred over considerable distances through the use of regional transfer centers.

In the Japanese system, all post offices handle transfer transactions, but 28 regional transfer offices maintain records of individual accounts and actually effect the transfers. A person desiring to open an account applies to any post office, pays a small fee, and upon approval by the regional transfer office an account is opened in his name at that regional office. He may make deposits to the account by filling out a form and paying in the amount (plus a fee) to a post office. The post office then sends a copy of the form to the regional office and the amount is credited to the individual's account. The regional office then sends the owner a statement of account together with the original deposit slip.

The diagram illustrates how transfers are made between accounts held in different regional transfer offices. In the first step, the payer submits a regular payment order form to his post office, stating the amount of the payment and the name and account number of the payee. The post office forwards the payment order to the payer's regional transfer office, which deducts the amount from his account, sends him a new statement of account, and forwards a payment advice to the payee's regional office. The payee's regional transfer office adds the amount to the account of the payee and sends him a copy of the payment advice form together with a new statement of his account. If time is an important consideration, the payer may request a telegraphic transfer.

Commercial bank giro systems vary greatly, with particular organizations determined primarily by the size and structure of the banking system and by the degree of centralization desired. In most cases there are few problems involved in handling transfers between branches of a single bank, although the exact procedure may depend upon the organization and accounting system of the bank. But methods of effecting transfers between offices of different banks are greatly influenced by the degree of centralization. The most highly centralized systems have common central institutions that manage the entire giro service as well as the funds deposited in individual accounts. On the other hand, some systems have no central institution at all, and each branch receiving a giro order is responsible for making transfers to other banks and branches that may be involved. In these systems, transfers between banks may be settled through correspondent balances or through clearing house settlements.

The organization of the Swedish Bank giro falls somewhat between these extremes. All commercial banks in Sweden contribute to a central giro institution located in Stockholm, but individual accounts are kept at branch offices and sums deposited are administered by these offices. The central institution settles transactions between banks and maintains central offices, but it does not control the money it handles. There is a daily settlement between the central institution and each bank that is a member of the system.

CHARGES FOR GIRO SERVICES

Charges for giro services vary from country to country and from system to system. The proposed charges for the British Post Office giro, which is now in the process of being established, are probably representative of charges by postal giro systems generally. In the British system, there will be no charge for regular transfers of funds such as those described above. Deposits by an account holder to his own account will also be free, but deposits by non-account holders will involve a fee of about ten cents. Fees on withdrawals by account holders or on cash payments to third parties will depend upon the amounts involved, with payments over 50 pounds to cost about 28 cents. Postage to the giro will be free.

Because many transactions are free and only nominal fees are charged on some others, income from charges is expected to cover only a relatively small part of the operating costs of the British system. Interest is not paid on deposits, however, and it is hoped that the investment of accumulated funds will provide sufficient income to cover the difference between charges and costs. Whether this hope will be realized will depend to a considerable extent upon the number of users of the system, the average size of the accounts, and the activity in the accounts.

ELECTRONIC DATA PROCESSING

Advocates of the development of a giro transfer system for the United States base their arguments chiefly on the grounds that this system possesses characteristics which make it particularly suitable for the use of electronic data processing equipment. Unlike check payments systems, transactions in the giro system take place entirely within the individual bank, or if more than one bank is involved, entirely within the banking system. Thus, when a depositor instructs his bank to make payment to another giro account holder, his bank receives all the information needed to complete the transaction — the identification of both the payer and the payee, the amount to be paid, and the time at which payment is to be made.

Proponents of the giro system maintain that the entire transfer process could be handled almost instantaneously by computers. The payer's instructions to his bank could be fed into the bank's computer and if both the payer and payee are depositors of that bank the computer could perform all of the operations necessary to make the transfer, including the printing out of confirmation to the payer and advice of payment to the payee. If the payer and payee have accounts at different banks, the computer at the payer's bank could perform the operations necessary for its records and transmit the information to the second bank's computer, either directly or through a central institution, and settlement between the banks could be made as described above.

Although the transition to a completely computerized giro transfer system undoubtedly would not be without its pain and problems, the development of such a system appears to be entirely within present technical capabilities. Banks already make extensive use of data processing equipment in their operations, and a push-button type of telephone has been developed which permits a customer to communicate directly with his bank's computer.

Some possible applications of equipment already available are described in a recent issue of the Bell Telephone Magazine. Making use of the push-button telephone, the housewife of the future may pay the family bills at any time of day or night simply by tapping out instructions to her bank's computer. She may ascertain her account balance by making inquiry of the computer and the information will be provided to her in spoken form. When shopping, she may use a card obtained from her bank which, when inserted in the store's special telephone, will permit her to make payment by instructing the bank's computer to transfer the proper amount to the store's account. Or she may obtain a credit card from her bank which would permit purchases to be charged to a convenience or instalment credit account at her bank, thereby eliminating the necessity of opening charge accounts at numerous establishments and carrying a large number of credit cards.

A GIRO SYSTEM FOR THE UNITED STATES?

Despite these apparent advantages, it is still questionable whether the United States will ever have a fully developed giro transfer system. Arguing against such a development is the absence of most of the conditions that brought about the establishment of such systems in other countries. Commercial banks in this country have provided an efficient payments system and, unlike those in some countries, they have actively sought the accounts of small depositors.

Some elements of the giro system have already been adopted in this country. An increasing number of businesses are processing payrolls by instructing their computers to instruct their bank's computers to reduce their accounts and to credit their employees' bank accounts. Banks are already making limited use of the cards described above. The American Bankers Association has conducted seminars dealing with the possibilities of an automated payments system and is sponsoring research efforts along the same lines.

But the full development of the system envisaged would be a lengthy and costly process. The characteristics of the special telephone which make it adaptable for communication with business machines would necessitate major modifications in telephone central offices before these could be made available to the general public. Costs of data processing equipment would be substantial, not to mention the problems of obtaining competent personnel to operate this equipment. In addition, many serious technical problems doubtless would arise during the period of transition. Finally, the transition would inevitably encounter numerous obstacles posed by legal and customary technicalities involved in setting transactions.

But the ultimate benefits might more than offset these costs. In the words of George W. Mitchell, Member of the Board of Governors of the Federal Reserve System, "In the modi-

fied giro system . . . there will be no check sorting and re-sorting, no shipment of checks from bank-to-bank or bank-to-customer, no storage requirements for checks, no kited checks, no checks returned for insufficient funds, and no float." These are substantial benefits indeed.

Governor Mitchell believes that the adoption of some form of computerized giro system is inevitable and that it will occur much sooner than most observers expect. In any event, possibilities for significant economies have been opened up by the rapid technological advances of recent years. These possibilities create a standing incentive for commercial banks to make important changes in the payments services they offer to the public.

CHAPTER TWO

MONEY AND GOLD

5

GOLD, MONETARY MANAGEMENT, AND THE BANKING SYSTEM*

Allan Sproul†

The role of gold is still important in our domestic monetary system (see the section on gold near the end of Selection 2), although it is no longer nearly as important as it was forty years ago. The "gold standard," however, is still a subject of much heated argument.

By the full gold standard is meant a state of affairs in which a nation does three things: (1) defines its monetary unit in terms of gold, expressing the monetary unit, such as the dollar, as the equivalent of a certain fixed quantity of gold; (2) allows the free import and export of gold, permitting gold to move freely into or out of the country, without restriction; and (3) will buy gold from or sell gold to anyone who wishes it, at a fixed price.‡ This last means that gold can be bought and sold in unlimited amounts at the mint (at the fixed price) and in the general market (at the free market price, as determined by supply and demand). Since the Treasury will sell gold in unlimited amounts to anyone wishing to purchase it, all currency and demand deposits are, at least nominally, freely convertible (or fully redeemable) into gold.

In practice, two main types of gold standard have existed: the gold coin standard, as maintained in the United States before 1933, in which gold coins circulated as a medium of exchange; and the gold bullion standard, in which there are no circulating gold coins, but gold bars or bullion may be held by the public as a store of value. Aside from this difference, both types of gold standard are essentially the same, following similar rules and performing similar functions. Since 1933 the United States has been on a limited form of the gold bullion standard, sometimes called an international gold bullion standard. It is now illegal for anyone to have gold in his possession in this country, except for special purposes, unlimited convertibility having been halted in 1933.

Much of this chapter relates to arguments pro and con about the gold coin standard, particularly with respect to its domestic implications. We will turn to the international implications of the gold standard in Part 6 at the end of the book.

* Remarks of Allan Sproul at the Seventy-Fifth Annual Convention of the American Bankers Association, San Francisco, California, November 2, 1949. Reprinted from *Monthly Review* of the Federal Reserve Bank of New York (December, 1949). Reprinted by the courtesy of Mr. Sproul and of the Federal Reserve Bank of New York.

† President of the Federal Reserve Bank of New York, 1941–1956.

‡ It should be noted that for a nation to define its

Two groups of arguments for the reestablishment of a gold coin standard may be distinguished in the writings and speeches of those who propose it, one group relating primarily to the domestic economy and one to the probable effects on international trade and finance. In the first group the arguments run about as follows:

1. Replacement of our "dishonest," inconvertible currency with an "honest" money having intrinsic value would promote confidence in the currency, and encourage savings, investment, long-time commitments, and production.

2. Irredeemable paper money leads to inflation, whereas the upper limits imposed upon currency and credit expansion by a thoroughgoing gold standard serve as a restraining influence on irresponsible politicians and overoptimistic businessmen.

3. Present governmental taxing and spending policies are wrong, and dangerous. The gold standard would put a brake on public spending.

4. As a corollary of the preceding argument, since the gold standard would hinder further extension of government control and planning, it is a necessary implement of human liberty.

The second group of arguments, relating to the international advantages of a gold coin standard, generally make no distinction between the effects of a unilateral adoption of such a standard by the United States, and the multilateral establishment of an unrestricted gold standard by many countries, and of exchange rates fixed by such a standard. The arguments run somewhat as follows:

1. The existence of premium markets in gold abroad and the lack of gold convertibility at home creates — and is representative of — lack of confidence in the gold value of the dollar. In the absence of a thoroughgoing gold coin standard we cannot convince anyone that we may not devalue the dollar.

2. Restoration of "normal" patterns of international trade is being retarded by the inconvertibility of currencies in terms of gold and, therefore, one with another. This inconvertibility has led to tariffs, quotas, exchange controls, and to general bilateralism.

3. Under a managed paper currency system there is always the temptation to solve national problems by devices which lead to international disequilibrium. This, in turn, has led to domestic devices restrictive of foreign trade. The international gold standard, by eliminating the need for restrictive commercial policy, would increase the physical volume of international trade, resulting in an improved division of labor and higher standards of living for everyone.

First, let me say that I perceive no moral problem involved in this question of gold convertibility. Money is a convenience devised by man to facilitate his economic life. It is a standard of value and a medium of exchange. Almost anything will serve as money so long as it is generally acceptable. Many things have served as money over the centuries, gold perhaps longest of all because of its relative scarcity and its intrinsic beauty. In this country we still retain some attachment to gold domestically, and more internationally, but to carry on our internal business we use a paper money (and bank deposit accounts) which has the supreme attribute of general acceptability. There is no widespread fear of the soundness of the dollar in this country, no widespread flight from money into things. The constant cry of wolf by a few has aroused no great public response. Savings, investment, long-term commitments, and the production and exchange of goods have gone forward at record levels.

Much of the nostalgia for gold convertibility is based, I believe, on fragrant memories of a state of affairs which was a special historical case; a state of affairs which no longer exists. The great period of gold convertibility in the world was from 1819 to 1914. It drew its support from the position which Great Britain occupied, during most of the nineteenth century and the early part of the twentieth century, in the field of international production, trade, and finance. The gold coin standard flourished because the organization of world trade under British leadership provided the

---

monetary unit in terms of gold and to fix a price for gold are one and the same thing. For instance, in the United States today the dollar is defined as equivalent to 13.71 grains of fine gold, or 1/35 of an ounce of fine gold, since there are 480 grains in a troy ounce; since each dollar is defined as equivalent to 1/35 of an ounce of gold, the value of each ounce of gold is fixed at $35. By devaluation of the dollar in terms of gold is meant setting less than 1/35 of an ounce of gold as the equivalent of one dollar — which is the same thing, of course, as raising the price of an ounce of gold.

conditions in which it could, with a few notable aberrations, work reasonably well.

The ability of the British to sustain, to provide a focal point for this system has been declining for many years, however, and the decline was hastened by two world wars which sapped the resources of the British people. The heir apparent of Great Britain, of course, was the United States, but up to now we have not been able to assume the throne and play the role. And until some way has been found to eliminate the lack of balance between our economy and that of the rest of the world, other than by gifts and grants in aid, we won't be able to do so. This is a problem of unraveling and correcting the influences, in international trade and finance, which have compelled worldwide suspension of gold convertibility, not vice versa. The job before us now is to attack the problems of trade and finance directly. We should not deceive ourselves by thinking that gold convertibility, in some indefinable but inexorable way, could solve these underlying problems for us.

Nor is it true, of course, that gold convertibility prevented wide swings in the purchasing power of the dollar, even when we had convertibility. Within my own experience and yours, while we still had a gold coin standard, we had tremendous movements in commodity prices, up and down, which were the other side of changes in the purchasing power of the dollar. What happened to us in 1920–21 and 1931–33 under a gold coin standard should prevent a too easy acceptance of that standard as the answer to the problem of a money with stable purchasing power.

When you boil it all down, however, and try to eliminate mythology from the discussion, the principal argument for restoring the circulation of gold coin in this country seems to be distrust of the money managers and of the fiscal policies of government. The impelling desire is for something automatic and impersonal which will curb government spending and throw the money managers out of the temple, as were the money changers before them. To overcome the inherent weakness of human beings confronted with the necessity of making hard decisions, the gold coin standard is offered as an impersonal and automatic solution. Through this mechanism the public is to regain control over government spending and bank credit expansion. It is claimed that whenever the public sensed dangerous developments, the reaction of many individuals would be to demand gold in exchange for their currency or their bank deposits. With the monetary reserve being depleted in this way, the government would be restrained from deficit financing through drawing upon new bank credit; banks would become reluctant to expand credit to their customers because of the drain on their reserves; and the Federal Reserve System would be given a signal to exert a restraining influence upon the money supply. In this way, Congress, the Treasury, and the Federal Reserve System would be forced by indirection to accept policies which they would not otherwise adopt.

In effect, under a gold coin standard, therefore, the initiative for over-all monetary control would, through the device of free public withdrawal of gold from the monetary reserve, be lodged in the instinctive or speculative reactions of the people. No doubt some people would take advantage of their ability to get gold. There would be many reasons for their doing so. Conscientious resistance to large government spending, or fear of inflation, might well be among these reasons. But speculative motives, a desire for hoards (however motivated), and such panic reactions as are generated by unsettled international conditions or temporary fright concerning the business outlook or one's individual security — all of these, and more — would be among the reasons for gold withdrawals. The gold coin mechanism does not distinguish among motives. Whenever, for any reason, there was a demand for gold, the reserve base of the monetary system would be reduced. Moreover, if only the United States dollar were convertible into gold while practically all other currencies were not, hoarding demands from all over the world would tend to converge upon this country's monetary reserves. Circumvention of the exchange controls of other countries would be stimulated, and dollar supplies which those countries badly need for essential supplies or for development purposes would be diverted to the selfish interests of hoarders.

Even if a particular reduction in the reserve base did occur for useful "disciplinary" reasons, the impact of such gold withdrawals upon the credit mechanism is likely to be crude and harsh. Since the present ratio between gold reserves and the money supply is about one-to-five, and since some such ratio will be in effect so long as this country retains a fractional reserve banking system, a withdrawal of gold coins (once any free gold is exhausted) will tend to be multiplied many times in its contractive effect on bank credit and the money supply.

It was, in part, to offset such arbitrary and extreme influences upon the volume of credit, and to make up for the inflexibility of a money supply based on gold coins (in responding to the fluctuating seasonal, regional, and growth requirements of the economy), that the Federal Reserve System was initially established. During the first two decades of its existence, the System devoted much of its attention to offsetting the capricious or exaggerated effects of the gold movements associated with continuance of a gold coin standard. We had an embarrassing practical experience with gold coin convertibility as recently as 1933, when lines of people finally stormed the Federal Reserve Banks seeking gold, and our whole banking mechanism came to a dead stop. The gold coin standard was abandoned, an international gold bullion standard adopted, because repeated experience has shown that internal convertibility of the currency, at best, was no longer exerting a stabilizing influence on the economy and, at worst, was perverse in its effects. Discipline is necessary in these matters but it should be the discipline of competent and responsible men; not the automatic discipline of a harsh and perverse mechanism. If you are not willing to trust men with the management of money, history has proved that you will not get protection from a mechanical control. Ignorant, weak, or irresponsible men will pervert that which is already perverse.

Here, I would emphasize my view that the integrity of our money does not depend on domestic gold convertibility. It depends upon the great productive power of the American economy and the competence with which we manage our fiscal and monetary affairs. I suggest that anyone who is worried about the dollar concentrate on the correction of those tendencies in our economic and political life which have brought us a deficit of several billion dollars in our federal budget, at a time when taxes are high and production, employment, and income are near record levels. I suggest that, going beyond the immediate situation, they address themselves to the difficult problem of the size of the budget, whether in deficit or surplus or balance. At some point the mere size of the budget, in relation to national product, can destroy incentives throughout the whole community, a dilemma which is even now forcing curtailment of government expenditures by the Labor government in Great Britain. These are problems gold coin convertibility cannot solve under present economic and social conditions. Gold has a useful purpose to serve, chiefly as a medium for balancing international accounts among nations and as a guide to necessary disciplines in international trade and finance. It has no useful purpose to serve in the pockets or hoards of the people. To expose our gold reserves to the drains of speculative and hoarding demands at home and abroad strikes me as both unwise and improvident.

6

A REPLY TO MR. SPROUL ON THE
GOLD STANDARD*

Walter E. Spahr†

Walter E. Spahr is executive vice president and treasurer of the Economists' National Committee on Monetary Policy. This is a group, mainly of economists, one of whose purposes is "educating the public as to the desirability of an early return to a gold standard." Professor Spahr's response to the preceding statement of Mr. Sproul follows.

Elsewhere Professor Spahr has briefly presented the positive case for a return to a gold coin standard. The interested reader is referred to A Proper Monetary and Banking System for the United States, *edited by James Washington Bell and Walter Spahr, published by Ronald Press in 1960.*

When a president of a Federal Reserve Bank recommends an irredeemable currency for the people of the United States, the nature of his contentions deserve scrutiny, since an irredeemable paper money is the worst form of currency devised by man. Its record demonstrates this. The fact has been illustrated in an endless number of ways, for centuries and today, that a vague unfulfilled promise to pay cannot possibly be equal to gold, which is a self-sufficient liquidator of financial obligations, not dependent for its value on the promise of any man or institution. The history of the world's experiments with irredeemable paper money is one of tragedy. A people have never indulged in the use of irredeemable promises to pay without suffering injury in some form; often the result has been a catastrophe. That is to be expected since a promise to pay is no better than the promissor, whereas gold is free of all uncertainties in men's promises.

In the face of these thoroughly-established facts, Mr. Allan Sproul nevertheless recommended for the United States an irredeemable currency, as a part of our restricted international gold bullion standard. In respect to the continuation of our domestic system of irredeemable currency he says: "I perceive no moral problem involved in this question of gold

* From *The Commercial and Financial Chronicle*, November 10, 1949. Abridged with the permission of the publisher and the author.

† Professor Emeritus, New York University.

convertibility." He really did not face the issue involved in the question of morality but went on with a series of assertions as to why our system is proper and desirable.

Regardless of what Mr. Sproul's concept may be as to what is or is not moral, a simple fact that should be beyond argument is that the Treasury and Federal Reserve Banks issue promises to pay which they do not redeem. If dishonesty has any meaning that is an act of dishonesty. We have built a large body of contract law designed to compel people to fulfill their obligations and their promises to pay — to eliminate dishonesty in so far as it can be done by law. If the Treasury and Federal Reserve Banks are to be exempt from responsibility for fulfillment of promises to pay, then we have one standard of obligation for them and another for all other people. It would be a case of granting to them privilege without corresponding responsibility, an arrangement for which there is apparently no valid defense.

Mr. Sproul says that "the principal argument for restoring the circulation of gold coin in this country seems to be distrust of the money managers and of the fiscal policies of government." That is one of the fundamental arguments, undoubtedly. His plea is that monetary management be left in the hands of "competent and responsible men" and his warning is that if "you are not willing to trust men with the management of money, history has proved that you will not get protection from a mechanical control."

Aside from the implication involved in his statement that the issue is one of mechanical control versus management by "competent and responsible men" — which is not a correct presentation of the issue — the fact is that this is the argument of every government dictator. It is, in essence, the argument that "the people's money and purse should be left in our hands; we know best; we are responsible men; and we should be trusted." Mr. Sproul advocates discipline in monetary matters but "it should be the discipline of competent and responsible men; not the automatic discipline of a harsh and perverse mechanism." In other words, but accurately, "competent and responsible men" should discipline the people but the people should not be permitted to discipline these officials since that "mechanism" is "harsh and perverse."

The simple fact of the matter is that no man or group of men can be trusted to "manage" properly an irredeemable paper money or the people's purse when the managers deprive the people of all means of putting any effective brakes on these managers.

Mr. Sproul says: "Nor is it true, of course, that gold convertibility prevented wide swings in the purchasing power of the dollar, even when we had convertibility."

We have a substantial body of well-tested knowledge to the effect that business and price fluctuations are not, and cannot be, the consequence of a single cause, and that the causal factors are many and appear in a great variety of combinations. Therefore, to imply a single causal factor, and to imply further that a convertible currency, if a good device, should prevent "wide swings in the purchasing power of the dollar," is to offer assumptions that have no standing among competent authorities in this field.

Conversely, there is no valid basis on which to rest a supposition that a managed irredeemable currency can smooth out or prevent fluctuations in the price level. The worst fluctuations the world has ever seen have been under irredeemable currencies. That is to be expected since they provide a means that makes runaway prices and extreme currency depreciation possible.

But, if a steady price level could result from currency management, that fact would not demonstrate the desirability of either the price level or the management. A steady index of a price level can result from the averaging out of a multitude of instabilities and disequilibria in the economic system, and, in such cases, a steady price level (or purchasing power of the dollar) proves nothing as to the health of the economy. We had an unusually steady average of prices from 1923–29 and then plunged into a severe and long recession and depression.

These are elementary facts in our reputable studies on business and price fluctuations. But Mr. Sproul expands still further in his observations in this field. "Within my own experience and yours," he says, "while we still had a gold coin standard, we had tremendous movements in commodity prices, up and down, which were the other side of changes in the purchasing power of the dollar. What happened to us in 1920–21 and 1931–33 under a gold coin standard should prevent a too easy acceptance of that standard as the answer to the problem of a money with stable purchasing power."

If Mr. Sproul would search the evidence produced by the most experienced, careful, and reputable authorities in the field of money or business fluctuations he should find that there is no basis for regarding any monetary standard as "the answer to the problem of a money with a stable purchasing power" for the reason that there is no such thing as a single causal factor in business or price fluctuations. Still further, no such authority would recommend a "stable purchasing power" except as it is the natural result of harmonious relationships in the economic system.

Mr. Sproul's assumption is that the gold standard was in some way responsible for what happened to us in 1920–21 and 1931–33. That not only implies a single causal factor and fails to deal with the real causes but it belongs to the following type of inferences: We went to war under our Constitution, therefore let us abolish it and permit "competent and responsible men" to manage us without a Constitution; we had a train wreck on a railway, therefore let us abolish railways; we had a bad accident in a Cadillac automobile, therefore let us adopt cheap cars or walk; we went to war when we had peace, therefore let us have no more peace.

Mr. Sproul criticizes the gold standard because it does not prevent man from engaging in the abuse of credit and because it calls a halt on him when he goes too far in his foolishness. But he is silent about the infinitely greater price fluctuations, and the currency depreciations, devaluations, and collapses which have commonly characterized an irredeemable currency which he attempts to defend.

Mr. Sproul says that "The gold coin standard flourished because the organization of world trade under British leadership (during most of the nineteenth century and early part of the twentieth century) provided the conditions in which it could, with a few notable aberrations, work reasonably well." He then goes on to say: "The heir apparent of Great Britain, of course, was the United States, but up to now we have not been able to assume the throne and play the role." As to the problems interfering with our assumption of this role, he says: "We should not deceive ourselves by thinking that gold convertibility, in some indefinable but inexorable way, could solve these underlying problems for us."

Mr. Sproul's position seems to be that the gold standard caused, or at least did not save us from, our problems of 1920–21 and 1931–33, and that it did not contribute to England's world position of 1819–1914. It flourished, he says, "because the organization of world trade under British leadership provided the conditions in which it could. . . ." He has no place for the consideration that if England played such a role under the gold standard perhaps we could "assume the throne and play the role" too if we had a thorough-going gold standard. At least, a gold standard did not prevent England from playing that role; and it should be quite obvious that no nation with an irredeemable currency can play it very long. ". . . up to now," says Mr. Sproul, "we have not been able to assume the throne and play the role," but in his argument our irredeemable currency system has nothing whatever to do with this situation.

Now the simple fact of the matter is that a gold standard, in so far as a money system can facilitate exchange, has done, and does, more to open up trade than any instrumentality thus far known, provided other obstructions are removed. Conversely, irredeemable currencies tend to block it, and they do that even though other obstructions be removed. The nearest thing to a "one world," of which we talk so much and which is so widely advocated these days, existed to its greatest extent when most countries were on, or were linked to, a gold standard. With most countries now employing irredeemable currencies, with the greatest international medium of exchange known obstructed by money managers, international trade and investment are distorted and ill. Mr. Sproul's recommendations would perpetuate this illness. He would not permit nature, operating through a gold standard and redeemable currencies, to provide its curative powers; the job is for the "managers" who should "attack the problems of trade and finance directly" — whatever that means.

Says Mr. Sproul further: "In effect, under a gold coin standard . . . initiative for overall monetary control would, through the device of free public withdrawal of gold from the monetary reserve, be lodged in the instinctive or speculative reactions of people." He wants none of this; he wants the money managers to be free of any pressures for redemption except as these come from central banks and governments.

The basic question that arises here is this: On what proper ground can a government or central banking system deprive a people of the right to exchange their goods or labor for gold, if they prefer it, and require them to accept instead irredeemable promises to pay?

Mr. Sproul refers to the instinctive or speculative reactions of people and says, "The gold coin mechanism does not distinguish among motives." There is no reason why it should. If one holds a promise that is payable upon demand, the holder is under no obligation to provide reasons for his demand for payment; but the promissor is under obligation, without right to question the demand. That is as it should be. But Mr. Sproul wants his bank and the

Treasury free to issue promises while the recipient must not be permitted to demand and get payment in an object of universal acceptability because, among other things, "The gold coin mechanism does not distinguish among motives." The problems inherent in the fractional reserve system on which banks operate are not to be solved properly by freeing banks of their obligations to meet in gold coin their liabilities payable on demand.

If a person has property he has a right, if a right means anything, to exchange it for something he prefers; and no government or bank can properly take to itself what he prefers and force him to take instead its promise to pay — particularly when it is irredeemable.

If the poorest newsboy, learning to work and save, accumulates $10 worth of pennies, why should he not be permitted, if he prefers, to invest it in a ten-dollar gold piece, which spells honesty and safety, rather than be compelled to accept an irredeemable promise to pay which on its face and in fact spells dishonesty and corruption and danger of depreciation? Honest men and women know that there is only one correct answer to this.

7

THE RESTORATION OF A GOLD-COIN STANDARD IN THE UNITED STATES

The Douglas and Patman Committees

Two significant Congressional inquiries were conducted into the functioning of our monetary system in the early post-war years. The first was the inquiry of the Douglas Committee (named after its chairman, Senator Douglas of Illinois), formally known as the Subcommittee on Monetary, Credit and Fiscal Policies of the Joint Committee on the Economic Report, which held hearings during 1949. The second was that of the Patman Committee (after Representative Patman of Texas), formally known as the Subcommittee on General Credit Control and Debt Management of the Joint Committee on the Economic Report, which held hearings during 1952.

Each inquiry devoted itself in part to a consideration of the gold standard and the role gold should play in our economy. Their unanimous conclusions follow.

I. THE DOUGLAS COMMITTEE*

We believe that to restore the free domestic convertibility of money into gold coin or gold bullion at this time would militate against, rather than promote, the purposes of the Employment Act, and we recommend that no

* From *Monetary, Credit and Fiscal Policies*, Report of the Subcommittee on Monetary, Credit and Fiscal Policies (Douglas Committee) of the Joint Committee on the Economic Report, U.S. Congress, 1950.

action in this direction be taken. We also recommend a thorough congressional review of existing legislation relating to the power to change the price of gold with a view to repealing any legislation that might be so construed as to permit a change in the price of gold by other than congressional action.

Since 1934 the United States has been on an international gold bullion standard; gold may be held or dealt in only in accordance with rules prescribed by the Secretary of the

Treasury, but in practice the Treasury sells gold freely to meet all bona fide demands for domestic industrial, commercial, and artistic purposes, and it provides gold for export to the extent necessary to prevent the dollar from declining in foreign-exchange markets. It does, however, place some limitations on gold exports and it prohibits the use of gold domestically for monetary or hoarding purposes.

Some have proposed the reestablishment of an unlimited gold-coin standard; they would require the government to provide unlimited redeemability of its money into gold and to remove all limitations on holding and dealing in gold. This proposal is usually supported by the following principal arguments: (1) Only a money that is freely redeemable in gold is an "honest" money. (2) To restore free redeemability would restore to the people of the country an effective method of preventing monetary and fiscal abuses by the government. In a statement presented to the subcommittee, Prof. Walter E. Spahr put this argument in the following terms:

Redeemability gives every individual with dollars the opportunity, to the extent of his purchasing power, to get the standard metal if he prefers that to the promises to pay it. This enables him to exercise some control over the use by his government and banks of the people's gold and over the amount of promises these agencies may issue. If either or both issue promises to an extent that invites lack of confidence, every individual, to the extent he has dollars, can express his lack of confidence. His demand for redemption is his right, if the promise means anything. It is his effort to protect his savings against men's uncertain promises. His demand for redemption is a red flag of doubt. If many red flags appear, the banks, the Treasury, and Congress receive warnings and must call a halt or exercise greater restraint in their use of the people's money. In this manner redeemability provides a people with control over the government's use of their purse.

The gold standard with provision for redemption in effect provides a system of golden wires to every individual with dollars, over which he can send messages of approval or disapproval to the central signal board. When our government took the people's gold and thrust irredeemable promises to pay on them, it cut all these wires to the central signal box. The people were cut off. The lights went out on the central signal system and the people were left helpless. Thus absolute con-

trol of the people's gold and public purse passed to their government. The latter had freed itself from receipt of signals of disapproval and from any effective check. The spending orgy is the result. Vote buying goes on and can go on without let or hindrance. The people are helpless; the government is the boss; irresponsibility is in the saddle and it cannot be checked. The understanding, concerned, and responsible men in Congress are in the minority and are helpless. Government spending and bureaucracy are out of control. Apparently this course cannot be brought to a halt except by restoring to our people control over their purse. That can be done only by the institution of redeemability of the promises to pay of the Treasury and banks.

And (3) for the United States to return to an unlimited gold coin standard would set a good example for the rest of the world and would hasten the reestablishment of a world-wide gold standard and of a system of free multilateral payments in international trade.

An "honest money" in the sense of a money that maintains a relatively constant purchasing power is essential to the attainment of the purposes of the Employment Act; maximum production, employment, and purchasing power cannot be continuously maintained over a period of time if either serious deflation or serious inflation is allowed to occur. But we do not believe that the restoration of unlimited convertibility of our money into gold would be either an appropriate or an effective method of promoting stability of price levels and of the purchasing power of the dollar. It probably could not prevent a serious inflation in this country if other pressures were inflationary.

In short, the restoration of free convertibility of our money into gold would be neither a reliable nor an effective guard against serious inflation. For this purpose there can be no effective substitute for responsible monetary, credit, and fiscal management. There is no reason to believe that a requirement of redeemability into gold would promote wise monetary and credit policies; in fact, past experience indicates that it would at times endanger such policies, for gold drains can be induced by deflation as well as by inflation. For example, the internal gold drains and gold hoarding in 1932 and 1933 probably contributed somewhat to deflationary pressures in this country. We concur in the following statement by the Chairman of the Board of Governors of the Federal Reserve System:

An overriding reason against making gold coin freely available is that no government should make promises to its citizens and to the world which it would not be able to keep if the demand should arise. Monetary systems for over a century, in response to the growth in real income, have expanded more rapidly than would be permitted by accretions of gold. In the United States today our gold stock, although large, is only 15 per cent of our currency in circulation and bank deposits, and less than 7 per cent of the economy's total holdings of liquid assets. The retention of a gold base is desirable in order to maintain international convertibility, and a gold-standard system has therefore evolved in which the various forms of money and near money in the country are ultimately convertible to gold, where that is necessary to meet the country's international obligations. Return to a gold-coin standard, however, would clearly expose the economy to the risk of drastic and undesirable deflation at times of high speculative demand for gold for hoarding, or else the government would have to withdraw its promise of gold convertibility. Conjecture as to the possibility of such a withdrawal would stimulate a speculative demand for gold and might precipitate the event feared. The long-run effect would be to weaken rather than to strengthen confidence in the dollar.

The restoration by other countries of the free redeemability of their moneys into gold coin for internal hoarding as well as for other purposes would delay and hinder, rather than promote, the abolition of exchange restrictions and the restoration of a system of free multilateral international payments, for it would mean that a part of the gold reserves of those countries would be drained off into private hoards and would not be available to meet adverse balances in international payments.

II. THE PATMAN COMMITTEE*

Since the passage of the Gold Reserve Act of 1934, the international value of the United States dollar has been definitely tied to a fixed

* From *Monetary Policy and Management of the Public Debt*, Report of the Subcommittee on General Credit Control and Debt Management (Patman Committee) of the Joint Committee on the Economic Report, U.S. Congress, 1952.

amount of gold. This amount of gold has been 1⁄35th of a fine ounce continuously since January 31, 1934. According to a legal opinion submitted to the Subcommittee by the counsel for the Board of Governors of the Federal Reserve System, it cannot be changed except by act of Congress, nor can the corresponding price of gold ($35 an ounce) be changed without act of Congress except for a narrow margin between the authorized buying and selling price set by the International Monetary Fund in accordance with the Articles of Agreement of that organization as approved by Congress in the Bretton Woods Agreements Act of 1945. This international value of the dollar is implemented by the willingness of the United States Treasury to sell gold to, and buy gold from, foreign governments and central banks in such amounts as may be necessary to maintain the international value of the dollar.

United States currency, however, is not redeemable in gold coin or bullion, either for domestic holding or for private holding abroad (as far as the latter comes directly under the purview of the United States at the time of export). This matter was considered by the predecessor subcommittee under the chairmanship of Senator Douglas, which said:

We believe that to restore the free domestic convertibility of money into gold coin or gold bullion at this time would militate against, rather than promote, the purposes of the Employment Act, and we recommend that no action in this direction be taken.

This Subcommittee has given further consideration to the advisability of restoring the free domestic convertibility of money into gold coin or gold bullion and concludes that such a policy would be unwise either at the present time or as an ideal for future action.

The advantages of the United States continuing on an international gold standard are manifest. Gold is the most generally acceptable medium for the settlement of international balances that the world has yet been able to devise, and the certainty that the United States will always pay or accept any balances due on international account in gold makes the dollar a universally acceptable means of payment in world trade. It is a major aim of the international economic policy of the United States to promote the sound growth of multilateral trade and to discourage bilateral and discriminatory trade practices. These are fostered by nonconvertible currencies, and one of the most important things which the United States can do to promote multilateral trade is to continue the international gold convertibility of its own currency and to encourage and assist other countries in making their currencies convertible. This is the effect of the present international gold standard of the dollar. The restoration of domestic convertibility — which would tend to draw additional gold stocks to the United States — would increase the difficulties in the way of other countries which are now striving to restore the external convertibility of their currencies and so would place further obstacles in the way of the healthy growth of multilateral world trade.

In the domestic field, however, the risks of gold convertibility are high and the advantages are questionable. The limited stock of gold relative to the possible demands on it if we should return to domestic convertibility is in fact the heart of the argument in favor of such a return, as the case is often put. A return to domestic gold convertibility is meant as a means of disciplining the Government. As Professor Walter E. Spahr said in his answer to a question of the earlier subcommittee under the chairmanship of Senator Douglas:

The gold standard with provision for redemption in effect provides a system of golden wires to every individual with dollars, over which he can send messages of approval or disapproval to the central signal board. When our Government took the people's gold and thrust irredeemable promises to pay on them, it cut all these wires to the central signal box. The people were cut off. The lights went out on the central signal system and the people were left helpless.

The Subcommittee rejects the view that the Government of the United States should be controlled by "a system of golden wires" and reaffirms its faith in the ballot box.

Experience shows, moreover, that these golden wires are more likely to be pulled to prevent the Government from relieving distress in a period of depression than to restrain inflation in periods of prosperity. The messages coming over the golden wires were not helpful during either the twenties or the thirties. They had often been wrong before. Wide extremes of boom and depression and of high and low prices occurred repeatedly during the many years of gold convertibility. During periods of expansion the messages coming over the wires were usually those of approval of expansionary policies; during periods of depression the messages were those of disapproval of all expansionary efforts toward recovery. Gold convertibility when we had it did not contribute to sound monetary policy, and it is sound monetary policy which promotes economic stability.

As Mr. Allan Sproul, President of the Federal Reserve Bank of New York, said to the Annual Convention of the American Bankers Association in San Francisco in November, 1949:

* * * We had an embarrassing practical experience with gold coin convertibility as recently as 1933 when lines of people finally stormed the Federal Reserve banks seeking gold, and our whole banking mechanism came to a dead stop. The gold-coin standard was abandoned, an international gold bullion standard adopted, because repeated experience has shown that internal convertibility of the currency, at best, was no longer exerting a stabilizing influence on the economy and, at worst, was perverse in its effects. Discipline is necessary in these matters but it should be the discipline of competent and responsible men; not the automatic discipline of a harsh and perverse mechanism. If you are not willing to trust men with the management of money, history has proved that you will not get protection from a mechanical control. Ignorant, weak, or irresponsible men will pervert that which is already perverse.

The Subcommittee agrees with Mr. Sproul; a return to the domestic convertibility of gold would be equivalent to a vote of no confidence in the monetary authorities of this country, including both the Treasury and the Federal Reserve System. It would represent an abandonment of the policy of the Employment Act of 1946 and the ideals for which it stands. It would turn the monetary navigation of the United States over to an automatic pilot which took no account in its computations of human suffering and unemployment. The Subcommittee does not believe either that a return to domestic convertibility is now opportune or that it should be accepted as an ideal for the future.

CHAPTER THREE

MONEY, DEBT, AND FINANCIAL MARKETS

8

THE SAVING-INVESTMENT PROCESS AND
THE MARKET FOR LOANABLE FUNDS

John G. Gurley[†]

When we analyzed the importance of the saving-investment process in Selection 1, we abstracted from the financial institutions which are so important in facilitating that process. Financial institutions — such as commercial and savings banks, savings and loan associations, credit unions, insurance companies, and others — are the intermediaries through which funds are transferred from ultimate savers (or lenders) to ultimate investors (or borrowers). The commercial banks accept funds (called deposits) and in turn make loans and investments. Savings and loan associations also accept funds (called shares) and also make loans and investments. Similar functions are performed by all the above-mentioned institutions. As a result of the existence of these institutions, savers who do not wish to "hoard" their cash under a mattress, but who feel that purchasing corporate bonds or mortgages would be too risky or too illiquid, are presented with an attractive alternative: they can "purchase" demand or savings deposits or savings and loan shares or insurance, as they prefer. And yet the corporations and potential home buyers can still sell their bonds and mortgages — to the financial intermediary rather than to the ultimate saver.

Thus the financial intermediaries channel funds from ultimate savers to ultimate investors by issuing their own debts (deposits, shares, and so forth) for the ultimate savers or lenders to buy, and in turn using these funds to buy the debts (corporate bonds, mortgages, and so forth) of the ultimate investors or borrowers. Were such financial intermediaries not in existence the flow of saving to investment outlets would be much smaller indeed, with profound effects upon the allocation of resources, the level of income and employment, and the rate of economic growth.

Before reading this selection, you should get a copy of The Two Faces of Debt and study it carefully. This pamphlet, published by the Federal Reserve Bank of Chicago, is a highly informative analysis of the role of debt and financial institutions in our economy. It should really be reprinted here, but space is short and you can get a copy free simply by dropping a postcard to the Federal Reserve Bank of Chicago, Chicago 90, Illinois.

[†] Stanford University.

I.*

AN ECONOMY WITHOUT FINANCIAL ASSETS

Suppose that there were an economic system that had no financial assets at all. There are at least two things that one could say about such an economy. First, without money, the economy would be subject to all the inefficiencies of a barter system. Second, without money or other financial assets, the economy would probably have a relatively low level of investment and would tend to misallocate whatever investment it had.

The second point requires elaboration. An economy without financial assets would require each economic unit to invest in real goods whatever part of its current income was not consumed, which is its saving. I neglect for the moment trading in existing real assets. No unit could invest more than its saving because there would be no way to finance the excess expenditures. And no unit could invest less than its saving because there would be no financial assets in which to put the excess saving. Each economic unit would be forced into a balanced budget position, with saving equal to investment. This sort of arrangement would quite likely lead to a relatively low level of investment and saving and hence tend to retard the rate of growth of national output.

The absence of financial assets, moreover, would bring about an inefficient allocation of resources. An ordering of investment opportunities by their expected rates of return would almost always imply investment by some economic units that exceeded their saving (that is, deficits) and investment by others that fell short of their saving (that is, surpluses). But without financial assets this efficient ordering of investment could not be achieved. Relatively inferior investment projects would be undertaken and many of the superior ones would go by the boards, simply because there would be no way to distribute investment projects among

* From an address before the 1959 Conference on Savings and Residential Financing, sponsored by the United States Savings and Loan League. From the *Proceedings of the 1959 Conference on Savings and Residential Financing*, May 7 and 8, 1959. Reprinted by the courtesy of the publisher (The United States Savings and Loan League) and the author.

economic units in a way that differed from the distribution of saving among them.

MONEY INCREASES INVESTMENT AND SAVING

Let us now introduce paper money into the economy; the government issues it when it purchases goods and services. A means of payment will, of course, allow the economy to get rid of the inefficiencies due to barter. But money will do more than that; it will increase the efficiency of resource allocation and it will most likely lead to a higher level of investment.

Consider, first, the new possibilities for private investment. Private economic units that have highly promising investment opportunities may now make investment expenditures in excess of their current saving by drawing down previously accumulated money balances. Others that do not have such promising investment opportunities can save in excess of their real investment by accumulating money balances. Thus, some promising investment projects can be undertaken that otherwise would not have seen the light of day; and other, inferior investments that otherwise might have been undertaken can now give way. Money allows investment spending to be distributed among economic units in a different way from saving. In allowing some specialization among economic units in investment and saving, it opens up the possibility for a more efficient ordering of investment throughout the economy.

Consider, next, the investment opportunities for government, the issuer of money. As private economic units increase their demand for money balances during output growth, the government can satisfy this demand by new issues of money. Since this money is issued by governmental purchases of goods and services, a rising private demand for money means that economic resources are turned over for government's use. These resources can be used to increase social capital or, through transfer payments, to finance private investment. The way is clearly opened up for an increase in investment and saving.

ELEMENTARY INNOVATIONS IN FINANCE

A financial system restrains growth if it ties the distribution of spending too rigidly to the distribution of income among economic units and if it does not make institutional provision for selective matching of budget surpluses in some sectors with budget deficits in others. Economic units can be expected to look for ways around such restraints. Indeed, in any economy, the financial structure is continually reshaped by the efforts of economic units to break out of the confines of existing financial arrangements. Before moving on to the more sophisticated efforts involving new financial assets, markets and institutions, let us look at a few elementary innovations in finance. For this purpose the early economic history of this country offers interesting illustrations.

Our economy in its early stages approximated the economy I have just pictured. Its leading financial asset was money; it had few, if any, financial institutions; and its markets for other financial assets were hardly developed. There were definitely financial restraints on real growth, and these were hurdled in very elementary ways.

For example, the formation of partnerships was a common device for mobilizing savings in the American colonies, before the emergence of corporate organization and of private markets in corporate securities. The merging of business budgets by partnership arrangements widened the range of investment opportunities for any given dollar of saving.

Another popular technique for raising funds in colonial times was the lottery, which has a long tradition the world over as a substitute for borrowing. The colonial governments used lotteries not only to gain funds for themselves but also to extend grants to private individuals and business firms. The colonies — and the states later on — also permitted individuals to conduct lotteries to finance designated investments. The lottery ticket may not be a perfect substitute for a bond or a stock certificate, but in many countries it has been one of the first steps along the road of financial development.

Governments have gained economic resources not only by issues of money and by lotteries but also by taxation, by sale of goods produced under government auspices, by direct appropriation of private output and in other ways. They

have used these resources for government investment projects and they have released some to private enterprise through numerous techniques of transfer. In our own colonies, these transfer techniques included bounties to encourage investment in preferred categories, premiums for output of exceptional quality and subsidies for desired enterprise that was slow to gain momentum.

All governments, both in primitive and advanced societies, have tried to increase private demand for money balances, for the purpose of obtaining economic resources. Money was early made receivable for taxes in this country and elsewhere and usually receivable for payment of debts, with penalties provided for creditors who preferred other means of settlement. In physical appearance, in denomination, in provisions for convertibility and in other ways, efforts were made to increase demand for money. Primitive price controls and rationing cannot be omitted from this list of devices.

Tangible assets may serve the same purpose as money balances. Any existing asset that a sector is willing to acquire as an alternative to spending on current output releases that output for other uses, including new investment. Public lands served admirably in this country, both in colonial times and later, to secure funds for development purposes. The most famous instances were the land grants to canal and railroad companies. To the extent that the companies sold the land, their need to obtain external funds by other means, including security sales, was reduced. Many savers certainly preferred to accumulate land instead of securities in those years, and the saving they released clearly was allocable to new investment.

PRIMARY SECURITIES

These elementary innovations, however, can carry us only so far. To make further progress we must allow our economic units to issue securities of their own. These are primary securities, or claims against nonfinancial economic units. In the early stages of development they usually take the form of face-to-face loans. An economic unit that wishes to borrow seeks out another that wants to lend, and a loan is negotiated on the spot. We may think of primary securities as initially taking this form.

The ability of economic units to borrow directly from one another affords those with highly productive investment projects more scope than before to bid away resources from others with less productive projects. Primary securities stimulate real growth by increasing the probability that alternative investments will be exploited in order of their productivity. They also more fully exploit financial incentives to saving and thereby make it more likely that the level of saving and investment will be raised.

DISTRIBUTIVE TECHNIQUES

Face-to-face loans, however, are not a good way of getting primary securities distributed from borrowers to lenders. Therefore the next step must be the development of distributive techniques. These include the broadcast of information to borrowers regarding the asset preferences of lenders and to lenders regarding the issues of borrowers. They include, too, a widespread network of communication that tends to overcome regional market barriers. Facilities for rapid contract and settlement of loan transactions — security exchanges — increase the resemblance of security markets to competitive commodity exchanges. Facilities for brokerage, for market support and seasoning of new issues, for dealer inventories and for future as well as spot deliveries are other familiar distributive techniques. The guaranty of private primary securities by governments and the issuance of government securities themselves in place of private securities are still other examples.

The effect of distributive techniques in widening security markets is to permit each borrower and lender a higher degree of diversification in his debt and financial assets. Investing in primary securities alone, each lender can spread his budget of financial assets over a greater variety of claims than he could acquire on local markets. He can enrich the packet of advantages associated with the marginal dollar's worth of "consumption" of primary securities.

And each borrower can diversify the form of his debts, reducing the real disadvantages associated with the marginal dollar's worth of indebtedness.

The development of distributive techniques, then, tends to raise the level of investment and saving by increasing the marginal utility of the last dollar's worth of financial assets to the lender and reducing the marginal disutility of the last dollar's worth of debt to the borrower. At the same time, such development tends to increase the efficiency of resource allocation by pitting more and more investment opportunities against one another for lenders to look over.

INTERMEDIATIVE TECHNIQUES

Distributive techniques get primary securities distributed efficiently from borrower to lender and from lender to lender. But no matter how efficient this process is, lenders still end up with primary securities. And the fact is that, although these securities may be tied with a red ribbon and sprayed with perfume, there has always been a conflict between borrowers and lenders, between the types of securities that borrowers can best issue and the types of securities that lenders desire to accumulate.

This is where financial intermediaries come in. These institutions place themselves between ultimate borrowers and lenders, purchasing the primary securities of the borrowers and issuing claims against themselves (indirect securities) for the portfolios of lenders. Financial intermediaries resolve in part the long-standing conflict between borrowers and lenders by "turning" primary securities into the types of financial assets that lenders want, at prices that do not inhibit growth unduly.

Intermediative techniques give lenders a wide variety of financial assets particularly suited to them and at the same time make it less necessary for borrowers to issue types of securities that are ill-adapted to their businesses. Like distributive techniques, then, intermediative techniques raise the marginal utility of the last dollar's worth of financial assets to the lenders and reduce the marginal disutility of the last dollar's worth of debt to the borrowers. In these ways they tend to raise investment and saving and to allocate scarce savings optimally among investment alternatives.

FINANCIAL TECHNIQUES SUMMARIZED

All of the things I have mentioned are financial techniques for raising levels of saving and investment and allocating resources efficiently. The role of financial intermediaries in the saving-investment process, then, is essentially the same as the earlier role of lotteries, public land sales, Jay Cooke's distributive techniques during the Civil War and so on. The financial development of our country can be thought of as a rather steady progression from the cruder to the more sophisticated techniques for solving a common economic problem, with the colonial governments' paper money issues at one end and modern intermediative techniques at the other.

II.*

THE DEMAND FOR LOANABLE FUNDS

During any year, nonfinancial economic units sell new issues of debts and equities in the market for loanable funds. These securities are purchased by other nonfinancial economic units, by the monetary system, and by nonmonetary intermediaries.

The net demand for loanable funds, during any year, is the planned net issues of primary securities by nonfinancial economic units — by consumers, business firms, and Government units. Primary securities are the obligations of these economic units, and they include Government securities, corporate bonds and stocks, mortgages, and a variety of short- and intermediate-term debt. The sellers of these new issues are ultimate borrowers.

Chart 1 illustrates that ultimate borrowers may sell primary securities through any of three channels: (1) Directly to ultimate lenders; (2) indirectly to them through the monetary system; or (3) indirectly to them through nonmonetary financial intermediaries.

(1) When primary securities are sold directly

* From John G. Gurley, *Liquidity and Financial Institutions in the Postwar Economy*, Study Paper No. 14 prepared for the Joint Economic Committee's *Study of Employment, Growth, and Price Levels*, U.S. Congress, January 1960.

to ultimate lenders, the latter acquire these securities rather than claims on financial institutions. These financial transactions may conveniently be called direct finance.

(2) When primary securities are sold to the monetary system, the ultimate lenders acquire money balances and time deposits instead of primary securities. This is called indirect finance through the monetary system. The monetary system comprises the monetary accounts of the U.S. Treasury, Federal Reserve banks, and commercial banks.

(3) When primary securities are sold to nonmonetary financial intermediaries, ultimate lenders acquire claims on these intermediaries — nonmonetary indirect assets — rather than primary securities. This is called indirect finance through nonmonetary intermediaries. These intermediaries include mutual savings banks, savings and loan associations, life insurance companies, credit unions, and similar institutions. Nonmonetary indirect assets are mutual savings deposits, savings and loan shares, policy reserves, and so on. For some purposes the time deposit departments of commercial banks should be included in the group of nonmonetary intermediaries.

CHART 1

The Market for Loanable Funds

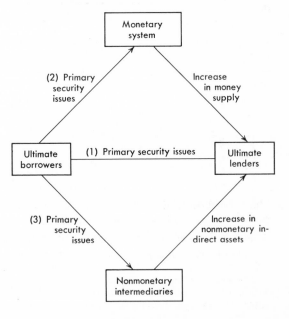

THE SUPPLY OF LOANABLE FUNDS

The net supply of loanable funds, during any year, is the demand for primary securities by ultimate lenders, the monetary system, and nonmonetary intermediaries.[1] When ultimate

[1] This is what the orthodox definition amounts to. In that definition the supply of loanable funds is:

Planned saving by economic units
+
Increase in stock of money
−
Increase in economy's demand for money (hoarding)

Assuming that saving and investment are done by different groups and that savers do not repay debts, planned saving is equal to economic units' increase in demand for primary securities, money, and nonmonetary indirect assets. The increase in the economy's demand for money minus that of economic units is the increase in demand for money by nonmonetary intermediaries. With these definitions, the supply of loanable funds becomes:

Economic units' increase in demand for
primary securities
+
Economic units' increase in demand for
nonmonetary indirect assets
+
Increase in stock of money
−
Nonmonetary intermediaries' increase in
demand for money

The second item above is equal to nonmonetary intermediaries' increase in demand for primary securities, neglecting gold. This yields my definition.

lenders supply loanable funds, they acquire primary securities. When the monetary system supplies loanable funds, it acquires primary securities and ultimate lenders accumulate money and time deposits. When nonmonetary intermediaries supply loanable funds, they acquire primary securities and ultimate lenders receive nonmonetary indirect assets. These relationships are shown in Chart 1.

MARKET EQUILIBRIUM

The market for loanable funds is in equilibrium when the demand for loanable funds is equal to the supply of loanable funds. It is in equilibrium, in other words, when issues of primary securities by ultimate borrowers are equal to the incremental demand for primary securities by ultimate lenders, the monetary system, and nonmonetary intermediaries.[2] When there is excess demand for loanable funds, interest rates on primary securities rise and other terms of lending tighten. When there is excess supply of loanable funds, interest rates on primary securities fall and other terms of lending are eased.

[2] This assumes an initial state of equilibrium — that the stock of primary securities is initially equal to the demand for this stock.

9

THE STRUCTURE OF THE FLOW-OF-FUNDS ACCOUNTS*

Lawrence S. Ritter[†]

The subject of debt involves as many confusions in the popular mind as does the subject of money. In fact, the two are closely intertwined in economic activity; frequently they are two aspects of the same process.

For example, it is the opinion of most laymen that in our society the superstructure of debt (and its other side, credit) is built upon the foundation of money. In fact,

* From the *Journal of Finance*, Vol. XVIII, No. 2 (May, 1963). Reprinted by the courtesy of the publisher (the American Finance Association).

† New York University.

however, the reverse is just as true: in a sense, money itself is the superstructure, built upon a foundation which consists of debt and, ultimately, faith in the integrity and solvency of the issuer of the IOU which we call money. For both currency and demand deposits, which are the money we use in our society, are fundamentally merely liabilities — or in other words, debts — owed by some institution. Thus money is built upon debt rather than debt upon money.

It is important to realize that every debt must have its credit counterpart somewhere. For every debt which someone owes — that is, for every liability — there must exist someone else to whom these funds are owed, someone who has a credit or an asset of equal value. The fact that we are willing to hold debts of others as our assets enables our complex economic system to function, since funds are transferred from savers to investors primarily through the medium of debt.

In the field of finance, the Federal Reserve's flow-of-funds accounts are the counterpart of the Commerce Department's national income accounts. This paper attempts to explain the basic principles underlying the flow-of-funds accounts, since their construction involves a number of fundamental theoretical propositions of widespread interest and application.

I.

The flow of funds is a system of social accounting in which (a) the economy is divided into a number of sectors and (b) a "sources-and-uses-of-funds statement" is constructed for each sector. When all these sector sources-and-uses-of-funds statements are placed side by side, we obtain (c) the flow-of-funds matrix for the economy as a whole. That is the sum and substance of the matter.

The number of sectors is a technical, rather than a fundamental, question. While there must be more than one, in order to permit transactions between sectors, the maximum practical number depends solely on such factors as the homogeneity of groups of decision-making units in the economy, the availability of raw data, and ease of handling. Too few sectors are likely to hide significant relationships, while too many are likely to become unwieldy. In the national income accounts, the Department of Commerce divides the domestic economy into three sectors: households, business firms, and governments. In the flow-of-funds accounts, the Federal Reserve prefers four main domestic sectors, with financial institutions added to the above three. These main sectors are in turn divided into a number of subsectors. In any case, the sectoring should be exhaustive, i.e., the entire economy should be included, if necessary by the use of a residual "all other"

category. In our discussion below we confine ourselves to a closed economy throughout.

A *sector "sources-and-uses-of-funds statement"* is a hybrid accounting statement which combines that sector's balance sheets and income statement and is derived directly therefrom. Fundamentally, it does not involve any concepts not already present in the balance sheet and the income statement. The construction of model sector sources-and-uses-of-funds statement occupies most of the remainder of this paper. We proceed from the balance sheet as the first step.

A. A generalized balance sheet, applicable to any sector, would appear something like the following:

(1)	Assets	Liabilities and Net Worth
	Financial assets:	Liabilities:
	1. Money	1. Short-term
	2. Near-monies	2. Long-term
	3. Other	
	Real assets	Net worth
	$\Sigma = \Sigma$	

A balance sheet similar to the above can be drawn up for each sector. The only differences between them would be in the characteristic items that would appear under each heading.

As is well known, each real asset in the economy appears on only one balance sheet, that of its owner. However, each liability, by its very nature as a debt, must necessarily imply the existence of financial assets of equal amount on some other balance sheet(s). Similarly, each financial asset, by its very definition as something due to that sector, must necessarily imply the existence of a liability of equal amount on some other balance sheet.[1] Thus, although for any one sector its liabilities are not likely to equal its financial assets, if we take all the sector balance sheets for the entire economy and consolidate them into one, the total of liabilities would conceptually equal the total of financial assets. The net worth (wealth) of the economy as a whole is therefore equal to the value of real assets in the economy.[2]

For present purposes it is helpful to rearrange and consolidate Balance Sheet 1 as follows:

(2)	A	L and NW
	Real assets	Net worth
	Financial assets	Liabilities
	Money	
	$\Sigma = \Sigma$	

Sector Balance Sheet 2 is identical with 1 except for some consolidation and rearrangement of the entries. Since money is a financial asset, it should, strictly speaking, be included under that heading. However, economic theory has traditionally treated money as unique, so that it is entered separately. The entry "financial assets" must therefore be understood as standing for "financial assets other than money."

B. A balance sheet, of course, shows stocks as of a moment in time rather than flows over a period of time. However, by comparing the balance sheets of a sector at two different points in time and noting the changes that have taken place over the intervening time span, balance-sheet data can be converted from stock to flow form. Comparison of a sector's balance sheet

as of December 31, 1961, with that for December 31, 1962, for example, would show the net changes that have taken place between the beginning and the end of 1962.

If we confine ourselves to financial assets and liabilities for the moment, ignoring real assets and net worth, such a comparative sector statement, indicating the net changes that have taken place between two dates in Balance Sheet 2, could be presented as follows:

(3)	Financial Uses	Financial Sources
	Δ Financial assets	Δ Liabilities
	Δ Money	

Such a statement is a sector *financial* sources-and-uses-of-funds statement. It need not balance, since it is derived from partial rather than complete balance sheets. A financial source of funds for a sector is, by definition, an increase in its liabilities: households, business firms, governments, and financial institutions can obtain funds by increasing their liabilities (borrowing). A financial use of funds for a sector is, by definition, an increase in its holdings of financial assets or money: households, business firms, governments, and financial institutions can utilize their funds to buy financial assets (lending) or to build up their stock of money (hoarding). Thus 3 could be re-written as follows:

(4)	Financial Uses	Financial Sources
	Δ FA (lending)	Δ L (borrowing)
	Δ M (hoarding)	

However, the above alternatives do not exhaust the possible financial sources or uses of funds. For example, another source, other than borrowing, by which a sector might acquire funds is by selling financial assets or by dishoarding. And another possible use of funds is the repayment of one's debts. These did not appear on 4 because only net changes were considered and it was assumed that these were positive.

In gross form, a sector financial sources-and-uses-of-funds statement would have slots for negative as well as positive changes:

[1] See Kenneth Boulding, *Economic Analysis* (3d ed.; New York: Harper & Bros., 1955), pp. 257–61. The term "liabilities" is usually defined in the flow-of-funds accounts as including equities (stocks) as well as debt claims (bonds).

[2] This conclusion pleases conservatives because it implies that printing money cannot in and of itself make an economy wealthier. However, by the same token, it also implies that increasing an internally held national debt cannot in and of itself make an economy poorer.

(4′)	Financial Uses		Financial Sources	
	Δ FA ↑	(lending)	Δ FA ↓	(selling securities)
	Δ M ↑	(hoarding)	Δ M ↓	(dishoarding)
	Δ L ↓	(repaying debts)	Δ L ↑	(borrowing)

In this framework it becomes clear that lending and borrowing are not opposites, as is usually assumed. Instead, the opposite of lending, which is the purchase of a financial asset, is the sale of a financial asset. And the opposite of borrowing is the repaying of one's debts. Also evident is the similarity, in purpose and in impact on the financial markets, of borrowing and selling off financial assets; both increase the market supply of securities, the former by the sale of one's own liabilities and the latter by the sale of someone else's.

Useful analytically as 4′ is, it is difficult to collect data on a gross basis. As a result, most published data are in the form of 4, with each pair netted; by convention, if the net change in any entry turns out to be negative over a period, it is kept on the side where it presently appears in 4 but preceded by a minus sign. Net dishoarding, for example, would be recorded on the uses side but preceded by a minus sign and referred to as a negative use.

C. We have thus far ignored changes in the first pair of entries on 2, namely, changes in real assets and in net worth. This is because we have confined ourselves thus far to considering only financial sources and uses of funds. But, in addition to financial sources and uses, a sector is also likely to have "non-financial" sources and uses. These may arise from transactions on *capital* account or from *current* transactions.

Non-financial transactions on *capital* account, as in national income accounting, refer to changes in real assets and in net worth. A change in real assets over a period, the acquisition of capital goods, is usually termed real (in contrast to financial) investment. The purchase of a capital good is obviously as much a use of funds as the purchase of a bond or a stock. Investment may be reckoned on either a net or a gross basis, in the sense that depreciation may or may not be deducted from the change in the value of a sector's holdings of real assets.

The change in a sector's net worth over a period could now be derived as a residual, if

one wished to do so. Net worth, by definition, is equal to total assets minus total liabilities. A change in net worth over a period must therefore equal the change in total assets minus the change in total liabilities. If we insert the change in real assets into 4, we will have accounted for all changes in assets and in liabilities and could derive the change in net worth as the difference between the two. However, this procedure might obscure the fact that the change in net worth for a sector over a period is identical with what is usually termed the "saving" of that sector during the period.

The saving of any sector is, by definition, the excess of its current receipts over its current expenditures. But an excess of current receipts over current expenditures (flows) must necessarily imply either a buildup of (stocks of) total assets or a reduction of liabilities (or some combination of the two) equal in amount to the excess of current receipts over current expenditures. Thus the saving of any sector must be equal to the change in its total assets minus the change in its liabilities, which in turn equals the change in its net worth.

The net changes for a sector between two dates in the first pair of entries on Balance Sheet 2 can thus be presented as follows:

(5)	Non-financial Uses on Capital Account	Non-financial Sources on Capital Account
	Δ Real assets (investment)	Δ Net worth (saving)

Just as 4 did not have to balance, since it was derived from partial balance sheets, neither is 5 likely to balance. An individual unit or sector may invest an amount equal to its current saving, but it may also be in deficit, investing more than it saves, or in surplus, saving more than it invests. However, if 4 and 5 are combined into one, as 6, it must necessarily balance:[3]

Statement 6 is the most widely used form of sources-and-uses-of-funds statement and is fre-

(6)	Uses	Sources
	Δ RA (investment)	Δ NW (saving)
	Δ FA (lending)	Δ L (borrowing)
	Δ M (hoarding)	
	$\Sigma = \Sigma$	

[3] As would also, of course, be true if 4′ and 5 were combined into one, which could be called 6′.

quently labeled that, although, strictly speaking, it is incomplete. It contains financial sources and uses of funds (i.e., 4) and non-financial sources and uses on capital account (i.e., 5), but does not take explicit account of *current* transactions. That is, it does not include current receipts as a source of funds or current expenditures as a use, except insofar as the difference between the two (saving) is included as a source of funds on capital account. Nevertheless, as it stands, 6 is useful — since it must balance — in showing that a deficit sector, with investment greater than saving, *must* borrow, dishoard, or sell financial assets in an amount equal to its deficit; and that a surplus sector, with saving greater than investment, *must* repay debts, hoard, or lend an amount equal to its surplus.[4]

Although 6 is in wide use, it is difficult to recognize unless one has been forewarned. There seems to be a deep-seated aversion on the part of those who publish statistics to the establishment of consistency in either the titles or the form of the tables they issue. For example, the Department of Commerce regularly issues data in a table entitled "Sources and Uses of Corporate Funds," which is, as one would expect, statement 6 for the corporate business sector. The same department also issues data in a table entitled "Disposition of Personal Saving." This turns out to be the same thing for the household sector, although neither the titles nor the arrangements of the two tables bear any obvious relationship to each other.

D. A complete sector sources-and-uses statement, as mentioned above, must also take account of *current* transactions: of current receipts accruing during a period as a source of funds, and of current expenditures as a use of funds. In other words, the income statement has thus far been neglected.[5]

A generalized income statement, applicable to any sector, would, in skeleton form, be something like the following:

	Non-financial Uses on Current Account	Non-financial Sources on Current Account
(7)	Current expenditures	Current receipts
	Saving (addition to NW)	
	$\Sigma = \Sigma$	

The excess of current receipts over current expenditures is generally termed "saving" when it applies to the household sector, a "budget surplus" when it applies to the government sector, and "retained earnings" (or addition to net worth or to surplus) when it applies to the business sector.

As a "use" of funds on current account, saving takes the form of non-spending, of accumulation or retention. As such, it becomes available as a source of funds for capital account and represents an addition to net worth.[6] As with investment, saving may be reckoned on a net or a gross basis, in the sense that depreciation charges may or may not be deducted from the addition to net worth. It should be noted, however, that even if depreciation is deducted, so that saving is measured on a net basis, depreciation would still be a source of funds for capital account, since it represents a non-cash expense rather than an actual current outlay of funds.[7]

---

[4] It is also useful in providing a demonstration alternative to the usual Keynesian one that, ex post, saving must equal investment for the economy as a whole. It was noted above with respect to 1 that if all sector balance sheets were consolidated into one, the total of liabilities would equal the total of financial assets, so that the net worth of the economy as a whole must necessarily equal the value of the real assets. It follows that if all the sector-sources-and-uses statements, such as 6, were consolidated into one, the total of borrowing would equal the total of lending plus hoarding, so that, for the economy as a whole, ex post saving must necessarily equal ex post investment. See footnote 5 in Selection 1.

[5] Capital expenditures, which have been discussed above, do not appear on an income statement.

[6] Saving may also be negative, of course, and thereby represent a subtraction from net worth. Furthermore, net worth may also change for other reasons than those discussed in this paper, such as by revaluation of assets (capital gains or losses).

[7] For example, assume that a firm's current receipts exceed current expenditures by exactly the amount of depreciation charges, so that net saving (and the change in net worth) is zero. This zero change in net worth is not consistent with the fact that real assets must be written down by the amount of the depreciation; on this latter basis, net worth should be lower by the amount of depreciation. The firm must have, for example, "involuntarily" accumulated cash equal to the depreciation charges, which cash can be spent to restore real assets to their former value *or for any other purpose the firm chooses.*

E. A complete sector sources-and-uses-of-funds statement, including transactions on current and capital account, as well as financial transactions, would combine 6 and 7:[8]

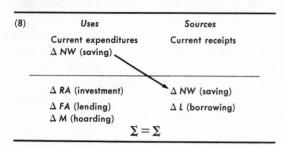

(8)	Uses	Sources
	Current expenditures	Current receipts
	Δ NW (saving)	
	Δ RA (investment)	Δ NW (saving)
	Δ FA (lending)	Δ L (borrowing)
	Δ M (hoarding)	
	$\Sigma = \Sigma$	

Complete sector sources-and-uses-of-funds statements, such as 8, are the basic backbone underlying the flow-of-funds accounts. Since the income statement (above the thin line) must balance, and the changes in the balance sheet (below the thin line) must also balance, the summation of all the sources must equal the summation of all the uses of funds. Also, since saving (or the change in net worth) on the income statement must necessarily be the same as the change in net worth (or saving)

on the balance sheet, saving could be deleted from both sides without disturbing the equality of total sources and total uses.[9] If this were done, the statement would simply express the logical necessity that the funds a sector receives during a period from current receipts and borrowing must necessarily be disposed of in some way, and must therefore equal the sum of its current expenditures, capital expenditures, lending, and hoarding.[10]

F. As mentioned at the beginning of this section, the flow-of-funds matrix for the economy as a whole merely consists of all the sector sources-and-uses statements placed side by side. Initially, in 1955, the published matrix showed the complete sector sources-and-uses statements in the form of 8. Since the 1959 revision, however, it has consisted of only partial statements in the form of 6, i.e., only that part of 8 below the dashed line.

Assuming a total of three sectors and omitting some detail, the current presentation of the flow-of-funds matrix for a specified time period appears essentially as follows.

(9)	Sector A		Sector B		Sector C		All Sectors	
	U	S	U	S	U	S	U	S
Saving (ΔNW)								
Investment (ΔRA)								
Lending (ΔFA)								
Hoarding (ΔM)								
Borrowing (ΔL)								

This complete matrix, or summary statement of the flow of funds, forms an interlocking self-contained system. It shows, for a specified time period, the balanced sources-and-uses-of-funds statements for each sector, the interrelations among the sectors, and the aggregate totals of saving, investment, lending, hoarding, and borrowing for the economy as a whole.

Any one sector may invest more or less than it saves, or borrow more or less than it lends. However, for the economy as a whole, saving

must necessarily equal investment, and borrowing must equal lending plus hoarding.[11] Thus deficit sectors, which invest more than they

---

[8] Or the combination of 6' and 7 into 8'. See footnote 3.

[9] Thus just as the Keynesian analysis can be presented without explicit reference to the concept of saving, since it is implied once consumer spending is determined, so the flow of funds can also be presented without saving appearing explicitly.

[10] More precisely, the funds a sector receives during a period from current receipts, borrowing, selling financial assets, and dishoarding must necessarily equal the sum total of its current expenditures, capital expenditures, debt repayments, lending, and hoarding (see footnotes 3 and 8).

[11] See footnote 4 and the related text.

save, necessarily imply the existence of other surplus sectors. This is not only because the economy-wide total of saving must equal investment, but also because a deficit sector *must* finance its deficit by borrowing, dishoarding, or selling off securities. This implies the existence of surplus sectors to do the lending, hoarding, or buying of the securities.[12] Similarly, surplus sectors, which save more than they invest, necessarily imply the existence of other deficit sectors.

If particular types of financial instruments are specified in the flow-of-funds matrix (as government obligations or corporate bonds), as in fact they are, the financial interrelations among the individual sectors can often be observed in even greater detail, in terms of which particular surplus sectors directly or indirectly finance which particular deficit sectors.

II.

It is not the purpose of this paper to delve into the technicalities involved in constructing the accounts. The literature on that is extensive and thorough. Nevertheless, it is worth calling attention to some of the main differences between the Federal Reserve's flow-of-funds accounts and the Department of Commerce's national income accounts. Four differences are of particular interest.

First, the national income accounts confine themselves exclusively to non-financial transactions. They contain no data on borrowing, lending, or hoarding. Second, the income accounts are designed to measure the current

output of final products; so far as possible, duplicative transactions and trading in already existing assets are eliminated in order to avoid double counting. This is not true of the flow-of-funds accounts. Third, the income accounts treat all real investment, or capital expenditures, as a business activity; neither consumers nor governments, as such, can invest. In the flow-of-funds accounts, consumer purchases of durable goods are treated as investment and are shown both gross and net of depreciation. This has the effect of removing the purchase of consumer durables from the category of current expenditures and thereby greatly increasing the volume of consumer (and national) saving. Finally, the sectoring is much more detailed in the flow-of-funds accounts than in the national income statistics, making integration and reconciliation of the two a rather complicated matter. In principle, one should be able to move easily from one set of accounts to the other, but in practice the sectoring and the treatment of various transactions are so different as to make it awkward and cumbersome to do so.

The potential usefulness of the flow-of-funds accounts as a theoretical tool is still largely unrealized. In the flow of funds we now have a complete and internally consistent body of data on financial flows, interlocked with national income data. Data on the financial markets are meshed with data on the goods and services markets. However, these still consist of logical ex post identities. Upon this foundation, we need to proceed to the even more important job of testing alternative hypotheses regarding the interaction between the financial and non-financial variables, with the ultimate objective of moving from the logical identities to the construction of a set of behavior relationships possessing explanatory value.

[12] The existence of deficit (or surplus) sectors in an economy thus requires a rather advanced financial structure to permit the requisite financial transactions to take place and, indeed, to facilitate them. See the lucid exposition of John G. Gurley in Selection 8.

PART 2

COMMERCIAL BANKING

CHAPTER FOUR

SOURCES OF BANK FUNDS: COMPETITION
FOR SAVINGS

10

SOURCES OF COMMERCIAL BANK FUNDS:
AN EXAMPLE OF "CREATIVE RESPONSE"*

Federal Reserve Bank of Cleveland

Part 2 of this book is concerned with commercial banking as a business, with the individual commercial bank as a profit-making (or at least profit-seeking) firm and with commercial banking as an industry, much like the steel industry or the soft-drink industry.

Looked at this way, banks acquire inputs (sources of funds) and transform them into outputs (uses of funds), just as General Motors acquires steel and rubber and transforms them into automobiles. An individual bank, as we have seen, must have excess reserves if it is to make loans. To get reserves, however, it first has to acquire deposits (its inputs). And for a good part of the postwar period banks have been losing in the race for deposits, losing to savings and loans and other competing financial institutions.

One of the reasons banks fell behind in the race for deposits is the existence of Regulation Q — the Federal Reserve's regulation governing the maximum interest rates commercial banks are allowed to pay to attract time and savings deposits.

In recent years, however, the Federal Reserve has raised the Regulation Q ceiling rates on commercial bank time and savings deposits sufficiently high so that banks have been able to compete vigorously for time deposits. The result has been a remarkable upsurge in this source of funds. The following two articles explore the background and some of the implications of this recent trend.

One further note: the negotiable certificates of deposit (CDs) mentioned below as having been such an important factor in the growth of commercial bank time deposits are merely receipts evidencing that a time deposit has been placed in a particular bank. Such pieces of paper can be bought and sold and are thus highly marketable (i.e., highly liquid). You can obtain a good description of them, and of other money market instruments, by writing to the Federal Reserve Bank of Cleveland, Cleveland, Ohio (44101) and asking for the booklet Money Market Instruments. *It is free.*

* From *Economic Review*, Federal Reserve Bank of Cleveland (November, 1965). Reprinted by the courtesy of the Federal Reserve Bank of Cleveland.

This article considers the growing importance of newly innovated sources of commercial bank funds. It thus is concerned with the "creative response"[1] of an industry — in this case, commercial banking — to a new environment in which old or traditional ways of conducting business will no longer produce the same results. In other words, the article examines what banks have done to attract funds in a period when traditional ways proved less than adequate.

Innovation, which is doing something new or doing something old in a new way, arises usually out of need. This is true of innovations in managerial structure, in production, in marketing, and in finance — to mention only a few areas of activity closely associated with the economic process. The case of commercial banking conforms to the pattern of doing something new or doing something old in a new way.

COMMERCIAL BANKING SINCE WORLD WAR II

Since the end of World War II, commercial banks have declined in importance relative to other financial institutions, continuing a trend that originated around the turn of the century.[2] While commercial banks have grown in size and are still the nation's leading financial intermediary, their growth has not kept pace with that of other private deposit-type financial institutions.[3] Whereas over the 20-year period since World War II, total sources of funds of commercial banks rose about 120 per cent, those of mutual savings banks more than tripled, those of savings and loan associations increased more than twelvefold, and those of credit unions, though still relatively small in absolute size, increased some twenty fold.

Put otherwise, while commercial banks at

[1] The term is borrowed from Joseph A. Schumpeter, "The Creative Response in Economic History," *Journal of Economic History*, Vol. VII, November 1947.

[2] See Raymond W. Goldsmith, *Financial Intermediaries in the American Economy Since 1900* (Princeton, New Jersey: Princeton University Press, 1958).

[3] In this article, commercial banks are compared only with other deposit-type institutions. A broader comparison with nondeposit-type financial institutions, for example, insurance companies and pension funds, would yield conclusions similar to those of this article.

the end of 1945 had held 86 per cent of the financial resources of all deposit-type financial institutions, the share had dropped to 65 per cent at the end of 1964. In each year through 1963, financial resources of commercial banks — the total of liabilities and capital — constituted a smaller proportion of the total resources of all deposit-type institutions. In 1964, however, there was the first sign of a change in this pattern. Thus, in 1964 for the only time since World War II, commercial banks succeeded in maintaining — in fact, slightly improving — their relative position. As a result, at the end of the year, sources of funds of commercial banks comprised a slightly larger portion of the total resources commanded by all deposit-type institutions than at the end of 1963 — 65.37 per cent in 1964 against 65.35 per cent in 1963.

The primary factor underlying the relatively poor showing of commercial banks in the postwar period perhaps has been the change in attitude of both businesses and individuals toward holding demand deposit balances. Both have become increasingly aware of the income foregone by holding temporarily idle funds in the form of "money" or, more specifically, as demand deposits; both have correspondingly become increasingly disinclined to do so. This is evidenced, in part, by the rapid growth of other deposit-type claims, which in turn reflects the public's desire to hold liquidity in income earning forms. Thus, demand deposit liabilities of commercial banks over the last 20 years have grown at an average annual rate of only 2.1 per cent; this contrasts sharply to average annual growth rates of 7.5 per cent for time and savings deposits at commercial banks, 6 per cent for mutual savings deposits, 14 per cent for savings and loan shares, and nearly 17 per cent for credit union shares. On the other side of the ledger, and as shown in Table I, demand deposit and currency holdings of nonfinancial corporations have grown less rapidly than have their holdings of total financial assets (which include demand deposits and currency). Thus, the ratio of demand deposits and currency to total financial assets of nonfinancial corporations declined from nearly 29 per cent in 1946 to 12.5 per cent in 1964.

TABLE I

Holdings of Financial Assets by Nonfinancial Corporations

Year	1 Demand Deposits and Currency (billions of dollars)	2 Total Financial Assets (billions of dollars)	3 One as a Percent of Two
1946	$21.2	$ 74.0	28.6%
1947	23.4	81.2	28.8
1948	23.6	86.6	27.3
1949	24.7	90.7	27.2
1950	26.2	107.5	24.4
1951	27.9	116.1	24.0
1952	28.7	122.1	23.5
1953	28.8	125.2	23.0
1954	30.9	130.3	23.7
1955	31.9	147.7	21.6
1956	32.1	153.0	21.0
1957	32.1	158.1	20.3
1958	33.5	170.0	19.7
1959	32.5	183.4	17.7
1960	32.1	191.4	16.8
1961	33.7	208.4	16.2
1962	34.5	224.4	15.4
1963	32.0	241.7	13.2
1964	32.5	260.7	12.5

Source: Flow of funds data, Board of Governors of the Federal Reserve System.

FACTORS ASSOCIATED WITH THE DECLINING DEMAND FOR CASH

The slower growth of demand deposits, reflecting as it does greater reluctance on the part of the public to hold idle money, is due in part to relatively high and generally rising interest rates that have characterized much of the postwar period.[4] An additional influence in this connection has been the absence of severe alternations in the level of economic activity since the end of World War II. Unlike the previous past when financial and industrial crises periodically gripped the nation's economy, the relative stability characterizing the two most recent decades has enabled business to plan their financial affairs better and hence to minimize unprofitable idle cash balances. Other factors might perhaps be cited, but whatever the causes of slower growth of demand deposits, commercial banks had to find ways of holding on to existing deposits[5] and of attracting newly generated funds.

TRADITIONAL RESPONSE

Though commercial banks did react to the changing environment, responses — until the past few years — were pretty much along traditional lines. As a general matter, commercial banks tended to limit their competition

[4] Lower and/or declining interest rates would not necessarily reverse the trend. One observer of the financial scene is probably correct in arguing that "once companies and individuals begin to economize on cash and place surplus funds into earning assets, the process is hard to reverse even though the return available from this economizing of cash may decline." See Paul S. Nadler, *Time Deposits and Debentures: The New Sources of Bank Funds* (New York: C. J. Devine Institute of Finance, Graduate School of Business Administration of New York University, 1964), p. 30.

[5] Shifts of funds out of demand deposits and into interest-bearing claims issued by nonbank financial intermediaries do not result in a decline in the demand deposits of the banking system — only a transfer of ownership. But, such shifts create losses for *particular* banks and increase the *volatility* of deposit balances in general. Moreover, if carried to an extreme, commercial banks would evolve into check clearing facilities — not a useless function, but certainly not one that is particularly profitable.

for loanable funds — to the extent possible under limitations imposed by Regulation Q — to raising interest rates paid on time and savings deposits, and to narrowing the differential between interest rates paid on such deposits and on deposit-type claims issued by other financial institutions as well as to advertising. In each year from 1952 through 1964, the effective rate paid on interest-bearing claims issued by deposit-type financial institutions exceeded the rate of the previous year. Commercial banks conformed to this pattern, reflecting both a willingness to compete for funds — albeit along traditional lines — and permissive actions by the regulatory authorities in progressively raising the ceiling on Regulation Q.

Banks were successful, after 1956, in narrowing the unfavorable differential between interest rates paid on their claims and interest rates paid on the claims of major competitors. Thus, whereas rates paid by savings and loan associations between 1952 and 1956 exceeded rates paid on time and savings deposits of commercial banks by more than 1.5 percentage points, this differential had narrowed to about ¾ of a percentage point by the end of 1964.[6]

Commercial banks have also sought to compete in the money market for the highly mobile short-term funds of both corporations and well-to-do individuals. Thus, as it became increasingly apparent that corporations and individuals were less likely to continue to hold large demand deposit balances, commercial banks attempted, as a second best alternative, to induce such depositors to keep funds on deposit as either time or savings deposits by making interest rates more attractive. In these efforts, particularly in the period beginning in 1957, some success was achieved.[7] Commercial

---

[6] Various factors enable commercial banks to compete successfully for loanable funds (particularly long-term savings) despite payment of lower effective rates of interest. One reason, for example, is that only commercial banks offer complete banking services and, hence, convenience.

[7] From 1936 through the end of 1956, maximum interest rates payable on commercial bank time and savings deposits under Regulation Q remained unchanged. As of January 1, 1957, maximum interest rate ceilings were raised on all types of time and savings deposits, excepting 30-to-89-day time deposits. This action by the regulatory authorities was initiated in recognition of the general rise in interest rates beginning in 1951.

banks were able to retain, often with the same deposit ownership, a portion of the funds formerly held in demand balances that might have sought profitable investment outside banks, as well as to attract a share of newly generated loanable funds.

Total time and savings deposits have increased at a much faster rate since the end of 1956 than have demand deposits — the former increased by 1.5 times as compared with the less than 25 per cent increase of the latter. At the end of 1956, demand deposits contributed almost 67 per cent of total sources of funds of commercial banks; by the end of 1964 the proportion had dropped to only slightly more than 50 per cent. Time and savings deposits, on the other hand, gained in relative importance, rising from less than 25 per cent to 37 per cent over the same period.[8] No particularly pronounced changes in the magnitudes of bank capital and other miscellaneous liabilities appeared in this period; at the end of 1956, the two components combined accounted for 9.1 per cent of total sources of funds of commercial banks as compared with 11.2 per cent at the end of 1964. However, recent innovations affecting these sources of funds have potentially important implications for the future, which are discussed later.

CREATIVE RESPONSE

To date, the 1960's have seen commercial banks become considerably more aggressive in their competitive efforts. This has been made possible in part by the greater leeway given by the monetary authority to commercial banks in the setting of interest rates.[9] But, in addition, commercial banks have found new ways of competing for funds — ways which likely will play a major role in determining the fortunes of commercial banking in coming years.

Prior to the early 1960's, commercial banks, as a general matter, apparently had been con-

---

[8] These percentages are for *total* demand and *total* time and savings deposits, as reported on bank balance sheets. The proportions thus differ from those usually derived from adjusted deposit data. Both sets of data, however, reveal similar patterns over time.

[9] Permission to raise rates payable on various types of time and savings deposits has been granted in every year since 1961.

tent to attract funds from traditional sources and by traditional means, with rising interest rates as the primary lure. The past few years, however, have witnessed a considerable change, with innovation now playing a dominant role in terms of both characteristics of claims issued by banks and the markets to which these claims are meant to have appeal.

Most important thus far of the debt instruments recently introduced by commercial banks — at least in terms of magnitude — is the negotiable certificate of deposit. In sharp contrast to the past when many banks discouraged or refused corporate-owned time deposits,[10] negotiable CDs were issued primarily to halt the movement of demand deposit funds from large commercial banks by corporate money managers into investment in various money market instruments, for example, Treasury bills, commercial paper, and bankers' acceptances. Certificates of deposit were not unknown prior to 1961, when leading New York City banks announced that they would offer such instruments to both corporate and noncorporate customers and a leading Government securities dealer indicated that it would maintain a secondary market for such instruments. But negotiable CDs totaled only slightly in excess of $1 billion at the end of 1960. By the end of 1964, this almost insignificant figure had grown to more than $12.5 billion — by August of 1965 to over $16 billion.

Negotiable CDs clearly have grown considerably faster than the total of time and savings deposits. While at the end of 1960, negotiable CDs constituted just 1.5 per cent of total time and savings deposits, by the end of 1964 they accounted for almost 10 per cent. Of the $54-billion increase in time and savings deposits between the end of 1960 and the end of 1964, negotiable CDs contributed more than one-fifth. Since negotiable CDs are a form of time deposit (as distinct from savings deposits[11]),

their increase has contributed far more significantly to the growth of time deposits. And it is the time deposit component in recent years that has evidenced most of the growth recorded in the total of time and savings deposits. From the end of 1961 to the end of 1964, time and savings deposits together increased by about 55 per cent. Time deposits alone, however, expanded about 2.3 times. The growing volume of negotiable CDs accounted for almost 45 per cent of the nearly $26 billion increase in time deposits over the period.

The appeal of negotiable CDs reflects in part their attractive yields; it also reflects their marketability, something the traditional time deposit lacked. However, while having much appeal to money managers, negotiable CDs are not necessarily as pleasing to bankers. For one thing, CDs tend to be highly sensitive to interest rates — to the extent that adverse differentials between interest rates paid on CDs and on other money market instruments could cause a loss of CDs and, hence, a loss of funds to the banks involved.

Interest rate considerations aside, there also exists the possibility of holders failing to renew maturing CDs, for example, because holders may want back their funds for working capital purposes. This is not a surprising situation in that, in many cases, CDs represent *temporarily* idle funds which in former years might have contentedly remained in demand balances. Negotiable CDs are therefore a potentially volatile source of funds, in contrast to the traditional savings, or even time, deposit. In this respect, CDs bear a strong resemblance to demand deposits.[12] Moreover, not only must legally required reserves and adequate capital be kept against CDs (as in the case of other deposits), but bankers may often feel queasy about investing such funds in high-yielding relatively illiquid assets. In short, negotiable CDs can easily become a rather volatile and expensive source of funds.

The issuance of negotiable CDs has probably been the most widely discussed aspect of the renewed vigor with which commercial banks

---

[10] A view in the past often was (and in some cases still is) that the buildup of interest-earning time deposits owned by corporations would be at the expense of demand deposits which earn no interest.

[11] Time deposits are generally held by businesses and well-to-do individuals, and include: time deposits open account, time CDs (negotiable and non-negotiable), and other special accounts. Savings deposits, as evidenced by the ownership of a passbook, represent generally the savings of the public-at-large.

[12] See George R. Morrison and Richard T. Selden, *Time Deposit Growth and the Employment of Bank Funds* (Association of Reserve City Bankers, 1965), Chapter III.

have sought to strengthen their commanding position as a financial intermediary. Of less quantitative importance thus far — but also possessing significant implications for the future — are new sources of funds showing up in the capital and miscellaneous liability accounts of commercial banks. Of particular interest are subordinated debentures and capital notes, and more recently unsecured short-term promissory notes, which were first issued in September 1964 by the First National Bank of Boston. The outstanding volume of subordinated debentures and capital notes rose from a level of only $21 million in mid-1963 to over $800 million at the end of 1964. In relation to total bank capital of nearly $28 billion at the end of 1964, $800 million is an inconsiderable amount. Yet, in the absence of regulatory restraints, there is reason for believing that the total could increase sharply and to significant proportions.

From a bank's point of view, debentures and capital notes have much to recommend them as a source of funds. To the extent that they substitute for additional sales of common stock, and to the extent that the rate of interest on them is less than the rate of return on invested capital, present stockholders stand to benefit from higher earnings per share and possibly higher market values of their equity holdings. But, aside from use as a substitute for the issuance of additional common stock, unsecured debentures and capital notes may also substitute for and/or supplement deposits (demand and time and savings) as a source of loanable funds to commercial banks.

Compared with negotiable CDs, for example, debentures and capital notes possess several distinct and widely accepted advantages. First, neither debentures nor capital notes require the maintenance of legal reserves, while as a deposit liability, CDs require such reserves. Second, debentures or capital notes do not require supporting equity capital or, at least, not to the extent that CDs or the more traditional deposit liabilities would require it. Third, neither debentures nor capital notes are subject to a Federal Deposit Insurance Corporation assessment; as a form of time deposit, CDs are subject to a 1/12 of one per cent annual assessment. Finally, because funds secured through debentures and

capital notes are likely to remain for a relatively long period of time, there is less need for maintaining secondary reserves, such as Treasury bills and other low-yielding though highly liquid assets. Thus, nearly all the proceeds from debentures and capital notes can be placed in loans and longer maturity investments.

In the absence of regulatory restraint, it is likely that unsecured short-term notes will become an increasingly important source of funds for commercial banks. Having some of the advantages of debentures and capital notes, short-term notes, in addition, are not burdened with similar marketing problems.*

CONCLUDING COMMENTS

Having said this, however, it should be remembered that, if not handled properly, that is, with full appreciation of the costs and risks involved, these "new" sources of funds could present serious problems to commercial banks.[13] Thus, it should not be surprising that the supervisory authorities have demonstrated prudent caution in evaluating such sources of funds. Nevertheless, the fact that new sources of funds have been "innovated" does suggest that commercial banks are seriously seeking to revitalize their position as a financial intermediary. The ultimate success of any single innovation is perhaps not important. What is important is that creative innovation has been reintroduced

* Editorial note: In January of 1966 the Federal Reserve redefined unsecured notes as "deposits", thus for the time being at least effectively stunting the growth of this instrument.
[13] Acquisition of substantial amounts of loanable funds through the issuance of capital notes and debentures commits the issuing bank to fixed interest payments over extended periods of time. Should market rates of interest subsequently decline, the bank's earning power may become jeopardized. An additional source of possible difficulty arises from the relatively high interest rate paid on these sources of funds. At, say, a 5 per cent rate of interest on debentures, proceeds from this source could hardly be placed in shorter-term loans and investments. Thus, it might become necessary to place these funds in longer-term and less liquid loans and investments. At some point the desire for profit might conflict with prudent behavior. For additional discussion see L. Wayne Dobson, *The Issuance of Capital Notes and Debentures by Commercial Banks* (Kentucky Bankers Association, 1965), pp. 22–26.

to commercial banking. And this virtually guarantees that the business of banking will never again be the same — as it probably should not

since change happens all the time in the various segments of U.S. business and financial enterprise.

11

IMPLICATIONS OF THE BIG TREND IN BANKING*

E. Sherman Adams†

The Big Trend in banking is plain for all to see. Time deposits are pouring into the commercial banks at the rate of more than a billion dollars a month. Bankers are aware that their banks are becoming more and more savings institutions. But how many have really thought through all the implications of this trend for bank management policies?

For what we are witnessing is a banking revolution. As recently as 1952, time deposits constituted less than one-fourth of total commercial bank deposits. Today they account for around 40% and are far more important than that as a source of loanable funds.

Bankers have been making some adjustments to this influx of time money, of course. They have had to. Last year the increase in interest paid on time deposits caused an unprecedented rise in bank expenses. To counter this, banks stepped up their mortgage and instalment lending and added substantially to their holdings of municipal securities.

These moves, however, were largely automatic. They showed that bankers have fast reflexes but do not necessarily prove that they have fully reoriented their thinking, their policies, their habitual attitudes, their hard-earned

prejudices, to the transformation that is taking place in the banking business.

DEPOSIT TRENDS SINCE THE WAR

Let's analyze what has been happening since World War II. As can be seen from Chart 1, commercial bank time deposits have expanded

CHART 1

The Surge of Time Deposits
(Billions of dollars)

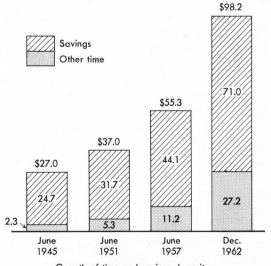

Growth of time and savings deposits—
all insured commercial banks

* Address by E. Sherman Adams, Vice President, First National City Bank, New York, at the Annual Convention of the New Hampshire Bankers Association at Wentworth-by-the-Sea, New Castle, N.H., on June 21, 1963. Reprinted by the courtesy of the author.
† First National City Bank of New York.

by more than $70 billion since mid-1945. This increase is equal to more than twice the total volume of all types of deposits of the entire commercial banking system only 30 years ago. More than half of this expansion has taken place within the past five years. A few months ago the total of these funds pushed past the hundred billion dollar mark.

Chart 2 shows the rate of expansion of time and also of demand deposits since 1945. Time deposits have increased over 200%, in contrast to only 60% for demand deposits. The rate of increase of time deposits has accelerated almost without interruption since 1950. It has more than doubled over the past two years.

As a result, as Chart 3 indicates, the proportion of time deposits to total deposits has increased substantially. Just within the past three years, it has risen from 31% to 38%.

The simple ratio of time to total deposits understates the relative importance of these funds to commercial banks. Almost all of these deposits can be productively employed — for member banks, all but the 4% required cash

CHART 3

The Big Trend

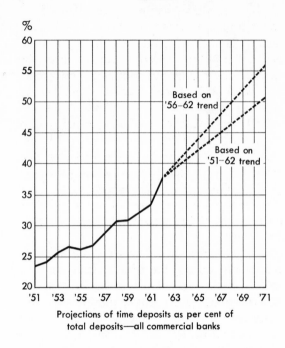

Projections of time deposits as per cent of total deposits—all commercial banks

reserves. In the case of demand deposits, employable funds are considerably reduced by float and by higher cash reserve requirements. At the present time, time deposits contribute 47% of the employable deposits of all member banks after allowing for required reserves and float.

REASONS FOR THE BIG TREND

Why has the Big Trend developed? One big reason, of course, is that, as shown by Chart 4, the volume of demand deposits relative to Gross National Product rose sharply during the 1930's and then became further inflated by the Treasury's wartime financing. Since the war, the economy has been growing up to this inflated money supply and we have been getting back to a more normal relationship between demand deposits and GNP.

The relative shrinkage of demand deposits has been accelerated by the rise in interest rates. This has given corporate treasurers strong incentive to keep their funds as fully invested as possible. Chart 5 shows the sharp decline that has taken place in the cash balances of business

CHART 2

Rate of Deposit Growth

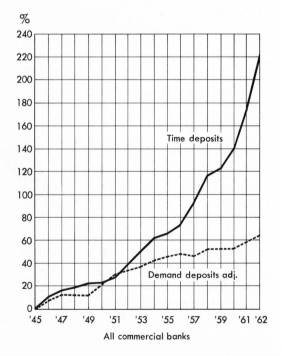

All commercial banks

firms in relation to their sales volume — a decline from almost 10% in 1940 to less than 5% in 1962.

Also, of course, business firms have been coming to the banks for loans in unprecedented numbers. Deplorable as it may seem to bankers, a company that is borrowing at the bank has little disposition to keep more money on deposit than necessary as a compensating balance.

Meanwhile, the volume of personal savings has been rising rapidly, and commercial banks shared in this expansion. This has been particularly true in recent years as more and more bankers have reached the conclusion that this is the most promising source of funds for future growth and have competed more aggressively for savings money.

Other time deposits, which expanded only moderately during the 1950's, have approximately doubled since the introduction of negotiable certificates of deposit a little over two years ago. Basically, this new instrument is a means of attracting back into the banking system funds that had been flowing into other short-term investment media — Treasury bills, commercial paper, and the like. It is estimated that the value of this new type of deposit is

CHART 5

Working Balances Work Harder

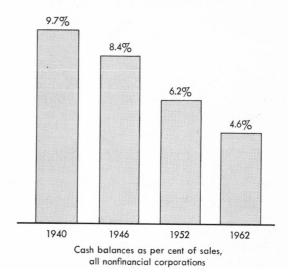

Cash balances as per cent of sales,
all nonfinancial corporations

now around $8 billion. This is an excellent beginning toward restoring commercial banks to their proper role as the major intermediary in the short-term money market.

FUTURE DEPOSIT TRENDS

What of the future? Will the Big Trend accelerate, slow down, level off, or what?

Chart 3 presents two different projections for the ratio of time to total deposits, one based on the 1951–62 rate of increase, the other based on the faster 1956–62 rate. On the basis of the latter, time deposits would constitute 50% of total deposits by the end of 1968. Even on the basis of the somewhat slower rate of increase for the entire period, they would pull even with demand deposits before the end of 1971.

Chart 6 shows projected rates of growth (on a ratio scale) for demand as well as time deposits. Here we see demand deposits projected on the basis of the average annual increase over the past eleven years, namely, 2½% per year. Again we have projections for time deposits on two bases: — the average rate of 9% a year for the entire 1951–62 period and the average rate of 11% a year over the past six years. Again we see time passing demand deposits by 1971 even at the slower rate.

CHART 4

Demand Deposits and G.N.P.

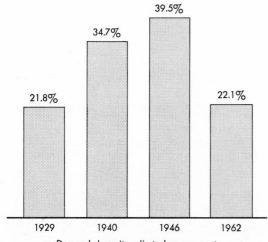

Demand deposits adjusted as per cent
of Gross National Product

CHART 6

Future Deposit Trends

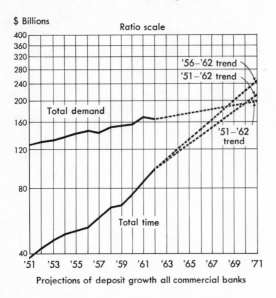

Projections of deposit growth all commercial banks

This is shown graphically by Chart 7. The total volume of bank debits naturally moves very closely with Gross National Product, as you can see. Bank debits can be analyzed in terms of the volume of demand deposits and their rate of turnover — deposits times rate of turnover equals bank debits. Since 1946, as Chart 7 indicates, deposits have risen more slowly than GNP because turnover has been rising. In the future, assuming a continuing rise in GNP, deposits should rise more rapidly as the rate of increase in turnover levels off, as it eventually must.

So we can conclude, it seems to me, that demand deposits will probably expand at a somewhat faster rate in the future than during the years since World War II. Indeed, we may already be entering a period when more and more corporations will decide that they need to carry larger cash balances to keep pace with expanding production and sales.

Will the Federal Reserve authorities permit a faster expansion of demand deposits? I think

Are these simple projections realistic indicators of what will actually happen? In the case of demand deposits, it is noteworthy that the ratio of these funds to GNP is now back to the 1929 level. Over a period of years, the volume of demand deposits has a tendency to keep pace with the growth of the economy. Their slow rate of increase since the war should not be regarded as permanent.

Some corporate treasurers will doubtless continue to work out more ways of economizing on their cash. However, many firms cannot make their working balances work very much harder than they have in recent years. The rate at which corporate treasurers can become increasingly economical is bound to slow down. When that happens, companies whose volume is expanding will increase their balances.

RISE IN TURNOVER MAY SLOW DOWN

Put it another way. The turnover of demand deposits has been rising rapidly since 1946. It cannot possibly continue indefinitely to rise at this rapid rate. Even a slowing down in the rate of increase in deposit turnover would tend to accelerate deposit expansion.

CHART 7

Future Growth of Demand Deposits
(Ratio scale)

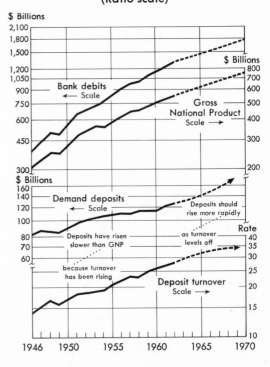

there is no question but that they will, assuming that business needs more cash with which to operate. One of the Fed's basic responsibilities is to accommodate the needs of the economy for money.

WILL THE BIG TREND CONTINUE?

Turning to time deposits, there is some question whether we should expect a continuation of the 1956–62 rate of increase. This period included two unusual factors: the dramatic boosting of interest rates paid by commercial banks and the introduction of negotiable certificates of deposit. On the other hand, although commercial bank savings deposits have slowed down a little since their big spurt in the first half of 1962 after the change in the rate ceilings, the pace of their expansion since then has remained considerably better than before the change in Regulation Q. Over the coming years, commercial banks should be able to continue to win a larger share of the rise in personal savings than they did during the 1950's.

And it should be remembered that personal savings will undoubtedly expand at a much faster rate than the growth of the economy. Over the past decade, the expansion of deposit-type savings has amounted to 150% compared with a rise of 60% in Gross National Product.

What about other time deposits? In this area, the negotiable certificate of deposit is the dynamic element. More than two-thirds of all negotiable C/D's are held by businesses. Chart 8 indicates what an enormous potential market this is for money-market instruments. It also shows the impressive start that negotiable C/D's have made over the past two years in competing for this vast reservoir of short-term corporate funds.

Just how fast and how far negotiable C/D's will expand, it is obviously impossible to say. To date, however, they have been going like a house afire, and they apparently still have a long way to go.

Putting all these considerations together, it seems plain that the Big Trend is not a fleeting phenomenon. It has all the earmarks of being

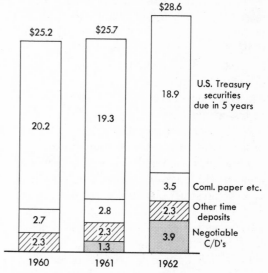

CHART 8

Big Market of C/D's
(Billions of dollars)

Money market instruments held by corporations

a permanent revolution. On this basis, let us examine some of its manifold implications for bank management policies.

IMPACT ON BANK LIQUIDITY NEEDS

Probably the most crucial area is asset management. Two basic factors underlying the lending and investment policies of every commercial bank are its liquidity requirements and its earnings position. Both are importantly affected by the Big Trend.

As for liquidity, let's start with the fundamental proposition that the average bank needs very little liquidity against savings deposits, especially when these funds exhibit a strong upward trend as they do in most banks today. This means that as savings deposits become relatively more important, banks need less in the way of liquid assets in relation to total deposits.

There is nothing novel about this statement, of course, but the fact remains that commercial banks typically have not invested savings deposits in the same types of assets as savings institutions. This did not matter much when savings deposits were relatively small, but it becomes important — more important than is generally realized — when savings deposits increase to 20, 30 or 40% of total deposits.

One caveat at this point. For many banks, a goodly part of the increase in their savings in recent years has been in large accounts — investment-type savings. These funds are potentially vulnerable to a sustained rise in short-term interest rates. In analyzing his liquidity requirements today, therefore, the banker must consider the composition as well as the amount of his savings deposits.

What about the negotiable certificates of deposit? How volatile will they prove to be? Some bankers contend that with $8 billion or more of these funds outstanding, the Federal Reserve must permit rates on them to fluctuate freely with other money-market rates. Some have even jumped to the extreme conclusion that they will never again have to worry about running out of money because they will now be able to go out and get all they want by means of C/D's.

I do not share this extreme view, and would not share it even if Regulation Q were put on stand-by or completely eliminated. The invention of the negotiable C/D did not impair the ability of the Federal Reserve to control the quantity of bank reserves and bank credit. Since the Fed can still tighten the availability of bank credit as conditions dictate, individual banks cannot expect to be immune from the effects of such a tightening.

But this does not mean that all C/D's should be regarded as hot money. Corporations will undoubtedly continue at all times to hold large amounts of liquid assets and I see no reason why an increasing proportion of these assets should not be in the form of "bankers' certificates." Nevertheless, a banker cannot assume that the volume of his corporate time deposits will never decline.

OTHER LIQUIDITY CONSIDERATIONS

Another point that is sometimes overlooked is that demand deposits today are far less volatile than they used to be. For the most part, these funds now consist of needed working balances. Most of the fluff has flown. The great bulk of the demand deposits of the average bank today is stable, hard-core money.

To be sure, bankers must be concerned not only with possible fluctuations in deposits but also with future loan demands, especially from business customers. However, to the extent that a commercial bank becomes increasingly a savings institution, the relative significance of this consideration is reduced. Moreover, the ability of a bank to meet an increase in business loan demand is enhanced by a strong upward trend in its savings deposits, not to mention the added flexibility of negotiable C/D's.

In general, therefore, commercial banks have considerably less need for liquidity today than they had 10, 15 or 20 years ago. The adequacy of a bank's secondary reserves should be measured primarily in relation to its demand deposits rather than total deposits. Old rules-of-thumb with respect to a bank's loan-deposit ratio and other broad measures of liquidity obviously need to be revised.

IMPACT ON BANKING EARNINGS

The Big Trend has also greatly changed the earnings picture of the average bank. In 1962, member banks paid out over $2 billion in interest on time deposits, more than eleven times their interest payments in 1946. As Chart 9 shows, the rise in interest paid on deposits has been responsible for a substantial part of the rise in total bank operating expenses, especially over the past several years. Since 1956, it has accounted for 68% of the sharp rise in operating expenses per $100 of deposits from $2.34 to $3.43.

This rising trend of bank expenses will undoubtedly continue, though probably not at the same pace as last year. At the same time, bank lending rates, which have more than doubled since 1946, have definitely been leveling off, as the chart shows. This points to a continuing and probably intensifying squeeze on bank profit margins — not necessarily this year but over a period of years.

An important corollary is that the rise in bank expenses has raised the floor under bank lending rates. This largely explains why these rates have become less sensitive to the influence

CHART 9

Bank Expenses and Lending Rates

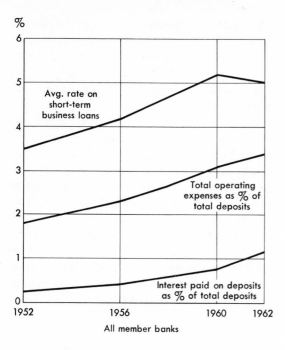

All member banks

This may come as a shock to many bankers and bank directors who have become accustomed to continuously rising per-share earnings year after year. Some have come to regard this as a top priority goal, as a symbol of good bank management. In the future, they may have to learn to take dips in earnings in stride.

IMPLICATIONS FOR ASSET MANAGEMENT

Rising expense ratios obviously mean that banks must seek higher-yielding assets, and since 1946 there has been a massive shifting by banks from lower-yielding into higher-yielding assets. In general, bank earnings have been well maintained — thanks partly to rising interest rates. But what will happen as the Big Trend continues — and especially if interest rates have passed their peaks? Banks cannot continue indefinitely to shift into municipals at the rate they did last year. Will they be able to maintain their present profitability in the face of the persistently rising cost of interest on time deposits?

Some of the evidence on this question is not reassuring. Various studies have shown that,

of monetary policy, especially on the down side. Banks are simply not in a position to afford much reduction in their lending rates from present levels.

THE RISE IN OPERATING RATIOS

Chart 10 shows the sharp impact that the Big Trend has had on bank operating ratios over the past six years. Prior to 1956, banks enjoyed a gradually declining trend in the ratio of their operating expenses to operating earnings, reflecting a continuing improvement in operating efficiency. Since 1956, however, the rapid rise in interest expense has reversed this favorable trend and pushed operating ratios up from less than 61% to almost 70% in six years' time.

Over the coming years, the Big Trend will probably cause some further rise in the average bank's operating ratio. The higher this ratio goes, the more sensitive net earnings become to changes in gross income. This enhances the likelihood of sharper fluctuations, downward as well as upward, in net operating earnings.

CHART 10

Bank Expense Ratios

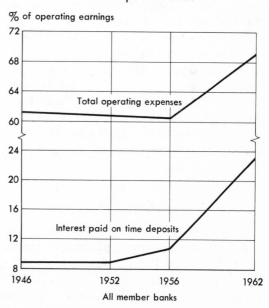

All member banks

on the average, banks with a higher proportion of savings deposits earn less than other banks of comparable size and location which have a low proportion of savings deposits. This would suggest that as the Big Trend continues, bank profitability may tend to decline.

This evidence is certainly sobering, but, fortunately, it is not conclusive. For one thing, we should not forget that many banks could not operate profitably without savings deposits and their prospects would be bleak indeed if it were not for the expansion potential of these balances. Also, there are doubtless some banks that can invest new savings deposits more profitably today than they could years ago. Finally, even more significant, there are plenty of adequately capitalized banks with relatively large savings deposits which are earning a good return on invested capital.

Examination of the figures for individual banks reveals that there are wide disparities in their operating results and correspondingly wide differences in their asset management policies. For the most part, banks with inadequate earnings have simply failed to make the adjustments in their lending and investment policies which they need to make to earn a good return. And most of them appear to have ample leeway for making such adjustments.

One thing that stands out is that these disparities are most significant among banks whose savings deposits range from 20 to 40% of total deposits. Let us call them the 20-to-40 percenters. Banks in this group show marked differences in lending and investment policies and in their profitability. Generally speaking, banks with more than 40% in time deposits have learned long ago how to operate profitably as part savings institutions. Those with less than 20% do not need to learn. Among the 20-to-40 percenters, some have learned and some have not, and it shows.

FACTORS IN BANK PROFITABILITY

For example, Chart 11 presents two significant asset ratios for two different groups of banks in the 20-to-40% class, one being a sampling of 94 banks with high profitability in terms of earnings in relation to assets, the other

being a sampling of 99 banks with low profitability. As can be seen, the high profit banks had a considerably higher average loan ratio than the low profit bank. Perhaps even more significant, the ratio of personal instalment loans of the high profit banks was more than 50% higher than that of the low profit banks. These were apparently two of the principal factors which accounted for the great disparity in their net earnings.

It is pertinent to note that the average rate of interest paid on time deposits by these two groups of banks was identical. It is also noteworthy that in the case of these two particular groups of banks, their proportionate holdings of mortgages were not significantly different. This evidence, admittedly fragmentary, would suggest that perhaps the importance of mortgages has been overstressed and the importance of instalment loans not fully appreciated. And at the present time, of course, the return on new mortgages is less attractive than it has been in the past.

Today most commercial banks are in the critical 20-to-40% class. Many have moved into this class within the past few years. Chart 12 gives an indication of the high proportion of

CHART 11

Factors in Bank Profitability

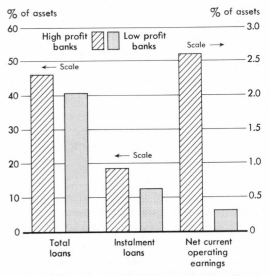

Ratios of samples of high and low profit banks with time deposits ranging from 20%–40% of total deposits

CHART 12

Middle Class Explosion
Most banks have now become 20 to 40 percenters

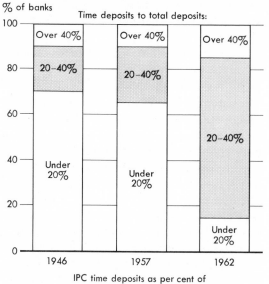

IPC time deposits as per cent of
total deposits of 20 large banks

larger banks that have become 20-to-40 percenters just since 1957. The evidence indicates that while most banks in this class have made some adjustments in their asset management policies, many may still have further adjustments to make. Unless and until they do, their earnings positions may progressively deteriorate.

REAPPRAISAL OF CAPITAL REQUIREMENTS

Many banks may not be fully aware of their need for better earnings because they have not maintained their capital positions. Their reported earnings per share have continued to rise but the increase in their capital accounts has not kept pace with their deposits. Some banks have not yet faced up to the fact that the expansion of their time deposits has been increasing their capital requirements.

I know of no valid reason for assuming that, as a general proposition, less capital is needed against savings than against demand deposits. In fact, one could easily argue the exact opposite on the grounds that savings are more fully

invested in a higher proportion of risk assets. The continuing surge of time deposits means that many banks should right now be carefully reappraising their present and future needs for capital.

Such a reappraisal will confront them with the importance of earning at least as much per $100 of additional time deposits as they are presently earning per $100 of existing deposits. If they fail to do so, then, assuming they maintain their present capital ratios over the years ahead, they will gradually dilute the earning power of the capital presently invested in their institutions.

It is significant, and ominous, that for all member banks, earnings per $100 of deposits declined 9% in 1961 and 8% further in 1962. Granted that the rise in expenses in 1962 was unusual, these figures still suggest that many banks are not investing their mounting time deposits profitably enough to avoid an eventual erosion of the return earned on invested capital.

POLICIES WITH RESPECT TO SAVINGS

Entirely aside from the matter of the employment of savings deposits, other policies with respect to a bank's savings business have now assumed far greater importance than formerly. Take interest rate policy. An adequate interest rate policy has become essential to healthy growth. On the other hand, an excessively liberal rate policy can be a serious drag on earnings. Today's banker must formulate his interest rate policies on the basis of careful study and must thoroughly reexamine them periodically in the light of changed conditions.

Or take the matter of small, unprofitable savings accounts. Most bankers are aware that a substantial portion of their savings accounts are unprofitable, but in the past they have not had to give much attention to this problem. But now perhaps they should.

Chart 13 shows a breakdown of one large commercial bank's savings deposits by size of account. As you can see, accounts under $500 constitute well over half of the total number of accounts but comprise only 3½% of total savings balances.

CHART 13

How Many Accounts Are Unprofitable?

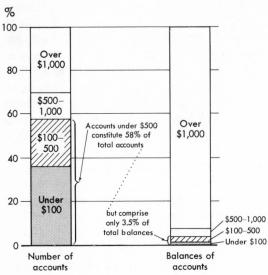

Breakdown of savings accounts of a large bank
by size of account

Unquestionably most of these small accounts are unprofitable, and this is true for the average bank. To be sure, a bank has a public responsibility to encourage thrift. Also, some small accounts will eventually become larger, profitable accounts. But most of them will remain small. Many of them are not truly savings accounts at all; they are pocketbook accounts. What, if anything, should a bank do to give less encouragement to accounts of this kind or to make more of them profitable?

There are plenty of other questions with respect to savings policies that will become increasingly important as the Big Trend continues. They are questions that most banks can no longer afford to ignore or to answer off the cuff.

In formulating policies with respect to savings, most banks need better estimates of the profitability of their savings business than they have at the present time. They need to know not simply what they are earning on their existing savings deposits, but also the incremental costs and marginal profitability of taking on and investing additional savings deposits in the future, taking into consideration the availability

of various types of assets and the returns they will yield.

Good estimates of this kind are essential to the formulation of wise policies with respect to a bank's savings business. Ignorance of costs and profitability have led many banks to pay rates they cannot afford on the basis of present incomes.

ASSET ALLOCATION TECHNIQUES

This brings us inevitably to the controversial subject of asset allocation, a subject which the Big Trend is making more timely every day. Asset allocation is regarded by some as anathema, by others as a panacea. Actually, of course, it is neither. Intelligently applied, asset allocation techniques can be a useful tool of bank management. Unintelligently applied, they can do more harm than good.

There are three major areas in which asset allocation techniques can be useful: (1) in current liquidity management, (2) in long-range asset planning and (3) in determining the profitability of savings deposits. All of these areas have now assumed critical importance to 20-to-40 percenters. Many bankers are today studying asset allocation for the first time because they have for the first time become 20-to-40 percenters.

Take current liquidity management. As the Big Trend continues, a bank needs to keep less of its resources in liquid assets. How much less? Asset allocation techniques may help the banker to arrive at a sensible answer.

Similarly, for banks whose deposit mix is changing rapidly, long-range asset planning has particular significance. For instance, over the next five years, should your bank expand your mortgages and consumer loans by as much as 50%, or perhaps even more, in order to find profitable employment for your increasing savings deposits? If so, you had better decide this soon so you can make plans for achieving this objective. Asset allocation techniques may help you reach the right decision.

How long should you continue to pay 4% on over-one-year savings? Yields on mortgages and on municipal securities have declined considerably since you went to 4%. How much will you earn over the coming year on the deposits you attract or retain with that 4% rate? Again, asset allocation techniques can help supply the answer.

Some bankers assume that asset allocation is necessarily a rigid formula, that it is proposed as a substitute for judgment. This is a false assumption. Bankers should not reject asset allocation techniques without taking the time to understand them and to investigate their potential usefulness. This applies particularly to bankers who have recently joined the ranks of the 20-to-40 percenters.

BANKING FOR EVERYMAN

It would be a mistake to think of the banking revolution solely in terms of the growth of savings deposits. Actually, this is simply one aspect of a broader development, namely, the expansion of retail banking. Commercial banks are becoming less and less commercial, they are increasingly becoming financial department stores for the American family.

This calls for a reorientation of many banking policies in addition to those we have already mentioned. Public relations is an obvious example. Time was when many banks dealt chiefly with business firms and the carriage trade. Today everyone owns a carriage, and banks must seek to project a favorable image among all segments of the population, a far more complicated job.

This applies also to bank advertising and marketing problems. Bankers must learn completely different sales techniques if they are to become successful retailers. And this includes training all of their personnel who come in contact with the public to become effective sales people too.

Retail banking requires many skills and capabilities which the traditional bank lending officer or operating officer does not have. People who possess these talents need to be found and must then be given adequate authority, support and official recognition.

IMPLICATIONS FOR PUBLIC POLICY

The Big Trend also has many implications for public policy which we can touch on here

only briefly. Take reserve requirements against savings deposits. There is widespread agreement today that the primary function of member bank reserve requirements is to serve as part of the mechanism for regulating the money supply. Since savings deposits are not part of the active money supply, it can logically be argued that they should not be subject to cash reserve requirements. It is obviously discriminatory to require member banks to maintain cash reserves against savings when competing thrift institutions are not subject to the same requirements. The Big Trend has made this inequity a matter of increasing concern.

Or take the practice of requiring banks to pledge specific assets as security for public deposits. At the present time commercial banks have pledged for this purpose more than $25 billion of their assets, consisting largely of relatively low-yielding U.S. Government securities. The Big Trend makes it necessary for banks to earn a higher rate of return on their loans and investments than in the past. The archaic practice of pledging assets to secure public deposits became increasingly burdensome as the Big Trend continues.

CONCLUSION

In conclusion, let us summarize briefly. We have seen that the Big Trend has a major impact on bank liquidity requirements and on bank earnings. Hence it requires basic revisions in bank lending and investment policies. It has a significant effect on bank capital requirements, and it has increased the importance of all of the policies banks follow with respect to their savings business. All of these factors make it timely for bankers to study the possible use of asset allocation techniques as an aid to policy formulation. Finally, the expansion of retail banking requires changes in many other areas such as public relations, marketing and personnel policies.

In short, the Big Trend has far-reaching implications for almost every aspect of bank management. It has special significance for banks that are 20-to-40 percenters, but there are few banks that are not affected by it to some degree.

This means that all banks need carefully to reexamine all of their existing policies in the light of the sweeping changes that are taking place in the banking industry. If they fail to do so, the next big trend in banking could be a trend toward lower earnings. On the other hand, for banks that do adapt their policies to the new realities of banking life, the future is bright with opportunity both for profitable growth and for greater service to the public.

12

COMPENSATING BALANCE REQUIREMENTS: THE RESULTS OF A SURVEY*

Nevins D. Baxter and Harold T. Shapiro†

Commercial bank practice with respect to the requirement that compensatory or minimum deposit balances be maintained by borrowers is an important aspect of bank management. This survey revealed a substantial amount of information on this subject.

The compensating-balance requirement is an arrangement between commercial banks and their customers, which provides that the customer must hold a certain deposit to compensate the bank for granting him a loan (perhaps at a privileged rate of interest), or for establishing a line of credit, or for performing certain services, such as check collection. Recently, requirements of this type appear to have become increasingly important in commercial-bank operations. Parallel to this development, there have been several attempts in the literature to provide a theoretical analysis of the nature of these requirements.[1]

There have been few attempts, however, to investigate contemporary banking practices with respect to these requirements, and to determine how these practices vary from area to area and among banks of different deposit sizes. One such survey was made in the mid-1950's by the Federal Reserve Board as part of their "Survey of Bank Loans for Commercial and Industrial Purposes." This survey provided some limited information about the extent to which compensating-balance requirements were employed and gave some indication of their magnitude.[2] It seemed clearly desirable to us that more up-to-date and comprehensive information concerning actual banking policies be

* From *Journal of Finance*, Vol. XIX, No. 3 (September, 1964). Reprinted by the courtesy of the publisher (the American Finance Association) and the authors.
† University of Pennsylvania and the University of Michigan, respectively.

[1] See, for example, J. Guttentag and R. Davis, "Compensating Balances," *Monthly Review* of the Federal Reserve Bank of New York, December 1961; *idem*, "Are Compensating Balance Requirements Irrational?" *Journal of Finance*, March 1962; *idem*, "Balance Requirements and Deposit Competition," *Journal of Political Economy*, December 1963; D. Hellweg, "A Note on Compensating Balance Requirements," *Journal of Finance*, March 1961; D. Hodgman, "The Deposit Re-

lationship and Commercial Bank Investment Behavior," *Review of Economics and Statistics*, August 1961; T. Mayer and I. O. Scott, "Compensatory Balances; A Suggested Interpretation," *National Banking Review*, December 1963; H. T. Shapiro and N. D. Baxter, "Compensating-Balance Requirements: The Theory and Its Implications," *Southern Economic Journal*, January, 1964.

[2] C. Cagle, "Credit Lines and Minimum Balance Requirements," *Federal Reserve Bulletin*, June 1956, pp. 573–579. See also F. P. Gallot, "Why Compensating Balances?" *Bulletin of the Robert Morris Associates*, August 1958, and Mayer and Scott, *op. cit.*, both of which provide some quantitative information on compensating balance practices.

made available with regard to compensating-balance requirements.

The present study was designed to find out precisely how widely compensating-balance requirements are used today, the exact nature of these requirements, their importance as a variable in the bank-customer relationship, and how the requirements vary under changing money-and-credit conditions. Section I discusses the design of our commercial-bank sample and our survey technique. Section II presents and analyzes the results of the study, and Section III discusses the relation of the results to the theory.

We find that compensating balances are widely applied, but are most popular both in large banks and with respect to large borrowers. Specifically, we conclude that there are significant differences in the behavior of large and small banks, but that banks in urban areas tend to behave rather uniformly regardless of size. In most cases, practices are fairly homogeneous throughout the country. Moreover, banks generally do not apply compensating-balance requirements according to hard-and-fast rules, but rather as a flexible variable in the bank-customer relationship.

I. DESIGN OF THE SAMPLE AND SURVEY PROCEDURE

The unit banking system in the United States, and the complex of state and federal laws, have rendered the structure of American banking divergent from state to state. Largely because of the concentration of deposits in money-market centers and the varying regulations governing branch banking, there is little correlation between the volume of deposits and the number of independent banking units in any given state. Because of this factor we constructed our sample to account for both the amount of deposits and the number of banks (independent decision units) in each state.

A target sample size of 500 was allocated among the states on the following basis. The percentage of the total banks in the nation located in a given state was averaged with the percentage of the deposits in that state. The resulting figure was multiplied by 500, this giving the preliminary "quota" sample size for

each state. The "quotas" were modified in two respects. First, in general, a minimum of five banks was chosen from each state. Second, the "quotas" were often slightly altered when it seemed appropriate to do so in view of the actual banking structure of the state. This was done to insure adequate representation from each state of both rural and urban areas and of large, medium, and small banks. The fifty largest banks in the country and the largest bank in each state were automatically included. The sample covers approximately 4 per cent of the banks in the country, but includes well over half of all deposits in the nation.

In order to investigate whether differences in banking practices exist in various areas of the country, among banks of different size, and between rural districts, each bank was classified according to geographic location, deposit size, and character of urban area. Banks were placed into one of eight geographic areas and seven deposit groups, and also differentiated on the basis of whether their head office was located in a major financial center, in other urban areas, or in rural districts.[3]

An initial survey questionnaire was prepared and then pre-tested in interviews with banks in the New York and Philadelphia Federal Reserve districts. From these interviews a final multiple-choice questionnaire was developed (see Appendix A) and sent in February 1963 to all the banks (526) in our sample. After a two-month period, questionnaires were again sent to those banks which had not yet responded; 66 per cent of the banks responded to the initial questionnaire, and an additional 14 per cent to the follow-up, making a total of 420 respondents in all.

II. RESULTS OF THE SURVEY

DISTRIBUTION OF RESPONDENTS

Of the 80 per cent response to the survey, banks of all sizes and from all geographical areas were well represented. In fact, although the poorest percentage response came from the

---

[3] Major financial centers include "Reserve cities" and cities containing at least one bank with deposits in excess of $400 million. Urban areas are those cities with over 50,000 population which do not qualify as major financial centers.

TABLE I

Sample Size and Percentage Response by Area and Deposit Groups

Region	North-East	Mid Atlan-tic	South	Mid-West	Great Plains	Texas	Moun-tain	Pacific	Entire Sample
Sample Size	77	74	64	115	59	54	36	47	526
Percentage response	79%	84%	75%	81%	76%	82%	78%	83%	80%

$Millions							
Deposit Size	Under 20	21–50	51–100	101–200	201–500	501–1,000	Over 1,000
Sample Size	190	89	74	55	57	38	23
Percentage response	75%	76%	80%	89%	82%	87%	91%

smallest banks (deposits under $20 million), over 75 per cent of this group responded; this compares with the better than 90 per cent response from the group containing the country's largest banks (deposits over $1 billion). Similarly the response geographically was uniformly excellent, ranging from 75 per cent in the South to 84 per cent in the Middle-Atlantic States. The response was slightly higher for banks in major cities as compared to banks in rural areas. Table I gives the sample size and percentage response by area and deposit group.

WHO USES COMPENSATING BALANCES?

Compensating-balance requirements are generally employed throughout the country.[4] These requirements are least prevalent, however, in those areas of the country where the economy is predominantly agricultural and where the average size of bank is small. It appears that large banks, which by nature have diversified loan portfolios, almost invariably apply compensating-balance requirements to at least some of their customers. It is interesting to note that small banks located in large urban areas tend to follow the practices of their larger competitors in that they employ compensating balances to a greater extent than do rural banks of the

[4] A notable exception is the state of Vermont, where they were declared illegal in 1961.

same deposit size.[5] Table II summarizes the affirmative response pattern.

The use of compensating-balance requirements has become more widespread in the last decade. For the nation as a whole, about one half of the banks now requiring compensating balances did so before 1951. Before 1951, however, their use was mainly confined to the larger banks. This is illustrated by the fact that 80 per cent of the banks with deposits over $1 billion who now use balance requirements did so before 1951, against 15 per cent for banks with under $20 million of deposits.[6]

The years immediately following the March 1951 Accord saw little increase in the use of compensating-balance requirements. Interest rates were still relatively low and the banking system had an adequate volume of reserves to meet borrowers' demands. In contrast, the pe-

[5] Of our 420 respondents, 346 banks replied to the questionnaire at first request and 74 to the follow-up. It is interesting to note that 78 per cent of the original group used the requirement, whereas only 69 per cent of the followup respondents did so. This information might indicate that a larger proportion of the non-respondents do not use compensating balances than of the respondents, and that our results have therefore slightly overstated the prevalence of the requirement.

[6] Even in this earlier period, however, small banks in urban areas, like their larger competitors, had already begun to use the requirement; in fact, about half of such banks did so.

TABLE II

Affirmative Response Pattern
(percent of total respondents)

$ Millions Under 20	21–50	51–100	Deposit Size of Bank 101–200	201–500	501–1,000	Over 1,000
42	85	93	100	100	100	95

Major Financial Centers	Urban Areas	Rural Districts
98	96	50

riod 1955–1958 showed a marked increase in the application of the requirement, noticeably among smaller banks, which as a group had previously virtually ignored these practices. Since 1958 the importance of compensating balances has continued to grow, but at a slower rate.

THE NATURE OF THE COMPENSATING-BALANCE REQUIREMENT

The compensating balance is generally not a hard-and-fast requirement, but is instead a flexible variable, the nature of which differs from bank to bank and customer to customer. Typically, the compensating deposit is 10 per cent of total negotiated credit lines and an additional 10 per cent on that part of the line in use. Often the alternative of maintaining an average deposit of 15 per cent of the entire line of credit may be selected.

Compensating-balance requirements are generally applied to lines of credit, direct loans, and sometimes appear in lieu of service charges to non-borrowing customers who utilize other bank services such as payroll accounts. It appears that compensating balances are most prevalent in the negotiation of lines of credit. Over four-fifths of those banks employing the requirement indicated their primary importance in line arrangements.

In the overwhelming majority of cases, the compensating-balance requirement is negotiated directly between the bank and individual customer, a great deal of flexibility being left to the loan officer involved. The next most prevalent, but much less common practice, has the balance requirement set in advance and the same for all loans to which it applies. Other practices, such as having the requirement set in advance for each category of loan, or for each category of borrower, or both, are also employed to a lesser extent. It appears that no significant differences in negotiation practices exist among banks of different sizes or in different areas of the country.

METHOD OF FULFILLING THE COMPENSATING-BALANCE REQUIREMENT

The compensating-balance requirement need not always be fulfilled by maintaining a balance which is at times at least as great as the requirement. This fact assumes special importance when we consider that the compensating deposit may therefore be an asset with some degree of liquidity.[7] The extent of the liquidity will be greater the longer the period over which the customer is allowed to average the size of his deposit to meet the requirement. In cases where the compensating deposit is treated as an average over a period of a year, such an asset can serve important seasonal purposes, if the borrower is willing to maintain high balances at those times of the year when he is "in funds."

It appears that about half of the banks employing compensating-balance requirements allow some sort of averaging. This practice, however, is employed by better than 80 per cent of those banks with deposits in excess of $500 million, as compared with some 30 per cent of those with deposits under $50 million. Therefore the compensating deposit in the smaller banks should be viewed as a less liquid asset for the depositor.

Typically, the compensating deposit can be averaged over a period of a year. Other meth-

[7] This factor is important in considering the profitability of compensating-balance requirements. See Section III below.

ods, which are used to a lesser extent, include averaging the deposit over periods of less than a year and averaging over the period through which the loan is outstanding. Some banks do apply different methods to different types of borrowers. Geographically, there seems to be little difference in the frequency with which these methods are employed.

TO WHOM ARE
COMPENSATING BALANCES APPLIED?

Compensating balances are applied to a greater or lesser extent to virtually all types of borrowers, but the category and size of customer are important factors in influencing the degree to which these requirements are employed. Compensating balances are most common with respect to credit extended to finance companies and commercial-and-industrial firms and are least common in agricultural and consumer loans. (See Tables IIIA and IIIB.) As regards each category of borrower, the requirement is invariably and significantly more prevalent for the larger businesses.

Tables IIIA and IIIB present data on the application of compensating-balance requirements by deposit and area group, respectively. The upper section of each table gives the percentage of affirmative respondents who applied

compensating balances by category of loan, and the lower by size of loan.

The tables exhibit many apparent differences in the extent of the application of compensating-balance requirements by different groups of banks. A large portion of these discrepancies is to be explained not by different attitudes toward the requirement, but instead by differences in the composition of loan portfolios. Compensating balances are applied much more widely by larger banks. This is due in part to the fact that smaller banks are generally less diversified and may have virtually no loan customers in certain categories. The much lower frequency of the balance requirement for Security loans among smaller banks is a case in point. Consumer loans is the only case where the requirement is apparently more important for smaller banks; and this might be expected, given their portfolio emphasis. As regards real-estate loans, the much higher prevalence of compensating balances in urban banks on the Pacific Coast can also be explained by the much higher portion of this type of loan in their portfolios.

The compensating-balance requirement, as has been stressed throughout, is generally applied with a great deal of flexibility and is not usually of a contractual nature. There are, how-

TABLE IIIA

Application of Compensating-Balance Requirements by Deposit Group
(percentage of affirmative respondents)

(Deposits, in Millions of Dollars)	Total	Under 20	21– 50	51– 100	101– 200	201– 500	501– 1,000	Over 1,000
Category of Loan								
Finance								
Companies	91	83	83	98	94	96	97	95
Commercial and								
Industrial	86	82	78	84	96	85	94	95
Real Estate								
Loans	46	47	38	42	45	40	64	60
Security Loans	37	27	28	36	43	28	61	65
Agricultural								
Loans	21	30	19	13	18	13	36	25
Consumer Loans	15	25	14	11	16	11	12	10
Size Category of Loan								
Small	65	52	52	67	75	62	94	85
Medium	88	77	74	96	98	87	97	95
Large	94	82	93	100	98	96	97	95

TABLE IIIB

Application of Compensating-Balance Requirements by Area Groups
(percentage of affirmative respondents)*

Area	Total	New Eng- land	Mid- At- lantic	South	Mid- West	Great Plains	Texas	Moun- tain	Pacific
Category of Loan									
Finance Companies	91	98	87	81	95	93	94	100	84
Commercial and Industrial	86	95	81	84	82	83	85	79	100
Real Estate Loans	45	54	39	46	41	24	41	24	81
Security Loans	37	45	41	38	25	28	47	11	59
Agricultural Loans	21	25	11	19	16	21	32	26	31
Consumer Loans	15	11	17	11	10	14	27	16	22
Size Category of Loan									
Small	66	77	56	65	77	62	50	63	66
Medium	88	98	89	76	93	79	85	79	88
Large	94	100	94	89	99	86	91	79	100

* The figures give no indication of the percentage of customers to whom the requirement is applied but merely of the percentage of affirmative respondents who apply it to at least some of their customers in each category.

ever, certain significant exceptions, the most important of which concerns finance companies. These companies often maintain large unused credit lines as insurance against fluctuations in their commercial-paper outstanding. Moreover, because the average volume of direct bank borrowing by finance companies is small relative to their total negotiated lines of credit, and because their borrowing is generally subject to large and unpredictable fluctuations, the interest payments on borrowings by finance companies may be insufficient to compensate the banks for the "costs" of maintaining these credit lines. Compensating balances are rigidly employed to make the finance-company relationship profitable for the banks. One aspect of this policy is that finance companies are often not allowed to average their compensating deposits. The requirement is also strictly enforced when credit is extended to various types of nondepositors. These would include out-of-town borrowers, national credit lines, and participation loans.

BANKERS' ATTITUDES TOWARD COMPENSATING BALANCES

Bankers decide whether or not to employ compensating balances for a variety of reasons. As Table IV indicates, important explanations

TABLE IV

Banker's Reasons for Employing Compensating Balances
(percentage of affirmative respondents)

To increase deposits	83.2
To increase net earnings	69.5
To increase lending capacity	53.7
To change the effective rate of interest	49.3
To compensate to the bank in lieu of service charges	40.3
To increase quality of loan asset	40.3
To lend to a larger number of customers at the prime rate	17.4

suggested by those banks using the requirement are the desire to increase deposits, net earnings, and lending capacity, but these explanations seem to be somewhat more important for larger banks than for small.[8] An explanation for this lies in the fact that small banks in rural areas often have more than sufficient reserves to satisfy their loan demand. Moreover, competition in these areas may often be such that an individual bank may have the bulk of local deposits and cannot attract new reserves by the imposition of a compensating-balance requirement. Another reason offered by the banks for employing compensating-balance requirements is their desire to increase the quality of their loan assets by assuring the working-capital position of the borrower. This is not done so much to provide default insurance as to strengthen the liquid position of the customer. And, as has been noted above, banks frequently employ compensating balances in lieu of direct charges for services rendered, especially for non-borrowing customers.[9] This practice appears most common among the largest banks.

Often compensating balances are employed in order to change the effective rate of interest without altering the contract rate. This practice, which is common when interest rates are for any reason inflexible, is least prevalent among the largest banks. An example of interest inflexibility is the desire of many banks and borrowers to increase the number of loans made at the prime rate. The imposition of a compensating deposit allows the bank to lend to non-prime borrowers at the price rate.[10] Interestingly enough, the State of Vermont has made the practice of compensating-balance requirements illegal precisely to avoid the possibility of making "a deposit in lieu of a specified payment."[11] The results of the survey indicate that the overwhelming majority of banks not requiring compensating balances are small and located in rural districts. (See Table V.) An important reason cited by those banks not using

---

[8] The goals of increasing deposits and lending capacity may be fully consistent with a long-run desire to increase net earnings.

[9] A bank is often asked by its correspondent to maintain a compensatory deposit; this is largely in payment for services rendered but is also common against paper which is discount with the correspondent.

[10] Cf. D. Hodgman, *op. cit.*

[11] "Vermont Laws Relating to Banks, Development Credit Corporations . . ." reprinted from *Title 8 and Others, Vermont Statutes Annotated*, p. 164.

TABLE V

Banks Not Requiring Compensating Balances (distribution of the 98 banks not using the requirement)

Deposit Group ($ million)		Urban Classification	
Under 20	83	Major financial	
21–50	10	centers	2
51–100	4	Urban areas	5
101–200	0	Rural districts	91
201–500	0		
501–1,000	0		98
Over 1,000	1		
	98		

compensating balances is that their competitors do not do so.[12]

This factor, together with the generally insufficient loan demand in certain rural areas, puts the customer in a good bargaining position relative to his bank. These banks, therefore, cannot afford to place additional requirements on a potential borrower.

A final factor is that the most common loans in rural areas are generally agricultural or to consumers. The normal cash flow in these situations is such that compensating balances are often impracticable. Such requirements, which in these cases unduly complicate the loan contract, might prove unacceptable to many customers.

COMPENSATING-BALANCE REQUIREMENTS AND CREDIT CONDITIONS

An overwhelming number of banks in our sample indicated that the increased application of compensating balances during the past decade can be associated with the increased monetary restraint in that period. This conclusion applies to banks of all sizes and in all areas of the country but is especially true for the larger banks. Changes in compensating-balance policy, however, are only infrequently directly associated with changes in the prime rate or other such indicators. Instead, such changes appear

---

[12] Small banks in urban areas have attitudes similar to those of their larger competitors in employing the requirement. Bankers' attitudes in this regard seem to be more a function of the competitive situation than of the size of the bank.

to result from increased reserve pressures on the individual banks, which hope, in turn, to attract new reserves through the requirement.

The greater importance of compensating-balance requirements in periods of tight money is reflected in at least three ways. The actual size of the requirement is sometimes increased, they are applied to a greater number of loan customers and, most frequently, the requirements are enforced more rigorously. Those banks which actually increase the size of the requirement usually also apply them more widely and enforce them more strictly. For less than one-fifth of the banks using the requirement did compensating-balance policy bear little relation to changes in business-and-credit conditions.[13]

III. PRACTICE AND THEORY

The results of the survey, together with theoretical considerations set forth elsewhere, help us to evaluate the rationale for compensating-balance requirements as a tool of commercial-bank policy.[14]

The two most interesting theoretical problems considered in the literature are first, whether compensating-balance requirements present a profitable alternative to explicit interest-rate adjustments; and second, whether the requirements should be viewed as a competitive or an oligopolistic phenomenon. Although our survey was not designed to test the various theoretical arguments directly, the evidence gathered is useful in relating banking practices to the various theories. The results of the survey are consistent with the following two hypotheses: one, that compensating-balance requirements arise out of competition between banks for deposits; two, that the requirements are profitable. In addition, the evidence can help explain the rationality of compensating balances in certain special circumstances.

As regards the use of compensating-balance requirements as a competitive weapon, the survey reveals that their imposition is far more prevalent in urban areas where the competition for deposits is keener and where borrowers have access to a relatively large number of banks. This observation is underscored by the fact that small banks in urban areas tend to employ compensating balances to a greater extent than do their rural counterparts. On the other hand, banks not using the requirement very often indicated that competition for deposits was not an important factor in their area. It would seem that the above factors support the conclusion that compensating balances are largely a competitive phenomenon. Whether they are rational in this context, however, becomes the next consideration.

The theoretical literature has shown that in order for compensating balances to be profitable, they must succeed in drawing reserves into the bank, except in the case where the requirements are met by normal deposit balances.[15] If we assume that the imposition of compensating-balance requirements does not affect net reserve flows between banks, it has been shown by Davis and Guttentag that bank competition for customers with large voluntary balances relative to borrowing needs will result in a situation where compensating balances are in fact equal to the normal balances. In this circumstance, the requirements are a profitable tool of commercial-bank policy.[16] Davis and Guttentag then deduced that compensating balances would be most prevalent on those firms with large working balances. With the striking exception of finance companies, to be discussed below, the results of our survey con-

[13] Insofar as compensating deposits are a less liquid asset than are normal deposits, their increased application in times of monetary restraint would, cet. par., tend to enhance the effectiveness of monetary policy.

[14] See Footnote 1.

[15] H. T. Shapiro and N. D. Baxter, op. cit., "Compensating-Balance Requirements: The Theory and Its Implications," Southern Economic Journal, January, 1964. By profitable we mean that the short-run gross income of the bank is increased. Because it is by nature almost impossible to relate profit and reserve flows to specific factors (such as the imposition of a compensating-balance requirement), the information derived from the present survey does not allow us to test the theory directly. The survey results however do enable us to determine whether the profitability conditions specified by the theory seem to hold in actual practice. Therefore, assuming the theoretical arguments to be correct, we can establish the extent to which compensating balances may be profitable.

[16] R. G. Davis and J. M. Guttentag, "Balance Requirements and Deposit Competition." The Journal of Political Economy, December 1963.

firm this contention, the requirement being quite common in commercial-and-industrial loans and least common in connection with consumer and agricultural loans.

It has been demonstrated, however, that compensating-balance requirements may indeed draw new reserves into the bank providing that the compensating deposits possess some degree of liquidity to their owners.[17] Such "liquidity" can be attributed to compensating deposits where averaging is allowed. The widespread use of averaging revealed by the survey thus allows for the possibility of reserve inflows to the bank. In addition, the survey results also imply that many banks employ compensating balances "to increase lending capacity," a phrase which bankers probably associate with inducing an inflow of new reserves into the bank.

Whether a compensating-balance policy is always successful in inducing reserve inflows is not clear. Small banks in rural areas are unlikely to attract new reserves, as they probably already hold a substantial portion of the total reserves in the area. Even in the more competitive urban areas, the possibility of inducing net reserve inflows may be slight. In this situation the first bank to impose the requirement in a given market may initially gain new reserves in exchange for interest-rate concessions. Competitors, however, will then be forced to also impose the requirement as a defensive move to protect their reserve positions. Once all competing institutions in an area use the requirement, compensating-balance policy is unlikely to induce net reserve shifts among them. And, as noted above, without these reserve shifts, the requirement as a competitive device, in excess of normal working balances, cannot be profitable to any bank. This situation is analogous to the well-known tariff paradox: while it may very well be to the advantage of any single country to impose a tariff, when all other countries retaliate everyone is worse off. Any country acting alone may not find it profitable to remove its tariffs, just as any bank acting alone may not find it advantageous to remove its compensating-balance requirement.

There exist, in addition, important practical

---

17 H. T. Shapiro and N. D. Baxter, *op. cit.*

situations where compensating balances are rational even though no large normal deposits are present and no reserve flows are anticipated. First, the most significant of such situations, and quantitatively the most important area in which compensating balances are applied, involves the relationship between banks and finance companies. The existence of the requirement in this case should be looked upon largely as reflecting the peculiar nature of finance-company business, which was discussed in Section II above.[18] Second, where rigidities in the rate of interest exist, the compensating balance can be used as a device to alter the effective rate of interest without changing the contract rate. The survey has indicated that the requirements often serve this function. Also, as noted above, compensating balances are employed in lieu of certain service charges and are rational in this context.

Despite the well-known drawbacks of questionnaire techniques, we believe that our survey has provided significant information concerning commercial-bank practices with regard to compensating-balance requirements. The requirements are widespread, responsive to money-and-credit conditions, flexibly employed, and may be a very rational tool of commercial-bank policy.

APPENDIX A

QUESTIONNAIRE ON COMPENSATING-BALANCE REQUIREMENTS

Instructions: Questions are to be answered by checking as many choices as are appropriate. In the event that any elaboration would seem desirable, you are invited to do so.

1. Do you employ compensating-balance requirements under any circumstances?

     _____ yes

     _____ no

     Question 2 Is To Be Answered By Only Those Banks Who Do *Not* Employ Compensating-Balance Requirements.

---

18 It is also conceivable the widespread uniformity with which the compensating-balance requirement is applied to finance companies reflects the exercise of market power by the banks.

2. (a) Compensating-balance requirements have
_____ been instituted but discontinued
_____ never been instituted
 (b) The use of compensating-balance requirements has been discontinued or rejected because:
_____ of lack of customer acceptance
_____ administrative costs prohibitive
_____ they unduly complicate the loan contract
_____ adjustment of interest rates presented a superior alternative
_____ competitors do not use them
_____ other, please specify.

3. (a) Compensating-balance requirements became an important factor in bank operations
_____ before 1951
_____ between 1951 and 1954
_____ between 1955 and 1958
_____ since 1958
or _____ have never been important.
 (b) Have compensating-balance requirements become increasingly important in the last decade of relatively tight money?
_____ yes   _____ no

4. To indicate the category of borrower to whom compensating-balance requirements are applied, place an X in as many of the boxes in the table below as are appropriate. For example, you would mark boxes 1, 2, 3, and 9 if compensating-balance requirements apply to all commercial-and-industrial loans and to real-estate loans for large borrowers, but not to others. Determine what you consider to be small, medium or large according to your own banking operations and capital structure.

5. Compensating-balance requirements are employed (check as many as apply):
_____ to be able to lend a larger number of customers at the prime rate
_____ to change the effective rate of interest without altering the contract rates
_____ to increase deposits
_____ to increase net earnings
_____ to reduce clearing drains
_____ to increase lending capacity
_____ to compensate the bank for check clearing and other services rendered
_____ to increase quality of loan assets by assuring borrower's working capital position.

6. Is the required compensating balance
_____ negotiated separately for each individual loan contract
_____ set in advance for each category of loan (e.g., commercial-and-industrial, agricultural, etc.)
_____ set in advance with respect to size of borrower (i.e., small, medium, large)
_____ set in advance with respect to both category of loan and size of borrower (small commercial-and-industrial, etc.)
_____ set in advance and the same for all loans to which it applies.

7. (a) In a period of tight money compensating-balance requirements (check as many as apply)
_____ are usually increased
_____ are usually applied to an increased number of loan customers
_____ are usually enforced more rigorously

SIZE OF BORROWER

TYPE OF LOAN	Small	Medium	Large
Commercial and Industrial	1	2	3
Agricultural	4	5	6
Real Estate	7	8	9
Consumer	10	11	12
Securities	13	14	15
Finance Companies	16	17	18

_____ are usually decreased, applied to fewer customers and enforced less rigorously

_____ none of the above; compensating-balance policy bears little relation to change in business-and-credit conditions.

(b) Changes in compensating-balance policy *usually*

_____ precede changes in the prime rate

_____ occur at approximately the same time as changes in the prime rate

_____ follow changes in the prime rate

_____ bear no relation to changes in the prime rate.

8. In which of the following cases are compensating-balance requirements most important?

_____ in negotiating direct loans

_____ in negotiating lines of credit

_____ other, please specify.

9. The compensating-balance requirements must be fulfilled by

_____ holding a deposit, at all times not less than the requirement

_____ holding an average of daily deposits calculated over a period of a year not less than the requirement

_____ holding an average of daily deposits over a six-month period not less than the requirement

_____ holding an average of daily deposits over a three-month period not less than the requirement.

13

A RUN ON THE BANKS*

Marriner S. Eccles†

Most business firms and individuals have liabilities which they must pay off when they come due. But commercial banks are unique; much of their liabilities are in the form of demand deposits and these, as their name implies, are all payable on demand. Therefore, more than most businesses, commercial banks require a high degree of "liquidity," i.e., a large volume of assets which are actually in the form of cash or which can quickly be turned into cash with little or no loss.

The greatest calamity that can befall a bank is to experience a "run" by its depositors — a large and sustained demand for cash by many of its depositors. In the ordinary course of events a bank expects a certain number of its depositors to demand currency on any one day, or in any one week. But it also expects that others will be depositing funds with it, so that on balance there will be little net change except for expected seasonal movements. If a large number of depositors unexpectedly demand currency, and the drain continues or gathers momentum, the bank is in trouble, for it is not likely to keep that much cash on hand, nor is it likely to have enough liquid asset that can be quickly sold to obtain more cash. Just how much trouble a bank will be in under such

* Reprinted from *Beckoning Frontiers* by Marriner S. Eccles, by permission of Alfred A. Knopf, Inc., and the author. Copyrighted 1950, 1951 by Marriner S. Eccles.

† Chairman of the Board, First Security Corporation. Member of the Board of Governors of the Federal Reserve System from 1934 to 1951 and Chairman from 1934 to 1948.

circumstances is dramatically illustrated by the experience of Marriner Eccles and his banks during the early 1930's, a period when many thousands of banks were forced to close their doors and go out of business.

During 1930 I awoke to find myself at the bottom of a pit without any known means of scaling its sheer sides.

Since the crash of 1929, men I respected assured me that the economic crisis was only temporary and that soon all the things that had pulled the country out of previous depressions would operate to that same end once again. But the weeks turned to months. The months turned to a year or more. Instead of easing, the economic crisis worsened. The pit grew deeper and I found myself in it.

On the morning of the awakening, I saw for the first time that though I'd been active in the world of finance and production for seventeen years and knew its techniques, I knew less than nothing about its economic and social effects. Yet, by itself a confession of ignorance led nowhere. Friends whose estates I managed, my family, whose interests I represented, and the community at large, in whose economic life I played a sensitive role, all expected me to find the way out of the pit. Yet all I could find within myself was despair. Having been reared by my father to accept the responsibilities of wealth and having been placed by circumstances at the helm of many enterprises, there were times when I felt the whole depression was a personal affront.

Wherein had I been at fault?

Night after night following that head-splitting awakening I would return home exhausted by the pretensions of knowledge I was forced to wear in a daytime masquerade. I would slump forward on a table and pray that by a supreme act of will the answers would somehow be revealed. As an individual I felt myself helpless to do anything. I heard grassroots talk that "the government ought to do something." But why the government? Wherein is the government different from the individual? Is it not just a sum of all individuals? Or, granting there is a difference, what specifically should the government do?

For instance:

What should be done in a situation where the dollar was so painfully sound when measured by its power to buy goods and services that when prices fell and unemployment increased, the dollar somehow got "sounder"?

What was to be done in a situation such as I faced in our lumber mills, where we would operate at a loss even if men worked without pay?

What was to be done by our banks when loans on homes, farms, livestock, and securities or to business and industrial enterprises could not be paid because values had drastically declined?

What was to be done when the pressure on the banks to "get liquid" so as to meet depositor claims caused a situation where the liquidation of debts made it impossible to pay off debts?

What was to be done when men on the farms and in the cities, who needed each other's goods, were stranded on opposite river banks without the consumer purchasing power by which they could navigate a crossing for trading?

These were not academic questions. They were intimately connected with day-to-day dangers, and particularly the danger of a sudden run on the banks. It didn't matter where the run started. A weak bank that closed its doors could create community tensions of a sort that could close the doors of sound banks as well.

Fortunately, the banks of the First Security Corporation kept their doors open throughout the depression. No depositor lost one penny. But time after time the life of our organization was imperiled by failures or imminent failures in neighboring banks. Physical nearness alone tended to involve all banks in the fate of any one of them. I still grow weak when I think of the runs or threatened runs with which we had to deal.

The first one occurred in 1931 in Ogden. Here one of the most highly regarded and oldest banks in the entire state was the Ogden State Bank. Under the management of the Bigelow family it had served the community well for over forty years. In size it was only slightly smaller than our Ogden banks. But the officers of our banks were, like myself, young men or men relatively new to the community. We didn't have the sort of public confidence enjoyed by the Ogden State Bank. If it got into trouble, what could the community expect of a bank managed by much younger and less experienced men?

I had advance warning of trouble when Archie Bigelow, the president of the Ogden State Bank, revealed to Bennett and me that his bank was facing great losses on its loans due to the deflation, that its capital and surplus were impaired, and that it was losing deposits. But Bigelow felt his bank could be saved if it was merged with our Ogden banks.

Examination of the imperiled bank showed that it was so far gone it would pull down our banks if they were linked to it as a life-saver. Came the week-end in the late summer of 1931 when doom could no longer be staved off. Word reached us that the Ogden State Bank would not open its doors on the coming Monday.

We knew we could expect a severe run on our Ogden banks; we also knew that when word of it got around, the effect would extend to other areas where the First Security Corporation owned banks. These others had to be alerted and prepared for imminent developments, and because our Ogden banks were the central institutions in our banking complex, it was imperative that they break the run as quickly as possible and stay open at all costs.

The Sunday preceding the Monday when the Ogden State Bank did not open, I called together all the officers and directors of the First National and the First Savings banks. Having a list of all the important commercial accounts held by the Ogden State Bank, I pointed out to the directors and officers of our banks that the firms represented on the list would be without banking facilities on Monday morning when the Ogden State Bank remained closed. Yet they would need to make deposits, get currency, borrow money, and issue checks. The directors of our banks were to pick out the firms on the list with whom they had close personal or business dealings. Then on Monday morning they were to call the heads of these

firms, invite them to deposit their funds on hand with our banks, and say that if they needed a loan or currency we would be glad to take care of their pressing needs. I wanted not only to gain an inflow of deposits but to develop confidence among the employees of those firms. They would be paid in checks drawn on our banks, and the combined incoming traffic would help reverse the current of the outgoing traffic we knew was to be expected on the next day.

The officers and directors went at this job with zeal and set in motion what it was hoped would happen.

While this plan was formed to stabilize our commercial accounts held locally, we had cause to fear a concealed run on our commercial and bank accounts that could start at distant points. Specifically, like other city banks, we held balances of many outside corporations as well as of independent country banks in the area. We knew that if the officials of these outside concerns heard of a run on our banks, they would take precautionary measures to avoid getting caught short. They would either ask for a direct transfer of funds or they would make a draft or checks on our banks and deposit them with other banks.

I'd seen this happen many times. I'd also seen its aftermath. The process by which large corporations, for instance, withdrew funds from the hinterland and concentrated them in New York and other large cities hastened the collapse of countless country banks. Having this danger in mind, we felt we had a fighting chance to overcome it if, first, our outside accounts were warned in advance of an imminent run, and, second, if they heard the news directly from us and not from press reports or from some other source. That Sunday night a telegram was drafted for delivery the first thing Monday morning to each of our outside accounts.

The telegram read:

THE OGDEN STATE BANK WILL NOT OPEN ITS DOORS THIS MONDAY MORNING. THIS WILL CAUSE SOME DEMANDS FOR WITHDRAWAL OF FUNDS ON OUR OWN BANKS. WE

HAVE ANTICIPATED THIS FOR SOME TIME AND ARE FULLY PREPARED TO MEET ANY AND ALL DEMANDS WHICH ARE MADE UPON US. WE FELT IT DESIRABLE THAT YOU SHOULD GET THIS INFORMATION FIRST HAND.

Fortunately, there was not a single transfer of funds from among the accounts that received these telegrams.

While we made this bid to shore up the confidence of our commercial accounts, we realized that the greatest potential danger lay with the savings group. If they were thrown into panic by a run on our savings bank, the effect would not be self-limiting. Our national bank shared the same premises with our savings bank; a run on the latter would certainly be duplicated in a run on the former. In view of this, all officers and employees of the national and savings banks were contacted that Sunday and asked to be at work the next morning at eight o'clock.

When they assembled the next morning, I told them what they would have to face in a few hours. "If you want to keep this bank open," I said, "you must do your part. Go about your business as though nothing unusual was happening. Smile, be pleasant, talk about the weather, show no signs of panic. The main burden is going to fall on you boys in the savings department. Instead of the three windows we normally use, we are going to use all four of them today. They must be manned at all times because if any teller's or clerk's window in this bank closes for even a short time, that will stir up more panic. We'll have sandwiches brought in; no one can go out to lunch. We can't break this run today. The best we can do is slow it down. People are going to come here to close out their savings accounts. You are going to pay them. But you are going to pay them very slowly. It's the only chance we have to deal with the panic. You know a lot of depositors by sight, and in the past you did not have to look up their signatures, but today when they come here with their deposit books to close out their accounts, you are going to look up every signature card. And take your time about it.

And one other thing: when you pay out, don't use any big bills. Pay out in fives and tens, and count slowly. Our object is to pay out a minimum today."

The tellers and clerks ably carried out their part of the act despite the crowd that surged through the doors of the bank the moment they were opened. Someone with an objective turn of mind could have learned much that day about the degree to which banking is understood by the community at large. I recall one depositor, for instance, who in great anxiety closed his savings account and with the currency given him promptly bought a cashier's check. He did not know that if the bank closed, his check would be worth no more than his deposit. But amidst the pushing and shoving inside the bank there was little time to reflect on matters of this sort.

At two o'clock that afternoon Bennett, my brother George, and I met to decide what should be done when the regular three-o'clock closing hour was reached. The crowd in the bank was as taut as it was dense. Some people had been waiting for hours to draw out their money. If we tried to close at three, there was no telling what might happen. But, as in all other things, a poverty of alternatives made us adopt the boldest one. We decided to make an exception of this one day and to remain open so long as there were people who wanted to get their money.

In the meantime a call had been put through to the Federal Reserve Bank in Salt Lake City to send currency to our Ogden banks as well as to all others in the First Security Corporation. The armored car that brought funds to us in Ogden arrived on the scene as in the movies when the Union cavalry charges in to save all from the Indians. The guards strode through the crush inside the bank, and all made way before them.

Of equal importance in the events of the day, Morgan Craft, the deputy manager of the Federal Reserve Bank in Salt Lake City, had been a passenger in the armored car that raced to Ogden. When he entered our bank, I grabbed his arm and led him through the crowd to a black and gold marble counter in the officers' section of the savings bank. Mounting the counter, I raised my hand and called for attention:

"Just a minute!"

There was instant silence.

"Just a minute!" I repeated. "I want to make an announcement. It appears that we are having some difficulty handling our depositors with the speed to which you are accustomed. Many of you have been in line for a considerable time. I notice a lot of pushing and shoving and irritation. I just wanted to tell you that instead of closing at the usual hour of three o'clock, we have decided to stay open just as long as there is anyone who desires to withdraw his deposit or make one. Therefore, you people who have just come in can return later this afternoon or evening if you wish. There is no justification for the excitement or the apparent panicky attitude on the part of some depositors. As all of you have seen, we have just had brought up from Salt Lake City a large amount of currency that will take care of all your requirements. There is plenty more where that came from." (This was true enough — but I didn't say we could get it.)

"And if you don't believe me," I continued, "I have here Mr. Morgan Craft, one of the officers of the Federal Reserve Bank, who has just come up in an armored car. Mr. Craft, say a few words to the folks."

I pulled him up to the top of the counter. He not only said a few words, but threw in one or two for extra measure.

"I just want to verify what Mr. Eccles has told you," he said. "I want to assure you that we have brought up a lot of currency and there is plenty more where that came from."

This, again, was perfectly true. But he didn't say the currency belonged to us. Nevertheless, the mood of the day was so unreasoning that men were heartened by words as meaningless as those which caused them fright. In a split instant the faces before me relaxed in relief. The edge in all voices seemed to vanish. Some people stepped out of line and left the bank. And a happy buzz replaced the waspish one heard earlier. The word was passed to the crowd outside the bank: "They are going to stay open. They are going to stay open."

But the danger had not yet been averted. There is another bank in Ogden, called the Commercial Security Bank, headed at that time by Harold Hemingway. Because of what had happened to the Ogden State Bank, the Commercial Security Bank was also experiencing a deadly run on that Monday. It suddenly occurred to me that if our banks remained open past three o'clock and Hemingway closed his at the usual hour, the contrast would lead to an unjust implication that the Commercial Security Bank was unsound. On Tuesday the run at Hemingway's bank would be even more severe. He would in all probability be forced to close his doors, and this in turn would intensify the run on our banks, which likewise might be irresistible. We had been competitors for business, but this was one time when either we had to hang together or we would hang separately.

I called Hemingway on the phone and told him that we were going to remain open as long past three o'clock as was necessary. I asked him to do the same. He told me he couldn't do that since he had very little currency left. Fortunately, the work of the officers of our banks in bringing in new commercial accounts at the beginning of the day had produced a situation where by three o'clock we had taken in nearly as much in the commercial bank as we had paid out in the savings bank. This, plus the money brought in from Salt Lake City, and the way our tellers did their work, enabled us to lend forty thousand dollars to Hemingway so that he could remain open beyond three o'clock. In this way the first day's storm was weathered. But we knew there was more trouble to come.

At the close of the day I called together the personnel of the banks for another conference.

"Now listen," I said. "A lot of people who've been at work will only hear about this run for the first time when they get home tonight. Tomorrow there will be the makings of another crush, and we are going to meet it by doing the opposite of what we did today. Instead of opening at ten, we are going to open at eight. Nobody is going to have to wait outside of the bank to start any sort of line. When people come in here, pay them very fast. Don't dawdle over signatures. Pay out the accounts in big bills. Above all, don't let any line form. It will mean a continuation of the panic."

This tactic was a homely application of how a compensatory economy worked. On Tuesday the amount we paid out exceeded that of the first day, but the important objective was reached. No lines formed to inspire a hysterical belief that the bank was in trouble. On Tuesday customers came into the doorway of the bank, looked furtively around the lobby, and, seeing that things were peaceful and serene, walked away. And that was the end of that run. I thanked God for the nerves I inherited from my father and mother.

CHAPTER FIVE

USES OF BANK FUNDS:
LOANS AND INVESTMENTS

14

CONTINUOUS BORROWING THROUGH
"SHORT-TERM" BANK LOANS*

Federal Reserve Bank of Cleveland

Commercial banks are business firms and, as such, are constantly striving to make a profit. They attempt to do this mainly by making loans and, what is really the same thing, purchasing securities, such as government or private bonds. In the process, each bank thus acquires a portfolio of "earning assets" — of bonds, promissory notes, and other instruments certifying someone else's indebtedness to the bank — which yield an interest income. It is in the management of these earning assets, that is, in the making of loans and the purchasing of securities, that the banks both earn their profits and exert a vital impact upon the economy.

Bank loans form the largest part of commercial bank assets. According to traditional commercial banking theory (known as the "real bills doctrine") banks should make only short-term business loans. These should reflect the processing of real goods and should enable the borrowing business firm to repay the bank when the underlying transaction has been completed, as when the goods have been processed and then sold. It was thought that if banks confined themselves to this type of short-term self-liquidating loan they would both insure their own liquidity and best accommodate the needs of trade; business firms should do their long-term borrowing through bond flotations rather than by commercial bank loans.

However, presently well over one-third of the dollar volume of member bank business loans are so-called "term loans," that is, with a maturity of over one year. These hardly qualify as short-term self-liquidating loans. Furthermore, a special survey undertaken by the Federal Reserve Bank of Cleveland in 1955 revealed that in that District (the Fourth Federal Reserve District) many of the ostensibly short-term loans were in fact longer-term loans, having been continuously renewed. The findings of this special survey and the conclusions drawn therefrom by the Federal Reserve Bank of Cleveland follow.

* From *Business Review*, Federal Reserve Bank of Cleveland (September, 1956). Reprinted by the courtesy of the Federal Reserve Bank of Cleveland.

Over the past thirty years, the growing importance of intermediate-term loans by commercial banks to business borrowers has brought about a fundamental change in the nature of bank credit. In addition, the practice of continuous renewals of nominally short-term loans has added to the extent to which the banking system is providing credit for fixed-asset purposes to the business community.

Although the growth of business loans with original maturities of more than one year has been widely recognized, very little has been available, in the way of comprehensive data, concerning the actual extent of continuous renewals of business loans. The survey of business loans at member banks, conducted by the Federal Reserve System in October, 1955, has provided important new information on the subject of continuous indebtedness of business borrowers at Fourth District member banks.[1]

The discussion which follows is designed to show how the majority of business loans, although nominally of short maturities, have been converted into longer-term credit in effect through the practice of continuous renewals. Thus, one-half of the volume of commercial and industrial loans was outstanding to borrowers who had been continuously in debt to the same banks for 2 years or more, while one-fourth of the loan volume represented continuous borrowers of 5 years or longer, as of the date of the survey.

Finally, an examination will be made of the reasons for and the significance of this fundamental change in banking practice.

TRADITIONAL VIEW

A certain view of the fundamental nature of commercial banking, which was almost undisputed in this country until the 1920's, has left its imprint upon our institutions and our thinking, even though the passing decades have eroded the theoretical structure. That is the view that loans by commercial banks are characteristically, and should be, short-term and self-liquidating in character.

The view was justified, in theory at least, on the grounds that the bulk of bank liabilities consists of demand deposits. It was argued that, by restricting themselves to the financing of short-term working capital for commerce and industry, banks could achieve the liquidity necessary to meet the requirements of deposits withdrawable on demand. The most liquid bank assets were thought to be loans arising out of transactions which would normally provide the borrowers with funds for repayment within a short time — i.e., business loans based on physical goods in the process of production or marketing.

Such a view in its most clear-cut form was the so-called "real-bills" doctrine, based largely on English banking practices. Under the name of "commercial loan theory of credit", the same general view came to be followed to some extent in American banking practices. In spite of a considerable formal adherence to the principle of short-term loans, however, American banks have long been faced with the fact that their customers often require funds for longer periods than the traditional maximum of three months as usually specified in the "commercial loan theory." Notwithstanding the theory, therefore, American banks in practice have generally departed from the exclusive holding of short-term, self-liquidating, working-capital loans. The extension of longer-term loans for fixed-asset purposes has become increasingly important since the 1920's, for reasons to be discussed later.

Even when business loans continued to be short-term in form, it was recognized as early as 1918 by some acute observers that banks in large cities at that time were often called upon to renew between 40 and 50 per cent of short-term unsecured business loans, thus providing longer-term credit in substance.[2] How far has this practice been extended under present-day conditions, and what are its implications? Before analyzing the reasons for

---

[1] No comparable data on continuous indebtedness of business borrowers is available for member banks nationally, since the question on this subject was a special addition to the survey in this District. Thus, while it is not possible to make comparisons with other parts of the country, there is no reason to believe that the picture would be markedly different as between the Fourth District and other Federal Reserve districts.

[2] Moulton, H. G., "Commercial Banking and Capital Formation," *Journal of Political Economy*, 1918, p. 658.

and the significance of such a fundamental change in banking, the extent of continuous indebtedness among banks' business borrowers will be outlined, as it applies in the Fourth Federal Reserve District.

SURVEY FINDINGS

The best measure of the extent of continuous renewals of business loans is a comparison of the age of the outstanding promissory notes with the length of time in which the same borrowers have been continuously in debt on commercial and industrial loans to the banks holding the notes.[3]

The business loan survey disclosed that while only one-third of the amount of notes was over one year old, nearly two-thirds of the dollar volume of commercial and industrial loans was outstanding to borrowers who had been continuously in debt on such loans to the same banks for one year or more. Similarly, while only 22 per cent of the amount of notes was 2 years old or more, half of the amount of notes represented borrowers continuously in debt for 2 years or longer.

At the extremes of "age," although over one-third of the dollar amount of notes was less than 3 months old, only 8 per cent of the dollar volume represented borrowers who had been in debt to the same banks for as little as 3 months. At the opposite extreme, while only 6 per cent of the amount of notes showed an age of 5 years or more, no less than 25 per cent of the dollar volume of loans was outstanding to borrowers who had been continuously in debt to the same banks for five years or longer.[4]

---

[3] The age of note is equal to the number of months elapsed between the time the note was made or *last renewed* and the survey date (Oct. 5, 1955). The period of the borrower's continuous indebtedness is equal to the number of months elapsed, as of the survey date, since the date of the borrower's last zero loan balance at the same bank on commercial or industrial loans (excluding business-purpose loans secured by real estate and non-business purpose loans).

It is important to note that the "period of continuous indebtedness" in this article is viewed from the standpoint of the lending bank only, and not from that of the borrower. An examination of the borrower's records would undoubtedly show continuous use of bank credit for longer periods in many cases, since some borrowers pay off loans at one bank while immediately borrowing from another bank.

[4] There is one important explanation to be made in connection with the above data dealing with the period

Not only notes recently made, but notes of all ages showed evidence of having been renewed often. It is thus apparent that any distribution of commercial and industrial loans by nominal age or nominal maturity seriously understates the "true" period of continuous use of bank credit by business borrowers. When attention is focused on the length of continuous indebtedness, the results strongly suggest that a much larger share of bank credit to business is used for fixed capital purposes (such as plant and equipment) than generally believed.

The discussion thus far has dealt with total commercial and industrial loans of all District member banks. Additional insight may be gained through a breakdown of continuous borrowing according to the line of business, size, and corporate status of the borrower and also by the size of bank.

Type of Business. Borrowers continuously indebted for one year or longer to the same bank accounted for 83 per cent of the loan volume to transportation, communication, and public utility firms and for 72 per cent of the loan volume to manufacturing and mining concerns. In both of the above categories, investment in fixed assets tends to be relatively heavy, thus indicating a need for relatively large amounts of capital loans.

On the other hand, continuous borrowers for a year or more accounted for only 16 per cent, in each case, of the loan volume outstanding to commodity dealers and sales finance companies. In both of these lines, loans for short-term, seasonal inventory purposes dominate the pattern of their bank borrowing.

Construction firms, along with manufacturers of textiles, apparel, and leather goods were the only other lines of business in which less than half of the loan volume was outstanding to borrowers continuously in debt to the same bank for over one year.

---

of the borrower's continuous indebtedness to a given bank. Within that period, it is very probable that the amount of indebtedness did not remain constant, but fluctuated from time to time. In the survey results, the dollar volume of loans according to which the relative concentration of borrowers' continuous indebtedness is measured consists of the *original* amount, when made or *last renewed*, of commercial and industrial loans outstanding on the survey date. The method thus gives effect to the *most recent high point* in the amount of the indebtedness.

The heaviest concentration of longer-term indebtedness to banks was in manufacturing and mining concerns (other than the textile-leather-rubber group). Of the loan volume outstanding to manufacturers of food, liquor, and tobacco products, 60 per cent went to continuous borrowers of 3 years or more, and 44 per cent to those of 5 years or over. The corresponding figures for metal and metal products manufacturers were 46 per cent — 3 years or longer, and 25 per cent — 5 years or over.

In the transportation-communication-public utility group, 58 per cent of the loan volume represented borrowers continuously in debt for 3 years or longer, and 37 per cent for 5 years or over.

Finally, it may be noted that in those lines of activity where small business tends to predominate, there was a heavy concentration of continuous borrowing amounting to one year or more — namely, in wholesale and retail trade, construction and real estate concerns, and firms providing various consumer services.

Size of Business.   When classified by size of business, the period of continuous indebtedness did not show as wide a variation as was the case when grouped by type of business. There were some important distinctions, however. In general, the smaller the size of the borrower, the greater was the per cent of loans outstanding to firms whose continuous indebtedness was under 2 years. Conversely, the larger the borrower, the greater was the share of loans outstanding to firms whose continuous indebtedness exceeded 3 years.

Corporate Status.   When classified by the form of business organization, loans to unincorporated borrowers tended to show relatively longer continuous indebtedness than in the case of corporate borrowers.

In the case of unincorporated firms, loans to borrowers continuously indebted for less than a year accounted for only 28 per cent of the dollar volume, while the corresponding figure for corporate firms was 39 per cent. Conversely, continuous borrowers of 3 years or longer accounted for 43 per cent of the loan volume outstanding to unincorporated firms, but only 36 per cent in the case of incorporated borrowers.

The above distinctions might have been expected. Since unincorporated borrowers with needs for intermediate term credit have no access to the capital market for sale of stocks or bonds, it is natural that their demands would focus on the banking system.

Size of Bank.   When classified by size of bank, the relative concentration of borrowers' continuous indebtedness showed no clear pattern. For example, the largest banks (those with total deposits of $250 million and over) had the highest share of loans outstanding to borrowers showing continuous indebtedness of 3 years or longer — about 43 per cent. The next largest size group of banks, however, with total deposits of $100 million to $250 million, had the lowest share of loans to borrowers continuously in debt for 3 years or over — about 19 per cent. At the same time, small banks (deposits of $2 million to $10 million) came close to matching the record of the largest banks in respect to the share of loans going to continuous borrowers of 3 years standing or longer.

Similarly, while there were wide variations among various bank size-groups as to the per cent of loans outstanding to borrowers who had been in debt less than one year, the variations were not clearly related to bank size, either directly or inversely. Evidently the business and corporate status of borrowers tend to outweigh the influence of size of borrower (which tends to be closely related to size of loan and therefore to size of bank) in determining which banks concentrate in continuous loans to business borrowers.

CHANGE IN BANKING DOCTRINE

The frequency of loan renewals and the pattern of continuous indebtedness of business borrowers represent a marked change in the nature of bank credit over the past several decades. In addition, the initial maturities of business loans have been extended in length during the same period. As of 1955, 43 per cent of commercial and industrial loans outstanding at all Fourth District member banks had an original maturity exceeding one year, in contrast to only 26 per cent in 1939 at weekly-reporting member banks in the District. The combination of longer initial maturities and increased frequency of renewals has largely destroyed any resemblance of present-day business loans to the classic tradition of short-term self-liquidating credits.

Why did such a major change come about? In part, the answer lies both in defects of the "commercial loan theory" and in unfavorable experience with its application in the United States in furnishing liquidity to the banking system in periods of crisis. A brief review of these matters is necessary in order to judge whether or not the longer-term nature of business loans today poses a major threat to the ability of banks to meet potential withdrawals by depositors.

A self-liquidating loan is one which will normally be repaid out of the income resulting from the transaction financed by the proceeds of the loan. But when the source of liquidity of short-term business loans is examined closely, it turns out that the borrower's ability to repay depends in large part on the willingness of other banks to extend loans to the purchasers of the goods produced by the first borrower. Reliance on this source of liquidity thus breaks down during any type of banking crisis.

The increased importance of bank holdings of investment securities during the 1920's and 1930's gave rise to a new "shiftability" doctrine of liquidity — namely, that banks could protect themselves agaits large deposit withdrawals by holding credit instruments for which there is a highly organized and ready market. The emphasis on the shiftability theory of bank liquidity was strengthened by the growth during the 1930's and 1940's in the volume of U.S. Government obligations, particularly Treasury bills. Short-term Government obligations can generally be converted into cash very quickly and with very little danger of loss. During the 1920's, when a relatively large volume of bank loans was based on securities collateral, shiftability depended on the normal functioning of the securities market. In any event, the "shiftability" of any securities held by a bank normally depends on the willingness of other banks or customers of other banks to purchase them. Thus, the liquidity of bank assets, whether of the "shiftable" type or the "self-liquidating" type, presumes a normal functioning of the whole banking system.

Since the bulk of present-day bank loans is

in the form of term loans to business, loans to consumers, and mortgage loans to home-owners, the liquidity of such loans is measured by the borrower's ability to meet instalment payments out of income. The increasing importance of these types of loans has given rise to a third concept of bank liquidity, based on the "anticipated income" of the borrower.

While all three doctrines of bank liquidity noted above — "commercial loan theory", "shiftability", and "anticipated income" — have a certain validity when applied to any given bank during normal periods, they all break down when applied to the commercial banking system as a whole in crisis periods. Regardless of the types of credit extended by banks, any wholesale attempt on the part of the banking system to meet deposit withdrawals by a liquidation of loans and investments, unaided by a central bank, is bound to fail. Any attempt by a given bank to improve its own liquidity position under such circumstances would worsen its own position, as well as that of other banks, by hastening the collapse of values. During periods of crisis, the liquidity of the banking system as a whole depends on the existence of a central bank which can purchase or make loans on commercial bank assets by issuing new currency. This lesson, learned by bitter experience in the early 1930's, was recognized by legislation in 1935 which permits the Federal Reserve System to purchase, or accept as collateral for a loan, any "sound" asset offered by member banks.

In addition, a major change in bank examination standards, known as the Uniform Agreement, was adopted in 1938 by the three Federal bank supervisory agencies — the Comptroller of Currency, the Board of Governors of the Federal Reserve System, and the Federal Deposit Insurance Corporation — and agreed to in principle by the executive committee of the National Association of State Bank Supervisors. The principal changes in bank examination procedure were the abandonment of the "slow" classification of bank loans and the recognition of the principle that bank investments should be judged in the light of inherent soundness rather than on the basis of day-to-day fluctuations in market values. Under the new standards, according to an official statement, "the principle is clearly recognized that, in making loans, banks should be encouraged to place emphasis upon soundness and intrinsic value rather than upon liquidity or quick maturity, and examiners are expected to follow this principle in their examinations."

Since that time, the extension of longer-term credit to business has proceeded both in form, through longer initial maturities, and even more in substance, through the practice of continual renewals of nominally short-term loans.

While the relative shift in uses of bank loans to business from short-term working capital purposes to longer-term fixed capital purposes certainly has not improved the liquidity position of commercial banks, at least it has not worsened it. (Rather, it is the growing proportion of loans to deposits which has reduced bank liquidity, as noted below.) On the basis of past experience, so-called self-liquidating short-term loans to local borrowers were often the least liquid part of a bank's assets during crisis periods when liquidity needs were greatest.

CONCLUSIONS

Several decades have now elapsed since the time of the fundamental change in banking doctrine and practice with respect to loan maturities. A brief appraisal of the past effects of the change and its implications for the future may be in order. The important questions relate to the appropriate uses of bank credit and the fundamental banking problems of solvency and liquidity. The following conclusions on these matters are tentatively suggested.

(1) With respect to appropriate uses of bank credit, the shift to longer-term business loans, both in form and in substance, has constituted an important contribution of commercial banks in meeting vital credit needs of the business community. This is especially true in respect to new, small, or unincorporated firms, whose access to sources of intermediate and long-term external financing, other than bank credit, is very slight or nonexistent. The device of term loans, and the practice of continuous renewals of nominally short-term loans, make up a part of the wide variety of credit practices adopted by banks to meet the financing needs of small business.

On the unfavorable side, however, the rapid growth of business loans during periods of inflationary pressures may aggravate the situation if the proceeds of the loans are used to finance capital expenditure programs rather than to finance short-run, seasonal inventory requirements. There is some evidence that this has been the case.

(2) With respect to bank solvency, the shift to longer-term business loans poses a potential threat. This is particularly true since other types of bank loans have also tended to become longer-term in nature and to rely more on the anticipated income of the borrower over extended periods.

It is obvious that the longer the period over which income is anticipated and repayment schedules based, the greater is the risk of unforeseen adverse developments. To be sound therefore, the practice of granting longer-term credits must be matched by vigorous efforts of banks to build up their capital funds in keeping with the greater credit risks involved in current loan practices. This is vitally important in order to insure the continuity of the bank's operation during periods when it might become necessary to write off unsound assets, as well as to provide an adequate "cushion" of owners' equity in the bank to protect depositors against losses.

Although bank capital funds have grown rapidly in the postwar period, some authorities have expressed doubt as to whether they have grown fast enough to keep pace with the expansion in bank loans, both in amount and as a proportion of total bank assets.

(3) With respect to the need for bank liquidity, the trend toward longer-term business credits, while desirable in important respects, has not repealed the overriding fact that commercial banks are institutions with over 90 per cent of liabilities payable on demand or on short notice. *The trend in the direction of longer-term loans, combined with the rising proportion of total loans to total deposits, thus becomes sound only if balanced by adequate holdings of secondary reserves — i.e., liquid assets that can be quickly converted into cash with virtually no danger of loss.*

In determining the form of secondary reserves, the "shiftability" doctrine of bank liquidity, with one major qualification, is a sound guide. Secondary reserves must be assets that can be shifted easily from one bank to another in normal times in order to meet individual bank needs for cash, but they must also be assets which the commercial banking system as a whole can shift to the central banking system in periods of crisis. For several reasons, short-term Government securities seem to be the only major credit instrument which can fulfill this need. First, such securities are the only type of money-market instrument available in sufficient quantity to meet the needs of all commercial banks. Secondly, short-term Governments are the only securities (with minor exceptions) which the Federal Reserve System freely buys or sells, under both past and present policy.

Mainly because of the accidental circumstance of World War II, the banking system acquired an enormous volume of U.S. Government securities which fulfilled the need for secondary reserves. By 1945, bank holdings of such securities far exceeded total bank loans, so that the question of bank liquidity was largely academic.

Since that time, however, a rapid reversal has taken place in bank holdings of Government securities. Banks have disposed of huge sums of Governments in order to finance the unprecedented demand for loans in the post-war business boom.

As an illustration of how far these trends have gone, the ratio of total loans to total deposits at all Fourth District member banks has risen from 28 per cent in 1950 to 45 per cent at present. For many individual banks, loans already constitute over half of total deposits. Conversely, the ratio of U.S. Government securities to total deposits at all District member banks has declined from 50 per cent in 1950 to 34 per cent at present, and is even lower for individual banks.

How long can this pace be maintained without reducing secondary reserves below a prudent level needed for sound banking? While no answer can be given that is applicable to all banks, it may be suggested that this is one of the most important problems that must be met by bank management in order to insure a strong and healthy banking system in the years ahead.

In the last analysis, each bank will have to set its own minimum standards of liquidity, as well as need for capital funds, based on a careful analysis of the behavior of its own deposits and the nature of its loan portfolio. The time may be ripe for a thorough reappraisal of such fundamental factors.

15

HOW HIGH CAN THE LOAN-DEPOSIT RATIO GO?*

David P. Eastburn†

The ratio of bank loans to deposits has traditionally been used as a measure of bank liquidity: a high loan-deposit ratio implying a low degree of bank liquidity, a low ratio corresponding to a high degree of liquidity. The previous selection noted that in the

* From the *Business Review*, Federal Reserve Bank of Philadelphia (May, 1966). Reprinted by the courtesy of the Federal Reserve Bank of Philadelphia and the author.

† Vice-President, Federal Reserve Bank of Philadelphia.

> mid-1950's the loan-deposit ratio had reached about 45 per cent, and questioned how much higher it could possibly go (see the last few paragraphs of the previous selection).
>
> Now, about a decade later, the loan-deposit ratio is above 60 per cent for all commercial banks in the aggregate and above 70 per cent for some individual banks. And still the question is being asked: how much higher can it go? The answer involves a consideration of all the many and varied forces which influence bank portfolio policies.

As credit demands press harder and harder on supplies, a recurring question in board rooms and executive dining rooms of commercial banks is "how high can the loan/deposit ratio go?" Bankers look at a ratio of 62 per cent for all commercial banks and ratios of 70 per cent and above for many individual banks and conclude that the ceiling can't be very far away.[1]

Older bankers with long memories, of course, may recall even higher ratios back in the 1920's. As Chart 1 shows, the ratio for all commercial banks was just under 80 per cent early in the twenties, and at the end of the decade was still as high as 70 per cent. But memories tend to be short, and as top positions of more and more banks are taken by younger men whose experience is limited to post-Depression years, the present ratio is, to all intents and purposes, a new peak. The broad rise from 17 per cent in 1944 to 62 per cent today seemingly just can't continue at the rate it has been going.

WHAT HAS MOVED THE RATIO IN THE PAST?

The future of the loan/deposit ratio will depend on the same basic forces that have shaped its past. As Chart 1 also shows, putting the question in terms of loans as a percentage of total loans and investments gives the same general picture as loans as a percentage of total deposits. This is a much more fruitful way of · looking at the question because the most important factor determining the loan/deposit ratio is the *kinds* of assets bankers decide to put their funds into. As Chart 2 shows, bankers ever since World War II have chosen to acquire loans rather than Federal Government securities. This accounts for the broad rise in the loan/deposit ratio during that period. The broad decline through the 1930's and World War II was caused by the opposite movement

[1] Some calculate the ratio by deducting uncollected items from deposits and expressing loans as a percentage of "adjusted" deposits. This produces a ratio for all commercial banks of 67 per cent.

CHART 1

The LOAN/DEPOSIT RATIO has experienced two broad swings in the past 45 years — declining from 1920 to 1944, and then rising since World War II. The ratio of loans to loans and investments has moved generally the same way.

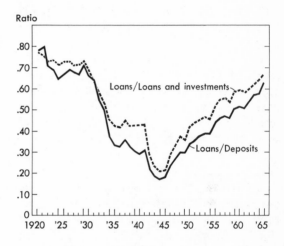

CHART 2

Changes in EARNING ASSETS HELD BY COMMERCIAL BANKS help to explain ups and downs in the loan/deposit ratio. The rise in the ratio in recent years results from the increase in loans relative to Governments and municipals held by banks.

CHART 3

Changes in earning assets of banks are strongly influenced by changes in NET PRI-VATE AND PUBLIC DEBT OUTSTANDING. As private debt has expanded in recent years relative to Federal and state and local government debt, much of this private debt has found its way into bank portfolios in the form of loans.

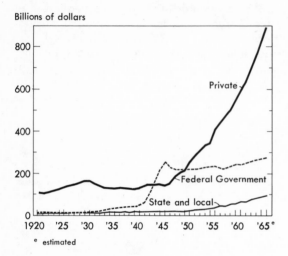

Billions of dollars

e estimated

CHART 4

The COMMERCIAL BANK SHARE OF OUT-STANDING DEBT also helps to explain behavior of the loan/deposit ratio. In the past few years, banks have acquired a larger share of outstanding private debt, thus pushing up the loan/deposit ratio even faster than would have resulted from shifting debt patterns alone.

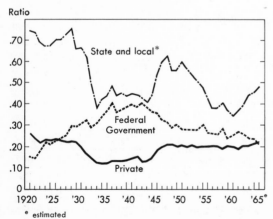

Ratio

e estimated
* Ratio of "other securities" to state and local government debt

— acquisition of Government securities at a rate greater than loans. Bank holdings of municipal securities were a relatively neutral factor during most of the earlier period, but after World War II began to become more important and in the last five years have really spurted.[2]

Individual bankers consider many things in deciding the kinds of assets to acquire, and in this, of course, lies much of the art and skill of commercial banking. But in a broad sense, their decisions are made for them by events over which they have little or no control. Among these are wars and the general state of the economy.

These affect the banker's decisions by influencing the kinds of instruments *available* for him to acquire. Trends in major types of debt outstanding in the economy, presented in Chart 3, show a striking similarity to trends in bank assets in Chart 2. During the Depression and World War II, Federal Government debt increased more rapidly than private and state and local government debt. As bankers took large amounts of Federal Government securities into their portfolios, this kind of instrument became a much larger proportion of total earning assets.

In the postwar period, on the other hand, bankers have responded to, and indeed contributed to, the tremendous surge of the private economy. Their acquisitions of loans have been part of the process which has generated such a rapid increase in private debt. In contrast, growth of Federal debt has been relatively limited and helps to explain the decline in bank holdings of Government securities. The expansion in state and local government debt has offered more opportunities for banks to acquire this type of instrument.

In broad terms, then, the types of assets which bankers decide to *hold* have been influenced strongly by the types of debt instruments *available*. When Federal Government debt has risen more rapidly than state and local and private debt, banks have acquired *Government securities* relative to other assets. When, as in

[2] Throughout this article, data on municipal securities actually are "other" (i.e., other than Federal Government) securities held by banks. Municipals constitute the great bulk of "other securities."

the postwar period, private debt has risen more rapidly than Government debt, banks have increased the importance of *loans* relative to investments. This fact, probably more than anything else, explains the behavior of both the ratio of loans to loans and investments and the ratio of loans to deposits.

The picture is much more complicated than this, of course, but here let's consider only one refinement. This has to do with the *share* of outstanding debt which commercial banks, *vis-á-vis* other investors, acquire. Chart 4 shows commercial banks' share of outstanding debt since 1920. It indicates that banks in recent years have acquired a rising share of private debt, but a declining share of Federal Government debt. Another way of putting this is that the ratio of loans to loans and investments and the ratio of loans to deposits have grown even faster than one would expect simply on grounds of the growth in outstanding debt; bankers have hurried the trend along in recent years by acquiring an increasing share of outstanding private debt.

OUTLOOK FOR 1970

This review of forces at work in the past brings us back to the question posed at the outset: how much higher can the loan/deposit ratio go? Without making any predictions, it is possible to figure how high it *might* go by, say, 1970, assuming certain conditions. These conditions involve: (1) trends in the various kinds of debt outstanding; (2) commercial banks' share of that debt. Some of the many possible assumptions that could be made are shown in the table on the next page.

In the first column, we assume simply that trends continue as they have been going in recent years. Private debt would keep rising very rapidly and commercial banks would continue to get a rising share of it. State and local government debt also would rise rapidly, and the commercial bank share would expand at the exceptionally fast rate of recent years. While Federal Government debt also would rise, commercial banks would reduce their share, as they have been doing for some time.

Any banker who expects things to keep going as they have been, in other words, can get an

	Assumed trend to 1970	
Outstanding debt —		
Private	Continues trend of recent years	Increase ¾ as fast as in recent years
Federal Government	"	Increases as fast as in recent years
State & local government	"	Increases as fast as in recent years
Commercial bank share of —		
Private debt	"	Increase ¾ as fast as in recent years
Federal Government debt	"	Declines ¾ as fast as in recent years
State & local government debt	"	Increase ¾ as fast as in recent years
Ratio of loans/loans & investments	72%	70%
Ratio of loans/deposits*	66%	64%

*Estimated from relationship to ratio of loans/loans & investments in recent years.

idea of the loan/deposit ratio in 1970 by looking at the bottom of the first column. This shows a ratio of about 66 per cent. This, of course, is higher than the ratio today. But it is not as high as one would expect simply by projecting the trend of the loan/deposit ratio in recent years. The reason, primarily, is the very rapid growth of municipals in bank portfolios. If this were to continue for the next several years, municipals would become an increasingly important part of bank earning assets and tend to hold down the rise in the loan/deposit ratio.[3]

The second column is intended for those bankers who may not be content to assume simply a continuation of recent trends. In this column, we assume that private debt will not rise as rapidly as it has been, nor will commercial banks increase their share of it as rapidly. On the other hand, Federal Government debt

[3] Municipals would rise from 14.7 to 18.0 per cent of total earning assets. The importance of assumptions about the behavior of municipals is illustrated by the fact that if all trends are assumed to continue as in recent years except that commercial banks' share of municipals is assumed to level off at the present percentage, then the loan/deposit ratio would rise to 68.5 per cent.

is assumed to keep growing at the recent rate and commercial banks do not reduce their share of it quite so rapidly. State and local government debt would also continue to rise as fast as it has been, but commercial banks would not increase their share of it quite so rapidly. Given these assumptions, the loan/deposit ratio would come out to about 64 per cent.

Bankers who foresee other possibilities will get other loan/deposit ratios. More extreme assumptions would tend to produce more extreme results. But the odds are against either extreme — either a very high, or very low ratio — as we look ahead. A very high ratio would suggest boom conditions in the private economy until 1970, with commercial banks extending their competitive position; at the same time, municipals and Governments held by banks would have to increase much more slowly or decline relative to loans. While these conditions are possible, they don't appear to be the most likely.

It seems still clearer that a *decline* in the ratio of any size is quite remote. As Chart 1 shows, the ratio has not dropped consistently and substantially since the 1930's and World War II. The only developments which could bring about such a drop would seem to be an international crisis or a depression. Either of these would require a major step-up in Federal Government spending which would produce a large flow of Government securities into commercial banks.

The greater likelihood is that the loan/deposit ratio will rise higher by 1970 than it is now, but not as fast as it has in recent years.

IN THE SHORTER RUN

Of course, 1970 is still some time away. In shorter periods the loan/deposit ratio responds, more than anything else, to fluctuations of the business cycle. As Chart 5 shows, the ratio rises during economic expansions and declines during recessions (shaded portions). The reason, of course, is that loan demand is strong when business is good. At the same time, supplies of funds get tight and, in order to meet needs of their customers, banks sell Government securities. Their holdings of municipals have tended

to grow more steadily, picking up in recent years as banks have sought higher-yielding investments.

What this look at cycles indicates is that on top of the longer upward drift of the loan/deposit ratio are superimposed particularly rapid spurts during periods of strong credit demand, such as the present. It is during these periods that concern about the ratio mounts. Bankers see their holdings of more risky and less liquid assets rising and their holdings of less risky and more liquid assets declining. As they look ahead to still further demands on their resources, they examine their risk and liquidity positions more and more closely and tend to

CHART 5

SHIFTS IN LOANS AND INVESTMENTS over business cycles explain short-run changes in the loan/deposit ratio. Banks move into Governments when loan demand falls off in recessions (shaded portions) and out of Governments when loans pick up again.

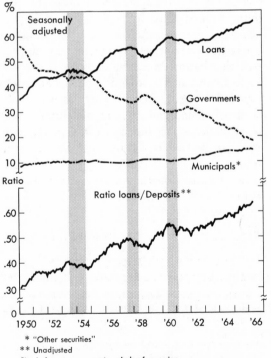

* "Other securities"
** Unadjusted
Shaded areas represent periods of recession.

become more selective in meeting further demands.

Bankers may not find much comfort, therefore, in the longer-run projections presented
above. Nor are they urged to. Sometime in the
future they may look back on today's ratio and
regard it as fairly comfortable. Bankers have
changed their views about customary levels of

the ratio in the past and may well change them
again in years to come.

But right now, and looking to the immediate
future, they feel squeezed by the rising ratio.
To the extent this feeling induces them to look
twice at demands for credit, it serves a useful
purpose of relieving pressures in our current
full-employment economy.

16

THE PRIME RATE*

Albert M. Wojnilower and Richard E. Speagle†

*Just as the volume of loans made is important, so — it goes without saying — is the price
charged for making them.*

Of all the interest rates charged by banks,
only one is widely publicized and uniform
throughout the country — the prime rate on
business loans. The prime rate is the rate that
banks charge their most credit-worthy customers; other borrowers must pay more. Rightly or
wrongly, changes in the prime rate are often
regarded by the public and the banks as one
of the chief indexes of credit conditions. This
article reviews the history of the prime rate,
assembles the available statistical evidence concerning its role in the lending process, and discusses changes in the prime rate and their
causes.

THE EVOLUTION OF THE PRIME RATE

While banks have always had rates reserved
for their best customers, a nationally publicized

* From *Essays in Money and Credit* (Federal Reserve Bank of New York, 1964). Reprinted by the
courtesy of the Federal Reserve Bank of New York and
the authors.
† The First Boston Corporation, and St. John's University, respectively.

and uniform rate apparently did not emerge
until the depression of the 1930's. The rate
set in that period of slack loan demand and
swollen reserve positions, 1½ per cent, represented a floor below which banks were said to
regard lending as totally unprofitable, given the
administrative costs involved. The rate remained unchanged through the war and until
December 1947, at which time it was raised to
1¾ per cent. In the ensuing years, there have
been only eighteen changes in the rate (all but
four of these upward). The current (August
1964) rate of 4½ per cent has been in effect
since August 23, 1960.

Prime rates are "officially" posted only by the
largest banks; changes in the rate become effective by means of announcements by these
banks. Normally one bank announces a change
in rate, and the other banks follow suit within
a day or two. On all but one occasion, the
bellwether has been a New York City bank,
and three such banks — First National City
Bank, The Chase Manhattan Bank, and Bankers Trust Company — have initiated fourteen

of the nineteen changes recorded. Through August 1956, rate changes were in steps of ¼ of a percentage point; subsequent movements have been in steps of ½ a point.

Evidently the prime rate is not a sensitive, open market rate (such as, for example, Treasury bill rates) fluctuating constantly in response to the changing intensities of demand and supply channeled into, and measured by, a national market. Movements in the prime rate lag appreciably behind changes in the general business situation and open market money rates. The practice of moving only in half-point steps has lengthened this lag, since it has meant that larger shifts in open market rates and credit conditions became a prerequisite for a change in the prime rate.

The lag, however, appears to be characteristic of bank loan rates in general, rather than of the prime rate in particular. Loan rates were "late" movers relative to other business and credit market indicators long before the rise to prominence of the prime rate. According to the figures of the National Bureau of Economic Research, fluctuations in loan rates charged by banks have been trailing cyclical changes in business at large since at least 1919, when the statistical record begins. The median lag in the post-World War II period has, however, been somewhat longer than in earlier years.

Until late 1953, the prime rate was almost always lower than the prevailing yield on new issues of high-grade corporate bonds, by and large the most important alternative source of outside financing available to prime borrowers. After 1953, however, the prime rate came at times to exceed the yield on new issues of Aaa-rated corporate bonds, and since mid-1961 it has been almost continuously higher. Bond yields have generally turned upward or downward ahead of the prime rate, but the differential between the two interest rates has been at most ½ of 1 per cent and normally much narrower.

The prime rate has generally been in the range of 1 to 2 percentage points above the Federal Reserve discount rate. Changes in the prime rate have been less frequent than changes in the discount rate, which has been more closely related to short-term open market rates,

but the general pattern of movements has been similar.

WHO PAYS THE PRIME RATE?

The criteria that borrowers must meet if they are to qualify as "prime" cannot be precisely defined. On average, at banks in the nineteen cities included in the Federal Reserve Quarterly Interest Rate Survey, approximately half the total dollar volume of reported short-term business loan extensions (and renewals) has carried the prime rate.[1] This proportion is much higher, however, for large loans and far lower for small loans (detailed figures are given later in this article), so that the number — as opposed to the dollar amount — of loans granted at the prime rate is much less than half the total. Since large loans are normally made to large businesses, and small loans to small firms, it is clear that, whatever the formal standards that may be required of a "prime" borrower, the prime rate is extended principally to large firms. Indeed, interest rates on loans exceeding $200,000 are dominated by the prime rate. Since 1951, the differential between the prime rate and the average interest rate on these large loans has never been larger than 0.5 of a percentage point and usually smaller, normally ranging from 0.20 to 0.35 of a percentage point. Differentials between the prime rate and average interest rates on smaller loans have been much larger and more variable, as shown in Table I.

TABLE I

Differentials Between the Prime Rate and Average Interest Rates on Short-Term Business Loans

Size of loan	Range of differentials, 1951–64 (in percentage points)
$200,000 and over	0.15 to 0.50
$100,000 to $200,000	0.43 to 0.97
$ 10,000 to $100,000	0.66 to 1.49
$ 1,000 to $ 10,000	0.92 to 2.24
All loans	0.27 to 0.71

Source: Quarterly Interest Rate Survey of the Board of Governors of the Federal Reserve System.

[1] This proportion is subject to cyclical fluctuations described later.

As mentioned earlier, a formal prime rate is apparently posted only by the larger banks. The question therefore arises whether the short-term rate levels and changes established by the leading banks are adhered to by smaller banks as well. Data for average new loan rates from the Federal Reserve Commercial Loan Surveys of 1955 and 1957 suggest that loans to large firms were then being made principally at the prime rate by small banks as well as by large.

The Quarterly Interest Rate Survey does not analyze term loan rates in the same detail as short-term rates. No national data are published. Results for New York City imply, however, that a large proportion of term loans is made at the prime rate. Since 1951 the average rate on new term loans in New York City has only once exceeded the prime rate by more than ½ per cent (March 1954), and then by an insignificant margin. Indeed, on several occasions in the 1956–60 period, the average rate on new term loans in New York was *below* the prime rate, apparently because loans were being taken down under fixed-interest commitments entered into at previous times of lower rates. Since then, there has been an effort to avoid such occurrences through the more frequent use of "escalator" clauses that tie the rate on term loans to some fixed relation with the prime rate at the time of take-down.

THE PREVALENCE OF THE PRIME RATE

The argument is sometimes made that the posted prime rate may be a façade hiding a much more flexible interest rate structure. The available statistical evidence, however, suggests the contrary. Changes in the prime rate seem to be a reliable index of what is happening to the average level of business loan rates paid; indeed, prime rate fluctuations are generally larger than changes in rates on non-prime business loans. The following discussion explores the relevant evidence and its implications.

Since the prime rate moves infrequently, later than other rates, and only in sizable steps, one might expect "shading" of the rate to become fairly prevalent from time to time. Unpublicized discounts might be offered at times of slack demand, with "gray market" premiums appearing when supplies are tight. This, at least, is what is fairly commonly observed in other markets where the published "list price" is established by a few large sellers, but where there are also many small sellers, as well as numerous large and small buyers. With respect to the prime rate, however, such unpublicized concessions appear to be rare. While there are always a few short-term loans (ranging up to about 2 per cent of the total at the banks reporting in the quarterly survey) which are extended at rates nominally below the prime rate, these often result from special arrangements in which the effective interest cost is easily shown to be at least as high as the prime rate.

After 1960, with the prime rate remaining unchanged in an environment of prolonged monetary ease of varying degrees, one might suppose that rate "cutting" in individual transactions became more common. There seemed to be more frequent rumors of such instances, but no evidence of any significant increase is to be found in the figures.

The equivalent of rate "shading" could, of course, be accomplished through adjustment of one or more of the many other dimensions of a loan contract. An obvious expedient, virtually equivalent to a rate change, would be the variation of the standards established for the "prime" rating. If loan demand were slack, for example, these standards might be lowered, making more borrowers eligible for the prime rate. The average level of rates actually paid would thereby be reduced, even though the prime rate remained unchanged. Conversely, these standards might be stiffened at times of tight money, resulting in a higher level of rates actually paid.

Such accommodations to market forces could also occur through a multitude of other nonrate factors. Some of these, such as changes in the compensating deposit balances required of borrowers could, at least under some circumstances, be used as rather obvious substitutes for rate adjustment. For others, such as the duration and amounts for which loans are granted, the collateral required, and the services the bank undertakes to render, the relation to interest rates is less clear cut. Furthermore, it is conceivable that, at those times when the market is "moving away" from the prime rate, rates to less-than-prime borrowers are adjusted while prime borrowers are left untouched, so that the level of the prime rate becomes less representative of the true loan rate structure.

Nevertheless, the available evidence, including that obtained in interviews, suggests that systematic undermining of the prime rate, through those nonrate aspects that affect true interest costs in an obvious and easily measured way, has not played a generally prominent role except for certain classes of bank customers, notably sales finance companies. The statistical evidence, moreover, indicates that lending at the prime rate — which is of course a minimum rate — actually tends to be less pervasive in periods of relatively easy money and more pervasive in periods of relatively tight money. This statement, perhaps surprising at first sight, is explored in the next section.

FLUCTUATIONS IN THE PROPORTION OF LOANS QUALIFYING FOR THE PRIME RATE

The proposition that a smaller proportion of loan volume qualifies for the prime rate when money is easy and a larger proportion when it is tight, can be tested against data collected in the Quarterly Interest Rate Survey as to the amounts of business loans extended at various interest rates.[2] Because of the irregular fluctuations, little can be said about changes in the proportion of prime loans during periods when the prime rate remained unchanged. What does seem clear, however, is that periods of tight money and rising rates have most often been times when the proportion of total lending volume made at, or close to, the prime rate has increased. Conversely, periods of easy money and reduced prime rates have been accompanied by declines in the proportion of loan volume transacted at the prime rate. When money is tight, more of the loan volume carries

the prime rate; when it is easy, a smaller proportion of the dollar volume of loans qualifies. Thus, changes in the prime rate appear to overstate rather than understate the extent of actual changes in the average rate level.

The same finding holds not only for total loan extensions, but also "within" each of the loan-size classes distinguished by the statistics. Table II illustrates the prevailing pattern for two periods of credit ease and tightness. The same pattern held for the whole period under review. In all size groups, a larger proportion of the dollar volume of loans qualified as prime when the prime rate was rising, while a smaller share qualified when the prime rate was low.

The growth in the proportion of prime loans when rates rise, as well as its contraction as rates fall, appears to reflect two major influences. One is the cyclical behavior of bank loan demand by prime borrowers. At times of business expansion and rising interest rates, credit demand by these borrowers increases and, because they are preferred customers, is more likely to be satisfied than loan requests by other firms. Thus, the proportion of prime loan volume rises within each loan-size category (and the dollar volume of large loans, which contains the highest proportion of prime loans, rises relative to the volume of smaller loans). Conversely, at times of economic slack these borrowers normally make repayments, reflecting larger net cash flows and the often greater availability of other means of financing, such as open market (commercial) paper. The share of these borrowers in the loan total is thus reduced.

A second important factor is the traditional "stickiness" of loan rates. When the prime rate is raised from, say, 3½ to 4 per cent, some borrowers who previously paid 4 per cent are apparently allowed to renew loans at the same rate, expanding the proportion of prime rate loans in the loan total. Conversely, when the prime rate falls, some borrowers may not have their rates reduced; as a result, the proportion of prime loans drops. While the influence of the demand and stickiness factors cannot be completely segregated, bank interviews as well as the statistics on average rates paid strongly suggest that both factors are significant.

---

[2] The Federal Reserve Quarterly Interest Rate Survey gives information on the average interest rate, for various loan sizes, charged by the sample banks (or branches) on short-term business loans made during the first fifteen days of each end-of-quarter month. Data are also compiled giving the percentage distribution of the dollar volume of loans extended at selected interest rate levels.

TABLE II

Short-Term Business Loans Extended at the Prime Rate
at Times of Credit Tightness and Ease

Percentage of loan volume extended at the prime rate (or less)

Size of loan	September 1957 (tightness)	June 1958 (ease)	June 1959 (tightness)	December 1960 (ease)
$200,000 and over	73	60	69	66
$100,000 to $200,000	31	21	28	25
$ 10,000 to $100,000	12	6	11	8
$ 1,000 to $ 10,000	5	1	6	2
All loans	62	48	59	56

Percentage of loan volume extended at no more than 0.5 per cent above the prime rate

Size of loan	September 1957 (tightness)	June 1958 (ease)	June 1959 (tightness)	December 1960 (ease)
$200,000 and over	89	75	86	83
$100,000 to $200,000	67	44	62	52
$ 10,000 to $100,000	45	20	44	28
$ 1,000 to $ 10,000	23	5	24	12
All loans	82	64	79	74

Source: Quarterly Interest Rate Survey of the Board of Governors of the Federal Reserve System.

THE PRIME RATE AND RATES ON OTHER BUSINESS LOANS

Comparison of the behavior of the prime rate with average interest rates on new business loans yields similar results. When the prime rate has advanced, the average rate also has increased, but by a smaller amount. Thus, when the prime rate rises, rates on nonprime loans do not increase correspondingly. Conversely, when the prime rate has been lowered, the average rate for all loan extensions has not declined to the same extent; rates on nonprime loans have fallen by less than the prime rate. To summarize, changes in the average level of rates charged have always been smaller than the prime rate change. Moreover, there has been little movement in average loan rates except at times of a change in the prime rate.

These relations also hold within each loan-size class taken separately; changes in the actual average rate have been smaller than changes in the prime rate. The pattern is illustrated in Table III for two characteristic periods, during one of which the prime rate rose 1 per cent, while during the other it fell 1 per cent.

It is evident that, when the prime rate falls, small-loan rates do not drop as much as large-loan rates. Conversely, when the prime rate rises, small-loan rates do not increase correspondingly, partly because they may be close to the legal rate ceilings prevailing in many areas. Indeed, the pattern of a narrowing in rate differentials as rates rise, and a widening as they fall, is observable over the entire historical span of loan rate statistics, which begins in World War I.

To some extent, the pattern of these rate changes merely reflects the cyclical changes in the proportion of lending at the prime rate (in combination with the greater prevalence of the prime rate for larger loans) already described. If in any loan aggregate the proportion of prime (low-rate) loans rises, the average rate for that group must fall, and conversely. Since the proportion of prime loans has declined when interest rates were falling, we should expect that a 1 per cent drop in the prime rate would lower average rates by something less than 1 per cent. Conversely, a 1 per cent rise in the prime rate would raise the over-all rate average of any loan group by less than that amount. The actual degree of rate sluggishness was found to be clearly greater, however, than could be accounted for by such shifts in loan distribution

TABLE III

Changes in the Average Interest Rate on Short-Term Business Loans

Size of loan	December 1957-June 1958 Fall in average rate (as prime rate fell 1 percentage point)	March 1959-December 1959 Rise in average rate (as prime rate rose 1 percentage point)
$200,000 and over	0.76	0.92
$100,000 to $200,000	0.61	0.80
$ 10,000 to $100,000	0.41	0.65
$ 1,000 to $ 10,000	0.21	0.46

Source: Quarterly Interest Rate Survey of the Board of Governors of the Federal Reserve System.

(as shown by certain calculations that are not reproduced in this article). Thus, rate stickiness appears to be an independent factor tending to stabilize rates.[3]

FINDINGS AT INDIVIDUAL BANKS

These results based on statistical aggregates do not imply, of course, that all banks behaved uniformly. Investigation of the behavior of a few New York City banks as regards fluctuations in the proportion of loans made at the prime rate revealed a degree of diversity but, on the whole, gave results consistent with the broad statistical findings. Thus, at one large institution, the proportion of loans granted at the prime rate moved in accord with the national pattern. The same was true of term loans at a second bank (this was the only class of loans studied at this bank). At a third institution, however, the 1960 cut in the prime rate was followed by an increase in the proportion of new loans made at the prime rate, contrary to the pattern shown by the aggregate statistics. Nevertheless, officers of this bank agreed, a larger proportion of loans *normally* carries the prime rate when money is tight than when it is easy, and conversely. This was explained in terms of the difficulty of raising rates that are already at, or close to, the 6 per cent statutory ceiling. On the other hand, rates on such loans are not reduced when the prime rate falls.

[3] It is conceivable that, in addition to the cyclical rise and fall of prime loans relative to nonprime loans, nonprime loans also rise and fall cyclically relative to others of still lower quality. Should this be the case on a large scale, all the stickiness might be explained away. But the data and the interview results make it appear unlikely that this actually happens.

TERM LOANS

Rates charged on term loans behaved somewhat differently. Comparing the New York City average rate with the out-of-town averages, which probably include relatively fewer large and/or prime borrowers, it appears that, as in the case of the short-term rate, a rise in the prime rate exerts its largest impact on rates paid by prime borrowers and has less effect on rates paid by others.

A divergence between short-term and term loan rates occurred during the latter part of rate upswings, as in mid-1953, mid-1956 to mid-1957, and mid-1959 to mid-1960. Short-term rates advanced in step with the prime rate at these times, but term loan rates rose more slowly. As a result, there were long periods in which the average rate on new term loans was lower than that on even the largest ($200,000 or more) short-term loans. Since 1960, rates on term loans appear to have been more responsive to general interest rate movements than rates on short-term loans.

NONRATE ASPECTS OF BANK-CUSTOMER RELATIONS

Although the present study was not directly concerned with the nonrate aspects of bank loan allocation, it provided some insights consistent with the results of other recent studies. In particular, a critical factor considered by banks in ruling on particular credit requests seems to be the past and expected profitability of the customer relationship as a whole, including prominently its deposit as well as its loan aspect. Just as bank loans often have special advantages for borrowers, so lending to prime borrowers often yields banks substantial returns, in the form of deposits or additional business, over and above interest receipts. At one large bank, for example, the rise in the proportion of prime loans as money tightened was attributed partly to the fact that "many good customers [depositors], nonborrowers for years, seemed to come in for loans". Conversely, when deposits are abundantly available, the banks become less concerned about the deposit side of the customer arrangements and more willing to make loans to other credit-worthy borrowers. Much more investigation into lending terms and practices is needed, however, to justify any firm conclusions on these points. Indeed, there may be considerable differences in basic philosophy and policy among individual banks and among banks of different sizes.

It is vital to recognize, however, that the importance of nonrate factors in individual transactions does not necessarily imply that rate changes play an insignificant role in the aggregate. Borrowers with access to several sources of funds, such as large utilities and finance companies, are often quite sensitive to rates and rate differentials. Their reaction to rate movements may at times substantially affect the over-all loan situation. Moreover, all borrowers may be marginally influenced by rate levels, and anticipations of rate changes, in the size of their bank loan requests. Since most loan proceeds are quickly spent on goods and services, even a relatively small response of the pace of loan extensions to a change in interest rates can have significant effects on total economic activity.

CHANGES IN THE PRIME RATE

We now turn to changes in the prime rate and their causes. The behavior of the prime rate is subject, of course, to a great variety of influences, some essentially long run in nature, others cyclical. To explain the timing of particular prime rate changes, furthermore, one must take into account the complex decision-making process in the banks that exercise rate leadership and the competitive relations among these institutions.

Although it is only about seventeen years since the first change in the prime rate, the general pattern of the forces to which it is subject seems fairly well established. The basic trend of the rate during these years, like that of other interest rates, has been upward. Demand for bank loans has expanded greatly, reflecting the growth of the economy and the drawing-down of liquidity reserves accumulated during World War II. Moreover, although most prime borrowers have access to other means of financing, bank loans offer significant advantages in terms of the flexibility of amounts, timing, and other arrangements. Even the highly rate-sensitive national sales finance companies are careful to maintain their bank credit lines at all times.

Viewing the postwar period as a whole, the growth of bank deposits has not kept pace with loan demand. Loans were replacing Government securities in bank portfolios, while the total size of bank assets and deposits increased comparatively slowly. Each business upswing saw loans rise to occupy a more prominent position in bank portfolios than in the preceding expansion, and these increases were only partly reversed during recessions. In the business expansion that began in early 1961, the rise in loans relative to deposits has been much more gradual than during the expansions of the 1950's. By August 1964, nevertheless, the ratio of loans to total deposits at weekly reporting member banks (which include generally the largest banks) was slightly above its 1960 peak.

In order to obtain funds for lending, banks have had to step up competition for deposits. Already in the latter 1950's, and of course even more so in the 1960's, a relatively large share of deposit gains consisted of time deposits on which, in contrast to demand deposits, banks must normally pay interest. In turn, the rates banks charge, including the prime rate, also had to go higher. The rise in the prime rate during the postwar years appears to have been of the same order of magnitude as the increase in the yields on other outlets for bank funds.

During the 1950's, pressure of growing demand on relatively limited supply was probably more severe on the large banks in New York and Chicago that "make" the prime rate than on any other group of banks. These city banks have traditionally taken the lead in servicing the national firms that make up much of the prime borrower group. During the 1950–60 period, total deposits at these banks increased only about 20 per cent, compared with a rise of some 50 per cent at all other insured commercial banks. Over the same period, the bank debt of large manufacturing corporations (with assets of over $100 million) more than tripled.

This situation changed markedly after 1960. Reflecting cash flows larger than financing needs, bank debt of large manufacturing corporations declined between the end of 1960 and 1963. At the same time, deposit growth in New York and Chicago accelerated to a rate ahead of the national average. These banks thus had more money to lend, just when loan demand from their national customers declined.

Also after 1960, loan-deposit ratios at large "outside" banks as well as at smaller banks rose relative to New York and Chicago. In contrast to the decline in borrowing by large corporations, bank debt of smaller corporations, many of them customers of smaller banks, continued to expand. If these trends persist, it will be interesting to observe whether leadership in establishing the prime rate may perhaps pass away from New York, or alternatively whether the prime rate may lose its unique national status.

CYCLICAL FACTORS

Viewing the postwar period as a whole, the direction and timing of changes in the prime rate have been determined largely by the ramifications of the cyclical behavior of loan demand and supply. The fact that the prime rate rises and falls later than most other business-cycle indicators seems due at least in part to the time it takes for shifts in the business situation and monetary policy to be translated into changes in the loan supply-demand balance. Because of the nature of bank credit and of the market in which it is sold, the prime rate responds only to shifts in the credit situation that are unmistakable and are expected to persist.

The demand for new loans waxes and wanes roughly in rhythm with the cyclical swings in private investment, particularly investment in inventories. The supply of additional loans

that a bank can extend, on the other hand, depends primarily on the growth of its deposits and, with a given deposit volume, the extent to which it is willing to liquidate other assets to accommodate loans. The aggregate of deposits for all banks is, of course, significantly influenced by Federal Reserve policies, as a result of which the rate of growth of bank deposits has tended, on the whole, to be faster in times of economic weakness and slower in times of boom. During recession periods, in sum, loan demand is slack but the supply of bank funds is growing; in boom periods, by contrast, peak loan demands are pressing on a limited credit supply.

The ratio of loans to deposits, referred to earlier, is a convenient summary measure of the shifting balance over the cycle between loan demand and availability, and is known to play a significant role in the formation of loan policy by individual banks. Some margin of the deposit liabilities must be invested in assets that, in contrast to loans, can be quickly converted into cash. Consequently, a high loan-deposit ratio, whether for an individual bank or for the banking system, indicates a state of being largely "loaned up"; considerations of liquidity then dictate restraint in lending. Conversely, a low ratio suggests that a bank may be having difficulty in finding acceptable loans and is probably more receptive to new requests. Of course, the loan-deposit ratio is only an approximate measure of liquidity, since loan portfolios may be more or less liquid depending on the types and turnover rate of the loans involved while the deposits themselves may be more or less volatile.

As a result of the relationship between loan and deposit movements over the cycle, the loan-deposit ratio shows pronounced cyclical swings (Chart 1). The ratio falls during recessions, when loan volume contracts while deposits generally increase. The ratio rises during business expansions, when loan volume is growing while deposits generally increase relatively slowly. During the 1950's, as Chart 2 shows, the relation between the loan-deposit ratio of larger banks — indicating the pressure of loan demand on supply — and the prime rate was quite close.

To the extent that the prime rate and loan-

CHART 1

The Prime Rate and Various Credit Indicators

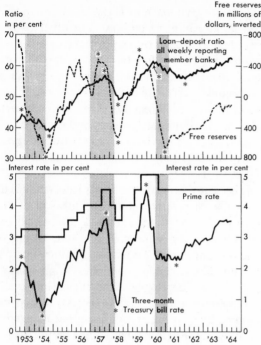

Note: Treasury bill rates are monthly averages of daily market yields, free reserves are three-month moving averages of monthly figures. Shaded areas are business-cycle contractions, according to the chronology of the National Bureau of Economic Research. Asterisks mark the apparent cyclical turning points in the various series.
Source: Board of Governors of the Federal Reserve System.

CHART 2

The Prime Rate and Loan-Deposit Ratios
Weekly reporting member banks

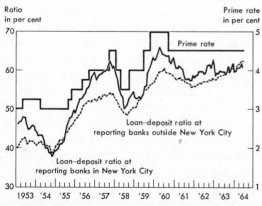

Note: Loan-deposit ratios equal loans (adjusted) less loans to brokers and dealers as a percentage of total deposits less cash items in process of collection. Ratios are based on averages of Wednesday figures.
Source: Board of Governors of the Federal Reserve System.

deposit ratios are related, some of the "laggardness" of the prime rate is explained. Loan-deposit ratios do not respond immediately to changes in the direction of monetary policy (Chart 1). At least since 1953, turning points in the cyclical course of loan-deposit ratios have in almost all instances lagged several months behind turns in free reserves, and at times also behind Treasury bill rates. At business-cycle troughs (and at the 1957 peak), turns in loan-deposit ratios also have trailed behind the turning points in business at large.

The effects on the prime rate of the cyclical fluctuations in the balance of loan demand and supply are reinforced by movements in the more sensitive, open market interest rates. While the path of open market rates, like that of loan-deposit ratios, reflects primarily the over-all credit situation, each rate is also subject to forces and anticipations specific to its own market. As a result, differentials among the various open market rates and loan rates are by no means constant. Interviews with leading banks indicate that the actual and anticipated standing of other relevant interest rates, along with loan-deposit ratios, plays a key role in decisions to change the prime rate. Long-term rates, such as those on corporate bonds (including rates on private placements with insurance companies and other nonbank investors), are considered by some banks to be more relevant than short-term rates.

When credit demand is expanding, rates on the various instruments through which borrowers may obtain access to nonbank funds — such as commercial paper and bond issues — rise promptly, and further rises are normally anticipated. With the prime rate still low, borrowing from banks becomes more attractive and pressure develops on the available supply of bank funds. At the same time, the costs banks must incur to raise additional funds increase. Rates on time deposits tend to rise toward the legal maxima. Sales of securities, at rising rates (declining prices), mean capital losses. Temporary reserve deficiencies become more frequent and must be offset at higher Federal funds or Reserve Bank discount rates. Such conditions appear ripe for the raising of the prime rate.

When credit demand is contracting, the sequence is reversed. As open market rates fall, borrowing at the established prime rate becomes less attractive. Some outstanding loans may be prepaid with the proceeds of open market financing. For the banks, the costs of attracting new deposits, and the returns offered by other investment outlets, decline. Sooner or later, the prime rate gives way.

The stability of the prime rate since 1960 is not out of keeping with the forces outlined above. During these years, with money relatively easy and business loan demand moderate, there was little upward pressure on the rate. Indeed, banks were by and large searching for loans. On the other hand, there were also economic forces working against a lower prime rate. These included high loan-deposit ratios, the marked rise in interest costs on time deposits and in the share of such deposits in the deposit total, and the relatively high return available on short-term investments as a result of official policies to boost such rates for balance-of-payments reasons. Even though the threshold at which a prime rate change is tripped off has not been crossed in recent years because of these offsetting influences, the mechanism that explains the earlier rate changes may well remain intact.

INDIVIDUAL BANK DECISIONS TO CHANGE THE PRIME RATE

The preceding broad considerations describe the environment propitious to a change in the prime rate. They are not sufficient, however, to predict with any confidence the precise timing of rate changes. The changing of the rate represents a major decision. A considerable time interval may elapse between the conclusion by some officials of a given bank that a rate change is appropriate and the decision of its management to take action. Elements of "gamesmanship" are necessarily involved, both among competing interests within a given institution and with respect to efforts to anticipate the reaction of customers and competitors. The attention which officials and the public have in recent years paid to "administered prices" also may have played a part in slowing down the response of bank managements to market conditions that might have warranted moving the prime rate.

Any actual change must be initiated by one particular bank. This is a risky step, for if the others do not follow, the lead bank faces a flood of loan requests perhaps in excess of lending capacity (if its rate is below the market) or a rapid exodus of customers to other banks (if its rate is above the market). It is not surprising, therefore, that most prime-rate moves have been initiated by the two largest New York banks, The Chase Manhattan and First National City. These two banks have been particularly prominent in initiating changes upward. Three of the four rate reductions during the postwar period, on the other hand, originated with other, somewhat smaller banks.

It is clear that a bank assumes leadership in a rate change only upon considerable deliberation among its top officials, whose views need by no means be unanimous. In one instance studied, two and a half months intervened between the initial proposal by a high official that the rate be changed and the ultimate action. However, less than two weeks elapsed in another case, in which consideration of a rate shift was reportedly touched off by a change in the Federal Reserve discount rate. At times noneconomic motives, such as the desire for leadership or publicity, appear to play an important part. Once some other bank has announced a change, on the other hand, the decision to follow along can normally be taken promptly and with little travail.

There was some indication that, at times when the existing rate seemed out of line, a move in the Federal Reserve discount rate might be interpreted as calling for, or giving sanction to, a changing of the prime rate. At other than such pivotal times, however, judging from the statistical record, discount rate changes have had little influence.[4]

---

[4] It may be pointed out that, in many financially advanced foreign countries, the rate structure of bank lending tends to be anchored to some key rate. In the United Kingdom, for example, the equivalent of the prime rate by custom stands in a fixed relation to the Bank of England's discount rate. For prime private borrowers, the rate is set ½ per cent above the discount rate (with a minimum of 5 per cent), but most private firms pay 1 per cent above the discount rate. In France, the authorities prescribe a minimum loan rate for the commercial banks, which the banks are permitted to adjust to the extent of one half of any central bank discount rate change. In Germany, the structure of bank loan rates is governed by officially

Bankers as well as the public tend to view the prime rate as the principal index of conditions in the bank loan market. So far as the interest rate on such loans is concerned, this view appears to be accurate: the extent and timing of all types of business-loan rate changes is governed closely by changes in the prime rate. It is doubtful, however, that the prime rate, taken by itself, is a reliable indicator of fluctuations in loan availability, which reflects, in addition to rate, other credit terms, standards of credit-worthiness, and the like.

Quite strikingly, the prime rate is among the last indexes of the credit situation to register a change in the credit climate. A number of reasons explains this. Because of the many dimensions of a loan agreement, rate is probably a less significant factor in a business-loan transaction than in other large-sized credit transactions. Since every loan is to some extent unique

and since, as a related matter, there is no secondary market in which existing loans may be traded, there are no standard reference points or market quotations to which rates on new loans can be mechanically geared. Moreover, changes in the supply-demand balance in the loan market, as reflected by loan-deposit ratios, do not occur until after turning points in reserve positions and short- and long-term rates. A further lag is introduced by the necessarily cautious and complex price-making procedure of a market in which leading banks compete for the business of large national borrowers.

In sum, changes in the prime rate do not normally occur ahead of, or even concurrently with, shifts in the credit situation. Rather, a change in the prime rate may usually be interpreted as confirming that a sizable shift has already taken place and that no early reversal is expected.

17

FIRST STEPS IN BANKING*

Punch

The following selection from Punch, *the British humor magazine, requires no introduction.*

Q. *What are banks for?*
A. To make money.
Q. *For the customers?*
A. For the banks.
Q. *Why doesn't bank advertising mention this?*

A. It would not be in good taste. But it is mentioned by implication in references to Reserves of £249,000,000 or thereabouts. That is the money they have made.
Q. *Out of the customers?*
A. I suppose so.
Q. *They also mention Assets of £500,000,000 or thereabouts. Have they made that too?*
A. Not exactly. That is the money they use to make money.
Q. *I see. And they keep it in a safe somewhere?*
A. Not at all. They lend it to customers.

prescribed maximum rates linked to the central bank discount rate. In Canada, on the other hand, the prime rate is set by the chartered banks in consultation with each other and is not changed frequently — partly because in periods of tight credit it has been close to the 6 per cent legal maximum on interest rates in general.

* From *Punch*, April 3, 1957. Copyright *Punch*. Reprinted by the courtesy of the publisher.

Q. *Then they haven't got it?*
A. No.
Q. *Then how is it Assets?*
A. They maintain that it would be if they got it back.
Q. *But they must have some money in a safe somewhere?*
A. Yes, usually £500,000,000 or thereabouts. This is called Liabilities.
Q. *But if they've got it, how can they be liable for it?*
A. Because it isn't theirs.
Q. *Then why do they have it?*
A. It has been lent to them by customers.
Q. *You mean customers lend banks money?*
A. In effect. They put money into their accounts, so it is really lent to the banks.
Q. *And what do the banks do with it?*
A. Lend it to other customers.
Q. *But you said that money they lent to other people was Assets?*
A. Yes.
Q. *Then Assets and Liabilities must be the same thing?*
A. You can't really say that.
Q. *But you've just said it. If I put £100 into my account the bank is liable to have to pay it back, so it's Liabilities. But they go and lend it to someone else, and he is liable to have to pay it back, so it's Assets. It's the same £100, isn't it?*
A. Yes. But . . .
Q. *Then it cancels out. It means, doesn't it, that banks haven't really any money at all?*
A. Theoretically. . . .
Q. *Never mind theoretically. And if they haven't any money where do they get their Reserves of £249,000,000 or thereabouts?*
A. I told you. That is the money they have made.
Q. *How?*
A. Well, when they lend your £100 to someone they charge him interest.
Q. *How much?*
A. It depends on the Bank Rate. Say five and a half per cent. That's their profit.

Q. *Why isn't it my profit? Isn't it my money?*
A. It's the theory of banking practice that . . .
Q. *When I lend them my £100 why don't I charge them interest?*
A. You do.
Q. *You don't say. How much?*
A. It depends on the Bank Rate. Say half a per cent.
Q. *Grasping of me, rather?*
A. But that's only if you're not going to draw the money out again.
Q. *But of course, I'm going to draw it out again. If I hadn't wanted to draw it out again I could have buried it in the garden, couldn't I?*
A. They wouldn't like you to draw it out again.
Q. *Why not? If I keep it there you say it's a Liability. Wouldn't they be glad if I reduced their Liabilities by removing it?*
A. No. Because if you remove it they can't lend it to anyone else.
Q. *But if I wanted to remove it they'd have to let me?*
A. Certainly.
Q. *But suppose they've already lent it to another customer?*
A. Then they'll let you have someone else's money.
Q. *But suppose he wants his too . . . and they've let me have it?*
A. You're being purposely obtuse.
Q. *I think I'm being acute. What if everyone wanted their money at once?*
A. It's the theory of banking practice that they never would.
Q. *So what banks bank on is not having to meet their commitments?*
A. I wouldn't say that.
Q. *Naturally. Well, if there's nothing else you think you can tell me . . .?*
A. Quite so. Now you can go off and open a banking account.
Q. *Just one last question.*
A. Of course.
Q. *Wouldn't I do better to go off and open a bank?*

CHAPTER SIX

COMPETITION IN FINANCIAL MARKETS

18

THE CHANGING STRUCTURE OF FINANCIAL INSTITUTIONS*

Marvin E. Rozen[†]

In a sense, Chapter Six is a continuation of Chapter Three ("Money, Debt, and Financial Markets"). In Chapters Four and Five we looked almost exclusively at commercial banks. And although commercial banks are particularly important — because they create money — other financial institutions are also important. For they, as well as commercial banks, create credit. Only commercial banks can create money, but any financial institution can create credit. (So can non-financial institutions, too, for that matter. Indeed, you can create credit. If you lend someone a dollar you have created credit.)

So now we return to financial institutions and financial markets in general, and examine them a bit more closely than we have thus far.

Recent changes in the structure of our financial institutions raise issues of considerable interest. Heightened concern with problems of economic growth has led to a reappraisal of the process whereby financial institutions are affecting, and being affected by, the development of the economy. Shifts in the relative importance of financial institutions have raised new problems for economic control policies. Difficult issues of equity emerge in connection with the impact of various kinds of regulation on the circumstances of the different financial institutions. A broad reconsideration of the causes of change in our financial structure should help place these complex issues in proper perspective.

* From *Quarterly Review of Economics and Business*, Volume 2, No. 4 (November, 1962). Reprinted by the courtesy of the publisher and the author.
† Pennsylvania State University.

In brief, I shall argue as follows: large and significant changes, involving great shifts in the relative importance of the different kinds of financial institutions, have occurred in our financial structure. For the most part, these changes reflect the powerful real forces of variation in patterns of expenditure and in the acquisition of financial assets by households and businesses. At the same time, however, environmental constraints of an organizational, asset-liability, and regulatory nature, through their effect on the competitive responses of financial institutions, contribute to shaping our financial structure. The evolution of the structure of such institutions is thus marked by continuous interaction between the forces of economic change and the reactive capabilities of the various institutions. In a sense, change in financial structure is an index of accommodation to processes of economic transformation.

CHANGES IN THE RELATIVE IMPORTANCE OF FINANCIAL INSTITUTIONS

Table I reveals the extent of postwar change in the financial structure in terms of the share of total assets held by each kind of financial institution; Table II provides some historical perspective. The explanation of these broad movements will be deferred to the next section. Relative positions based on asset rankings are something less than a complete indicator of importance and power. Assets are, of course, not the same thing as net worth, and there are substantial differences in the nature of the liabilities offsetting the assets of the various financial institutions. Moreover, measurement of importance in terms of assets overlooks the impact of those types of institutions having small asset holdings but nonetheless great influence over the flow of financial investment. Investment and mortgage bankers, brokers, and financial counselors have a disproportionate weight in financial markets relative to their size as measured by assets. Partly this is because of their position in advising actual holders of financial assets and, in general, in widening and broadening participation of others in financial markets so as to reduce the share of financial institutions; in this role they may be termed "knowledge intermediaries." Partly it is due to the importance of turnover — financial institutions differ greatly in their activity and those whose portfolios are constantly changing are bound to have a greater effect.

Another deficiency of any table of shares of total assets held by different types of financial institutions is the neglect of intra-institutional financial change. First, there are likely to be, over time, significant variations in the internal interrelationships within any particular kind of financial institutions, e.g., changes in the number and size distribution of firms. Thus a commercial banking system dominated by large branch systems and giant unit banks would behave differently from one composed of small unit banks. (Changes in internal structure, moreover, are likely to coincide with shifts in relative importance because the accelerated, or decelerated, industry growth such shifts imply also creates the most favorable environment for rearranging the interfirm relationships.) Second, although names remain the same, the

TABLE I

Percentage Shares of Total Financial Assets Held by Private Financial Institutions, 1945–60[a]

Institution	1945	1946	1947	1948	1949	1950	1951	1952	1953	1954	1955	1956	1957	1958	1959	1960
Commercial banks	61.20	57.79	56.70	54.71	52.73	51.65	51.16	50.00	48.25	46.73	44.60	43.45	42.58	41.97	40.34	39.35
Mutual savings banks	7.30	8.10	8.11	8.19	8.14	7.87	7.64	7.61	7.69	7.63	7.56	7.63	7.66	7.55	7.30	7.13
Savings and loan associations	3.59	4.29	4.70	5.07	5.38	5.76	6.13	6.73	7.47	8.13	9.00	9.71	10.34	10.87	11.76	12.42
Credit unions	0.17	0.22	0.25	0.28	0.30	0.35	0.39	0.45	0.51	0.58	0.66	0.74	0.81	0.85	0.93	0.96
Life insurance	18.75	20.30	20.72	21.25	21.63	21.42	21.27	21.06	21.21	20.95	20.77	20.85	20.90	20.32	20.11	19.85
Other insurance	3.89	4.20	4.49	4.79	5.19	5.30	5.38	5.48	5.59	5.82	5.89	5.77	5.56	5.67	5.80	5.69
Private pension funds	0.99	1.22	1.37	1.56	1.70	2.07	2.39	2.67	3.02	3.30	3.62	3.97	4.39	4.63	4.97	5.46
Finance companies	0.86	1.40	1.79	2.28	2.61	3.13	3.15	3.45	3.74	3.59	4.50	4.54	4.61	4.19	4.57	4.86
Investment companies	0.56	0.57	0.58	0.60	0.72	0.84	0.98	1.18	1.17	1.60	1.90	2.08	1.91	2.66	2.99	3.02
Security brokers and dealers	2.67	1.92	1.29	1.28	1.60	1.62	1.51	1.36	1.34	1.65	1.51	1.27	1.23	1.31	1.23	1.24

[a] Totals will not add to 100 per cent because of rounding.
Source: Federal Reserve Board, flow-of-funds data.

TABLE II

Percentage Distribution of Assets of Private Financial Institutions, 1900, 1929, 1945, and 1958[a]

Institution	1900	1929	1945	1958
Commercial banks	52.9	41.8	56.5	39.5
Demand deposit business[b]	47.3	29.5	45.8	28.7
Savings and time deposit business[b]	5.6	12.3	10.7	10.8
Mutual savings banks	12.7	6.2	6.0	6.2
Savings and loan associations	2.6	4.7	3.1	9.1
Credit unions			0.1	0.7
Finance, mortgage, and loan companies	1.1	2.1	0.7	3.4
Life insurance companies	9.0	11.0	15.8	17.8
Other insurance companies	2.6	3.5	3.3	5.0
Private pension funds		0.3	0.8	4.1
Investment companies[c]		4.7	1.3	3.3
Personal trust departments[d]	15.9	18.9	10.2	9.3
Security brokers and dealers	3.2	6.7	2.1	1.6

[a] Details may not add to totals because of rounding.
[b] Allocated in proportion of deposit liabilities.
[c] Includes investment holding companies.
[d] Includes common trust funds.
Source: **Money and Credit: Their Influence On Jobs, Prices, and Growth,** Report of the Commission on Money and Credit (Englewood Cliffs: Prentice-Hall, 1961), p. 155.

operational behavior of financial institutions is likely to show considerable flexibility. Indeed, one of the most significant changes in financial structure is the extent to which financial institutions are capable of internal regeneration — taking on new functions and sloughing off old. With these qualifications in mind, let us turn to the explanation of the changing financial structure.

DETERMINANTS OF FINANCIAL STRUCTURE

Changes in the financial structure can be explained in terms of three factors: (1) the basic supply-demand dispositions underlying the various financial markets and the real forces (preference shifts, resource availabilities, technological changes) producing them, (2) the specific environmental conditions surrounding particular markets and financial institutions, and (3) the competitive responses of financial institutions themselves.

Supply-Demand Forces. Fundamental supply-demand factors determine the kinds of claims economic units are prepared to issue and the kinds they wish to hold. This is highly relevant to the position of the different financial institutions because it affects directly the growth rates in different financial markets and indirectly how these markets are shared. If

the public wants more housing, the supply of residential mortgages will rise relative to other financial assets; yields on mortgages will increase relative to other yields; institutions specializing in mortgages will be able to attract more funds because of their ability to pay more for their use; and thus they will tend to grow faster. Similarly, if the public becomes more thrifty, thrift institutions will expand at a more rapid rate and those markets in which they employ most of their funds will also grow faster.

Thus the growth and diffusion of real income has led, on the one hand, to the large increase in thrift, thereby benefiting savings institutions, and on the other hand and more recently, to the rise of the small investor via mutual fund participation. The increasing concern for security has sustained the position of insurance companies, and aided by other factors, has contributed to the rapid expansion of pension funds. The greater importance of consumer "investment" in housing and durables combined with changing public attitudes toward personal indebtedness has led to the growth of consumer credit institutions. Private placement, increasing reliance on internal sources of funds, leaseback arrangements, and trade credit extensions have changed the pattern of corporate.finance. The expanded role of the federal government in deposit insurance, mortgage guarantees, monetary control, and the maintenance of full employment has greatly influenced the behavior of economic units in their financial asset and liability choices. All of these changes and more have left a heavy imprint on the structure of our financial institutions. The long-run effect of these broad economic forces should be emphasized; at the same time, their secular nature permits institutional flexibility and adaptiveness to offset adverse trends. To what extent, however, the different financial institutions will possess these needed qualities depends to a considerable degree on precisely those organizational, asset-liability, and regulatory changes which are now to be discussed.

Institutional Differences. There is a clear line of influence leading from specific institutional traits to the reactive capabilities of the various types of financial institutions. This section will focus on three distinct but related kinds of institutional differences: organizational, asset-liability, and regulatory.

ORGANIZATIONAL STRUCTURE

(1) The legal form of enterprise will vary both within any single type of financial institution and between different types. The distinction between the corporate and mutual form is perhaps the most obvious and, because of the taxation controversy, has been commented upon most extensively. Mutual savings institutions were allowed to accumulate out of current earnings a reserve fund of up to 12 per cent of their deposits without such earnings being liable for income tax. Because mutual savings institutions have experienced rapid growth in their liabilities (deposits) relative to earnings, their tax liability has been exceedingly small. As a result, commercial banks, which are treated differently in this respect, assert that they are at a competitive disadvantage because of the more favorable tax treatment of mutual institutions.[1] If mutual institutions were taxed as heavily as commercial banks, it is argued, they could not afford to pay higher rates on savings, and thus they would grow appreciably slower and commercial banks appreciably faster. Like-

wise the impact of tax considerations on portfolio choice, by inducing institutions having large tax liabilities to look for tax-exempt securities and capital gains, also affect the growth possibilities and patterns of market participation of the several financial institutions.

Other distinctions of legal form also affect business decisions. The persistence of closely held corporations and family-and/or individual-dominated firms in many financial markets reflects the influence of personal service and personal contacts in highly localized markets. Recent gains by financial holding companies and captive finance companies are likewise reminders that new forms of legal organization can confer distinct advantages on their users, and thus can be vehicles for increasing one's market share.

(2) Spatial and locational differences are important in determining the ability of financial institutions to react flexibly.[2] Some intermediaries are organized along nationwide lines with numerous offices; others are local one-office institutions limited to and serving a single market; still others may be limited in their physical location but nevertheless function in a geographically dispersed market. Some draw funds locally and lend nationally; others draw funds nationally and lend locally. The changing character of local markets and the restrictions on the mobility of some financial institutions tend to work to the disadvantage of those financial institutions which are more dependent on local conditions.

Differing rates of regional growth and the resultant patterns of regional savings surpluses

---

[1] Briefly, the justification for differential tax treatment lies in the theory that the reserve fund accumulated by mutual institutions provides a cushion, analogous to the role played by capital and surplus in a corporate organization, to protect the depositors against asset depreciation. In practice the distinction has evolved from the desire to aid mutual institutions because of their origins as self-help and cooperative undertakings. The differential treatment has been a serious bone of contention and perhaps the best safeguards might be in a prepay insurance premium scheme which takes care of losses after they occur instead of attempting to protect against possible loss by building up a fund before the event. Recent legislation, however, has produced a compromise formula which will increase somewhat the tax liabilities of mutual thrift institutions.

[2] As is true of many other organizational differences, in part they reflect the impact of regulatory control. Differences in regulatory treatment, however, are sufficiently important and distinctive to merit separate discussion in a later section.

and deficits magnify these basic spatial differences. Financial institutions in areas of surplus depend for their expansion on their ability to overcome the immobility of capital; thus mutual savings banks in eastern states have welcomed the development of nationally acceptable mortgage instruments. Financial institutions in deficit areas are handicapped by persistent shortages of funds, and their growth depends on successfully finding external sources of funds. Accordingly, savings and loan associations in California advertise nationally and employ brokers to turn up funds.

(3) Closely allied to locational differences are entry conditions. Here, too, regulation is all-important. For instance, a restrictive chartering policy coupled with an easier branching policy can lead to preemptive branching, thereby making entry much more difficult for outsiders as compared with expansion by existing firms. Another important distinction may be found in the ability of financial institutions which depend on salesmen to enter new markets by expanding their selling operations easily and quickly, as, for example, mutual funds and insurance companies have done. In this connection, the low incremental cost of loading additional kinds of financial services on to an existing sales force creates considerable pressure for also expanding into related fields. Finally, as a result of high short-term interest rates and vigorous activity by "knowledge intermediaries," material changes have occurred in the market for large, short-term balances. Wherever non-holding intermediaries are most active, they will be a force widening markets and pushing forward the entry of outsiders, since their earnings are very sensitive to the volume of operations.[3]

[3] The expansion of brokerage activity always confronts asset-holding intermediaries with a difficult choice; in many cases they can also engage in brokerage, but only at the expense of infringing on their more normal activities. Thus if they react, they may jeopardize their usual role; if they remain passive, they find their market share being nibbled away. Another layer of complexity is added when it is realized that many broker-type activities perforce have large inventory requirements (either because the brokers are traders too or because of industry practice) and therefore have large demands for short-term finance. Thus it is not unusual to find a situation where, say, money brokers are competing with commercial banks, and at the same time are dependent on banks for carrying their inventories. In

(4) There are significant relative and absolute size differences. Absolute size matters because, on the one hand, substantial economies of scale are attainable for financial institutions, and on the other hand, participation in many financial submarkets is a function of size alone. For the latter reason, relative size within a single kind of financial institution is also a determinant of submarket participation, and contributes thereby to the establishment of a more finely drawn division of labor. The combination of size differences and economies of scale is very conducive to mergers, as is quite apparent, for instance, in commercial banking. Size disparities raise some especially acute problems in regulated industries because of the difficulties of framing rules of conduct for a non-homogeneous population. Likewise, great size differences, as in commercial banking, make it very difficult for industry-wide organizations to speak with one voice; the internal conflicts spill over into public disagreement on issues affecting the industry.[4] Again this is much more significant for a regulated industry because of its great dependence upon the actions of legislative and public bodies.

(5) Still another important difference has to do with whether financial institutions are engaged primarily in providing financial services or in pure intermediation. The public's demand for financial assets is of a dual nature. In some cases, for example, checking accounts, insurance-security protection, and, partly, thrift, a service is purchased and considerations of yield are either absent or distinctly secondary. In pure intermediation, yield dominates all else. Financial assets in which yield dominates are likely to be more sensitive reflectors of market pressures, whereas financial assets acquired through service transactions will be partly insulated from market forces and will reflect, to a greater extent, slowly changing public attitudes toward the particular service provided. There is a mechanism operating, it seems, as follows: pure intermediaries tend to specialize

such causes, brokers appreciate the diversity in commercial banking.

[4] I submit that savings and loan associations lobby much more effectively than commercial banks precisely because less glaring size disparities lead to a much greater degree of internal unity.

in areas of most rapid growth (mortgages, consumer credit) and obtain their funds by offering a yield inducement to potential suppliers. The rising demand for the commodity to be financed causes a widening spread between rates paid and yields that can be obtained and thereby provides pure intermediaries with both the means and the incentive to compete successfully for funds by raising the price they are willing to pay. They pass on, as it were, the public's increased desire for particular commodities in the form of increased demand and higher rates for money to accommodate this primary market shift. Service-oriented intermediaries, on the other hand, possess more steady and assured sources of funds, obtained by providing their primary service. They seek to place this reliable stream wherever yields appear most attractive, subject of course to statutory restraints and (slowly changing) customary portfolio practices. Thus some financial institutions have money to invest, and within given operating constraints they search for the most profitable outlets. Others have found or specialize in growing and favorable markets and seek funds to employ therein by offering yield inducements based on the profitability of the ultimate outlet.

This distinction has an important implication for the growth rates of the two types of intermediaries. In times of excess demand for money, the advantage lies with those who stimulate and induce rather than those who passively accept, unless, as with pension funds, the passive type of intermediary has struck a new and rich vein of consumer demand. In times when demand slacks off, the passive intermediaries, one expects, gain at the expense of the active ones. The explanation for this lies in the preference structure of the public with respect to financial assets. The passive intermediaries cater to some fairly basic demands of the public for security, insurance, checking services, and the like. The flow of money to these intermediaries, therefore, is not likely to be as income-sensitive as is the flow to specialist and risk-bearing intermediaries. Nor, likewise, is there much scope for yield blandishments as a means of increasing the flow of the public's savings into their hands. As a consequence, when yields rise, the more

volatile and spread-sensitive intermediaries are activated and start positively bidding for funds. The rise in rates deflects funds to them, and other financial institutions must await the day when the return they offer will once again appear attractive.

(6) Another difference to be found among financial institutions lies in the character of the other side of their market. Some financial intermediaries predominantly serve consumers; others deal mostly with nonfinancial enterprises; and some deal in large part with other financial intermediaries. Some financial institutions of course deal with all three, either obtaining money from households and supplying it to business and government, or obtaining funds from, and providing funds for, whomever they can. Transactions in consumer markets are likely to be smaller in size, more diffuse, and less organized; transactions with business and government are of larger magnitudes, and on the whole the bargaining parties are more evenly matched. One important development is the captive consumer market — the tendency to deal with ultimate consumers with respect to the financing of durables and housing through the selling agent of the particular commodity. This will affect relative growth by enabling some financial institutions to have access to rapidly growing consumer credit markets which would otherwise be excluded from such markets because of lack of direct contact with consumers.

This catalogue of organizational differences should not be considered exhaustive; for some purposes a much finer breakdown is necessary. For instance, variations exist in willingness to bear risk, engage in extensive selling effort, and innovate. Enough has been said, however, to make the general point that organizational dissimilarities do have a strong influence in determining the reaction of the various financial institutions to changing economic conditions.

ASSET-LIABILITY DIFFERENCES

The financial structure of the institutions themselves is of obvious importance, defining as it does the nature of intermediary activity. Intermediaries exhibit great differences in their sources of funds. Some have predominantly quick liabilities; others can predict with actuarial certainty the long-range translation of their liabilities into actual claims. Some rely on highly predictable and regular sources; others attract funds in extremely irregular movements, and their efforts to smooth the flow are conspicuously unsuccessful. Intermediaries differ greatly in ability to control the inflow of funds by their own actions; some can be very adept at matching flow to opportunity for use; others are more prone to feast or famine, and not always at appropriate times. Some rely predominantly on the general public as a source; others have specialized and fewer sources; still others depend on other financial intermediaries to a significant extent. Some, as we have seen, obtain their funds on a strictly yield basis; others receive funds in connection with the provision of financial services.

Likewise, there is great variation in the asset holdings of financial institutions — owing in no small measure to the need for matching assets with their pattern of liabilities. Some intermediaries must prize liquidity very highly; for others, this is not an important consideration. Portfolios differ widely in maturity structure and in riskiness. Some intermediaries confine their holdings to a single major type; others hold a wide variety of financial assets. Readiness to shift from one kind of asset to another varies greatly among intermediaries. There are correspondingly great differences in unit size of transactions. Thus, on both sides of the balance sheet, financial institutions will be subject to differential constraints arising out of dissimilarities in the structure of their assets and liabilities.

REGULATORY TREATMENT

The third, and final, factor affecting the responses of financial institutions is differences in degree and kind of regulation and in the ability to influence such regulation. As indicated in the discussion of organizational structure, regulation is significant and pervasive in establishing what financial institutions will and will not do. Now, however, the focus is on the general problems associated with regulation rather than on its specific incidence. In part, the impact of regulation is due to its inability to keep pace with a rapidly changing economy. Moreover, the regulation of financial institutions has been

exceedingly detailed. No doubt the fiduciary responsibilities of financial institutions have motivated such extreme care, but nevertheless it has made for rigidity and thereby has greatly circumscribed intermediary freedom of action. Economic change erodes specific regulation at a much faster rate than regulation framed along more general lines and allowing more supervisory discretion. The diversity of regulatory authority is another factor which produces large variations in the scope and freedom of intermediary action. The same type of financial institutions can be, and different kinds of financial institutions are, subject to different regulatory authorities. Some intermediaries may be regulated strictly; others may be subject to merely nominal and perfunctory regulation, or to none at all. Enforcement can be sporadic or continuous. The aims of regulation vary from maintaining fiduciary integrity to achieving credit control objectives. Thus differences are found in regulatory treatment as well as in the statutory framework of regulation.

Equally important is the ability to influence regulation and regulators, for not only existing regulation and its interpretation are relevant, but also the possibilities for changing regulations and for getting sympathetic treatment from regulatory authority. The preceding discussion has suggested that the erosion of regulation by economic change makes revision imperative. In this connection, the power structure within the financial community plays a large and significant role. The size and quality of legal and lobbying staffs, the importance and geographical representation of the particular intermediary, and its relative size will determine what kind of hearing legislators and regulators will give to requests from the several financial institutions. I do not mean to imply that the large and the powerful will always have their way; even less do I wish to suggest that any hint of wrongdoing or improper influence is involved. I simply mean that, all things considered, any regulated industry operating within some basic statutory framework will continually run up against complex problems arising out of this special status; and the more resources available for pleading its case before regulatory and legislative bodies, the better. For similar reasons, a class of financial institution with a high degree of internal cohesion among its constituent firms will be better placed to achieve legislative or regulatory reform than one which has great internal divisions.

Reactive Capabilities. Differences in organizational and financial structure and in regulatory treatment thus determine the nature and scope of market participation, and when set in the context of rapid and uneven economic change, play a large role in shaping the responses of the several financial institutions. Not all financial institutions are equally well placed in their ability to adapt and alter their mode of operation consequent to unfavorable change, and naturally, any particular economic change is unlikely to have an equal and uniform impact on all financial institutions. Where economic change has an adverse effect, an attempt is of course made to eliminate those factors responsible for the competitive disability. Such a response is made more difficult for some than for others, however, because rigidities and immobilities of organizational and financial structure and lags in regulatory change are also not distributed uniformly.

In this way nonuniformities, both in the incidence of economic change on financial institutions and in their ability to respond, affect relative positions; variation in ability to react, within broad limits laid down by the direction of economic change, thus determines the relative situations of the different financial institutions. True, all firms find it difficult to make structural adjustments and are subject to economic change; in these respects, financial institutions are not different. Luck is always pleasant, change hard, and resiliency, flexibility, and adaptability are the guarantors of competitive success. Regulatory restraint, however, places financial institutions in a different category; to the extent that regulation impairs the maneuverability of intermediaries in a nonuniform way, economic change provides opportunities for some but harms others. For this reason, regulation must be conscious of the equity issues it raises.

SPECIFIC EXAMPLES

Having asserted that organizational, asset-liability, and regulatory differences affect the ability of financial institutions to react to economic change, perhaps it may prove fruitful to trace some of the ways in which our financial structure has evolved and the specific reasons which account for this pattern of development. Institutions which have experienced enormous growth in the postwar period include such different types as mortgage companies, pension funds, mutual funds, and credit unions. The explanations for the rise of these institutions are correspondingly diverse.

Mortgage companies have mushroomed as a joint result of the housing boom and the impact of federal intervention upon the nature of the mortgage instrument. Federal underwriting and standardization have produced a security which can attract funds from afar, and the crucial role of originating and servicing mortgages has been the necessary complement to increasing the mobility of capital of institutional lenders. Mortgage companies were ideally suited to perform these functions. Other possible developments were for traditional, local mortgage lenders to expand their originating and servicing departments and for large institutional lenders to integrate forward instead of relying on local contacts. Although some progress was made in each of these directions, it was not on the scale that attended the growth of mortgage companies. There are several reasons for this: mortgage holders face potential conflict-of-interest problems if they also act, in effect, as brokers of mortgages; local mortgage holders may be reluctant to send mortgages outside the locality because of the consequences for positions of local market power if they contribute to the extension of the market; commercial bank holders of mortgages are also the chief sources of finance of mortgage companies themselves, and therefore may feel constrained not to compete with their customers or may believe that the arrangements reflect an agreeable division of labor; local mortgage holders traditionally prefer low-risk conventional mortgages, whereas servicing and origination are largely in government-underwritten mortgages; finally, custom plays a role —local mortgage holders conceive of their job as getting and holding mortgages, not servicing them. Forward integration, on the other hand, has been deterred largely by the legal complexities of doing business in the different states and the complex and nonuniform legal environment surrounding the mortgage contract. In addition, relationships with mortgage companies have simplified the problem of portfolio shifts and irregular savings flows with respect to regular sustained mortgage lending. In essence, the problem of reconciling the desire for mortgages with the flow of mortgage money has been shifted, for a price, onto the backs of the specialized institution.

The evolution of the mortgage company, however, is a continuing process, and it is still too early to see where it will end. As Goldsmith has written:

Will mortgage companies remain essentially an ancillary institution, an originating and service organization for institutional investors in government-insured and -guaranteed home mortgages, using short-term bank credit to carry a temporary inventory of mortgages already spoken for by institutional clients? Or will they, by adding operations characteristic of some companies prior to the days of mortgage insurance, broaden into a more diversified and independent type of institution — a sort of general mortgage dealer and underwriter — handling mortgages of all types, placing them with individual as well as institutional investors, and carrying a general inventory of uncommitted mortgages for sale? Are they likely, as well, by expansion or amalgamation, to increase their general real estate operations blurring further the distinction between mortgage companies and real estate investment, brokerage, and development companies? Finally, will they remain within their generally local spheres of operation, or will many of them develop, as a few have, into organizations working to a considerable extent through branch offices on a regional or even a nationwide scale?[5]

The growth of the other financial institutions mentioned can also be explained by specific circumstances surrounding each. Pension fund growth reflects, basically, the desire for security among industrial workers and the ability to achieve this end through collective bargaining. Mutual fund growth is based on the spread of income and wealth, the consequent diversification of relatively small savers into more risky fields, and vigorous selling activities. In both cases growth was largely a re-

sponse to and implementation of strong underlying real trends which demanded a novel kind of financial institution rather than outright extension or adaptation of existing ones. But though new financial institutions took root and grew, at the same time the management of pension funds and the creation of mutual funds, and the provision of investment advisory services to both, became grounds on which existing kinds of financial institutions actively competed. The growth of credit unions reflects a somewhat different emphasis. Although consumer credit too has undergone a rapid increase, the improvement of the position of credit unions is due, on the one hand, to the ability to take advantage of and undercut the relatively high consumer credit rates prevailing, and on the other hand, to the natural associational ties on which the movement was founded. Competitive opportunities plus unique natural advantages were important factors in the more rapid expansion of credit unions. In all four cases, the growth of the financial institution reflected the strong real trends at work. On the whole, regulation was minimal and exercised little constraint.

Another institution which has shown a rapid advance in the postwar period has been the savings and loan association. In this case, growth has been influenced to a greater extent by very favorable regulatory action. Savings and loan associations have successfully striven, in recent years, for regulatory action on participation mortgages, permission to engage in site-development finance, controls over premiums and give-aways, restriction of funds obtained through brokers, and 90 per cent loan-to-value ratios for mortgages. Regulatory authorities can thus be sensitive to, as well as obstacles in the way of, the need for change. Favorable regulatory treatment is, however, still only part of the story. The housing boom and the pull of favorable interest rate differentials supply the rest. The former emphasizes our dependence on real trends; the latter reflects aggressive competition and the imposition of interest-rate ceilings on their chief competitors.

The evolution of commercial banking over a generation of bankers is another piece of substantial evidence showing adaptability and flexibility on the part of financial intermediaries.

[5] Raymond W. Goldsmith, in the Foreword of Saul B. Klaman, *The Postwar Rise of Mortgage Companies*, Occasional Paper No. 60 (New York: National Bureau of Economic Research, 1959), p. vii.

The growth of and emphasis on consumer banking, both in searching for deposits and in consumer loan activity, the rise of interim real estate financing, the refinement of time-deposit certificates, the spread of term-lending, and the expansion of bank services in general add up to an extraordinary amount of change compressed within a short period of time. Here, too, regulatory authority has been both permissive and restrictive. For instance, under the press of wartime circumstance and postwar expansion, supervisory authorities have allowed risk asset-capital ratios to rise. On the other hand, the requirements of monetary control have undoubtedly damped the growth of demand deposits, and ceilings on savings deposit rates have weakened the competitive position of banks in relation to other thrift institutions. The share of financial assets held by banks would have fallen much further if banks had not adjusted their activities to such a great extent.

Finally, consideration of various proposals for changes in the legal and regulatory framework of financial institutions provides some insights into the forces working to produce structural variation. Insurance company pressure for the variable annuity, changes in the legal and tax status of real estate syndicates, central mortgage banking facilities, the packaging of mortgages for the pension fund market, the federal chartering of mutual savings banks, and the question of the tax-exempt status for state and local securities have been and are live issues and portents of change to come. Such healthy ferment is hardly a sign of ossification; yet it can also be seen to what extent change depends upon the ability to persuade regulatory authority of its desirability. As indicated earlier, the importance of this factor makes the evolution of financial structure distinctive.

CONCLUSIONS

In its broad dimensions the changing structure of financial institutions reveals a familiar picture. Within the general constraints of institutional and regulatory differences, the force of economic change shapes the pattern of development. The organizational, asset-liability,

and regulatory differences among financial institutions provide the basis for their varied responses. Thus the impact of exogenous economic change is reflected mainly in intra-financial institution rivalry and shifts in relative importance. Our financial institutions tend to have a small impact on economic growth itself precisely because they can be so flexible and accommodating in the aggregate. In the process, however, the shape of this aggregate undergoes recognizable transformation as the direction of real change and institutional adaptability jointly determine its structural evolution. This result is not as startling as might appear at first glance. After all, it is supremely important to emphasize, as Warren L. Smith has done, that "the basic function of financial institutions is the mobilization of the financial resources of the economy in support of economic activity." But the implications of this process for the changing shape of our financial institutions have not been adequately realized. The extent to which our financial structure changes form is a measure of both the capabilities and resourcefulness of our financial institutions when faced with challenges to institutional survival and growth, and their limited power to affect significantly the real growth path of our economy.

Two important corollaries derive from this argument. The first is that to the extent that our financial control measures are predicated on a restricted and limited view of the proper area for their exercise, that part of our financial machinery not covered will be sure to work against the purposes of control. Furthermore, the very changes in the structure of our financial institutions will undermine our ability to control because these changes are themselves an offset to our control measures. The second corollary is an issue of equity: differences in regulatory treatment, as we have seen, affect the competitive position of financial institutions. Thus it is necessary to review our regulatory procedures with a view to deciding between the conflicting considerations of equity and effective control. Both equity and efficiency are likely to be served by more comprehensive (but less detailed) regulation applied more consistently to all financial institutions.

19

IS THE PORTFOLIO CONTROL OF FINANCIAL INSTITUTIONS JUSTIFIED?*

Thomas Mayer†

We have stressed from time to time that financial institutions are business firms, just like automobile manufacturers and supermarkets. However, they are subject to far more regulatory controls than most business firms: controls over their portfolio decisions, over the prices they can charge, over the prices they can pay — over almost every aspect of their business.

The present selection inquires into the justification for one area of these controls, namely limitations on their uses of funds. Would we be better off if most of the restrictions on what financial institutions can do with their money were removed, and their decisions were left more to the free play of market forces?

While most firms are allowed to select their assets freely, financial intermediaries are severely limited in their asset choices. I shall attempt here to see whether one can justify this disparate treatment and whether I can reconcile my intuitive feelings in favor of portfolio control with my libertarian conscience. Let us therefore see whether a justification for asset control can be provided by the reasons usually given for interfering with the free play of market forces. The most important of these are (1) absence of sufficient competition,[1] (2) consumer ignorance of the nature of the product, (3) economic instability, inflation, and underemployment, (4) external economies and diseconomies, and (5) "wrong" choices by the consumer.[2]

I.

Let us now see to what extent, if any, these five factors provide a justification for limiting the asset choices of financial intermediaries. The first — lack of competition — is not a significant reason for interfering with these choices, since asset regulation has generally not dealt with this problem.[3]

A much more important reason for controlling the portfolios of financial intermediaries is the existence of consumer ignorance. The rea-

* From *Journal of Finance*, Vol. XVII, No. 2 (May, 1962). Reprinted by the courtesy of the publisher (the American Finance Association) and the author.

† University of California, Davis.

[1] This category includes the problems created by increasing returns to scale.

[2] This differs from the previously mentioned consumer ignorance. Consumer ignorance of the nature of the product may be consistent with the consumer wanting the "right product," though he does not know how to purchase it. By choosing the "wrong" product, I mean that the consumer may know the quality of the product but that he prefers one which, by some imposed value judgment, is considered wrong. For exam-

ple, in the drug industry there is a problem of consumer ignorance as here defined — the consumer wants what most people would consider the "right" product, an effective medicine, but does not know how to choose it. On the other hand, if we make the value judgment that being learned is better than being drunk, a drunkard makes the "wrong" choice — he certainly knows that drinking leads to drunkenness and reading to being learned, but, given his "wrong" value judgments, he decides to drink rather than read.

[3] The monopoly problem has been of significance for asset regulation in only one respect, and this is in the regulation of life insurance companies. It has been argued that to allow life insurance companies more leeway in buying common stock may result in their holding a controlling share of assets in some industries. Even proponents of more stock purchases by life insurance companies have expressed concern about this problem and have suggested limitations on stock purchases within any one industry.

son for this is that, to a considerable extent, the very existence of financial intermediaries results from consumer ignorance, for one of the reasons that households do not buy primary securities is that they cannot evaluate the borrower's credit standing, or could do so only at excessive cost.[4] Not only commercial banks but other financial intermediaries, too, exist because they can substitute their known credit standing for the ultimate borrowers' unknown one.

One of the important products of financial intermediaries is, therefore, safety. Now safety is a product which is very difficult for the consumer to evaluate. In this respect, deposits in financial institutions differ from other products, where the problem of consumer ignorance is relatively minor and a requirement of honesty in advertising suffices, since the consumer is able to evaluate the product while using it. But in the case of deposits in financial institutions, experimentation is too costly, for, by the time the consumer notices that his assets are no longer safe, it is generally too late. Thus government enforcement of safety — i.e., "product quality" — might lead to a better allocation of resources than unregulated competition would. Basically the reason for this is that government control of product quality, while limiting consumer choice in one way by banishing the low-quality product, at the same time creates another product, namely, a certified one. Hence asset control does not necessarily limit the choice of consumers.

Another reason that may justify exercising some control over financial intermediaries is the attempt to attain price stability and full employment. Clearly, the frequent bank failures, which were so common a part of American recessions until 1933, made these recessions worse than they otherwise would have been. Maintaining the safety of financial institutions is therefore an important, perhaps the most important, contribution that the government can make to economic stability. In addition, it has been argued that non-bank financial in-termediaries complicate the task of monetary management. If non-bank financial intermediaries *really* do offset in good part the effects of a tight-money policy, this *may* provide a justification for controlling their growth rate, but it does not provide a case for controlling the particular assets they buy and hence is not relevant, since asset control is not a good way of controlling their growth.

Apart from the stabilization problem, another important reason for controlling the assets of financial institutions is the existence of external economies. This consideration seems to lie at the back of one of the most important types of regulations, namely, those which try to influence asset selection in the direction of "socially desirable" investment. The most important of these are regulations favoring investment in mortgages. It appears to be public policy in the United States to stimulate home-ownership, presumably because it is felt that property ownership leads to "better citizenship" and to a better environment for the future generation.

There is a strong feeling in some parts of the country that local capital should be kept "at home," i.e., that there are external economies in increasing the area's capital stock. This feeling is responsible, at least in part, for the regulation limiting mortgages of federal savings and loan associations to a radius of 50 miles from the head office and for the limitation on the purchase of out-of-state mortgages by savings banks.

Another argument for regulation which can be fitted into the "external economies" rubric is the argument that certain non-bank financial institutions — savings banks, for example — should be encouraged to expand at the expense of commercial banks, for a specialized thrift institution, it is claimed, tends to promote saving to a greater extent than does a "department-store" institution like a commercial bank. This argument implies that the gains to the economy resulting from saving exceed the interest paid to the depositor, which is a frequently accepted proposition.[5]

---

[4] It is possible, of course, that, in the absence of government regulation, consumer ignorance would have been reduced by the market mechanism. Thus one can well imagine a private organization like Consumers Union evaluating the soundness of financial institutions.

[5] For a good recent discussion of this problem see A. K. Sen, "On Optimizing the Rate of Saving," *Economic Journal*, September, 1961, pp. 479–96.

Finally, for better or for worse, we sometimes interfere with the market mechanism to influence the consumer's choice for his "own good" — witness our prohibition of narcotics, for example. Hence two of the factors just mentioned — the pressure toward mortgage investment and the desire to increase saving — need not be wholly based on the external economies argument. Thus it may be that one of the reasons we subsidize homeownership is because we feel that the consumer does not "really appreciate" the full importance of good housing, and, similarly, some people may feel that, because of myopia, consumers tend to save less than they "should." Since the value judgments underlying public policy are not made explicit, it is difficult to see to what extent supporters of increased housing and increased saving are relying on the "guiding the consumer" argument rather than the "external economies" argument. But I will make the rather arbitrary assumption, part value judgment, part positive judgment, that this argument does not furnish a valid ground for asset control. This is not because I think that consumers have adequate knowledge but rather because I feel that the decisions of government officials are not based on adequate knowledge either.

To summarize, there are several possible reasons that can be given for interfering with the free market and regulating the assets held by financial intermediaries, when at the same time we leave other business relatively unregulated. First, there is the existence of consumer ignorance. This can be used to justify the imposition of certain standards of safety. Second, the economic stability goal also warrants measures to insure the safety of financial institutions. Third, external economies may justify certain regulations. Finally, if one assumes, as I shall not do here, that consumers should be protected from their own errors, then one can again accept all sorts of regulations, including portfolio control over financial intermediaries.

Thus asset control may lead to a more efficient resource allocation than would a completely free market. But it does not follow that portfolio control is necessarily desirable, for there may be some more efficient ways of achieving the same results. Let us therefore compare the efficiency of portfolio control with that of other devices.

II.

As just pointed out, both consumer ignorance and the stabilization problem warrant increasing the safety of financial intermediaries. But it may well be that financial intermediaries are at present *too* safe. Safety, after all, is not a free good but has the opportunity cost of lower earnings for the financial institution. In an ideal financial system, entrepreneurs would not be prevented from assuming risky ventures, since any risk can be financed at *some* risk premium. Similarly, households could allocate their assets among instruments of different risk, so that the household's marginal rate of substitution between risk and yield would equal the entrepreneur's marginal rate of transformation between risk and yield.

Although we hear many discussions of the difficulty of financing risky ventures (e.g., the lack of equity capital), allowing households a choice among instruments with different degrees of risk is also important, for households may have risk preferences or aversions. Indeed, Friedman has argued that it is possible that differences in incomes among households can be explained in part by differences in attitude toward risk.[6] An important function of the financial system consists, therefore, in providing households with assets having different risk coefficients. One way in which a financial system can allow households to reach their preferred risk position is to provide a large number of instruments with different degrees of risk, thus allowing each household to hold assets having the degree of risk it wants. This does not require a large number of risk-differentiated assets but could be accomplished through provision of as few as two assets with widely different risk coefficients. Households could then hold mixed portfolios of these two assets. One may therefore question our present policy of requiring all financial intermediaries to be extremely safe.

It may still be argued that differences in the

[6] M. Friedman, "Choice, Chance, and the Personal Distribution of Income," *Journal of Political Economy*, August, 1953, pp. 277–90.

degree of risk among financial intermediaries are undesirable because households are not sufficiently knowledgeable to evaluate correctly risk differentials. However, this argument is open to the objection that a policy of preventing risk differences among financial intermediaries drives into the stock market a number of households who, in terms of this argument, should not be there. Hence, even aside from the ethical question whether people should be prevented from taking risks, it is by no means clear that the damage done by consumer ignorance is reduced by allowing a "risk gap." Thus the case for imposing rigid risk restrictions on all, or most, financial intermediaries is much weaker than the case for imposing them on only one or a few intermediaries.

Moreover, our current rigid control over asset holdings is not the only possible way of providing for safety. After all, in the case of insured institutions, portfolio control protects in nearly all cases not the depositor but rather the insuring institutions. But these can be protected by rules other than our present rule of prohibiting the purchase of risky assets. We could allow financial institutions to purchase risky assets at the cost of paying a higher insurance premium; in other words, by adopting the methods of life insurance companies who insure low-grade risks at a higher premium than high-grade risks. If the insurance premiums are set accurately, this system would tend toward an optimal amount of risk taking.

The second reason for controlling the portfolios of financial institutions is the economic stabilization effect; as pointed out, this is a powerful argument for making these institutions safe. Moreover, unlike the consumer-ignorance argument, it does not have to be qualified by the proviso that some intermediaries should be allowed to run considerable risks.

The third justification of asset control is the existence of external economies. But here, too, there may be better ways of achieving the same result. For example, if there really are external economies to homeownership, direct subsidies, particularly if directed to the marginal homeowners, would be more efficient than regulations inducing financial intermediaries to purchase mortgages. To be sure, some people would lose by a shift to such a system, but they could be compensated. Similarly, the desire to "keep capital at home" mentioned earlier provides only a dubious justification for asset control, for it can easily be shown that, given the other conditions for optimal resource allocation, allowing financial institutions freedom in making "foreign investments," together with a system of compensatory payments to those who would be hurt by this, would increase economic welfare. It could, of course, be argued that, since other conditions necessary for welfare maximization are not met, regulations limiting capital mobility are not necessarily bad.[7] For example, if there is more unemployment in one state than in another, then regulations limiting capital exports from the former state may be desirable.[8] But, in actuality, there is little reason to assume that regulations are drawn up with such wisdom that they keep capital in those states which have above-average unemployment.

The final example of the external economies argument mentioned earlier is the stimulation of saving by having specialized thrift institutions. But again, if we really want to encourage the growth of specialized thrift institutions at the expense of commercial banks, we can do this better by subsidies and special taxes than by imposing restraints on the types of assets that commercial banks may hold.

In summary, then, consumer ignorance provides some justification for controlling the portfolios of financial intermediaries but does so with two important limitations. First, not all financial intermediaries should be subjected to such control, and, second, safety can be obtained by a device less restrictive than present controls, namely, the use of a variable insurance premium. The economic stabilization goal furnishes a second reason for insuring the safety of financial institutions, and, unlike con-

[7] For a discussion of this problem in general see K. Lancaster and R. G. Lipsey, "The General Theory of Second Best," *Review of Economic Studies*, XXIV, 11–32.

[8] See W. C. Ballaine, "New England Mutual Savings Bank Laws as Interstate Barriers to the Flow of Capital," *American Economic Review*, March, 1945, p. 158.

sumer ignorance, it does not provide a presumption for the exemption of some types of institutions. However, as before, a variable insurance premium plan could eliminate some of the rigidity of current controls. The existence of external economies and diseconomies does little to justify asset control, because a more efficient method of handling these external effects is

available. The final reason for asset controls — the consumer's inability to choose what is "best" for him — was discarded rather arbitrarily at the outset. Thus I can reconcile my desire for portfolio control and my libertarian conscience only by advocating safety regulations which are less stringent than current regulations.

20

COMPETITION, CONFUSION, AND COMMERCIAL BANKING*

Almarin Phillips†

How important is competition in financial markets? What are its implications for the allocation of resources? If it is important, is there sufficient competition now, or do we need more? And if we need more, how should we go about getting it?

The recent interest in competition in the commercial banking industry is a strange turn of events. Not long ago it was customary to refer to banking as one of the "regulated" industries — an industry in which competition had to be restricted by public authority to preserve the liquidity of the payments mechanism and to provide safety for depositors. Competitive (or antitrust) policy, it was thought, had very limited applicability to banking because of its regulated character.[1]

Rather suddenly, competition in banking has emerged as an ostensibly relevant public policy consideration. What some have regarded as a "wave" of mergers and holding company formations is in part responsible.[2] Fears of monopoly and of a substantial lessening of competition have arisen with regard to an industry which hitherto few had regarded as competitive in the first place. Congress responded with the Bank Holding Company Act of 1956 and the Bank Merger Act of 1960. The Department of Justice has brought Sherman and Clayton Act charges, and the courts — *because* of the regu-

* From *Journal of Finance*, Vol. XIX, No. 1 (March, 1964). Reprinted by the courtesy of the publisher (the American Finance Association) and the author.

† University of Pennsylvania.

[1] See, for example, Adolf A. Berle, "Banking Under the Antitrust Laws," *Columbia Law Review*, vol. 49 (1949). As recently as 1959, Carl Kaysen and Donald F. Turner classed commercial banks among those industries for which conventional antitrust policy was inapplicable. See their *Antitrust Policy: An Economic and Legal Analysis* (Cambridge, Mass., 1959), pp. 42–43, 291. For a brief discussion of regulations, see *National Banks and Future*, Report of the Advisory Committee on Banking to the Comptroller of the Currency (Washington, 1962).

[2] The recent "wave" has been an increasing one. In the 1940's, the average annual number was 81. For the period 1950–59, the average number was 150. Since the passage of the Bank Merger Act of 1960, the rate has been about 160 per year. These rates, however, are far below those of the late 1920's. See Charlotte P. and David A. Alhadeff, "Recent Bank Mergers," *Quarterly Journal of Economics*, vol. 69 (November, 1955); *Annual Report of the Comptroller of the Currency* (Washington, 1960); *Annual Report of the Federal Deposit Insurance Corporation* (Washington, 1960, 1961, 1962).

lations rather than *irrespective* of them — have found that commercial banking is to be treated as any other industry under the basic antitrust laws.[3]

In this paper, I shall argue on the one hand that commercial banking markets are typically not competitive enough to assure the efficient social performance of the industry. Evidence will be offered to demonstrate certain inefficiencies of the present banking structure which suggest the need for more intensive competition.

On the other hand, it will be contended that the existing complex of public policies with respect to banking, given the character of the industry, makes it quite impossible to achieve through conventional antitrust policies a type of competition which would be conducive to significantly improved performance. Public regulation and private organizational and institutional market characteristics make the performance of the industry insensitive to differences in market structure. As a result, orthodox policies aimed at maintaining or increasing competition by controlling the banking structure — as, for example, by preventing mergers — verge on the metaphorical "tilting at windmills." The performance of the industry will not be much affected by such policies so long as the regulatory and institutional characteristics remain unchanged.

The performance of banking markets could be improved, however. To achieve this, the most important changes in public policy would involve a relaxation of regulations and supervision to encourage more freedom of decision-making for *individual* banks, and to permit market forces to reward efficiency and to penalize inefficiency. The prohibition of such private competitive restraints as are inimical to the efficient functioning of the industry is also in order.

Paradoxically, it appears that, while the prevention of mergers cannot do much to maintain or increase competition, the increase in market rivalry signaled by changes in market organization would *foster* mergers and other types of consolidations. One of the virtually certain results of policies aimed at improving performance would be a slow but significant reduction in the number of banks in the country. This reduction in number would reduce the amount of inefficiency in banking but, because of the oligopolistic and locally-monopolistic structure of banking markets, because of remaining regulations, and because of the private organization of the industry, active price competition cannot and likely should not be achieved.

THE EVIDENCE OF INADEQUATE COMPETITION

Competition is desirable because of its effects on market performance and the allocation of scare resources. Bankers, as is true of other businessmen, will not be persuaded by the academic scribbler who charges that competition does not prevail.[4] For to them — understandably — competition appears primarily as rivalry with other banks and financial institutions and in concern over profits, market shares, and growth. The relationship between competition and efficient resource allocation is not their concern.

Assessing the degree of competition in a specific industry is typically difficult. With respect to commercial banking, however, the evidence is unusually persuasive, attesting really to the effectiveness of public policy in preventing the types of competition which would produce bank failures and market instability. Thus, the principal evidence consists of: (1) the low failure rate and general stability in the structure of the industry; (2) the persistence of firms of less than the optimal scale; and (3) price performance which is inconsistent with the results of multilateral market competition.

STABILITY OF THE BANKING STRUCTURE

During the ten years 1953–1963, there were only 91 voluntary bank liquidations and suspensions in an industry composed initially of about 14,000 firms.[5] Some of the liquidations may

---

[3] *United States v. Philadelphia National Bank*, 374 U.S. 321 (1963). In addition several Sherman Act cases alleging conspiracy in restraint of trade have been brought.

[4] For example, see the discussion of competition in *The Commercial Banking Industry*, American Bankers Association (New York, 1962), Ch. 1.

[5] "Changes in Banking Structure, 1953–62" *Federal Reserve Bulletin* (September 1963).

not have reflected adverse operating results. During the same period, there were 1,669 bank disappearances through mergers and absorptions, a small portion of which may have been motivated by "failing firm" considerations, but most of which occurred for other reasons. Thus, the rate of forced withdrawal from the banking industry has been remarkably low compared with other industries characterized by a large number of geographically dispersed firms.[6] Banking has either been blessed with exceptionally able management which has prevented withdrawals due to shifts in market conditions, inefficiency and management errors or, more likely, has been afforded some shelter from dynamic market forces. Bank failure, in itself, is of course not a goal of effective competition, but the risk of failure and, often, a turnover of firms are concomitants of competition. The higher bank failure rates prior to recent decades — and prior to extensive regulation and supervision — illustrate this point.[7]

The low failure rate is especially interesting in view of the size distribution of banks. Of the 12,933 insured commercial banks in existence at the end of 1962, 7,370 of them had total deposits of less than $5,000,000.[8] At the other extreme, only 314 banks had deposits of more than $1,000,000,000; 64 had deposits of over $500,000,000. The size distribution is highly skewed.

The same sort of distribution exists in many local and regional markets. In Chicago, for example, there were 154 banks in 1960, with the largest three having 48.1 per cent of total deposits. Similar figures for New York are 51 banks and 49.0 per cent; Philadelphia, 21 banks and 63.7 per cent; San Francisco, 18 banks and 50.6 per cent.[9] In these cities — and in many smaller ones — small banks frequently operate side-by-side with larger ones without apparent tendencies for the larger to force the smaller from the market. Larger banks, even without economics of scale, must possess some potential competitive advantage because of their greater assets and advantageous cross-elasticity of demand relationships. It would be expected, in other words, that without private or public sanctions moderating and rationalizing price rivalry, or without product differentiation sufficient to accomplish the same thing, there would tend to be more failures, especially among the smaller firms.

SCALE ECONOMIES

In effectively competitive markets, firms of less or greater than optimum scale are forced to make scale changes or to fail — though not necessarily in a short period of calendar time. It has become a commonplace, but certainly not an empirically proven fact, that there are economies of scale in banking.[10] In view of the conceptual difficulties involved in defining bank output, in treating product-mix and in separating the effects of branch and holding company operations in measuring scale, it is unlikely that the precise extent of these economies will be unearthed for some time to come. Nonetheless various estimates suggest that the economies are substantial up to at least $5,000,000 in deposits, and then perhaps plateau over size ranges up to the very largest of banks.[11] If it is true that economies extend only to the $5,000,000 deposit size, there would remain some 57 per cent of all commercial banks of less than optimal scale. If the economies extend to larger sizes, the percentage is even higher.

Such global figures may be misleading. In the first place, as of the end of 1962, 7,705 banks outside of metropolitan areas operated in one-bank towns.[12] Many of the smaller-than-optimum banks are found in this group. In some

[6] The rate of failure — and of new entrants — of retail and wholesale firms are many times this rate. For all industrial and commercial firms the failure rate is about 60 per month per 10,000 concerns.

[7] Anticipating a later argument, the consequences of these failures raise questions as to whether competition can be tolerated in banking.

[8] *Annual Report of the Federal Deposit Insurance Corporation* (1962), p. 134.

[9] Data developed in the Banking Markets Unit, Board of Governors of the Federal Reserve System, based on the principal county (or counties) of the cities, not on the entire S.M.S.A.

[10] David A. Alhadeff, *Monopoly and Competition in Banking* (Berkeley, 1954); Lyle E. Gramley, *Scale Economies in Banking* (Kansas City, 1962). But see also Paul Horvitz, "Economies of Scale in Banking," an unpublished paper for the Committee on Money and Credit, which questions the existence of economies of scale.

[11] David A. Alhadeff, *op. cit.*

[12] "Changes in Banking Structure, 1953–62" *loc. cit.*

onebank towns, the breadth of the market may be so restricted that the optimum scale cannot be achieved. Second, since the economies (or diseconomies) of branching operation and of the scale of branches are unknown, it could be argued that many of these small banks are still the most efficient of the alternatives practically available, and that no lack of competition is indicated.

This counter argument is not entirely convincing. While the breadth of the market in many towns may preclude even a single bank of optimum scale, competition would allow no more than one such bank. Yet, at the end of 1962, 1,800 banks operated in two-bank towns and 362 banks operated in three-bank towns.[13] Many of these banks are smaller than the apparent optimum, and market forces which foster the growth of one of them at the expense of the others are rarely observed. In addition, the fairly rapid development of branch operations in the wake of legislative changes in states such as Virginia and New York, and the premiums paid for the acquisition of small banks, especially where *de novo* entry is barred, are evidence that, at least in some types of operations, branch banking is more efficient than is unit banking.

PRICE BEHAVIOR

For some industries, the behavior of prices is used as a prime indicator of the degree of competition. To be useful for this purpose, price data on individual transactions are typically necessary and very little of this sort of data is available for banks. The Federal Reserve's *Business Loan Surveys* of 1955–57 and its quarterly *Survey of Short-Term Business Loans* contain limited data on interest rates charged on individual commercial loans, but no full scale analysis of the competitive implications of these surveys has been released.[14] For rates on other types of loans, and for rates paid on time deposits, for checking account service charges, and other miscellaneous prices, all one has for individual banks is published announcements — from which there are fre-

quent deviations — and collected personal experience.

With these caveats, what can be said? First, it can be observed that individual banks charge different rates to different customers for what seem to be the same type and size of loan. These may be due in part to different risk factors and to other dimensions of the product being sold — the type of collateral, the timing of repayments, the amount of compensating balances required, etc. One gains the suspicion, however, that these factors would not account for the existing variance in rates,[15] and that the bank and individual customers are, in fact, in bilateral rather than openly competitive bargaining postures. The customer with the greater alternatives, including the alternative of not borrowing because of his excellent financial standing, is apt to get lower rates than the customer with fewer or no alternatives. To the extent that this is true, the bank can, within limits, operate as a discriminating monopolist.

The alternatives available to buyers would certainly be greater were they willing and able to "shop" among banks and other financial institutions for the best terms. If this occurred in substantial proportions, the variance in rates charged by individual banks for particular types of loans would tend to be small and there would tend to be only small differences in rates among banks in the same market. In other words, the monopoly power of sellers is inversely related to the ability of customers to "shop."

The data on interest rate variations within and among banks are indicative, yet not proof, of very little actual "shopping" by bank customers. To some extent it may be necessary for the bank-customer relationship to be a continuing one, but it also seems obvious that banks discourage their customers from seeking alternative sellers in ways which lower the effective cross-elasticity of demand among banks.[16]

---

[13] *Ibid.*
[14] Reference is made below to some unpublished studies.

[15] For example, rates charged on business loans of $1,000–$10,000 by a single bank at a given time ranged from 5 to 6.5 per cent according to the FRB quarterly *Survey of Short-Term Business Loans.*
[16] Cf. "Maintaining an Effective Bank Relationship," a speech by Charles A. Agemian before the 1963 Eastern Area Conference of the Financial Executives Institute, reported under "Required Reading," *American Banker* (August 5, 6, and 7, 1963).

As a result, different banks in the same city are able to charge different rates for ostensibly identical loans. Price competition, which tends to generate uniform prices for the same product in a given market, is not very strong.

It is arguable that the lack of competition displayed by interest rates is a result of structural problems in the industry. With the conventional hypotheses of market theory, one would anticipate that rates would be somewhat lower and possess less variance in markets in which the number of banks is large, no one bank is of dominant size, and the distribution of size is not highly skewed. One might also conjecture that unit banks offer more attractive rates than do branch system and holding company banks if these forms of organization create or are associated with monopoly power.

There is little to support such hypotheses in banking markets. In a study of short-term loans to business by large banks in 19 major cities, the Banking Markets Unit, Board of Governors of the Federal Reserve System, has failed to find that market structure variables are associated with interest rates in any significant way. For small business loans ($1,000–$10,000) — a type of lending for which there are few alternatives outside of commercial banking — interest rates were found to vary significantly by the region of the country in which the cities covered by the study were located. After accounting for the regional effect, there was a slight but significant tendency for the rates charged by individual banks to decrease as the share of the market possessed by the bank increased.[17] The number of banks in the markets, the size of the largest bank, and the proportion of the market accounted for by the three largest banks, all possessed no explanatory value, even when checked for interaction effects.[18]

For large business loans ($200,000 and more), total variance in rates was found to be as large as that for the small loans. The regional influence was still significant — casting doubt on the idea that a truly national market exists for such loans. The larger banks tended to charge slightly but significantly lower rates than did the smaller banks. As with the small loans, the number of banks and the proportion of total deposits held by the three largest banks were not significant. There was no evidence that banks in a branching system charged rates different from those of unit banks.

Finally, in a smaller and admittedly less reliable study of small banks in several Minnesota towns, the Banking Markets Unit inquired into differences in interest rates depending on whether there were one, two or three banks in the town. The results indicated that the number of banks was unimportant in explaining rates charged even after the effects of loan mix, bank size, city size, level of income, and rate of change in city size and income were removed.[19] Interest rates paid on time deposits did not vary significantly with the number of

---

[17] This may well be due to the larger banks selecting the higher quality loans.

[18] Mr. Frank Edwards, using data from the 1955 Business Loan Survey, reports a statistically significant but absolutely very small positive relationship between interest rates and concentration for 1955. Data for 1957 do not confirm this relationship. His study uses the average rate paid on business loans, including term loans, by city by asset size class of borrower as the dependent variable in a multiple correlation test. The study by the Banking Markets Unit uses the average

rate paid on short-term business loans by bank by city. Variance in rates among banks within a city is thus included in the latter, but not in the Edwards study. It is possible that it is the inclusion of inter-bank as well as inter-city variances which causes concentration ratios to fail the tests of significance in the Banking Market Unit study. If this is the reason for the difference in findings, the conclusions based on total variance including inter-bank, intra-city variance seems to be the better. Edwards argues that the null results for 1957 are due to a "ceiling effect" which reduces total variance during periods of high interest rates. This argument would be as valid for 1960, the time of the FRB study, as for 1957.

It is interesting to note that the Supreme Court, in United States v. Philadelphia National Bank, was willing to conclude from simple and untested structural hypotheses that performance improves as the number of banks increases. "Specifically, we think that a merger which produces a firm controlling an undue percentage share of the relevant market and results in a significant increase in the concentration of firms in that market, is so inherently likely to lessen competition substantially that it must be enjoined in the absence of evidence clearly showing that the merger is not likely to have such anticompetitive effects." The Court, relying on Kaysen and Turner, op. cit. and others, observed that "[C]ompetition is likely to be the greatest when there are many sellers, none of which has any significant market share." (374 U.S. 321, at 363).

[19] This is contrary to the findings of Irving Schweiger and John S. McGee, Chicago Banking (Chicago, 1961).

commercial banks, but did tend to be higher in towns in which savings and loan associations were large relative to commercial banks. While neither rates charged nor rates paid varied significantly with size of bank, net earnings per dollar of earnings assets tended to increase slightly as the size of banks increased. Net earnings per dollar of earning assets tended to decrease as the number of banks increased, implying — since neither rates charged nor rates paid varied significantly with number of banks — that the competition associated with numbers of banks may result in higher costs rather than lower prices.

PUBLIC REGULATION AND PRIVATE RATIONALIZATION OF COMPETITION

The apparent lack of strong price competition, the continued existence of many banks of less than optimal scale and the insensitivity of market performance to market structure are not difficult to explain. They arise because of a vastly complex system of public regulation and supervision working in conjunction with a well-developed, yet generally informal, private market organization.[20] Most of the public regulation appears in the guise of instruments designed to protect the safety of banks and the liquidity of the payments mechanism — that is, to prevent bank failures and banking practices which might lead to failures. Much, but not all, of the private rationalization of competition is a side effect of certain cooperative arrangements among bankers — clearing houses, loan participations, and correspondent relations, for example — which add to the efficiency of the system. The point is not that there are conscious efforts to arrange conspiracies in restraint of trade, but rather that public regulation has the express purpose and private organization has the necessary effect of producing essentially non-competitive results.

Since public regulation is not pervasive of all facets of bank operations, and the private organization is typically informal, their restraining effects may not be obvious in those market

areas in which the number of banks is reasonably large and there is such a lack of concentration that the possibility of strong leadership is absent. As already noted, however, a substantial portion of all commercial banks operate in communities in which there are no more than three banks. The relevant market of some of these banks undoubtedly extends to areas outside their own communities, thus making the effective number of banks in the market larger than the community count of banks indicates. Still, to the extent that the geographic market for any bank service contains only a small number of sellers, conventional oligopoly theory is relevant. Without formal agreement and without direct communication concerning prices to be charged and market areas and customers to be served, tacit understandings quite similar to those which would be achieved by overt agreement are apt to arise. In the case of banks, the tacit understandings — which, parenthetically, may not be consciously recognized as such by the participants — are abetted by public regulation and supervision which helps to assure that no individual bank will behave in a way which would have a strong competitive impact on others.[21]

PUBLIC REGULATION

Very little of the public regulation of banks positively requires identical pricing. The most obvious instances relate not to output prices — rates charged — but to the prices paid for inputs — rates paid for funds. Here regulations require that no interest be paid on demand deposits and establish an upper limit to interest paid on time deposits. Until recent years, the latter was low enough so that the maximum rate was also typically the actual rate, though this is no longer so generally true.[22]

Control of input prices may have profound effects on the degree of competition for output.

[20] See Donald R. Hodgman, *Commercial Bank Loan and Investment Policy* (Champaign, Illinois, 1963), pp. 158–160, for a similar view.

[21] See *ibid.*, pp. 116–135, 159–160, for an excellent discussion of the "administered" and oligopolistically set New York prime rate and its effects in restraining competition. See also David C. Motter, "Bank Mergers and Public Policy," *National Banking Review*, vol. 1 (September, 1963), p. 96, especially fn. 23.

[22] See Caroline H. Cagle, "Interest Rates on Time Deposits, Mid-February 1963," *Federal Research Bulletin* (June 1963).

There have been numerous instances in industrial markets in which an anti-competitive pricing system for output developed and was maintained through the control of input prices. The crux of the *Socony Vacuum* case[23] was that major oil companies agreed to purchase "hot oil" and gasoline refined from this oil in an effort to prevent some of themselves and independent, non-integrated, companies from having significantly different costs. Without the condition of equal costs, the tacit agreement to follow the output price leadership of Standard of Indiana tended chronically to breakdown. Other cases in which cost identity was important in rationalizing output competition can be found in the beet sugar,[24] milk distribution,[25] and cigarette[26] industries.

In banking, it would be unwarranted to conclude that the regulation of interest paid on deposits creates a tight system of collusive output prices. However, they have — purposely — been instrumental in the general moderation of competition. The regulations prevent considerable price competition for funds, both among banks and between banks and other financial institutions. One consequence has been the prevention of what would otherwise have been a form of cost-increasing rivalry for funds and, for this reason, the erection of a protective shield for the less efficient and often smaller banks. In addition, the lack of competition for funds has been an important ingredient in eliminating cost differences which, especially in local markets, would be apt to get translated into more active competition in the output market. Banks, being unable to attract customers by paying higher rates on deposits, have had no alternative but to use non-price forms of rivalry. The resulting product differentiation — based on location, convenience, advertising, loan accommodations, etc. — have likely reduced the desire and ability of customers to shop among banks. The expenses involved in advertising and the proliferation of branches

may in some instances have resulted in higher bank operating costs than would prevail with more rate competition. Moreover, since even the most aggressive banks have been restricted in their ability to use deposit rates as a competitive weapon, tacit understandings to compete only with non-price techniques are made more viable. In short, the regulations tend to create more identical "value systems" among banks and, hence, to prevent the outbreak of open price rivalry.[27]

Similar tendencies for an identity of value systems arise from other aspects of regulation. Only a few of the regulations go directly to prices and terms for deposits and loans. Most have a more subtle effect. Limitations on mortgage lending and ownership of stocks, along with supervisory rules governing the risk asset ratio, standards for lending, and for accounting procedures, make for similar asset compositions and for similar views with respect to "sound" banking practices. Bankers, that is, are encouraged to conform to an established and, in many respects, non-competitive pattern of market behavior.

Finally, state and Federal regulations prevent various forms of entry into the markets of existing banks. Whether nationally or state chartered, banks cannot establish branches across state lines even though the economic market does not accord with these political boundaries. With respect to both entry by new banks and entry by existing banks through merger or *de novo* branching, the "adequacy" of the existing banks to meet the convenience and needs of the market is considered. The question of convenience and needs of a market very often reduces to the question of whether existing banks would be injured if they shared their market with another, not to whether there are economic reasons for the establishment of a new bank. These regulations facilitate tacit market sharing and reduce the likelihood that "maverick" bankers — those who might upset the status quo of a market — will enter.

The entry problem is a more difficult one in

[23] *United States v. Socony-Vacuum Oil Co.*, 310 U.S. 150 (1940).
[24] *Mandeville Island Farms, Inc. v. American Crystal Sugar Co.* 334 U.S. 219 (1948).
[25] *Pevely Dairy Co. v. United States*, 178 F.2d 363 (8th Cir. 1949).
[26] *American Tobacco Co. v. United States*, 328 U.S. 781 (1946).

[27] For a more complete discussion of the role of differences in costs and other aspects of "value systems" of firms on competition, see Almarin Phillips, *Market Structure, Organization and Performance* (Cambridge, Mass. 1962) pp. 32–40.

banking than in other industries, however. Entry performs its valuable role in allocating resources efficiently because of its effects on long-run supply. While in local markets a new bank may increase supply and tend to force down prices (if the new bank does not adopt the same non-competitive behavior of the existing banks), in the aggregate the total supply of bank credit is loosely fixed by monetary authority. For the entire economy, more banks do not mean a larger total supply in the same sense as is the case in other industries, or in the same sense as they do for local and regional bank markets. Rather, if the number of banks increases and supply of bank credit is fixed, the size of the average bank decreases and, assuming the existence of scale economies, the system moves away from the most efficient allocation of resources. If the competitive force of new entrants is to be relied upon to achieve efficiency, free entry in banking must take the two-way meaning attached to it in competitive theory — freedom of entrance and freedom of exit (failure or forced disappearance through merger). Forced exit, of course, is precisely what regulation and supervision, including restrictions on entry, are designed to prevent. As a result, the banking structure has responded very slowly to inefficient operations and to geographical shifts in demand.

PRIVATE ORGANIZATION

Public regulation is not the only source of rationalized competition among banks. It may not be even the primary source. The rationalization which comes from the organizational and institutional aspects of banks themselves is more difficult to see but probably no less important.

The informal organization of oligopoly in local markets was mentioned above. There are also several more formal types of horizontal relations. Of these, the clearing house is the most familiar. Its function of clearing balances is a necessary one, but one which does not require either the ownership of or active participation in the clearing house by the member banks. The functions beyond those of clearing which are performed are something of a mystery to any save the members, but no one would be surprised if matters such as hours of

business, service charges on checking accounts, and perhaps even interest rates charged and paid, were occasionally discussed.

Commercial banking, as other industries, has its trade associations — local, regional, state and nationwide bankers associations. These associations undoubtedly perform valuable informational and educational services. They also provide a forum for communication among bankers and an opportunity for those high in the organizational hierarchy — the leaders of the industry — to make known their views on sundry subjects. This sort of communication can hardly result in formal conspiracy among bankers; there are too many members in the group, the subject matter is too complex, and the disciplinary power is too weak. Still, the associations have their purpose. When problems arise, established channels of communication are available. And communication, especially when it comes from those at the top of a power hierarchy, tends to facilitate conflict resolution. Perhaps a great deal should not be made of this, but competition is a form of conflict and, in the present context, conflict resolution is a form of restraint on competition. If nothing more, the communication makes it easier to know what is expected of a "good" banker; easier to conform to "sound" banking practice.

In addition to horizontal relations there is in the organization of banking an explicit vertical relationship among banks. It is found in correspondent banking. It is well-recognized that a system of vertical affiliations among firms may restrain competition. This is probably one effect of correspondent banking, but the restraint is perhaps a mild one. Unlike resale price maintenance, in which the vertical relations may operate in a manner identical to that which would occur with full, horizontal agreement among distributors, correspondent relations exert a less obvious influence. There is no commodity flowing from the correspondent to corresponding bank which is resold. And it is general practice that the several banks in one community correspond with different banks in others.

The correspondent system tends to pyramid from a large number of banks in small cities and towns upward to a smaller number of banks in a few larger cities and upward again to a small number of banks in one or a few financial centers. Detailed knowledge of the full role played by correspondent banks is lacking and generalizations are hazardous. It is known that corresponding comprises much more than a holding of deposit balances and a clearing operation. Services and information flow from correspondents to the corresponding banks, in a direction opposite to that of the deposits. These often include advice with respect to portfolio, credit advice, and a sort of management consulting service. There are, in addition, loan participations which alter the otherwise vertical relation to a horizontal one.

To reiterate, this does not completely foreclose competition. But, as argued above, the banks in each of the cities involved have an implicitly recognized community of interest which arises from their horizontal and frequently oligopolistic market relations. Even while banks in one town generally correspond with different banks in the city at the next level up, the horizontal relations at each level are such as to produce substantial uniformity of behavior. The correspondent relations provide another system of communication among banks and easy access to information which allows and encourages all the banks in the system to conform to established modes of behavior.

The unique combination of formal and informal organization in commercial banking — partly associated with public regulation and supervision and partly with private, institutional arrangements — explains the lack of competitive market performance and the failure of that performance to vary with the market structure. This organization is by far the most pervasive factor in determining performance. "Good" banking practices are equated with "quiet," non-price forms of rivalry in the view of both bankers and the regulatory agencies.

IMPROVING COMMERCIAL BANKING PERFORMANCE

It would be possible and, within limits, it probably is desirable to improve the performance of commercial banking markets. It appears, however, that the role of conventional antitrust policy — the prevention of mergers and combinations in restraint of trade — in achieving this result is an extremely limited one, because of the continuing necessity for some public regulation and supervision and also because of the impossibility of altering substantially the oligopolistic structure of the typical banking market.

The most obvious need for public intervention is to preserve the liquidity of the money supply which, in the absence of deposit insurance, requires supervision and regulations to prevent bank failures. With deposit insurance, the liquidity of the payments mechanism depends not on the liquidity and solvency of the banks themselves, but rather on the liquidity of those to whom the banks owe debts — the depositors — which it is the function of the insurance to maintain. Nonetheless, deposit insurance does not make possible the elimination of bank regulation and supervision. If the insuring agency did no more than examine banks for the purpose of discriminating in premiums on the basis of risk, *de facto* regulations would continue to exist. Moreover, given the highly leveraged position of bank capital and the liquidity of bank liabilities, continued supervision and regulation will be necessary to prevent systemic failures and their generally disrupting influence.

Regulation, then, will continue, but the nature of regulation requires modification. If it is accepted that the organization, rather than the structure, of the industry is the controlling variable in determining performance, it follows that the primary means of altering performance is through changing the organization, especially that part which emanates from regulations.

The most important single policy would be to permit freer entry. This would involve making new charters available on a less restrictive basis than is done on the current "needs and convenience" criterion, removing arbitrary limitations on *de novo* branching and branching by merger, and ending the prohibitions against branching over state lines. Efficient independent banks and those smaller banks which offer differential services for which there is market demand would not be forced from the market by these changes. Inefficient banks would have to improve their efficiency, merge, or fail; the market power of locally monopolistic or oligopolistic banks would be effectively constrained.

The elimination of restrictions on interest rates paid on deposits would be another important step. This, especially if accompanied by steps to equalize the reserve requirements of all banks, regardless of size,[28] would remove what amounts to protective subsidization of smaller banks. In addition, bank supervision could be modified to permit banks greater freedom in establishing their own credit and risk standards. Increased price competition would not likely arise from permitting banks to experiment with new types of credit or to specialize in particular lines, but there would be encouragement for a constructive type of nonprice competition. Competition through advertising, promotion, and location would to some degree be supplanted by competition through new and improved loan and deposit services.

The removal of interest rate restrictions and the relaxation of regulations would also tend to reduce the number of banks. The increased cost of funds, while good for the industry as a whole and its relations with other financial institutions, would tend to increase operating costs. Some banks, because of the cost increase and because of management errors in the extension of credit, would experience operating difficulties; some would fail, perhaps to be absorbed by another bank or to be succeeded by a new firm.

These are not small changes in policy. Accomplishing them would require the establishment of a *national* policy for what should be a *national* industry. Uniform chartering and branching policies, uniform and less compulsory supervisory standards, uniform reserve requirements and free interstate banking would spell the end of the dual banking system as it now exists. Moreover, while the social benefits appear to merit such changes, they are radical enough to suggest that they should be accomplished in small steps over a period of years. The opposition of bankers to the proposals probably is assurance that no change will be rapid!

Finally, some sort of antitrust policy would still be necessary. While clearing houses, loan participations and correspondent relationships are necessary to the industry, there is no obvious reason why other horizontal and vertical combinations in restraint of trade should be accorded special Sherman Act exemption. That is, the private organization of the industry should be left intact except where it has no purpose other than to restrain trade. A necessary caution here is that the sometimes extremely difficult distinction must be made between those kinds of cooperative endeavors which are necessary because of the character and structure of the industry — and, hence, are "reasonable" restraints — and those which are unnecessary and operate to the detriment of society. This calls for the antitrust standard used by Judge Medina in the *Morgan* case[29] rather than the usual *per se* procedures for restraint of trade cases. Too, it should be recognized in antitrust proceedings that the classical type of atomistic competition cannot be made to prevail in banking markets. The most that can be sought is oligopolistic competition for differentiated products, constrained by freedom of entry and the ability of existing banks to innovate.

Similarly, while legislative barriers to mergers should be removed to encourage competition, competitive policy for the industry should, at the same time, include the prohibition of mergers and holding companies which may tend to lessen competition substantially. This is a difficult standard to apply, however, and even when enforcement is in the antitrust agencies — as it should be — rather than lodged with regulatory authorities, there is danger that the policy could evolve into the protection of small and inefficient competitors rather than a policy to promote competition.[30] An extremely strict merger policy would make it difficult to realize scale economics and the benefits of freer entry.

[28] Including for this purpose interbank deposits and vault cash in reserves.

[29] *United States v. Morgan*, 118 F. Supp. 621 (S.D.N.Y. 1954).

[30] It can be argued that the trend of enforcement of the amended Section 7 of the Clayton Act has already turned in this direction. In particular, see *Brown Shoe v. United States*, 370 U.S. 294 (1962). *United States v. Philadelphia National Bank*, 374 U.S. 321 (1963) may have similar overtones despite the testimony of small bankers that they favored the merger. A more competitive market environment could easily alter their views.

PART 3

THE INSTRUMENTS OF
CENTRAL BANKING

CHAPTER SEVEN

WAR FINANCE AND ITS AFTERMATH

21

WAR AND POSTWAR MONETARY AND DEBT MANAGEMENT POLICIES*

The Douglas Committee

In any economy, at any one time, there exists only a limited quantity of the resources useful for producing goods and services, only a limited volume of the factors of production — land, labor, capital equipment, human knowledge, and entrepreneurship. There is thus a maximum output which can be produced when all the factors are fully employed. The output of a fully employed economy can be compared to a huge pie: part of the total product is in the form of consumer goods; usually a much smaller slice in the form of capital goods and equipment; and the remainder in the form of government goods and services.

War is an inflationary process. The government demands more and more of the pie, diminishing the share of resources going into the production of consumer goods and services — while increasing the stream of money flowing into consumers' bank accounts. The government demands an ever-increasing slice of the pie to finance the production of the means of battle; consumers find themselves with larger incomes and more money, but less consumer goods available for purchase. Prices will rise and inflation ensue to the extent to which consumers bid against each other for the scarce supply of goods. Thus anti-inflationary war finance requires that the government tax its citizens heavily and persuade them to save, perhaps by buying government bonds, in order to reduce their spending.

When the United States entered World War II there was still a substantial volume of unemployment — over 8 million men were unemployed in 1940, about 15 per cent of the labor force, and this remained at close to 6 million men in 1941, almost 10 per cent of the labor force. Once we entered the war, however, this slack was rapidly eliminated. Unemployment was less than 2 per cent of the labor force by 1943, bringing us up against the production ceiling imposed by full employment and the resulting inflationary pressures described above.

World War II involved the United States Government in expenditures which totaled about 400 billion dollars. A government can raise the money it needs in any of several ways: it can (1) print the money; (2) borrow from the banking system, either from the commercial banks or the Federal Reserve Banks; (3) borrow from the public; or (4)

---

* From *Monetary, Credit and Fiscal Policies*, Report of the Subcommittee on Monetary, Credit and Fiscal Policies (Douglas Committee) of the Joint Committee on the Economic Report, U.S. Congress, 1950.

acquire it by legal compulsion, that is, taxation. There are two equally important aims to government wartime finance. First, and most obvious, to raise the needed funds. Second, to reduce the money in the pockets of consumers and businessmen, thereby reducing their ability to spend and push prices higher. Evaluating the above-mentioned four alternatives from the point of view of these dual objectives, it is obvious that the first two achieve only the goal of raising the funds for the government. They do not drain money from the public. (The banks, as we have seen, create money when they lend.) The third and fourth, in varying degrees, achieve both objectives. It is thus desirable to finance a war by the third and fourth methods so far as possible.

The World War II record of the United States in this respect was only fair: about 45 per cent of the 400 billion dollars was raised by taxation, 35 per cent (about 130 billion dollars) by borrowing from the nonbank public, and 20 per cent (or 80 billion dollars) by borrowing from the banking system.

The Treasury and the Federal Reserve generally acted in concert during the war. One of the main features of the wartime financing effort was a joint agreement between the Federal Reserve and the Treasury to maintain stable prices and yields on government securities. An announcement was made early in 1942 that the existing pattern of interest rates on government securities would be maintained for the duration — that pattern was an interest rate of ⅜ per cent on Treasury bills, ⅞ per cent on 9 to 12-month certificates, about 2 per cent on 10-year bonds, and 2½ per cent on the longest bonds. This was done to encourage investors to buy bonds promptly (rather than having them wait and postpone bond purchases in the hope interest rates might rise) and to hold down the interest cost to the government of raising the huge sums required.

This frozen yield structure, however, was to give rise to numerous postwar problems. At the end of the war the national debt amounted to a staggering 260 billion dollars. In 1940 it had been less than 50 billion dollars. Faced with the task of managing this huge debt, the Treasury insisted that the Federal Reserve continue its policy of maintaining low interest rates by buying securities at stated prices from all who wished to dispose of them. This meant that Federal Reserve open market operations had to be devoted to maintaining the prices of government securities rather than to altering member bank reserves.

Before reading this selection it would be helpful to review the relevant pages in Selection 2 on open market operations by the Federal Reserve System. There we saw that if the Federal Reserve wants to reduce member bank credit creation it must sell government securities. Buying only adds to member bank reserves and increases their ability to expand loans. The conflict between these principles and the postwar demands made upon the Federal Reserve should be clear.

The problem led to the formation by Congress of the Douglas Committee in 1949, known formally as the Subcommittee on Monetary, Credit and Fiscal Policies of the Joint Committee on the Economic Report. (See editorial introduction to Selection 7.) The Committee surveyed the history of the problem and explored the implications of alternative solutions, as detailed in this selection.

In view of the fact that it will be mentioned frequently, it is advisable to have firmly in mind the important relationship between the rate of interest and the capital value (or price) of an income-earning asset. A perpetual transferable private or government bond which carries a fixed dollar interest income of $5 per year and costs $100, obviously yields an annual rate of interest 5 per cent. If the price of the security were to fall to $50, however, the effective rate of interest received would no longer be 5 per cent, but $5/$50 or 10 per cent. And if the price of the security were to rise to $200, the effective rate of interest would fall to 2½ per cent. A fall (or rise) in the price or capital value of a fixed dollar income security is reflected in a rise (or fall) in the effec-

tive rate of interest it yields. To put the same thing somewhat differently, a rise in the effective rate of interest to 10 per cent must mean that, since the security yields but $5 per year, its value has fallen to $50. Anyone intent on obtaining 10 per cent on his money would pay $50 for it. And a fall in the effective rate of interest to 2½ per cent must mean that, since the security yields $5 per year, its value has increased to $200. Anyone interested in obtaining 2½ per cent on his money, would pay $200 for it.

All this can be put briefly in the form of an equation: $r = Y/CV$, where r = the annual effective rate of interest, Y = the annual dollar income return, and CV = the price or capital value of the security. If the dollar income is contractually fixed, as is usually the case with debt instruments, the effective rate of interest and the price of the security must move inversely.

Therefore, in reading the following selection it should be kept in mind that to let the price of government bonds fall or to let the rate of interest on government securities rise are but two different ways of saying the same thing; to say that the Federal Reserve wished to keep the price of government securities from falling and therefore had to stand ready to purchase them at a fixed price if the price were not to fall, is equivalent to saying the Federal Reserve was committed to not allowing the rate of interest to go up.

We believe that an appropriate, flexible, and vigorous monetary policy, employed in coordination with fiscal and other policies, should be one of our principal instruments for achieving and maintaining economic stability. For several reasons we reject the idea, held by a few economists and others, that for stabilization purposes little or no reliance should be placed on monetary policy and that we should rely exclusively on other measures, such as fiscal policies. (1) It is highly doubtful that fiscal policy would be powerful enough to maintain stability in the face of strong destabilizing forces even if monetary policy were neutral, and a conflicting monetary policy could lessen still further the effectiveness of fiscal policy. (2) Monetary policy is strong precisely where fiscal policy is weakest; it is capable of being highly flexible. It can be altered with changes in economic conditions on a monthly, daily, or even hourly basis. (3) It is a familiar instrument of control and thoroughly consistent with the maintenance of our democratic government and our competitive free-enterprise system. It is certainly much to be preferred over a harness of direct controls. (4) Our monetary history gives little indication as to how effectively we can expect appropriate and vigorous monetary policies to promote stability, for we have never really tried them.

For example, the effectiveness of these policies during the late 1920's was seriously reduced by the Federal Reserve's lack of powers for the selective control of security loans. After 1929, a vigorous easy-money policy was not adopted until bank reserves had been allowed to shrink for more than two years, thousands of banks had failed, and general business confidence had dwindled; and after World War II its use as a restrictive measure with which to combat inflation was very seriously hampered by considerations relating to the management of the federal debt. With our improved banking structure and the benefit of our past experience, we should be able to look forward to more effective monetary management characterized by timely, vigorous, and flexible actions.

The essential characteristic of a monetary policy that will promote general economic stability is its timely flexibility. To combat deflation and promote recovery, the monetary authorities must liberally provide the banking system with enhanced lending power, thereby tending to lower interest rates and increase the availability of credit. To retard and stop inflation they must restrict the lending power of banks, thereby tending to raise interest rates and to limit the availability of credit for private and government spending. And these actions must be taken promptly if they are to be most effective.

Flexibility is an essential characteristic of a monetary policy that will promote general economic stability. To combat deflation, it must make money and credit more available at lower cost; and, to curb inflation, it must restrict the availability and raise the cost of money and credit. During World War II and the postwar period, however, the Federal Reserve and the Treasury did not vigorously restrict credit in order to fight the current inflation. Instead, monetary policy became virtually fused with federal borrowing and debt-management policies and was used to prevent or limit increases in the yields and decreases in the prices of federal securities. General credit restriction could not be vigorously tried out because of the strong desire to maintain low interest rates and yields on government securities and to prevent or at least to hold within very narrow limits any decline in the prices of governments. This raises, we believe, the most important current question in the field of monetary policy: "To what extent should the use of a restrictive monetary policy to curb inflation be inhibited by the desire to hold down the yields and to hold up the prices of federal securities?" A short sketch of the development of this policy will help bring out the issues involved.

Between early 1937 and our entrance into World War II, the Federal Reserve on several occasions bought and sold federal securities not for the primary purpose of affecting the volume of bank reserves and aggregate lending power but for the express purpose of influencing the prices of governments, and especially the longer-term issues, in order "to maintain an orderly market" for them. In justifying these actions the Federal Reserve did not mention the needs of the Treasury, but stressed that its principal purposes were: (1) To "exert a steadying influence on the capital market, which is an essential part of the country's economic machinery, and disorganization in which would be a serious obstacle to the progress of economic recovery" and (2) to safeguard the large government portfolios of member banks against "unnecessarily wide and violent fluctuations in price." In short, by the time we entered World War II, "the maintenance of an orderly market for government securities" had already become an important objective of Federal Reserve policy. But not

yet had the Federal Reserve reached the point of "pegging" government prices at stated levels and standing ready to buy all securities offered to it at the pegged prices. It was "maintaining an orderly market for governments" in the sense of preventing "disorderly" changes in their prices and yields, but it was not yet maintaining a rigid yield pattern.

The next phase was entered at the time of Pearl Harbor. The Federal Reserve assured the nation that it could and would see that the Treasury was supplied with all the money that it needed for war finance, and in March, 1942, its Open Market Committee agreed with the Treasury to maintain for the duration of the war approximately the then-existing structure of yields on governments. These promises were completely fulfilled. Two facts about the frozen-yield structure are very significant. The first was the very low level of the entire yield structure. Partly because of the depressed demand for credit and partly because of the huge volume of excess bank reserves all interest rates, but especially those on short-term safe paper, had fallen greatly since 1929 and the early 1930's. The second fact was the very low level of yields on short-term paper relative to yields on the longer maturities. The pattern above which yields were not to be allowed to rise ranged from three-eighths of 1 per cent on 90-day Treasury bills, through seven-eighths of 1 per cent on 9–12 month certificates of indebtedness, through about 2 per cent on 10-year bonds, and up to a maximum of 2½ per cent on the longest-term marketable issues.

Though several measures were employed to prevent a rise of these yields above the agreed-upon pattern, by far the most important one, and the only one that needs to be mentioned here, was the agreement of the Federal Reserve to buy all the governments that others were unwilling to hold at yields not in excess of those agreed upon with the Treasury. In effect, therefore, the Treasury and the Federal Reserve fixed the pattern of prices and yields at which the Federal Reserve would be a passive buyer, and the Federal Reserve relinquished control over the volume of its government holdings to the Treasury as issuer and to others as buyers and sellers. And, of course, its purchases of these securities both added directly to the money supply and supplied the commercial banks with additional reserves on the basis of which they could create money. What happened to Federal Reserve holdings of governments as a result of this passive policy is that their total holdings rose from a little more than $2 billion at the beginning of 1942 to about $24 billion at the end of 1945, and virtually all of this increase represented the rise in Federal Reserve holdings of bills, certificates, and other short-term governments on which the yields were very low. Private investors were "playing the pattern of the rates"; with the safety and liquidity of the longer issues greatly enhanced by the Federal Reserve price support program private buyers tended to concentrate on the purchase of them and to leave to the Federal Reserve the purchase of the short-term, lower-yield maturities. In fact, during 1945 and 1946 the great private demand for the longer-maturities bid down markedly their yields.

As the war ended, therefore, the Federal Reserve was following a rigid policy of preventing the yields on governments from rising above the agreed-upon pattern, and it was accomplishing this by passively purchasing — and monetizing — all of these securities that others were unwilling to hold at yields not above those on the pattern. In effect the Federal Reserve had relinquished control over the amount of the federal debt that it would monetize in order to prevent yield increases. Having committed itself to this policy, it could not refuse to buy and monetize governments at the agreed-upon price, for to do so would have been to let the price of the security fall and the yield rise. This policy was continued without significant change until July, 1947, nearly 2 years after V-J day. But in mid-1947 some upward flexibility began to be introduced; in a series of steps the yield on bills was increased to about 1.16 per cent by late 1948, the yield on certificates to 1.25 per cent, and long-term yields by lesser amounts. In 1949, as inflationary pressures abated and the private demand for credit declined, yields were allowed to fall somewhat. Though the policy from July, 1947, until

late 1948 did indicate an ability of the Federal Reserve and the Treasury to agree upon a reintroduction of some upward flexibility in yields and interest rates, it does not by any means indicate that the concern for "maintaining an orderly market in governments" has been abandoned and that the use of a restrictive monetary policy to combat future inflations will not be seriously hindered by a concern for preventing or limiting decreases in the prices and increases in the yields on governments. In fact, throughout this period the Federal Reserve made it clear that it was continuing its policy of maintaining an orderly market for governments, the rise of even short-term rates was never allowed to proceed very far, and in no case was the price of a government security allowed to decline below par. The following press release by the Federal Reserve on June 28, 1949, indicates, according to Chairman McCabe, that policy in the future will be flexible:

The Federal Open Market Committee, after consultation with the Treasury, announced today that with a view to increasing the supply of funds available in the market to meet the needs of commerce, business, and agriculture it will be the policy of the committee to direct purchases, sales, and exchanges of government securities by the Federal Reserve banks with primary regard to the general business and credit situation. The policy of maintaining orderly conditions in the government security market, and the confidence of investors in government bonds will be continued. Under present conditions the maintenance of a relatively fixed pattern of rates has the undesirable effect of absorbing reserves from the market at a time when the availability of credit should be increased.

But in interpreting this statement, two facts are important: (1) The June, 1949, decision had the effect of lowering interest rates, thereby facilitating Treasury finance. The Treasury might not have assented so readily had the policy been toward higher interest rates. And (2) the statement did not, and of course could not, indicate the extent of flexibility that will be employed in the future. The range of flexibility may prove to be so narrow as to limit very seriously the effectiveness of a restrictive monetary policy.

Treasury and Federal Reserve officials have advanced a number of reasons for the policy of holding down the yields and supporting the prices of governments in the face of inflation: (1) Such a policy holds down service charges on the federal debt. The Secretary of the Treasury stated to the subcommittee:

The interest cost of the debt to taxpayers is another of the many considerations which must be taken into account in debt-management policies. It is estimated that the interest charge on the public debt during the fiscal year 1950 will be $5,450,000,000. This item represents over 13 per cent of the federal budget for the year. The interest cost is likely to grow over a period of time — in the absence of substantial debt reduction — because the rate of interest on savings bonds increases as the bonds are held to maturity, and because an increasingly large proportion of the debt represents the accumulation of trust funds invested at rates set forth in the law which are higher than the present average interest rate on the debt.

A general rise in interest rates would bring about a further rise in the budget charge for interest payments. An increase of as little as one-half of 1 per cent in the average interest paid on the debt would add about $1,250,000,000 to this charge. The Treasury was able to finance the last war at an average borrowing cost of less than one-half the borrowing cost of World War I. If this had not been done, the interest charge at the present time would be more than $10,000,000,000 a year instead of $5,000,000,000 a year. It is clearly evident that this $5,000,000,000 annual savings in the taxpayer's money is a highly important factor in the budget picture of the Federal Government.

(2) The maintenance of relatively stable prices on governments helps to maintain confidence in the public credit and facilitates Treasury sales of securities for both new financing and refunding purposes. This looms important to the Treasury, with about $50 billion of its marketable debt maturing within a year and with large volumes of outstanding nonmarketable issues, especially savings bonds, payable on demand. (3) The maintenance of stable security prices protects investors against capital depreciation and prevents any loss of public confidence in financial institutions, including banks, that might result from a serious decline of these prices. (4) Any marked decline in the price of governments would be communicated to other parts of the credit market and might bring about unemployment and deflation by interfering with the flotation of new private securities. And (5) any feasible rise of the yields on governments would be so ineffective as an anti-inflationary measure as not to be worth its cost. Though Federal Reserve and Treasury officials, and especially the latter, seem to have been greatly influenced by the objectives of holding down the service charges on the federal debt and of facilitating Treasury security flotations it is well to remember that there were also other considerations behind the postwar policy, such as those relating to protecting individual and institutional investors against capital depreciation, prevention of a financial panic, and avoidance of restrictive policies that would be so vigorous as to reduce employment and production.

The principal argument against a monetary policy of preventing or narrowly limiting the increase of yields on governments is that it seriously limits, if it does not completely prevent, the use of restrictive monetary policy as an instrument for combating inflation. It is no hindrance to the use of a liberal monetary policy to fight deflation and unemployment; the very same low-interest, easy-money policy that will be conducive to business recovery also holds down service charges on the federal debt and facilitates security sales by the Treasury. But in periods of inflation the objective of preventing or narrowly limiting increases of yields on governments may conflict directly with that of combating inflation; the former objective requires a policy of continued easy credit and low interest rates while the latter requires a lessened availability of credit accompanied by higher interest rates.

That the Federal Reserve is powerless to restrict credit in general while maintaining low yields on governments is brought out by two facts: (1) All holders of governments, both individual and institutional, retain complete freedom to buy or sell at will any or all of these securities, of which their holdings are tremendous. At their own option they may sell these securities to acquire money to spend for consumption, to finance capital purchases, or to lend to others. Any tendency for interest rates on private obligations to rise relative to those on governments tends to induce investors to sell governments in order to make funds available to private users. And (2) in order to prevent yields on governments from rising above any given level the Federal Reserve must stand ready to buy at those yields all the government securities that others do not wish to hold. In this way all holders of governments, not merely member banks, are given access to new money from the Federal Reserve. They get this money by selling governments, and the cost of the money to them is the yield that they sacrifice on the securities sold. Thus for the Federal Reserve to maintain low yields on governments by passively purchasing them in unlimited quantities is to assure that money for other uses will continue to be cheaply available in large amounts.

Such a policy of maintaining low yields on governments negates or seriously reduces the effectiveness of every Federal Reserve instrument for general credit restriction: (1) Open market operations are likely to be useless; the Federal Reserve is not free to refuse to buy or actually to sell governments in order to restrict credit in general but must purchase these securities in such amounts as are required to prevent undesired rises in their yields. Even if the Federal Reserve should sell governments in an attempt to restrict credit it would be compelled, under this policy, to buy them back again to prevent a rise of yields. (2) Increases in Federal Reserve discount rates are likely to be largely ineffective as positive restrictive measures, for banks will not need to borrow so long as they can secure funds at will by selling governments to the Federal Reserve. Even the psychological effects of increases in discount rates are much reduced by the fact that banks are largely out of debt to the Federal Reserve and know that they can remain so. (3) The restrictive effects of increases in member-bank reserve requirements are greatly reduced by the fact that the banks can easily repair their reserve positions and restore and even expand their lending power through the sale, at their own option, of governments to the Federal Reserve.

It appears to us impossible to prescribe by legislation highly specific rules to guide the determination of monetary and debt management policies, for it is impossible to foresee all situations that may arise in the future. The wisest course for Congress to follow in this case is to lay down general objectives, to indicate the general order of importance to be attached to these various objectives, and to leave more specific decisions and actions to the judgment of the monetary and debt management officials. We believe that specific policies should conform to the following broad principles: (1) They should prevent "disorderly" movements in the prices and yields of governments while avoiding the maintenance of such inflexibly low yields as to reduce seriously the effectiveness of monetary policy for anti-inflation purposes. A few people, but apparently only a very small minority, have argued that the Federal Reserve ought never to enter the market to influence the behavior of prices and yields on governments. This position is, we believe, untenable. It is a central function of the Federal Reserve to influence the behavior of yields in general, and the behavior of yields on more than $250 billion of securities, making up more than half of all public and private debt in this country, can hardly be ignored. The Federal Reserve should prevent not only panicky declines in the prices of these securities but also other disorderly, erratic, and overly rapid changes. A part of the technique of central banking is to avoid excessively harsh restrictive measures. Declines of the magnitude that occurred after World War I, when long-term governments fell to about 80, serve no useful purpose. On the other hand, the Federal Reserve and the Treasury should not allow their concern for holding down yields and supporting the prices of governments to prevent a vigorous use of restrictive monetary policy to combat inflation. To continue to maintain an easy availability of credit at low interest rates in the face of inflation is not to be neutral; it is to feed the fires of inflation. (2) The advantages of avoiding inflation are so great that they should be pursued even if the cost is a significant increase in the service charges on the federal debt and a greater inconvenience to the Treasury in its sale of securities for new financing and refunding purposes. In general, the government ought not to use its monetary policy to maintain easy credit and to facilitate the management of its own debt if that monetary policy is not conducive to the maintenance of general economic stability. Exceptions to these principles should occur only at times of serious national emergency. In emphasizing the desirability of using a restrictive monetary policy, which must entail some rise of interest rates, to combat future inflations we are not arguing for a secularly higher interest rate structure. There is good reason to believe that secularly low interest rates will be in the national interest for they will stimulate private capital construction. We favor interest rates as low as they can be without inducing inflationary pressures. But flexibility of interest rates, without which a flexible monetary policy is impossible, should be restored.

Also involved in this broad problem of the relationship between monetary and debt management are questions relating to the division of authority. Who should determine and administer these policies? The traditional position in this country has been that power and responsibility for monetary policy should be lodged in the "independent" Federal Reserve System, which though accountable to Congress should not be responsible to the executive branch. To assure the maintenance of this independence the members of the Board of Governors were given 14-year terms, the Secretary of the Treasury and the Comptroller of the Currency were removed from the Board, and a certain amount of decentralization of authority within the Federal Reserve System was continued. On the other hand, power and responsibility for debt management within very broad limitations laid down by Congress is delegated to the Treasury Department. In theory, therefore, the Federal Reserve exercises the powers of monetary management while the Treasury exercises the powers of debt management. But this is hardly a realistic description of the actual location of these powers. The Federal Reserve has always exercised an influence on debt management policies through its general monetary policies and in recent years, as noted above, monetary management has been an integral part of debt management. Moreover,

the Treasury has monetary control powers; it can tend to ease or tighten the money market by shifting its general balance from the Federal Reserve banks to commercial banks and vice versa, its purchases and sales of securities for the account of its trust funds have general effects similar to those of Federal Reserve open-market operations, and at times in the past it has had discretionary powers relative to gold and silver. But in recent years the Treasury has exercised its greatest influence on monetary policy through its debt management policies, and especially through its power to fix the various terms, including interest rates, on its new issues.

As a practical matter there will be at any time an approximate equality between the yields fixed by the Treasury on its new offerings and market yields on comparable outstanding Treasury issues, the latter reflecting the general monetary policy being followed by the Federal Reserve. The Treasury will not be able to sell its new issues at yields below the market yields on comparable issues already outstanding, and it is not likely to offer significantly higher yields on the new issues. But who determines the levels at which the yields on the outstanding and new issues will be equalized — the Federal Reserve or the Treasury? Do Federal Reserve officials determine the general level of interest rates, including yields on governments, that they will establish so that the Treasury in fixing rates on new issues must conform to the decisions of the Federal Reserve? Or do Federal Reserve officials conform their general credit policies, including their support levels for governments, to the pattern desired by the Treasury? The evidence presented to the subcommittee indicates that there is no simple answer to these questions. Federal Reserve and Treasury officials and staff members are in frequent consultation, and many decisions are agreed upon by the two agencies without marked differences of opinion. On some occasions when there were originally differences of opinion the Treasury has "gone along" with Federal Reserve requests for higher interest rates. But the evidence indicates that in a majority of the cases where the judgments of the two agencies differed it was the judgment of the Treasury that prevailed; the Federal Reserve was not willing to assert its independence and force market yields to rise above the yields that the Treasury wished to set on its new issues, thereby embarrassing the Treasury. It appears that in the absence of strong Treasury influence the Federal Reserve would have initiated a tighter monetary policy somewhat earlier and that this policy would have been carried further. Allan Sproul, who as president of the Federal Reserve Bank of New York and vice chairman of the Federal Open Market Committee participated in negotiations with the Treasury, offered this testimony at our hearings:

It is important that better means be found, if possible, for reconciling potential differences between the Treasury and the Federal Reserve System, so that action in the credit sphere may be taken promptly, as needed, in reasonable harmony with the action being taken by the Treasury in the sphere of debt management.

The record of cooperation in the postwar years has been better than might have been expected, and so has the record of our economy, whatever connection there may be between the two. But agreed action, in my opinion, has most often been too little and too late, so far as the aims of an effective monetary program were concerned.

For example, the System wanted to discontinue its preferential discount rate on government securities maturing within 1 year, before the end of 1945; Treasury acquiescence, and the action, did not come until April, 1946.

From the closing months of 1945 through all of 1946, the System was pressing for discontinuance of its artificially low buying rate — three-eighths of 1 per cent — on Treasury bills; the action finally came, with Treasury agreement, in July, 1947.

From that point on, as inflationary pressures increased, the System wished to follow a program of credit restraint which would have necessitated small but, perhaps, frequent increases in short-term interest rates which would have meant similar increases in rates on Treasury bills and certificates, and some increase in the yield of other short and intermediate government securities.

The Treasury did a large part of the job, of course, by devoting its substantial cash surpluses to the retirement of debt in such a manner as greatly to aid in achieving the common objective; but the Treasury was generally several months behind in accepting the implications of a tightening policy for the interest rates on its short-term securities.

The general thesis of the following statement to the subcommittee by Marriner Eccles, a member of the Board of Governors and formerly its Chairman, appears to be justified.

The Treasury . . . is not responsible to Congress for monetary and credit policy and has had for a long time a general easy-money bias under almost any and all circumstances. As long as the Federal Reserve policy must be based upon this criterion, it could not pursue a restrictive money policy to combat inflationary pressures.

Decisions regarding management of the public debt set the framework within which monetary and credit action can be taken. As the size of the debt grew through the period of deficit finance in the thirties and particularly over the war period, Treasury needs came to overshadow and finally to dominate completely Federal Reserve monetary and credit policy. When the Treasury announces the issue of securities at a very low-rate pattern during a period of credit expansion, as it did last Wednesday, the Federal Reserve is forced to defend these terms unless the System is prepared to let the financing fail, which it could not very well do. To maintain a very low-rate pattern when there is a strong demand for credit, the System cannot avoid supplying Federal Reserve credit at the will of the market.

Under these conditions it can hardly be said that the Federal Reserve System retains any effective influence in its own right over the supply of money in the country or over the availability and cost of credit, although these are the major duties for which the System has statutory responsibility. Nor can it be said that the discount rate and open-market operations of the System are determined by Federal Reserve authorities, except in form. They are predetermined by debt-management decisions made by the Treasury. This will be true as long as the System is not in a position to pursue an independent policy but must support in the market any program of financing adopted by the Treasury, even though the program may be inconsistent with the monetary and credit policies the System considers appropriate in the public interest.

There have been many proposals for altering the division of authority and responsibility for monetary and debt management in the interest of securing more appropriate policies. These range all the way from proposals that all monetary and debt-management powers be lodged in the Treasury or in a newly created department of money and finance directly responsible to the government to proposals that all these powers should be lodged in the Federal Reserve. We do not favor either of these extreme proposals. We oppose the concentration of all these powers in the Federal Reserve primarily because we doubt the wisdom of placing one authority in the position of borrower and of determiner of the monetary and credit conditions under which its borrowing will be done, but also because it seems inappropriate to entrust the technical details of managing the debt to an independent agency. We oppose concentration of all these powers in the Treasury, or in a new department responsible to the President, because we fear that considerations relating to service charges on the federal debt and to the ease of refunding would be weighed too heavily and would create a bias toward inflexibly low interest rates and continuously easy money. Moreover, we see only a limited value in proposals designed merely to bring Federal Reserve and Treasury officials into frequent consultations; such consultations already occur.

We recommend that three general methods be employed to secure more appropriate monetary and debt-management policies. In the first place, every effort should be made to build up the quality and prestige of Federal Reserve officials. Measures for this purpose should include (a) decreasing the number of members of the Board of Governors from seven to not more than five in order to make the position attractive to more capable men and to lessen the temptation to appoint men of lesser stature, and (b) raising the salary of the Chairman of the Board of Governors to the same level as the salaries of Cabinet members — namely, $22,500 — and raising the salaries of other Board members to $20,000 a year. Inability to extend such salary increases to certain other officials engaged in bank supervision and examination should not be allowed to prevent Board members from receiving salaries more commensurate with the importance of their functions.

In the second place, we recommend that Congress by joint resolution issue general instructions to the Federal Reserve and the Treasury regarding the objectives of monetary and debt-management policies and the division of authority over these policies. These instructions need not, and in our judgment should not, be detailed; they should accomplish their purpose if they provide, in effect, that, (a) in determining and administering policies relative to money, credit, and management of the federal debt, the Treasury and the Federal Reserve shall be guided primarily by considerations relating to their effects on employment, production, purchasing power, and price levels, and such policies shall be consistent with and shall promote the purpose of the Employment Act of 1946; and (b) it is the will of Congress that the primary power and responsibility for regulating the supply, availability, and cost of credit in general shall be vested in the duly constituted authorities of the Federal Reserve System, and that Treasury action relative to money, credit, and transactions in the federal debt shall be made consistent with the policies of the Federal Reserve. We believe that the issues involved here are of such great importance to the people of the United States that Congress should at this time give these further instructions to the Federal Reserve and the Treasury to guide them in the performance of their functions.

In the third place, we recommend that the Secretary of the Treasury and the Chairman of the Board of Governors of the Federal Reserve System be made members of the National Monetary and Credit Council which we recommend elsewhere in this report.

The "independence" of the Federal Reserve does, of course, create the possibility that the Federal Reserve System might follow policies which were directly at variance with important policies of the executive department and which might tend to defeat an over-all economic program that met the approval of a majority of the American people. In practice, however, this is not a real danger, and seriously adverse effects from any such development can be guarded against without making the Federal Reserve System more directly responsible to the executive department. Federal Reserve officials are kept fully informed as to the government's policies; the executive department is perfectly free to make its views and wishes known to the Federal Reserve, and Congress can always use its investigatory and legislative powers to bring about a change in Federal

Reserve policies if these should at any time prove to be seriously at variance with important national policies.

The effectiveness of monetary and debt-management policies in simultaneously maintaining relatively stable price levels and maximum production and employment is greatly influenced by the appropriateness of other economic policies, and especially those relating to prices and wages. For example, widespread monopolistic increases in prices and a widespread insistence upon unduly large increases in money wage rates could make it impossible for the monetary authority both to maintain relatively stable price levels and maximum production and employment. If in the face of such price and wage policies it refused to supply more money and credit to finance a rise of price levels, it might produce unemployment. And if it supplied the additional money and credit needed to maintain maximum employment and production it might be financing an upward spiral of prices. The monetary authorities may face such a dilemma in the future unless the attitudes of employers and employees are such that wage and price bargains can be arrived at within the framework of a relatively stable general price level.

22

THE CLIMAX OF THE TREASURY–FEDERAL RESERVE DISPUTE*

Marriner S. Eccles†

The Douglas Committee held hearings in late 1949 and issued its report (see Selection 21) in January, 1950. It concluded that "the advantages of avoiding inflation are so great and a restrictive monetary policy can contribute so much to this end, that the freedom of the Federal Reserve to restrict credit and raise interest rates for general stabilization purposes should be restored even if the cost should prove to be a significant increase in service charges on the Federal debt and a greater inconvenience to the Treasury in its sale of securities. . . ."

But this pronouncement did not end the dispute between the Federal Reserve and the Treasury. Another full year elapsed before they would sign a treaty of peace that would in effect implement the recommendations of the Douglas Committee. In the interim, the struggle grew even more intense. In the following selection Marriner Eccles, writing but a few days before the Treasury-Federal Reserve "Accord" of March 4, 1951 (see Selection 23), details the dramatic events that preceded that historic agreement.

* Reprinted from *Beckoning Frontiers* by Marriner S. Eccles, by permission of Alfred A. Knopf, Inc., and the author. Copyright 1950, 1951 by Marriner S. Eccles.

† Chairman of the Board, First Security Corporation. Member of the Board of Governors of the Federal Reserve System from 1934 to 1951 and Chairman from 1934 to 1948.

This is being written during the first part of March 1951. In Korea we are heavily involved in a war with the Chinese Communists. In Europe we now mean to give muscular strength to the skeleton of the North Atlantic Alliance. Here at home we are accelerating a defense production program to provide for our own needs and help meet the needs of other free countries.

The cost of that program has yet to be determined. Let us hope that when the decision is made, it is directly related to our economic potential. I have emphasized this point before. Heretofore, when we mobilized our military strength for war and accepted the regimentation of our entire economy, we could still look forward to a return to "normalcy" when the war ended. We can hold no such hope under present world conditions. In the first place, we are not mobilizing for war; we are mobilizing to deter an enemy from starting a world war. In the second place, there is no termination for our defense preparedness program. It must continue as long as aggressive Communism threatens the peace of the world.

Under these circumstances, what we contribute to the common defense must be planned in relationship to what our economy is willing to pay for currently. The events of the last five months have not in any way changed this basic necessity. The limitation of our human and material resources still make it imperative that we get the greatest possible benefits out of our technological superiority. Only by doing this can we maintain the strength of our position as the arsenal of democracy and thereby carry out our commitments to other free countries of the world while defending ourselves.

Nor have recent events altered the fact that a sound domestic economy is of paramount importance in any adequate defense against Communist aggression. Our diplomats may be able to stave off a third world war. Our fighting men may be able to win such a war if it is forced on us. But whether we avoid the battlefield or triumph on it, we can still lose our domestic freedoms. The very system our defense program is designed to protect can be lost through a complete regimentation of our economy; a regimentation imposed in an effort to prevent the inevitable inflation from either war or a defense program that is beyond our resources or ability to pay for currently. The death toll of inflation in other nations was succinctly described by Senator Paul H.

Douglas in the Senate on February 22, 1951, when he said:

> By wiping out the middle classes and separating society into two classes of the propertyless on the one hand and the rich speculators on the other [inflation] paved the way for fascism and communism on the continent of Europe. It is a destroyer almost as evil as war itself. In the eyes of those who want to destroy democracy and capitalistic institutions it is a cheap way of achieving their collapse. It costs the enemy nothing in lives and treasure. It is really a supreme folly for a nation which is arming against the threat of invasion from without to let this invader, inflation, bring ruin from within.

Have we avoided this supreme folly? The answer is that we have not. In the five years between V-J day and Korea the repeated efforts the Federal Reserve made to deal with a prime source of inflation got nowhere. Within the Administration, the Treasury Department, with its chronic institutional bias toward cheap money, had the final say on monetary and credit policies. Within the Congress, the repeated requests made by the Reserve System for congressional recognition and support of its inflation-control program met with an inadequate and ineffective response. I favored a cheap-money policy during the depression, when millions were unemployed and facilities everywhere lay idle. I reluctantly went along with a cheap-money policy during the war years when we faced the need to finance huge budgetary deficits. But there was no justification for such a policy in the period between V-J day and the present, when we had budgetary surpluses and lived under mounting inflationary pressures. There was no justification for the Treasury's insistence that the Federal Reserve System adhere to a policy of purchasing government securities at the will of the holders and at fixed prices. Such action did not assure confidence in the credit of the government. Instead, it fostered the unwarranted growth of bank reserves that fed the inflationary fires; and these fires slowly consumed the real purchasing power of the dollar. As the Reserve System has repeatedly noted, the credit of the government is determined by the willingness of the public to buy and hold government securities.

When, with this in mind, the Reserve System asked to be free of the Treasury's demand that it buy all securities offered it at fixed prices, this in no way implied a preference for higher interest rates, which would increase the income of all holders. The Federal Reserve was not interested in higher interest rates as such. It is mischievous error to present the issue in these terms. We simply wanted to curb the sale of government securities to the Federal Reserve which add to the reserves and deposits of the banking system; to curb those sales by making the market more self-supporting and less dependent on Federal Reserve purchases. As Dr. E. A. Goldenweiser expressed the issue in the *Wall Street Journal* for February 2, 1951:

. . . An anti-inflationary influence was not expected to be exerted by the rise in short-term rates but by the reduction in funds at the disposal of banks for lending or investing. If rates advanced as a result of the tightness, this would not be the object of policy, nor in itself a means of carrying it out. It would be an incidental result of general credit restriction. Whether desirable in themselves or not the advances in rates would be secondary in importance to the imperative need of restraining the flow of money into buyers' hands.

Furthermore, we at no time urged a completely free market that would be subject to manipulation by private interests. What we wanted was an *orderly* market in which the Federal Reserve maintained control, but where freedom of action would be permitted so as to reflect more nearly the real demand by private investors. Maintenance of an orderly market is not the same thing as maintaining a fixed pattern of rates irrespective of inflationary conditions. It should be remembered that continued support of government securities at fixed prices, of par or above, makes call money, or interest-bearing currency, out of the marketable public debt. If these conditions are to prevail, then the rest of governmental financial policy is illogical. Specifically, what justification is there for various issues of marketable government securities, with their wide variations of maturities and interest rates? Why should the government discriminate against holders of savings bonds by paying them less

interest if they cash them prior to maturity, and at the same time see to it that the holders of remarkable bonds are protected against loss of principle or interest if they sell them before maturity? Why should the so-called "marketable" bonds bear such a designation if prices are not permitted in any degree to reflect market demand?

Questions of this sort met a uniform answer from the Treasury. It cited its paramount need to keep interest rates low and thereby reduce the cost of managing the public debt. If this policy was not justified in the period between V-J day and the Korean war, there was far less justification for it in the months following our involvement in that war. In the period between June 1950 and February 1951 the cost of living rose 7 per cent; wholesale prices, 17 per cent; wholesale prices of farm products, 22 per cent; textile products, 32 per cent; basic raw materials, 50 per cent. These increases were not caused by the production of armament. Thus far, armament production has been small in volume. Neither were they caused by an excess of government spending over receipts. During the second six months of 1950, when prices shot upward, the federal government's receipts exceeded its expenditures by almost $2 billion. To this degree the government's fiscal policies have been a deflationary and not an inflationary force. In fact, increasing congressional support for a vigorous fiscal policy, calling for sharp reductions in nondefense expenditures and a pay-as-you-go tax program, is one of the few hopeful events at the present time.

The price increases in the last seven months of 1950 were due to two interrelated factors. First, there was an increase in the use of the existing excessive supply of money. Second, this existing supply was greatly expanded by an abnormal and rapid growth in bank credit made possible by the Federal Reserve supporting the government security market on the basis of the Treasury's cheap-money policy. Specifically, Reserve System purchases of government securities from nonbank as well as bank investors in this seven-month period created reserves that enabled the banking system to expand its loans and investments by 20 per cent, or about $10 billion, and brought on an estimated 8-per-cent increase in the money supply in the form of deposits.

The significance of this process was not lost on the general public. The resistance of the Reserve System to the Treasury requirement that it support government securities at prevailing fixed prices at last won outside interest and aid. There was a growing awareness that the government was not selling new security issues, nor was it engaged in deficit financing. The budget, instead, showed a surplus for the past year. Yet the volume of money and credit grew sharply. An increasing number of people understood, furthermore, that the growth was directly attributable to the fact that those who held marketable government securities (as distinguished from savings bonds) could readily convert them into money, and in most cases at premium prices. This was made possible by the support policy.

What I've just described was the background for an extraordinary event in the history of relations between the Treasury and the Federal Reserve. At a luncheon meeting of the New York Board of Trade on January 18, 1951, Secretary of the Treasury Snyder announced a policy of debt management for the duration of the emergency. Its manifest purpose was to freeze the existing pattern of rates. The Secretary said:

In the firm belief, after long consideration, that the 2½ per cent long-term rate is fair and equitable to the investor, and that market stability is essential, the Treasury Department has concluded, after joint conferences with President Truman and Chairman McCabe of the Federal Reserve Board, that the refunding of new money issues will be financed within the pattern of that rate.

The announcement came as a special shock to the Federal Reserve System. But it also was a shock to the investment and money market. It gave the impression that Chairman McCabe, and hence the entire Federal Reserve, had agreed to the announced policy. I understand that McCabe neither agreed nor knew that the speech was going to be made. In any case, he could not speak for the other eleven members of the Federal Open Market Committee, who are responsible only to Congress for carrying out their statutory responsibility. Four days after the Snyder announcement, Edward H. Collins, the leading and able financial writer for the *New York Times* began what was to be an increasing public protest. "All that Mr. Snyder has proved," Collins wrote, "would seem to be that he is still top dog at the White House. But this was enough to convince him that he has been right all along, and all this nonsense about short-term money rates and their application to inflation was just so much high falutin book talk, important only for purposes of theoretical debate by central banking authorities."

Collins continued:

More shocking, fundamentally, than this absurd dictum, however, was the simple fact of what seemed to be the Secretary's mission. Central banks in their general policies may from time to time make concessions to the temporary needs of the Exchequer, but when and if they do they announce the fact themselves. In the opinion of this writer, last Thursday constituted the first occasion in history on which the head of the Exchequer of a great nation had either the effrontery or the ineptitude, or both, to deliver a public address in which he has so far usurped the function of the central bank as to tell the country what kind of monetary policy it was going to be subjected to. For the moment at least, the fact that the policy enunciated by Mr. Snyder was, as usual, thoroughly unsound and inflationary, was overshadowed by the historic dimensions of this impertinence.

While criticisms of this sort were being re-echoed throughout newspapers of the nation as well as by economists generally, the Federal Reserve officially observed a discreet silence. However, Allan Sproul, President of the New York Federal Reserve Bank, and the ablest man in the System, replied by indirection to Snyder in the course of a speech before the New York State Banking Association on January 22. Reading between guarded lines, the press correctly interpreted Sproul's remarks as a challenge to Snyder's views. I was less guarded. I restated the Reserve System's case when, at the request of Senator Taft, the ranking Republican member on the Joint Committee on the Economic Report, I was invited to appear before that body on January 25. The Administration leaders on the committee did not want me as a witness; they wanted Chairman McCabe instead, but he begged off because he could foresee the difficult position in which he would be placed. He could not defend the Treasury's position; as Chairman, it would be difficult for him to oppose it publicly without resigning.

Though it appears to have been Secretary Snyder's intention to present the Reserve System with a *fait accompli*, the vigor of the counterattack evidently led him to make a further attempt to get the Federal Reserve committed to the Treasury's announced debt-management policy. On the morning of January 31 the Federal Open Market Committee met in Washington as scheduled. Chairman McCabe advised us shortly after the meeting began that the President wanted him to bring the entire committee to the White House for a conference at four o'clock that afternoon. Notice of the scheduled visit was made public; the press corps who had been following developments closely became very much interested. The committee naturally assumed it was being called to the White House in regard to the Treasury-Reserve controversy. We prepared no formal statement of our position. It was agreed, however, that Chairman McCabe would be the only spokesman of the group and would make no commitments for the committee as to open-market policy.

This was the first time in the history of the Federal Reserve System that a President called either the Reserve Board or the Federal Open Market Committee to the White House for the purpose of discussing or influencing their policies. Until this instance the dictum laid down by Woodrow Wilson and reported by Senator Carter Glass in his book *An Adventure in Constructive Finance*, had been adhered to by all our chief executives. Glass had asked Wilson, the "father" of the Reserve System, why he did not establish closer relations with the Reserve Board he had created. To this Wilson is quoted as saying: "The very moment that I should attempt to establish close re-

lations with the Board, that moment I would be accused of trying to bring political pressure to bear."

What took place at the White House meeting is described in the memorandum that appears directly below. (Though I shall have more to say later about the memorandum, here I merely add that it was written by Governor R. M. Evans at the request of the full Federal Open Market Committee, made that day immediately after we returned to the Federal Reserve Building. It was later approved by the members of the committee after some minor suggested changes were made. Then, on February 3, under extenuating circumstances to be related presently, I released it to the press on my own responsibility and without the knowledge of others on the committee.) The memorandum reads:

The full Federal Open Market Committee met with President Truman in the Cabinet Room shortly after 4 p. m., on Wednesday, Jan. 31, 1951. Chairman [Thomas B.] McCabe had met with the President in his office a few minutes earlier and came into the Cabinet Room with him. The President shook hands cordially with everyone present.

The President stated that during the past few weeks he had met with many groups in the Government because he wanted them to know the seriousness of the present emergency and to ask for their full assistance and co-operation. He stated that the present emergency is the greatest this country has ever faced, including the two world wars and all the preceding wars.

He gave a brief sketch of the difficulty of dealing with the Russians.

The President emphasized that we must combat Communist influence on many fronts. He said one way to do this is to maintain confidence in the Government's credit and in government securities.

He felt that if people lose confidence in government securities all we hope to gain from our military mobilization, and war if need be, might be jeopardized.

He recalled his wartime experience when he bought Liberty Bonds out of his soldier's pay When he returned from France and had to sell his bonds to buy clothes and other civilian things, he got only $80 or a little more for his hundred dollar bonds and later they were run up to $125. He said he did not want the people who hold our bonds now to have done to them what was done to him.[1]

He stated that most politicians would not ask for higher taxes prior to election but that he had vetoed a reduction in taxes before election and won anyway. If it had not been for that irresponsible reduction in taxes, he said, the Federal budget would have been in balance all these years.

He stated that he wanted to levy all the taxes necessary to pay the cost of the defense effort which he felt would be between 100 and 120 billion dollars over the next few years. He stated that he had just met with the Congressional leaders and asked for sixteen and one half billion dollars in taxes and that he expected to get this in two bites — a quick tax bill yielding about ten billion and the other six and one half billion to come after more careful study. He wanted us to understand that he is doing all he can on the tax front to combat inflation.

The President gave each member of the committee a copy of "the Federal Budget in Brief," expressed the opinion that the budget had been pared to an irreducible minimum. He said that he had participated in the preparation of sixteen budgets and felt he was competent to judge and understand them. Maybe something could be cut out but it would make a hole in the defense effort, and that he would not do.

The President said that he felt we had done a good job and wanted us to continue to do a good job in maintaining the financial structure of the country. He further stated that he had had a number of conferences with our chairman but this was his first opportunity to meet and talk with the entire committee. He made no mention of recent differences of opinion with the Treasury.

Chairman McCabe thanked the President for receiving us and indicated that we all share his concern for the maintenance of the Government credit. He stated that although the support of the Government bond market was something in the nature of an extra-curricular activity for the Federal Open Market Committee, it had performed this service for the past nine years or more and had done a very good job.

He stated that the committee had always carefully weighed its responsibilities to the Government and to the general economy as well and that these are statutory responsibilities which it could not assign if it would.

The President interjected that he was familiar with that, but wanted the committee to continue

its good work during the defense period. He emphasized that he was speaking of the defense period only.

Chairman McCabe referred to the fact that in the last few days the Government bond market had gone up a few thirty-seconds and then had come down a few thirty-seconds, which he considered to be a proper market operational technique. The President said he would not undertake to discuss details of that kind, that he was principally concerned with maintaining the confidence of the public in Government securities as one way of presenting a unified front against communism. He did not indicate exactly the details of what he had in mind, but he reiterated that we should do everything possible to maintain confidence in the Government securities market.

The chairman outlined concisely some of the responsibilities with which we were charged, principally to promote stability in the economy by regulating the volume, cost, and availability of money keeping in mind at all times the best interests of the whole economy.

The chairman turned to the members of the Federal Open Market Committee and said the President could depend on every one in the group to do what they could to protect the Government credit.

Chairman McCabe stated that with a group of men such as those composing the Federal Open Market Committee, there would, of course, be differences of opinion as to just how the best results could be obtained.

The President nodded, indicating that he understood this. The chairman suggested the following procedure: that we consult frequently with the Secretary of the Treasury, giving him our views at all times and presenting our point of view strongly, and that by every means possible we try to reach an agreement. If this could not be accomplished, he (the chairman) would like to discuss the matter with the President.

The President said this was entirely satisfactory and closed the meeting on the same note as it was opened — namely, that he wanted us to do everything possible to maintain confidence in the credit of the Government and in the Government securities market and to support the President of the United States in achieving this end.

The chairman stated at the end of the meeting that he presumed that any statement concerning this meeting would be made by the President. The President said he would have no objection to our making a statement and thought that it might be a good thing.

The chairman then asked him what would be the general nature of the statement and he said it

[1] Unlike the marketable bonds of World War I, the savings bonds of World War II are non-marketable and redeemable at predetermined values. Hence present holders of savings bonds are assured against price fluctuations.

can be said that we discussed the general emergency situation, the defense effort, budget and taxes, and that he had stressed the need for public confidence in the Government's credit. He said further that he would be talking to the press the next morning and that he would be prepared to answer questions that might be raised.

Since the President indicated that he would be discussing it with the press the chairman said he felt it would be best for us not to issue any statement to the press at this time. The President did not seem to be particularly concerned about whether or not a statement was issued. The press conference scheduled for the following morning was canceled because of General Eisenhower's appearance at the Capitol.

And that is all that happened.

When the members of the committee returned to the Federal Reserve Building, it was agreed after full discussion that no commitments had been made or, for that matter, sought either directly or indirectly to support the policy Snyder announced on January 18. It was thought advisable, however, that a memorandum should be made of what had happened at the White House. Thereupon the committee adjourned to meet again in two weeks.

Around noon of the next day the following release appeared on the ticker tape:

WASHINGTON (AP) — The Federal Reserve Board has pledged its support to President Truman to maintain the stability of Government securities as long as the emergency lasts.

White House Press Secretary Joseph Short announced this today, saying there have been reports of differences of opinion between the Treasury and the Federal Reserve Board.

"This is to quiet those rumors," Short said.

Members of the Federal Reserve Board conferred with Mr. Truman yesterday. Secretary of the Treasury Snyder did not attend the meeting.

Almost immediately thereafter a second story appeared on the ticker tape. Its source was identified as a "Treasury spokesman," and he translated the White House statement as an approval of the position Secretary Snyder took in New York on January 18. The story read:

WASHINGTON (AP) — A Treasury spokesman said that the White House announcement means the market for government securities will be established at present levels and that these levels will be maintained during the present emergency.

As a result of the White House and Treasury statements I received a call from Alfred Friendly of the *Washington Post* and from Felix Belair, Jr., of the *New York Times*. They both observed that the stories on the wires indicated that the Reserve System, under pressure from the President on the previous day, had capitulated to the Treasury. They wanted to know whether this was true. I replied that it was not. There were no commitments and there was no pressure. I indicated briefly what was the sense of the White House meeting. This was reflected in the accounts the two men wrote for the next day's editions of their newspapers. They made it plain that despite the White House statement indicating a truce in the long-standing controversy over credit policy between the Treasury and the Federal Reserve, the dispute had not been settled.

At the time I spoke to Friendly and Belair, I did not know that the interpretation placed on the White House meeting by the Treasury spokesman was being confirmed in a letter that was evidently prepared in the Treasury for the President's signature; it was on its way to McCabe that Thursday afternoon. On Friday morning, at the request of Governor James K. Vardaman, the Board of Governors went into an executive session. Vardaman had read the Friendly article in the *Post* and wanted to know who provided him with the information it contained. "An article like that could only come from someone who was present at the White House," Vardaman observed. I at once said that I gave Friendly the information from which he could write his story. I do not believe Vardaman expected this prompt and frank admission. His only response was that what I did was inappropriate. I said that under ordinary circumstances I would fully agree with him and would be equally critical of any such disclosure; nevertheless, I felt that, in view of the real facts, the White House press release and particularly the Treasury interpretation of it called for a prompt denial.

On this same morning individual members of the Board of Governors were shown the letter McCabe had received from the President the day before. Addressed to "Dear Tom," its most significant passages read:

Your assurance that you would fully support the Treasury defense financing program, both as to refunding and new issues, is of vital importance to me. As I understand it, I have your assurance that the market on Government securities will be stabilized and maintained at present levels in order to assure the successful financing requirements and to establish in the mind of the people confidence concerning Government credit.

I wish you would convey to all the members of your group my warm appreciation of their cooperative attitude.

It would understate our reaction to say we were surprised by what we read. After some informal discussion, it was felt that the only way the matter could be handled was to have McCabe see the President as soon as possible, show him the memorandum Governor Evans had prepared at the direction of the Federal Open Market Committee, and then request that the letter be withdrawn, since it did not reflect the understanding of the committee. This could be done without embarrassment at this time since the letter had not been released. Meanwhile the stories in the morning editions of the *Washington Post* and the *New York Times* no doubt alerted the Treasury (and possibly the White House) to the fact that the Open Market Committee would continue to resist any pressure to support the Treasury's announced policy. With the apparent intention of ending both this resistance and the doubts raised in the press as to future Federal Reserve policy, late Friday afternoon the President's letter to McCabe was publicly released without notice either to McCabe or to anyone connected with the Reserve System. Other members of the Reserve Board and staff had left their offices for the week-end. Around seven o'clock in the evening I, too, was preparing to leave my office in the Reserve Building. But my plans were changed when Felix Belair of the *New York Times* called me on the phone.

He began: "I thought you said the Open Market Committee hadn't agreed at the White House Conference to support the market for government securities at present levels."

"That's right," I replied.

"Well, then, listen to this."

He proceeded to read me the text of the President's letter to McCabe.

"Where did you get that?" I asked him when he was through. "I thought that was a confidential letter."

"Why, the White House has just released it to the world," Belair said. "What have you got to say to that?"

"I don't know," I said. "Let me think about it. I'll call you later."

The pattern of recent events made it clear that the release of the letter was a final move in a Treasury attempt to impose its will on the Federal Reserve. If swift action was not taken to offset the effect of the move, the Federal Reserve would no longer have a voice in deciding monetary and credit policies. It would lose the independent status Congress meant it to have and, in its most important function of open-market operations, it would be reduced to the level of a Treasury bureau. I resolved that this would not happen. At a loss for any better means available at that moment, I felt the best chance that the System had to preserve any of its independence was to release the confidential memorandum covering the meeting with the President. Any objective-minded person who read it could not escape the conclusion that the President's letter to McCabe did not reflect what was said at the White House. But the memorandum had to be released promptly if it was to be effective. I felt that McCabe, whom the President had chosen to head the Board of Governors, could not release the memorandum without at the same time submitting his resignation as Chairman. In any case, McCabe was at his home in Pennsylvania. I also knew it would be impossible to bring together the full Open Market Committee until the first part of the week. I doubted whether the committee would release the memordandum even at that time, or whether it would be appropriate for it to take such official action. (As I've already intimated, whatever their private views, no other member of the committee, with the exception of Allan Sproul, voiced any public protest against the policy announced by Snyder on January 18.) The logic of fairly recent events pointed to me as the one who might be expected to assume the initiative in this matter because more than a year before, in testimony before the Douglas subcommittee investigating Treasury-Reserve relations, I had noted the imperative need to clarify what appeared to be a conflict of responsibility. Again, in testimony before the Joint Committee on the Economic Report on January 25, 1951, I critically pointed out the inflationary effects should the Reserve System support Secretary Snyder's debt-management policy as he announced it on January 18.

Another aspect of this decision should be mentioned. Three days before, I had written but not yet submitted my letter of resignation to the President. It was to be effective March 1, and would mark the end of seventeen years in the government, of which sixteen years were spent as a member of the Reserve Board. In the months immediately preceding the writing of that letter I had also completed plans to return to my home in Utah and to private business interests in the West. But it was evident that if I released the memorandum, I could not submit my resignation without making it appear that I was running from an unpleasant situation I had precipitated. I therefore postponed sending it.

The only copy of the committee's memorandum was in the hands of Sam Carpenter, the secretary to the Board of Governors. I called him at his home and told him what I had learned through Belair. I then asked Carpenter if he could come to the Federal Reserve Building and show me the memorandum so that I could see whether it in any way justified the President's letter to McCabe. After an interval Carpenter reached my office. The pages he showed me bore penciled notations, representing the minor changes agreed to earlier in the day. At my request, he left his memorandum with me, though I did not tell him what I meant to do with it.

By the time my secretary had copied the text, it was eleven o'clock. I then called Belair and told him I might have a statement to make, but wanted to sleep on it. I promised to get in touch with him the next morning. A night's sleep did not change my view. In response to my call on Saturday morning, Belair appeared at my apartment in the Shoreham Hotel. He repeated his question: "What is your view of the President's version of his meeting with the Federal Open Market Committee as explained in his public letter to Chairman McCabe?" In reply I handed him a statement I'd prepared. It read:

I'm astonished. The only answer I can make is to give you a copy of the record of what took place at the White House meeting, as agreed upon by the other members of the Federal Open Market Committee and from which I have deleted only certain references which deal with the international and military situation. Any other comment would be superfluous. I am giving you this solely upon my own responsibility and without the knowledge of other members of the Committee. It is most unfortunate that this vitally important matter of money and credit which Congress has placed in the Federal Reserve System has been raised in a manner which only needlessly adds to confusion.

At my request, Belair gave a copy of the statement and the memorandum to the editors of the *Washington Post* and the *Washington Evening Star*. It was front-page news on Sunday, February 4. In these, as in all other newspapers throughout the country that carried the story, the universal judgment was that the record of what had happened at the White House did not support the version expressed in the President's letter to McCabe. The memorandum contained no reference to the maintenance of the government-securities market to present levels, to the pattern of rates announced by Secretary Snyder, or to the refunding of new issues. It indicated that President Truman declined to discuss the behavior of the government-securities market and that he simply spoke in general terms about the need to maintain confidence in the government's credit. All this aside, without understanding the technical details of the controversy, the public gained the impression that the White House was putting pressure on an organization that was meant to be independent of political influences. As a result of this, public sentiment, and hence congressional sentiment, swung to the support of the Federal Reserve.

By Monday morning the fat was in the fire. Rather than wait for the scheduled meeting on February 13, McCabe called the Open Market Committee to meet the next day, Tuesday, February 6. The purpose was to consider what should be done in view of the week-end development. With the exception of Allan Sproul, no one at the meeting either approved or criticized my action in releasing the memorandum. Sproul expressed the view that what goes on at a Presidential conference should not be disclosed until the President gives it out, but when the President does that, he should give an accurate report of what has happened. It was the Board's memorandum and not the President's letter to McCabe that accurately represented what actually was said and the spirit in which it was said. For this reason, Sproul continued, he was glad I had taken individual action in releasing the memorandum; it temporarily retrieved our place in the financial community and with the public. In my reply I expressed regret that the situation had developed to the point where releasing a confidential document seemed absolutely essential. I purposely avoided telling anybody what I was going to do because I did not want to involve anyone else in any way.

Turning to the larger question that justified the release of the memorandum, I said that it was as important for the Open Market Committee to do everything in its power to try to prevent inflation as it was important that a successful defense program be carried out. "If we fail in this task," I said, "history may well record that we were responsible in great measure for helping to bring about the destruction of the very system our defense effort is designed to protect. We should not delay action; in retrospect I think we have been derelict in not acting more aggressively, particularly since Korea. We know what *we* should do in this inflationary situation. We should publicly inform the President, the Treasury, and the Congress of what we propose to do, and then do it. Otherwise the public will get the impression that we have capitulated and lack the courage to discharge our responsibilities. If Congress objects to our actions it can change the law; but until it does that, we have a clear responsibility to check inflation — in so far as we can do this within the framework of our authority — by preventing a further growth in the supply of money and credit at this time."

At the suggestion of Allan Sproul, the committee agreed that a letter would be sent to the President to get the current issue back on an official basis; also, that another attempt be made to resume negotiations with the Treasury along the lines McCabe had suggested to the President at our White House meeting. Before the day was over, the proposed letter to the President was drafted and approved, as was the second letter to the Secretary of the Treasury reopening the door for further discussion of debt-management policies. It was our hope that the White House would release our reply, since it clearly stated the reasons underlying the committee's position and was a complete answer to the President's letter to McCabe. Our reply was approved by every member of the Open Market Committee except one, who had close White House connections. However, when reporters later pressed the President with questions about our letter, he replied that he had not yet seen it. Meanwhile, efforts were made by Administration leaders and by members of the White House staff to get the Open Market Committee to withdraw what we had written. The committee was unwilling to do this.

At this writing, at a time when there is widespread concern over inflationary dangers, it is difficult to predict the long-run significance of bringing the controversy between the Treasury and the Federal Reserve out in the open for public and congressional discussion. As for myself, I am mildly hopeful that the System will exercise a greater degree of independence in the use of its powers in helping to maintain economic stability. The Federal Reserve has a very difficult role to play in this undertaking. Its actions are seldom popular. If it is to succeed in its mission, it will need great internal strength in its composition, great courage in its action, and a sustained public and congressional understanding of the role it should play in our society of democratic capitalism.

23

THE TREASURY—FEDERAL RESERVE ACCORD*

The Patman Committee

The Federal Reserve-Treasury dispute ended with a joint announcement by the two agencies on March 4, 1951. The effect of the agreement, known as the "Accord," was to restore the independence of the Federal Reserve to pursue flexible monetary policies. Purchases of short-term securities were promptly discontinued. Although the Federal Reserve continued to buy Treasury bonds for a brief period, they were bought at a gradually declining scale of prices (that is, at higher interest rates) and soon ceased altogether.

The Treasury-Federal Reserve accord of March 4, 1951, was described to the Subcommittee in identical language by the Secretary of the Treasury and the Chairman of the Board of Governors of the Federal Reserve System. This description is as follows:

Throughout the period from August 1950 to February 1951, there were frequent consultations between Federal Reserve and Treasury officials, and on some occasions with the President, concerning the coordination of monetary and debt management policies. These discussions preceded the working out of the accord between the Treasury and the Federal Reserve concerning policies that deal with their related problems.

The following joint announcement was made on March 3, 1951, for publication March 4, by the Secretary of the Treasury and the Chairman of the Board of Governors and of the Federal Open Market Committee of the Federal Reserve System:

"The Treasury and the Federal Reserve System have reached full accord with respect to debt-management and monetary policies to be pursued in furthering their common purpose to assure the successful financing of the Government's requirements and, at the same time, to minimize monetization of the public debt."

This statement reflected agreements that had been reached, following extended discussion between representatives of the two agencies, regard-

* From *Monetary Policy and Management of the Public Debt,* Report of the Sub-committee on General Credit Control and Debt Management (Patman Committee) of the Joint Committee on the Economic Report, U.S. Congress, 1952. (Italics supplied.)

ing their mutual and related problems. The presumed area of difference had become greatly magnified in the newspaper and other public discussion and there was urgent need to reassure the public that the Treasury and the Federal Reserve were in agreement as to proper debt management and monetary policies in the situation then existing.

The Treasury and Federal Reserve felt that everything possible should be done to terminate the unwholesome situation that had developed *and to coordinate the debt management responsibility of the Treasury with the Federal Reserve responsibility for restraining credit expansion.* It was the immediate object of the Treasury to restore conditions in the market that would be favorable to refinancing the large volume of maturing obligations, as well as financing several billions of new money required during the remainder of the year. It was the immediate object of the Federal Reserve to endeavor to curb the unprecedented inflationary loan expansion that had continued uninterruptedly since Korea *by minimizing the monetization of the public debt and by making it necessary for member banks to borrow from the Federal Reserve in order to obtain additional reserves.* With these basic objectives in view, representatives of the fiscal and technical staffs of the Treasury and the Federal Reserve had been designated to engage in a series of discussions and to formulate a proposal which might serve as a basis for policy decision.

The discussions between the Treasury and the Federal Reserve had made it clear that there were many areas of agreement between the Federal Reserve and the Treasury with respect to the solution of these problems; that the cooperation between the Treasury and the Federal Reserve had been of exceptionally high order on most matters of mutual concern; that there are bound to be differences of opinion now and then between agencies, as there are between individuals in the same agencies; but that such differences could be diminished by closer, regularized liaison with respect to mutual problems. It was agreed that there were both immediate and long-run factors which had to be taken into account in arriving at an accord, and that the purpose of the negotiation was to reach agreement upon policies that would reduce to a minimum the monetization of the public debt without creating an adverse market psychology with reference to Government securities.

First, consideration was given to the matter of long-term bonds overhanging the market and at the time being offered for sale daily in large amounts. It was agreed that a substantial portion of these bonds could be taken off the market by a Treasury offer to exchange for them a non-marketable 2¾ per cent, 29-year bond, redeemable at the holder's option before maturity only by conversion into a 5-year marketable Treasury note. The purpose of offering this new security, as announced by the Treasury, *was to encourage long-term investors to retain their holdings of Government securities, in order to minimize the monetization of the public debt through liquidation of outstanding holdings of the Treasury bonds of 1967–72.* The Federal Reserve agreed to help the Treasury in explaining to large institutional investors the nature and purpose of this new issue. The extent of the acceptance of the offering testified to the success of this joint endeavor.

Second, there was the problem of the long-term Government securities which private holders might try to sell on the market after the terms of the exchange offering became public. It was agreed that a limited volume of open market purchases would be made after the exchange offering was announced; and that if sales on the market were excessive, *the situation would be assessed daily, the market would be kept orderly, and open market purchases, if any, would be made on a scaledown of prices.*

Third, the pending task of refunding the large volume of short-term securities maturing or callable in the near future presented difficult problems both for the Treasury and for the Federal Reserve. *It was agreed that the Federal Reserve, in order to minimize monetization of the debt, would immediately reduce or discontinue purchases of short-term securities* and permit the short-term market to adjust to a position at which banks would depend upon borrowing at the Federal Reserve to make needed adjustments in their reserves. This contemplated a level of short-term interest rates which, in response to market forces, would fluctuate around the Federal Reserve discount rate. It was expected that during the remainder of the year the Federal Reserve discount rate, in the absence of compelling circumstances not then foreseen, would remain at 1¾ per cent and that the Federal Reserve would operate to assure a satisfactory volume of exchanges in the refunding of maturing Treasury issues.

Fourth, the raising of new funds by the Treasury to finance the defense mobilization program presented other problems. It was recognized that there were no substantial amounts of nonbank funds seeking investment, and that it would be some time before such funds would accumulate. It was agreed that more frequent conferences between the Treasury and Federal Reserve officials and staff should be held so that the Federal Reserve might collaborate more closely with the Treasury in working out a joint program of Government financing as well as in maintaining orderly markets for Government securities.

CHAPTER EIGHT

OPEN MARKET OPERATIONS

24

THE SIGNIFICANCE AND LIMITATIONS OF FREE RESERVES*

Peter D. Sternlight and Robert Lindsay†

One of the most frequently used concepts in present-day analysis of Federal Reserve policy is that of member bank "free reserves," defined as member bank excess reserves less their borrowings from the Federal Reserve Banks. The following article from the Monthly Review of the Federal Reserve Bank of New York explains the background and implications of the concept.

Each Friday morning, in the financial pages of major newspapers, there appears an item on member bank reserve positions. And, more often than not, the emphasis in these stories falls heaviest on the recent change in "free reserves" — or, as it is termed when negative, "net borrowed reserves." The prominence given this measure of reserve availability reflects in part the desire to find a single measure for interpreting Federal Reserve policy actions that are necessarily complex. While changes in the availability of bank reserves, and the resulting pressures exerted upon the liquidity of banks and their capacity to expand credit, lie at the heart of monetary and credit control, there is an understandably human tendency at times to oversimplify. It is therefore important that the meaning of the free reserves concept be

thoroughly understood, and its limitations always kept in mind. Especially is it important to realize that a specific level of free reserves (negative or positive) may be associated with one degree of credit restraint or ease at one time, and with significantly different credit conditions in other periods.

THE MEANING OF FREE RESERVES

The concept itself is, of course, an outgrowth of the legal requirement that member banks hold reserves equal to a specified percentage of their deposits. Member bank reserve balances in excess of these required reserves are known as "excess reserves," and as such they are an indicator of surplus primary liquidity in the banking system. However, when member banks are obtaining a relatively large proportion of their reserves by borrowing from the Federal Reserve to meet temporary reserve needs, a given volume of excess reserves does not have the same significance, in terms of reserve availability and credit expansion po-

* From *Monthly Review*, Federal Reserve Bank of New York (November, 1958). Reprinted by the courtesy of the Federal Reserve Bank of New York and the authors.

† Now Deputy Undersecretary of the Treasury for Monetary Affairs, and Professor of Finance at New York University, respectively.

tential, as when the banks have little need for recourse to borrowing. This stems from the fact that member bank borrowing from the Reserve Banks, although it is a source of reserves and therefore potential backing for bank deposits, may be undertaken only temporarily by any single bank. For the individual bank it is a stopgap. Rather than resort too frequently or on too large a scale to the "discount window," a member bank must take other steps to maintain or restore its reserve position — perhaps through liquidating investments or restricting loan volume. Thus a bank in debt to the Federal Reserve is always under pressure, because it is necessarily in search of funds in order to repay.

In the early years of the Federal Reserve System, the volume of member bank borrowings was widely used as an index of money market pressures, particularly after the mid-twenties, as the realization grew that changes in this volume moved in close tandem with interest rate changes. During most of the 1930's, however, member banks held large amounts of excess reserves, and did little or no borrowing at the Reserve Banks after the "bank holiday" in 1933. Attention thus shifted to excess reserves as a measure of reserve availability and potential credit expansion. In more recent years, many member banks have again found it necessary to borrow frequently, even while excess reserves existed elsewhere in the banking system. Indeed, near the close of a reserve-accounting period, the same member bank might simultaneously be holding excess reserves and borrowing additional reserves from the central bank in order to meet a reserve deficit accumulated earlier in the period. Thus, taken alone, neither excess reserves nor borrowings can provide an adequate continuing measure of credit availability.

To meet the need for such a measure, the concept of "free reserves" — defined as excess reserves less member bank borrowings from the Reserve Banks — was developed. By the same token, "net borrowed reserves," or "negative free reserves," exist when total member bank borrowings from the Federal Reserve Banks are larger than excess reserves.

The fluctuations in free (or net borrowed) reserves, excess reserves, and borrowings from the Reserve Banks are shown in Chart 1 for the period since 1949. It may be noted that, while excess reserves have been fairly stable, free reserves have moved over a wide range, marking out the major swings between monetary ease and restraint. Because excess reserves tend to vary to a relatively small extent, it is sometimes satisfactory to use member bank borrowings alone, rather than free reserves, as a measure of greater or less credit restraint. At times, however, there will be sizable movements (or small, but still significant, movements) in excess reserves that are automatically picked up by the free reserves-net borrowed reserves concept, but that might be lost from sight if borrowings were the sole criterion.

The volume of free reserves in the banking system is affected by a number of influences. First, there are what may be grouped together as technical market or operating factors, which affect mainly the reserve base, and include among others the volume of Federal Reserve float, the amount of currency in circulation, and various international transactions. Secondly, there is the amount of required reserves, as determined by the volume of bank deposits (which in turn reflect primarily the amount of bank credit outstanding). Finally, there are Federal Reserve operations, either in the form of open market operations or in the form of changes in reserve requirement percentages. The latter are usually made only at infrequent intervals to effect massive changes in reserve availability. Open market operations are conducted flexibly from day to day and often are directed only at offsetting the effects of other influences on the reserve base, but they are also used to bring about major shifts in the availability of reserves and hence in credit conditions.

Obviously, such major policy shifts are reflected, at different times and under different conditions, in different levels of free reserves. When free reserves are both positive and relatively high, member banks would usually find themselves actively seeking to acquire earning assets, and hence increasing the money supply.

CHART 1

Excess Reserves, Borrowings, and Free Reserves, 1950–1958
Annual averages of daily figures

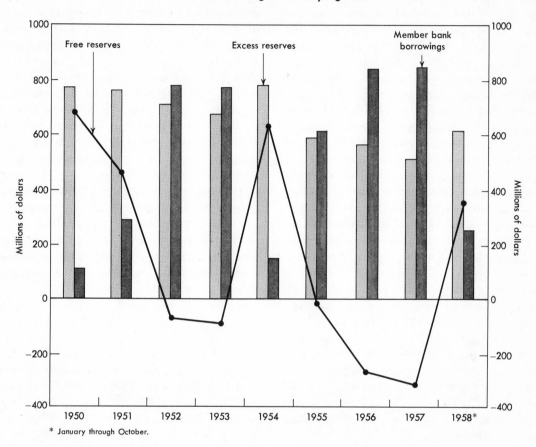

* January through October.

But the level of free reserves at which such results may be expected is not fixed and immobile. The figure would have to be higher, for example, when the national total of free reserves included a heavy concentration in those member banks that habitually maintain substantial excess reserves (usually "country" banks). Money market banks are generally more aggressive in seeking outlets for excess funds than are country banks, so that the significance of any national total of free reserves, or of net borrowed reserves, must depend in part upon the distribution of the total. The significance of any level of free reserves is clearly also influenced by such other factors as the existing state of bank liquidity and the strength of current demand for loans, both na-

tion-wide and among classes of banks. At times when banks have, for example, higher ratios of loans to deposits, or of long-term loans to short-term loans, they may be less responsive to higher levels of free reserves. Should the demand for bank credit be unusually strong, somewhat lower levels of free reserves might well produce a suitable influence upon credit availability, and an appropriate rate of growth in the money supply.

When free reserves are held for some time at a relatively high level, member banks will not only continue to make loans available to their customers — and probably more readily available than at lower levels of free reserves — but they are also likely to seek out new investment opportunities aggressively, acquiring Treasury securities and other debt instruments as a means of putting these additional funds to work. But a time of credit ease and large free reserves is also a time of slackened business activity, so that the demand for loans that banks are willing to make may be weak. For this reason, banks will tend to increase their holdings of securities relative to loan assets. Thus a period of substantial free reserves is likely to be a time when banks are enhancing their secondary liquidity. In the course of this process, securities prices will be bid up, and the entire structure of money market interest rates will move lower — from yields on Treasury bills to rates on business loans. At the same time, as the banks acquire investments, and deposits increase correspondingly, the money supply expands, the liquidity of the nonbank public is increased, and interest rates on bonds and mortgages tend to decline. It is in this way, through the pressure of an enlarged supply of bank funds seeking investment against a reduced demand for bank credit, that there is a tendency for a high level of free reserves to be associated with falling interest rates, increased liquidity in the banking system, expansion of credit, and growth in the money supply.

In a similar way, the maintenance of free reserves at relatively low levels (and especially levels going well down into the negative range) sets in motion an opposite set of reactions. To avoid becoming too deeply or too steadily indebted to the Reserve Banks, member banks tend to finance the expansion of their loans by liquidating secondary reserve assets. Under this continued selling pressure, securities prices generally fall and interest rates rise. Or in some cases, as securities prices fall, banks may become increasingly unwilling to take the capital losses entailed in selling their investments and may turn instead to limiting the extension of loans. In any event, the result of sustained net borrowed reserves is restraint on bank credit, a lessened expansion (or possibly a moderate contraction) of the money supply, and a curbing of liquidity both within and outside the banking system.

It is important to realize, in addition, that the easing or restraining effects are related primarily to the level of free reserves that is being maintained and are not dependent upon continuing further changes in that level. To be sure, as noted above, a given magnitude of free reserves may induce different degrees of ease at different times, depending on a variety of influences. But, in maintaining whatever degree of ease or restraint has been achieved under the conditions prevailing at any particular time, it is not necessary for free reserves or net borrowed reserves to rise continuously to higher and higher levels, as has sometimes been supposed. For example, when a level has been found at which banks genuinely "feel easy," they will continue adding securities to their portfolios, thus increasing their own secondary liquidity and the money supply, as long as their reserve balances continue (in the aggregate and on average) to increase sufficiently to cover the growth in their required reserves. This process does not necessarily require any further increase in the average volume of free reserves.

LIMITATIONS OF THE CONCEPT

It is the loose fit of any specific level of free reserves to any degree of credit ease or restraint that creates the basic limitation of the concept as a precise indicator of actual credit conditions. For this reason, along with other more technical considerations, it is a mistake to assume a rigorous correspondence between, on the one hand, any given level of free reserves and, on the other hand, the availability of reserves to banks or the availability of bank credit to the nonbank public.

LIMITED MEASURE OF RESERVE AVAILABILITY

Suppose, for example, that the Federal Reserve authorities were to try to rely on this measure alone, and elected to maintain a constant level of free reserves, well above any levels previously attained, as a sure sign of genuine ease. As banks make use of existing free reserves to enlarge their investment or loan portfolios, deposits and thus required reserves will rise, thereby reducing the level of free reserves. So long as the monetary authorities wish to maintain the target level for free reserves, they must continue to create new reserves (probably through open market purchases) to match the increase in required reserves. And each new injection of reserves may simply disappear into required reserves as the banks lend or invest even more. There thus may be a continuing increase in total reserves, the money supply, and the liquidity of the economy, without any appreciable rise in the averages of free reserves. Relatively constant free reserves at this "disappearance" level would not imply a constant level of reserve availability (or of bank credit).

This description applies equally well, it may be noted, to periods of Treasury financing. During such periods, the central bank usually attempts to maintain an "even keel," so far as its own operations are concerned. With the provision of reserves sufficient to enable the banks to fulfill their underwriting function, and initially carry the bulk of the securities by means of temporary credit creation, the end result, so far as free reserves are concerned, may be little or no change. Moreover, once the distribution phase begins, reserves may be reabsorbed in whole or in part by the central bank, while the bank-held securities are dispersed into the hands of ultimate investors. Thus, it is quite possible that a well-integrated program of central bank aid to the market and the Treasury, during the technical phase of subscription and initial redistribution, may result in substantial changes up and down in total reserves, without any appreciable change in the averages of free reserves from week to week.

An illustration of this general limitation of the concept may be found in the experience of the first half of 1958. Following a steep rise in late 1957 and early 1958, as credit policy shifted from restraint to ease, aggregate free reserves remained around $500 million from March through July 1958. Yet Treasury bill yields and other short-term interest rates continued to head lower for several months after the plateau in free reserves was reached, as did loan-deposit ratios for weekly reporting banks. The nation's money supply also expanded considerably further after the first quarter of the year. Thus, a process which resulted in a relatively steady (though indeed high) level of free

reserves meant the continuous supplying of reserve balances, and fostered greater and greater liquidity and an expansion of the money supply.

LIMITED MEASURE OF BANK CREDIT AVAILABILITY

However, the mere existence of additional reserve balances will not by itself insure that member banks will be willing to extend additional credit to the nonbank public. Judging the availability of bank credit merely on the basis of the free reserve level might be compared to weighing the liquidity of a corporation simply on the basis of its current cash balance and some particular segment of its current short-term debt. Obviously, a variety of other assets and liabilities, as well as records of past performance, must also be taken into account. Thus, in judging the availability of credit from the banking system, consideration must be given to such factors as the distribution of bank assets among loans and investments of varying degrees of liquidity, the size and composition of bank liabilities, and the level and structure of interest rates. In addition, explicit consideration must be given to the manner in which the banking system has responded to past patterns of free reserves.

In the latter part of 1956, for example, credit availability was generally under pressure even though net borrowed reserves declined markedly (that is, free reserves rose). The maintenance of restraint in this case was partly a result of the usual seasonal buildup of demand for bank credit. However, is was also an outgrowth of the increasing pressures that had been brought to bear on the banking system through 1955 and 1956, as the Federal Reserve System sought to limit the rapid expansion of credit. In particular, bank liquidity had been steadily diminishing. Moreover, new uncertainties were injected into the money and capital markets by the Suez crisis and the approach of a national election.

Accordingly, it was considered desirable, in order to avoid unduly heightening the degree of restraint, to ease up somewhat on the level of free reserves. Thus, free reserves rose (or, more accurately, net borrowed reserves declined) substantially in the last several months of 1956 while, nonetheless, Treasury bill rates and other money market yields moved considerably higher.

VOLATILITY

At a more technical level, the usefulness of free reserves-net borrowed reserves as an indicator of credit conditions is limited by its tendency to fluctuate sharply in short periods. To some extent, these swings occur because the factors that affect reserves cannot always be fully foreseen and offset by Federal Reserve open market operations. For example, the pre-Christmas outflow of currency into circulation might proceed more rapidly than usual, causing an unexpected tightening of reserve positions. Usually, if the unforeseen easing or tightening lasts for only a very short time (say for a few days), the effects on credit conditions will be quite small, perhaps extending only to the market for Federal funds and the shortest dated Treasury bills. But if the "aberration" lasts for a longer time, or if market psychology at the time is for some reason particularly sensitive to hints of possible changes in credit conditions, the reaction may be considerably greater.

Not all of the fluctuation in free reserves is a result of such unexpected developments; at times, relatively large short-term movements are foreseen but not offset. For the most part, as noted above, very short-run changes in the statistics have little material effect on the credit climate; indeed, the attempt to smooth out each wiggle in the statistics might have much more disturbing market repercussions than the fluctuation in free reserves itself. For example, there is typically a rise in free reserves (or decline in net borrowed reserves) at about the third week of each month, coinciding with the regular monthly rise in float and return flow of currency. To offset fully the reserve bulge caused in this way would require a rapid succession of reversals in the direction of Federal Reserve open market operations, which would tend to upset and confuse the money market. To a considerable extent, the more alert participants in the market have become accustomed to an increase of free reserves in the third week of the month; since the condi-

tion is recognized as being only temporary, it does not produce the credit-easing effects sometimes associated with higher free reserves. Offsetting action often is taken but never mechanically, and only rarely would the fluctuation be fully counteracted.

GEOGRAPHIC DISTRIBUTION

Probably the most frequent cause of week-to-week variability in the condition of the money market is not the aggregate volume of free reserves but rather changes in the geographical distribution of these reserves. For example, a dealer in Government securities located in the central money market, might see from the weekly figures published on Friday morning that total member bank free reserves averaged $500 million in the statement week ended the previous Wednesday, and then wonder why he had experienced any difficulty in arranging bank loans to finance his firm's securities holdings. More often than not, the answer will be that free reserves were concentrated in country banks or possibly in some of the reserve city banks as well, while the larger banks in other centers and the New York money market banks had little or none to spare.

CONCLUSION

For all its limitations, the free reserves concept remains a useful guide to the interpretation of credit policy. It cannot stand alone, as a single, all-purpose indicator of liquidity or credit availability, but for that matter neither can any other measure. Even changes in the discount rate, although often taken by the general public as a signal of central bank intentions, may signify nothing more than a technical adjustment to prevailing market rates of interest. However, viewed together with other factors, such as the banking system's ratio of loans to deposits, the size and turnover rate of the money supply, the volume and growth of bank credit, and trends in various market interest rates, and with due regard for regional differences around the country, the amount of free or net borrowed reserves can give a useful lead in the interpretation of changing credit conditions. Clearly, it is more meaningful than either excess reserves, or total borrowings, taken alone, and represents another in the continually unfolding series of aids that can be used in analyzing current monetary developments and Federal Reserve policy.

25

RECENT MONETARY CONTROVERSY*

Paul A. Samuelson†

Since open market operations are acknowledged as the main weapon of the Federal Reserve System, a considerable amount of controversy has been generated in recent years by the Federal Reserve's 1953 decision to limit its open market operations to the purchase and sale of short-term Government securities, mainly Treasury bills. From 1953 to 1961 the Federal Reserve deliberately eschewed buying or selling intermediate or long-term securities.

In the following selection Professor Samuelson reviews the history of the Federal Reserve System. Against that background, he discusses the doctrine of operating only in short-term securities, frequently termed the "bills only" or "bills usually" policy.

Voltaire defined history as a fable agreed upon. In this sense of the word I can briefly sketch the history of American central banking as a background for discussion of current monetary issues.

1. INSTITUTIONAL DEVELOPMENTS

In the first years of this century we had periodic crises and panics in the money market. These pathologies were diagnosed as being due to the *inelasticity* of our National Banking system. So, after a decade of hot debate, in 1913 the Federal Reserve System was established.

Characteristic of our American distrust in centralisation was the decision to create twelve regional Federal Reserve Banks. This agreeable fiction of decentralisation and regionalism has many small advantages in terms of communication with the hinterland: it provides listening posts for grass-roots public opinion; it improves the architecture of some of our great cities; and it provides honorific posts for representatives of industry, agriculture, banking and the public. But very soon it became clear to all that we had indeed created a central bank, inevitably and not improperly dominated by New York and Washington. And this trend toward centralisation continues even into the present day. To illustrate: If I find myself in violent disagreement with current monetary policy, my friends at the local Boston Federal Reserve Bank would think me mad to subject *them* to bitter criticism. The privilege to be criticised bitterly is recognisably located in Washington and New York, and in that order.

It is more than forty years since the Federal Reserve was founded. Most of the giants who then walked the earth are now gone. Only their children, principally daughters, remain. And most of these, it would seem, make great

* From *The Three Banks Review*: a publication of the Royal Bank of Scotland, William Deacon's Bank Limited and Glyn, Mills & Co., No. 29 (March, 1956). Reprinted by the courtesy of the publisher and the author.

† Massachusetts Institute of Technology.

claims on behalf of their sires for *the* basic idea underlying the Federal Reserve. This gives rise to an adding-up problem in which the imputed claims add up to more than 100 per cent of the whole — surely an harmonious and harmless social solution. But what is perhaps more notable is the fact that people seem most anxious to claim credit for that basic feature of the Federal Reserve System which has come in time to be almost completely repudiated. I refer to the notion that the Federal Reserve exists for the purpose of providing automatic *elasticity* of our currency and credit through its mechanism of providing new reserves to the commercial banks whenever they bring to its 'rediscount window' the endorsed promissory notes of their customers as collateral for a loan or rediscount. I do not know whether Glass, or Warburg, or Willis, or President Wilson himself is primarily responsible for this clever gadget by which the monetary supply can be made infinitely elastic in response to the 'legitimate needs of industry and trade.' In any case, by the 1920's President (or 'Governor') Benjamin Strong of the New York Federal Reserve Bank, who was the first of our three great American central bankers, had come to realise that the essential function of the Federal Reserve Authorities is to thwart both automatic inelasticity and automatic elasticity of the credit system, replacing these by discretionary actions hoping to moderate unemployment and inflation.

After the First World War the Federal Reserve stumbled on to a second and more powerful weapon of monetary control: open-market operations in government securities to expand or contract member bank reserves and deposits. And fortunate this was, since in the years following the 1929 Stock Market crash the supply of promissory notes to be rediscounted and the desire of the member banks to rediscount them almost completely dried up. The basic reforms of the Federal Reserve Act in 1933 and 1935 made government securities eligible as collateral for advances, with the result that rediscounts ever since have been on the basis of government securities as collateral. But even this fundamental reform could not keep the rediscount mechanism from withering away to nothing in the twenty years after 1933. The

rediscount rate itself became a dead letter; use of the rediscount privilege was negligible from 1934 until the end of the war, and it came again to be of some significance only since 1950.

It is easy to see why this was the case. During most of the 1930's and early 1940's the commercial banks had excess reserves. If you were a sensible banker, the last thing in the world you would have thought of doing would be to pay interest in order to get more of such idle reserves. Then during the Second World War, when the structure of yields on government securities of different maturities was assured by Secretary of the Treasury Henry Morgenthau, our central bank always bought enough of the newly issued war debt to keep the commercial banks adequately supplied with enough reserves to purchase that part of the new war debt which the insurance companies and general public were unwilling to buy.

It is true that in recent years the Reserve officials have had to sweep the dust off the rediscount window and scurry around for old clerks who remember its mechanisms and procedure. Specifically, the Accord of 1951 recognised the independence of the Federal Reserve from the Treasury and its freedom to stop pegging government securities' prices; during much of the time since then, the Federal Reserve Open Market Committee has deliberately kept the reserves of the banks so low as to force them into the rediscount window, with late 1952 being a strong case in point and this last year being another.

The British boast of having an unwritten constitution. American institutions too grow like Topsy and in wonderful and mysterious ways undreamed of by their legislative founders. Thus, in private a present-day Federal Reserve official may speak of the banker who 'flagrantly abuses' the rediscount privilege in almost the same indignant tones that I might use in referring to a scoundrel who steals from the church or to a traitor who tramps on the flag and damns Motherhood. And to whom is he thus referring? To one who brings forged or stolen collateral to the window for rediscount? Not at all: simply to a commercial banker naïve enough or brassy enough to think he can augment his investible funds by con-

tinual or continuous use of the ancient rediscounting 'privilege.' I daresay that whoever it
was who really originated the built-in elasticity
of the Federal Reserve rediscount mechanism
must be turning over in his grave when he hears
of this fundamental — and from the economist's viewpoint, salutary — change in Federal
Reserve philosophy and practice.

Nor did the founding fathers of the Federal
Reserve System envisage the frequent use of
what, after open-market operations, has become
the principal monetary weapon of American
central banking — namely, changes in the legal
reserve requirements that member banks are
required to hold at the Federal Reserve Banks
in proportion to their demand deposits. Prior
to the great depression the legal reserve ratio
of all city and country member banks averaged
about 10 per cent of demand deposits and was
fixed by statute. In 1936, a year after Congress
gave the Federal Reserve Board power to
double the required reserve ratios, the Board
became apprehensive over inflationary pressures
and over its inability to exercise tight control of
the member banks when they were possessive
of so much excess reserves. It therefore ordered
drastic increases in legal reserve ratios in order
to mop up excess reserves. Anyone having more
exaggeratedly romantic notions about the potency of monetary policy than I do would have
to put much of the blame for the 1937 recession
on the hardening of interest rates that came
about early in that year as a result of the increased reserve requirements. (The authorities
themselves were not fully prepared for what
followed from their actions because they had a
shallow theory of liquidity preference; according to this theory, excess reserves were truly
'excessive' in the eyes of the commercial banker,
so that one could expect that he would indif-
ferently give up these excess reserves and refrain
from attempting to replenish any part of them
by security sales.) As an objective historian I
must mention without comment that all this
was going on while (i) there was some noticeable tendency for the cost of living to be rising
at a rate of about 5 per cent per year, and at
the same time that (ii) the economy was en-
joying sizable unemployment at the rate of
perhaps 15 per cent of the labour force, with
the index of physical production being some

25 per cent below what in retrospect appears
to be the long-run trend of our producible potential.

Throughout the war and most of the postwar years the legal reserve ratios bumped
against the ceiling levels that the Reserve Board
was legally able to prescribe. At one time in the
post-war period when inflation seemed particularly virulent, many members of the Board
wanted Congress to increase this discretionary
ceiling, thereby restoring to the Board two-way
freedom, to contract or expand reserve requirements. (The regional Reserve Banks and the
banking community generally took a dim view
of this way of strengthening the Reserve Authorities' powers to fight inflation, for the
prudent reason that use of this weapon would
lower bank earnings.)

In the last few years, the Board has so frequently changed reserve requirements as to
make it necessary for us to begin to wonder
whether we were right in thinking that this
weapon of monetary control is one to be used
only at infrequent intervals. For, after all, the
purpose of the monetary authorities is to put
different amounts of predictable and unpredictable pressure upon the member banks' availability of credit, and is there any logical reason
why this should not be done by frequent
changes in legal reserve ratios?

In mid-1953, when the Board rightly feared
that the hard-money crusade of the early Eisenhower Administration had gotten out of hand
and might be held responsible for any ensuing
recession, it dramatically lowered reserve requirements. Less understandable in terms of
the older doctrine of sparing and once-and-for-
all use of changing reserve ratios was the further lowering of requirements in 1954 when the
economy had long been in a mild recession and
when the Federal Reserve wanted to intensify
the easiness of money.

Congressional critics of the 'Fed' hasten to
attribute the lowering of reserve requirements
to its desire to increase bank earnings or, as
the critics prefer to put it, bank profits. Such
critics are right in pointing out that the same
degree of monetary tightness or ease can often
be achieved either by open-market operations
or by reserve requirement changes; in a real
sense, therefore, the 'Fed' is like a public utility

commission which passes on the desirable or fair level of earnings that it will allow the companies under its jurisdiction; and in appraising the degree to which the banks and other interests in the economy are to be given representation in the Federal Reserve structures, this element of self-interest must be given its proper weight. None the less, until Congress legislates an increase in the reserve requirements that the Board is empowered to prescribe — and you'd lose your money if you bet that this was likely to happen in the foreseeable future — a case can be made for the Board's gradually working down the required reserve ratios toward the middle of its discretionary range, so that it again has two-sided freedom in the use of this powerful weapon of monetary control.

2. THE PRIMACY OF OPEN-MARKET OPERATIONS

For the present purpose there is no need to go into the other less-important credit weapons of the Reserve Authorities. They do have the power to set margin requirements for loans on listed stocks: e.g., this last year the government became fearful of a speculative bull market, and the Board raised margin requirements from 50 per cent to 60 per cent and again to 70 per cent, the present figure. (This means that I can borrow from my broker or banker only 30 per cent of the value of listed stocks; if I certify to my banker that my loan is not made for the purpose of 'carrying listed securities,' I might be able to avoid this restriction.)

Also, in the past the Board has had the power to regulate down-payment terms and length-of-contract terms of instalment purchases (so-called Regulation W) and of house mortgages (Regulation X). There is a good deal of evidence that these selective credit controls had great potency, but they have now lapsed.[1] The Federal Reserve Board has never appeared to be very comfortable exercising these selective controls, which are philosophi-

cally at variance with its general belief in overall non-discriminatory credit control; and there is no fundamental reason why these regulatory powers should have to be given to the Central Bank rather than to an administrative agency of the Executive Branch of the government.

Concerning 'moral suasion', the last of the traditional weapons of central banking, I don't know quite what to say. When it is recalled that the American banking system consists of some 14,000 separate banks, with no few banking chains having a dominant position, a case can be made for the traditional American view that this weapon has no potency. I must confess that mine is a minority view in having doubts on this matter: I suspect that there is some considerable potency in the short run in verbal statements made by the Authorities to the banks; for bankers after all operate in a less-than-perfectly-competitive industry and are notoriously sensitive to public opinion. Since Central Bankers live from day to day and week to week in a series of short runs, even limited potency of moral suasion can be of social importance.

What does our review of the changing institutional structure of the Federal Reserve System leave us with? Primarily with the recognition of *open-market operations as the important weapon of monetary policy*. Whether or not frequently changing reserve requirements could play an important role, we have not yet arrived at a time when they are likely to do so. And the recently revived rediscount mechanism owes its effectiveness to prior contractionary Federal Reserve open-market sales, which cut down on commercial bank reserves and force them to the rediscount window, where they come under the whip-hand of the 'Fed' and become subject to real moral suasion.[2] In a literal

---

[1] President Allan Sproul of the New York Federal Reserve Bank, our third great Central Banker (after Strong and Eccles), asked at the end of 1955 that the power to regulate instalment credit be restored; and President Eisenhower in his Economic Message (January 1956) has asked Congress to consider stand-by powers to regulate instalment credit.

[2] Some writers, here and abroad, have alleged that a change in the rediscount rate will itself have great announcement effects conducive to stability: men will interpret a rise to mean that the end of the boom is in sight, and will thus be led to cut down on their spending and to confirm their expectation. Careful observation of our money market suggests that this announcement effect would not, by itself, be of the desired potency. For when money is becoming tight in a boom, the market is getting new signals of this fact every day and the rediscount rate is only one of the following many signals: weekly changes in bill rates, commercial

sense, rediscounting operates as an offset to open-market operations rather than as a reinforcing weapon: when open-market sales tighten bank reserves, bank borrowing from the rediscount window tends to relieve the stringency and hence to serve as an offset; similarly, when the banks are in debt to the 'Fed', open-market purchases aimed at expanding bank loans and real investment may be partially thwarted by the natural tendency of the banks to use at least part of their new reserves to repay their borrowings.

Recognising this 'perversity', some critics have criticised the 'Fed' for leaving rediscount rates so low as to cause the rediscount mechanism to come back into effectiveness. Without denying their offsetting tendency, I think a defence can be made for use of rediscounts. They do provide an important safety valve, and without this safety valve the authorities might not dare to apply as much contractionary or expansionary pressure. My old teacher, Joseph Schumpeter, was fond of pointing out that good brakes make cars go faster, an analogy which applies perfectly to the present point.

I think it important to have inferred from our review of developments the primacy of open-market operations. Indeed, speaking teleologically, one might say that the whole evolution of the Federal Reserve System has been towards a perfecting of the open-market operations weapon of credit control. Yet, since 1952,

paper rates, bond yields, banks' published reserve position and Reserve Banks' open-market reports, etc. The rediscount rate moves as a result of these, though admittedly its movement does serve to confirm the suspected movement and to initiate some further moves. Only gullible textbook writers attach full weight to the rediscount rate and to the postulate that the Central Bank is certainly going to achieve what it sets out to do; the men in the market-place are too eclectic to believe in one simple theory or one key indicator.

Moreover, with each passing year of flexible monetary policy there is a developing tendency for announcements of monetary tightness to be given an interpretation just opposite to that relied on by the older writers. Today, financial men know that the Federal Reserve 'leans against the breeze', tightening money when it thinks the forces of expansion are strong and easing money when deflation seems a threat. Therefore it is rational for an investor to say, 'Aha! the "Fed" is raising interest rates; they must know that the current outlook is very bullish, and if that is going to be so, I'd better expand my operations'. Conclusion: announcement effects are often ambiguous.

a fundamental debate has been raging over the proper use of this weapon. A new doctrine has been formulated and been given a measure of official acceptance. This new doctrine would alter seriously the traditional use of the open-market weapon. Many economists think it would weaken seriously the potency of monetary policy; and to these critics the hamstringing of the open-market weapon, which had been developed after a long evolution, is rather like the case of a higher ape who, having come down from the trees, and having learned over the aeons to use his thumb and brain, then appoints an *ad hoc* committee, which negates the evolutionary development by a decision to limit the use of thumb and brain.

3. THE NEW DOCTRINE OF OPERATING ONLY IN SHORT-TERM ISSUES

Economists and the general public first learned of the new Federal Reserve Doctrine from the *Fortieth Report* (1953) *of the Board of Governors of the Federal Reserve System*. There had been no previous full-scale discussion and debate over the issues. Even the brief statement in that Report might have escaped appropriate notice if there had not been an almost unprecedented eruption into print of the controversy that had been taking place within the system, as a result of the forthright dissent registered by President Sproul of the New York Federal Reserve Bank.

It was then remembered that there had been earlier set up an *Ad Hoc* Sub-committee on the Government Securities Market, which after much labour and investigation had prepared a Report in November 1952. The new doctrine embodied in this Report, to cease open-market purchase and sales of intermediate- and long-term government securities, has been badly in need of a name. It has been referred to as the Craft Doctrine, after Robert H. Craft, the New York banker who took leave of absence to serve as its full-time technical consultant. It has been called the *Ad Hoc* Doctrine. I have even heard it referred to in academic circles as the 'Riefler Doctrine', in honour of the distinguished monetary economist Winfield W. Riefler, who as an adviser to Chairman Martin is held, perhaps unfairly, to be the good or evil genius behind the doctrine. I think it would be more appropriate to attribute the doctrine to Chairman of the Federal Reserve Board William McChesney Martin, Jr., formerly the president of the New York Stock Exchange and holder of many high offices under the Democratic Administrations. Therefore, I christen it the 'Martin Doctrine' and shall so refer to it.

Once economists heard about the new doctrine, its split vote, and the New York Federal Reserve Bank criticism of it, we were of course anxious to get hold of a copy of the *Ad Hoc* Report; but it was tantalisingly unavailable, and we had to conduct our investigations of the doctrine in the dark as to the exact arguments advanced in its favour. (It was subsequently learned that the questions about the government securities market had been addressed solely to financial specialists; only about one and one-half of the names in the interrogated list would be regarded as economists by members of our exclusive guild.)

Finally, in December 1954, the two-year veil of secrecy was pierced when the so-called Flanders Hearings on monetary policy[3] forced the Federal Reserve System to make public the *Ad Hoc* Committee Report. Since that time there has sprung up in our academic journals a lively discussion over the merits of the Martin Doctrine and the Sproul objections to it. Undoubtedly, this is only the beginning and the score cannot yet be given; but up until now almost all the academic discussants have been critical of the new doctrine. Specialists in the money market, who might be expected to favour a doctrine explicitly designed to foster growth of their function, have been divided: particularly in the hard-money debacle of Spring 1953 was there much criticism of the new policy, and this at the same time that the Reserve Board was congratulating itself on the

[3] *U.S. Monetary Policy: Recent Thinking and Experience*, Hearings before the Sub-committee on Economic Stabilization of the Joint Committee on the Economic Report. Congress of the United States. Eighty-third Congress, Second Session. See also articles by Alvin H. Hansen and Sidney Weintraub in the 1955 *Review of Economics and Statistics*, and by Deane Carson in the 1955 *Quarterly Journal of Economics*.

smoothness of the new régime. Since then, though, I think I can discern a move in the New York money market towards more favourable acceptance of the Martin Doctrine, and I confidently predict that the specialists will come to favour it unanimously if it is allowed to remain in effect for a number of years.

What about the United States Treasury? The Democratic Secretaries, Morgenthau, Vinson and Snyder, had all wanted the Reserve System to help keep government security prices orderly and to support the government bond market directly or indirectly. Their reasons for wanting this were various, ranging from a childishly vain desire to have government bonds over-subscribed, to the desire to keep interest costs on the public debt down, to a concern for the capital values in bank and insurance company portfolios and to fear of disorderly market avalanches. I do not wish to go into the merits of the struggle between the Treasury and Federal Reserve. Let me simply state dogmatically that the Secretary of the Treasury should be just as concerned for the nation's stability as the Central Banker. He is not appointed to have a pleasant life, either as a taxer or a borrower. This being the case, there is no legitimate clash between Treasury and Central Bank policy: they must be unified or co-ordinated on the basis of the over-all stabilisation needs of the economy, and it is unthinkable that these two great agencies could ever be divorced in function or permitted to work at cross purposes. (In particular it is nonsense to believe, as many proponents of monetary policy used to argue, that fiscal policy has for its goal the stabilisation of employment and reduction of unemployment, while monetary policy has for its goal the stabilisation of prices. In comparison with fiscal policy, monetary policy has no differential effectiveness on prices rather than output.)

Fortunately for analytic clarity — I hesitate to say, for the country — there has been no clash between the Treasury and the Central Bank during the Eisenhower Administration. W. Randolph Burgess, the Deputy Secretary of the Treasury who went twenty years ago from the Federal Reserve System to become a leading New York banker, was in 1953 even more disposed toward tight money than the Reserve Authorities.

The Martin Doctrine has many facets: (i) the decision to confine operations to the short end of the market; (ii) the negation of any target of desired yield patterns, with 'intervention in the Government securities market . . . solely to effectuate the objectives of monetary and credit policy (including corrections of disorderly markets)'; (iii) the tentative decision not to aid new Treasury financing directly.

I wish to concentrate on the important core of the doctrine — that it is legitimate for a Central Bank to affect credit by open-market operations in short-term governments — principally bills — and that all other intervention is illegitimate. I have already asserted that the Treasury and Central Bank have to be co-ordinated in the interests of national stability, so I am little interested in the division of labour between them. Hence the December 1955 support of a new government issue, which represented an apparent departure from the Martin Doctrine or a use of its escape clause relative to 'disorderly markets', I do not find as exciting an incident as have the Board's Congressional critics. I prefer to stick to fundamentals.

What are the arguments for the Martin Doctrine? Really it stands or falls on the basis of one major premise. Deny that premise, and all the subsidiary arguments concerning the desirability of developing a more 'self-reliant' money market having the oft-repeated properties of 'depth, breadth and resiliency' cease to be relevant to the issue. The major premise is this:

By confining operations to short terms, the monetary authorities can realise all the desired effects on credit and spending and can do this in the manner that is philosophically most compatible with the ethical goals of a free society.

It will be seen that this premise has in it an assertion about the facts of the modern money market — namely an alleged close relationship between induced changes in (i) short-term interest rates and in bank reserves and the resulting changes in (ii) long-term interest rates, credit availability, and investment spending.[4] It also has in it an ethical assertion that is neither open to scientific proof nor disproof, but whose feasibility and costs in terms of other ethical ends will depend very much on questions of fact and logic.

I do not think we need spend much time on the question of tradition and legitimacy. As far as precedent goes, there are Central Banks of the present and past which could provide a precedent for anything that someone might suggest doing, however fantastic or collectivistic. Even if we look to the Great Tradition of Central Banking, whether it be in the England of Queen Victoria or in the United States of Governor Strong, we are merely re-posing our problem. My account of the organic evolution of Federal Reserve could be used by one unsympathetic to the Martin Doctrine to brand it as a departure from tradition; and an Edmund Burke, if he were alive today, might in eloquent terms damn the new doctrine on this account alone. Moreover, in its deduction of broad policy principles by logical syllogisms from fixed axioms, the Martin Doctrine is at odds with the pragmatic and even fuzzy development that has characterised Anglo-Saxon institutions, here and abroad. If the Doctrine is right, no appeal to legitimacy is needed; and if it is wrong, such an appeal cannot save it.

Another red herring should be cleared away from the argument. The issue is not between pegging or aiming at some definite structure of interest yields as against adopting the Martin Doctrine of dealing in shorts only. Few of the critics of the Washington view propose any pegging. The genuine issue is between feeling free when the occasion seems to call for it to put pressure *directly* on the whole spectrum of interest rates rather than to abdicate this freedom by a self-imposed restriction requiring you to operate in shorts alone, in the belief that

[4] Some defendants of the Doctrine ride a horse in two directions on this technical issue. After asserting that intervention in the long-term market is bad because it will affect capital values and open the way for espionage and venality as investors try to learn in advance the course of policy, in the next breath they assure us that the effects of short-term purchases on long-term yields are immediate and strong!

your pressure will be indirectly applied to longs with the desired speed and potency.

Nor is anyone against the development of the money market. Without the Martin Doctrine, the pursuit over a period of time of flexible monetary policy was bound eventually to strengthen the dealer mechanism, for the simple reason that there would be an increasing function for such dealers and therefore an opportunity for entry and competitive profit making. The notion that such a development could not come into existence so long as the 'Fed' operates in long-terms is, in my judgment, incorrect inference and forecasting: if there is money to be made in the long run from taking risks, dealers in a free market will increasingly take these risks.[5] If the Martin Doctrine were deemed wrong on the basis of the stability needs of the nation and our philosophical ethical goals, it would be wicked to adhere to it for the purpose of creating the vacuum into which bond specialists increasingly are pulled.

4. CONCLUSION

I have now laid out what seems to be the important background considerations to the debate. What is my own evaluation of the issue? Any reader by now must have guessed that my studies have led me to favour the New York view and to regard the Washington Martin Doctrine as a backward, and unnecessary, step. My reasons are simple and can be briefly stated.

First, there is the ethical issue. I do not wish to force my own philosophical beliefs on anyone, but will simply posit that the greatest feasible amount of freedom is our goal. Yet experience tells us: Freedom is a scarce commodity, not a free good; it is to be conserved; to maximise over-all freedom, you do not try to maximise it in every direction, instead you

[5] Lessening the 'Fed's' power to create uncertainty in the minds of the men in the market is to rob the New York Federal Reserve writers of one of their choicest weapons. While I am not sure that Allan Sproul, Robert V. Roosa and John H. Williams themselves always knew quite what they meant when they preached the virtues of creating uncertainty, this device may have its place in the Central Banker's arsenal and should not be thrown away or limited without careful consideration.

must 'spend' a little of it wherever that will add to the sum-total.

This is the *rationale* for Central Banking (and for that matter, for stabilising fiscal policy). For its own sake, no one wants a Board of men to decide on over-all quantitative monetary measures — any more than we desire price-fixing boards or utility-regulation boards for their own sake. Conservative political philosophers have become resigned to Central Banking itself as one of the necessary costs of a stable economy. The Washington philosophers — and in this area the opinions of money-market philosophers have no expert standing — take the curious view of 'this far and no farther'. It is legitimate to infringe liberty and freedom by selling short-term securities and affecting reserves, so long as you stay within some semantically meaningless definition of 'neutrality' with respect to your effects on the structure of interest yields; debt management operations that directly affect the structure of interest rates are all right, but only as long as they are carried on by the Treasury and only so long as they are operations in connection with new offerings and refundings; the momentary and ever-changing liquidity preferences of the market-place are to be taken as sacred, and if you affect them more than indirectly, you are being paternalistic and are heading down the road to serfdom. So go the arguments. One slip of the pen and the Federal Reserve philosophers are in danger of slitting their own throats, since Professors Ludwig von Mises and Milton Friedman, who claim to know what freedom really requires, use as impeccable logic to prove that all Central Bankers should be abolished.

The enemies of monetary policy, who may or may not be opponents of freedom, are of course delighted with the Martin Doctrine. They know that the more the Federal Reserve circumscribes its own powers, the greater the probability that selective credit agencies will spring up elsewhere in the government — in the fields of housing, small business finance, farm credit and elsewhere.

And this leads finally to the technical non-ethical question. Can the Central Bank achieve all it ever wants to achieve, or ought to achieve, by operating in short-terms alone? I am inclined to think that since the beginning of the 1953–54 Recession, adherence to the Martin Doctrine has done no particular harm or good. True, the policy of active ease had to push short-term rates down farther than would have been needed to achieve the same expansion of long-term credit, but that is no great social evil. None the less, the fact that long and short markets have been rather intimately connected in these prosperous times should not blind us to the lessons of experience. We may devoutly hope that private investment demands and stabilising fiscal policies will always be so fortunate as to leave to monetary policy only the minor problem of contributing modestly to over-all stability. (That, wishful thinking aside, is the considered claim that can be made for monetary policy in the last few years.) We may hope that a great depression like that of the 1930's will never have to be faced; and we can even be optimistic that our new powers of fiscal and monetary control will handle such a situation if it were to arise. But we forget at our peril how during the great depression our short-term interest rate was forced down essentially to zero, how banks were flooded with excess reserves by the inflow of gold from abroad, and yet how slow long-term interest rates were to fall and how unavailable credit was to risky capital formation.[6] What then

[6] Had not the New York Bank quoted, tongue in

was the interconnection of long and short markets? In any such future depression, how much of the life-blood of capitalism will have to be lost before the Martin Doctrine is repudiated?

I end, as I began, with a quotation. A couple of years ago I received a communication from a scholar, who said that he had been looking for the source of the quotation: "Those who ignore history are condemned to repeat it." He finally traced it down to my *Economics*. Though flattered, I had to disclaim priority. Was it from Action? Buckle? From whom? To my surprise I could not find it in any of the standard reference works. (Actually, it was later discovered to be due to the philosopher Santayana.) So I asked Professor Crane Brinton of Harvard, thinking that if any historian would recognise it, surely he would. He answered: "I don't know the source of your quotation, but I'll improve on it for you." And this is what he said. "Those who are ignorant of history are condemned to repeat it. And those who know history are condemned to repeat it too."

I hope in the field of monetary policy Professor Brinton is wrong.

cheek, an earlier finding of Reifler on the interconnection of markets, I should not have dared cite the National Bureau study which he headed, and which showed the perverse and recalcitrant depression pattern of low short rates and high long. See *Occasional Papers*, Nos. 3 and 6, of the National Bureau of Economic Research. Aside from these, there is a vast literature on the general subject.

26

THE "BILLS ONLY" POLICY: A SUMMARY OF THE ISSUES*

Otto Eckstein† and John Kareken‡

In 1959 the Joint Economic Committee of the Congress conducted an intensive "Study of Employment, Growth, and Price Levels." The following two staff memoranda were prepared for the congressmen in connection with the Committee's Study. They provide a concise summary of the issues involved in the Federal Reserve's "bills only" policy.

I.

To: Members of the Joint Economic Committee.
From: Otto Eckstein and John Kareken.
Subject: A background memo on the Federal Reserve's "bills only" policy.

A. THE PREACCORD SITUATION

In order to finance World War II efficiently, the Treasury and the Federal Reserve agreed early in 1942 that the latter would hold all interest rates on Treasury securities at fixed levels; in other words, the System took on the job of "pegging" the market for Treasury securities. Of course, it was recognized at that time that this pegging operation would tie the System's hands, but this consideration was subordinated to the needs of wartime finance.

B. THE ACCORD

The pegged markets were continued far into the postwar period. But whereas this arrangement made considerable sense during the war and the reconversion period, it made much less sense after 1947; as the years went by, the Federal Reserve's power was continuously curbed even though the forces of economic expansion were gathering strength. Thus, in March 1951, the Treasury and the Federal Reserve reached their famous "accord," which returned to the System the power to regulate the money supply.

* From *Employment, Growth and Price Levels*, Hearings before the Joint Economic Committee, U.S. Congress, July 1959. Reprinted by the courtesy of the authors.
† Harvard University.
‡ University of Minnesota.

C. BEYOND THE ACCORD: THE POLICY OF MINIMUM INTERVENTION

Having the freedom granted it by the accord, the Federal Reserve continued after mid-1951 to move its policy in the direction of less and less direct intervention in the market. In late 1952 and early 1953 it put into effect the so-called policy of minimum intervention, which included the much-discussed "bills only" policy. The policy of minimum intervention is made up of the following principles:

1. The System should buy or sell Treasury securities only to influence bank reserves in accordance with general policy, and not to influence the interest rate on a particular type of security, except when the market becomes "disorderly";

2. System open-market operations should be conducted entirely in short-term securities, preferably bills, and the open-market account should not engage in "swapping" operations (for example, trading a block of bonds for an equal volume of bills);

3. No direct support should be given Treasury financing operations.

D. ACTIONS TAKEN COUNTER TO THE DOCTRINE

The policy of minimum intervention has not been always adhered to, but there have been only three occasions when the System has violated the above principles. In December 1955 the System bought certificates as well as bills in support of a Treasury financing. In the first part of 1957, the Federal Reserve sold certificates, presumably because it was almost out of bills. In July 1958, a relatively large volume of Treasury securities of different maturities was purchased in support of securities prices.

E. THE ARGUMENTS IN DEFENSE OF BILLS ONLY

Those arguments which have been set down on paper, and may therefore be taken as official, are:

1. That private decisions about investment and spending should be made on the basis of a structure of interest rates which are determined, not by the System, but by the free market.

2. That the private market for Treasury securities can only be made strong enough to support necessary System open-market operations if dealers are guaranteed against arbitrary official actions. This guarantee is given by "bills only."

3. That sales or purchases of long-term securities give rise to pronounced expectations about future interest rates, and are therefore more likely to obscure the "true" supply-demand relationship and so mislead the System into an incorrect policy.

An unofficial, but nonetheless oft-heard argument is that if the System deals in securities other than bills —

(a) It is much easier, as a matter of politics, to return again to a world of pegged interest rates; and

(b) Policy may really be made in New York, at the open-market trading desk, for policy directives from the Federal Open Market Committee can never be sufficiently detailed to guide fully actual open-market purchases and sales.

F. THE ARGUMENTS AGAINST "BILLS ONLY"

1. Leaving the determination of interest rates entirely to the free market sometimes means speculative excesses, which is why official intervention is occasionally required, even in the long-term securities markets. (See point D above.)

2. Because the flow of funds between the long- and short-term markets is anything but free and easy, operations in bills produce gluts and stringencies in the short-term market but have only a delayed influence on long-term interest rates; moreover, the response of long-

term interest rates to open-market operations in bills is extremely difficult to predict, except when bill operations are very large and hence dangerous for other reasons.

3. A strong market for Treasury securities can be best achieved by a policy which maintains relatively stable securities prices and thus encourages investment by all types of private lenders, not merely dealers in Treasury securities.

4. The "bills only" policy denies the Treasury the type of underwriting support which is employed in private financing operations.

II.

To: Members of the Joint Economic Committee.
From: Otto Eckstein and John Kareken.
Subject: A background memo on Federal Reserve swapping operations.

A. THE SIGNIFICANCE OF THE SWAPPING OPERATION

A "swapping" operation is, by definition, simply a trade of Treasury securities of different maturities by the Federal Reserve which leaves its total holdings of such securities unaffected. For example, the System Open Market Account might buy X billion dollars worth of Treasury bonds and simultaneously sell X billion dollars worth of Treasury bills. Under reasonable assumptions, therefore, the impact of this sort of swapping operation on bank reserves is zero. But the impact on relative interest rates (that is, the difference between the rates on bills and bonds) is not zero; a simultaneous sale of bills and purchase of bonds will increase the bill rate and decrease the going interest rate on bonds.

It is this combination of properties — neutrality with respect to bank reserves, but not with respect to relative interest rates — which makes the swapping operation of such potential usefulness as a tool of monetary control even during periods of inflationary pressures. Specifically, it can be used to support a particular sector of the market for Treasury securities when the economy is expanding because the support will not produce more bank reserves.

B. SOME EXAMPLES

Our own postwar history demonstrates how the swapping operation works out in practice. For example, in the latter part of 1947 Treasury bond prices began to fall, partly as a response to previous speculative activity; in December 1947 and thereafter downward pressure was even greater, for the Federal Reserve lowered its bond support price. To prevent bond prices from falling very considerably the System had to buy large quantities of bonds. But because it was able to sell large amounts of bills at the same time, total System holdings of Treasury securities rose by much less than otherwise would have been the case.

Nor is this the only example of swapping operations. We have another, though opposite, instance in the 1948–49 recession when the System sold bonds to offset bill purchases — just as it did in a limited way in the early postwar period. Indeed, bank reserves were expanded so little in the period before the Treasury-Federal Reserve accord in large part because the System made so much use of swapping operations.[1]

C. SWAPPING OPERATIONS AND "BILLS ONLY"

It must be emphasized that the possibility of making greater use of swapping operations cannot be separated from the question of whether or not "bills only" is a wise policy. Limiting open-market operations to short-term securities, preferably bills, obviously precludes the kind of swapping operations used in the past. Moreover, the broad Federal Reserve philosophy of minimum intervention includes as one of its principles an explicit prohibition against swaps. And the reason given for this prohibition is essentially that given for the entire doctrine of minimum intervention; when it adopted this prohibition (December 1953) the Federal Open Market Committee argued:

"* * * if the System open market account were to engage in purchases and sales in the open market without altering total holdings of securities in the portfolio, the objective of such transactions would not be clearly discernible to the market and thus might cause confusion and uncertainty as to credit and, in so doing, militate against the depth, breadth and resiliency sought in the Government securities market" (40th Annual Report of the Board of Governors of the Federal Reserve System, p. 104).

Again, then, swapping operations cannot be undertaken so long as bills only is in force. Or put another way, if swapping operations are desirable, then bills only cannot be a wise policy.

D. THE CURRENT APPLICABILITY OF SWAPPING OPERATIONS

Today, of course, the natural question is whether or not this type of open-market operation by the Federal Reserve represents an alternative to raising the legal interest rate ceiling on Treasury bonds. What this would mean presumably is that instead of having Congress remove the interest ceiling, the System would buy long-term Treasury securities in the open market and simultaneously sell short-term obligations, thus lowering long-term rates relative to short-term rates and easing the way for long-term Treasury financing. Equivalently, the System could purchase Treasury bonds directly on issue. Either procedure has the same effect, however, as short-term Treasury financing. Therefore, no answer can be given to the question of using swapping operations before it is decided whether countercyclical debt management is wise or foolish — that is, whether issuing long-term securities during periods of economic expansion is wise or foolish.

But this is not all there is to this matter. Some economists doubt that the problem of the interest rate ceiling would have arisen at all if in 1958, when Treasury bond prices started to fall, the Federal Reserve had quickly given some temporary support to this sector of the market by means of a swapping operation. These economists argue that even small purchases of bonds (fully offset, say, by sales of bills) would have broken the force of what

[1] It must be rememberd, however, that during much of the preaccord period, particularly in the early postwar years, debt retirement went on at a goodly pace; this helped make it possible for the System to support a segment of the Treasury market without creating unwanted bank reserves.

was essentially a speculative movement. They argue further that such action would have in no way involved a return to pegged markets, and that long-term interest rates would be lower today if appropriate action had been taken in 1958. Whether or not this argument is true is a difficult matter to decide, but it is a widely held point of view.

27

THE CURRENT DEBATE ON THE TERM STRUCTURE OF INTEREST RATES*

Frederick M. Struble†

In February of 1961 the Federal Reserve announced that it was abandoning its "bills only" policy because of balance of payments considerations. They thereupon began to conduct open market operations throughout the entire maturity range of government securities, in an effort to raise short-term interest rates (to prevent the outflow of short-term funds to foreign countries, attracted there by higher yields on short-term securities), while simultaneously holding long-term interest rates down (to stimulate domestic business expansion). Such "swap operations" have come to be known as "Operation Twist" or "Operation Nudge" — i.e., twisting the yield curve by nudging short-term rates higher and long-term rates lower.

There is no way to tell whether the Federal Reserve would return to "bills only" were balance of payments considerations to become less pressing. Nothing the Federal Reserve has said, however, would lead one to conclude that "bills only" has been shelved for good.

At present, in any case, the Federal Reserve does operate throughout the entire maturity structure, purposefully attempting to "twist" or "nudge" the term structure of interest rates (i.e., the yield curve) to its liking. How effective is it likely to be in this effort? The answer depends on the forces which determine the term structure of interest rates — the relationship among interest rates on varying maturities of securities — and how amenable these forces are to Federal Reserve open market operations and other policy measures. The following article examines current theories regarding the forces which determine the shape of the yield curve, i.e., the relationship between short- and long-term interest rates.

Can the monetary authorities — the Federal Reserve System and the U.S. Treasury — alter the relationship among maturity yields on Gov-

* From *Monthly Review*, Federal Reserve Bank of Kansas City (January-February, 1966). Reprinted by the courtesy of the Federal Reserve Bank of Kansas City and the author.

† Economist, Federal Reserve Bank of Kansas City.

ernment securities by changing the maturity composition of Government securities outstanding? For many years, two different theories — the expectations theory and the segmented markets theory — have been used as a basis for answering this question.

The expectations theory contends that a change in relative supplies of securities with different maturities will not affect maturity yield relationships unless, in the process, it brings about a change in market expectations of future interest rates. On the other hand, the segmented markets theory argues that maturity yield differentials are caused by an imbalance between the maturity composition of debt demanded by lenders and supplied by borrowers. From this it follows that a shift in the maturity composition of supply will affect relative yields. The segmented markets theory acknowledges that market expectations of future interest rates may be changed as relative supplies in the various maturity sectors are altered, thus augmenting the change in yield differentials brought about by this operation. In general, however, most discussions of the segmented markets theory have emphasized the direct effects that changes in relative supplies will have on relative yields apart from any possible changes which might occur in expectations of future interest rates. Discussions of the expectations theory similarly have played down the possible effects that changes in the maturity composition of debt might have on interest rate expectations. As a result, the theoretical controversy has been clearly defined.

Although each of these theoretical positions has a long history, it seems a safe judgment that the segmented markets theory has been and continues to be the theory most generally accepted by market analysts. However, the degree of consensus on this question has been reduced considerably as a result of recent research. Older statements of the expectations theory have been reinterpreted incorporating more plausible behavioral assumptions and the more rigorous modern formulations have added clarity to the meaning of the expectations hypothesis. On an empirical plane, several of the more sophisticated tests have provided strong support for the expectations theory.

This article reviews the current state of this controversy. To simplify the discussion, references to specific studies have been avoided. The reader interested in pursuing the topic further is referred to the brief bibliography of the major works on this question at the end of this article.

THE SEGMENTED MARKETS THEORY

Although the term segmented markets is used here to identify one theory of the term structure of interest rates, in other discussions this theory has been identified by several other terms, including institutional, imperfect substitutes, and hedging. Each refers to a type of balance sheet decisionmaking complicated by legal restrictions and traditional practices such as the matching of the maturity structure of one's assets with the maturity structure of one's liabilities — presumably in order to avoid risk. It is argued that because major groups of borrowers and lenders prefer to match assets and liabilities in this way, the market for credit instruments is partly compartmentalized, or segmented, according to the maturity of debt instruments. As a result, loans with different maturities are imperfect substitutes in the aggregate as well as for individual investor and borrower groups in the sense that different rates of return are required to hold securities with different maturities, and also, the size of the difference in rates of return varies with changes in the maturity composition of asset portfolios. This means that maturity yield differentials are determined by an imbalance between the maturity structure of debt demanded by investors and the maturity structure of debt supplied by borrowers.

Since the alternative theoretical position to be discussed in the next section of this article stresses the importance of interest rate expectations, it is worthwhile to note that discussions of the segmented markets theory generally have limited the influence of interest rate expectations to possible effects that *changes* in expectations of future interest rates can have on *current* interest rate relationships. This is quite different from the primary role assigned to expectations in the expectations theory. For, briefly, the expectations theory asserts that *current* differences in the maturity yields exist because the market expects interest rates to change over future periods of time. Moreover, it contends that it is possible to determine from a given yield relationship the pattern of future interest rates predicted by the market.

Discussions of the segmented markets theory have either ignored this issue or have asserted that a current yield structure is not affected by interest rate expectations in this manner.

Several facts appear to provide strong support for the segmented markets theory. In particular, the behavior of many institutional lenders accords with the assumptions about investor behavior made by this theory. For example, commercial bank portfolios are heavily weighted with assets of short maturity while assets held in the portfolios of insurance companies and savings and loan institutions are predominantly long term. Many examples of borrower behavior also may be cited which conform to the assumptions underlying the segmented markets theory. Consumers usually finance purchases of houses with long-term mortgages and purchases of less durable consumer goods with shorter-term debt agreements. In a similar manner, business firms generally attempt to match the maturity of their liabilities with the durability of their assets — inventories are financed by short-term loans while plant and equipment investments are financed by longer-term loans. These examples clearly are far from exhaustive. Presumably, it is the pervasiveness of such practices that makes the segmented markets theory so compelling to many analysts, particularly those involved in the day-to-day operations of credit markets.

Against this evidence supporting the segmented markets theory, the results of recent empirical studies have been surprising. One study after another designed to measure the effects of the maturity composition of debt on maturity yield differentials was unable to discern a substantial relationship between these variables. Consequently, these findings have cast doubt on the segmented markets theory.

These empirical studies have not been entirely convincing, however. In attempting to estimate the implications of changing supply conditions, all but one study ignored the possible consequences of simultaneous shifts in demand. Most studies assumed that the demand for loans with different maturities remains relatively stable over time. If this is the case, then changes in maturity yield differentials can be attributed to changes in relative supply. If, however, conditions of demand change concurrently with changes in relative supplies, this would reduce the correlation between relative supplies and relative yields. The failure of most studies to consider this problem reduces their significance. The fact that the one study which did consider this problem came to essentially the same conclusions as the others, however, suggests that failure to consider this contingency may not have been an important deficiency. In addition, on an *a priori* basis, it seems unlikely that changes in demand would vary inversely with changes in supply so consistently that an actual relationship between relative supplies and relative yields would be entirely obscured.

THE EXPECTATIONS THEORY

The consistent findings that changes in relative supplies of securities with different maturities have only small effects on maturity yield differentials not only cast doubt on the segmented markets theory, they also provide indirect support for an alternative theoretical explanation of the term structure of interest rates. Both the pure expectations theory and the version of this theory which contends that liquidity preference is partly responsible for the establishment of maturity yield differentials, agree on one vital point: that the maturity structure of outstanding debt does not affect the maturity structure of yields.

The basic assertion of the pure expectations theory is that loans with different maturities, that are similar in all other respects, are perfect substitutes to investors in the aggregate. This means that the relationship among current prices and yields on securities with differing maturities are adjusted so that the rates of return on this debt — calculated to include capital gains and losses where applicable — are expected to be equal for any given period of time; and that the maturity composition of outstanding debt does not affect maturity yield differentials. From these assertions it follows that maturity yield differentials exist because the market is expecting interest rates to change over the future — to change in such a way that apparent differences in return which might be inferred from yield differentials are wiped out in the process — rather than because it expects the rates of return on loans with different maturities to differ. Moreover, any process which alters the maturity composition of investor portfolios, but does not change expectations of future interest rates, will not affect the existing structure of yields on loans with different maturities.

It should be emphasized that loans with different maturities may be perfect substitutes in the aggregate even though not every investor views them as such. Credit markets may be dominated by a relatively small but well-financed group of traders who treat loans of different maturities as perfect substitutes. If this is the case, the investors, whose actions are offset by these traders, would have no influence on security prices and yields. Security prices and yields would be established by traders willing to adjust their holdings of securities with different maturities until they expect the realized rates of return on the securities to be equal over any given period.

Still another possibility exists for rationalizing that certain securities in the aggregate are perfect substitutes. The preferences of different investor groups may overlap so that all securities within one maturity range may be perfect substitutes for one investor group, while securities in another maturity range may be perfect substitutes for another investor group. For example, banks may consider debt instruments over a certain range of short-term securities to be perfect substitutes while savings and loan associations, insurance companies, and other investors may view longer maturity dates as perfect substitutes. If the maturity ranges of different investor groups overlap sufficiently, the structure of yields would be adjusted as if each investor believed all securities to be perfect substitutes.

However one views the process which leads to loans with differing maturities being perfect substitutes in the aggregate, the essential point is that the yields and prices are determined by investors who expect the rates of return on these securities to be the same over any given period of time. It is necessary to qualify this statement moderately, since most presentations of the expectations theory do recognize that such factors as market impediments and transactions costs may result in some inequality in expected rates of return and may cause some distortion between actually established yield structures and those which would be established if these factors did not exist. In general analysis, however, it seems a valid practice to ignore these factors, for yield differentials change rather substantially over time, and it is highly unlikely that this behavior could be attributed in any significant way to changes in transactions costs or other market impediments.

There are two compatible ways to look at the equality of expected rates of return. An existing long-term rate can be conidered equal, roughly speaking, to an average of a current short-term rate and the short-term rates which are expected to be established over time until the long-term loan matures. On the other hand, a current long-term rate can be viewed as standing in a specific relationship to a current short-term rate such that its price is expected to change just sufficiently so that its rate of return will equal the short-term rate over the period required for the short-term loan to mature.

In either case, any yield differential represents a market prediction that interest rates will change over the future. For example, consider two loans with 1 and 2 years to maturity that are selling to yield 2 per cent and 3 per cent, respectively. According to the pure expectations theory, this interest rate relationship indicates a market prediction that the price of the 2-year loan will fall by roughly 1 per cent over the year. Or, it indicates that the market is expecting the yield on a 1-year loan to be roughly 4 per cent 1 year in the future. This prediction is implied because the average of the current 1-year yield of 2 per cent and the expected 1-year yield of 4 per cent is roughly equal to the current 2-year maturity yield of 3 per cent. In short, the expectations theory contends that differences in yields on loans with different maturities are established not because the market expects to receive a higher return on one security than on another, but instead, because the market expects the rates of return on the two securities to be the same over an equal period of time.

To view this conception from a broader perspective, consider the relationship among a whole range of yields on loans with differing maturities. This relationship is usually depicted by a yield curve, a curve which provides a general picture of the relationship among all maturity yields on a particular date. Three prevalent types of yield curves have been established during this century. The first is an upsloping curve with yields rising as maturity lengthens and then generally becoming flat in the range of longest maturity dates. The second is a downsloping curve with yields declining as maturity lengthens and then generally becoming flat in the range of longest maturity dates. The third is a flat yield curve with all maturity yields equal.

According to the expectations theory, the unsloping curve indicates that the market is expecting all yields to rise over future periods of time, with the greatest increases expected among short-term yields. The downsloping curve reflects market expectations that all yields will fall over future periods of time, with the greatest declines expected in shorter-term yields. The flat curve reflects market expectations that all yields will remain unchanged.

As might be expected, yield curves tend to vary over the business cycle and the types associated with the various phases of the business cycle lend plausibility to the expectations theory. For example, upsloping yield curves are usually observed during recessions and throughout the early part of a business expansion. It seems quite plausible that borrowers and lenders would be expecting interest rates to increase at such times. Conversely, down-sloping yield curves generally have been established at or near the peaks of business expansion. With interest rates generally high historically, it is at least plausible that investors would be expecting to see yields decline in the future.

THE LIQUIDITY PREFERENCE VERSION OF THE EXPECTATIONS THEORY

Several discussions of the expectations theory have concluded that expected changes in yield relationships provide only part of the explanation for the existence of yield differentials. They have argued that lenders generally prefer to hold short-term loans as assets because the price of these assets tends to vary minimally. This preference is reflected in the willingness of investors to forego some expected return in order to hold short-term assets. As a result, longer-term assets generally provide a liquidity premium and their expected rate of return tends to be higher. To put this another way, it is asserted that the level of longer-term yields is always higher than it would be if the structure of yields was determined solely by market expectations. The fact that yield curves have sloped upward considerably more often than they have sloped downward since World War II often is cited as evidence of the existence of a liquidity premium on longer-term securities. It should be noted, however, that the predominance of upsloping yield curves is not necessarily inconsistent with the pure expectations theory. If the market generally had expected yields to rise over this period — and yields did rise — the larger proportion of yield curves would have had an upward slope. It will be remembered that at the outset of the postwar period interest rates were at historically low levels.

Although the liquidity preference variant of the expectations theory contends that rates of return on loans with different maturities are expected to differ, it does not view credit markets as being segmented. Instead, the size of the presumed liquidity premium is held to be unrelated, or essentially unrelated, to the maturity composition of outstanding debt. Thus, the position of the liquidity preference approach is the same as the pure expectations approach on this vital point. In addition, the liquidity preference theory asserts that, in general, changes in yield differentials imply that the market has changed its expectations about the future course of interest rates. Here, again, the liquidity preference approach is in accord with the pure expectations approach and in conflict with the segmented markets approach. For these reasons, it is possible to consider this position as a variant of the expectations theory.

IMPLICATIONS OF
EMPIRICAL EVIDENCE

The expectations theory has never been widely accepted outside of academic circles. Until recently, one reason was the inability of analysts to develop a test which supported this theory. In fact, early studies which purported to test this theory concluded that it had no empirical validity. This conclusion was based upon the demonstration that yield predictions derived from a structure of yields in accordance with logic of the expectations theory were usually wrong. Recent presentations of this theory have made it clear, however, that this is not a valid test. A test of the market's ability to form accurate forecasts of future interest rates does not constitute a test of whether an existing yield structure depends upon market expectations of future interest rates. All that is asserted by the expectations theory is that yield differentials exist because the market expects interest rates to change. It is not claimed that the predictions of the market necessarily will be accurate. In addition to this clarification, recent studies have generated new evidence in support of the expectations approach. And, although these findings taken individually are not overwhelmingly compelling, as a group they do serve to increase the degree of acceptance of the expectations theory.

It is impossible in the short space available to describe these tests in detail, but their general approach may be outlined. First, hypotheses about how interest rate expectations are formulated at one point in time or how they are altered with the passage of time are developed. Maturity yield relationships established at various points in time and the subsequent changes in these relationships, with the passage of time are then compared with this independent evidence of market expectations. A high degree of correlation has been found between these variables.

Another approach has been to draw inferences about the validity of the expectations approach by comparing actual interest rates established over a certain period of time with forecasted interest rates as implied by yield structures established in the past. The criterion used for judging the results was not whether market predictions always turned out to be correct, however, as it was in earlier tests of this kind. Rather, it was one of determining whether actual rates turned out *on the average* to be above or below forecasted rates. The presumption has been that if, on the average, actual rates were equal to forecasted rates, this suggested that the pure expectations theory was correct. The findings in several studies that forecasted rates generally exceeded actual rates has been the principal source of support for the assertion that a liquidity premium on long-term debt must be recognized as a factor in determining maturity yield relationships.

Although most recent empirical studies of the expectations theory have proceeded along the lines described above, it should be noted that some investigations have approached the problem from a different perspective and have found evidence which casts doubt on this theory. One piece of evidence of this kind has been the inability to identify a group of balance sheet units that behave like the hypothetical speculators assumed in some presentations of the expectations theory. Moreover, objections have been raised as to the possibility of the type of speculative activity ascribed to traders because of technical deficiencies in the market with regard to short-selling. Additional evidence, which would appear to be particularly damaging to the overlapping markets version of this thory, was the finding in one recent study that interest rate expectations were not uniform among different market observers. This conflicts with one of the assumptions usually made in presenting the expectations theory which is that interest rate expectations of all investors tend to be uniform.

SUMMARY AND CONCLUSIONS

The problem of explaining maturity yield relationships remains unresolved. The implications of recent empirical findings, although far from being one-sided, have shifted opinion away from the segmented markets theory and toward either the pure expectations theory or this theory modified to include the existence of a liquidity premium on long-term debt. Perhaps the most compelling evidence produced by these studies was the consistent finding that changes in the maturity composition of debt have little, if any, effect on the maturity structure of yields. This, of course, constitutes not only a direct challenge to the segmented markets approach but, in addition, provides indirect support for the alternative theory. Other direct tests of the expectations hypothesis have added further support for this theory. In fact, on the basis of the results of these two groups of tests, a strong argument has been made for rejecting the segmented markets theory and accepting the expectations theory. However, all the evidence does not point in one direction. The generally acknowledged fact that major groups of borrowers and lenders are constrained either by legal restrictions or personal preferences from viewing securities with different maturities as perfect substitutes, the inability to identify economic units performing as speculators, and the evidence of diverse interest rate expectations all serve to temper any inclination to discard the segmented markets approach and accept the expectations theory. Perhaps the best appraisal at this time is that, as a result of recent research, the expectations approach has won an important skirmish, but the outcome of the war remains in doubt.

BIBLIOGRAPHY

Conard, Joseph W. *An Introduction to the Theory of Interest.* Berkeley and Los Angeles: University of California Press, 1959.

Cootner, Paul H. "Speculation in the Government Securities Market," *Fiscal and Debt Management Policies,* a series of research studies prepared for the Commission on Money and Credit. Englewood Cliffs, N.J.: Prentice-Hall, 1963, 267–310.

Culbertson, J. M. "The Term Structure of Interest Rates," *Quarterly Journal of Economics,* LXXI (November 1957), 485–517.

de Leeuw, Frank. "A Model of Financial Behavior." *The Brookings Quarterly Econometric Model of the United States,* ed. J. S. Duesenberry *et al.* Chicago: Rand McNally & Company, 1965, 465–530.

Kessel, Reuben A. *The Cyclical Behavior of the Term Structure of Interest Rates.* (Occasional Paper 91, National Bureau of Economic Research.) New York: Columbia University Press, 1965.

Malkiel, Burton G. "The Term Structure of Interest Rates," *American Economic Review,* LIV (May 1964), 532–543.

Meiselman, David. *The Term Structure of Interest Rates.* Englewood Cliffs, N.J.: Prentice-Hall, 1962.

Okun, Arthur M. "Monetary Policy, Debt Management and Interest Rates: A Quantitative Appraisal," *Stabilization Policies,* a series of research studies prepared for the Commission on Money and Credit. Englewood Cliffs, N.J.: Prentice-Hall, 1963, 331–380.

Scott, Robert H. "Liquidity and the Term Structure of Interest Rates," *Quarterly Journal of Economics,* LXXIX (February 1965), 135–145.

28

THE STRATEGY OF OPEN MARKET OPERATIONS*

Jack M. Guttentag†

The modus operandi of open market operations, so simple to understand as explained in Selection 2 and in most money and banking textbooks, turns out to be somewhat more complicated than it appears at first glance, as this selection brilliantly demonstrates.

The view is gaining ground that there is something wrong with the procedures used in open market operations. These procedures have recently come under academic attack, largely on the grounds that they do not provide firm control over the money supply, and they have also been subjected to soul-searching within the Federal Reserve (some minor modifications have been introduced since 1960). I do not believe, however, that the crux of the difficulty, as opposed to its myriad symptoms, is well understood.

Confusion regarding procedures has stemmed partly from lack of a conceptual framework for examining open market operations, and partly from a lack of explicit and detailed knowledge regarding the procedures actually employed. The concept of an "open market strategy" is introduced in Section I and used in Section II to describe and assess the "money market strategy," which was used exclusively during 1953–60 and in modified form thereafter. The main weakness of the strategy, and this is the main argument of the paper, is its incompleteness, i.e., the fact that the Federal Open Market Committee (FOMC) does not set specific quantitative target values, for which it would hold itself accountable, for the money supply, long-term interest rates, or any other "strategic variable" that could serve as connecting link between open market operations and system objectives; rather it tends to rationalize the behavior of these variables after the fact. This results in innumerable problems in-

cluding inadvertent changes in long-term interest rates and in the money supply. Section III compares my proposal for a complete strategy with some alternative proposals, while Section IV considers modifications in strategy that have actually occurred since 1960.

I. THE CONCEPT OF OPEN MARKET STRATEGY[1]

The deliberations of the Federal Open Market Committee culminate in an instruction given either to itself or to the manager of the System Open Market Account at the Federal Reserve Bank of New York. An instruction includes open market *targets* and *constraints*. A target is something the FOMC aims at, while a constraint is a limiting value of something else the Committee is concerned with. The time period to which the target value applies is the control period. For example, if the Committee instructs the manager to hit weekly average free reserves of $100 million subject to the proviso that 90-day bill rates at daily closings are not to fall below 3 per cent, then free reserves are a target, 90-day bill rates are a constraint, and the control periods are a week and day, respectively. An *open market strategy* can be considered the set of open market targets, constraints, and control periods that is being employed at any one time.[2]

---

[1] The concept of an open market strategy, which is the author's and not the Federal Reserve's, is used both to describe and to evaluate open market procedures. The purpose will be evident from the context.

[2] Under some conditions a strategy would also specify *routes*, namely, the maturity range within which purchases or sales are to be made. Until 1961, however, this element of strategy was frozen by the "bills only" policy. This policy has been thoroughly raked over in the literature and will not be examined in this paper.

* Reprinted by permission of the author and the publisher from *The Quarterly Journal of Economics*, Vol. LXXX, No. 1 (February, 1966). Cambridge, Mass.: Harvard University Press, Copyright 1966 by the President and Fellows of Harvard College.

† University of Pennsylvania.

Open market strategy should be distinguished from *policy formulation*. The latter is the process of setting specific values ("dial-settings") for open market targets and constraints. The factors consulted by the FOMC in setting open market target dials can be considered *policy determinants*. Whereas only a small number of targets can figure in an open market strategy, the number of possible policy determinants is almost limitless.

An open market strategy may include several targets having control periods of different length. For example, one possible strategy would include a nonborrowed reserve target on a weekly basis (total reserves less borrowing from the Reserve Banks), total reserves on a monthly basis, and total commercial bank credit on a quarterly basis. The ordering is in terms of the extent to which the targets are under open market control.

Several characteristics of a good strategy may be noted (others will emerge as we proceed).[3] First, a strategy should have no more than one target for a given control period. The function of the target is to facilitate control over the next target in the sequence, and the one target that is best for this purpose should be used. Second, targets and constraints should be precise and quantifiable. Third, it should be possible to relate the final target in the strategy — the one with the longest control period — empirically to the system's objective(s) (say GNP). If this is not possible, the strategy is "incomplete."

There are no doubt a number of strategies that would meet these specifications including liquid asset strategies (the final target is some measure of the public's liquidity position), and long-term interest rate strategies. No attempt is made here to appraise the various alternatives, despite the obvious importance of this question. A rational choice would be heavily influenced (though not exclusively determined) by one's views on the mechanism through which monetary policy affects the economy — a

subject on which there is no consensus within the profession.

The Federal Reserve cannot, on the other hand, avoid using *some* open market strategy. For various reasons that will be developed later the Federal Reserve prefers not to face up to this. As a result, the strategy employed has been obscure and difficult to unravel. Still, it must be unraveled if it is to be fairly appraised.

II. THE MONEY MARKET STRATEGY

The open market strategy described below is a hypothetical construct. In addition to published sources, it is based on a study of the official minutes of the Federal Open Market Committee and its Executive Committee during the period 1951–60, which were recently made available to the public;[4] and on the author's own observations and experience inside the Federal Reserve.[5] The conceptions offered are consistent with a wide range of public statements in official and quasi-official publications, some of which will be cited. In good part, however, the real test of the conception is its usefulness in making order out of seeming chaos. The construct differs from a recent attempt in the same direction by Brunner and Meltzer[6] in its focus on operational aspects, i.e., on what the system does rather than on the views of system spokesmen regarding monetary theory and the causal processes through which open market operations affect the economy. These views sometimes have little relationship to open market strategy.[7]

---

[3] A good strategy, it may be noted, is no guarantee of good policy any more than a bad strategy precludes it. An appropriate analogy is to formal organizational structure in a large institution. A sound organization encourages and facilitates effective decision-making while a poor structure creates unnecessary roadblocks and distractions.

[4] Federal Open Market Committee, *Minutes of the Committee 1936–1960, and its Executive Committee, 1936–55* (hereafter cited as *Minutes*), The National Archives, Washington: 1964 (microfilm).

[5] The writer was an economist at the Federal Reserve Bank of New York during the period 1954–62.

[6] Karl Brunner and Allan H. Meltzer, *Some General Features of the Federal Reserve's Approach to Policy*, a Staff Analysis for the Subcommittee on Domestic Finance of the House Committee on Banking and Currency, Feb. 10, 1964; in the same series, *The Federal Reserve's Attachment to the Free Reserve Concept*, May 7, 1964; and *An Alternative Approach to the Monetary Mechanism*, August 17, 1964.

[7] The expressed view that open market operations affect GNP by influencing, say, variable x, may or may not mean that the FOMC issues instructions to achieve specific values of variable x.

A. OPEN MARKET TARGETS

Under the money market strategy the principal open market target is the condition of the money market. This is evident from the published record of Committee meetings,[8] from the comments (as reported in Committee minutes) of the Board Chairman, whose "consensus" — customarily given at the close of a meeting — is a sort of instruction; and from the reports to the Committee of the manager of the System Open Market Account on operations transacted during the period between meetings. The last is, indeed, the crucial evidence, since targets are in the final analysis what the manager understands them to be.

By market condition is meant the complex of interest rates on short-term claims — usually ranging from overnight credit (federal funds) to three-month Treasury bills — and the availability of credit in the different segments of the market at quoted rates. It must be emphasized that it is the condition of the *entire market* that is the target. Since the market as a whole is something of an abstraction, it is usually defined qualitatively in terms of various degrees of "ease" or "tightness." The control period is variable, ranging from one day to several weeks.

Actual assessment of market condition is based on a wide range of quantitative and other information: by the complex of quoted rates; by member bank free reserves (excess reserves less borrowing from the Reserve Banks), which are correlated with short-term interest rates; by statistical data on the financial position of market participants; and by direct communication with such participants (or with sources who themselves have contact with them), sometimes called the "feel of the market." One very important element in the feel of the market is the report of nonbank government securities dealers to the trading desk at the New York Reserve Bank regarding the availability to them of overnight financing for carrying their portfolios.

Free reserves have a dual function in the stra-

tegy.[9] First, the measure is a quantitative proxy for money market condition. It is, in fact, the only gauge of market condition that is both quantifiable and considered generally indicative of the condition of the money market as a whole. Despite the fact that it is imperfectly correlated with overall market condition, therefore, it plays a key proxy role in the money market strategy. Second, free reserves are employed as an independent target; discussion of this function will be deferred until later.

B. MONEY MARKET CONDITION AND FREE RESERVES

The proxy role of free reserves in the money market strategy can be illustrated with a model that assumes that there is an interest rate relevant to the abstract money market. The banks' demand for free reserves (F) and the public's demand for deposits (D) are assumed to be functions of this rate (r); the volume of nonborrowed reserves (N) and the reserve ratio (k) are controlled by the Federal Reserve, the first by open market operations and the second by fiat; and the supply of deposits (S) is derived from k, N and F.

$$F = f(r)$$
$$D = g(r)$$
$$S = \frac{1}{k}(N{-}F).$$

A geometrical representation of the model is shown in Figure I. Note that since each supply curve is drawn with reference to a fixed amount of nonborrowed reserves, movements along a supply curve imply changes in free reserves. Each supply curve implies a unique schedule of desired free reserves, shown in the right-hand panel, but the reverse is the case only for specified levels of nonborrowed reserves.

Suppose, now, that no direct information is available on the actual money market rate (which is the case) but the Committee has some desired rate in mind (say, R_1 in Figure I), and also know the function F. It will then instruct the manager to achieve free reserves

---

[8] For example the record of the June 17, 1958 meeting notes ". . . that for the next three weeks no action should be taken to cause the tone of the market to get materially easier or tighter" (1958 *Annual Report of the Board of Governors,* p. 52).

[9] Free reserves are referred to as "net borrowed reserves" when borrowing exceeds excess reserves. The earliest reference to free reserves in the Committee minutes is in the meeting of Oct. 6, 1953. During the prior two years or so borrowing from the Reserve Banks was used in a similar way.

FIGURE I

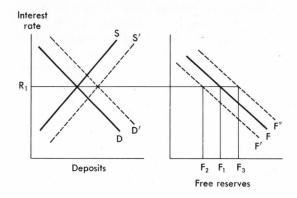

of F_1 which is the level associated with the desired rate. In this way free reserves serve as proxy for the condition of the abstract money market.

The Committee's judgment regarding the function F is based on the relationship between free reserves and the degree of market ease or tightness (as indicated by other measures) in the recent past — perhaps over the three weeks prior to the Committee's regular meeting.

Ordinarily the Committee would not set a single free reserve value (F_1) as a hard and fast target but as the midpoint of a range within which the manager may exercise discretion. Discussion at the committee meeting may indicate, with varying degrees of explicitness, the magnitude of the target range. One important determinant of the range is the Committee members' judgments regarding impending shifts in the level of free reserves associated with the desired condition of the money market. The range needed to maintain a steady market tone of R_1 in Figure I would be $F_2 - F_3$, for example, implying that desired free reserves are expected to fluctuate within the limits $F' - F''$.

Sometimes the account manager can employ the repurchase agreement as a sort of quasi-automatic mechanism for maintaining the desired condition of the money market in the face of shifts in desired free reserves. As indicated above, the availability of dealer financing is an important clue to market condition. If free reserves appear to be on target, for example, but dealer financing is available under conditions that are more restrictive than is consistent with the desired money market tone,

the desk may provide such financing under repurchase agreements, thus easing the pressure and raising free reserves above the target level. In the opposite case, dealers may exercise their option to repay outstanding repurchase agreements and free reserves will fall.

A second determinant of the free reserve target range is the magnitude of probable errors in reserve projections. From the manager's vantage point, errors in the data are (*ex ante*) indistinguishable from shifts in desired free reserves, and he responds to them in the same way. Suppose, for example, that the target range is set at $F_2 - F_3$ in Figure I; that the reserve projections indicate that free reserves will be F_1 in the absence of open market operations; but that the manager discerns greater tightness than is normally associated with that free reserve level. He accordingly allows free reserves to rise to what is then projected as F_3. It is later revealed, when final data become available, that free reserves initially had been overestimated, that they would have amounted only to F_2 in the absence of operations, and actual free reserves turn out to be F_1 after all. This means that the open market purchases designed *ex ante* to raise free reserves served *ex post* to correct an error in the reserve projection.

A third determinant of the free reserve target range, which has the effect both of narrowing and blurring its limits, is the amount of discretion the Committee is prepared to delegate to the manager to "feel the market";[10] the wider the range the greater the discretion. The reluctance of some Committee members to delegate wide discretion may result in a *de facto* free reserve target range narrower than the range required to maintain a constant market tone in the face of shifts in desired free reserves. Where this is the case free reserves be-

[10] During 1953–60 some Committee members opposed such delegation as a matter of principle. For example, ". . . he [Malcolm Bryan] would like to express the judgment that a directive to feel the market is not the sort of directive that a principal can appropriately give to his agent or that an agent can wisely accept from his principal." (*Minutes*, Dec. 7, 1954). And "Mr. Robertson said that he also believed that too much reliance on 'feel of the market' as seen in New York could be disastrous in the conduct of operations to carry out Committee policy. . . ." (*Minutes*, Oct. 22, 1957). The President of the Federal Reserve Bank of New York, on the other hand, tended to emphasize the need for granting the manager wide latitude.

come an independent target as well as a proxy for market condition.

C. TREATMENT OF OPERATING TRANSACTIONS

The money market strategy implies that the account manager will offset changes in non-borrowed reserves from so-called "operating transactions" such as changes in currency in circulation, Federal Reserve float, Treasury gold transactions, and the like. Use of a free reserve target implies such offsetting. If the target is F_1 in Figure II, for example, and a drain of reserves from gold outflows would shift the supply curve from S to S', free reserves would fall from F_1 to F_4 unless the manager supplies enough reserves to hold the supply curve where it is. The largest part of system transactions reflect offsetting of this type. During the period 1954–63 the Federal Reserve purchased $68 of securities for every $100 drained by net operating transactions on a weekly average basis (see Table I); in 1962 and 1963 the figure was over $90.

The treatment of operating transactions implied by the money market strategy marks a significant advance over the more primitive practice, signs of which were still evident in 1953, of issuing instructions in terms of purchases and sales. The latter procedure requires the Committee to involve itself in the purely technical problem of projecting changes in reserves.

Open market operations for the purpose of offsetting operating transactions, which are often called "defensive," tend to stabilize the money market and also the flow of money and credit, since they moderate changes that would

TABLE I

Multiple Regression, Weekly Changes in Federal Reserve Security Holdings on Changes in Required Reserves and in Operating Transactions

Year	b — Coefficient		Partial Correlation Coefficient		R^2
	RR	OT	RR	OT	
1963	.86	−.95	.90	.98	.96
	(.07)	(.03)			
1962	.83	−.92	.86	.97	.94
	(.07)	(.03)			
1961	.65	−.75	.67	.91	.82
	(.10)	(.05)			
1960	.67	−.71	.58	.82	.66
	(.13)	(.07)			
1959	.76	−.63	.75	.84	.71
	(.10)	−(.06)			
1958	.84	−.76	.83	.88	.81
	(.08)	−(.06)			
1957	.95	−.41	.71	.68	.58
	(.13)	(.06)			
1956	.96	−.55	.66	.70	.50
	(.16)	(.08)			
1955	.99	−.52	.58	.70	.47
	(.20)	(.08)			
1954	.40	−.24	.34	.35	.12
	(.16)	(.09)			
1954–63	.78	−.68	.64	.81	.67
	(.04)	(.02)			

Source: Federal Reserve Bank of Philadelphia.
Note: Standard errors are in parentheses.

otherwise occur in total member bank reserves. The use of any reserve target, it may be noted, implies similar treatment of operating transactions, though the offset period could be different. Under the money market strategy the offset period is a week, comparable to the control period for free reserves.

D. TREATMENT OF CHANGES IN REQUIRED RESERVES

Under the money market strategy changes in required reserves are accommodated by the Federal Reserve. Such accommodation is implied by use of a free reserve target.[11] This aspect of

[11] The open market purchases needed to hit a specified free reserve target are calculated as follows:
$$O = F_t - [F_a + \Delta OT - \Delta RR]$$
where O = open market purchases
F_t = target level of free reserves
F_a = actual free reserves in the preceding period
ΔOT = the projected increase in nonborrowed reserves from operating transactions
ΔRR = the projected increase in required reserves (including those stemming from ΔOT).

FIGURE II

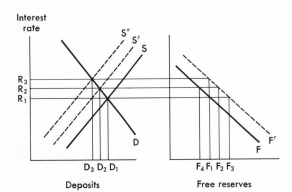

Interest rate

Deposits

Free reserves

the money market strategy is unique and has important implications.

1. Money Market Stability and Money Supply Instability. First, it implies short-run stabilization of free reserves and the money market but destabilization of the flow of money and credit. This is because accommodation of changes in required reserves is tantamount to accommodation of changes in the demand for deposits. If the free reserve target is F_1 in Figure I, for example, and the demand for deposits increases from D to D', enough nonborrowed reserves would be provided to shift the supply curve from S to S'. In effect the Federal Reserve allows nonborrowed reserves to increase by the amount of the rise in required reserves generated by the increase in deposits. Interest rates and free reserves remain unchanged, as the bulge in demand is accommodated by open market purchases.

Changes in required reserves are a rough measure of the pressures that would impinge on banks to alter their free reserves in the absence of accommodation by the Federal Reserve. These changes are often substantially larger than even the largest policy-induced changes in free reserves. For example, during the period of sharp transition in policy from "ease" to "tightness" between mid-1958 and mid-1959, the average weekly change in free reserves between the beginning and end of the period was less than $20 million per week. In contrast, the weekly changes in required reserves exceeded $100 million in twenty-nine separate weeks and ranged up to $440 million.

System accommodation of changes in required reserves moderates seasonal and erratic swings in short-term interest rates. Such stabilization has positive social value but its importance is hard to assess. Perhaps the most important beneficiary is the federal government, which would otherwise incur rate penalties when it sold large blocks of securities. The other side of the coin is that short-run instability in the money supply is given free play. The implications of this will be discussed in Section III C below.

2. Biased Relationship Between Money Supply and Reserve Base. Since under the money market strategy the Federal Reserve more or less automatically accommodates changes in the demand for deposits — in effect the system "feeds in" reserves as the banks demonstrate they are prepared to use them — an association is generated between actual changes in deposits and in nonborrowed reserves (or related reserve base measures). The result is a high statistical correlation found by Brunner and Meltzer and by Meigs between money supply and various reserve base measures. These high correlations are deceptive insofar as they are taken to imply the possibility of close short-run control over the money supply.

3. Neutralization of Shifts in Deposit Mix. Accommodation of changes in required reserves under the money market strategy implies that shifts in the demand deposit-time deposit mix have no effect on total deposits. A shift from demand deposits to time deposits, for example, tends, other things being equal, to release reserves because of the lower reserve requirement against time deposits, and in the absence of open market operations this would lead to additional bank credit expansion. Under the money market strategy, however, the system automatically absorbs these reserves.

The same result would be obtained, of course, through an equalization of reserve ratios against demand and time deposits, but so long as the reserve ratios differ this function of the strategy is desirable. I am inclined to believe that it has been of real, if unappreciated, value to the Federal Reserve in recent years when shifts in deposit mix have been quite pronounced. Time deposits grew very sharply during 1961, for example, following the decision by New York City banks to issue certificates of deposit, and also in early 1962 following the rise in the maximum allowable interest rate on time deposits under Regulation Q. There is no reason why shifts of this sort should influence the rate of growth of total deposits.[12]

E. TREATMENT OF CHANGES IN DESIRED FREE RESERVES

As noted earlier, free reserves not only serve as a proxy for the condition of the money

[12] Shifts in deposit mix that reflect changes in the public's demand for real assets show up in other economic indicators (unemployment rate, GNP, etc.) and are taken into account in setting the dials on open market targets. This will be discussed further below.

market but to some extent are an independent target. In part the independent role of free reserves reflects the preference of Committee members for a quantitative target, as well as a disinclination by some to delegate authority to the manager to "feel the market." In part it reflects a presumed relationship of free reserves to the "degree of credit restraint."[13]

The independent and proxy roles involve the same open market operations in the face of changes in operating transactions and shifts in the demand for deposits, but divergent operations in the face of shifts in the demand for free reserves. Suppose, for example, desired free reserves in Figure II rise from F to F'. The proxy role (wherein the initial free reserve target F_1 stood for Rate R_1) implies open market purchases to raise free reserves to F_3 while the independent role implies open market sales to restore free reserves to F_1. The independent role implies a change in interest rates and deposits (to R_3 and D_3 in the example) while the proxy role does not.

It is not clear, either from my own observations, from the minutes or from the statistical data I have looked at, that either the proxy or independent role of free reserves has priority when desired free reserves shift. The money market strategy includes no operational criteria for determining the proper course of action, and the most likely result is *ad hoc* compromise. Compromise occurs automatically if the system does nothing. Passivity in face of the shift to F' in Figure II, for example, would involve a rise in free reserves and in interest rates (to F_2 and R_2), and a decline in deposits to D_2. An actual case is given further below.

F. POLICY DETERMINANTS

A policy determinant is anything that affects open market dial-settings. Three broad types of policy determinants may be distinguished. The most important, as is well known,

is current data on business conditions — GNP, industrial production, price indices, unemployment and the like (including in recent years the balance of payments). This requires no elaboration here.

A second policy determinant, relevant only to marginal changes in policy, is the "market." The Committee minutes contain many references to "allowing" the market to ease or tighten from "natural" forces. The Committee generally specifies the direction in which the change is to be tolerated. If an imminent recession is suspected, for example, the market will be allowed to ease but not to tighten.[14]

Under the money market strategy, strategic variables such as money supply, bank credit, long-term interest rates, etc., constitute a third set of policy determinants. The Committee may change the dial-settings toward greater ease, for example, if it feels the money supply is growing too slowly, or long-term rates are too high. The behavior of these variables is always reported and often discussed at Committee meetings. Yet the overwhelming impression gained from the Committee minutes is that these variables carry an effective weight close to zero. The basic reason is that typically the Committee does not hold firm views as to what constitutes appropriate behavior of these variables; within rather wide limits it is prepared to rationalize whatever behavior materializes.

Thus, under the money market strategy, the value of strategic variables is, within wide limits, indeterminate. Indeterminacy implies the possibility of inadvertent (unplanned) changes in these variables in response to irrelevant causes, i.e., developments that are unrelated to the appropriate values of these variables.

---

[13] It has never been clear whether this has meant the elasticity of the supply of bank credit function, or the rate of bank credit expansion. A tendency to confuse the two is pervasive in the published record of policy actions by the FOMC. On the other hand, a clear recognition of the distinction is found in some official sources. The minutes suggest that most Committee members have thought in terms of elasticity.

[14] Assuming the dynamic factor at work in the market is a change in the demand for deposits, this procedure might be rationalized on the grounds that current data on business conditions provide insufficient basis for, say, easing policy but a movement toward ease by the market, if it occurred, would provide sufficient additional evidence that business conditions had weakened, as to warrant the policy shift. If the dynamic factor at work in the market is a shift in desired free reserves, however, the procedure is indefensible, although it is better than following free reserves. References to "natural" forces in the minutes do not distinguish changes in the demand for deposits from changes in desired free reserves.

A shift in the banks' desired level of free reserves is such a development.[15]

Monetary policy during the second half of 1959, which was widely criticized for being too tight, is probably a good example. There is reason to believe that the sharp rise in interest rates and contraction in money supply during this period was at least partly inadvertent, the result of a change in desired free reserves.[16] Each of three regression equations used by A. James Meigs to explain free reserves shows a drop in the "predicted" ratio during this period,[17] while actual free reserves were rising, indicating that the desired free reserve function was drifting to the right.[18] In the face of this shift, the system "compromised" by allowing free reserves to rise and the money market to tighten (see Table at right).[19]

1959	Average Rate on Three-month Treasury Bills (Per cent)	Average Level of Free Reserves (Millions of Dollars)	Seasonally Adjusted Change in Money Supply (Billions of Dollars)
July	3.24	−556	.8
August	3.36	−536	−.5
September	4.00	−493	−.3
October	4.12	−459	−.4
November	4.21	−433	−.1
December	4.57	−424	−.7

Source: Federal Reserve Bulletins.

There is no evidence in the published record or in the Committee minutes of an explicit rationale for this compromise, the system describing its posture during this period as one of "steady pressure."[20] Similarly, there is no indication in the official minutes that the Federal Reserve intended the money supply to decline. On the contrary, toward the end of the year some Committee members became concerned about the decline in money supply, but policy was not changed.[21]

[15] The problem is analogous to that of a fractional reserve banking system with *no* central bank, where the total money supply is influenced by developments affecting the public's desired composition of money as between deposits and currency.

[16] The problem of indeterminancy may be distinguished from loss of control, where the limits of the Committee's indifference are exceeded. The 1959 decline in money supply was tolerated by the Committee with misgivings. By February 1960, however, a majority of the Committee had swung to the view that the money supply decline should be arrested, yet for a number of reasons it was unable to accomplish this objective (see IV below). For a short period the money supply was out of control.

[17] Free reserve levels calculated from Meigs's equations T35 and T36 are charted in his *Free Reserves and the Money Supply* (Chicago: University of Chicago Press, 1962), p. 75, and the levels calculated from his T34 are in Giorgio Basevi, "Vault Cash and the Shift in the Desired Level of Free Reserves," *Journal of Political Economy*, LXXI (Aug. 1963), 411.

[18] Cyclical changes in desired free reserves may reflect persistent changes in the opposite direction in bank portfolio liquidity. The liquidation of government securities and expansion of loans during 1959 pushed loan-deposit ratios progressively higher during the year to levels banks had not experienced since the 1920's.

[19] I am not suggesting that the rise in desired free reserves was the sole factor working toward higher interest rates during this period; credit demands also were rising. The point is that if the Federal Reserve is maintaining a "steady policy" (under the money market strategy), as it claimed to be doing during the latter part of 1959, a rise in credit demands will be largely accommodated and a sharp rise in interest rates avoided by keeping free reserves steady, as explained earlier. To the extent that the dynamic influence on rates is a rise in desired free reserves, however, the system can prevent rates from rising only by allowing

free reserves to rise. My argument is that the rise in free reserves needed to prevent a run-up in rates in late 1959 far exceeded the increase that the FOMC would have considered consistent with its "steady policy." It thus allowed rate increases much larger than those it would have tolerated if the upward pressure on rates had originated elsewhere than with the banks.

[20] The uneasy nature of the compromise is suggested by the following explanation in the *1959 Annual Report of the Federal Reserve Bank of New York* (p. 28): "In the face of divergence between statistical indications of somewhat reduced pressures on reserves and the fact of continued tightness in the money markets, the System sought, through its open market operations, to keep the tone of these markets from changing significantly in either direction."

[21] In late November "Chairman Martin said he shared some of the apprehension that had been expressed about the money supply and the relationship of credit to growth, but he did not believe this was the time to correct it." (*Minutes*, Nov. 24, 1959). And in the following month the Chairman noted that ". . . the System is doing well . . . This was not in any sense to say that the Committee should disregard Mr. Mills' basic point regarding the quantity of the money supply. Personally, he did not know just how to measure the money supply . . . he was unable to make heads or tails of the money supply on either a quantitative or a qualitative basis." (*Minutes*, Dec. 15, 1959)

G. COMMUNICATIONS AND INTERNAL CONTROLS

A Federal Reserve "insider" has noted, with regard to certain parts of my description of the mechanics of the money market strategy, that it is "my interpretation," implying that there is room for other interpretations. This is correct and it is also revealing. It bespeaks a looseness of the strategy as one of its hallmarks. A good strategy is not subject to different interpretations.

Ambiguity in the strategy arises from the following sources:

1. Free reserves have an ambiguous role, as noted above.

2. The words used in the first instance to define current policy are imprecise.

Chairman Martin referred to Mr. Rouse's comment that the market had been "tight but not too tight," and he enquired whether it would also be correct to say that it had been "easy but not too easy."

Mr. Rouse responded that this statement also would apply.[22]

3. Even if a given set of words always meant some well understood condition of the money market, they could not have the divisibility and precise ordering that is characteristic of numbers.[23]

4. The underlying reality to which the words refer is not completely clear. "The" money market is a series of individual submarkets which, although closely interrelated, are also partially segmented. On a weekly average basis rates on federal funds and on 90-day Treasury bills, for example, often diverge sharply. Free reserves would be only partially satisfactory as a proxy for the overall condition of the money market, even if it were used solely and explicitly for this purpose.

5. "Market developments" or "natural forces" are sometimes allowed to affect open market dial-settings without specification as to the source of such developments.

Ambiguity inherent in the money market strategy generates a problem of communicating policy to the public. Analysts interested in something more precise than words — which are not regularly available on a current basis in any case — have naturally seized upon free reserves. It has been the only quantitative expression of the FOMC's objectives and it is available to the public in a weekly press release. System spokesmen complain intermittently that free reserves are unduly emphasized by the public but the complaints are futile so long as they offer the public nothing else.[24]

Ambiguity also generates a problem of accountability within the Federal Reserve. Since the instruction to the manager of the System Open Market Account is loose, it is difficult for the FOMC to hold him to account for carrying it out. Brunner and Meltzer have argued that the result of this has been that the manager has himself often introduced policy changes which have subsequently been ratified by the Committee.[25] My own impression is that this does not happen. It is prevented by periodic detailed reports required of the manager, and by close over-the-shoulder surveillance of the manager's actions by the Committee and by senior Board staff.

This method of control, however, is extremely

[22] *Minutes*, Jan. 25, 1955.

[23] Very ingenious semantic devices have been employed to denote the fine gradations called for by a flexible policy. For example, a favorite terminological tactic to indicate finer gradations of policy within broad categories of ease or restraint is to leave the basic nomenclature unchanged but to add that "doubts are to be resolved on the side of ease (or restraint)." The task is essentially hopeless, however, since there are more policies than words to describe them.

[24] Chairman Martin has stated publicly that he rues the day that data on free reserves were first published. Joint Economic Committee, *January 1963 Economic Report to the President. Hearings*, January 28 to February 6, 1963, Part I, p. 357.

[25] See (*The Federal Reserve's Attachment to the Free Reserve Concept, op. cit.*, pp. 31–50). Brunner and Meltzer base their view on the supposed finding that ". . . movements of free reserves quite frequently precede rather than follow decision of the FOMC." Their interpretation of this evidence is, however, largely impressionistic. No criteria are presented for distinguishing turning points in free reserves from random variations, and no justification is provided for comparing turning points in free reserves with the date of "major" policy changes rather than with the earliest date of a policy change. The finding that free reserves change "in advance of the decision by the FOMC" at five of six cyclical turning points, for example, is reduced to two of six if the earliest date of a policy change is used. Nor is account taken of the proxy role of free reserves, whereby the manager may allow free reserves to change in order to maintain a given tone of the money market.

clumsy, requiring that the Committee or its staff involve itself to some extent in day-to-day developments, and that the manager spend a great deal of time on reports to the Committee. These reports, moreover, do not provide as valuable a flowback of information as they might because of their generally defensive tone and their ambiguities. They are defensive to the extent that the manager, not being sure exactly what the Committee wants him to do, finds it necessary to convince the Committee that what he did was what they wanted. The reports are ambiguous to the extent that the original instruction to the manager is ambiguous.[26]

H. THE ORGANIZATION OF KNOWLEDGE FOR USE IN POLICY FORMULATION

Since the money market strategy does not include any targets that can be related empirically to Federal Reserve objectives, the FOMC has no analytical framework for translating the complex of factors consulted in policy formulation into an open market directive. The translation is a matter of "art."

The scope and volume of information employed in this process, including special research projects on problems of current concern, is truly impressive. Difficulty arises in using this material not because it is short-run (as Brunner and Meltzer allege), but because there is no explicit procedure for tying it all together. In effect each of the myriad pieces of data and research reports is sorted into one of three piles: a pile that argues for more ease, a pile that argues for more restraint and a pile that argues for no change (or does not argue at all; as I noted above, this is almost always true of information on strategic variables.) The weights attached to the items in the piles exist in the minds of the Committee members and it is no exaggeration to say that there are as many systems of weights as there are members.

---

[26] It is natural and a type of poetic justice that the words used by the Committee in giving instructions to the manager are thrown back to the Committee. If the Committee instructs him to follow an "even keel tipped on the side of ease," for example, he can report back that he "maintained an even keel. . . ." and the Committee is not in a position to complain that it does not understand what these words mean.

I. FOUNDATIONS OF THE MONEY MARKET STRATEGY

Meigs and Brunner and Meltzer attribute the system's operational procedures to a particular intellectual conception of the monetary process; practice follows theory. They term this conception the "free reserve (or reserve position) doctrine" and trace its origins back to the 1920's.

System experience during this early period indicated that borrowed and nonborrowed reserves were inversely correlated — when the system sold securities the banks repaid borrowings — while the volume of borrowed reserves was directly related to short-term interest rates. The Federal Reserve thus found it could influence short-term rates by controlling the volume of borrowed reserves through open market operations, and Riefler, Burgess and others articulated this into a theory of open market control.

A more detailed historical study than has yet been made would be necessary to determine whether the money market strategy as it developed in the 1950's owes very much to the monetary doctrines of the 1920's, or whether the strategy is largely a "rediscovery" under roughly similar conditions. In either case, the money market strategy has certain "advantages" to the central bank relative to alternative strategies that are not often appreciated by outsiders, and which the system is loath to relinquish.

1. The money market strategy stabilizes the money market, and the Federal Reserve values such stability. In part this reflects the system's heritage (underlying one of its stated purposes, the provision of an "elastic currency," was the strongly felt need to moderate seasonal swings in interest rates). In part, concern with stability reflects a tendency to be solicitous of the market's welfare, perhaps because the system depends upon the market so heavily.

2. The money market strategy provides targets that can be employed over very short periods, which is the first priority for an institution that lives in the short run. The system's front line exposure to sizable short-run fluctuations in the demand for deposits suggests that such measures as money supply,

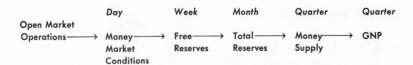

	Day	Week	Month	Quarter	Quarter
Open Market Operations⟶	Money Market Conditions ⟶	Free Reserves ⟶	Total Reserves ⟶	Money Supply ⟶	GNP

bank credit and even total reserves are unsuitable as short control-period targets.[27] The system is convinced, and no evidence has ever been presented to the contrary, that the attempt to control such variables in the short run would accomplish nothing (except to destabilize the market). This does not explain why the system does not set target values for money or any other strategic variable over longer control periods.

3. The main reason is that a more complete strategy would widen the range of system commitments, potential "failures" and exposure to external attack. The money market strategy minimizes the system's commitments, and maximizes its apparent wisdom. By not setting explicit longer-run targets for anything, the Federal Reserve can appear to "take account of everything." Maximum opportunity is afforded (in *Annual Reports*, for example) to shift emphasis from one strategic variable (say money stock) to another (say bank credit) after the fact, depending on hindsight assessment of their behavior during the period.[28]

The system's propensity to minimize commitments while appearing restrospectively all-wise gives it a sort of vested interest in obscuring its strategy. As one small but revealing piece of evidence, the word "target" is anath-

[27] Prior to 1960 money supply data pertained to one day a month (the last Wednesday) and the time series of such data were extremely erratic and difficult to use. Because of large intra-monthly fluctuations, the one-day series sometimes sent out false signals for three or four months running. Revisions were sometimes quite sizable, moreover, and on at least one occasion — in 1957 — revisions altered the direction of movement of the series for a period of seven months. In 1960 the one-day series was replaced by the much-improved daily average series. Bank credit data, however, have always been on a one-day basis.
[28] The Federal Reserve has often been criticized for being more concerned with "credit" than with "money." It is true that in *Annual Reports* and other *ex post* analyses of Federal Reserve policy credit usually takes up more pages. I suspect, however, that this merely reflects the fact that credit lends itself to sectoral disaggregation (there is more to write about). From an operational point of view, neither credit nor money is used as a target, and neither carries any significant weight as a policy determinant.

ema to the Federal Reserve; I have never seen it in an official published document. My proposal for a complete strategy necessarily overrides this unsavory feature of the money market strategy.

III. RECOMMENDATIONS FOR PROCEDURAL CHANGE

A. TOWARD A COMPLETE STRATEGY

The central weakness of the money market strategy is that it is incomplete; the basic targets of the strategy cannot be related to system objectives. As a matter of emphasis my recommendation for a complete strategy stops short of specifying its form. There appears to be much support in academic circles for a money supply strategy, but other plausible possibilities exist and in the last analysis it may not make much difference which is chosen. Only one complete strategy is needed.

A complete strategy would not replace the money market strategy; rather it would enlarge upon it by adding additional target variables with longer control periods. A money supply strategy, for example, might look something like the diagram at the top of the page.

A complete strategy would accomplish the following:

1. It would force the FOMC to formulate views regarding appropriate behavior of the strategic variable included in the strategy and to ask why deviations had risen, when they did arise, between target and realized levels. The strategic variable in the strategy would no longer be indeterminate, and changes in desired free reserves could no longer influence policy.

2. It would resolve the problem of communications and internal accountability. Policy would be defined quantitatively in terms of the longest-run target included in the strategy. Over-the-shoulder surveillance by the FOMC of day-to-day operations could be relaxed since these operations would be constrained by the necessity of hitting the longer-run target.

3. It would provide an analytical frame-

work for bringing directly to bear on policy formulation the immense flow of information available to the Federal Reserve. Though it is doubtful that the element of art can ever be eliminated from policy formulation, an effort should be made gradually to reduce its scope in favor of analytical procedures. The adoption of a complete strategy would focus the powerful intellectual and informational resources of the Federal Reserve on *the* relevant question: What value of the longer-run target variable included in the strategy should be sought in order to accomplish system objectives?

This proposal may be compared with some other recent suggestions for the reform of open market procedures.

B. SCRAP FREE RESERVES

The reform that appears to command almost universal assent is that free reserves (as a guide, target, theory, or whatever) should be scrapped in favor of some reserve base measure.[29] This is based largely on the finding that free reserves have a much lower degree of correlation with the money supply than do various reserve base measures.

Accepting for argument's sake the assumption that a money supply strategy is desirable, this recommendation is nevertheless based on a series of misconceptions.

1. It is implicitly assumed that free reserves and reserve base targets are exclusive alternatives. For a given control period this is the case — only by coincidence would targets for each be mutually consistent. There is nothing inconsistent, however, about using them both as targets for control periods of different length. Using free reserves as a short-run target retains

the stabilizing feature of the money market strategy.[30]

2. It is not clear that free reserves would be less effective than a reserve base measure in controlling money (the latter could turn out to be a fifth wheel in a money supply strategy). Studies by Meigs and Brunner and Meltzer show that the relationship of free reserves to money supply is very low on a monthly basis, but they do not show that such short-run control of the money supply is necessary. If the appropriate control period for money is three months or longer, the available evidence regarding the best method of control is inconclusive. When money supply is regressed on free reserves and other money market measures using three-month and twelve-month data, quite respectable coefficients are generated (see Table II).[31] Coefficients obtained from regressions in which money is related to reserve base

[29] See the studies by Brunner and Meltzer, cited above, and William G. Dewald, "Free Reserves, Total Reserves and Monetary Control, *Journal of Political Economy,* LXXI (April 1963), 141–53. By a peculiar quirk of fate academic economists discovered free reserves about the time the Federal Reserve abandoned "bills only," and the former bids fair to replace the latter as a focal point of academic criticism. Some good samples are found in the 1964 Patman Hearings, for example, the comments by O. H. Brownlee and Dudley Johnson (House Committee on Banking and Currency, *The Federal Reserve System After Fifty Years, Hearings,* Feb. 11–Mar. 25, 1964, Vol. 2, pp. 1062 and 1439).

[30] It may be wondered why the use of a seasonally adjusted total reserve target would not also stabilize the market and obviate the need for free reserves. First, the seasonal in desired free reserves is not fully or even correctly registered in total reserve series that cover the period when the Federal Reserve was using a money market strategy. Second, although seasonal changes in the demand for deposits are registered in the series, weekly seasonal factors (which are needed to stabilize the market) are inherently crude because of the shifting dates of Treasury financings, corporate tax payments, and the like. Third, erratic changes in the demand for deposits are not registered in the seasonals. The seasonally-adjusted total reserve target could, of course, be adjusted on a current *ad hoc* basis to take account of erratic changes and shifting seasonals, but this would in effect convert it into a free reserve target. For example, if a total reserve target is adjusted to accommodate an erratic rise in the demand for deposits, the impact of this demand on required reserves must be estimated, and this additional amount provided to the banks, which is exactly what is done in maintaining a free reserve target.

[31] I am indebted to Richard G. Davis for these data. Davis' data indicate that it is possible to generate negligible coefficients of multiple determination between free reserves and money *only* by using monthly unadjusted data, or by including the pre-accord period in the computations. All the tests used by Brunner and Meltzer in examining the "modified free reserve doctrine" did one or the other (*The Federal Reserve's Attachment to the Free Reserve Concept, op. cit.,* pp. 56–62). In testing their alternative hypothesis, however, (the "modified base conception" advanced in *An Alternative Approach to the Monetary Mechanism*) they employ annual changes between corresponding quarters of adjacent years, a procedure that would have generated much higher coefficients for the "modified free reserve doctrine" if they had used it.

TABLE II

R^2, Money Supply and Related Monetary
Flows on Free Reserves and Other Money
Market Measures
January 1953 — August 1963

Dependent Variables	Independent Variables		
	Free Reserves		Distributed Free Reserves and Bill Rate-Discount Rate Differential 12 Month
	3 Month	12 Month	
Money Supply	.30	.19	.51
Money Supply plus Time Deposits	.38	.50	.70
Required Reserves	.30	.58	.63
Bank Credit	.44	.62	.77

Source: Richard G. Davis.
Note: Dependent variables in three-month and twelve-month equations are three-month averages of monthly per cent changes (seasonally adjusted data), and per cent changes over corresponding months in previous year (unadjusted data) respectively. Independent variables are monthly levels and twelve-month average levels respectively. Distributed free reserves involve three separate variables for central reserve city, reserve city and country banks. All R^2's are significant at the 99 per cent level.

measures are usually higher but because of the accommodation aspect of the money market strategy (see Section II D above), they are subject to an upward bias of unknown extent.

This is not to extol free reserves but simply to indicate that existing research provides little real basis for choosing between free reserves or some reserve base measure as the best intermediate target for controlling money. Additional research is needed on the relevant control period for money supply; on possible disaggregation of money into more easily predictable components;[32] on the degree of system control over the independent variables included in existing regressions; and on the pattern of errors generated by the relationships. Emphasis on statistical regressions tends to obscure the fact that the system may be able to "improve

on the fit" operationally by progressively adjusting its short-run targets to take account of errors as they unfold.[33]

C. REDUCE THE VOLUME OF "DEFENSIVE" OPERATIONS[34]

Some observers feel that system policy would be more effective if the volume of reversible open market operations was sharply reduced. In most cases this view is based on the suspicion that these operations simply do not accomplish anything, and may be distracting. Robertson refers to "... a great deal of monkeying around in the marketplace for very little net effect." But Brunner and Meltzer make the more serious charge "that the so-called defensive operations . . . impart substantial variation to the changes in money supply." If they are right, a cessation of defensive operations would free the system from short-run distractions, and stabilize money and credit. My view, in contrast, is that the Federal Reserve accommodates variability in the demand for deposits and in the money stock but does not cause it.

The regressions of weekly changes in system securities holdings on changes in required reserves and in operating transactions, shown in Table I, shed some light on this. If changes in required reserves originate mainly on the demand side, the coefficient for required reserves, assuming system accommodation is incomplete,[35] should be less than 1.0. If system operations are the main cause of short-run instability in required reserves, on the other hand, the coefficient for required reserves should be

---

[32] The currency component of money, for example, is not related to free reserves but can be predicted quite closely using other approaches. (See Irving Aurbach, "Forecasting Currency in Circulation," Federal Reserve Bank of New York, *Monthly Review*, Feb. 1964). Similarly, some work I have done relating free reserves to various components of bank credit growth indicates that the relationship with investments is substantially higher than the relationship with loans.

[33] Autocorrelated errors provide scope for such adjustments. If errors are random and unpredictable, of course, the system cannot improve on the fit but the degree of its control will increase as the time period lengthens.

[34] The term "defensive" in this context can be taken to mean both offsets to operating transactions and accommodation of changes in required reserves. It is not clear whether or not Roosa, who coined the term, meant it to embrace accommodation operations (see *Federal Reserve Operations in the Money and Government Securities Markets, op. cit.*, p. 76).

[35] This assumption cannot be proved but its intuitive plausibility is supported by the fact that the coefficient for operating transactions is less than 1.0. Since the system only partially offsets changes in reserves from operating transactions, it is highly unlikely that it would fully accommodate changes in required reserves.

greater than 1.0. This is because a rise in required reserves resulting from open market
operations cannot exceed, and on a weekly
basis would almost certainly fall short of, the
reserves provided through open market operations. The coefficient for the period 1954–63
was .78 and the standard error .04.[36] The coefficients were less than 1.0 in every one of the
ten years calculated separately.

If short-run variability in money stems from
the demand side of the market, a cessation of
accommodation operations would accomplish
little or nothing. The "noise" generated by
transient fluctuations in demand is no less distracting when the system sits on the sidelines
than when it engages in accommodation operations. The system cannot eliminate the noise;
what it can and should do is set itself a clear
signal to listen for through the noise, in the
form of longer-run targets.

By the same taken, a policy of nonaccom-
modation would not lead to any significantly
greater stability in money and credit, since the
pressures now eased through open market operations would impinge on the discount window.
Recognizing this, Brunner and Meltzer would
impose stability on money and the reserve base
by using the discount window for accommodation purposes (at a penalty rate), while *offsetting* the resulting defensive changes in borrowed reserves using open market operations.
Paradoxically enough, the volume of reversible
open market operations required to smooth out
the reserve base and money supply could be
many times larger than that now required for
accommodation purposes, while marked short-
run fluctuations in interest rates and credit
availability would be reintroduced by the
agency created to eliminate them. There is no
evidence that such constant whipsawing of the
market is necessary to assure Federal Reserve
control of the money supply.

[36] The results are not conclusive, however, since I
cannot rule out possible bias in the coefficient. One
possible source of bias is changes in desired free reserves, which can affect both required reserves and open
market operations. If the Federal Reserve was passive
in the face of a shift in the banks' demand for free
reserves, the coefficient for required reserves would not
be affected. System operations either to stabilize the
market or to stabilize free reserves, however, would
affect the coefficient.

D. RESEARCH ON THE MONETARY MECHANISM

Brunner and Meltzer attribute much of the
shortcomings of monetary policy to the Federal
Reserve System's failure to understand how the
money supply is determined and to provide a
meaningful theoretical conception of the process. This allegation has some truth, but it is
much too indiscriminate.

1. The system *has* shamefully neglected research on problems central to its concern, including the mechanism of money supply determination. Indications are that this is now
being rectified.

2. Nevertheless, research on the best method
of controlling money clearly is subordinate to
the question of whether money should be controlled. I suspect that the system knows
enough now to control the money supply over
periods of reasonable length if it were prepared
to set money supply targets. The customary assumption of monetary theory, that the central
bank controls the money supply, has been incorrect more because the system has not had
the intention to do so, than because it has not
had the technical know-how.

3. The system is properly subject to criticism
for not having an explicit and complete open
market strategy, but the precise nature of that
strategy remains an open question. Brunner
and Meltzer provide no evidence for their insistence that the money supply is the only
strategic variable worth considering.

4. Ambiguity in the system's monetary theory
reflects conflicting views on the channels of
monetary influence within the economics profession, and should not be taken too seriously.
So long as there are alternative theories of
respectable lineage, we should expect a public
agency in its own theoretical statements to
cultivate the black art of double meanings. But
this is no defense of an ambiguous open market
strategy. We should be lenient of ambiguity
in the system's monetary theory but intolerant
of ambiguity in its open market strategy.

IV. RECENT TENDENCIES IN
OPEN MARKET STRATEGY

The minutes of the FOMC reveal that in
1960 the Committee was in ferment over pro-

cedures. The precipitating factor was the Committee's growing belief that the decline in the money supply that had begun in mid-1959 should be brought to a halt and its seeming inability to accomplish this objective.[37] Malcolm Bryan, President of the Atlanta Reserve Bank, who had long pressed for the use of a total reserve target, argued that

. . . by inadvertence we have not done what we intended. It does not seem to me in the slightest accurate to say that a single one of us, in the last two and one-half months, has wanted to enforce an actual diminution of the money supply or to effect an actual diminution of the seasonally adjusted reserves of the banking system.[38]

Long an isolated voice, Bryan now found strong support from, among others, Delos Johns of the St. Louis Bank.

The time had come, in his opinion for the Committee to subordinate its consideration of net borrowed reserves and other money market pressures to objectives expressed in terms of total reserves or the money supply. He did not mean to say that the Committee thereby would have adopted a system that would assure the avoidance of mistakes, but the use of such a technique would

[37] The reason the money supply continued to decline in the face of an easing in policy is the subject of another paper. In brief, upper turning points in general (and the 1960 one in particular) are associated with a decline in the demand for demand deposits. (The effect of this decline on money supply swamps an expansionary tendency from a shift to the left in the desired free reserve function.) Whether very substantial countermeasures by the Federal Reserve could avert the decline is not clear but it is clear that very vigorous action is not in fact taken. This lack of action reflects the FOMC's propensity for gradualism. Conflicting views on policy by individual Committee members, which are especially likely around turning points, must be compromised. (In 1960 particularly, a tendency for caution was natural in view of the fact that the first steps toward ease were taken well before the cyclical peak in May.) Gradualism means small changes in policy, which implies small changes in the targets included in open market strategy. Since money supply is not included, the FOMC finds it difficult to make the large changes in free reserves needed to prevent the money supply decline without appearing to contradict the prior decision to change policy only slightly. It is doubtful that the Committee's expressed concern over the money supply in 1960 had any impact at all on open market dial-settings. Realization of this by the Committee was, indeed, the main stimulus for changing procedures.

[38] *Minutes*, Mar. 22, 1960.

help to avoid doing things to total reserves and money that the Committee did not intend.[39]

A. THE "DISCOVERY" OF RESERVE FLOWS

The 1960 episode resulted in considerable soul-searching within the Federal Reserve and to re-examination of long-held preconceptions. The most important tangible consequence was a heightened interest in reserve flows and their incorporation into open market strategy. In May 1960 the manager of the System Open Market Account began for the first time to report current data on total reserves and nonborrowed reserves to the FOMC. A great deal of technical statistical work began on these series and a new synthetic series termed "available reserves" was developed.[40] This series began to appear in FOMC policy directives beginning December 19, 1961.

Instructions to the account manager continue to run in terms of free reserves and the condition of the money market (including bill rates), but the Committee sets rough growth objectives for available reserves which have appeared in its formal policy directives.[41] The

[39] *Ibid.* In addition to the *Minutes* valuable information on the 1960 episode is contained in *Review of Annual Report of the Federal Reserve System for the Year 1960*, cited above. It was fortuitous that the Joint Economic Committee investigation of a number of issues connected with the Board of Governors' *Annual Report* happened to focus on the 1960 *Report*. In a critical memorandum on the Report to Chairman Patman, John Gurley noted reference in the record of FOMC policy actions to the "disappointing" behavior of the money supply during 1960 (*ibid.*, pp. 116–17). This led Gurley to raise a number of relevant questions regarding implementation procedures, the replies to which (*ibid.*, pp. 147–61) are revealing as to the thinking of the Board Staff at that time.

[40] Available reserves consist of seasonally-adjusted required reserves held against private deposits plus total excess reserves unadjusted. In the July 1963 *Federal Reserve Bulletin* a number of other reserve flow series were published in seasonally-adjusted form for the first time.

[41] This paper must pass quickly over a second development in open market strategy which is much better known and which affects my main thesis only marginally. This is the emergence in 1960 of the balance-of-payments problem as a matter of policy concern, and the abandonment of "bills-only" in early 1961. While these developments were widely interpreted to mean that the system would aim at reducing long-term rates while holding up short-term rates ("operation twist"), neither long rates nor short rates have become an open market target. Rather short-term rates, specifically the three-month Treasury bill rate,

desk keeps these measures under surveillance on a weekly basis and deviations from the desired growth rate are brought to the Committee's attention for possible adjustment of the short-run targets. The Committee, however, continues to view the condition of the money market as the primary target.

The "discovery" of reserve flows has been associated with an extraordinary concern over possible overemphasis of free reserves. System spokesmen have joined academicians in criticizing the measure and they have gone to great pains to emphasize that the Federal Reserve does not rely on free reserves exclusively or even primarily.[42]

The adoption of a reserve flow target is a reform of questionable value. Available reserves cannot be related to GNP, and therefore open market strategy remains incomplete. True, the use of available reserves (or any of several related measures) reduces the probability that the FOMC will lose control of the money supply. The problem of money supply control, however, arises only when the Committee knows what it wants the money supply to do,

and, judging from the 1953–60 record, this is the exception rather than the rule. If the Committee does not have an explicit objective for money supply (or related measures), available reserves are of no help. The development of a reserve flow strategy might, of course, be viewed as a stepping stone toward a money supply or related strategy but the Federal Reserve has placed the cart before the horse.

B. WHY NOT ALL THE WAY?

The system is manifestly reluctant to go all the way. It has three objections that should be squarely faced:

First, it is argued that the Federal Reserve should not restrict itself to consideration of one or a few strategic variables; rather it should be eclectic and take account of many. The tendency to make a virtue of eclecticism, however, is based on confusion between policy formulation and open market strategy. (The money market strategy breeds this confusion as noted earlier.) Some amount of eclecticism might be a virtue in formulating policy; the amount of information that the FOMC can fruitfully consider is limited only by its ability to sift, analyze and weigh. But ultimately an instruction must be issued and it cannot be eclectic (it can, of course, be ambiguous).[43]

Second, it is argued that even if the system wanted to restrict itself to one final target, it would not know which specific one to choose (a public agency should not play favorites). This reluctance to declare for one specific final target among the competing alternatives rests on the illusion that the system can choose *not* to have such a target. This alas is not the case. If open market strategy does not include any long-control period targets, then the short-run targets become the long-run targets as well. Nor is there point in being immobilized in choosing

---

have become a *constraint* while purchases of long-term securities have been made for the purpose of meeting reserve targets without forcing short-term rates below constraint levels (see Stone, "Federal Reserve Open Market Operations in 1962," *op. cit.*, p. 432; and Deming, *op. cit.*, p. 11). One might expect that the increasing importance of a specific segment of the money market (along with increasing emphasis on reserve flows) would result in a corresponding de-emphasis of the abstract money market; but the 1962 and 1963 records of FOMC policy actions indicate quite clearly that this is not the case.

[42] For example, see Harry Brandt, "Controlling Reserves," *Monthly Review*, Federal Reserve Bank of Atlanta, Sept. 1963. This concern over free reserves was nothing new. The FOMC minutes reveal that the Committee began to worry about free reserves as they came to rely on them, and by 1957 its general attitude had become strongly ambivalent. The Committee did not like the measure but it didn't know how to do without it.

"Chairman Martin stated that he still considered the limitations of the net borrowed reserve figures to be too great to make them of use as more than a target. . . .!" (*Minutes*, Oct. 10, 1957, my exclamation point.)

It was not until 1960 that the system's concern over free reserves came to focus on its relationship to money supply growth. In earlier years the Committee's concern was largely that free reserves were not a reliable indicator of money market condition.

[43] One good indication of this confusion is the system's firmly held view that it is essential that the manager attend meetings of the FOMC. "To assist him in carrying out the necessary operations, the manager has the benefit of the full discussion at the meeting at which a policy decision is reached" (*Review of Annual Report of the Federal Reserve System for the Year 1960*, p. 149). In my view the manager should be barred from meetings except to report on operations. In this way the Committee would force itself to issue a clear instruction.

between, say, money supply including and excluding time deposits, since the empirical relationships employed to implement the strategy would be based on the specific concept used. When two bridge sites appear equally plausible, one is nevertheless chosen.

Third, it is argued that even if the system made a choice it would have little or no basis for setting quantitative target values. Would it not be prudent to hold off until better empirical bridges are built? No. Open market strategy is based on *some* presumption regarding the relationship of final targets to GNP. If we know all too little about the relationship of GNP to, say, money supply, we know much less about its relationship to free reserves, money market condition or available reserves. The choice of a strategy, furthermore, is a vital stepping stone toward the development of the empirical relationships needed to implement it; it provides both the focus and the incentive for research effort. The history of the money market strategy suggests that so long as the system is not committed it will build no empirical bridges.

V. CONCLUDING COMMENT

The real barrier to the adoption of a complete strategy is largely psychological. The Federal Reserve would have to relinquish the illusion that it "takes account of everything," while exposing its real objectives nakedly to public scrutiny. This could be risky. There is much unreasonable hostility to monetary policy to begin with, and it is likely that in some cases further exposure would merely invite more vigorous attack. My own view, however, is that this would be more than offset by heightened support and help from other (and particularly academic) quarters. The Federal Reserve inadvertently encourages a great deal of hostility by failing to provide constructive outlets to monetary economists on the outside — most of whom view the Federal Reserve as "their" institution and would like to identify with it if they could. Let the system shout "5 per cent in the second quarter," and I suspect that much hostile and irrelevant carping would be rechanneled into pertinent econometric and other analytical exercises.

CHAPTER NINE

THE DISCOUNT RATE AND DISCOUNT POLICY

29

REDISCOUNTING*

Milton Friedman†

The rediscount rate was considered the main instrument of central banking throughout the nineteenth and for the first three decades of the twentieth century. In 1931 the Macmillan Committee reported in England that discount rate policy "is an absolute necessity for the sound management of a monetary system, and it is a most delicate and beautiful instrument for the purpose."

Rediscounting fell into disuse in this country during the 1930's and 1940's, when the discount rate had only nominal significance. As Selection 23 indicates, however, the Treasury-Federal Reserve Accord of 1951 signaled its re-emergence as an important part of Federal Reserve policy, and it has remained so ever since.

*In the following selection, Professor Friedman presents a dissenting view from the Federal Reserve's position on the role and the value of the discount mechanism.***

The Federal Reserve System was created by men whose outlook on the goals of central banking was shaped by the money panics during the national banking era. The main problem requiring solution seemed to them to be banking crises produced by, or resulting in, a widespread desire on the part of the public to shift from deposits to currency, generally because of a loss of confidence in banks arising out of a few notable bank or commercial failures. Under a fractional reserve banking sys-

tem, widespread conversion of deposits into currency requires either an increase in high-powered money or a drastic shrinkage in the total amount of money. Prior to the Federal Reserve System, a sizable increase in high-powered money generally could come only from gold imports. This took time and required a fairly drastic incentive. In consequence, a serious liquidity crisis could seldom be met in this way in the first instance. An individual bank might be able to convert its assets into currency; the system as a whole could not do so. The attempt by many individual banks to do so produced pressure for wholesale liquidation that led to contraction of the total money supply. Unless the process were halted fairly early, the attempted liquidation would drive down the prices of bank assets and render most banks technically insolvent.

* From Milton Friedman, A *Program for Monetary Stability* (Fordham University Press, 1960), pp. 35–45. Reprinted by the courtesy of the publisher and the author.

† University of Chicago.

** For an exposition of the Federal Reserve's views on these subjects, see the Forty-Fourth *Annual Report* of the Board of Governors of the Federal Reserve System, Covering Operations for the Year 1957, pages 7–18.

The therapeutic device that developed was the so-called suspension of payments — an agreement among banks, generally through their clearing house associations, that they would honor all requests to transfer deposits "through the clearing house," but would refuse to convert deposits into currency on demand, though continuing to do so for some purposes and for some customers. The suspension of payments in this sense did not involve even the temporary closing of the banks on any large scale or the cessation of their financial operations — as occurred during the much more drastic Banking Holiday of 1933. It meant rather the creation of two only partly convertible media of payments, currency and deposits, with deposits only imperfectly convertible into currency and hence with currency at a premium in terms of deposits. Once adjustment was made to the use of two such media of payments convertible into one another at a flexible rather than a fixed rate, the suspension could continue for months on end, as it did at times, without producing an economic breakdown and indeed in conjunction with economic revival.

The solution to the problem of panics embodied in the Federal Reserve Act was, in the words of its title, "to provide an elastic currency." Federal Reserve money was designed to differ from other forms of money by being subject to substantial change in quantity over short periods of time for reasons other than the immediate profitability of either the issuer or, as with specie, the importer or exporter. In this way, when depositors wished to convert deposits into currency, additional high-powered money could be made available in the form of Federal Reserve notes. Fundamentally, "elasticity" was aimed at not in the total amount of money but in the amount of one kind of money — currency — relative to another — deposits — though there was of course much confusion then as now between these two kinds of elasticity. Rediscounting was designed as the means whereby additional high-powered money could be put into circulation and subsequently retired. By rediscounting their assets, banks could convert them into the currency which their customers were demanding without reducing the reserves of other banks. The Reserve System was to be a "lender of last resort," ready to provide liquidity in a time of crisis to satisfy a widespread demand for currency that otherwise would produce either suspension of payments or a substantial decline in the total stock of money.

Rediscounting was therefore not originally intended to be used continuously to determine or alter the total stock of money. When the Act became law, the gold standard ruled supreme. It was taken for granted that it would continue to do so and that it would dominate the longer-term movements in the total stock of money. This view is reflected in the gold reserve ratios that were incorporated in the Federal Reserve Act. During and after World War I, the gold standard changed its character and the gold reserve ratio became a largely irrelevant guide for short-term movements. Rediscounting then developed into one of the two blades of the scissors continuously controlling the stock of money, open market operations being the other. In the 1929–33 contraction, the kind of situation developed that had been contemplated when the System was established and that an elastic currency issued through rediscounting had been designed to handle. In the event, these tools did not enable the System to cope with the crisis. Whether they need have been inadequate if differently managed is a moot question.

One result of the banking collapse was the enactment of federal insurance of bank deposits. Its purpose was to protect depositors against the kind of cruel losses they had experienced during the preceding years, not primarily to solve the problem of bank panics. It has, however, succeeded in doing so where rediscounting failed. Although deposits are technically insured only up to $10,000, bank failures involving losses to depositors have become almost a thing of the past. Banks still become insolvent, but they no longer fail. Instead, they tend to be merged with other banks or to be reorganized, with the Federal Deposit Insurance Corporation assuming responsibility for the bad assets. An indirect result has been to prevent any chain reaction such as used to occur. Even if a bank fails or is reorganized, there is no reason for depositors in other banks to become concerned. Changes in the ratio of deposits to currency still occur as a result of changed preferences. Such changes, however, even if sizable, tend to be gradual and do not involve runs on individual banks. A liquidity crisis involving such runs on a widespread scale is now almost inconceivable. The need for rediscounting in order for the Reserve System to serve as "a lender of last resort" has therefore become obsolete, not because the function has been taken over by someone else but because it no longer needs to be performed. To avoid misunderstanding, I should perhaps add that while federal deposit insurance has performed a signal service in rendering the banking system panic-proof, it does not seem to me the most desirable method of achieving this end.

Having lost its initial function, rediscounting has acquired three very different and less critical roles. In the first place, it is a means whereby member banks can obtain funds from time to time at a lower cost than by alternative devices. In this respect, it involves special governmental assistance to a particular group of financial institutions. It is hard to see why it is appropriate or necessary for government to render such assistance or why commercial banks should be singled out to receive it. The capital market is a well-functioning and sensitive market, and banks can readily manage to provide for special needs in other ways — as for example they did throughout the later 1930's when, for reasons I shall mention shortly, rediscounting was hardly resorted to.

In the second place, rediscounting is a means whereby member banks can readily adjust their reserve balances to conform to reserve requirements when they unexpectedly discover that they are likely to be in deficit. Other means are however available and widely used for this purpose, the most notable among them in recent years being the Federal Funds market. In consequence this function, like the preceding, is solely a convenience offered to member banks.

In the third place, as already noted, rediscounting is a means whereby the Reserve System can influence the total amount of high-powered money in existence and thereby the total stock of money. This is its major current function and the function in terms of which

it must basically be judged. And it so happens that rediscounting is a technically defective tool for this purpose.

The distinctive feature of rediscounting is that the initiative to rediscount is in the hands of the member banks. In consequence, the Reserve System cannot itself determine the amount of money it creates through the discount window or, for that matter, by a combination of the discount window and the open market. It can affect the amount of discounting by exercising discretion with respect to the banks for whom it will discount and the amount of discounting it will do for individual banks, or by changing the discount rate and thus the incentive on the part of banks to discount. The exercise of discretion is an undesirable kind of specific credit control that involves detailed intervention into the affairs of individual banks and arbitrary decisions by governmental officials. Moreover, it is incapable of being applied in a sufficiently sensitive way to produce predictable results over short periods. Hence, it is not even an efficient tool for controlling the amount of rediscounting. Most of the time, it has been held in abeyance. It has been brought into play generally only when the System has wished to avoid using its major weapons of discount rates or open market operations; notably in 1919, when the rediscount rate was being kept unchanged under Treasury pressure; in 1928 and 1929, in connection with the use of direct pressure to discourage so-called speculative loans; and in 1950–51, when the bond-support program was in effect. Whatever else is done about rediscounting, this feature should be changed. If rediscounting is retained, it should be a right, not a privilege, freely available to all member banks on specified terms.

The discount rate is the primary means used to influence the amount of discounting, so much so that "discount policy" is generally regarded as concerned exclusively with setting the discount rate. In practice, the discount rate has been used as a discontinuous instrument, changes being made only at substantial intervals and by sizable amounts. This operation by fits and starts introduces unnecessary instability into the economy. It also means that changes in the discount rate are newsworthy and attract attention. There is speculation about what they will be and much significance is read into them when they occur. If the System could predict accurately the future course of events and could establish an unambiguous connection between changes in the discount rate and its predictions, these "announcement effects" might be highly desirable, since individuals would then be led to behave in a way that would reinforce the System's action — though in that case, the same result could almost surely be attained simply by publishing the System's predictions. As it is, the "announcement effects" are an additional source of uncertainty in the economy.

A second defect of the discount rate is the extreme difficulty of predicting the effect of a change in the rate on the amount of discounting, let alone on the stock of money. The effect on the willingness of member banks to borrow is very different under different circumstances, depending on such factors as the level of other rates of interest, the state of the demand for loans and the supply of funds from other sources, the investment opportunities available, and so on.

A closely related defect is, in my view, much the most important. The discount rate is something that the Federal Reserve System must continually change in order to keep the effect of its monetary policy unchanged. But changes in the rate are interpreted as if they meant changes in policy. Consequently both the System and outsiders are led to misinterpret the System's actions and the System is led to follow policies different from those it intends to follow.

The key point underlying these perhaps cryptic statements is one that became familiar in the course of the discussion of the post-World War II bond support program: a constant absolute rate of interest, whether it be the yield on government securities or a discount rate, does not in any relevant sense mean a constant monetary policy. If market rates rise, while discount rates do not, the incentive to discount is increased. This will tend to produce an increase in the amount of credit extended through discounting, an increase in the total amount of Federal Reserve credit outstanding, and a faster rate of growth of the

stock of money than would otherwise have occurred. Conversely, if market rates fall, while discount rates do not, the incentive to discount is reduced, which will tend to reduce discounting and the amount of Federal Reserve credit outstanding, and to reduce the rate of growth of the stock of money. The same discount rate can thus correspond to "easy" money or "tight" money, however those ambiguous terms are defined, depending on the level of market rates; and maintaining the discount rate constant may imply a shift from "easy" money to "tight" money or conversely. In order to keep the degree of "ease" or "tightness" constant, the discount rate must be continuously changed.

Failure to recognize this point, and a tendency to regard the absolute level of the discount rate — or its level relative to some earlier date — as a measure of "tightness" or "ease" has been perhaps the single most pervasive source of confusion and error in the System's experience. In 1920, this fallacy was one reason why the System followed an unduly tight policy and maintained it too long. The discount rate of 6% imposed by all the Reserve Banks in January-February of 1920 and perhaps even the 7% imposed by the New York and three other Reserve Banks in June 1920 would probably not have been high enough to have prevented the money stock from rising if they had been imposed in 1919. By late 1920, these rates were forcing a drastic monetary contraction, yet they were maintained, becoming increasingly "tight" in their effects, until May 1921. The mild reduction at that time still meant a relatively "tight" policy.

From 1929 to 1933, the System kept repeating that it was following an "easy money" policy, pointing to the successive declines in discount rates — aside from the disastrous rise in the fall of 1931. Yet market rates were falling so much more rapidly that by any relevant test the System's policy must be adjudged exceedingly tight — certainly if either the behavior of the money supply or the condition of financial institutions is taken as the guide.

The System has been widely regarded as following a very "easy" money policy in the later 1930's. In fact, the discount rate, though low in an absolute sense by historical standards, exceeded market rates on short-term funds by a wider margin than at any previous time, with the exception only of a few months before the 1933 Banking Holiday, when the discount rate was even farther above short-term market rates. As a result, discounting fell into almost complete disuse in the later 1930's. The substantial and relatively rapid increase in the money stock from 1934 to 1936 and again from 1938 to 1940 owed nothing to easy money policy: it reflected entirely a large gold inflow. The gold inflow in its turn was produced at first mostly by the Treasury's gold and silver purchase programs reinforced by the flight of capital from Europe after Hitler's accession to power, then mostly by the flight of capital to the United States as the threat of war increased, reinforced by the gold and silver purchase programs.

The ill-fated bond support program of World War II and the post-war years is the most widely recognized example of the fallacy in question.

A more recent and more sophisticated version of the fallacy is the emphasis that was placed for a time on "free reserves" as a criterion of the "ease" or "tightness" of monetary policy, and to some extent still is. "Free reserves" are defined as the difference between the reserve balances of member banks and the sum of their required reserves and their borrowings from the System, or, equivalently, the difference between "excess reserves" and "borrowings." Arithmetically, it is clear that any given level of free reserves is consistent with either a rapid increase in the money supply or a rapid decrease. Both excess reserves and borrowings can remain constant, yet total and required reserves rise or fall at any rate, and excess reserves and borrowings can both change, yet their differences remain the same. Economically, there is presumably some level of free reserves that banks desire to maintain at any given time, a level that they try neither to increase by liquidating assets nor to decrease by acquiring assets. I shall call this level "desired free reserves." If the Reserve System tries to maintain a higher level by open market operations, the banks will seek to use the excess to add to their assets and in the process will increase the money supply and required reserves, and so reduce free reserves. The System can frustrate the banks by creating still more

high-powered money, which will produce a continued increase in the money supply. Conversely, if the System tries to maintain a lower level of free reserves than desired, it can do so only by forcing a decline in the money stock. At any given time, therefore — and this is the element of validity in the free reserves doctrine — there is a level of free reserves consistent with no change in the money supply; higher levels imply an increase in the money supply and the higher the level, the more rapid the increase; and conversely for lower levels. But the levels corresponding to constant, increasing, or decreasing money supply do not remain the same over time. What matters is the size of free reserves relative to desired free reserves, not their absolute size. And the level of free reserves that banks desire is not itself a constant. It depends on the conditions of demand and supply for funds, on market rates of interest and their relation to the discount rate. Let the discount rate be unchanged, but market rates fall, and banks will desire to maintain larger free reserves. A level of free reserves that formerly was consistent with, let us say, a rate of rise in the stock of money of 3% a year, may now imply a rate of rise of 0% — this is the way in which the crude fallacy about discount rates enters in this more sophisticated analysis. I rather suspect that something like this is what happened in 1957 and accounts for the System being as tight as it was in the final months of that year.

As the 1957 example suggests, the fact that the same discount rate or the same level of free reserves implies different rates of monetary expansion, is particularly unfortunate at cyclical peaks. The System like the rest of us is unlikely to recognize that a decline is under way until some time after it has begun. In the meantime, the maintenance of the same discount rate or the same level of free reserves implies deflationary monetary pressure. In this way, there is an automatic tendency for a peak in business to produce a reduction in the rate of increase in the stock of money, just the opposite of the automatic reaction that most students would regard as desirable.

A final disadvantage of the use of the discount rate to control the amount of rediscounting is that it tends to promote confusion between what might be called the "monetary" effects of monetary policy — the effects on the stock of money — and the "credit" effects — the effects on recorded rates of interest and other conditions in the credit market. It is easy to see why these two should be confused. In modern financial systems, the creation of money is linked with lending and investing activity and changes in the stock of money generally take place through the credit markets. There is, however, no necessary connection. In an economy with a pure commodity money for example, changes in the stock of money would take place through the purchase and sale of a commodity and not through credit markets at all. In practice, the actual link between the stock of money and credit conditions has varied widely. But the fact that there is a link has tended to lead to undue emphasis on the means whereby the money stock is changed rather than on the change itself. An ancient example of the confusion is the "real bills" fallacy. More recently, the change in economic ideas associated with the name of John Maynard Keynes led to an almost complete neglect of the "monetary" effects of monetary policy and concentration on the "credit" effects. Changes in the stock of money were treated as if they had no effect except insofar as they led to changes in a limited range of recorded market interest rates and thereby to changes in flows of spending. Analysis of the effects of monetary policy, both inside and outside the System, have therefore tended to be restricted to the level of recorded interest rates and movements in them to the complete neglect of changes in the quantity of money.

It is analytically possible to treat all effects of changes in the quantity of money as taking place via changes in interest rates and their effects in turn on flows of spending. But to do so in a comprehensive way requires taking account of a much broader range of rates of interest than "recorded market" rates, for example, implicit rates entering into consumer decisions about stocks of durable goods to hold.

The confusion between the "monetary" and the "credit" effects of Reserve policy is an evil regardless of the views one may hold about the economic importance of changes in the stock

of money or the channels through which such changes exert their influence. The Federal Reserve System occupies a commanding role under present circumstances in determining the stock of money — it can make the stock of money whatever it wants within very wide limits and to a high degree of precision. By contrast, it is one of many institutions in the capital market. It may be able to fix the yield on a few securities but only by sacrificing its control over the stock of money and even then only within fairly narrow limits. It cannot for long determine the whole structure of yields on capital assets. These propositions have surely been adequately demonstrated by postwar experience in this and other countries. Hence even if one were to believe — as I do not — that changes in the stock of money are relatively unimportant in their economic effect compared to changes in the capital market, and exert their influence predominantly by affecting recorded rates, the Reserve System's role is to control the stock of money. Its tools should be judged by their efficiency in enabling it to do so, though one might then wish to determine what changes it should make in the stock of money on the basis of the changes it was desired to produce in recorded interest rates. The fact that discounting means the setting of a specific interest rate fosters the belief that the System is directly controlling rates of interest and that its aim is to do so. This leads both the System and outsiders to misjudge its policy. It also inhibits Reserve policy because the Reserve System is attributed credit or blame for matters that are in fact outside of its control. It is described as aiming at a "higher" or "lower" level of interest rates when in practice any effects on interest rates may be entirely incidental to its purpose. It may, and I would say should, be raising or lowering discount rates not in order to affect interest rates but to affect the rate of change in the stock of money.

To avoid these disadvantages, rediscounting should be eliminated. The Federal Reserve would then no longer have to announce a discount rate or to change it; it would then have direct control over the amount of high-powered money it created; it would not be a source of instability alike by its occasional changes in the discount rate and by the unintended changes in the "tightness" or "ease" of policy associated with an unchanged rate, nor would it be misled by these unintended changes; and it would be less subject to being diverted from its main task by the attention devoted to the "credit" effects of its policy.

If rediscounting were eliminated, one minor function now performed by the discount rate would need to be provided for in some other way. Since required reserves are calculated after the event and need to be estimated in advance, some discrepancies between required and actual reserves are unavoidable, yet some penalty must be imposed on such discrepancies to enforce the reserve requirements. Currently the penalty is generally a charge equal to interest on the deficit at a rate equal to the discount rate plus 2 percentage points. The simplest alternative would be a fixed rate of "fine." To avoid discrepancies becoming an indirect form of discounting, the "fine" should be large enough to make it well above likely market rates of interest. The fine would then become the equivalent of a truly "penalty" discount rate — to use the language that was the source of so much discussion in the early days of the System — except that no collateral, no eligibility requirements, or the like would be involved.

An alternative to the complete abolition of discounting is to follow the Canadian precedent of tying the discount rate automatically to a market rate — currently the Canadian rate is set each week at ¼ of one per cent above the latest average tender rate for Treasury bills. If the differential were sufficiently high, this would be equivalent to abolishing discounting. Otherwise, while such a device would eliminate some of the disadvantages I have enumerated, it would be decidedly inferior to the abolition of rediscounting, and would leave much room for the authorities to affect the discount rate through the amount of bills offered for sale, or similar devices if some other rate were used.

30

A COMMENT ON THE ROLE OF THE DISCOUNT WINDOW IN CREDIT POLICY*

Robert V. Roosa†

The following two selections are in effect a reply to Selection 29. In the process of explaining how the "discount window" is administered they also explain why, in the authors' view, the rediscounting facility is an essential part of the American banking scene and why the Federal Reserve has not seen fit to emulate the "penalty rate" as employed by the central banks of Canada and England.

* Reprinted by permission of the author and the publishers from *The Quarterly Journal of Economics*, Vol. LXIII, No. 2 (May, 1959). Cambridge, Mass.: Harvard University Press, Copyright, 1959, by the President and Fellows of Harvard College.

† Partner, Brown Brothers Harriman and Company. Formerly Vice President, Federal Reserve Bank of New York.

There seem to be some serious misconceptions abroad to the effect that Federal Reserve Banks, on their own initiative, ration credit at the discount window, refusing one bank or accommodating another, as a sort of credit control. This is of course not done. In determining the validity of borrowing requests, the stress is on good banking practices; no attempt is made to orient each borrowing bank's position into the broader policy aims of current Federal Reserve credit control. Any bank with a good record can be virtually certain that it will get a loan.

Perhaps part of the confusion, and it exists in some banking circles as well as in the world outside, comes from the compulsion many of us feel to classify decisions rigidly into two categories — the "yes" and the "no." From that often follows the arbitrary determination that whatever is not unequivocally "no" must be "yes." Without returning to the philosophy classroom, one might hope to find agreement that it is no more arbitrary to turn this quite around, so that whatever is not unequivocally "yes" must be considered "no." And on this equally dubious scale, there would be no difficulty in finding scores, if not thousands, of rejections. A bank that would not hesitate to present a note (supported by ample collateral) for a sum equal to, say, 10 per cent of its reserve balances, or perhaps 20 per cent of its capital accounts, would be most apprehensive in asking for a sum several times larger than this, regardless of the collateral, and would expect to provide an explanation in an effort to justify the amount on a very temporary basis. A bank that wanted to borrow for more than a few days, even in relatively small amounts, would know that no note can run for more than fifteen days, that a renewal request would be scrutinized closely to judge the adequacy of the provision being made to pay off shortly with funds obtained in other ways, and that its chances of full accommodation would be particularly slim if it had been borrowing in several other reserve-computation periods during recent months.

The truth is, of course, that the discount window is never either wide open nor tightly closed. Insofar as human frailties permit, it is always the same window, open in the same way at all times for borrowers of the same circumstances. What makes the impact of these continuous standards seem to vary is that the circumstances of the banks themselves change. In some part, nearly all of the time, the changes reflect what has been done to the reserve base, as a whole, by the open market operations or other actions of the Federal Reserve. Hence the continuous interest, at the policy level within the Federal Reserve System, in the interactions between the degree of general pressure as individual banks find themselves, more often or less often, in need of temporary borrowing assistance to average out their required reserves.

The crucial point is that the central bank should not give up the ultimate initiative for control over the creation of bank reserves. In the American setting, the fact that banks borrow only as a privilege means that even though any individual bank can temporarily, in effect, cause the creation of reserves by borrowing at the discount window, that same bank simultaneously takes on an obligation to find ways of extinguishing those reserves — the more promptly the better, in order to preserve its privilege for use again when unexpected reserve drains occur. Thus, as a general rule, the larger the aggregate volume of bank borrowing from the Federal Reserve, the greater will be the effort then going on, through the banking system, to limit credits and bring reserves into balance with the requirements against deposits. But the pressure exerted on credit extension is gradual and not precipitate. Time is allowed for any one bank to shift some of its burden of adjustment to others, rather than undergo the full shock alone, if an unexpected reserve drain has left it far short of requirements in a single reserve-computation period.

There are sharp contrasts, of course, between the role of discount operations in the American unit banking system and the purposes served by discounting in most other countries. In many, the absence of an active trading market in the instruments of short-term liquidity (Treasury bills, bankers acceptances and the like) prevents the central bank from relying upon open market operations, and discounting becomes the principal means of supplying central bank credit (i.e., bank reserves) to the banking system. In such countries, there must be a substantial amount of discounting in existence all of the time, and effective variations are induced by changes in the borrowing ceilings established for individual banks, by changes in the margin applied in valuing some kinds of collateral, by changes in the discount rate, or by other means. Within rather wide limits, borrowing at the central bank becomes a right; not, as in this country, a privilege — carrying an implication that early repayment is necessary in order to preserve the widest latitude for later use of the borrowing facility at times of large and sudden reserve strains.

In other countries, fortunate enough to have a money market, the banking structure usually consists of only a few, large branch banks. There, the reserve losses of one branch office may be netted against the gains of another, as deposits move about the country, without any net strain visible in the total reserve position of the parent bank as a whole. In the United States, these inescapable physical by-products of a check-payment mechanism are all brought out into the open. No individual bank can feel assured that it will get back from others, each day or each week, a volume of deposits equal to those withdrawn. There may be an evening out over time, or through seasons, but the short swings for any single bank can be very wide indeed. So long as there are frictions in redistributing reserves, with some banks always ending their reserve-computation periods in a deficient position, and unable to tap promptly all of the excesses lodged in other banks elsewhere, there will be need for borrowing at the Federal Reserve. And because this is, within reasonable limits, merely a mechanical facility, aiding the smooth functioning of the deposit-money process, no purpose would be served by trying to fend off borrowing by using a stiff "penalty rate" concept of the discount rate in this country. On the contrary, banks faced with unexpected withdrawals might, if the discount rate were set well above going money market rates, be induced to make abrupt curtailments of other loans or investments, in an effort to meet their reserve requirements, with upsetting, or at least capriciously disturbing, effects in their local communities.

Yet the same facility which many banks may need in meeting the unavoidable exigencies of deposit shifts, as money moves about from day to day in doing the nation's business, might also be tapped, if there were no frictions imposed upon access to the discount window, for the more obvious purpose of borrowing at a lower rate in order to lend (or invest) at a higher rate of return. That is why, in the administration of the discount window, and in the exercise of bank supervision, banks are continually reminded that they cannot rely upon any funds borrowed from the Federal Reserve as a permanent, or quasi-permanent, addition to their own resources. It is to make certain that the discount window is used, and only used, to meet actual needs for temporary assistance in maintaining reserves at the required levels that surveillance becomes necessary. It is very difficult to say where the influence of surveillance begins, and the influence of the traditional reluctance to borrow runs out. But there is really no need to try. Both are certainly present; and whenever the check imposed by tradition might begin to falter, the limits imposed by surveillance would begin to take hold. Quite understandably, more-over, at times when Federal Reserve policy is aimed at limiting the overall growth of bank credit and the money supply, more banks will be running their reserve positions very close to the margin, and deficiencies in these positions will occur more frequently, and in a larger aggregate total for the country as a whole, as deposit shifts continue to work their uneven incidence among individual banks from day to day. It is for that reason, and not because there is any wholesale breakdown in the reluctance to borrow, or in the surveillance, that the volume of borrowing tends to rise when Federal Reserve policy is restrictive.

When an increase in borrowing is going on, the policy arm of the Federal Reserve will be trying to judge, very broadly, whether the total volume of borrowing that has emerged is exerting too much pressure toward the limitation of bank credit, or not enough, or perhaps is about right. If the general diffusion of pressure seems too great, in the light of overall credit policy objectives, then, without any need to decide that one bank should have more reserves at the discount window, or another less, the Federal Reserve can make a change that will result in some of the banks, somewhere, borrowing less. It can release new reserves into the banking system, and would ordinarily do so through open market operations. As these funds begin to flow from bank to bank, some banks will find themselves able to repay borrowings without having to sell other investments or reduce other credits, and there will be fewer banks (or at any rate a smaller aggregate of borrowing requests) stepping in to take their place in the next round of borrowings at the discount window.

With no changes in the criteria used at the discount window, an additional release of reserves through open market operations, while other conditions remain the same, will bring about a reduction in the volume of borrowing. The "pressure component" in the total volume of bank reserves will have been reduced. But at no time, either when total borrowing was high, or after it had been reduced, would the Federal Reserve have been in any danger of losing control over the creation of bank reserves. It is, in effect, the decisions made with respect to open market operations that determine, within rough limits, the volume of borrowing that will emerge within the unchanging framework of lending criteria applied at the discount window. And it will normally be the combined influence of the forces released by open market operations, and those generated by the persistent urge to repay borrowings, that together determine the degree of pressure toward further expansion of credit, or toward a limitation upon such expansion, that may exist in the commercial banking system at any given time.

31

FEDERAL RESERVE DISCOUNT POLICY AND ITS CRITICS*

Murray E. Polakoff†

Since the Federal Reserve System's inception in 1914, controversy has surrounded its use of the discount mechanism as an instrument of credit and monetary policy. Early criticism tended to center around the profitability aspects of bank indebtedness and to suggest that discretionary discount policy would be ineffective during periods of rapid expansion unless a penalty rate was imposed on member banks. Contemporary criticism has evoked essentially similar theoretical arguments bulwarked by the additional claim that frequent discount rate changes tend to produce adverse psychological effects on the credit markets. On the policy level, however, many of the postwar critics have sharply parted ground with their predecessors insofar as they have advocated the abandonment of discretionary discount policy. This seems to be part of a more general trend among some economists in the postwar period to substitute rules for discretion in the exercise of monetary policy.

I. INTRODUCTION

The Federal Reserve System, throughout its history, has tended to be both eclectic and pragmatic in its analysis and use of the discount mechanism. While it has not moved boldly enough on many occasions, nor with sufficient

* From *Banking and Monetary Studies*, edited by Deane Carson (Irwin, 1963). Reprinted by the courtesy of the publisher and the author.
† New York University.

vigor and imagination, there has been a tendency to take note of what it deemed valuable in the strictures of its critics and to modify, if sometimes with a considerable time lag, its own philosophy and approach as circumstances seemed to warrant. Nonetheless, one of the many problems besetting System policy has been its failure to integrate successfully the various theories of discounting in such a manner as to maximize the utility of the discount mechanism.

Parts II and III of this essay trace briefly the evolution of discounting and discount theories in addition to examining in some detail the postwar criticisms of discount policy as exemplified in the writings of several critics who advocate a nondiscretionary approach to discount policy. Part IV attempts to integrate some of the current theories of discounting and to ascertain the extent to which the discount window serves as an escape mechanism from System efforts to control inflationary pressures. The results are such as to suggest that, on balance, there is no need to do away with an active and discretionary discount policy so long as the System has the moral courage to use effectively the tools already at its disposal as well as the willingness to continue to experiment and innovate in line with changing conditions.

II. DISCOUNT THEORIES AND THE EVOLUTION OF DISCOUNT POLICY

Any analysis of member bank borrowings from the Fed must proceed, for the sake of conceptual clarity and policy decision making, on some assumption or set of assumptions regarding the attitude of the former toward borrowing from the latter. Prior to World War II, several views were advanced which continue to form the theoretical underpinnings for much of the controversy surrounding contemporary discussions of discount policy.

A view heard early in the System's history was that member banks, as profit-maximizing private institutions, borrowed primarily for profit considerations whenever they had the opportunity to obtain a favorable differential between market rates and the discount rate.

Given the existence of a "profit spread," the banks would have a continuous incentive to borrow in order to acquire higher yielding assets. Therefore, it was argued by some System critics, some penalty rate was necessary if banks were not to abuse the discount privilege during periods of credit stringency.

While System officials viewed with sympathy the notion of a penalty rate such that the discount rate would lead the market upward and follow it downward, thereby placing a continuous penalty on obtaining central bank credit, there was no more agreement in those early years than now as to what the relevant rate should be against which to compare the discount rate. Initially, the idea of a penalty rate seemed to refer to a comparison between the discount rate and the rate on eligible commercial paper presented at the discount window for security behind the loan. However, since the type of paper presented offered no real clue as to the uses made of the proceeds — uses which might include loans and investments with higher yields than those on the eligible collateral — opinion within the System was divided over what constituted the pivotal rate. Among the diverse rates suggested were: those charged by member banks on customer loans; some average rate of return on total earning assets; the highest yield on open-market paper; and the lowest rate of return on the bank's investment portfolio. Actually, the only penalty rates enforced during the early 1920's were those on some types of open-market paper. To rationalize its failure as a lender of last resort, a false analogy was drawn between the Bank of England's bank rate and the discount rates set by the Reserve Banks.[1]

With the development of open-market operations as an instrument of national credit policy in the 1920's, a new official doctrine promul-

[1] The reason for suggesting that the analogy is a false one lies in the different institutional arrangements in both countries. In Great Britain, it is the bill dealers and not the commercial banks that borrow directly from the Bank of England. Since the former specialize in a particular kind of asset — formerly commercial bills and now Treasury bills — and since the Bank rate is higher than the rate on bills, the discount rate in that country truly can be considered to be a penalty rate when dealers are forced to seek accommodation at the central bank.

gated later in the decade squarely took issue with the profitability thesis and its policy implications. The Riefler thesis, as it came to be known, suggested that penalty rates, however defined, were unnecessary for the proper execution of discount policy.[2] Briefly, the hypothesis stated that borrowings occurred primarily when banks, for brief and unexpected reasons, found themselves short of reserves. In such circumstances they tended, in the main, to borrow out of "need"; i.e., they were not motivated basically by relative profit considerations but rather reluctantly resorted to the discount window to meet adverse clearing balances and unanticipated seasonal loan demands and then tended to repay their outstanding debts to the System as quickly as possible. Such aversion to indebtedness by member banks was explained by a tradition among them antedating even the establishment of the Federal Reserve System as well as their own psychology which suggested that continuous borrowing was a confession either of weakened financial condition or of poor management. Open-market and customer loan rates were, to a large extent, a function of central bank credit with marginal bank borrowings constituting the decisive influence on money market rates. Given the tradition against borrowing, the larger its volume the greater would be the efforts of member banks to contract loans and repay indebtedness. This would be accomplished through the sale of open-market paper, increasing its yield and dampening inflationary pressures.[3]

From the standpoint of monetary policy, the Riefler thesis suggested that the way to initiate a credit tightening action was through the employment of open-market sales which, by decreasing the reserve base, would force member banks to the discount window. Once money rates rose, the Reserve authorities might then raise the level of discount rates to keep them in line with increases in the rest of the rate structure. However, since discount rates did not exert a direct influence on the volume of borrowings, no penalty rate was necessary. Policy emphasis was to be shifted from the discount mechanism to open-market operations. It is small wonder that the new doctrine was welcomed, given the force and clarity of the "need" thesis with its attendant implications that Reserve Banks could continue to serve their individual banks in reserve arrears while not, at the same time, losing control over the aggregate volume of credit through failure to impose a penalty rate. In spite of subsequent modifications through the years, including a crisis of confidence in the efficacy of the reluctance principle during the 1950's, it has continued to serve as the capstone for official discount policy to the present time.[4]

The late 1930's witnessed the emergence of a significant variant of the profitability thesis which has since gained considerable favor as a purported explanation of member bank borrowing behavior.[5] Actually, while Turner's definition of profit borrowing was broad enough to encompass borrowing from the Fed for the express purpose of relending such funds at higher market rates, his analysis was confined

---

[2] Named after the most influential exponent of the doctrine, namely Winfield W. Riefler of the Board of Governors. See his *Money Rates and Money Markets in the United States* (New York: Harper & Bros., 1930), chap. ii, pp. 16–36.

[3] Conversely, during deflationary periods when borrowings were low, funds would be offered by the banks through the purchase of such paper, thereby driving down their yields. Consequently, over the course of the business cycle there would tend to exist a high degree of positive correlation between open-market rates and the volume of bank borrowings.

[4] Current official thought still is dominated by the Riefler notion that, given the reluctance of banks to borrow, the larger the aggregate volume of such borrowings brought on by open-market sales, the greater will be the degree of pressure placed on borrowing banks to limit credits and bring reserves into line with deposit requirements. Consequently, a large volume of bank indebtedness constitutes presumptive evidence of credit rationing by member banks and higher market rates, both helping to contain inflationary pressures. If this were unequivocally so, however, there would appear to be little or no rationale for the System's constant emphasis on discount rate changes and discount administration as necessary techniques for *limiting* the volume of borrowings, an unnecessary and even perverse preoccupation if increases in the latter always elicited the type of responses presumably following from bank reluctance to borrow. The Riefler doctrine currently may be found incorporated under the System's concept of free reserves. Presumably the level of free reserves (excess reserves minus borrowings) serves the Fed as a measure of tightness or ease in the money market.

[5] R. C. Turner, *Member Bank Borrowing* (Columbus, Ohio: Ohio State University Press, 1938).

almost exclusively to choices of alternative courses of action in the adjustment of required reserves, such choices being dictated by the relative spread between yields on short-term open-market paper and other secondary reserves and the discount rate. Regardless of the initial reasons for additional reserves, the *extent* to which member banks availed themselves of the discount window rather than the open market in satisfying their desire for funds depended upon the profit spread; i.e., the cost differential between borrowing at the discount rate or selling secondary reserves thereby foregoing their yield. Adjustment of bank reserves thus became a function of the relative profitability of the two alternatives, the banks preferring the least costly method. Starting out from a position of equilibrium, if the discount rate should fall relative to open-market rates, the banks would respond by increasing their borrowings from the System, since they would now find the price of such marginal borrowings relatively more attractive for adjustment purposes than the liquidation of secondary reserves. Presumably the greater the spread, the larger would be the volume of borrowings, at least within some fairly wide range of spreads. The statistical findings for the 15-year period covered by Turner from 1922 through 1936 appeared to corroborate his analysis, since high positive correlation coefficients were found between the level of discounting and profit spreads on open-market loans. While Turner concluded that his variant of the profitability thesis appeared to offer at least a partial explanation of changes in the volume of borrowing, he was also willing to grant that the tradition against borrowing appeared to set some upper limit to such borrowings even in the presence of increasing spreads. Furthermore, he pointed out that nowhere did the empirical data suggest that discounts tended to lead and the profit spread to follow. The tendency in every case was either for synchronous movements, or for the profit spread to lead and discounts to follow. Since this indicated to him that the causal pattern was not the sort envisaged by Riefler, Turner recommended that discount policy should once again place more emphasis on the discount rate in regulating the overall volume of bank bor-

rowings. If reasonable stability in the volume of borrowings was desired, open-market operations should be used simply as an offset to net changes in all the other factors beside discounts influencing the supply and use of total member bank reserves. If a contraction of discounting was desired during a tight money period, a "penalty rate" should be enforced, the discount rate being above open market rates.

The Turner version of discount theory and policy was to lie dormant for many years, in part because of official satisfaction with the Riefler thesis, in part because the 1930's and 1940's were characterized by the virtual cessation of borrowings by member banks. Excess reserves tended to be plentiful during the depressed 1930's as a result of decreasing loan demand and heavy gold inflows. When they began to disappear around 1944 due to wartime monetary expansion, the price support program for government securities by the Fed insured the banks' ample reserves without recourse to borrowing. However, with the decision of the Fed to return to classical monetary techniques after the Treasury-Federal Reserve Accord in 1951, the need for an effective discount policy again came to the fore. It can reasonably be inferred from subsequent events that the immediate post-Accord experience led the Fed to accept, at least in part, the importance of the Turner thesis if not the type of discount policy advocated by him.

The final quarter of 1952 saw the Treasury bill rate rise above the discount rate by a good one half of 1 per cent while, at the same time, quarterly averages of daily borrowings rose rapidly to nearly $1.5 billions, well above any comparable figure since 1921. This relatively large volume of bank indebtedness in the face of long-held official insistence upon the efficacy of the tradition against borrowing appears to have caused considerable consternation within the System. The result was an official inquiry into the discount mechanism, an inquiry which subsequently resulted in a decision to reinforce the banks' tradition against discounting through the employment of nonprice criteria in judging bank requests for credit as well as greater reliance on the discount rate as a cost factor. With regard to the latter, the

Riefler doctrine which had guided Fed discount policy for a good quarter of a century was modified in the sense that the System increasingly became convinced that as the spread between the bill rate and discount rate widened the reluctance of banks in general to borrow from it tended to grow weaker.

However, acceptance of the importance of the discount rate as a cost factor would appear to have posed a dilemma for official discount policy in the mid-1950's. Policy demanded that consideration be given to having discount rate action take the lead in applying a policy of credit restraint, instead of following the prewar practice of bringing pressure on bank reserves through open-market operations until such time as general market rates rose, and then raising the discount rate. Only then would sufficient pressure be maintained on bank reserves through open-market operations so that the bill rate would follow the discount rate but would not go above it, thereby keeping the discount rate at all times in the position of being a "penalty rate." Such a substantial modification of the Riefler doctrine, however, ran into the objection that even if the discount rate were kept above the bill rate at all times through moderate open-market operations, it would still be considerably below the yields on other secondary reserves. Furthermore, choice of the bill rate as the pivotal rate would tend to pose problems since fluctuations in its yields were as much due to erratic influences, such as temporary investment of the proceeds of large corporate issues, as to prevailing pressures in the money market. Hence, it was argued that such a policy provided no "effective" penalty rate at all and, unless enforced at substantial adverse spreads, would still leave the Fed powerless in the face of inflationary pressures. The results seem to have been a compromise; while subsequent advances by the Fed in "discount rates represented an adjustment to changes that had occurred in market rates rather than an attempt to lead market rates," a more active discount rate policy was followed both in 1955–57 and 1958–60, than in 1952–53, with rates raised on 12 different occasions in those years as compared with only one increase in the earlier period. More-

over, the discount rate, while lagging behind changes in the bill rate, nevertheless remained above the latter for most of the later periods. Apparently the System hoped that keeping the discount rate attuned to changes in market rates, when further implemented by the revised Regulation A and a deliberate educational campaign geared to refurbishing the tradition against borrowing, would be sufficient to keep the level of discounting within manageable bounds.

III. RULES VERSUS DISCRETION IN DISCOUNT POLICY

While the System had been struggling during the decade of the 1950's for a viable posture related to discounting, academic criticism in the post-Accord period has tended, for the most part, to center around the issue of discretion versus nondiscretion in the execution of discount policy.[6] Many of the arguments favoring lack of discretion have ranged, frequently within the same individual, from technical criticisms of current policy to philosophic positions which eschew deliberate intervention in a market economy coupled with a distrust of those in positions of power. Thus, Professor Simmons has voiced resentment against deliberate use of the discount window through "non-price rationing to control the amount of lending done by the central bank" and, for the same reason, has stated that the "present discount mechanism seems poorly suited to serve as a monetary control in a market economy."[7] Similarly Professor Friedman has opposed continuance of System administrative action on the grounds that the "exercise of discretion is an undesirable kind of specific credit control that involves detailed intervention into the affairs of individual banks and arbitrary decisions by

[6] Actually, some critics have taken the issue much further into a critique encompassing all of discretionary monetary policy. See Milton Friedman, *A Program for Monetary Stability* (New York: Fordham University Press, 1960); also, E. S. Shaw, "Money Supply and Stable Economic Growth," in *United States Monetary Policy* (New York: The American Assembly, 1958), pp. 49–71.

[7] Edward C. Simmons, "A Note on the Revival of Federal Reserve Discount Policy," *The Journal of Finance*, Vol. XI, No. 4 (December, 1956), pp. 414, 420.

government officials."[8] Whatever the specific criticisms of official discount policy, the results have been reflected in a spate of suggestions ranging from advocacy of a nondiscretionary penalty rate to complete abandonment of the discount mechanism.

A leading advocate of a nondiscretionary discount policy is Professor Warren Smith. While Smith accepts completely Turner's reasoning on the importance of the cost impact of discount rate changes and, therefore, criticizes official discount policy in the expansion phase 1954–56 for its failure to maintain a penalty rate, he adds a new dimension to the controversy by concentrating on the so-called "announcement effects" accompanying discount rate changes. In so doing, he takes issue with the Fed that the market psychologically interprets discount rate changes in line with System intentions and reacts accordingly. In his opinion, frequent rate changes do tend to be destabilizing on both the supply and demand sides of the market. For example, increases in the discount rate during periods of expansion may misfire inasmuch as instead of supplying a note of caution they may accelerate optimism on the part of businessmen concerning the economic future and so lead to rapidly increasing demands for credit instead of inhibiting investment decisions. More important is the fact that lending institutions which do pay careful attention to System actions may become confused by discount rate changes and so react perversely, since, at times, they may attribute to upward changes a marked tightening of monetary policy, whereas such changes may merely represent technical adjustments to changes in other market rates. At other times, failure to make such adjustments may create expectations of a fundamental change in monetary policy, thereby enhancing credit availability and a decline in long-term rates. The result may be such as to bring forth a flood of capital issues previously kept off the market. On the other hand, a technical readjustment misinterpreted by market lenders as a sign of increasing pressure by the Fed may lead to sharply increasing long-term yields and

credit rationing, thereby forcing the System to offset its current policy unwillingly through temporary easing of restrictive open-market operations. Given the failure of System policy to enforce a penalty rate augmented by potentially destabilizing "signal" effects, Smith advocates abandonment of discretionary discount policy and the establishment of a fixed relationship between the discount rate and the Treasury bill rate. The former automatically would be adjusted each week so as to maintain a constant differential of 1 per cent or more between it and the auction rate on Treasury bills.

As Smith himself admits, changes in the discount rate are only one, and not a very important kind of information on which business expectations are formed. Furthermore, empirical data for the period 1955–59 would not tend to support the notion that discount rate changes lead to destabilizing actions on the part of businessmen. Thus, changes in business loans from commercial banks as well as public offerings and private placements of corporate security issues during that period tended to precede, rather than follow, initial changes in the discount rate. Again, there was little correlation between changes in the discount rate and registration of new corporate issues. On the supply side, it is difficult to believe that knowledgeable financial institutions, aware of the fact that changes in discount rates in recent years have followed, rather than led, changes in money market rates would react strongly and perversely to discount rate changes. Also, they necessarily make use of many other indicators in forming and confirming their expectations of prospective economic and financial developments, including other aspects of monetary policy such as the free reserve position of member banks. Finally, fluctuations in long-term rates are much more influenced by other forces than uncertainties associated with the discount rate. At the very least, systematic empirical research should be undertaken as to the likely effects of discount rate changes on the money and capital markets before the expectations argument is made the basis for abandonment of discretionary discount policy.

Quite apart from the validity of the expec-

[8] Friedman, op. cit., p. 39.

tations argument, a nondiscretionary penalty rate would prevent the System from altering the relative cost of borrowing at times when changing economic conditions might be such as to make it important to encourage a change in the willingness of member banks to borrow. Furthermore, to the extent that discount rate changes have any adverse psychological effects, deliberate manipulation of the discount rate by the System for the purpose of confounding market expectations would be impossible under a nondiscretionary policy.

An extreme variant of the nondiscretionary approach would go so far as to abolish discounting completely as a credit control weapon. While Professor Friedman is more aware than most of the potentially inhibiting effects on borrowing of System administrative action, nevertheless he opposes its continuance on philosophic grounds as well as on the grounds that it cannot be applied in a sufficiently sensitive manner in the short run so as to produce "predictable" results.[9] So far as official discount rate policy is concerned Friedman, like Smith, agrees that frequent changes in the discount rate tend to be destabilizing in terms of market expectations. However, such changes are necessary if the System is to keep its monetary policy unchanged. This involves the Fed in changing the discount rate as open-market rates change, a purely technical adjustment but nevertheless one which is interpreted by the market as meaning a change in policy.[10] Nowhere does Friedman evaluate the reluctance of banks to borrow as a possible deterrent to the excessive use of the discount window. Given his strictures against discount administration and discount rate policy, he would substitute for present practices a fixed fine "large enough to make it well above likely market rates of

interest." Such a fine would be necessary to prevent discrepancies between required and actual reserves from becoming an indirect form of discounting. By setting the fine sufficiently high so that it would be punitive for those individual banks failing to meet their reserve requirements, it would then become the equivalent of a true penalty rate except that no collateral, eligibility requirements, or criteria of appropriate borrowing would be involved.

One of the arguments in favor of retention of the discount facility, whether on a discretionary basis, is that it serves as a safety valve for those individual banks temporarily in reserve arrears. Such banks can always obtain reserve accommodation provided they are willing to pay the going rate. Friedman, however, feels that the federal funds market already serves as an effective substitute for discounting. Moreover, other substitutes would become available under the push of profit incentives should rediscounting be discontinued. While there may be considerable merit to these contentions, nevertheless it must be remembered that market imperfections may continue to exist to an even greater degree among such substitutes than through direct access to the discount window. Some of the arguments which can be mustered against criticism of the "safety valve" feature of discounting are as follows: (1) The discount mechanism is particularly well suited to supplying a portion of reserves for seasonal needs and reserve losses and supplying them directly and immediately to the points where they are most needed. This is not true of open-market operations, the sole instrument of credit control which Friedman would have the Fed retain. (2) Given our unit banking system, it is inevitable that during periods of strong inflationary pressure the very mechanics of our check-payment mechanism would be such as to cause sharp swings in the reserve positions of individual banks as payments were accelerated. A punitive fine in place of the borrowing privilege and failure to borrow in other markets and from other banks faced with similar problems might only lead to abrupt curtailment of earning assets by the deficient banks, thereby resulting in disturbing effects in their local communities and in the money and capital markets. (3) It is a fact

[9] Friedman, op. cit., p. 39. Surely "predictable" in this context does not imply lack of any systematic relationship between the extent of borrowing and discount administration, even in the short run. The real problem, therefore, becomes one of the extent of slippage rather than the existence of slippage itself. Obviously, slippage exists in all economic phenomena in the sense that deviations exist between predicted and actual values. Furthermore, the System has never attempted to experiment with such possibilities as may be inherent in discount administration as an anticyclical credit control weapon.

[10] The same evaluation of the "expectational" view previously given would apply to Friedman's analysis.

that frictions do exist in the credit markets. Thus, only a small minority, and those the larger banks in the System, are in a position to avail themselves fully of the federal funds market in order to tap excess reserves lodged elsewhere to meet their temporary reserve deficiencies. On the other hand, discounting serves as a safety valve for *all* member banks faced with an unexpected deficiency in their reserve positions.

IV. IN DEFENSE OF DISCRETION

It is interesting to note that the Fed, as well as its critics, appeared to be agreed on one major issue during the debates of the 1950's: namely, that the spread was a critical variable in explaining member bank borrowing behavior and, further, that should it widen substantially during an expansionary period there would appear to be little or no ceiling to the volume of indebtedness incurred by member banks in the aggregate. Thus, Simmons, Aschheim, Friedman, and Kareken assume that member bank demand for reserves borrowed from the System is highly or perfectly elastic with respect to market interest rates. Even Smith, who like Turner before him, recognizes a borrowing constraint in the form of the tradition against borrowing as well as the deterrent impact of the policing activities of the System upon bank borrowings, nevertheless fails to *integrate* such constraints with his least cost thesis. What he does is to compartmentalize "need" and "profits" in such a manner that the former is applied only to the goals of bank borrowing, whereas the latter becomes important simply as a means of attaining such ends. This assumed ambivalence in bank borrowing behavior leads him to ignore the reluctance motive when explaining the *extent* to which member banks make use of the discount window. When translated into prescription, it tends to exaggerate the importance of the cost element and to minimize the effects of nonprice constraints in affecting the amount of discounting so that the only practical alternative appears to be the abandonment of discretion and a fixed penalty rate.

Similarly, the Fed during the 1950's, while continuing to emphasize the importance of the reluctance motive in influencing the course of member bank borrowing, nevertheless appeared convinced that, given increasing spreads during periods of inflationary pressures, the reluctance of banks in general to borrow from it tended to grow weaker relative to increasing profitability. The logic of the argument seemed to imply that unless the discount rate in such periods could be raised often and high enough so as to keep it in line with changes in the bill rate, borrowings would escape from the confines of being a safety valve and merely would become transformed into an engine of inflation. Hence, the inner agonizing within the System during the middle 1950's resulted in revision of Regulation A and the frequent use of discount rate changes. As indicated earlier, during the expansion phase 1955–57 the discount rate was raised on seven different occasions while it was increased five times during the period 1958–60.

A recent study made by the writer suggests that both the Fed and its critics may have underestimated radically the effectiveness of the reluctance motive and administrative action by the Fed in influencing the actual path of member bank borrowings.[11] Scatter diagrams for the period 1953–58 indicated that the general shapes of the borrowing curves clearly were not those that one would infer from the profitability and Fed hypotheses. Rather they showed either a tendency for borrowing to taper off as the bill rate rose relative to the discount rate or even the possibility of a downturn in the outstanding volume of indebtedness in the face of increasing spreads. Similar results were found for the expansion phase 1954–57. Subsequently, the writer fitted linear and second degree parabolic functions by the method of least squares to the data for 1954–

[11] "Reluctance Elasticity, Least Cost, and Member-Bank Borrowing: A Suggested Integration," *The Journal of Finance*, Vol. XV, No. 1 (March, 1960), pp. 1–18. That the reluctance motive is real is indicated by a recent study which shows that for the period 1956–59 the number of banks borrowing at any time in a quarter as a proportion of all member banks ranged from a low of 14.7 per cent in the third quarter of 1956 to a high of only 21.6 per cent in the third quarter of 1959. Furthermore, only a fraction of these banks had to be contacted by the Fed for violating some aspect of Regulation A. "Answer to Question XVI of the Commission on Money and Credit," *op. cit.*

FIGURE I

Short-Term Interest Rate

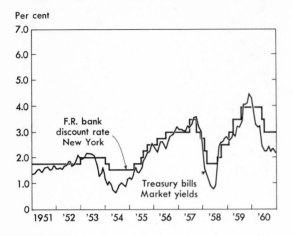

FIGURE II

Relation of Member-Bank Borrowings to
Least-Cost Spread,
April, 1958, through May, 1960
Monthly averages of daily figures

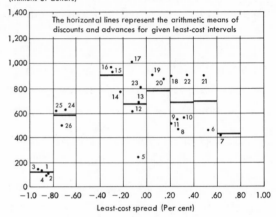

57. Analysis of variance tests were then performed. At the 5 per cent level of significance, it was found that a simple linear regression was inappropriate. However, when a second degree function was employed it was found to give an acceptable fit to the data. This tended to confirm the impression of nonlinearity of the borrowings path for 1954–57 found in the scatter diagram.[12]

Figure II suggests the borrowing path for the expansion phase 1958–60. For the period as a whole there would appear to be the same tendency for the marginal propensity to borrow to decline as spreads increase followed by an absolute decline in indebtedness after a spread of −.2 is reached. However, the chronological distribution of the monthly averages of daily borrowings during 1958–60 was such as to indicate the possibility of a structural shift between the earlier and later phases of the period. Accordingly, it was broken up into two phases, that of April, 1958–March, 1959, and April, 1959–May, 1960. The data were then plotted in

the scatter diagram to be found in Figure III. They tend to confirm the upward shift in the borrowings curve.[13] At the same time, however, both borrowing slopes appear to be curvilinear rather than linear. The early period shows an absolute downturn in indebtedness beyond a spread of .4. The later period indicates a tapering off of borrowings with a net borrowings ceiling established within a relatively wide range of spread values. The slopes of both curves do not appear to be consistent with either the profitability or Fed hypotheses.

A theoretical explanation which the writer believes is consistent with the empirical slopes of the expansion paths. is one which, unlike the least-cost hypothesis, initially assumes *both* reluctance and relative cost to be mutually operative in the adjustment of member bank reserve positions.[14] Given the end or ends of bank

---

[12] For the linear function F was found to be 3.07 as compared with an $F_{.05}$ of 2.92. For the second degree polynomial, however, F came to 1.17 as compared with and $F_{.05}$ of 3.32. The values found for the quadratic were $Y = 806.163 + 210.855\ X - 1,319.629X^2 + u$. The index of determination was .58. However, the results, like those in the scatter diagram, are, at best, suggestive since no attempt was made at the time to test for the existence of autocorrelation in the error term.

[13] The upward shift in the borrowings curve clearly implies that one or several other variables besides spread were involved in the determination of member bank borrowings during this period. Currently the writer is experimenting with several multiple regression equations with a view toward ascertaining the nature of the shift variable.

[14] In fact, the banks' aversion to borrowing should be thought of as being composed of (*a*) their own tradition against such action and (*b*) the administrative action of the Fed under the Foreword to Regulation A.

FIGURE III

Relation of Member-Bank Borrowings to Least-Cost Spread, April, 1958, through May, 1960
Monthly averages of daily figures

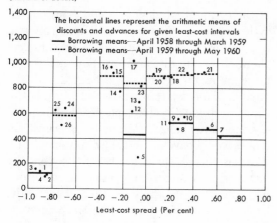

Discounts and advances
(Millions of dollars)

The horizontal lines represent the arithmetic means of discounts and advances for given least-cost intervals
— Borrowing means—April 1958 through March 1959
---- Borrowing means—April 1959 through May 1960

Least-cost spread (Per cent)

borrowing (i.e., need and/or profit),[15] the extent to which they will avail themselves of the discount window rather than the open market in satisfying their desire for such funds depends on the relationship between the degree of reluctance or disutility involved in borrowing from the Fed, on the one hand, and the favorable cost differential or utility between borrowing at the discount rate and the opportunity cost of disposing of Treasury bills, on the other. Moreover, it is further assumed that not only

[15] It should be noted that the writer does not concern himself with the ends of bank borrowing but rather with the choice of method by which member banks obtain additional loanable funds. Whether the initial desire for additional lendable funds stems from increases in customer loan demand and/or restrictive open-market operations by the Fed, and whether such desire is psychologically related to need or profit, the fact remains that, given such changes, banks do have a choice of the method they will employ in replenishing their reserves — i.e., whether they will borrow or sell bills — and such choice presupposes certain psychological costs *and* utilities involved in the act of using the discount window. Further, so far as the underlying motivations or ends of bank borrowing are concerned, the writer would be prepared to go so far as to state that all such previous efforts have been doomed to failure since it is virtually impossible to separate the need-to-serve-its-customers from the profitability component in bank loans.

are the banks reluctant to make use of the discount window as an avenue for obtaining additional loanable funds but that such reluctance tends to *increase* (rather than *decrease* as in the Fed analysis) relative to profitability as the differential widens and borrowings grow. Given both assumptions, it then follows logically that the nature of any empirical function depicting the relationship between spread and borrowings for member banks in the aggregate must be one which resembles the reaction curves found in Figures II and III. For example, starting from an initially low level of discounts and advances, as the spread widens and borrowings increase, the degree of reluctance begins to exceed considerations of relative cost. As this occurs, the slope of the curve begins to taper off since the marginal propensity to borrow is declining. Further increases in the spread can only result in a situation where the borrowings curve flattens out completely as the demand for additional funds becomes perfectly inelastic followed perhaps by an absolute decrease in indebtedness as banks proceed to repay a portion of their outstanding liabilities to the System.[16]

Under discount rate changes and open-market operations, administration of the discount window by the System is directed pri-

[16] It should be clear from all that has already been said that the above hypotheses, like the others heretofore presented, is at best only a partial, if important, explanation of the various and complex forces affecting bank borrowings. A complete explanation would have to take into account all variables affecting the reserve positions of member banks. Therefore, it would have to include all factors affecting the banks' total reserve positions as well as those determining their required reserves. The behavioral process might then be as follows: given a change in the total unborrowed reserves of member banks either as a result of market forces or Fed open-market operations, banks can adjust to such changes through changes in their assets, thereby changing their required reserves, and/or excess reserves, or they can discount with the Fed (or repay indebtedness to it), or a combination of both. This must be the case since if we let U denote total unborrowed reserves; TR, total reserves, B, discounts and advances; RR, required reserves; and E, excess reserves, then $U = TR - B$, $TR = RR + E$; $\therefore$ $U = RR + E - B$. Assuming no change in the reserve ratio and no excess reserves, then changes in U can only be offset by changes in RR and B. Whether such adjustments will be made through bill holdings, or through borrowing, depends on the least cost spread. For an excellent analysis of a closely related problem, see Meigs, *op. cit.*

marily toward avoiding undesirable operating practices on the part of each individual bank rather than toward controlling the overall volume of credit. As a former leading authority within the System has put it: "The stress (in discount administration, MEP) is on good banking practices; no attempt is made to orient each borrowing bank's position into the broader aims of current Federal Reserve credit control."[17] In spite of this "banking" approach, the tradition against borrowing implemented by discount administration was sufficient both in 1954–57 and 1958–60 to overcome "profitability" as spreads increased. As a result, an effective borrowings ceiling seems to have been established. Furthermore, unlike the 1952–53 period when quarterly averages of daily indebtedness rose to nearly $1.5 billions in two out of the eight quarters, no quarterly averages of daily borrowings in 1954–57 exceeded $1.0 billions. In fact, throughout the 36 month expansion phase 1954–57, monthly averages of daily borrowings barely exceeded $1.0 billions in four months while the record was even better in 1958–60 when monthly averages of daily indebtedness touched $1.0 billions in only one of 26 months. While part of this may be explained by increasing use of the federal funds market as an alternative to the discount window, it is a reasonable conjecture that much of the better performance in the 1958–60 expansion phase as compared with 1954–57 lies in the increase in the effectiveness of discount administration. While the revised Regulation A set out general borrowing criteria in February, 1955, it must have required some considerable time for the individual Reserve Banks to implement it by working out detailed criteria applicable to their districts and for their member banks to be informed, and thoroughly appreciative of, the limits of borrowing applicable to them. It would seem that the effectiveness of regulation and bank attitudes toward it have changed secularly. That the System currently faces the 1960's with more confidence in its ability to contain excessive borrowing demands with the discount tools now at its disposal may be inferred from one of its recent statements in

which, while downgrading the relative importance of spreads, it elevates discount administration to a position roughly comparable with the tradition against borrowing.

Furthermore, should the range of borrowings at different spreads become too wide in the future for System tolerance, it should be possible to counteract it through administration of the discount window in a conscious contracyclical manner. Such a policy offers an alternative approach to "penalty rates" or complete abolition of the discount function and yet retains the many advantages associated with the discount window. It also avoids any of the "adverse exceptional" effects posited for frequent discount rate changes. While the precise techniques would have to be studied in some detail, it seems reasonably clear that the System by increasing its degree of moral suasion as borrowings rose could, at the same time, increase the banks' aversion to discounting since such restrictive action would strongly reinforce their own tradition against borrowing. As a result, there would be a downshift in the borrowings path so that at each spread there would take place a smaller volume of borrowings than formerly. While the System appears to feel that it is impractical to use discount administration in an anticyclical manner, this is more in the nature of a pronunciamento than a serious attempt to study the possibilities of such a course of action should it be needed. As has been pointed out in a somewhat different connection, "there is no basis for thinking that nonprice rationing is in principle any less effective than price rationing in curbing unwanted expansions of System credit; . . . what has been wanting in Federal Reserve policy is a lack of will." Certainly the will to innovate must be included along with courage and judgment if one is to justify the use of discretionary monetary policy.

APPENDIX

The period chosen for Figures II and III represents the expansion phase April, 1958–May, 1960 (the initial and terminal dates coinciding with the trough and peak for the subcycle as measured by the National Bureau of Economic

[17] Roosa, *op. cit.*, p. 333.

Research's business cycle reference dates). The monthly spreads were obtained by subtracting the average monthly rediscount rates of all the Federal Reserve Banks during this period from the corresponding average yields on three-month Treasury bills. Such spreads were then correlated with monthly averages of daily borrowing by member banks. The numbers 1–26 found in the figures denote the chronological sequence such that number 1 stands for the initial month of the expansion phase, or April, 1958, while number 26 represents the terminal month, or May, 1960.

The technique employed in fitting the relationship between spread and borrowings is rather crude and should be considered only as a first step in fitting the function. Nevertheless, it has the basic merit of minimizing any preconceptions concerning the underlying shape of the curves while, at the same time, suggesting their general nature. The method is the relatively simple one of computing the arithmetic means of the dependent variable (discounts and advances) for given intervals of the independent variable (least-cost spread), the horizontal lines to be found in Figures II and III representing such arithmetic means. In Figure III the solid horizontal lines represent the arithmetic means of borrowing for the period April, 1958–March, 1959, while the dashed horizontal lines are the arithmetic borrowing means for April, 1959–May, 1960. So far as the use of horizontal lines to represent the means of the dependent variable for given intervals of the independent variable is concerned, it should be remembered that regression equations are basically only polynomials fitted to the means of arrays.

CHAPTER TEN

RESERVE REQUIREMENTS

3 2

100 PER CENT RESERVES*

Irving Fisher†

As we have already seen (Selection 2), the fact that commercial banks are allowed to hold only partial or fractional reserves against demand deposits gives them the power to create (or destroy) money. While the individual commercial bank cannot safely lend an amount greater than the amount of its excess reserves, the commercial banking system as a whole can expand its demand deposits (and loans) by a multiple of its excess reserves.

The general rule for the system as a whole was formulated in Selection 2 as follows: if the required reserve ratio is R, and excess reserves are E, the commercial banking system as a whole can expand its demand deposits by E/R. In other words, the system as a whole can expand demand deposits and loans by a multiple of its excess reserves, and the multiple by which it can expand is the reciprocal of the required reserve ratio. Assume excess reserves are $1 million: then, if the reserve ratio is 10 per cent, or one-tenth, demand deposits could expand by $10 million; but if the reserve ratio were 20 per cent, or one-fifth, demand deposits could expand by only $5 million.

What would be the power of the banking system to expand (or contract) demand deposits if reserve requirements were raised to 100 per cent? The general rule now applicable to the individual commercial bank (that it cannot lend an amount greater than the amount of its excess reserves) would then become applicable to the system as a whole. And since required reserves against demand deposits would be 100 per cent, excess reserves for even the individual bank would no longer automatically arise at the will of the bank whenever cash or cash-items (as checks) are deposited in it.

Some economist, therefore, anxious to take from the commercial banks the power to create or destroy money, advocate that the banks be required to hold reserves of 100 per cent against demand deposits. This would reduce them to the status of warehouses of cash and middlemen in the process of exchanging titles to cash (that is, demand deposits). The selection below, first published in 1935, is by a leading advocate of 100 per cent reserves.

* From Irving Fisher, *100% Money* (New Haven: The City Printing Company, 1945), pp. 3–20. The first edition was published in 1935. Reprinted by the courtesy of the executors of the estate of the late Irving Fisher.

† Professor Fisher of Yale University died in 1947.

INTRODUCTION

In the United States, as in a few other countries, most of our bills are paid by check — not by money passing from hand to hand.

When a person draws a check, he draws it against what he calls "the money I have in the bank" as shown by his deposit balance on the stub of his check book. The sum of all such balances, on all such stubs in the whole country, i.e., all checking deposits, or what we ordinarily think of as the "money" lying on deposit in banks and *subject to check*, constitutes the chief circulating medium of the United States. This I propose to call "check-book money" as distinct from actual cash or "pocket-book money." Pocket-book money is the more basic of the two. It is visible and tangible; check-book money is not. Its claim to be money and to pass as if it were real money is derived from the belief that it "represents" real money and can be converted into real money on demand by "cashing" a check.

But the chief practical difference between check-book money and pocket-book money is that the latter is bearer money, good in anybody's hands, whereas check-book money requires the special permission of the payee in order to pass.

In 1926, a representative year before the great depression, the total check-book money of the people of the United States, according to one estimate, was 22 billion dollars, whereas, outside of the banks and the United States Treasury, the pocket-book money — that is, the actual physical bearer money in the people's pockets and in the tills of merchants — amounted, all told, to less than 4 billion dollars. Both together made the total circulating medium of the country, in the hands of the public, 26 billion dollars, 4 billions circulating by hand and 22 by check.

Many people imagine that check-book money is really money and really in the bank. Of course, this is far from true.

What, then, is this mysterious check-book money which we mistakenly call our "money in the bank"? It is simply the bank's *promise to furnish* money to its depositors when asked. Behind the 22 billions of checking deposits in 1926, the banks held only some 3 billions in actual money. The remaining 19 billions were assets other than money — assets such as the promissory notes of borrowers and assets such as government bonds and corporation bonds.

In ordinary times, as for instance in 1926, the 3 billions of money were enough to enable the banks to furnish any depositor all the money or "cash" he asked for. But if *all* the depositors had demanded cash at one and the same time, the banks, though they could have gotten together a certain amount of cash by selling their other assets, could not have gotten enough; for there was not enough cash in the entire country to make up the 22 billions. And if all the depositors had demanded *gold* at the same time, there would not have been enough gold in the whole world.

Between 1926 and 1929, the total circulating medium increased slightly — from about 26 to 27 billions, 23 billions being check-book money and 4 billions pocket-book money.

On the other hand, between 1929 and 1933, check-book money shrank to 15 billions which, with 5 billions of actual money in pockets and tills, made, in all, 20 billions of circulating medium, instead of 27, as in 1929. The increase from 26 to 27 billions was inflation; and the decrease from 27 to 20 billions was deflation.

The boom and depression since 1926 are largely epitomized by these three figures (in billions of dollars) — 26, 27, 20 — for the three years 1926, 1929, 1933.

These changes in the quantity of money were somewhat aggravated by like changes in velocity. In 1932 and 1933, for instance, not only was the circulating medium small, but its circulation was slow — even to the extent of widespread hoarding.

If we assume that the quantities of circulating medium for 1929 and 1933 were respectively 27 and 20 billions and that its turnover for those years was respectively 30 and 20, the total circulation would be, for 1929, 27×30 equals over 800 billion dollars and, for 1933, 20×20 equals 400 billion dollars.

The changes in quantity were chiefly in the deposits. The three figures for the check-book money were, as stated, 22, 23, 15; those for the pocket-book money were 4, 4, 5. An essential part of this depression has been the shrinkage from the 23 to the 15 billions in check-book money, that is, the wiping out of 8 billions of dollars of the nation's chief circulating medium which we all need as a common highway for business.

The shrinkage of 8 billions in the nation's check-book money reflects the increase of 1 billion (i.e., from 4 to 5) in pocket-book money. The public withdrew this billion of cash from the banks and the banks, to provide it, had to destroy the 8 billions of credit.

This loss, or destruction, of 8 billions of check-book money has been realized by few and seldom mentioned. There would have been big newspaper headlines if 8 thousand miles out of every 23 thousand miles of railway had been destroyed. Yet such a disaster would have been a small one compared with the destruction of 8 billions out of 23 billions of our main monetary highway. That destruction of 8 billion dollars of what the public counted on as their money was the chief sinister fact in the depression from which followed the two chief tragedies, unemployment and bankruptcies.

The public was forced to sacrifice 8 billion dollars out of 23 billions of the main circulating medium which would not have been sacrificed had the 100% system been in use. And, in that case, there would have been no great depression.

This destruction of check-book money was not something natural and inevitable; it was due to a faulty system.

Under our present system, the banks create and destroy check-book money by granting, or calling, loans. When a bank grants me a $1,000 loan, and so adds $1,000 to my checking deposit, that $1,000 of "money I have in the bank" is new. It was freshly manufactured by the bank out of my loan and written by pen and ink on the stub of my check book and on the books of the bank.

As already noted, except for these pen and ink records, this "money" has no real physical existence. When later I repay the bank that $1,000, I take it out of my checking deposit, and that much circulating medium is destroyed on the stub of my check book and on the books of the bank. That is, it disappears altogether.

Thus our national circulating medium is now at the mercy of loan transactions of banks; and our thousands of checking banks are, in effect, so many irresponsible private mints.

What makes the trouble is the fact that the bank lends not money but merely a promise to furnish money on demand — money it does not possess. The banks can build upon their meager cash reserves an inverted pyramid of such "credits," that is, check-book money, the volume of which can be inflated and deflated.

It is obvious that such a top-heavy system is dangerous — dangerous to depositors, dangerous to the banks, and above all dangerous to the millions of "innocent bystanders," the general public. In particular, when deflation results, the public is deprived of part of its essential circulating medium through which goods change hands.

There is little practical difference between permitting banks to issue these book credits which perform monetary services, and permitting them to issue paper currency as they did during the "wildcat bank note" period. It is essentially the same unsound practice.

Deposits are the modern equivalent of bank notes. But deposits may be created and destroyed invisibly, whereas bank notes have to be printed and cremated. If eight billion bank notes had been cremated between 1929 and 1933, the fact could scarcely have been overlooked.

As the system of checking accounts, or check-book money, based chiefly on loans, spreads from the few countries now using it to the whole world, all its dangers will grow greater. As a consequence, future booms and depressions threaten to be worse than those of the past, unless the system is changed.

THE PROPOSAL

Let the government, through an especially created "Currency Commission," *turn into cash* enough of the assets of every commercial bank to increase the cash reserve of each bank up to 100% of its checking deposits. In other words, let the government, through the Currency Commission, issue this money, and, with it, buy some of the bonds, notes, or other assets of the bank or lend it to the banks on those assets as security. Then all check-book money would have actual money — pocket-book money — behind it.

This new money (Commission currency, or United States notes), would merely give an all-cash backing for the checking deposits and would, of itself, neither increase nor decrease the total circulating medium of the country. A bank which previously had $100,000,000 of deposits subject to check with only $10,000,000 of cash behind them (along with $90,000,000 in securities) would send these $90,000,000 of securities to the Currency Commission in return for $90,000,000 more cash, thus bringing its total cash reserve up to $100,000,000 or 100% of the deposits.

After this substitution of actual money for securities had been completed, the bank would be required to maintain *permanently* a cash reserve of 100% against its demand deposits. In other words, the demand deposits would literally be deposits, consisting of cash held in trust for the depositor.

Thus, the new money would, in effect, be *tied up* by the 100% reserve requirement.

The checking deposit department of the bank would become a mere storage warehouse for bearer money belonging to its depositors and would be given a separate corporate existence as a Check Bank. There would then be no practical distinction between the checking deposits and the reserve. The "money I have in the bank," as recorded on the stub of my check book, would literally *be* money and literally be *in the bank* (or near at hand). The bank's deposits could rise to $125,000,000 only if its cash also rose to $125,000,000, i.e., by depositors depositing $25,000,000 more cash, that is, taking that much out of their pockets or tills and putting it into the bank. And if deposits shrank it would mean that depositors withdrew some of their stored-up money, that is, taking it out of the bank and putting it into their pockets or tills. In neither case would there be any change in the total.

So far as this change to the 100% system would deprive the bank of earning assets and require it to substitute an increased amount of non-earning cash, the bank would be reimbursed through a service charge made to its depositors.

ADVANTAGES

The resulting advantages to the public would include the following:

1. There would be practically no more runs on commercial banks;

    because 100% of the depositors' money would always be in the bank (or available) awaiting their orders. In practice, less money would be withdrawn than now; we all know of the frightened depositor who shouted to the bank teller, "If you haven't got my money, I want it; if you have, I don't."

2. There would be far fewer bank failures;

    because the important creditors of a commercial bank who would be most likely to make it fail are its depositors and these depositors would be 100% provided for.

3. The interest-bearing government debt would be substantially reduced;

    because a great part of the outstanding bonds of the government would be taken over from the banks by the Currency Commission (representing the government).

4. Our monetary system would be simplified;

    because there would be no longer any essential difference between pocket-book money and check-book money. All of our circulating medium, one hundred per cent of it, would be actual money.

5. Banking would be simplified;

    at present, there is a confusion of ownership. When money is deposited in a checking account, the depositor still thinks of that money as his, though legally it is the bank's. The depositor owns no money in the bank; he is merely a creditor of the bank as a private corporation. Most of the "mystery" of banking would disappear as soon as a bank was no longer allowed to lend out money deposited by its customers, while, at the same time, these depositors were using that money as *their* money by drawing checks against it. "Mr. Dooley," the Will Rogers of his day, brought out the absurdity of this double use of money on demand deposit when he called a banker "a man who takes care of your money by lending it out to his friends."

In the future there would be a sharp distinction between *checking* deposits and *savings* deposits. Money put into a checking account would belong to the depositor, like any other *safety* deposit and would bear no interest. Money put into a savings account would have the same status as it has now. It would belong unequivocally to the bank. In exchange for this money the bank would give the right to repayment with interest, but *no checking privilege*. The savings depositor has simply bought *an investment* like an interest-bearing bond, and this investment would not require 100% cash behind it, any more than any other investment such as a bond or share of stock.

The reserve requirements for savings deposits need not necessarily be affected by the new system for checking deposits (although a strengthening of these requirements is desirable.)

6. Great inflations and deflations would be eliminated;

because banks would be deprived of their present power virtually to mint check-book money and to destroy it; that is, making loans would not inflate our circulating medium and calling loans would not deflate it. The volume of the checking deposits would not be affected any more than when any other sort of loans increased or decreased. These deposits would be part of the total actual money of the nation, and this total could not be affected by being lent from one person to another.

Even if depositors should withdraw all deposits at once, or should pay all their loans at once, or should default on all of them at once, the nation's volume of money would not be affected thereby. It would merely be redistributed. Its total would be controlled by its sole issuer — the Currency Commission (which could also be given powers to deal with hoarding and velocity, if desired).

7. Booms and depressions would be greatly mitigated;

because these are largely due to inflation and deflation.

8. Banker-management of industry would almost cease;

because only in depressions can industries in general fall into the hands of bankers.

Of these eight advantages, the first two would apply chiefly to America, the land of bank runs and bank failures. The other six would apply

to all countries having check-deposit banking. Advantages "6" and "7" are by far the most important, i.e., the cessation of inflation and deflation of our circulating medium and so the mitigation of booms and depressions in general and the elimination of *great* booms and depressions in particular.

OBJECTIONS

Naturally, a new idea, or one which seems new, like this of a 100% system of money and banking, must and should run the gauntlet of criticism.

The questions which seem most likely to be asked by those who will have doubts about the 100% system are:

1. Would not the transition to the 100% system — the buying up of the assets with new money — immediately increase the circulating medium of the country and increase it greatly?

Not by a single dollar. It would merely make money completely interconvertible; change existing circulating deposits of imaginary money into circulating deposits of real money.

After the transition (and after the prescribed degree of reflation had been reached), the Currency Commission could increase the quantity of money by buying bonds, and could decrease it by selling, being restricted in each case by the obligation to maintain the prescribed price level or value of the dollar with reasonable accuracy.

But it is worth noting that the maintenance of 100% reserve and the maintenance of a stable price level are distinct; either could, conceivably, exist without the other.

2. Would there be any valuable assets "behind" the new money?

The day after the adoption of the 100% system there would be behind the new money transferable by check the very same assets — mostly government bonds — which had been behind the check-book money the day before, although these bonds would now be in the possession of the Currency Commission.

The idea is traditional that all money and deposits must have a "backing" in securities to serve as a safeguard against reckless inflation. Under the present system (which, for contrast, we are to call the "10% system"), whenever the depositor fears that his deposit cannot be paid in actual pocket-book money, the bank can (theoretically) sell the securities for money and use the money to pay the panicky depositor. Very well; under the 100% system there would be precisely the same backing in securities and the same possibility of selling the securities; but *in addition* there would be the credit of the United States Government. Finally, there would be no panicky depositor, fearful lest he could not convert his deposits into cash.

3. Would not the gold standard be lost?

No more than it is lost already! And no less. The position of gold could be exactly what it is now, its price to be fixed by the government and its use to be confined chiefly to settling international balances.

Furthermore, a return to the kind of gold standard we had prior to 1933 could, if desired, be just as easily accomplished under the 100% system as now; in fact, under the 100% system, there would be a much better chance that the old-style gold standard, if restored, would operate as it was intended.

4. How would the banks get any money to lend?

Just as they usually do now, namely: (1) from their own money (their capital); (2) from the money received from customers and put into savings accounts (not subject to check); and (3) from the money repaid on maturing loans.

In the long run, there would probably be much more money lent; for there would be more savings created and so available for lending. But such an expansion of loans — a normal expansion generated by savings — would not necessarily involve any increase of money in circulation.

The only new limitation on bank loans would be a wholesome one; namely, that no money could be lent unless there was money to lend; that is, the banks could no longer *over*-lend by manufacturing money out of thin air so as to cause inflation and a boom.

Besides the above three sources of loan funds (bank capital, savings, and repayments), it would be possible for the Currency Commission to create new money and pass it on to the banks by buying more bonds. But this additional money would be limited by the fundamental requirement of preventing a rise of prices above the prescribed level, as measured by a suitable index number.

5. Would not the bankers be injured?

On the contrary.

(a) they would share in the general benefits to the country resulting from a sounder monetary system and a returned prosperity; in particular they would receive larger savings deposits;

(b) they would be reimbursed (by service charges or otherwise) for any loss of profits through tying up large reserves;

(c) They would be almost entirely freed from risk of future bank runs and failures.

The bankers will not soon forget what they suffered from their mob race for liquidity in 1931–33 — each for himself and the devil take the hindmost. Such a mob movement would be impossible under the 100% system; for a 100% liquidity would be assured at all times and for each bank separately and independently of other banks.

6. Would the plan be a nationalization of money and banking?

Of money, yes; of banking, no.

IN CONCLUSION

The 100% proposal is the opposite of radical. What it asks, in principle, is a return from the present extraordinary and ruinous system of lending the same money 8 or 10 times over, to the conservative safety-deposit system of the old goldsmiths, before they began lending out improperly what was entrusted to them for safekeeping. It was this abuse of trust which, after being accepted as standard practice, evolved into modern deposit banking. From the standpoint of public policy it is still an abuse, no longer an abuse of trust but an abuse of the loan and deposit functions.

England effected a reform and a partial return to the goldsmiths' system when, nearly a century ago, the Bank Act was passed, requiring a 100% reserve for all Bank of England notes issued beyond a certain minimum (as well as for the notes of all other note-issuing banks then existing).

Professor Frank D. Graham of Princeton, in a statement favoring the 100% money plan, says of President Adams that he "denounced the issuance of private bank notes as a fraud upon the public. He was supported in this view by all conservative opinion of his time."

Finally, why continue virtually to farm out to the banks for nothing a prerogative of government? That prerogative is defined as follows in the Constitution of the United States (Article I, Section 8): "The Congress shall have power . . . to coin money [and] regulate the value thereof." Virtually, if not literally, every checking bank coins money; and these banks,

as a whole, regulate, control, or influence the value of all money.

Apologists for the present monetary system cannot justly claim that, under the mob rule of thousands of little private mints, the system has worked well. If it had worked well, we would not recently have lost 8 billions out of 23 billions of our check-book money.

If our bankers wish to retain the strictly banking function — loaning — which they can perform better than the government, they should be ready to give back the strictly monetary function which they cannot perform as well as the government. If they will see this and, for once, say "yes" instead of "no" to what may seem to them a new proposal, there will probably be no other important opposition.

33

IS THE FEDERAL RESERVE SYSTEM
REALLY NECESSARY?*

Deane Carson†

Since you have just finished an article by an advocate of 100 per cent required reserves, here is the other extreme: zero required reserves.

Since 1964 marks the golden anniversary of the Federal Reserve System, the title of this essay may appear somewhat uncharitable to those who have come to think of the Federal Reserve in terms only slightly less affectionate than those accorded to the Old Lady of Threadneedle Street. I hasten to assure the reader that my heresy, if that is what it is, involves principally the word *System*; that is to say, I shall examine the need for a Federal Reserve *System* as it is presently constituted, quite apart

* From *Journal of Finance*, Vol. XIX No. 4 (December, 1964). Reprinted by the courtesy of the publisher (the American Finance Association) and the author.
    † Columbia University.

from the generally acknowledged need for central bank monetary policy. While this task might be thought properly to lie within the province of the political scientist, I shall show that, on the contrary, there are many important economic aspects involved in such an inquiry.

Central to the analysis which follows is the proposition that the success of the essential function of the central bank, monetary management, is independent of the structural arrangements that characterize its organization. This is to say, central bank policies can be executed within a variety of organizational structures, both internal as well as external vis à vis the commercial banking system. The Federal Reserve System *qua System* is but one of a number of such structural arrangements within which a monetary policy can be carried on.

Unfortunately, this fact is little appreciated. A fair sampling of money and banking textbooks, while explicitly silent on the point, leave one to infer that in some unique sense the existing system is a necessary adjunct to the pursuit of successful monetary management. After a chapter or two on the structure of the Federal Reserve System, the student is successively introduced to *functions* and to *policy*.

Out of this, or perhaps independent from this, have developed a mythology and a basic fallacy. The mythology has many aspects: it is generally believed that "member banks" are necessary to the conduct of monetary policy; it is generally believed not only that legal reserve requirements are necessary to the conduct of monetary policy but also that these reserves have to be held at the central bank; it is widely if certainly not universally believed that the Federal Reserve Banks serve many useful functions that could not and are not performed by private institutions, such as discounting, clearing of checks, and provision of vaults for the safekeeping of securities; and, without exhausting the mythology, a rather substantial sentiment exists to the effect that the whole pyramid of varying *authority* — the two hundred and sixty-one Directors of Federal Reserve Banks and their branches, the twelve-man Open Market Committee, the seven-man Board, and the twelve-man Federal Advisory Council — somehow formulates a monetary policy superior to that which could be conjured up by a single Governor of the calibre of Montague Norman or Benjamin Strong.

The fallacy that all this has fostered is simply this: monetary policy, being an extremely complex matter, requires a very complex *System* to make it operative, and the resources that we now allocate to monetary management are required to maintain a viable central banking function in relation to the goals we have assigned to the Federal Reserve. In opposition to this I would advance the proposition that a simple central banking structure is most conducive to successful monetary management, other things equal, and that we can reduce both its internal and its external costs by adopting certain basic reforms.

Basically, my proposals involve two such reforms which, while perhaps not interdependent at first glance, are closely related in fact. I propose, first, that membership in the Federal Reserve be placed on a completely voluntary basis; and, second, that compulsory legal reserve requirements be abolished. These, together with their corollary structural changes, are discussed in turn below.

I. THE CASE FOR VOLUNTARY MEMBERSHIP

At the present time, state-chartered banks may elect to become members of the Federal Reserve System; banks chartered by Federal authority must become members as a matter of law. This distinction between banks according to the source of charter was initially imposed on the grounds that the purposes of the Federal Reserve Act could only be carried out if a substantial fraction of the cash reserves of commercial banks were mobilized in the Federal Reserve District Banks, and if a substantial number of banks had access to the discounting privileges afforded by these regional arms of the Federal Reserve System. Fears that compulsory membership for all commercial banks would compromise the rights of the several states, together with the easy expediency of subjecting Federally chartered banks (which were already subject to Federal control) to captive membership in the System, were responsible for the distinction between banks as written into the Federal Reserve Act.

I shall demonstrate in this section that voluntary membership (1) would not, as some have alleged, destroy the effectiveness of monetary management, and (2) would reduce the discrimination against (particularly) smaller Federally-chartered banks that are now captive members. Initially, we assume that the second part of the suggested reform is not adopted, that is to say, member banks continue to be subject to compulsory legal reserve requirements which must be held with the District Banks. This assumption is dropped in Section II of the paper.

Our initial task is to estimate the probable results of legislation providing for voluntary membership in the Federal Reserve. Such an estimate is based upon the assumption that National banks of any given size would elect to remain in the System in the same proportion that State-chartered banks of that size are presently members. Since we have data at hand on the assets of member National banks, and member State banks in various size groups, estimates can easily be generated. Tables I and II provide the basic data for these estimates. By summing the totals for various classes of banks in Table I, we observe that insured bank assets totaled $310.8 billions at the end of December, 1963. Next, summing the totals of column 7

in each Table, we find that if all insured commercial banks were accorded the right to forgo System membership, something like $98.1 billion of commercial bank assets would be "outside" the Federal Reserve. This represents 31.5 per cent of total assets.

The effectiveness of monetary policy depends to some extent on the pervasiveness of its impact and possibly but not clearly upon the percentage of banking institutions that have access to the discount window. Any correlation between policy effectiveness and *number* of member banks, however, must certainly be weak,

TABLE I

Number and Assets of Insured Commercial Banks, by Size, December 1963
(dollar amounts in millions)

1	2	3	4	5	6	7
Deposit Size	National		State-Member		Insured Nonmember	
(millions of dollars)	No. Banks	Assets	No. Banks	Assets	No. Banks	Assets
Less than 1.0	132	$ 123	24	$ 22	630	$ 535
1.0 to 1.9	388	702	131	224	1,665	2,766
2.0 to 4.9	1,316	5,100	465	1,758	2,563	9,228
5.0 to 9.9	1,145	9,082	328	2,530	1,282	9,760
10.0 to 24.9	935	16,037	277	4,647	688	11,314
25.0 to 49.9	329	12,739	104	4,068	144	5,434
50.0 to 99.9	167	13,257	68	5,459	48	3,573
100.0 to 499.9	164	41,052	64	15,170	30	6,102
500 and over	39	72,143	27	57,337	1	677
Total	4,615	$170,233	1,488	$91,215	7,051	$49,390

TABLE II

Estimate of Assets of Nonmember
National Banks if Membership Were Optional
(dollar amounts in millions)

1	2	3	4	5	6	7
Deposit Size (millions of dollars)	Assets of Insured State Banks	Assets of Insured Non-member Banks	Assets of Insured Non-member Banks as Per cent of Insured State Banks	Assets of National Banks	Assets of National Banks that would be nonmembers (column 4 times column 5)	Cumulative Nonmember Assets
Less than 1	$ 557	$ 535	96.1	$ 123	$ 118	$ 118
1.0 to 1.9	2,990	2,766	92.5	702	649	767
2.0 to 4.9	10,986	9,228	84.0	5,100	4,284	5,051
5.0 to 9.9	12,290	9,760	79.4	9,082	7,212	12,263
10.0 to 24.9	15,961	11,314	70.9	16,037	11,368	23,531
25.0 to 49.9	9,502	5,433	57.2	12,739	7,285	30,816
50.0 to 99.9	9,032	3,573	39.6	13,257	5,244	36,060
100.0 to 499.9	21,272	6,102	28.7	41,052	11,776	47,836
500 and over	58,014	677	1.2	72,143	842	48,678

since the impact of scarce or ample funds would not appear to depend upon the presence of Federal Reserve stock in the portfolio of any particular bank. Furthermore, our highly developed system of correspondent banking relationships insures that monetary policy changes will be transmitted to the entire banking structure. I would certainly argue, in any case, that the effectiveness of monetary policy with 68.5 per cent of commercial bank assets covered will be no less than when 90 or 100 per cent coverage obtains.[1] Since the reasons for this are covered in the following section, they need not be considered here.

An alternative to the voluntary membership proposal discussed above would provide for compulsory membership of all insured commercial banks above a given size. The cutoff asset size that has been occasionally mentioned is $10,000,000. Under this proposal, obviously, larger non-member State banks would be required to join, while all National banks under the cutoff size would be afforded the choice now open to State-chartered banks. For the latest available data (end of 1963) I have calculated that this cut-off point would reduce "covered" assets by only approximately $6.2 billion under the extreme assumption that all National banks with less than $10 million total assets elect to forgo Federal Reserve membership. At the same time, voluntary membership would be extended to approximately 77 per cent of all insured commercial banks, from the present 66 per cent.[2]

On its face, this proposal would seem to be a superior alternative to completely voluntary membership. And indeed, it probably is a more satisfactory basis for discrimination than that found in the present law. On the other hand, its superiority to complete voluntarism can only be defended on the grounds that effective monetary policy requires that a large proportion of the reserves of the commercial banks be held in the form of compulsory balances at the Reserve Banks. More precisely, it requires the finding of a positive correlation between effectiveness of monetary policy and the percent of total bank reserves held within the System. Again this is properly a matter for consideration in Section II and is therefore postponed for the moment.

There are, however, clear advantages to the completely voluntary membership proposal. Certainly the most important of these is that it would enable all insured banks to choose between public and private suppliers of banking services to banks. In this connection it is worthy of note that large private banks, as correspondents, now provide a very wide range of such services on terms that are clearly superior to similar services provided by the Federal Reserve Banks. Among the more important of the latter are check-clearing arrangements, temporary loan accommodation, credit and operations analysis, and provision of economic information. Small National banks find it convenient to utilize these privately supplied services, against which they must carry correspondent balances, in spite of the fact that they must also carry legal reserves with the District Banks. In effect, compulsory membership imposes a discriminatory burden on these banks in the form of double cash balances.

Table III demonstrates the extent to which Federal Reserve membership leads to this result.

It indicates a consistent pattern of higher cash holdings to total assets for member banks than for nonmember banks. This is not due to lower reserve requirements for State-chartered banks; indeed, of the selected states, nine have substantially higher reserve requirements than those currently imposed by the Federal Reserve[3], six states impose legal reserve requirements that are substantially the same as System requirements,[4] and only two states[5] have reserve requirements that are substantially less than the Federal Reserve's 12.5 per cent and

---

[1] As a matter of fact, the middle 1920's are often considered years of effective monetary policy; at that time approximately 69 per cent of commercial bank assets were covered.

[2] Table I.

[3] Wyoming (20 and 10 DD and TD); Alaska (20 and 8); Idaho (15 per cent of all deposits); Kansas (12½–20 and 5); West Virginia (15 and 5); South Dakota (12–20 depending on size but one-third may be held in bonds); New Hampshire (15 and 5); Vermont (30 and 8); and Mississippi (15–25 and 7–10).

[4] New Mexico and New Jersey (12 and 4); Hawaii, Connecticut and Maine (12 and 5); and District of Columbia (12½ and 4).

[5] North Dakota (10 and 5); and South Carolina (7 and 3).

TABLE III

Cash and Balances with Banks as a Percentage of Total Assets of National, State Member, and State Non-Member Banks in Selected Areas[a]
June 29, 1963

State or Area	National Banks	State-chartered Member Banks	State-chartered non-Member Banks
United States	17.6	18.4	12.5
Alaska	12.9	—	13.0
Connecticut	17.5	18.3	10.4
District of Columbia	18.3	16.4	14.5
Hawaii	17.1	—	12.4
Idaho	11.8	12.4	11.7
Kansas	18.6	17.9	14.1
Maine	13.8	12.9	9.2
Mississippi	18.6	18.5	16.7
New Hampshire	17.6	—	6.2[1]
New Jersey	12.9	12.5	10.5
New Mexico	17.7	18.5	15.0
North Dakota	12.6	—	9.4[2]
South Carolina	20.3	16.4	15.2
South Dakota	13.4	13.6	11.3
Vermont	11.4	—	6.8
West Virginia	17.2	19.2	12.7
Wyoming	15.2	17.2	14.0

Source: FDIC Assets, Liabilities and Capital Accounts of Commercial and Mutual Savings Banks, March 18 and June 29, 1963.

(a) States were selected to exclude all those in which banks subject to Reserve City legal reserve requirements were in operation.

(1) Includes 20 banks, 1 of which was a member bank.

(2) Includes 115 banks, 2 of which were member banks.

4 per cent requirements against demand deposits and time deposits respectively.

The clear implication of these comparisons is that membership in the Federal Reserve leads banks to hold a higher proportion of their assets in cash than is considered necessary by banks that are not in the System. From this we deduce that compulsory membership of National banks, where it is due to a "locked-in" effect,[6] discriminates without economic justification against banks holding Federal charters. In effect, captive banks, particularly the smaller National banks, maintain sterile cash reserves required by law for which they receive few compensating benefits; in order to carry on

[6] All National banks, of course, could escape the burdens of membership by changing to State charters. The costs of this, however, are quite high in many cases. When a bank changes its charter it must also change its name, entailing considerable out-of-pocket expenses and loss of "good will." It is not reasonable to impose this cost in order to reduce other costs that have no economic justification, and where a reasonable alternative remedy is at hand.

their business, they also must carry correspondent balances which do bear a return in the form of needed services. Non-member banks, which may and almost invariably do make their legal reserves serve double-duty as service-generating correspondent balances, are placed in a position of competitive advantage.

While the inequity of present membership requirements would be somewhat modified if compulsory membership were adopted, discrimination would not be eliminated. Indeed, while discrimination by charter would be avoided, total inequity might well increase. Under compulsory membership all banks that find privately produced bank services to banks superior to those provided by the Federal Reserve would be deprived of the choice now accorded to State banks. Since it is principally the larger banks that find Federal Reserve membership attractive, such a plan would tend to discriminate against small banks in general rather than against a particular segment of this group.

II. THE NEED FOR RESERVE REQUIREMENTS AND RESERVE BALANCES AT THE FEDERAL RESERVE BANKS

Desired cash holdings of the banking system limit the marginal expansion of bank deposits and, to the extent that they are influenced by legal reserve requirements, it can be said that the latter serve as a fulcrum for credit control. More precisely, however, the monetary control mechanism operates *via* changes in the level of total reserves relative to desired cash holdings of the banking system. I shall contend in this section that the necessity for legal reserve requirements and minimum cash balances at Federal Reserve banks is a function of the particular objectives of Federal Reserve policy; I shall further argue that the locus of the banking system's cash reserves is of little significance with respect to either the structure of the Federal Reserve System, or its effectiveness as a central bank.

A. *The Functions of Reserve Requirements and A Proposal.* Reserve requirement changes are a substitute for open market operations. An initial justification for the existence of legal reserve requirements is, therefore, that their levels can be changed, and with them monetary and credit expansion potentials. It is not within the scope of this discussion to weigh the merits of changes in reserve requirements *versus* changes in the open market portfolio of the central bank. In a zero per cent reserve requirement banking system, however, it must be recognized that the substitute, imperfect as it now is from the standpoint of effectuating monetary control, would no longer exist.

It can be argued, therefore, that some future situation might arise that would call for the raising of reserve requirements, even though the Federal Reserve Board has not seen a need to do so since February 1951, thirteen years and several business expansions ago.[7] I recognize this possibility as a defect in the plan, but a defect which could be easily remedied through congressional action, given the compelling circumstances that would give rise to the need.

Quite apart from the above, a great deal of emphasis has been given to the *level* of legal reserve requirements as a base which limits the potential expansion of money and credit. Arithmetical exercises in standard textbooks "prove" that the height of reserve requirements determines the maximum expansion potential of any given amount of excess reserves, subject to assumptions that are usually specified.[8] It is not at all clear that this fact is relevant to the functionality of legal reserve requirements. In the first place, banks individually and in the aggregate would hold some level of desired cash reserves against deposits in the absence of legal requirements,[9] thus providing the "base" for monetary and credit expansion (or contraction).

In the second place, since the levels of reserve requirements have been progressively lowered (with few reversals) in the postwar period without appreciably affecting the performance of monetary policy, the question can be raised as to why they are at all necessary in the present context — that is, as a limitation on the potential expansion of money and credit.

Cash reserves can be controlled by open market operations, and the tone of the market observed by the simple device of central bank hypothecation of the market's desired level of bank cash reserves. Given continuance of reporting requirements, the device of "shadow reserve requirements" suggested here would enable the central bank to observe "excess reserves," "free reserves" and "net borrowed reserves" as indicators of money market conditions without the necessity of formal requirements.

The plan would work in the following way: suppose the Federal Reserve Board were to announce that it considered X per cent of deposits (details aside) an appropriate level of cash reserves for the commercial banks (or some seg-

---

[7] On November 26, 1960, the Board raised country bank reserve requirements from 11 to 12 per cent, while simultaneously permitting the calculation of vault cash in the reserve base. This increase was a technical adjustment to the inclusion of vault cash and therefore does not count as a monetary policy action.

[8] Zero desired excess reserves, and no change in cash in circulation.

[9] For example, state chartered banks in Illinois are not subject to reserve requirements, yet they keep something in the order of 12 per cent of their deposits in cash.

ment of the banking system).[10] Periodic reports to the Federal Reserve on actual cash holdings and deposits would give the monetary authorities precisely the same "feel of the market" that they now require to conduct defensive open market operations to offset very short-term disturbances in the money market.

It is of course a debatable question whether offsetting these changes is an appropriate objective of monetary control in the pursuit of longer range goals of full employment, price level stability, and economic expansion. Many would argue that day-to-day fluctuations in cash reserves need not interfere with the achievement of an appropriate level of change in the money supply which, after all, is the most important means of realizing the goals. Beyond this, it has been argued persuasively that free reserves are a misleading guide for monetary management.[11]

B. *Slippage Effects of the Zero Reserve Requirement Proposal.* The proposal set out in skeleton form above raises a very obvious question: will the abolition of reserve requirements increase the slippage that now exists between policy actions and policy results? Contrary to one's first inclination to answer affirmatively, it is not at all certain that this should be the case.

We are not concerned with slippages in general, but rather with one segment of the total lag between policy actions and their ultimate effects upon income and prices. This segment is the initial one, that which spans the sequence between a change in total cash reserves of the commercial banks and the employment of these reserves in loans and investments.

While this is basically an empirical question, intuition leads to the belief that if banks individually and collectively are in equilibrium (in the sense that their cash to deposit ratios are at the desired level), changes in cash reserves occasioned by open market operations will

elicit responses quickly and in the right direction. If the Federal Reserve purchases securities (presumably, but not necessarily with Federal Reserve notes), the banks will find actual cash in excess of desired cash, and will take steps (loans, investments) to return to equilibrium.

On the other hand, sales of securities by the central bank will push the banks into equilibrium in the opposite direction. If the Federal Reserve retains its discount window, the deficit banks could choose between "borrowing" from themselves and borrowing from the Federal Reserve Bank. As Sprinkel has pointed out, the discount window is itself an institutionally sanctioned source of slippage;[12] I would suggest that its usefulness would depart with the demise of legal reserve requirements.

In effect each bank would have its own discount window; but we know that banks eschew borrowing as sin, and there is no reason to believe that this attitude would change just because the lender was the bank itself. I suspect that loan and investment officers would keep an even sharper eye on the actual cash ratio than they now do on the free reserve position. Temporary departures from desired equilibrium would occasion furrowed brows in the Board room and charges to the operating officers to "get the cash ratio back where it is supposed to be."

Over the monetary cycle the banks might well change their levels of desired cash reserves relative to deposits in a way that would counteract monetary policy. But this is hardly a peculiar defect of the zero reserve requirement proposal, since in effect precisely the same thing occurs with existing legal reserve requirements.

III. CONCLUSIONS

I have presented the case for voluntary membership in the Federal Reserve and a system of zero required cash reserves. The Federal Reserve System has evolved in the past half century into a vast and cumbersome machine; a quasi-private organization, its regional staffs have grown far out of proportion to their importance in conducting monetary policy. The

[10] It is not necessary to make such an announcement to generate the statistical indicators. However, an announced level of appropriate reserves would benefit portfolio managers and managers of reserve positions in that it would remove one source of uncertainty as to central bank policy that would exist if the announcement were not made.

[11] Cf. A. James Meigs, *Free Reserves and the Money Supply*, (Chicago: The University of Chicago Press, 1962).

[12] Beryl Sprinkel "Monetary Growth as An Economic Predictor", *Journal of Finance*, September 1959, p. 342.

tourist business in Maine may indeed be an important area of economic inquiry, but it is difficult to see its connection with the goals of monetary control. The district Federal Reserve Banks engage in such irrelevancies simply because of the archaic notion of membership in the Federal Reserve System. Catering to the banks to induce them to retain membership diverts a good deal of the attention of our monetary authorities from the main business at hand.

Voluntary membership would go far toward a solution to this problem.

Reserve requirements are unnecessary to the effective conduct of monetary policy. They impose a tax on member banks that might well be levied in another way, if the revenue is needed or a need exists for penalizing this particular industry. Since they serve no liquidity purpose, it is extremely difficult to justify their existence.

34

COMMENTS AND REPLY*

Harmon H. Haymes, James W. Leonard,
George G. Kaufman, and Deane Carson

The present selection consists of three Comments on the previous selection, combined with a Reply by Deane Carson.

I. HARMON H. HAYMES†

In the title of his recent article, "Is the Federal Reserve System Really Necessary?" Deane Carson raised a provocative question, but nowhere in his article did he answer it. The title asks if the Federal Reserve is necessary. The article does not deal with the necessity or even the desirability of the Federal Reserve. It merely suggests, with no analytical justification, two so-called "reforms" for the System: (1) that membership in the Federal Reserve be made voluntary for national banks as well as for state banks, and (2) that legal reserve requirements be abolished.

As a basis for his proposals, Mr. Carson describes a "mythology" which allegedly has developed. He offers no citations to indicate

where or among whom the "mythology" exists. The first "myth" is the general belief "that member banks are necessary to the conduct of monetary policy." But this is not a myth. No one would argue that present membership arrangements constitute the only workable relationship, but some sort of coordination between the central bank and commercial banks is necessary if monetary policy is to function efficiently. At a later point in his essay, Mr. Carson presents his own proposal for monetary policy. His plan calls for "periodic reports to the Federal Reserve" from commercial banks indicating the amount of their cash and deposits. Some sort of formal relationship, whether it be called "membership" or something else, is necessary if such reports are to be required.

The second "myth" cited by Mr. Carson is the general belief "not only that legal reserve requirements are necessary to the conduct of monetary policy but also that these reserves

* From *Journal of Finance*, Vol. XX, No. 3 (September, 1965). Reprinted by the courtesy of the publisher (The American Finance Association) and the authors.
† Economist, Federal Reserve Bank of Richmond.

have to be held at the central bank." The first portion of this "myth" has some foundation in fact. If legal reserve requirements are not necessary to the conduct of monetary policy, they certainly facilitate it. But changes in legal reserve requirements are not, as Mr. Carson asserts later, merely "a substitute for open market operations." The policy role is only one of the functions of legal reserves. They are also required for other reasons. If they were not, why would state governments, which do not engage in monetary policy, impose legal reserve requirements on the banks they regulate? Moreover, there are no laws in the United States requiring any commercial bank to hold any reserves with the central bank. Any Federal Reserve member bank may hold all of its reserves in cash if it so chooses. Deposits with Federal Reserve Banks are voluntary.

Mr. Carson's third "myth" is that Federal Reserve Banks perform useful functions not performed by private institutions, such as discounting, clearing of checks, and providing vaults for safekeeping of securities. But is there such a myth? The Federal Reserve does perform these functions, and on a large scale, but no one with even a passing acquaintance with American banking could fail to know that commercial banks also engage in all of these activities. In fact, the use of Federal Reserve facilities is entirely voluntary. Any bank, member or nonmember, may get these services performed by other commercial banks if it so chooses.

The last "myth" is that "the 261 directors of Federal Reserve Banks and their branches, the 12-man Open Market Committee, the 7-man Board, and the 12-man Federal Advisory Council somehow formulate a monetary policy superior to that which could be conjured up by a single governor. . . ." The idea that this "myth" exists hardly deserves comment. It is similar to suggesting that a single dictator could make all of the laws for the nation better than all of Congress together.

Mr. Carson's "reform" proposals bear directly on the first two "myths" only. They suggest no remedy for the implied uselessness of the Federal Reserve's service functions or for its allegedly unnecessary leadership. The first

proposal, to make Federal Reserve membership voluntary for national banks, would according to his estimate raise the proportion of commercial bank assets outside the System to 31 per cent. His estimate is based on the assumption that national banks, if given a choice, would choose membership in the same proportion as state banks of about the same size. He states that "The effectiveness of monetary policy depends to some extent on the pervasiveness of its impact. . . ." but in the same paragraph argues ". . . that the effectiveness of monetary policy with 68.5 per cent of commercial bank assets covered will be *no less* [emphasis supplied] than when 90 or 100 per cent coverage obtains." If the coverage can drop this much with *no loss* of effectiveness, why not a drop of twice as much? Or four times as much? Unless he can prove that there is a critical point somewhere below 68.5 per cent at which the loss of effectiveness begins, he has contradicted himself.

Mr. Carson advocates voluntary membership principally on the grounds that required membership forces small member banks to carry higher reserves than they otherwise would. He say they must maintain a legally required reserve plus deposits with correspondent banks in order to receive correspondent benefits. He then attempts to demonstrate the extent to which Federal Reserve membership imposes a discriminatory burden in his Table III, which shows ". . . a consistent pattern of higher cash holdings to total assets for member banks than for nonmember banks." But Mr. Carson is a victim of the *"post hoc, ergo propter hoc"* fallacy. Table III does indeed show a higher percentage of cash holdings for member banks, but not necessarily for the reason he assumes. A more logical explanation is that member banks consistently hold more demand deposits than time deposits, and reserve requirements are much higher for demand deposits. For the banks in his sample the ratio of demand deposits to time deposits averaged 195 per cent at state-chartered member banks and 181.8 per cent at national banks, as compared with 123.4 per cent at nonmember banks. The table therefore provides no support for Mr. Carson's argument.

His proposal also suffers from the fact that national banks may at present withdraw from the Federal Reserve System at any time by switching from a federal to a state charter. He recognizes this in a footnote, but concludes that the tremendous loss of good will which would be incurred by dropping the term "national" from their names would be too costly to make it feasible.

Mr. Carson's second proposal is that legal reserve requirements for member banks be eliminated. His proposal is apparently based on the belief that the only reason for the existence of legal reserves is to carry out monetary policy, and that in the absence of legal requirements, commercial banks would voluntarily keep their reserves at some "desired" level specified by the Federal Reserve. Thus, according to Mr. Carson, all that would be necessary to assure the effectiveness of monetary policy would be a system in which all banks would report their reserve levels, just as they do now to meet the legal requirements. Although the Federal Reserve has not used its ability to change reserve requirements as a tool of monetary policy to any great extent, the existence of legal reserve requirements is useful in that it assures the policy makers of some minimum level of reserves at member banks. A purely voluntary system would eliminate that assurance, although, according to Mr. Carson, "banks eschew borrowing as sin," therefore "loan and investment officers would keep an even sharper eye on the actual cash ratio than they now do on the free reserve position." (We would note in passing that since free reserves are excess reserves minus borrowings, an individual bank does not ordinarily have a free reserve position.)

Mr. Carson concedes that "the banks might well change their levels of desired cash reserves relative to deposits in a way that would counteract monetary policy," but, he says, ". . . precisely the same thing occurs with existing legal requirements." But it does not. The legal requirements place a floor under reserve holdings, averaged over the settlement period, and the fact that member bank reserves earn nothing tends to restrict their expansion.

If member banks should, as Mr. Carson suggests, keep reserves just as constant on a voluntary basis as on a required basis, it would be difficult to see any practical difference in the operation of the proposed system and the existing system. Perhaps a clue to Mr. Carson's antipathy toward legal reserve requirements may be found in his apparent subscription to a popular misconception. He asserts that reserve requirements "impose a tax on member banks that might well be levied in another way, if the revenue is needed or a need exists for penalizing a particular industry." But of course, legal reserves are not a tax. No one pays them; no one collects them. Instead, they are assets of commercial banks, and serve a useful purpose as a liquidity cushion in addition to their policy role.

As to the question of "revenue needed," we can only assume that Mr. Carson is misinformed. No one derives revenue from member bank reserves. The reserves may be held in their own vaults if the commercial banks so desire, and the Federal Reserve Banks have no need of member bank reserve deposits to enable them to acquire earning assets. In fact, they purchase securities in the Open Market by creating new reserves. (Not with Federal Reserve notes, as Mr. Carson assumes. The physical volume of notes involved would make Open Market operations unreasonably cumbersome.) And the creation of reserves is the objective of most such purchases.

Much of Mr. Carson's reasoning is difficult to follow, but perhaps his most baffling argument is that "Catering to the banks to induce them to retain membership diverts a good deal of the attention of our monetary authorities from the main business at hand. Voluntary membership would go far toward a solution to this problem." If the monetary authorities spend an inordinate amount of time trying to induce banks to retain membership when membership is *required*, why should they spend less time if membership were *voluntary*? Probably only Mr. Carson knows the answer.

Constructive criticism of any institution is always to be desired. It is unfortunate that Mr. Carson's criticisms are undocumented, and that his "reforms" are actually attacks on straw men of his own creation.

II. JAMES W. LEONARD†

In his recent article Professor Deane Carson presented an argument for the elimination of legal reserve requirements and for making membership in the Federal Reserve System voluntary. Carson's proposals are based upon an alleged discrimination factor. The purpose of this paper is to present a theoretical analysis which shows that the discrimination factor is not important, and then to give some empirical support to the theoretical argument.

THE CARSON ARGUMENT

The argument presented by Carson for voluntary membership in the Federal Reserve System is based upon the proposition that member banks, especially the smaller ones, are placed in a position of competitive disadvantage. This disadvantage arises from the fact that member banks are required to hold a larger proportion of their assets in the form of cash. Member banks maintain balances with correspondent banks in order to obtain the services of the larger banks, and also must maintain legal reserves with the Federal Reserve Bank. The nonmember banks get double duty out of correspondent balances. Carson presents data which shows that nonmember banks have lower ratios of cash to total assets than member banks. Thus, the imposition of legal reserve requirements by the Federal Reserve tends to discriminate against member banks because they are forced to maintain a larger proportion of their assets in a nonearning form.

If the discrimination argument is to hold then it must be true that member banks are forced unnecessarily to sacrifice profitability for liquidity (or for correspondent services). The following analysis will show that no such sacrifice will be made.

THE COUNTERARGUMENT

We assume that member banks and nonmember banks are in an equilibrium position with respect to the amount of cash reserves, securities, and loans which they hold relative to deposits. The portfolios of each class of

† University of Illinois.

bank are assumed to be equally liquid. We assume that the Federal Reserve has decided to make additional reserves available to the banking system, and that these reserves are divided equally between the two classes of banks. Furthermore, we introduce the proposition that the member banks have decided to hold correspondent balances in exchange for the services which the larger banks provide.

After the Federal Reserve action the nonmember banks would still be in an equilibrium position. Reserves, securities, and loans would have risen sufficiently to maintain the same degree of portfolio liquidity as before. The member banks have used the additional reserves to establish correspondent balances. It seems logical to assume, however, that the member banks would also desire to maintain portfolio liquidity equal to the former equilibrium position. Reserves and deposit balances are more liquid than securities. Securities are more liquid than loans. Thus, the member banks are more liquid than the nonmember banks, and are more liquid than the original equilibrium position. This will cause the member banks to reduce the excess liquidity. This will be accomplished by decreasing securities and increasing loans.

After the reduction in securities and increase in loans, the portfolios of the member and nonmember banks will be equally liquid, even though the proportions of cash, securities, and loans differ. We could also expect the over-all rate of return to be the same. Therefore no sacrifice of profitability for liquidity has been made because of the decision to carry correspondent balances. Consequently the discrimination argument does not hold.

AN EMPIRICAL CHECK

The ratios in Table I are presented as evidence of the validity of the previous analysis. An examination of the data in Table I tends to confirm the analysis. The member banks have compensated for their heavier cash position by reducing liquidity in the other two parts of their portfolio. There is no reason to believe that banks consider one portfolio to be any more liquid than the other two. The rates of return tend to substantiate this conclusion,

TABLE I

Selected Rations (in percentages) of National Banks, State Member Banks, and Nonmember Banks

	National Banks	State Member Banks	Nonmember Banks
1. Cash Assets / Total Assets	17.58%	18.41%	12.75%
2. Government Securities / Total Assets	21.11	18.75	27.54
3. Loans / Total Assets	48.27	49.70	47.14
4. Net Income / Total Assets	.74	.70	.68

Source: FDIC Annual Report, 1963.

and are also consistent with commonly accepted principles of profitability and liquidity.

III. GEORGE G. KAUFMAN†

In a recent article in this *Journal*, Professor Carson questions "the need for a Federal Reserve *System* as it is presently constituted, quite apart from the generally acknowledged need for central bank monetary policy." Carson concluded that, in contrast with the existing complex structure, "a simple central banking structure is most conducive to successful monetary management, other things equal, and that we can reduce both its internal and external costs by adopting certain basic reforms." The two reforms discussed are voluntary bank membership in the Federal Reserve System and abolition of legal reserve requirements.

While these two frequently proposed reforms may be highly desirable on other grounds, I fail to see how they would either affect the structure of the Federal Reserve System or significantly reduce its costs. By removing the major "cost" of membership, the abolition of reserve requirements would permit a system of voluntary membership to be effective. However, as Carson correctly points out, banks would still have a demand for some cash re-

† Economist, Federal Reserve Bank of Chicago.

serves, at least part of which would be held in clearing accounts. In addition, most checks would continue to be cleared ultimately at regional Federal Reserve Banks or Branches. As a result, Federal Reserve employment and costs, which are functions not of the size of member bank reserve balances but of reserve activity, would be basically unaltered by the change. The relevant reform here, if a change in structure is to be the objective, is not the elimination of reserve requirements, but of Federal Reserve check-clearing operations.

Likewise, wholly voluntary membership can be expected to accomplish little more than at most reducing the size of the bank relations departments of the various Reserve Banks.[1] Since these departments are small — for example, bank relations accounts for only about 10 of the almost 2,400 employees, or less than one-half of 1 per cent of total employment at the Chicago Federal Reserve Bank — any cost savings achieved can hardly be considered significant.

IV. REPLY: DEANE CARSON†

A. *Harmon H. Haymes*' comment on my proposals to abolish legal reserve requirements and make membership in the Federal Reserve System voluntary may be likened to the boxer who, knowing he is losing on points in the final round and bleeding from cuts over the eyes, swings wildly in hopes of a knockout. Haymes not only fails to land a punch (with one exception noted below), but delivers himself several telling, and perhaps not altogether necessary, blows.

1. In defending legal reserve requirements, Haymes asserts that they "serve a useful purpose as a liquidity cushion in addition to their policy role." While such reserves may be used to meet adverse clearing balances over the reserve accounting period, and may fall below legal reserve requirements if counterbalanced

[1] It may be noted in passing that the case for at least some compulsory membership is not that nonmembers per se represent a monetary slippage, as Carson indicates, but that member banks may threaten to withdraw if they disagree with System policy. Thus, the degree of slippage would vary with the posture of monetary policy and cannot be taken as an exogenous variable.

† Columbia University.

by excess reserves and borrowings on the average, they are of extremely limited use as assets. Bankers generally consider *legally required reserve* balances as the most illiquid segment of their asset portfolio, useful over long periods only at a penalty rate of interest.

But why *legally* required reserve ratios are necessary to provide the sort of liquidity cushion that Haymes deems desirable is not stated. Banks will hold cash in vault to meet withdrawals and cash balances with correspondents to meet adverse clearings even if the Federal Reserve System did not exist. While there is a natural propensity for the regulator to assume that his ratios are superior to those that would be maintained voluntarily in the free market, such an assumption has no bearing on the function of cash as a source of liquidity. Indeed, without legal ratios it would appear that the "liquidity cushion" aspect of cash reserves would be enhanced.

2. We are left, then, with the "policy role" of reserve requirements. Haymes sheds no light on what this is and what mechanism is involved. Instead, he simply states that changes in reserve requirements and open market operations are not substitutes *because* the former play other (i.e., liquidity cushion) roles. This brings him full circle without making a dent in my position.

3. Haymes takes me to task for subscribing to a "popular misconception" that reserve requirements impose a tax on member banks for, as he puts it, "No one pays them; no one collects them." This is certainly a literal interpretation of what I meant by a tax; I trust that the theory of opportunity cost is not a popular misconception. Indeed, to the extent that legal reserve requirements are above the desired level of cash reserve to deposit ratios for commercial banks (and the evidence favors this assumption), the legal ratio imposes a cost on member banks equal to the forgone revenues that would accrue had the unwanted margin of cash been invested.

4. In a curious parenthetical remark, Haymes ridicules my statement that the monetary authority *could* purchase securities by issuing Federal Reserve Notes, asserting that "the physical volume of notes involved would make open market operations unreasonably cumbersome." I did not mean to suggest that payment be made in one-dollar bills. After all, how many zeros can a Federal Reserve Note contain?

5. On voluntary membership, Haymes attacks my position by declaring that "some sort of coordination between the central bank and commercial banks is necessary if monetary policy is to function efficiently." My observations are twofold: First, I do not understand Haymes' use of the word "coordination" except in the context of stimulus and response, which in any case operates through money and capital markets. What more is needed than my suggestion that commercial banks be required by law to report their balance sheets and other pertinent data to the monetary authority?

Secondly, one can reasonably infer from Haymes' defense of membership that it has contributed to the efficient functioning of monetary policy. What an indictment of the present System (and here I would include the elaborate superstructure of Federal Reserve officials) this is! Was the institutional arrangement responsible for such episodes as 1920–21, 1931, 1937, 1957, and 1960? If so, Haymes should be looking for alternatives.

6. Haymes states that my proposal for a simplified structure of monetary authority is tantamount to the belief that a dictator could make better laws than Congress. Here, he simply misses the point. Democratic procedures have much less to do with the number of people who are involved in decisions[1] than whether or not the people who make them are accountable to the public. The Federal Reserve System is structured to minimize accountability to the body politic and to its elected representatives, including the President of the United States.[2] This was accomplished by design, in order to insulate monetary policy from "political influence"; let us evaluate it on these grounds, rather than erroneously defending it as a means of

[1] If this were not the case, should we not double — or quadruple — the number of Congressmen and members of the Federal Reserve Board?

[2] On Federal Reserve "independence" see Chairman William McChesney Martin's statements in *Investigation of the Financial Conditions of the United States, Hearings*, Senate Finance Committee (Washington: GPO, 1957), Part 3, pp. 1361–63.

democratically arriving at "good" monetary policy.

7. I am not, as Haymes asserts, involved in contradiction when I state that the effectiveness of monetary policy depends in part upon its pervasiveness and then assert that it would be no less effective with 68.5 per cent of commercial bank assets covered by membership than with 100 per cent. To answer his question, pervasiveness of impact has nothing to do with the percentage of assets covered; the 68.5 per cent was an estimate of what would obtain if membership were made voluntary for all banks. Haymes might well have objected to my theory of slippages and offered empirical evidence to refute it, but he remains silent on this crucial point.

8. In my original article, I presented evidence to show that member banks tend to hold more cash relative to total deposits than nonmember banks. Haymes legitimately raises the point that this may be due to different deposit mix for member and nonmember banks. In my current empirical work I have included this variable, as well as several others, in the cash demand model.

Preliminary work on Illinois bank data reveals a strong tendency for member banks to have higher cash deposit ratios than nonmember banks, where the deposit mix is equal. From my two samples of 93 member and 94 nonmember Illinois banks, I have compared 58 pairs of banks, each pair of which had a virtually identical deposit mix. Forty-seven pairs (81 per cent of the total pairings) yielded nonmember banks with lower cash to total deposit ratios.[3] While this partially negates Haymes' criticism, other factors may account for the above results. Hopefully, the investigation of these factors will go far toward clarifying the controversy.

9. Haymes erroneously states that my proposal calls for commercial banks voluntarily to keep their cash reserves at a level *specified* by the Federal Reserve. How this interpretation emerged can only be surmised. What I did say was that individual banks would keep whatever cash ratios they desired and these would yield

[3] Data from April 12, 1961 call reports. Illinois nonmember banks are not subject to any legal reserve requirement.

an aggregate ratio for the banking system. Then, should the Federal Reserve require such concepts as excess and free reserves in conducting monetary policy, it could assume a hypothetical desired (by the Federal Reserve) ratio, thus providing, through the difference in actual and desired cash, the indicator.

10. Haymes reminds me that banks do not *ordinarily* [italics mine] have a free reserve position. This is nit-picking. If I may pick my own nit, positive excess reserve minus zero borrowings equal free reserves; negative excess reserves minus zero borrowings equal negative free reserves, etc.

To conclude, far from having attacked straw men of my own creation, Haymes provides ample proof that the title of my article should be given serious consideration.

B. *Professor Leonard's* criticism of the membership discrimination hypothesis is based upon an analysis that is somewhat obscured by (1) his failure to define what he means by "liquid" and "liquidity," and (2) by questionable assertions such as "*reserves and deposit balances* are more liquid than securities," and "securities are more liquid than loans."

As for (2) above, it is not altogether certain that reserves and deposit balances *are* more liquid (whatever that means) than securities. For the most part, member bank reserve balances are highly sterile; this is also true of correspondent balances where the correspondent requires some minimum balance in return for services rendered. On the other hand, Treasury bills can be sold with one-day payment lag without significant loss to the seller.

Furthermore, some loans are more "liquid" than some securities, in the sense that they can be realized more rapidly and with smaller loss (demand loans vs. long-term governments, for example).

As for (1) above, the failure to provide an objective definition of liquidity makes it impossible to evaluate the statement "after the reduction in securities and increase in loans, the portfolios of the member and nonmember banks will be equally liquid, even though the proportions of cash, securities, and loans differ." Apparently the author has in mind an objective criterion of trade-off between cash (wherever held), securities (with various maturities), loans (of various quality), and rates of return. In any case, the model is not adequately specified.

Professor Leonard interprets his empirical findings as favorable to the nondiscrimination hypothesis. Without further analysis of such factors as deposit mix, size, and location, however, the differences he finds in net income cannot be attributed to membership status.

C. *George Kaufman* argues that cost-savings would be small if my proposals were adopted. He bases this contention on the grounds that there would be little reduction in the check-clearing function of the Federal Reserve, which accounts for a substantial amount of System employment and cost.

At the present time, the Federal Reserve System (and ultimately, of course, the general taxpayer) subsidizes the clearing and collection of checks drawn on commercial banks. Kaufman suggests that significant cost reductions could be achieved through the elimination of this aspect of Federal Reserve operations.

The alternative to present arrangements (assuming the Federal Reserve went out of the check-clearing business) would be a private clearing system, either through large regional banks, or through new facilities established to meet the need that would arise. Assuming the former, clearinghouse banks would either explicitly bill users of this service or allocate costs by requiring minimum balances. In other words, the function of correspondent banks in this respect would simply expand; as a result of competition, regional clearinghouse banks would tend to emerge and specialize in this activity.

There is little reason to believe that this private system would be more efficient than the present one; it is generally recognized that check-clearing is efficiently handled in the Federal Reserve Banks and that a great deal of competition exists between District Banks to keep costs low. On the other hand, the reform proposal would allocate costs of clearing more directly to the users of checks rather than general taxpayers. In other words, social costs might well remain the same, although allocated in a different way.

This proposal would certainly alter the structure of the Federal Reserve System, and I am grateful to Kaufman for suggesting it. Together with my proposals, plus the currently strong Congressional demands to remove bank supervisory functions from the Federal Reserve System, we may some day have a central bank that is singularly devoted to monetary policy.

D. If one is permitted to criticize one's own article, it seems to me that my proposal to abolish reserve requirements could be attacked on welfare grounds: specifically, that it would tend to create an unearned capital gain for holders of bank stocks. As cash reserves were converted to earning assets, income would rise and therefore the capitalized value of the streams of income. Whether or not this bounty is defensible on any ground or whether or not it should be taxed away is properly the subject of another article.

PART 4

THE THEORY AND PRACTICE
OF MONETARY POLICY

CHAPTER ELEVEN

HOW EFFECTIVE IS MONETARY POLICY?

3 5

THE INFLUENCE OF MONETARY POLICY ON LENDERS AND BORROWERS*

Board of Governors of the Federal Reserve System†

How does monetary policy work? Through what channels does it affect economic activity? What categories of expenditure does it affect? The Subcommittee on General Credit Control and Debt Management (Patman Committee) of the Joint Committee on the Economic Report addressed a series of such questions to the Federal Reserve in 1952. The following essay is based upon the Federal Reserve's replies to those questions, modified and expanded for publication in the Federal Reserve Bulletin *in 1953. Notice the emphasis that the Federal Reserve places on the role of the availability of credit as well as its cost.*

Before World War II it was generally thought that monetary policy exerted its main effects through borrowers, who became more or less willing to borrow as the cost of borrowing (interest rates) moved down or up. It was concluded that the effectiveness of monetary policy depended almost entirely on the responsiveness of borrowers to changes in interest rates.

In postwar years, however, at least as much attention has been paid to the reactions of lenders, to their willingness to make credit more or less available as influenced by "easy" or "tight" monetary policies. If indeed monetary policy does work via the reactions of lenders, then "tight money" can be effective even if borrowers are insensitive to interest costs. For if credit is simply not available, then borrowers will not be able to borrow even if they are willing to pay the price.

SOME GENERAL OBSERVATIONS

Credit and monetary measures have widespread effects in encouraging or discouraging

* From *Federal Reserve Bulletin*, Vol. 39, No. 3 (March, 1953). Reprinted by the courtesy of the Board of Governors of the Federal Reserve System.

† This article was prepared under the direction of Ralph A. Young, then Director of Research of the Board's Division of Research Statistics.

expenditures. A general tightening of credit has its most direct effect in restricting the amount of spending with borrowed funds. Credit restraint also curbs the expansion of money, and so limits increases in the amount of cash balances held by individuals, businesses, and other spending groups.

Credit restraint, moreover, has important deterrent effects on spending out of existing cash balances and from funds obtained by the sale of assets, where no credit granting and no money creation are involved. These are indirect effects which come about in a number of ways. There may be a dampening of too optimistic expectations of businesses and consumers. A rise in interest rates produced by credit tightening will tend to reduce the value of capital assets, a development that will discourage some new investment in construction and in producers' equipment. Consumers and businesses may decide to save more, either because they are less sure that credit will be available for possible emergencies or to ensure fulfillment of future plans, or because the interest return on savings has become more attractive.

Easing of credit, on the other hand, tends to have opposite effects. It encourages spending with borrowed money. It also stimulates greater spending out of current income and past savings. Credit easing does this by promoting the belief that prices of goods will rise, by reducing interest rates and thereby both lowering the cost of borrowing and stimulating a rise in capital values, and by making it less necessary and less profitable for businesses and consumers to save.

Whether a tightening or an easing of credit will find a response in the demand for credit depends on the existence of a fringe of borrowing or potential borrowing. That is, greater difficulty in obtaining credit or increased cost of credit influences decisions of borrowers by deterring them from using credit for investments with marginal profitability or for consumption of marginal usefulness. It may also deter borrowers from using as much credit for other purposes as might have seemed profitable or useful had credit conditions remained unchanged. In a boom period, when credit is in great demand, there is always fringe borrowing which can be cut out either by greater selectivity in lending or by higher interest costs. If an easing of credit is to stimulate borrowing in a period of business recession, there must be a similar fringe of potential borrowing which will become effective when credit is more readily available and cheaper. Under most conditions such a fringe exists, and an easing of credit will stimulate borrowing in amounts or for purposes that were previously not regarded as profitable or useful, and for purposes for which credit could not previously be obtained.

This fringe of potential borrowing, however, may be very limited under special circumstances. In a period of inflationary boom, investment in plant and equipment (productive capacity) and in housing and purchase of durable goods may proceed so rapidly, unless checked somewhat, that future needs will be too far anticipated. Then, in case of a serious business downturn, many activities involving credit that would ordinarily have been greatly stimulated by an easing of credit may not respond, because for the time being the demand for them has already been filled in the previous boom. Other potential borrowers may feel so discouraged about profit possibilities as a result of the downturn that they too will not borrow, however cheaply and readily credit may be available. Once such conditions and attitudes have developed, the immediate effect of an easing of credit will be limited, although such an easing is still an essential measure in setting the stage for ultimate recovery. The ability to combat a recession with credit and monetary action, therefore, depends in large part on the extent to which restrictive credit action has been taken in the preceding boom, as well as on how early and aggressively easing action occurs after a downturn.

A general tightening of credit results from a reduction in the availability of credit relative to the demand for it. Such tightening may develop because the supply of credit has contracted without a corresponding reduction in demand, because the demand for credit has increased without a corresponding increase in supply, or from some combination of these. In a boom period, demand for credit typically increases and credit conditions tend to tighten even though there is an actual increase in the volume of credit granted. In order to keep credit from tightening under such conditions, reserve banking policy would need to permit the total credit and monetary base to expand at the pace set by the progress of the boom regardless of the inflationary or other unsound developments that might be occurring.

2

A general easing of credit results from an increase in the supply of credit relative to the demand for it. Easier credit conditions may generally be expected to develop in a period of economic recession, except when there are banking difficulties or extreme pressures for liquidity on the part of consumers and businesses. Credit and monetary policy in such a period should encourage the development of easier credit conditions.

EFFECT ON LENDERS

A general tightening or easing of credit affects lenders in all sectors of the credit market, from short- to long-term. In the short- and intermediate-term sectors of the market the major suppliers of funds are the commercial banks. Expansion or contraction of their loans and investments tends to expand or contract the volume of money. There are, however, many other lenders that supply a substantial volume of short- and intermediate-term credit through the investment in prime-grade marketable paper of cash balances not needed for current expenditures and of secondary reserve funds. The volume of such investment varies with the attractiveness of the interest return. The supply of bank credit is dependent on bank reserve positions, which in turn may be tightened or eased by reserve banking actions. The total supply of short-term credit is thus highly flexible.

In the market for long-term credit, the supply of funds is related to the volume of saving. Major lenders in this market, in addition to individuals, are insurance companies, savings banks, savings and loan associations, public and private pension funds, and nonprofit institutions. Commercial banks, although primarily short-term and intermediate-term lenders, also invest their time deposits in real estate loans and in long-term corporate, Federal, and State and local government securities. The supply of investment funds is relatively fixed at any time and does not adjust quickly to changes in demand. In a period of boom, however, increased demand for long-term credit tends to spill over into the short-term credit market, and in a period of recession lack of long-term credit demand may induce investment funds to seek short-term outlets. Conditions of availability and cost of short-term and long-term credit thus are constantly interacting. Moreover, the lending and investing activities of commercial banks bridge the markets and help to link them together.

Commercial Banks. Individual commercial banks obtain funds primarily from the deposits of working balances and savings of individuals and businesses. For the banking system as a whole, however, most of the deposits result from credits extended by banks. Commercial banks as a group can expand their credits only to the extent that they have or can obtain the reserves needed to support the resulting growth in deposits.

The availability of reserves is directly subject to Federal Reserve influence. Aside from a gold inflow or a return of currency from circulation, which can usually be counteracted by reserve banking action, and except for certain temporary technical factors, the volume of bank reserves can be increased only by bank borrowing at the Reserve Banks or through open market purchases of securities by the Federal Reserve.

Commercial banks consider borrowing a temporary expedient. They do not like to be long in debt. Individual banks can get additional funds to lend by selling Government or other securities or by permitting maturing issues to run off. As a group, however, banks cannot expand their total supply of loanable funds in this way except when such paper is being bought by the Federal Reserve System. Unless the Federal Reserve is buying securities and thereby supplying reserves, a reduction in security holdings by one or more banks will normally draw reserves from other banks and no net addition to reserves will occur. An attempt by banks as a group to obtain additional reserves by selling securities, or by allowing maturing issues to run off, will increase the supply of short-term paper for sale in the market, thus lowering prices and raising yields on such paper. Similar market pressure may result if banks draw upon balances with correspondents or call loans made in central credit markets in order to build up reserves.

At the lower prices and higher yields, Government and other short-term securities will be more attractive. Nonbank investors may be induced to buy more of them, using temporarily idle deposit balances. Sales of short-term paper by banks to nonbank investors and the use by banks of the proceeds to make loans will shift the ownership of deposits and may increase the activity of existing deposits, but such sales will not increase total bank reserves so as to permit an increase in total bank credit and deposits.

With prices lower and yields higher on short-term paper, banks are less likely to reduce their holdings of secondary reserve assets, notably short-term Government issues. Some banks may continue to do so, but others will stop selling or may buy. In the aggregate, the secondary reserve position of banks will tend to stabilize. This development is brought about in several ways. Many banks and other potential lenders are reluctant to sell securities at a loss. As the potential loss becomes greater, this reluctance deepens. Rising yields on short-term paper, moreover, make the credit outlook uncertain, and this uncertainty, together with the fact of potential losses on the sale of paper held, makes the secondary reserve positions of banks less satisfactory to bank managements. Hence, holdings of liquid assets that were previously viewed as adequate or even more than adequate come to be viewed with concern. The result is a greater unwillingness on the part of bank managers to reduce holdings of liquid securities in order to make more loans.

The key fact is that with a tightening in the credit situation banks cannot count with as much certainty on the ready availability of additional reserve funds and will therefore tend to be more restrictive in their lending practices and standards. This restraint both reflects and is a part of the process of credit tightening. As the credit and monetary climate thus changes, bankers will modify their expectations about the general outlook for business and commodity prices. Applications for loans, particularly inventory loans, will be more carefully screened. Businesses which obtain credit to accumulate inventories will be under pressure from their bankers to keep inventories more closely in line

with actual requirements. Bankers will also bring pressure for repayment on many borrowers with outstanding obligations. In general, they will be alert to find reasons for refusing credit requests or not meeting them fully and for accelerating repayment of outstanding loans, rather than eager to extend credit.

When credit conditions ease, more and more banks will free themselves from borrowing and, as reserves accumulate in excess of working requirements, they will become more aggressive in competing for loans and marketable paper. Other lenders and investors will also be under pressure to keep their funds employed. This change in the credit situation will find prompt response in declining yields in all sectors of the market. Uses of credit that under conditions of credit tightness were postponed or not cultivated by lenders will be promoted by them under conditions of credit ease.

Lenders and Investors in Long-Term Market. A tightening in credit and the accompanying increase in interest rates will significantly affect lenders and investors who operate primarily in the long-term credit market, including life insurance companies, mutual savings banks, savings and loan associations, and pension funds. They will become less willing to make any but the best grade loans and investments. They will generally exercise greater caution in accepting marginal applications for credit.

In part this change in attitude reflects the declining value of assets associated with rising interest rates. All income-producing assets yielding a fixed rate of return tend to decline in price when market rates of interest rise. This is true because they are valued in the market on the basis of expected returns, capitalized at the appropriate current rate of interest including allowance for risk. It is easy to see this relationship in the case of prime-risk securities, since their market value changes only with changes in interest rates; when interest rates rise, the value of such securities correspondingly declines. Actually the decline can be even more marked in the case of securities or other income-yielding assets of lesser grade. As interest rates increase, investors become less optimistic about the business outlook and therefore change their appraisals of risk positions. Such changes in appraisals of risk, combined with the general increase in interest rates, will result in an even greater decline in value for lesser grade securities than for prime assets.

Thus in a period of tightening credit, long-term lenders and investors, while at first attracted by the higher yields available on assets of less than top grade, gradually become more restrictive and selective. They become less willing to sell prime securities to acquire higher-yielding but more risky assets, partly because they can sell the prime securities only at a loss, which they hesitate to accept. They also become more interested in retaining in or adding to their portfolios the more liquid types of assets, because of concern about the decline in the market value of their entire investment portfolio and the general uncertainty about future developments. In addition, the higher interest rates on these more liquid assets in a period of tightening credit come closer to providing the average interest rate which institutional lenders must obtain on their earning assets in order to meet contracts with their own creditors.

In recent decades the flow of savings to non-bank institutional lenders, particularly insurance companies, has been increasing rapidly and the size of the investment problem of these lenders has grown accordingly. In order to ensure the ready placement of funds regularly becoming available for investment from new savings and from repayment of old loans, the major savings institutions have developed techniques for committing their funds in advance to corporate, mortgage, and other borrowers. Such commitments make it possible for potential borrowers to proceed with projects which they might not undertake without assurance of financing on satisfactory terms. But nonbank lenders will hesitate to commit themselves beyond the funds they expect to have coming in if they fear that interest rates may rise in the near future and that they may therefore have to sell securities at a loss to meet future commitments. As a result, when credit is tightening, some proposed projects requiring long-term credit may be deferred because a financing commitment cannot be arranged.

When interest rates decline, investors in the long-term market will find their positions more liquid. The yields available on high-grade securities will fall and the prices of such securities will rise. This development in itself will encourage long-term lenders to extend investment into areas with more attractive rates of return. Moreover, if institutional lenders are quite certain that interest rates will fall and that prices of high-grade securities will rise, they will be willing to commit themselves to future lending that will require the sale of high-grade securities in order to make loans with a more attractive interest return.

Underwriters and security dealers are important in the money and capital market, and their responses to credit tightness in turn affect the availability of credit. They are particularly sensitive to changes in interest rates because they customarily carry a large inventory of securities in the process of distribution. They risk large losses if they are holding large amounts of securities in a period of rising interest rates, since they may not be able to sell them except below cost or may have to carry the securities for some time on borrowed money. Thus underwriters and dealers may be expected to carry securities less readily and hence to discourage security flotations while interest rates are adjusting to higher levels. When yields are stable or are expected to fall, they will be more likely to encourage such flotations.

EFFECT ON BORROWERS

Restraint on borrowing exerted by tightening credit results in part, as already explained, from the increased difficulty of finding lenders and obtaining loans. It also results in part from the influence on the borrower of higher interest costs and from his greater uncertainty about future credit and business developments.

Borrowers for Business Investment. Much business is done on the basis of being able to borrow capital at rates of interest lower than the return that is expected to be obtained on the use of that capital. These margins will be affected by changes in interest rates and by changes in the profitability of the businesses concerned. Each change, though small, may influence borrowing for which the profit margin is narrow, while not affecting the bulk of economic enterprise. Such small effects, however, help to maintain economic balance.

The sensitivity of business borrowers to changes in interest rates varies widely, however. In certain fields of long-term investment, such as industrial and commercial construction, public utilities, and railroads (which are large and important fields), interest costs are particularly significant. In such fields comparatively small increases in interest rates can have a substantial effect in postponing the demand for capital. Even in other fields where interest costs are less important, fringe borrowers may be deterred from borrowing when interest rates rise, while other borrowers may decide to get along with less credit. The higher that long-term rates become, and the more likely that this condition is temporary, the greater will be the tendency for long-term borrowers to postpone investment expenditures because they expect to be able to borrow later at considerably lower interest costs.

An increase in interest rates does more than just affect the cost of credit to borrowers. It also reduces the market value of existing assets unless the actual or expected earnings on these assets rise, since earnings are capitalized at a higher rate of interest.[1] The liquidity position of all asset holders is adversely affected by this development, and their willingness to undertake new long-term commitments may be influenced.

A rise in interest rates also influences the utilization of productive resources, directing some activity away from production of long-

lived, slowly depreciating capital goods and thereby freeing resources for an immediate increase in output of consumption goods and of producers' equipment to make consumption goods.[2] An interest rate increase has this effect both by increasing the cost of long-term borrowing and by changing the relationship between prices of existing capital assets and the cost of producing new assets. In the fixed capital area these changes, together with changes in the outlook for profits and risks due to the altered credit and monetary situation, shift the balance of business decisions toward holding or buying old assets, and adapting old assets to new uses, rather than buying new ones.

How the changed relationship between prices of existing capital assets and costs of producing new ones occurs is illustrated below. The illustration pertains to hypothetical office buildings with a net income from rent of $100,000 a year.

Estimated cost of constructing
   new building $1,500,000
Capitalized market value of
   existing building with earnings from rent (net of all
   current costs and depreciation) of $100,000:
     If the current interest rate,
     with allowance for risk,
     is 6 per cent. 1,666,667
     If the current interest rate,
     with allowance for risk,
     is 7 per cent. 1,428,571

If the current interest rate for such investment, with allowance for risk, were 6 per cent, the capitalized value of the existing property would be more than the cost of constructing a new building with the same earning prospects. An investor in this type of real estate, instead of buying an existing building, would build a new structure, other things being equal. If, on the other hand, the relevant interest rate were 7 per cent, the decision would go the other way.

---

[1] In a highly developed economy such as the United States, the volume of accumulated capital assets is very great in relation to current income. Small percentage changes in the value of such assets involve large dollar amounts. In a recent study by Raymond W. Goldsmith, it is estimated that for the 145-year period 1805–1950 the average yearly rate of growth of reproducible tangible wealth in the United States was about 4¼ per cent, or about 2 per cent on a per capita basis. At the end of 1948 reproducible tangible wealth owned by individuals, businesses, and farmers was valued at approximately 600 billion dollars. Although not all of this represents assets whose value is directly affected by changes in interest rates, the figure serves to give some idea of the magnitude of reproducible assets involved. In addition, values of income-producing lands are affected, as are values of negotiable claims not represented by real assets.

[2] Accelerated tax amortization for a capital good shortens the book life of the capital asset and reduces the period of borrowing that may be involved in its purchase. Long-lived capital goods may thus be made, in effect, more equivalent in shorter-lived producers' equipment, both from the standpoint of the effects of credit tightness on their purchase and from the standpoint of the obsolescence risk involved.

Business borrowers in the short-term market may also be greatly influenced by changes in credit conditions. Inventory accumulation is normally financed in substantial part by short-term credit. When businesses have been building up inventory positions, a tightening in the credit and monetary situation removes some of the incentives for inventory accumulation. Uncertainty with respect to the possibility of renewing the credit, moreover, increases the possibility that inventory holdings may have to be sold under unfavorable market circumstances. This deters particularly inventory accumulations of a purely speculative variety.

Lower interest rates, through their effects on costs, capital values, and business anticipations, will encourage borrowers to make additions to physical property and also to accumulate inventory.

Consumer Borrowers. Use of credit by consumers is not subject to direct restriction by higher interest rates in the credit market. Consumer credits are generally extended on fairly standardized terms and at relatively high and inflexible credit charges. The rates paid for money at wholesale by the institutions that lend to consumers is only one of a number of important costs elements in the credit charge to consumers at retail. Thus changes in interest rates in the credit market have a less than corresponding effect on the charge for credit to consumers. Nevertheless, the interest cost is one important element in lenders' cost, and general credit tightness or ease tends to be transmitted to consumer credit through its influence on the strictness or leniency of credit standards applied by consumer-credit-granting institutions. Alteration of credit standards is a method by which lenders in this area control other important elements of their costs, namely, collection costs and losses by default. Because of the nature of the consumer credit market, selective credit regulation has been used in this field during emergency periods.

Residential Mortgage Credit. Mortgage borrowing for house purchases is considerably affected by increases in interest rates. Borrowing to buy houses is typically long-term and on an instalment-repayment basis. An increase in the interest rate, which adds to the monthly mortgage payment, raises the attractiveness of rental housing compared with ownership. Total spending for houses may thus be reduced, as some buyers are discouraged altogether and others are induced to buy cheaper houses. The effect of this on economic activity is felt most directly through the market for new houses. The size of the monthly payment on a mortgage, however, reflects the length of the borrowing term as well as the interest rate. By lengthening the period of mortgage repayment the restrictive effect in the housing sector of an increase in interest rates may be largely offset. It is, consequently, highly important to avoid encouragement of longer mortgage maturities during a period of boom when credit tightness is relied on to maintain economic stability and hold down inflationary pressures. The tendencies described, of course, work in reverse to stimulate house purchases during a period of recession.

Investors and Traders in Corporate Stock. The direct effect of changes in interest rates on demand for credit to finance purchases of corporate stocks depends largely on what is happening in the stock market. When stock prices are stable, credit tends to be used by regular investors and professional traders who deal in lots of substantial size and expect only small unit profits. Credit demand for such transactions may be sensitive to interest rates, since the increased cost of higher rates may wipe out profits, while lower rates will tend to add to profits. On the other hand, when stock prices are rising or declining under the impact of speculative pressures, the expectation of quick capital gains may be so strong as to make borrowing costs a matter of distinctly secondary importance. In such circumstances, selective credit regulation of margin requirements on loans to purchase or carry stocks can aid in restraining credit expansion in this area.

Tighter or easier credit conditions may indirectly affect borrowing on stocks through their influence on the pace of economic activity. The willingness of individuals to buy and hold stocks, both outright and on credit, is necessarily related to their judgments of business developments and prospects.

36

THE EFFECTS OF MONETARY POLICY ON THE MAJOR SECTORS OF THE ECONOMY*

Warren L. Smith†

In 1959 the Joint Economic Committee of the Congress conducted its third major post-war study of the financial system. In 1949 there was the Douglas Committee, in 1952 the Patman Committee, and in 1959 the "Study of Employment, Growth, and Price Levels." Again in 1959 the Chairman was Senator Paul Douglas; Professor Otto Eckstein of Harvard University was Staff Director.

The following discussion of the channels through which monetary policy influences the economy is from the chapter on monetary policy in the report of the staff to the Committee. It is, to say the least, somewhat more skeptical of the efficacy of monetary policy than the preceding selection, which was from the Federal Reserve itself.

I.

In the last few years, with the minor exception of controls over margin requirements for loans to purchase and carry securities, the Federal Reserve has relied exclusively upon so-called general or quantitative credit control instruments. These instruments include open market operations, changes in member bank reserve requirements, and changes in the discount rates charged to member banks for borrowing from the Federal Reserve. These controls are said to be general because they enable the System to control, at least approximately, the total supply of money and credit in the economy, but do not interfere with the allocation of credit among uses, which is left to the market to decide. Selective credit controls — of which the consumer credit controls used during World War II and on a few occasions since may be taken as typical — are designed to interfere with the allocation of funds without directly affecting the total supply available.

It is sometimes said — and the leading officials of the Federal Reserve System appear to adhere to this view — that the central bank should rely entirely (or almost entirely) on the gen-

eral credit controls, since the only legitimate function of the central bank is to control the total supply of funds, leaving to the market the task of allocating credit. General controls, it is said, are impersonal and nondiscriminatory, whereas selective controls are explicitly designed to discriminate, and the central bank should not be a party to discrimination.

However, recent experience suggests that general credit controls have different effects on different classes of borrowers, depending on the extent to which they rely on internal funds for financing, the variety of sources of funds available to them, their bargaining power in dealing with lenders, the types of markets — competitive, oligopolistic, and so forth — in which they sell their products, and so on.

Of course, even in a highly competitive economy, general credit controls would not affect everyone equally (whatever that means). But in such an economy the differential effects on different types of borrowers could be defended on the ground that they were merely a reflection of differences in consumer tastes, differences in the productivity of resources applied to different uses, and differences in the evaluation of risks associated with different business undertakings. But our economy certainly does not fit this model even approximately, since there are market imperfections in nearly all areas. In fact, defenders of general monetary controls have themselves emphasized at times the fact

* From *Staff Report* on Employment, Growth, and Price Levels, pp. 362–401. Prepared by the staff for the consideration of the Joint Economic Committee, U.S. Congress, December, 1959. Reprinted by the courtesy of the author.

† University of Michigan.

that interest rates are sticky and that the effects of monetary policy may arise mainly from private credit rationing which is made possible partly by the existence of market imperfections.

Instead of distinguishing between general and selective controls on the basis of principle, it seems better to admit that each policy instrument — general as well as selective and monetary as well as fiscal — has its own peculiar incidence on the economy. This is an especially important, indeed necessary, way to approach the problem of policies for promoting growth and stability in the context of the present report, with its emphasis on other structural aspects of the economy. In accordance with this approach, we shall attempt as best we can to assess the effects that monetary policy has had and is likely to have upon some of the major sectors of the economy.

A. RESIDENTIAL CONSTRUCTION

Residential construction is the area of the economy where there is clearest evidence that monetary policy has had a significant impact. When credit has tightened housing starts have declined and when credit has eased starts have speeded up, although there has been a lag in the process. The clearest case of the effect of monetary policy is perhaps to be found in the 1955–57 period. Housing starts began to rise under the stimulus of easy money and low interest rates during the 1953–54 recession, hit a peak of 1,443,000 units on a seasonally adjusted basis in December 1954, and then began to decline. The decline continued with some temporary interruptions throughout 1956 and 1957 as credit conditions became tighter and continued on into 1958, reaching a low point of 918,000 units in March of that year. At this point, chiefly due to the stimulus of easy credit and low interest rates, a pickup began which continued until April 1959, when the effects of high interest rates and tight money apparently began to have an effect once again. It is especially interesting to note that in the 1955–57 period of credit restraint, residential nonfarm construction was the only major category of GNP expenditures that showed a decline, dropping from $18.5 billion in the first quarter of 1955 to $17 billion in the third quarter of

1957, a drop of 8.1 per cent. When valued at 1954 prices, such expenditures dropped much more — 16.4 per cent — due to a substantial rise in the prices of houses.

Housing starts have exhibited very marked year-to-year fluctuations throughout the postwar period. For example, starts increased by 37 per cent from 1949 to 1950, dropped by 25 per cent from 1950 to 1951, rose by 13 per cent from 1953 to 1954 and by a further 9 per cent from 1954 to 1955, fell by 17 per cent from 1955 to 1956 and by another 9 per cent from 1956 to 1957, and rose by 15 per cent from 1957 to 1958. The volume of residential construction valued at constant prices has behaved in somewhat the same way as housing starts, although the fluctuations have been much less severe, due to the presence of a strong upward trend related to the propensity to build larger and more elaborate houses. The interesting thing about these fluctuations is that they have been distinctly anticylical, with residential construction rising when the rest of the economy was declining and declining when the rest of the economy was rising.

Prior to 1953, housing does not appear to have been influenced very much by general credit controls, for the simple reason that relatively little use was made of such controls. The pronounced impact on housing since 1953 is chiefly due to the existence of a rather peculiar but very simple mechanism. Due to ceilings on the interest rates that may be charged on mortgages insured by the Federal Housing Administration and guaranteed by the Veterans' Administration, a rise in yields on other competitive types of investments, such as corporate and Government securities, has tended to attract the supply of investment funds away from these mortgages. On the other hand, when credit conditions have eased and yields on competitive investments have fallen, the supply of investment funds has tended to flow back into the Government-supported mortgage programs. This is the essence of the mechanism, although the picture is clouded in detail by statutory and administrative changes in the interest rate ceilings and in the allowable terms (downpayments and maturities) on FHA-insured and VA-guaranteed mortgages, by the use of discounts as a means of giving some flexibility to the yields on insured and guaranteed mortgages, and by variations in the support given to the mortgage market by the Federal National Mortgage Association.

It would seem that if — as is frequently suggested — the ceilings on the interest rates that can be charged under the Government-supported programs are removed, the sensitivity of residential construction to monetary policy will depend primarily upon the interest elasticity of demand for residential housing. Unfortunately, we know nothing about this interest elasticity, and the existence of the interest rate ceilings impedes investigation of the question on the basis of recent historical data. Other factors would be involved too — including the preferences of institutional investors for mortgages as compared with competing investments under conditions in which interest rates are relatively free to move, and the elasticities of demand for funds on the part of borrowers (including corporations and municipalities) who compete with home buyers for funds. Little is known about these factors either, except for some indications, referred to below, that business investment demand appears to have little interest elasticity.

It does appear a reasonable conjecture that under a regime of freely fluctuating interest rates, unless some other selective control were substituted for the rate ceilings, residential construction would continue to show significant fluctuations. But instead of behaving in a contracyclical fashion, as has been the case in the last few years appears to have been affected by effect would dominate and the fluctuations would be procyclical, thus contributing to overall instability. However, the cyclical pattern would be disrupted by changes in the rate of family formation and other factors only partially related to current business conditions.

To sum up, residential construction in the last few years appears to have been affected by monetary controls more than any other sector, and despite changes that have been occurring in this field recently, a continuing high degree of sensitivity seems likely as long as the ceilings on FHA and VA interest rates remain in effect.

B. BUSINESS PLANT AND EQUIPMENT EXPENDITURES: GENERAL

In the traditional way of looking at things, monetary policy is supposed to exert its main effects on the economy through its influence on business expenditures for fixed investment. For example, the tightening of credit raises interest rates, and businessmen are supposed to decide how much investment to carry out by comparing the expected returns on the investment with the cost (explicit or implicit) of the funds needed to finance it. The rate of interest is viewed as the cost of funds, and when this cost rises, some marginal investments that would otherwise have been carried through are ruled out since they do not promise a high enough return to cover the cost of the funds.

Investment in plant and equipment is a highly complicated phenomenon, and our knowledge of its determinants is far from satisfactory. However, there is a fairly impressive accumulation of evidence that investment is, in general, not strongly influenced by interest rates. Moreover, in view of the general nature of investment decisions, there are some lines of theoretical reasoning which would suggest a priori that the effects might be expected to be weak. And, finally, there are some features of the institutional framework within which investment activity is conducted which tend to weaken the effects of interest rates on investment.

First let us take a rather crude look at the recent facts. Plant and equipment expenditures have generally moved in the same direction as interest rates in the postwar period. The clearest example of this is in 1955–57; from the first quarter of 1955 to the third quarter of 1957, plant and equipment expenditures increased steadily, the net increase for the period amounting to $12.1 billion or 46 per cent. During this same period, the yield on outstanding issues of high-grade corporate bonds rose from 2.93 per cent (in January 1955) to 4.12 per cent (in September 1957), a relative increase of 41 per cent, and from January 1956 (the first month for which data are available) to September 1957, the yields on newly issued corporate bonds of high quality rose even more — from 3.15 per cent to 4.73 per cent, a relative increase of 50 per cent . As the defenders of monetary policy are always quick to point out, this rapid and continuous growth of private investment at the same time that interest rates were rising substantially does not, by itself, demonstrate that credit restrictions did not have strong effects. Obviously, demand curves for capital goods were shifting outward under the impetus of the boom — this is evidenced by the very fact that there was simultaneously an increase in interest rates and an increase in investment expenditures. Conceivably investment would have increased much more rapidly than it did if credit had not tightened. One cannot prove anything by reference to crude statistics of this kind — nevertheless they are worth examining.

Such real evidence as there is concerning the sensitivity of investment to changing credit conditions lies elsewhere than in a consideration of the immediate statistics. In part, it can be found in a consideration of the nature of investment decisions, together with the institutional framework within which such decisions are typically made. In addition, there is a considerable amount of systematic empirical evidence which has been accumulated in recent years.

One fact, primarily institutional, which considerably weakens the effect of monetary policy on business investment is the predominance of internal financing. According to the Federal Reserve flow-of-funds estimates, for the corporate nonfinancial business sector, funds obtained from internal sources (capital consumption allowances and retained earnings) amounted to 68 per cent of total funds obtained from internal and external sources for the period 1953–58. In 1955, 1956, 1957, and 1958, funds derived from internal sources amounted to 124, 86, 82, and 92 per cent, respectively, of total plant and equipment outlays. In principle, decisions to invest out of funds obtained internally might be influenced by interest rates if businesses weighed the expected returns from plant expansion against the returns that could be expected from outside investments, but in fact it seems certain that such decisions are almost entirely independent of interest rates. The chief reasons for this are (*a*) prospective returns from capital projects that might be under consideration are so high relative to returns on safe financial assets (such as Government securities) that the comparison is of little relevance, and (*b*) outside investments involving substantial risk require continuous attention and divert the energies of management away from the firm's main line of business.

It is doubtful whether even investment financed from external sources is very sensitive to interest rates. It is interesting to note — although, again, such statistics by themselves do not prove anything — that total funds obtained by nonfinancial corporations from bonds, stocks, mortgages, and other loans increased even more rapidly than investment expenditures during the 1955–57 period. The amount increased from $5.7 billion in 1954 to $11.4 billion in 1956, a rise of 100 per cent, and in 1957 remained at about the same level as in 1956. Business investment decisions involve forecasts of many factors extending over the prospective life span of the investment, including product demand, wage rates and raw material prices, technological changes, possible obsolescence of the equipment, changes in the competitive position of the firm, movements of general business, and so on, often for a period extending many years into the future. Obviously such forecasts are subject to a great deal of uncertainty. In view of this uncertainty, it is difficult to believe that returns can be estimated with sufficient accuracy so that a decision to invest would be likely to be affected by a change of 1 or 2 percentage points in the corporate bond yield. Investments so marginal that their profitability would be imperiled by such changes in interest rates would scarcely have been under consideration in the first place.

A consideration of the methods that seem to be used by business firms — even large ones — in arriving at investment decisions also indicates little likelihood that their investment decisions will be affected in any clear way by the current rate of interest. Many firms use a so-called "payout period" type of analysis, under which investment projects are evaluated in accordance with the number of years that will be required to recover the initial investment, those investments with the shortest payout periods being ranked highest on the scale. In this kind of analysis, there is no place for the rate of interest. A more discriminating kind of evaluation involves the computation of an expected rate of return, which in its most sophisticated form represents the so-called "internal rate of return," i.e., the discount rate, which, when applied to the expected gross returns (before depreciation but after taxes) will make the discounted value of the project equal to its cost. This kind of calculation leads to an estimate of the yield on the investment that could be — but apparently seldom is — compared with the rate of interest. If any interest rate is used as a standard, it appears to be a conventional rate which is seldom changed to bring it into line with current market conditions. In fact, most of these calculations appear to be related to decisions as to how to allocate a given amount of funds among a number of potential investment projects rather than to decisions as to how much investment spending to do in total.

Another factor which reduces the sensitivity of investment to interest rate changes is the market structure and pricing policies that prevail in many of our largest industries. These industries, such as steel, automobiles, chemicals, and so forth, are characterized by oligopolistic market structures and rather rigid administered pricing practices which in many cases result in prices below levels which fully maximize short-run profits. The existence of unexploited monopolistic profit opportunities permits such companies to raise prices to their customers in order to pass along any increased interest costs they may incur. The increases in prices needed for this purpose would ordinarily be rather slight, since interest is a quite unimportant element of cost in most cases. Moreover, there would be at least a partially offsetting increase in aggregate demand due to the rise in interest incomes, which might be of some significance if during a period of rising interest rates many companies throughout the country increased their interest payments and passed the increases through into prices.

In addition to passing along the increased cost of funds obtained from external sources, firms possessing market control and unexploited monopolistic profit possibilities may raise prices, thus increasing profits, in order to have more funds available for internal financing of investment, either because they prefer internal to external financing or because external funds have become more expensive or difficult to obtain. Moreover, in other cases, dividends may be reduced — or not increased as much as they might otherwise be — in order to acquire internal funds.

Thus, there are a number of important reasons for expecting investment expenditures, in general, to be insensitive to interest rates. A considerable number of empirical studies seeking to isolate the determinants of business expenditures on plant and equipment have been carried out in recent years, and, by and large, they corroborate the expectation that interest rates are an unimportant factor. These studies are predominantly of two types. One type has relied upon answers by businessmen to questions addressed to them either in personal interviews or through mailed questionnaires. The other type has employed econometric or statistical analysis as applied to time series covering past periods, in some cases combined with cross-section data relating to different firms. The purpose in each case has been to find out the variables — interest rates, profits, sales, liquidity, and so on — which seem to be significantly associated with investment. In the space available here, it is not possible to review in detail the results of these studies. It seems fair to say, however, that the burden of evidence supports the view that investment is little affected by interest rates.

A few qualifications concerning the methods employed and the results obtained in these studies need to be pointed out, however. The surveys have been legitimately criticized on the ground that they have generally not been very scientifically conducted. Moreover, most of them — including the most widely known, the famous Oxford survey — have elicited a few answers from businessmen indicating that interest rates or credit availability might, under some conditions, have some effect on investment, although these factors are seldom if ever placed high on the list of determinants. Some of the studies — notably the Oxford survey — suffer from the defect that they were conducted before the war when economic conditions were markedly different from the present. Despite their shortcomings, however, the surveys do provide some valid evidence that investment demand is quite insensitive to interest rates.

There are also some difficulties about the econometric studies. One technical statistical problem is that profits and sales, which are commonly found to be the most important explanatory variables, are strongly intercorrelated with interest rates — that is, high profits and high interest rates have a strong tendency to appear together — and this makes it extremely difficult to disentangle the effects of interest rates from those of the other variables. It seems fair to say, however, that a strong interest effect, of present, would show up in the analysis, and that if an interest rate effect is present, it is almost certainly weak. A second difficulty relates to lags in the relationship. One study of investment in fixed capital in American manufacturing industries, by Franz Gehrels and Suzanne Wiggins, has come up with an interest rate effect but with a lag of 1 year. That is to say, according to this study, a change in the interest rate has an effect on manufacturing investment in plant and equipment a year later. It is possible that the reason other studies have failed to find such a relationship is that they have failed to introduce the proper lags. However, it may be noted that the existence of a lagged relationship of this kind is not much of a consolation for the supporter of monetary policy, since it introduces grave problems in connection with the timing of monetary action.

Recently considerable emphasis has been placed on changes in credit availability as the means by which monetary policy makes itself felt. It is argued that when credit tightens lenders may raise their credit standards and the conditions under which they will make loans. As a result, borrowers — especially marginal ones — find themselves unable to obtain funds

regardless of the interest rates they may be willing to pay. This argument has been applied especially to the commercial banking system. Doubtless there is something to it, although it may be noted that to the extent that credit controls work through this channel, the pinch is especially likely to be felt by smaller and weaker borrowers, a matter which is taken up more extensively below. In any case, its effectiveness appears to be seriously weakened if institutional investors, especially the banking system, are in a position to shift the composition of their portfolios from Government securities to private loans.

In this connection, the results of two surveys conducted by the American Bankers Association in 1955 and 1957 are of some relevance. The first of these surveys, in 1955, indicated only slight evidence of a tightening of lending standards, and it is not clear that such tightening as had occurred was due to monetary policy. The second survey, taken after a restrictive policy had been in effect for 2½ years, suggested that bank lending policies had become somewhat more selective, although two-thirds of the bankers replying indicated that the "greater selectivity" which had allegedly occurred had affected the increase in their loans since 1955 "hardly at all," and only a very small minority estimated the effect at more than 10 per cent. The ensuing discussion seems to imply that such effect as there was must have been chiefly in the field of mortgage credit.

The fact is that the supply of funds available to the private sector seems to be quite expansible under pressure, and it is not certain that many spenders will find credit unavailable when they need it. Moreover, some of the factors discussed above — such as the predominance and expansibility of internal sources of funds — are applicable whether monetary policy works through interest rates or through availability. And finally, to the extent that econometric studies are able to sort out the effects of interest rates from those of other closely correlated variables (such as profits or sales), such studies should be able to detect the effects of monetary policy whether these effects work through interest rates directly or through availability. At times when credit standards are raised and credit availability is reduced as a result of a policy of credit restraint, interest rates also rise. In fact, interest rates might be taken as an indicator of the degree of credit availability. This being the case, there should be a relationship between interest rates and investment expenditures, although, of course, the explanation of this relation would be different from the classical explanation based on the interest rate as a cost factor. The fact, therefore, that there is little evidence from econometric studies of any significant relation between interest rates and investment casts some doubt on the availability doctrine as well as on the more orthodox arguments emphasizing interest rates.

It seems fair to conclude that while changes in interest rates and credit availability brought about by monetary policy have some marginal influence over business investment expenditures, these effects are so weak that they are commonly swamped by the dynamic forces of innovation, surging business activity, and rising profits which almost invariably underlie a rapid growth of investment. For example, it is very doubtful whether restrictive monetary policy did more than touch the fringes of the private investment boom of 1955–57.

Interest rates and credit policy are likely to affect investment in some sectors more than in others. Two candidates for strong effects suggest themselves. One is public utilities which, being publicly regulated, are probably subject to somewhat less uncertainty than most other enterprises, and which employ a large amount of long-lived capital so that interest rates are a fairly large element of cost. The other is smaller business enterprises which are likely to be in a somewhat weaker position vis-a-vis the credit and capital markets than larger firms. Let us turn our attention to each of these sectors in turn.

C. PLANT AND EQUIPMENT: PUBLIC UTILITIES

Some investigations have been made of the determinants of investment in plant and equipment by electric power companies. One study by Lawrence Klein covering the interwar period (1921–41) found the interest rate to be a significant factor, along with profits and the stock of capital; Klein estimated the interest elasticity of investment in this industry to be 2.79, meaning that a relative decline of 1 per cent (of itself) in the rate of interest would result in an increase of 2.79 per cent in investment. On the other hand, a recent study by Kisselgoff and Modigliani, covering approximately the same time period as Klein's, arrives at an even more satisfactory explanation of investment by privately owned electric power companies by relating it to the rate of change of demand for electric energy and without making use of the interest rate. In fact, the authors tried out various formulations of the investment equation including the interest rate without success, and they conclude:

> On the basis of our statistical analysis, we cannot reach a definite conclusion concerning the influence of interest rates on investment; however, the evidence strongly suggests that even in this industry, where fixed assets are of great longevity, the cost of borrowed funds was not an important factor.

Another study by Michael Gort also suggests that the interest rate is not an important determinant.

Thus, the evidence (what there is of it) is not conclusive one way or the other. If interest rates are in fact not important in public utility investment, the explanation probably lies in certain peculiar features of the industry. Public utilities are supposed to make their services available throughout the territory they encompass. Although the practices of various regulatory agencies in setting utility rates vary considerably, most authorities apparently take interest costs into account in one way or another in setting rates and deciding what is a "fair return on invested capital." In view of the fact that the demand for electric power is apparently price inelastic in the short run for nearly all types of consumers, it appears that a company which is forced to pay a higher rate of interest for funds can hope to secure a rate increase and that the increase in rates will not appreciably reduce its sales. Under these conditions, the need to build up capacity to meet a growing demand may be the dominant consideration governing investment decisions, and the interest rate of decidedly secondary importance in the short run. At the same time, however, demand for electric energy is probably considerably more elastic in the longer run after households and businesses have had time to adapt their appliances and equipment to changed conditions. Thus, while the short-run effects of rising interest rates may be of little importance, a gradual upward drift of interest rates from one business cycle to another might significantly reduce investment by public utilities.

Investment in public utilities continued to rise in 1955–57 despite rising interest rates, and there is no obvious evidence that the increase in the cost of capital caused a reduction in investment. We may conclude that even in this field, where the conditions for a significant interest rate effect are, in some respects at least, unusually favorable, it is at least doubtful whether monetary policy has a very potent effect, particularly in the short run.

D. EFFECTS ON SMALL VERSUS LARGE FIRMS

Although general credit controls do not seem to affect business investment very much in the aggregate, there has been some discussion of the possibility that they may discriminate against smaller businesses. There are some plausible reasons for expecting such discriminatory effects, and some strong indications that under certain conditions they would be present. However, as to whether there has in fact been such discrimination in the last few years, the evidence is mixed, difficult to interpret, and highly unsatisfactory. It may be noted that there is considerable difficulty in deciding upon the proper definition of a small business — a subject which has generated a great deal of literature in the last few years — but we shall not worry about this problem in this necessarily brief discussion.

Fragmentary evidence suggests that smaller corporations rely upon external sources of funds somewhat more than do larger ones. In the case of unincorporated enterprises, the difficulty of disentangling the affairs of businesses from those of their owners makes it virtually impossible to measure the amount of internal financing. To the extent that small firms raise

funds externally, it is clear that they are more dependent on the banking system than large firms are, have fewer alternative sources of funds, and seem, in general, to be more vulnerable to the effects of tight credit. To the extent that larger firms do need to use bank credit, they have access to a larger number of banks, and the competition among banks for their business strengthens their bargaining position and probably enables them to get better terms, as well as greater assurance of getting the funds they need. Moreover, large firms have access to the open market as a source of short-term funds and to the organized security markets for long-term funds. Smaller firms are limited in their ability to utilize the facilities of the capital market, because they are not well known to investors except perhaps within a limited geographical area. New firms, as well as small firms, suffer disabilities in raising funds for growth and expansion. Established and profitable firms are able to finance a large portion of their needs from earnings retention. New firms in their early years may not have the necessary profits to finance expansion and their lack of credit standing makes it difficult to obtain funds from external sources. These same factors probably make new enterprises more vulnerable than existing ones to the effects of tightening credit. In addition, small (and new) firms which do not possess market control are likely to find it much more difficult to pass on increased interest rates to their customers through price increases than is the case with larger firms possessing a semimonopolistic market position. And they may similarly have more difficulty in raising prices in times of tight credit in order to obtain more funds from internal sources.

A satisfactory test of the hypothesis that smaller businesses are unduly affected by tight credit would require a careful study of investment broken down according to size of firm during periods of tight and easy credit. Unfortunately, satisfactory data for making such a test are not available. However, there are one or two small bits of evidence. The Federal Reserve flow-of-funds tabulations shows fixed investment expenditures for nonfinancial business firms, broken down between corporations and unincorporated enterprises. The behavior of these sectors in the 1955–57 period of credit restraint is of some interest. Investment by unincorporated businesses approximately kept pace with that by corporations between 1954 and 1955, but in 1956 and 1957, the period in which credit became noticeably tight, unincorporated businesses fell behind. From 1955 to 1956, unincorporated businesses increased their investment spending less than corporations, so that their share of total investment declined. And in 1957, while investment by corporations continued to increase, that by unincorporated enterprises actually declined.

The quarterly financial reports for manufacturing corporations prepared by the Federal Trade Commission and Securities and Exchange Commission show gross property, plant, and equipment accounts by size classes of corporations. The increase in these accounts during any period of time is a rough measure of gross investment. The increase in these accounts for all corporations between the third quarter of 1953 and the fourth quarter of 1954 — a period of relatively easy credit — amounted to $11 billion, of which $8.9 billion or 80 per cent of the total occurred in corporations having total assets of over $50 million. In the period of tight credit extending from the first quarter of 1955 to the third quarter of 1957, the total increase was $33.4 billion, of which $29.4 billion or 88 per cent of the total was credited to corporations with assets in excess of $50 million. Thus, these data suggest some gain in the relative position of large companies during the period of tight credit.

Obviously, these data are very sketchy. Moreover, even if it were clearly established that large firms did grow faster than small firms in the 1955–57 period, and that growth speeded up more for large firms as compared with the previous period of easy credit, it would not prove that smaller firms were unduly affected by tight credit. It is quite possible that the nature of the expansion during this period favored large firms — i.e., that the demand for products produced primarily by large firms underwent a disproportionate expansion. A conclusive study of the problem would require a careful and intensive analysis of the nature

of the shifts in demand and industrial structure that occurred during the period.

There is, however, some further evidence relating to the expansion of bank loans to small and large businesses during the 1955–57 period of credit restriction, derived from a detailed study by the Federal Reserve System. To summarize the results briefly, they indicate that business loans to large borrowers increased much more rapidly than loans to small borrowers during this period, although one cannot be sure whether this was due to a disproportionate effect of tight credit on the supply of funds to small businesses or to the fact that demands for funds on the part of large businesses were increasing more rapidly. It does appear that during this period interest rates on loans to large businesses rose substantially more than interest rates on loans to small businesses. In a sense, this was favorable to small businesses, but basically it probably hurt them by making loans to small business less attractive than loans to larger concerns. The reason for the narrowing of interest rate differentials apparently is that there are approximate ceilings on interest rates on business loans of 6 to 8 per cent due to usury laws and banking tradition in many parts of the country, and loans to small businesses, which involve more risk and expense, were closer to the ceilings at the beginning of the period so that they were able to rise only to a rather limited extent.

One of the Federal Reserve studies suggests that one way of solving the dilemma of distinguishing between large and small businesses is to divide firms into those that are large enough and sufficiently well-established to be able to obtain funds in the national credit and capital markets and those that are not able to utilize such facilities. The study then points out that the first group of firms will be able to borrow on a short- or long-term basis virtually at will provided they are willing to pay the going price for funds and will seldom encounter a problem of availability. The smaller firms, on the other hand, will have to rely mainly on trade credit and bank loans, which they must obtain from a limited number of banks on a customer relationship basis. This useful way of looking at the problem suggests, in view of the fact that the demand for credit appears to be quite inelastic within the range of rates we are accustomed to, that monetary policy is not effective unless it does have a strong impact on small business. *That is, if monetary policy works chiefly through availability and if availability is not a problem for large firms, it follows that when monetary policy is effective in curtailing business spending, its impact must fall mainly on small business.*

One final facet of the problem should be considered. Trade credit extended mainly by large firms to smaller firms is an important factor and may serve to reduce the pressure of credit restriction on smaller firms. During the 1955–58 period trade credit expanded very rapidly. Studies indicate that this is probably a systematic partial offset to whatever tendency there is for smaller firms to be unduly affected by restriction of bank credit.

E. STATE AND LOCAL GOVERNMENT EXPENDITURES

It has frequently been pointed out that State and local governments have been strongly affected by credit restrictions in recent years. Such restrictions would, of course, have their main effects on capital outlays of these governmental units, and probably the best available index of capital outlays is construction activity. Expenditures on new construction by State and local governments increased steadily during the period of tight credit in 1955–57 — from $7.8 billion in 1954 to $9.7 billion in 1957. In 1958 they remained at about the same level as in 1957.

The amount of new State and local government security issues sold for cash amounted to $7 billion in 1954, declined sharply in 1955 and 1956, reaching $5.4 billion in the latter year, then rose to $7 billion in 1957 and $7.4 billion in 1958. Actually, these figures substantially overstate the net amount of funds obtained through the capital market, since they make no allowance for the substantial amounts of old securities retired out of tax revenues by some governmental units. Expenditures on construction and land have been increasing about $1 billion per year. The current surplus — excess of tax receipts over other kinds of expenditures — increased each year up to 1958, so

that it was possible to finance increasing construction expenditures in 1956 and 1957 while at the same time reducing the net amount of funds raised by borrowing.

The high cost of funds and tightness in the capital market have unquestionably caused some borrowing by State and local governments to be canceled or postponed. A study by the Investment Bankers Association, covering the 9-month period July 1956 to March 1957, indicated that about $0.5 billion of bonds were not sold as scheduled, but a substantial portion of these were reoffered and sold at a later date during the period. However, all studies of this kind necessarily cover only issues which reached the offering stage — no one knows the volume of issues canceled at earlier stages of the borrowing process.

It is very difficult to judge the extent to which the cancellation or postponement of bond issues results in a corresponding reduction or postponement of State and local government spending. The proceeds of some issues may be intended for repayment of bank loans or refunding of outstanding securities. To the extent that the proceeds are designed to finance income-generating expenditures, some of these expenditures may be financed by drawing down liquid assets or by borrowing from the banking system or other sources. Furthermore, there is a lag between the raising of funds and their expenditure, and the postponement of issues may serve mainly to shorten the length of this lag. There are strong indications, however, that while these various adjustments may absorb some of the impact, substantial postponements of offerings do have an effect on expenditures.

There are signs that in some instances State and local governments and perhaps the electorate in voting on bond issues for public improvements are becoming more sensitive to interest costs, but there are also a great many instances where interest rates do not influence decisions at all. In some cases, there are legal ceilings on interest rates that can be paid by governmental units, but apparently these ceilings are commonly set at 5 or 6 per cent and are thus high enough so that they do not interfere with the raising of funds. Apparently, however, there have been instances in which interest rate maximums fixed in specific referendums have proved to be too low to make borrowing possible by the time the securities were offered.

There has recently been some indication of a contracyclical movement in contract awards by State and local governments. Awards leveled off in mid-1957 and then rose sharply at the same time that interest rates fell in late 1957 and early 1958; then late in 1958 they began a sharp decline which coincided with rising interest rates. The increase that occurred in 1958 has been cited as evidence of contracyclical stabilizing behavior on the part of State and local governments expenditures. A more complete study now in process finds evidence of systematic contracyclical behavior on the part of State and local government construction expenditures in recent years. This study, by Frank Morris, considers security offerings, contract awards, and construction put in place, and concludes that monetary policy has a contracyclical effect on State and local government construction expenditures which is approximately one-third to one-fourth as great as the effect on residential construction. It breaks expenditures into three categories — schools, water and sewer projects, and all other types of projects — and finds no substantial evidence of effects on schools and water and sewer projects, the entire contracyclical effect being felt in the "all other" category.

The large increments in the school-age population (ages 5 to 17) in recent years, in conjunction with the fact that school construction contract awards have shown little increase since 1954 and have actually been declining since mid-1958, suggest that money may have had some differential impact on school building, in contrast to the conclusions of the study referred to above. School construction rose roughly in pace with other types of construction during the post-war period up to 1954, but since that time has lagged distinctly behind other types of construction. In a period in which school facilities were generally recognized as inadequate to begin with, in which there have been increasing increments to the school-age population, and in which construction costs have been rising sharply, we find an apparent

decline in expenditures on school construction. One might surmise that the tight money that has prevailed during most of this period has had something to do with it.

During the last few years, yields on State and local government securities have been rising relative to yields on most other types of securities. The chief reason for this is apparently the fact that such securities are exempt from the Federal income tax, and, in order to market the greatly increased volume of issues during the postwar period, it has been necessary to appeal to investors in lower tax brackets to whom the tax exemption is of less value than to the wealthy investors who formerly constituted the bulk of the market for State and local government securities. It may be noted that commercial banks have in recent years become very important investors in these securities. It may be that tight money, by keeping the bank market from expanding more rapidly, has made it necessary for State and local governments to obtain funds from investors subject to lower tax rates than the 52 per cent applicable to commercial banks.

F. CONSUMER DURABLE GOODS

Consumer durable goods, particularly automobiles, have contributed significantly to economic instability during the postwar period. The rate of growth of outstanding consumer installment debt has been large, the debt having grown from $2.5 billion at the end of 1945 to $33.9 billion at the end of 1958. Some students of the problem have been worried about this rate of increase, feeling that it could not continue indefinitely and that when it slows down it will create problems in maintaining aggregate demand especially for consumer durable goods. However, an analysis of the growth of consumer credit on the basis of a life-cycle model, in which each year a new group of consumer borrowers in the early stages of household formation enters the market and a (smaller) one leaves the market (i.e., pays off its debt), indicates that a continuous geometric rate of growth of the absolute increments to outstanding debt is not an unreasonable possibility. In this situation, if we start from a condition in which the ratio of debt to income is very small (as was the case at the end of the war), this ratio will increase rapidly at first but the rate of increase in the ratio will gradually slow down and the ratio itself will eventually approach a constant. Apart from the fluctuations in consumer credit, the trend of growth since the end of World War II appears to be consistent with such a model.

Thus, it appears that it is the instability — the rapid accelerations and decelerations — in the growth of consumer credit rather than the high average rate of growth per se that constitutes the problem. Consumer credit has contributed to most of the fluctuations in economic activity since 1929. In the early postwar years, however, markets for consumer durable goods were dominated by special factors, including wartime shortages and the resulting need for replacement, the initially low level of consumer debt, large holdings of liquid assets, the rising supplies of durable goods during the reconversion period, and the temporary applications of selective controls from September 1948 to June 1949 and from September 1950 to May 1952. As a result, installment credit and durable-goods expenditures did not bear their usual relation to income; for example, during the 1949 recession, both durable-goods expenditures and the net change in installment credit outstanding continued to increase. Thus, installment credit appears to have had a stabilizing effect during most of this period. Since 1952, the procyclical behavior of earlier years has been resumed.

Fundamental to an explanation of the cyclical role of consumer credit appears to be the fact that such credit is largely used to finance the purchase of durable goods. The acceleration principle, applied in a somewhat loose fashion, provides a reasonably satisfactory explanation of the cyclical fluctuations in durable-goods buying. That is, if the demand for the services of durable goods is a function of the level of income, there will be an equilibrium stock of consumer durable goods corresponding to each income level. The demand for net additions to the stock will be a function not of the level but of the rate of change in income. Combined with various other relationships, such a relationship is capable of contributing to

(or even causing) cyclical fluctuations in economic activity. It seems likely that such a relationship (in a complex nonlinear form) does in fact exist and constitutes a basic explanation of the instability that characterizes the consumer-durable goods industries. The destabilizing effect of the accelerator is undoubtedly intensified in the downward direction by the fact that replacement can be postponed beyond the normal time and in the upward direction by the availability of consumer credit which permits rapid expansion of purchases to make up for postponement of replacement during the downswing, and consumer credit probably further intensifies the instability in several other ways:

1. It increases the demand for consumer-durable goods and enlarges the sector to which the acceleration effect is applicable.

2. The tendency of lenders to ease credit terms in upswings and tighten them during downswings because of changes in the attitude toward the risks of consumer loans may increase the amplitude of the swings.

3. The attitudes of consumer borrowers toward incurring debt to buy durable goods (as distinct from their attitude toward the goods themselves) may shift in a destabilizing fashion over the business cycle.

4. Required repayment of outstanding debt may constitute a severe drag on the shrinking total of consumer purchasing power during a period of declining activity.

5. If consumers are overburdened with debt when income falls and are forced to default, the solvency of financial institutions may be imperiled.

Some of these influences are obviously not likely to be important except in the case of a serious decline. Moreover, not all fluctuations in the demand for consumer durable goods are to be explained in terms of an accelerator relationship. For example, the sharp rise in automobile demand in 1955 and its subsequent sharp decline in 1956 were clearly due chiefly to autonomous forces such as a change in consumer tastes perhaps related to the new models of 1955.

Consumer credit is more important in connection with the purchases of automobiles than it is in connection with the purchase of other durable goods. During 1955–58, consumer credit extensions on automobile paper were 96 per cent of total consumer expenditures on automobiles and parts, while the ratio of credit extensions to consumer expenditures for all other durable goods combined was only 50 per cent. In view of the fact that automobiles have been more unstable than other durable goods, as pointed out above, this suggests that consumer credit does contribute to instability.

In view of the destabilizing fluctuations in consumer-durable goods and consumer credit, the question of the impact of general credit controls in this sector is an important one. There are a number of reasons for doubting the strength of the impact, although there are almost surely some effects. Several participants in the Federal Reserve study of consumer installment credit attempted to assess the sensitivity, and, although there were some differences in the conclusions arrived at, it seems fair to say that the consensus was that the effects of general controls are not very powerful in this sector. A high proportion of consumer credit emanates from commercial banks either directly or through the extension of bank credit to finance the activities of sales finance companies. As far as direct loans by the banks are concerned, the exceptional profitability of consumer loans, the possibility of selling Government securities in order to continue making loans when credit tightens, the fact that many banks have consumer credit departments which are not profitable unless a large volume of credit operations is maintained, and the possibilities of pressure from dealers in automobiles and other durable goods to continue making credit available are factors making for insensitivity. For sales finance companies, the great skill of these institutions in shifting nimbly among different sources of funds makes it difficult for credit restrictions to slow down their lending activity. And finally, the apparent insensitivity of consumer demand for durable goods and credit to changes in interest rates gives lenders considerable room for making upward adjustments in interest rates as costs of funds to them rise without affecting the quantity of credit extended. Consumers apparently are commonly quite ignorant of the finance charges they pay

and seem to be mainly influenced by the monthly payment they have to make. Moderate changes in interest rates on consumer loans do not affect the monthly payment much; and if they do, the effect can be compensated for by a slight increase in the term of the loan.

There is some support for the view that general controls do have a significant impact on consumer credit and a little evidence in support of this position. A recent study by Paul Smith, covering the period from mid-1955 to the end of 1956 when credit was tightening, compares the reactions of selected groups of banks (concentrating on banks which emphasize consumer lending) whose deposits increased during this period with other groups (similarly selected) whose deposits declined. The study finds that the declining-deposit banks — who by definition were under more pressure than the others — increased their consumer loans substantially less than the increasing-deposit banks. In general, the study shows that the declining-deposit banks reduced nearly all types of loans more than the other banks, while at the same time selling more securities, and that consumer loans were cut as much as other types. What the study does not show, of course, is the extent to which borrowers turned down by these banks were able to obtain loans from other banks or from sales-finance companies. Nevertheless, the results are of some significance.

It seems reasonable to conclude that, while general controls almost certainly have some effects on consumer credit, these effects are probably not very great. Moreover, there is another problem that arises when the movements in durable goods get out of phase with the economy as a whole — as in 1956–57 when the automobile industry was depressed at the same time that general business conditions were reasonably good. In such a situation, it may be desirable to tighten credit generally without having an effect on the depressed sector.

G. INVENTORY INVESTMENT

Changes in the rate of inventory accumulation and decumulation have been an important factor in business fluctuations in the United States during the postwar period. Inventory runups in boom times have set the stage for inventory disinvestment during periods of decline, and rapid inventory disinvestment has been an important factor in the recessions of 1949, 1953–54, and 1957–58.

The demand for inventory stocks in manufacturing appears to depend to a first approximation upon the current level of sales; this means that the change in inventories (which is inventory investment) depends upon the rate at which sales are changing. Thus, a decline in the rate of increase in sales can cause an absolute decline in inventory investment. Although the determinants of inventory investment are more complicated than this, the inventory demand relation is of this general type, and for this reason inventory investment is subject to exaggerated fluctuations which have a short-run destabilizing effect by magnifying fluctuations in final demand. From the point of view of economic stabilization, therefore, it would be desirable if inventory fluctuations could be damped. Since much inventory investment is financed by bank credit, some economists have put considerable emphasis on the role of monetary policy in regulating inventories. However, there is little evidence that monetary controls exert a strong influence on inventory investment. Inventories are usually held in order to maintain or increase output and sales or to profit from price speculation. In view of the short time periods for which they are commonly held, the interest rate is ordinarily a negligible element of cost. Accordingly, businessmen are ordinarily willing, if necessary, to pay an increased interest rate on inventory loans. If banks were to "ration credit" by simply turning down borrowers rather than by raising interest rates, this could have an effect on inventory investment. But inventory loans are precisely the types that, according to traditional theories of commercial banking, are most appropriate for banks to make. Moreover, banks feel an obligation to meet the temporary working capital requirements of their customers. In addition, as we have seen, banks commonly have substantial secondary reserves of Government securities which they can sell to obtain funds for lending. Finally, it is not certain that even if banks credit were less available, inventory investment would be strongly affected, since businessmen might be able to finance inventory investment by liquidating cash balances or Government securities or by borrowing elsewhere.

A recent study by Doris M. Eisemann of monetary policy in relation to inventories indicates, however, that inventories are sufficiently dependent on bank credit so that a policy that could effectively control bank loans might affect inventory investment. However, in addition to the problem of effectively controlling loans, this study suggests some other difficulties. One is that the durable goods industries, which have larger inventory fluctuations than nondurable goods industries, do not rely upon bank credit as much for financing inventories, and large firms, in general, have an unusually low ratio of loans to inventories. Moreover, in view of the time lag in making monetary policy effective and the difficulty of detecting the proper time for restricting inventory accumulation, the problem of timing monetary policy with a view to controlling inventories would be a difficult one.

In any case, there is certainly no evidence that monetary policy has had any appreciable effect on inventory investment and its fluctuations in the last few years.

H. LAGS IN MONETARY POLICY

Considerable evidence has accumulated in the last few years that whatever effects general monetary controls may have are likely to be realized only with relatively long time lags. A recent study by Milton Friedman, covering 19 business cycles from 1879 to 1954, has uncovered consistent and rather long timelags between turning points in the time rate of change of the money supply and turning points in general business conditions. At upper turning points, the lag averaged 16 months and ranged between 13 and 24 months for specific cycles. The average lag at lower turning points was 12 months with a range of 5 to 21 months. Another study by Thomas Mayer has attempted to measure, on a sector-by-sector basis, the lags that are likely to be present between changes in interest rates and credit availability and the effects on production, income, and prices. For example, for a construction project financed by borrowing, this lag would consist of the time elapsing between the raising of the funds and the accrual or payment of income to the factors of production. This would depend upon the speed with which orders were placed for materials, the extent to which the orders were filled out of existing inventories, the speed with which the rate of production was adjusted to make good the depletion of inventories and to keep pace with the change in sales, and a host of other factors, many of which would vary greatly from one industry to another and from one time to another, depending on business conditions. Furthermore, there would be secondary effects stemming from the spending of the income generated by the initial payments, and these effects would overlap those occurring in the first stage. The study referred to above estimates the lags at perhaps roughly 6 months for residential construction, something over a year for other types of construction, about 6 months for manufacturing equipment outlays, 2 months for consumer credit, and 3 months for inventories.

The lags are probably overstated in this study, although the inadequacy of the data, as well as conceptual difficulties, makes adequate appraisal difficult. In any case, the lags may well be long enough to be rather troublesome for monetary policy. Moreover, to the lags estimated in this study it is necessary to add the interval between the time when the monetary authorities take action and the time when this action affects interest rates and credit availability enough to produce a change in spending decisions; this interval may also be substantial.

It is often contended that the flexible administrative apparatus of the Federal Reserve gives monetary policy an advantage over fiscal or other stabilization policies because it is possible to take action quickly and to reverse the direction of policy without delay if it is necessary. However, this view overlooks the fact that in the case of monetary policy there may be a rather long lag between the time action is taken and the time its effects are felt.

It is possible that the effects of monetary policy are stronger than the analysis in the previous section of this chapter suggests, because most studies of the impact may not have made proper allowance for lags. In any case, the existence of the lags obviously complicates greatly the problem of the proper timing of monetary actions.

I. CONCLUDING COMMENT

In order to appraise the impact of monetary policy on aggregate spending, it is necessary to combine the sectoral impacts discussed above. In addition, it is necessary to take account of secondary changes in spending resulting from the operation of the multiplier. As indicated in the above discussion, the effects are obviously quite irregular — with some sectors (such as residential construction) being affected strongly and other sectors (such as fixed investment by large corporations) being affected very little. But for a period in which credit tightens and interest rates rise as much as in the 1955–57 period, for example, it seems likely that the total effect would be a matter of some consequence. However, the irregularity as between sectors raises problems, as does the presence of lag. And it is especially important to bear in mind that the effects seem to be weak in those sectors — such as plant and equipment expenditures, inventory investment, and consumer durable goods — that are prone to raid expansion and contraction and are consequently important generators of instability.

SUMMARY OF EFFECTS OF MONETARY POLICY ON MAJOR SECTORS OF THE ECONOMY

1. *It is clear that by far the greatest impact of monetary policy in the past few years has been on residential construction. Restrictive policies during periods of inflation have tended to reduce the rate of housing construction, while easy money policies in recession have stimulated it. The effect has been mainly, but perhaps not entirely, due to the existence of interest-rate ceilings on FHA-insured and VA-guaranteed mortgages, which have served to channel the supply of funds to and from residential construction as interest rates on competitive investments fall and rise.*

2. *Aside from this sector, the effects of monetary policy have probably been greatest on State and local government construction expenditures and on capital outlays by smaller businesses, although the evidence in these cases is far from definitive. The effects on plant and equipment expenditures of larger business con-*

cerns appear to have been very slight, and, as a result, monetary controls have not been very effective in dealing with booms powered by increases in fixed investment, as in 1955–57. Even in the case of public utilities, where conditions appear to be most favorable for monetary policy there is little evidence of a strong effect on investment. There has probably been some effect on consumer credit, although the impact here appears to be quite weak. Inventory investment has been affected very little.

3. It appears that such effects as monetary policy does have are felt by the economy only after fairly long time lags, although evidence on this matter is still rather sketchy. If the lags are as long as they appear to be, they create difficult problems in connection with the timing of monetary action.

4. Although the impacts are irregular as between sectors and appear with troublesome lags, the effect on aggregate spending resulting from vigorous credit tightening is a matter of some importance. However, the effects are weak in the sectors — including fixed investment, consumer durables, and inventories — which are subject to the greatest fluctuations and are the most serious generators of instability.

II.

In light of the difficulties suggested by the above analysis of monetary policy, there are several approaches that might be taken to increase its effectiveness. Unfortunately, however, there is no panacea, one reason being that our knowledge is not adequate to enable us to say with certainty that the diagnosis of the difficulties is correct. One thing that can be said with assurance is that there should be more intensive study of the effects of monetary policy. In this regard, we may hope that the studies now being conducted by the Commission on Money and Credit will throw useful light on the problems. *However, the Federal Reserve System should be encouraged to devote substantial research effort to such studies and to make the results, regardless of their implications, available to scholars outside the System.*

On the one hand, maintaining stability in a growing economy requires that aggregate demand should be permitted to grow in pace

with the aggregate capacity; that is, the level of output that can be produced when the labor force is fully employed. At the same time, as Charles L. Schultze has pointed out, changes in the composition of demand are important, particularly in an economy many sectors of which are characterized by downward rigidity of prices, since under such circumstances there is an inflationary bias built into the mechanism which we rely upon to reallocate resources in response to changes in demand.

In such an economy, large changes in demand which occur quickly cause considerable difficulties both in maintaining balance between the growth of capacity and the growth of demand and in preventing inflation. On the one hand, changes in demand tend to produce increases in the rate of investment as capacity is built up in the sector in which the demand has increased, and it becomes difficult to manage things in such a way that demand continues to grow in pace with capacity. Excess capacity tends to be built up in some sectors, and when demand fails to keep pace, the rate of investment slows down and unemployment results. In addition, prices tend to rise in the sectors to which demand has shifted, but, due to rigidities associated with market power, they fail to decline in the sectors where demand has declined. Instead, output and employment fall in these sectors. Policies which attempt to keep the price level stable by reducing aggregate demand may in turn strike areas where downward price rigidity prevails, and may be ineffective in dealing with inflation, and at the same time may result in further reductions in output and employment.

In this kind of economy, it is extremely difficult to design appropriate policies which will maintain stable growth of output and prevent inflation. One approach to the problem which may have merit within limits is to try to prevent some of the major shifts in demand which necessitate these complex adjustments. This approach cannot be pushed too far, since its extreme limit would be to keep the composition of demand constant. This would require a complex set of detailed controls, which, aside from being virtually impossible to administer effectively, would put the economy in a straitjacket and immobilize the machinery for reallocating resources to meet changing tastes and needs.

However, there are some changes in demand which it might be desirable to prevent or, more accurately, to check before they have been permitted to go too far. The record shows, for example, that investment in plant and equipment tends to develop in powerful surges, sometimes associated with expansion in one sector of the economy and sometimes another. A recent example is the investment boom of 1955–57. These surges seem to feed upon themselves, because investment goods production begets the need for more investment to expand the capacity of the industries which produce capital equipment. Thus, they tend to cause inflation centered in capital goods, which, due to downward rigidities of prices and wages, it is difficult to prevent by means of general controls which do not strongly affect the demand for capital equipment itself. Secondly, when these investment booms proceed beyond a certain point, it becomes difficult to keep demand growing in pace with capacity and thus prevent overcapacity and unemployment from developing. In addition to surges in the demand for capital equipment that occur autonomously, there are surges in demand that occur as a result of the operation of acceleration effects in consumer durable goods and business inventories. Such shifts in demand — or increases in aggregate demand centered in specific sectors of the economy — tend to cause difficult inflationary problems in themselves, and they also tend, via further acceleration effects, to set off or to accentuate booms in the capital goods industries. A case in point is the rapid rise in automobile demand, fed by consumer credit, in 1955, which reached a pace that could scarcely be sustained and probably was partly responsible for the capital goods boom of 1955–57.

Thus, there may be something to be said for the development of controls which are capable of dealing with specific destabilizing sectors characterized by strong accelerator effects, such as plant and equipment, consumer durable goods, inventories, and residential construction. All of these sectors, except residential construction, appear to be relatively insensitive to general monetary controls, according to our

earlier analysis, and the effects on residential construction have been due primarily to peculiar institutional relationships.

Serious consideration should be given to the development of selective credit controls in sectors of the economy which are the major sources or potential sources of instability, such as consumer durable goods, inventory investment, and residential construction. From a technical standpoint, it appears to be feasible to develop controls which would be reasonably effective in these areas. In the case of plant and equipment, both the feasibility and the wisdom of selective controls seem much more doubtful. Moreover, effective controls in the other sectors would probably reduce somewhat the scope for booms in capital goods.

Admittedly it is very difficult to develop satisfactory criteria for the administration of selective controls. However, many other countries which have made successful use of monetary policy during the postwar period have employed selective controls without difficulty; in fact, it has often been selective rather than general controls which have been most effective. Moreover, it should be noted that reliance on so-called general controls does not get us away from sectoral problems, and the more effective general controls are, the more acute these problems become. For example, suppose that in 1956 and 1957 general credit controls had been highly effective in the field of consumer credit. Would the monetary authorities have tightened credit to deal with general inflation and thus have made life still harder for the already depressed automobile industry? It is quite plain that if general credit controls affected all sectors equally (in some sense), they would still be quite unsatisfactory as a stabilization device, because we do not want equal effects everywhere at all times. If we want to improve the performance of stabilization policy significantly, it is necessary to move in the direction of greater selectivity. This has been apparent for some time, but the other findings of this study should increase our awareness of it. General controls are a mirage and a delusion. It is perhaps just as well that monetary controls have not been very effective; if they had been, they might have been disastrous.

37

A NEW THEORY OF CREDIT CONTROL:
THE AVAILABILITY THESIS*

James Tobin†

In Selection 35 above, which originated in 1952 in testimony by the Federal Reserve before the Patman Committee, substantial emphasis was placed on the influence of monetary policy over lenders and through them over the availability of credit.

This contrasts with traditional central banking theory, in which monetary policy is seen as exerting its effects mainly if not exclusively through borrowers and their reactions to variations in the cost of credit. Skeptics always questioned how much changes in interest rates (the cost of credit) influenced potential borrowers: would a business firm intending to borrow at 5 per cent interest cost not do so merely because the cost rose to 6 per cent?

The availability theory outflanks this objection to monetary policy's effectiveness by responding that even if borrowers are insensitive to interest cost they can't very well borrow if credit is simply not available because lenders won't lend.

In this selection, written at the time the availability thesis was first expounded, Professor Tobin traces the genesis of the new doctrine — which is still widespread today — and raises some pertinent issues.

The Patman inquiry inspired, both in written replies and in oral testimony, numerous expositions of the theory of monetary control. A large majority of the respondents assigned to general monetary controls considerable influence on the level of economic activity. Only a few voiced the skepticism of their effectiveness so common five or ten years ago. These volumes are impressive evidence of the "rediscovery of money," as Howard Ellis has called this reversal in economic fashion.

The important varieties of monetary theory espoused to the committee may be, with some violence to the individualities of some respondents, classified into three schools. One group, whose intellectual headquarters is Chicago, believes that aggregate spending is sensitive enough to the rate of interest, and hoarding insensitive enough, to make the quantity theory a good approximation. A second group agrees that the issue hinges on the sensitivity of

spenders and hoarders to interest rates. But this group is skeptical about the interest-elasticity of spending and is impressed more with the variability than with the constancy of monetary velocity. These two schools fit easily into the traditional framework of monetary discussion. Their disagreement, although it contributes to a marked difference in policy recommendations, is less a difference of theory than of empirical judgment. In the panel discussion Milton Friedman and Paul Samuelson represented ably these two points of view.

The third school, however, sets forth a new theory of monetary control which claims that both of the old schools are asking the wrong questions. Under the leadership of Robert V. Roosa[1] and others, the new theory has developed and spread rapidly in recent years. It has been inspired by postwar Federal Reserve policy, before and after the accord; the theory, in turn, inspires the policy. The Federal Reserve replies indicate that it is the offi-

* Reprinted by permission of the author and the publishers from *The Review of Economics and Statistics*, Volume XXXV, No. 2, May, 1953. Cambridge, Mass.: Harvard University Press, Copyright, 1953, by the President and Fellows of Harvard College.

† Yale University.

[1] See his essay, "Interest Rates and the Central Bank," *Money, Trade, and Economic Growth*, pp. 270–95. For the development of the doctrine, beginning with pre-war writings see pp. 275–76 of this essay and the works there cited.

cial rationale of current policy. Because of its intellectual interest and its evident practical importance, the new theory deserves careful examination. In the Patman inquiry only Professors Samuelson and Whittlesey gave it the critical attention which it merits.

According to this theory, monetary controls work much more through restricting the availability of credit than through increasing its cost, much more through restraints on lenders than through reactions of borrowers. It is possible, according to the theory, to curtail spending significantly by limiting the availability of bank reserves, without raising significantly market rates of interest. Some upward pressure on rates there is bound to be. But this is largely incidental, and one cannot judge the impact of a monetary restriction by the height to which it pushes interest rates. There are evidently two related parts to this proposition. The first is that it is possible to restrict reserves without raising interest rates appreciably. The second is that such restriction will curtail aggregate demand. Thus the new theory provides an answer to those of the other two schools who question the importance of fractional increases in interest rates. The significance of the new doctrine may be most clearly appreciated from the fact that it implies that monetary restriction will curtail aggregate demand even if the most extreme skepticism about the interest-elasticity of borrowing and spending were justified.

To put the theory in an over-formal but nonetheless perhaps an illuminating way, the substance of it is that an *increasing* yield on government bonds is an extremely good substitute for a *high* yield. At a given interest rate, the demand to hold government bonds, relative to other assets, will be higher if the interest rate is increasing or has recently increased than if it is stable. This is due to a combination of factors neglected in the older theories: first and most important, imperfections in the money markets which prevent the yields on other assets from adjusting to compensate for the increased attractiveness of government bonds; second, irrational and conventional behavior by financial institutions, so that portfolio decisions are not based wholly on yield compari-

sons but partly on considerations such as a reluctance to realize capital losses; third, uncertainties and expectations associated with increases in bond yields, which may make both borrowers and lenders appraise the economic future with more caution. Against these factors works the more familiar speculative effect: expectations and fears that interest rates will continue to rise tend to reduce the demand for bonds. But the new theory contends that if the favorable factors are skillfully exploited by the central bank, they will more than offset the speculative effect.

The consequences of a restriction of bank reserves are, according to the theory, as follows: The central bank restricts reserves by selling government securities or by lowering the price at which it will buy them. In either case there is some increase in their yield. This increase in yield deters banks and other lending institutions from selling government securities to make alternative loans and investments. It deters them for two principal reasons. First, they do not like to take a capital loss on government securities, even if an alternative asset offers a higher yield.[2] Second, and more important, the increase in yield makes government securities more attractive relative to alternative investments because the rates on other assets are kept from rising by institutional rigidities in the market. Lenders will, therefore, ration credit to private borrowers, and some willing borrowers will simply not be accommodated. For example, convention will keep the rate charged by banks to their commercial customers from rising; loan applications which previously would have been accepted will be refused. Again, the rate on mortgages will be sticky, in part because of government regulations; fewer mortgages will be bought. Similarly, corporations and state and local govern-

[2] The replies of insurance executives (*Compendium*, pp. 1234–44) do not provide unequivocal support to the view that they are irrationally "pinned in" to government securities by capital losses. (Neither do the figures on changes in insurance company portfolios since the accord.) Several executives explicitly denied that such losses were of any concern if higher-yielding investments were available. Others considered losses a deterrent, but it is not clear that they meant anything more than that higher yields on governments make them more competitive with other assets.

ments will find it impossible to float bond issues to finance investment projects. In all of these cases, it is argued, the disappointed borrower and spender does not have open to him in the market the alternative of offering a higher rate and obtaining the funds. Hence, even if borrowers are not likely to be deterred by higher interest charges, even if it is true that spending is insensitive to interest rate levels, monetary restriction is effective in curtailing spending.

This argument relies, as Professor Samuelson pointed out, on an increase in the imperfection of the market as a consequence of the initial rise in bond yields. There must be more rationing of credit than there was before. The importance of the argument depends on the persistence of the increase in imperfection. If the rates available to private borrowers are fixed for a long period, the theory uncovers important new potentialities for monetary control. If these rates are within a short time free to adjust upward to compensate for the increased yield and attractiveness of government securities, the contribution of the new theory is more modest. It points out some dynamic effects, neglected by the older theories, which temporarily enhance the influence of a monetary restriction. But as these effects wear off, the lasting influence of the restriction depends on the answer to the questions the older theories ask: how interest-elastic are the demands for the alternatives of bonds, goods and cash? As the transient effects die, lenders will satisfy the needs of borrowers who are willing to pay higher rates. In order to do so, they will shift out of government securities; and given the volume of bank reserves, security yields will rise. To the extent that the increase in bond yields induces corporations and individuals to hold securities rather than cash reserves, lenders are provided with funds to satisfy the needs of borrowers who were previously rationed out of the market. In the ultimate equilibrium, rates on different assets will stand in a normal relationship to each other; the former degree of market imperfection will be restored; and the effect on spending will depend on what the monetary restriction has done to the level of interest rates and how borrowers and spenders react to that. Even so, the transient effects

may be exceedingly useful to a central bank which wishes to dampen spending without raising interest rates much, or fears that demand is in any case not very responsive to the level of rates. If the inflationary pressure which the central bank wishes to oppose is itself temporary, the transient effects may be enough to do the job. Otherwise it would be necessary to administer successive doses of the medicine until the level of interest rates is pushed high enough to handle the situation.

The strength and persistence of these "availability effects" are empirical questions crucial to the new monetary theory. Inferences on the subject are drawn from events following the accord. But this should be done with great caution. Certainly the general economic stability of 1951 and 1952, compared with 1950, cannot be considered proof of the effectiveness of monetary policy, any more than it can be considered proof of the effectiveness of the direct controls introduced in 1951. Many other explanations of this phenomenon are at hand. But even if more specific evidence indicated that monetary policy should receive substantial credit for halting the inflation, the accord had unique characteristics which limit its usefulness as a basis for generalization. It was a departure from a policy and a rate to which the market had long been accustomed. It was natural for the market to react with confusion and imperfection and to transmit the change only slowly to the rates on private credit. Once the market is again accustomed to flexibility of basic rates, it may adjust with more speed. The first dose of the new medicine is likely to be the most effective, and it can only be administered once.

The evidence that the accord produced substantial effects of the kind envisaged by the new theory is not, in any case, impressive. Bank loans continued to grow. Insurance companies continued to dispose of government securities in favor of other assets, even though by 1951 they had reduced governments to something like a normal proportion of their portfolios. Although some new bond issues may have been postponed following the accord, the statistics of new issues suggest that it was not long before it was possible to place issues at rates acceptable to the market. (Professor Whittlesey argued also that anticipation of the accord greatly increased security offerings in the first quarter of 1951.)

In assessing the inflexibility of lending rates in the face of monetary restriction, it is essential to remember that lenders have at their disposal a number of devices for raising the effective rate of interest to the borrower while the nominal quoted rate remains the same. Bankers, for example, can be more insistent that borrowers keep certain amounts on deposit. Their replies to the committee indicate that in many cases this was in fact their reaction to monetary tightness in 1950 and 1951.

It is easy to understand why the new theory of monetary control should be eagerly seized as the rationale of Federal Reserve policy. For it offers the hope that monetary policy can be effective without the large fluctuations of interest rates which used to be considered essential. And even now, for better or for worse, the Federal Reserve is not realistically free to pursue a policy which disregards the prices of government bonds. A great deal of Federal Reserve and Treasury effort must still, as ever since the war, be devoted to increasing private investors' willingness to hold government securities by measures other than increasing their yields. The new theory reaches the cheerful conclusion that these measures will also be an effective curb on private spending, because they reduce the availability of credit to private borrowers.

Such a policy does not imply that rates must never rise; indeed occasional small changes in rates are, according to the theory, necessary to bring into play the effects on which the policy relies. It does require that, at any given level of rates, private willingness to hold government securities be as large as possible and, consequently, the supply of bank reserves and of money as small as possible. To this end the Treasury and Federal Reserve have available many devices, for example: judicious adjustment both of the types and maturities of public debt instruments and of the composition, in distinction to the size, of the Federal Reserve's government portfolio; "moral suasion" to prevent holders of government securities from selling — this went to extremes in 1950, and the Open Market Committee has now penitently forsworn its use; setting the rediscount rate in such relation to the short-term government rate as to induce banks in need of reserves to borrow them, so that both the traditional distaste of bankers for indebtedness and the Federal Reserve's discretionary powers in respect to the privilege of rediscounting may be exploited; "pinning in" private bond holdings by penalizing sales, redemptions, or conversions before maturity with capital losses; manipulation of market uncertainties and expectations about future rates. Experience with this kind of policy has led to increased awareness of lags, imperfections, and institutional conventions in the money markets. These the policy seeks to exploit to make monetary measures effective, at least temporarily. As the market adapts itself to one measure, the ingenuity of the monetary authorities may be taxed to find another.

Only the future will tell whether this kind of monetary policy will do the job to the satisfaction of the monetary authorities themselves, or whether in the end they will conclude that monetary control can only be successful through the more pronounced changes in interest rates on which central banks traditionally relied in the past.

38

THE LOCK-IN EFFECT:
BANK REACTIONS TO SECURITIES LOSSES*

Samuel B. Chase, Jr.†

In Selection 35 the Federal Reserve noted that when credit conditions tighten and interest rates rise, so that securities prices fall, "many banks and other potential lenders are reluctant to sell securities at a loss." This is one aspect of the availability thesis. It has come to be known as the "lock-in" effect or, as it was termed in the preceding selection, "the pin-in" effect. Much controversy has arisen as to whether or not such an effect actually exists; whether or not banks are really reluctant to sell securities merely because it would mean realizing a capital loss.

The importance of the controversy stems from the behavior of bank portfolios during the postwar years. During recessions, when reserves have been plentiful and loan demands weak, banks have purchased large amounts of government securities. Then, when recovery sets in and monetary policy tightens, they have typically sold off these securities to nonbank investors, thereby obtaining funds with which to make new loans despite restraining Federal Reserve policies. If banks always feel free to sell off their government securities in order to get funds with which to make new loans, it is hard to see how the availability of new credit is in any way restricted. Thus the lock-in effect occupies a key role in the availability doctrine.

The following selection is one of the few empirical investigations of the strength of this mechanism.

During 1959, and in certain other recent years, the prices of outstanding Government securities, other than short-term issues, declined markedly as heightened demands for borrowed funds brought an upward movement of interest rates. Since banks as a group hold sizable amounts of intermediate- and long-term Government issues, significant reductions in the market values of bank portfolios occur when interest rates rise abruptly.

The reaction of banks to changing prices of the securities they hold is important, both from the viewpoint of a bank's own profitability and from the viewpoint of the operation of restrictive monetary policies. Declining prices of Government securities tend to reduce the willingness of banks to extend additional loan credit, and are therefore an integral part of the operation of restrictive credit policies. But the precise implications of a decline in the market values

of bank investment portfolios have been a matter of debate. Few would argue with the propositions that a declining market value of a bank's investments, which serve partly as liquidity reserves, tends to inhibit sales of Government securities to finance an expansion of loan portfolios and that rising market yields encourage banks to hold Government securities. However, there is considerably less certainty concerning the validity of a third proposition — that banks are quite reluctant to sell securities when market values have declined because they wish to avoid showing the losses on their books. To the extent that banks refuse to sell securities because market values are below book values, they are sometimes said to be "locked in" to their existing investment portfolios.

The first part of this article deals with the logic of the "lock-in" argument as it applies to commercial banks. The second section presents certain data that throw light on the actual behavior of banks in the face of the 1959 decline in the market values of their Government securities portfolios.

* From *Monthly Review,* Federal Reserve Bank of Kansas City (June, 1960). Reprinted by the courtesy of the Federal Reserve Bank of Kansas City.

† Economist, The Brookings Institution.

REASONING BEHIND THE "LOCK-IN" ARGUMENT

Since Government securities are carried by banks at cost (less amortized premium and valuation reserves in some cases), a decline in their market value is not recorded on the banks' books unless the securities are sold. It is believed that bankers dislike showing securities losses on their books for a number of reasons. These reasons range from a desire to refrain from recording losses because they may be mistaken by depositors or others to be evidence of poor management, to the more concrete reason that it is advantageous for banks to maximize the current rate of accumulation in capital, surplus, and undivided profits accounts.

The accumulation in these accounts may be important because certain bank regulations are related to their size. For example, the aggregate amount of real-estate credit extended by a national bank cannot exceed 100 per cent of its unimpaired paid-in capital and surplus, or 60 per cent of its time deposit liabilities, whichever is greater. Similarly, the maximum amount that a national bank can loan to any one borrower is limited, with minor exceptions, to 10 per cent of its capital and surplus accounts. A bank that wishes to increase its loan limits may wish to avoid the recognition of losses that would result from selling securities in depressed markets because such a "book loss" would retard the current rate at which undivided profits accumulate and can be transferred to capital and surplus accounts.

However, against such possible advantages of maintaining the book value of its investment portfolio must be weighed two disadvantages, both of which may be significant in certain situations.

LOGICAL ARGUMENTS FOR PORTFOLIO FLEXIBILITY

For the purposes of portfolio management, the prices at which present holdings of Government securities were acquired is irrelevant to the determination of whether present securities portfolios constitute the optimum use of the funds represented by the market values. If a

bank can increase its ultimate earnings by selling the securities presently held and employing the proceeds of the sale in another use, it makes a distinct sacrifice by refraining from making the switch. Thus, for example, if two Government securities of similar characteristics should have unequal yields to maturity, computed on the basis of their market prices, a bank holding the security with the lower yield could increase the future income on its portfolio by switching its funds to the higher yielding issue. This would be true regardless of the effect of the switch on the book value of its investments.

On the same basis, it can be argued that a bank need not be deterred from expanding its loan portfolio simply because losses are realized when securities are sold to raise funds for the loan expansion. Such losses have been suffered whether or not the bank shows them on its books; a decline in the market value of security holdings is a fact that cannot be avoided by refraining from selling the issues.

If a bank is to maximize the earnings on its investible resources, the relevant question in determining whether it should continue to hold any security it now owns is whether, if it held funds equal to the market value of its holdings of the security rather than the security itself, it could find a more attractive alternative use for the funds. If so, the present pattern of investments can be improved upon by selling the security in question and putting the funds into the more attractive alternative uses. The only exception to this logical rule of profit-maximizing portfolio management involves the trading cost of switching investments. Switches from one use of funds to another would not be justified if the advantage of the switch, in terms of increased bank earnings, were so marginal as to be completely offset by the cost of making the change.

TAX TREATMENT OF BANK SECURITIES LOSSES

In addition to the fact that an unwillingness to engage in market transactions in Government securities because their prices are depressed may stand in the way of achieving the most profitable use of investible resources, the tax treatment of securities losses realized by banks may provide an important stimulus for establishing such losses by market transactions. Although banks are, like other taxpayers, allowed to treat profits on the sale of Treasury securities (other than discount obligations, such as Treasury bills) as capital gains for tax purposes, they are permitted to treat net losses on Government securities in any given year as stock-in-trade losses. This means that they may deduct net losses from ordinary income for that year without limit. Other corporate investors for whom such Government securities are classified as capital assets are allowed only to offset capital losses against capital gains. Noncorporate investors are, in general, allowed to deduct net losses from ordinary income only up to a maximum of $1,000 in any given year, with the privilege of carrying unused losses forward over a 5-year period.

Because of the unlimited deductibility feature of the income tax law as it applies to banks, the principles governing the advisability of bank transactions that establish securities losses differ from those applied to investors subject to restricted deductibility. The ordinary investor who incurs sizable losses on securities classified as capital assets is well advised to realize them through market transactions during a year in which he realizes capital gains, so as to be able to offset his losses against his gains. A bank has the more attractive alternative of taking securities losses in years other than those in which gains are realized. For a bank with net taxable income exceeding $25,000, after-tax losses are equal to only 48 per cent of the amount of losses recorded when the losses are deducted from ordinary income, but are equal to 75 per cent of the amount of losses recorded when the losses are offset against long-term capital gains.

For example, if at the end of 1959 a bank held 2⅝ per cent Treasury notes maturing in February 1963 that had been acquired at par value when they were issued, the bank could, by selling the securities at the December 31 market price of $92.875 per $100 par value, establish a loss of $7.125 per $100 par value of the notes it held. So long as the bank's securities losses exceeded its gains, it could deduct

the loss from ordinary income. The result would be to lower net income subject to tax at the 52 per cent rate (assuming net taxable income exceeds $25,000), reducing the bank's tax liability by 52 per cent of the amount of losses established. The tax saving would then be available for current investment. Supposing that the bank held $1 million par value of these notes, it could, by establishing a $71,250 loss on them, increase the market value of its holdings of securities by $37,050 (52 per cent of $71,250) if it reinvested both the proceeds of the sale and the tax saving. However, should the bank have experienced long-term capital gains sufficient to cover its securities losses during the taxable year in question, the loss on the Treasury notes would have to be offset against the gains. Since long-term gains are taxable at a maximum rate of 25 per cent, the reduction in the bank's current tax liabilities due to the $71,250 loss would be only $17,813.

Thus while it is always possible for a bank to reduce its current tax liabilities by realizing securities losses, the net tax advantage of recording the loss is considerably great when it can be deducted from ordinary income, which means that securities losses lead to a greater tax saving if they are established during years in which long-term capital gains are not realized.

DEVELOPMENTS DURING 1959

The advantages that may derive from liquidating securities, both in order to transfer funds into more profitable uses and to realize the tax savings made possible by the establishment of losses on Government securities during a year of generally falling securities prices, would seem to constitute an important deterrent to maintaining book values of securities by avoiding market sales. During 1959, financial developments were such as to put the strength of a "lock in" to a severe test.

In the first place, mounting loan demands during the year provided a strong inducement for banks, most of which experienced pressures on their reserve positions throughout 1959, to liquidate Government securities in order to expand their loan portfolios. Offsetting this inducement, and tending to retard a shift from Government securities into loans, were the reduced value of liquid assets held by banks that ensued from the decline in the market prices of Treasury issues, and the more or less steadily increasing return that could be obtained on Government securities. In addition, any reluctance banks might have to recognizing securities losses on their books may have played an important part in deterring loan expansion during 1959. These losses were particularly important in the case of longer-term Treasury securities such as the 2½ per cent Treasury bonds maturing in September 1972, of which banks across the Nation held well over $1 billion par value at the beginning of the year. The quotation on this bond fell to an all-time low of $79.3125 per $100 par value on December 30, 1959, down from a bid price of $85.5625 on the last day of 1958. If the "lock-in" effect was an important factor, banks that wished to expand loans, although they did not feel their liquidity positions were being strained, might still have been unwilling to liquidate Treasury securities on which prices had fallen sharply because of the book losses that such transactions would entail.

While aggregate figures for all banks in the Nation show that they did indeed liquidate substantial amounts of securities on which prices had fallen significantly, this fact cannot be interpreted as an indication that the "lock-in" effect was unimportant. It might be that, although banks were reluctant to establish book losses, they were willing to do so to some extent in order to provide for certain of the most desirable kinds of loan expansion but were still much less willing to extend loans than they would have been if the liquidation of investments could have been effected without recording losses.

However, in addition to the incentive to shift funds from Government securities portfolios to loan expansion, there existed the incentive to establish securities losses in order to reduce current tax liabilities. Banks that did not consider a decline in book values of securities (as distinct from the unavoidable fact of the decline in their market values) to be particularly undesirable might be expected to establish securities losses through market sales of Government is-

sues even if they did not wish to reallocate their resources from Government securities into loans. This is because the advantage of establishing securities losses traces to the immediate tax savings that result, and is the same regardless of how the funds are employed after the securities are sold.

Thus, a bank that considers the advantages of tax savings obtained by realizing losses on its holdings of Government securities to outweigh the disadvantages of showing the losses on its books may simply sell off its existing holdings and reinvest the proceeds in Government securities.[1] Such "tax switching" is practiced by a number of banks, but no evidence is available bearing directly on the extent of this practice.

LOSSES OF DISTRICT BANKS DURING 1959

Figures submitted by Tenth Federal Reserve District banks in their condition statements and their earnings and dividends reports for 1959 provide information that is helpful in gauging the extent to which they attempted to reduce their tax liabilities by establishing losses on Government securities. This information in turn provides a useful insight into the power of the "lock-in" effect, since banks that establish losses for tax purposes are clearly not "locked in."

[1] One technical feature of undertaking tax switches traces to the nondeductibility of securities losses obtained through wash sales. Whether a specific transaction constitutes a wash sale cannot always be determined in advance of a specific ruling by the Internal Revenue Service. In General, losses are not deductible under the wash sale rule when they are established on "substantially identical" securities in which both sales and purchases were conducted within a 30-day period. However, because of the large number of outstanding Government issues, there are many pairs of issues that may be satisfactory substitutes for one another in terms of bank portfolio management and that are not held to be "substantially identical." For example, the 2½ per cent bonds maturing in September 1972 and callable in September 1967 have been ruled not identical (for purposes of the application of the wash sale rule) with the 2½ per cent issue of December 1972, callable in December 1967. The differences between these two issues, aside from their 3 months' difference in maturity, are largely of a technical nature, and in general would not be such as to make banks unwilling to switch between them.

An examination of reports for nearly all member banks in the Tenth District indicates that of a total of 752 banks, 473 established net securities losses during the year in excess of .01 per cent of the average value of their investment portfolios as shown in their condition reports for December 31, 1958, June 6, 1959, and October 6, 1959. Of the remaining 279 banks, 61 reported net gains on securities in excess of .01 per cent of their average investments on the three call dates, while 218 banks showed net gains or losses amounting to less than .01 per cent of the average of their investment portfolios on the three call dates. Among the 473 banks showing net losses of more than .01 per cent, a majority (374 banks) had not losses ranging from .01 to 1 per cent of their investment portfolios. Sixty-eight banks showed net losses on securities amounting to between 1 and 2 per cent of average investment portfolios, while 22 banks recorded net losses of between 2 and 3 per cent. The remaining nine banks showed losses on securities in excess of 3 per cent of their average investment portfolios.

These figures indicate that bank reactions to the decline in the market values of their Treasury securities were subject to extreme variation. Although a complete examination of a banks' portfolio and a knowledge of its market transactions during the year would be necessary to know the precise extent to which it took advantage of the opportunity to establish securities losses for tax purposes, some insight is provided by the figures relating net securities losses to average investment portfolios. For example, one bank in the District that reported substantial securities losses stated in its annual report to stockholders that it engaged in extensive tax selling during the year, establishing a net after-tax loss on securities of almost $1 million on an investment portfolio that averaged $69 million. Its market transactions in securities maturing in over 1 year amounted to more than $48 million in 1959, a figure clearly in excess of the amount of sales necessary to finance the bank's loan expansion during the year.

Since for this bank the pre-tax losses on Government securities would be equal to slightly more than twice the amount of after-tax losses, the bank's net losses on Government issues amounted to something over 2½ per cent of its total investment portfolio. If the published information of this bank can be used as a benchmark, it would seem safe to conclude that other banks experiencing securities losses in excess of 2 per cent of their average investment portfolios during 1959 also engaged in considerable tax switching for the purpose of establishing losses. It is clear that banks selling for tax purposes did not consider themselves "locked in" to their holdings of Government securities, so that the decline in the market values of their portfolios below book values could not in itself have been a factor inhibiting them from financing an expansion of loans through securities liquidations.

Similarly, it would seem reasonable to presume that banks that established losses ranging from 1 to 2 per cent of their average holdings of Government securities probably did engage in at least some tax switching.

If this reasoning is correct, only 99 of the 752 member banks appear to have taken advantage, to any considerable extent, of the securities loss provisions of the Internal Revenue Code. It might therefore be concluded that most banks either were unaware of the advantages of establishing tax losses or did not consider them desirable, either because they entailed showing book losses, which was repugnant to the bank management, or because the banks did not feel it was worthwhile to devote the time and effort necessary to effect tax switches.

A lack of acquaintance with the provisions of the income tax laws concerning securities losses and a reluctance to devote the necessary time and effort to planning tax switches would presumably be more important factors for small banks than for large ones. Larger banks are likely to have specialized personnel whose time is devoted mainly to managing the securities portfolio. Thus it might be expected that the management of a large bank would be fully aware of the tax implications of establishing losses, and that the bank would be in a position to exercise the kind of careful planning necessary for the successful execution of tax switches. In addition, many smaller banks have net taxable incomes of less than $25,000, which puts them in the 30 per cent bracket of the corporation income tax, reducing the tax-saving advantages of establishing net securities losses.

From this point of view it is interesting to examine the securities losses of District member banks classified according to bank size. An examination of Table I shows that while only 6 per cent of the District member banks with deposits of less than $2 million established losses in excess of 1 per cent of their average investment portfolios, 32 per cent of the banks with deposits of over $50 million did so. In general the relative amount of net losses on securities tends to increase as the size of the bank increases.

This finding would seem to confirm the notion that the failure of at least some banks to realize the maximum possible securities losses can be traced to such factors as (1) the weaker incentive for smaller banks in the 30 per cent corporation income tax bracket to take advantage of tax provisions regarding securities losses, (2) an inadequate knowledge of these provisions, or (3) a less meticulous management of investment portfolios, perhaps because it does not pay smaller banks to employ specialists in portfolio management. Nevertheless, the evidence cited here indicates that the attraction of maintaining the book values of securities portfolios is strong. This is true even for larger banks which presumably exercise a close supervision over their portfolios and are

fully aware of the tax advantages of establishing securities losses. Only a minority of the largest banks in the District showed losses amounting to more than 1 per cent of their investment portfolios.

The hypothesis that many larger banks in the District carried substantial amounts of unrealized securities losses on their books at the end of 1959 may be further tested by an examination of portfolio figures for reserve city member banks, almost all of which have total deposits of $10 million or more. Figures for all central reserve city and reserve city banks in the Nation are also presented.

The declared book values of U.S. Government securities held by these banks, as they are shown on the December 31, 1959, statement of condition, can be compared with the market values of these holdings on the same date to determine the extent of their unrealized losses at the end of 1959. The market values of securities held by central reserve city and reserve city banks both for the Nation and for the Tenth District were computed by multiplying the par values of their holdings, as reported in the Treasury Survey of Ownership for December 31, by the ratio of market prices to par values of the securities on the same date. Table II shows the declared book values, together with the computed market values, of Treasury notes and bonds for District reserve city banks and for both reserve city and central reserve city banks across the Nation. In the third column of the table is shown the aggregate unrealized losses on each type of security,

TABLE I

Net Gains and Losses on Securities as Per Cent of Average Investment Portfolios
Tenth District Member Banks, 1959

Deposit Size	NET GAINS IN EXCESS OF .01%		NET GAINS OR LOSSES LESS THAN .01%		NET LOSSES						TOTAL	
					.01–.99%		1.0–1.99%		2.0% AND OVER			
	No. of Banks	Per Cent	No. of Banks	Per Cent	No. of Banks	Per Cent	No. of Banks	Per Cent	No. of Banks	Per Cent	No. of Banks	Per Cent
Under $2 million	10	5	115	53	77	36	10	5	3	1	215	100
$2–$10 million	36	9	90	22	233	57	35	9	13	3	407	100
$10–$50 million	10	10	12	11	53	50	20	19	10	10	105	100
$50 million and over	5	20	1	4	11	44	3	12	5	20	25	100
Total	61	8	218	29	374	50	68	9	31	4	752	100

TABLE II

Estimated Unrealized Losses on Marketable Treasury Notes and Bonds
December 31, 1959
(in millions of dollars)

	1		2		3		4	
	BOOK VALUES		MARKET VALUES		UNREALIZED LOSSES		UNREALIZED LOSSES AS A PER CENT OF BOOK VALUES	
	NOTES	BONDS	NOTES	BONDS	NOTES	BONDS	NOTES	BONDS
Tenth District								
Reserve City Banks	277.0	523.9	270.0	495.1	7.0	28.8	2.54	5.50
All Reserve City Banks	4,108.6	10,936.7	4,019.0	10,336.1	89.6	600.6	2.18	5.49
Central Reserve								
City Banks	1,744.3	4,183.1	1,718.2	3,985.0	26.1	198.1	1.50	4.74

Sources: U.S. Treasury Department, Board of Governors of the Federal Reserve System, and Federal Reserve Bank of Kansas City.

computed by subtracting the market values from the book values. Column 4 indicates, for each class of security, unrealized losses as a per cent of book values. One qualification that must be noted is that some banks carry valuation reserves against securities. The effect of building up such a reserve is to reduce book values below original costs, so that the figures shown understate the ·amount of unrealized losses somewhat. However, the practice of carrying valuation reserves against securities is quite limited; aggregate valuation reserves on securities for District reserve city banks at the end of 1959 amounted to only about $5 million, or less than .6 of 1 per cent of the book values of notes and bonds combined.

In the case of each group of banks the difference between book values and market values is sufficiently large to indicate that they bypassed the opportunity to realize considerable additional losses in 1959. This finding tends to confirm the conclusion that the maintenance of book values may be an important consideration even to larger banks, both in the Tenth District and throughout the Nation. It is notable that unrealized losses are a smaller proportion of book values for central reserve city banks than for reserve city banks, which tends to confirm further the judgment that larger banks are less likely to carry extensive unused securities losses than are smaller banks.

CONCLUDING REMARKS

Judging from the evidence presented concerning the practices of District banks, it appears that there is no hard and fast rule that banks are "locked in" to their holdings of Government securities when market values decline. The fact that many larger banks evidently engaged in tax switching during 1959 may be taken to mean that an aversion to showing book losses on securities was not a factor in limiting their willingness to extend loans.

Nevertheless, a majority of banks appear to have been reluctant to establish sizable net losses on securities, and it would seem correct to conclude that in these cases their willingness to extend additional loan credit was at least to some extent correspondingly tempered. Thus the evidence appears to indicate that the "lock-in" effect, though it is far from being a universal influence, is an important one.

39

DO CHANGES IN VELOCITY OFFSET
MONETARY POLICY?*

Lawrence S. Ritter†

Since the end of World War II, changes in the velocity of money (i.e., its rate of turn-over) have stimulated renewed interest in the behavior of velocity, and in its implications for the effectiveness of monetary policy. The Federal Reserve can control the quantity of money, but it has no similar control over its rate of turnover, the slowness or rapidity with which a given stock of money is spent. Consequently, the central bank's control over aggregate spending is imperfect. It can control the stock of money (M), but that is not the same thing as controlling the flow of spending (MV). In terms of the equation of exchange, MV = PT, if the Federal Reserve in pursuit of an anti-inflation policy reduces M by 10 per cent but as a result V rises by 15 per cent, then reducing the money supply has failed to achieve its presumed goal, namely the contraction of spending.

How serious is this avenue of escape? Does it in fact substantially impair the effectiveness of monetary policy? The answers that have been given to these questions are numerous and varied. Indeed, in some cases the same economist has given more than one answer to the same question, as the following two selections demonstrate all too well.

In the late 1950's a number of economists concluded that fluctuations in velocity did indeed largely nullify Federal Reserve anti-inflation efforts: reductions in M were simply met by a rise in V so that total spending (MV) continued unhampered.

In response to these views, the following selection — written in 1958 — defended the effectiveness of monetary policy. Its theme is that what at first glance appears to be offsetting fluctuations in velocity might in fact be helpful fluctuations, which actually assist the Federal Reserve in achieving its goals.

Recent changes in monetary velocity have led to renewed interest in its behavior and in the resulting implications for monetary policy. In particular, the view has been widely expressed that anti-inflationary monetary policy is unlikely to be successful, because of offsetting movements in velocity, no matter how effective it may be in controlling the volume of bank reserves and the supply of money. It is asserted that monetary restraint will for the most part be nullified by increases in velocity which permit total spending to continue unabated.[1]

* From "Income Velocity and Anti-Inflationary Monetary Policy," *American Economic Review*, Vol. XLIX, No. 1 (March, 1959). Reprinted by courtesy of the publisher (the American Economic Association).

† New York University. Chief, Domestic Research Division, Federal Reserve Bank of New York, at the time of writing.

[1] See, for example, Warren L. Smith, "On the Effectiveness of Monetary Policy," *Am. Econ. Rev.*, Sept. 1956, XLVI, 588–606; Hyman P. Minsky, "Central Banking and Money Market Changes," *Quart. Jour. Econ.*, May 1957, LXXI, 171–87; and John H. Kareken, "Post Accord Monetary Developments in the United States," *Banca Nazionale Del Lavoro Quarterly Review*, Sept. 1957, 322–51.

Smith writes, "I suggest that when credit conditions are tightened and the creation of new money through the banking system is restricted, the financial machinery of the country automatically begins to work in such a way as to mobilize the existing supply of money more effectively, thus permitting it to do most of the work that would have been done by newly created money had credit conditions been easier."

Minsky concludes, on similar grounds, that "the asserted asymmetry of monetary policy (that it is effective in constraining an inflation and ineffective in constraining a depression) is not true; monetary policy is of very limited effectiveness both in constraining an inflation and in counteracting a depression."

And to Kareken "the existence of a large public debt has served to reduce whatever effectiveness classical monetary policy had, since the traditional techniques cannot deal with attempts at a more intensive utilization of a given nominal money supply."

The 1955–57 experience is frequently cited in illustration: gross national product rose by 61 billion dollars (or 16 per cent) between the first quarter of 1955 and the third quarter of 1957, despite a total expansion in the money supply of only 4 billion dollars (or 3 per cent) over this period. The increased spending was primarily accomplished through a more rapid turnover of the money stock, with income velocity (defined as $GNP \div M$) rising from an annual rate of 2.93 in the first quarter of 1955 to 3.30 in the third quarter of 1957, a rise of 13 per cent. Conclusion: orthodox anti-inflationary monetary policy should be relegated to the sidelines as substantially impotent, rendered ineffective by offsetting swings in velocity. Fiscal policy and/or selective controls should be substituted in its stead.

Nevertheless, although on the surface they seem reasonable enough, these conclusions leave one uneasy. Is anti-inflationary monetary policy really of so little use? There is no doubt that there was pressure to economize on cash balances in the 1955–57 period, with funds relatively scarce; but is this a new phenomenon with which economists (including the monetary authorities) had had no previous experience? Cannot such factors be taken into account by the central bank in deciding upon the proper kind and degree of restraint required to achieve given ends? In brief, and with full awareness of the very real limitations of monetary policy, has not the case against its effectiveness been overstated?

The purpose of the present paper, however, is not to present a full-blown apologia for monetary policy, but rather more modestly to question whether these offsetting swings in velocity are actually as damaging as they appear at first glance. Might there not even be *advantages* in such velocity movements which could help rather than hinder the effectiveness of anti-inflationary monetary policies?

Data indicate that income velocity reached a peak of 3.30 in the third quarter of 1957. Although income velocity was about 4 in 1919, and again in 1929, it had not approached a level as high as that reached in the third quarter of 1957 since the 3.29 recorded in the year 1931. For the most part it remained below 3 during the years 1932–55, falling at one point to below 2. The record also reveals that short-run fluctuations in velocity have been frequent, with velocity generally rising when GNP has been rising and falling when GNP has been falling. At least this was generally true from 1920–32 and again from 1946–57, although from the mid-1930's to 1946 no such relationship existed. In those years of depression and war the money supply rose so substantially that velocity was usually decreasing, even when GNP was rising.

It should be no surprise that income velocity and GNP often move together and in the same direction, even though it is this very relationship which has led to the disillusionment with monetary policy cited above. After all, with income velocity defined as the quotient of GNP divided by the average stock of money (demand deposits plus currency outside banks), a counter-cyclical monetary policy which limited increases in the money supply when GNP was rising close to (or above) the full employment level, or which attempted to expand the money supply when GNP was falling, would be expected to result in velocity changes in the same direction as the movement in GNP.

I. RESERVE POSITIONS, INTEREST RATES, AND INCOME VELOCITY

The immediate impact of monetary policy, of course, is upon the banking system. As pressure is imposed upon reserve positions, short-term interest rates tend to rise, followed, perhaps with a lag, by longer yields. The clearest periods of restraint in recent years, for instance, were from about the second quarter of 1952 to mid-1953 and from the first quarter of 1955 through the third quarter of 1957. In both periods member bank free reserves (excess reserves less borrowing from the Federal Reserve Banks) declined to significantly negative levels, Treasury bill yields and long-term interest rates rose, and velocity increased. However, the total money supply did expand to a certain extent in each case; had it remained unchanged, interest rates and velocity might well have risen even further.

The income velocity of the money supply and the average issuing rate on Treasury bills

CHART 1

Income Velocity and Treasury Bill Rate
Quarterly, 1948–57

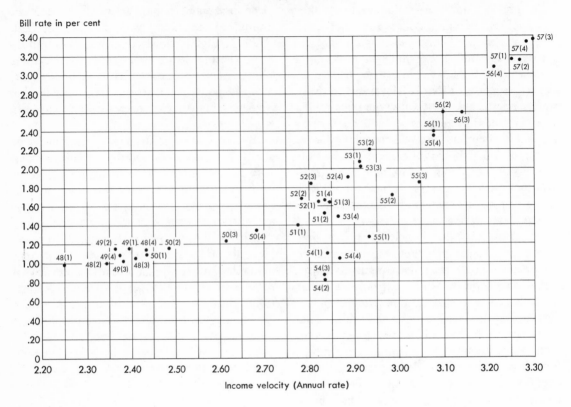

are plotted in the form of a scatter diagram in Chart 1 for the period 1948 through 1957. The above-mentioned periods during 1952–53 and 1955–57, when GNP rose while the expansion of the money supply was held in check by the central bank, clearly reveal the simultaneous rise in Treasury bill rates and income velocity; the close positive relationship between bill rates and income velocity taken in time sequence from mid-1952 to mid-1953 and from the third quarter of 1954 through the third quarter of 1957 is particularly striking.

These are in broad terms the very results that one would expect on the basis of generally accepted theoretical considerations. We assume that there is a fairly constant relationship in the short-run between the dollar value of GNP and holdings of "active" cash to be used for current and expected payments (essentially

Keynes' M_1).[2] As GNP rises, the volume of cash required for day-to-day household and business payments needs also increases; but if the money supply is held constant, the funds required to satisfy these "active" or transactions needs must be drawn from formerly "idle" holdings (M_2). Interest rates thus rise in order to attract these funds, inducing owners of idle balances to part with or economize on their cash holdings. This activation of idle balances is reflected in an increase in velocity, since observed income velocity varies directly with the ratio of active balances (M_1) to the total money supply (M).[3]

[2] The actual ratio of active cash to GNP depends at any one time upon such generally slowly changing institutional patterns as the stage of development of the monetary and financial system, the degree of industrial integration, the distribution of income and wealth, the frequency and regularity of receipts and

$$V = \frac{GNP}{M}$$

$$V = \frac{GNP}{M_1} \cdot \frac{M_1}{M}$$

$$V = k \cdot \frac{M_1}{M}$$

Thus, while monetary policy has its immediate impact upon the banking system, its effects soon spread through the myriad of interrelationships that comprise the financial mechanism to gradually pervade other areas of economic activity. The process is recognizable by such familiar features as persistent pressure on bank reserve positions, "shortages" of funds and continued tightness in the money and capital markets, a decline in bank and nonbank liquidity, an increase in the extension of "trade credit", and — last but not least — articles in the press and speeches before trade and labor groups denouncing the "tight money" policy.

It is impossible in fact to distinguish active from idle dollars, except by some rather arbitrary assumptions. And it is not necessary for present purposes to actually attempt to separate them statistically, since Chart 1 adequately demonstrates the significant relationships involved. Nevertheless, it is still interesting to make the alternative statement of the above principles in terms of the dollar volume of idle balances in existence over various periods of time. As noted above, the maximum level that income velocity has reached in about the past quarter-century has been a rate of almost 3⅓ times per year (1931 and 1957), although occasionally it had previously been as high as about 4 (1919 and 1929). During mid-1957 a number of signs, including sharp increases in money rates and capital market yields, seemed to indicate that velocity was approaching close

to the straining point, that the financial mechanism as then constituted was not geared to enable it to increase very much further. There are thus some pragmatic grounds for believing that present limits to velocity are closer to an annual rate of about 3⅓ rather than the peak of 4 times per year reached in the 1920's. An income velocity of 3⅓ means, as its reciprocal, a ratio of money supply to GNP of 30 per cent. For purposes of convenience the 30 per cent has been chosen as sufficiently close to illustrate the principles involved.

If we assume that at an income velocity of about 3⅓ times per year funds would be turning over at close to their maximum degree of rapidity, this implies that just about all cash would then be utilized for transactions purposes, with idle balances reduced to minimum levels. We can on this basis calculate the volume of active and idle balances in various periods by assuming that a money supply equal to 30 per cent of GNP is desired for transactions purposes, and that the excess of the money supply over this amount can be isolated as idle balances. The relationship between idle balances so computed and the bill rate is shown in the form of a scatter diagram in Chart 2. In this framework the 1952–53 and 1955–57 periods of restraint take the form of decreasing idle balances and rising bill rates, and again the movement in time sequence during these periods is particularly striking. From the first quarter of 1955 to the third quarter of 1957 GNP rose by 61.3 billion dollars, as mentioned earlier, increasing the transactions demand for cash by 30 per cent of 61.3 billion or 18.4 billion. But the money supply increased only 4 billion dollars, so that the remaining 14.4 billion required for additional transactions balances had to be drawn from formerly idle holdings. In consequence, the bill rate rose from 1¼ per cent to 3⅜ per cent, idle balances declined from 15.7 billion dollars to 1.3 billion, and the income velocity of the total money supply increased from 2.93 to 3.30.

II. IMPLICATIONS FOR MONETARY POLICY

Let us now return to our original query: to what extent is a restrictive monetary policy

---

disbursements, etc. However, it is recognized that at high interest rates there is likely to be some interest elasticity in the demand for transactions balances. See Alvin Hansen, *Monetary Theory and Fiscal Policy* (New York: McGraw-Hill Book Co., 1949), Chapter 4, and James Tobin, "The Interest-Elasticity of Transactions Demand for Cash," *Rev. Econ. Stat.*, Aug. 1956, XXXVIII, 241–7.

[3] Designating income velocity as V and assuming a fixed ratio k (in the short-run) between the dollar value of GNP and M_1:

CHART 2

Idle Cash Balances and Treasury Bill Rate
Quarterly, 1948–57

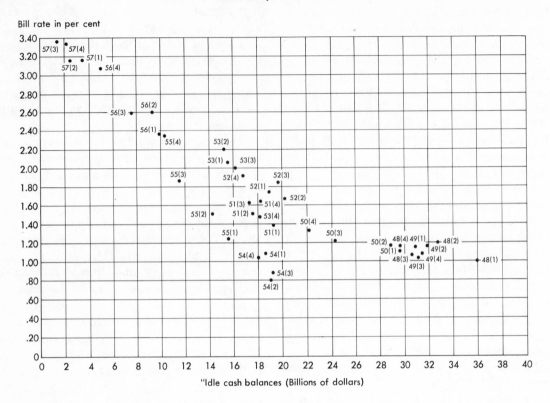

"Idle cash balances (Billions of dollars)

likely to be thwarted by offsetting increases in velocity? Are there any useful features to these variations which monetary policy can utilize to its advantage?

The problems of the monetary authorities are more complex than some would picture them. In particular, they must necessarily be continuously concerned not only with maintaining economic stability in the short run, but also simultaneously with allowing sufficient financial elbow room for the realization of potential real economic growth, even in periods when inflationary dangers threaten. It is not an adequate solution to check inflation by methods which also prevent desirable real growth. Furthermore, although hindsight is often characterized by a remarkable clarity, the day-to-day maintenance of economic stability is usually complicated by a considerable degree of uncertainty as to whether current economic trends are on balance inflationary or deflationary. In

light of these factors, changes in velocity, rather than subverting monetary policy, become an indispensible part of that policy.

With respect to the problem of maintaining economic stability, one of the main criticisms directed against orthodox anti-inflationary monetary policy has been that it is a very dangerous tool which cannot be used in moderation — that if effective at all, it is likely to be too drastically effective, precipitating an economic collapse through a shattering of confidence in the money and capital markets.[4] Changes in velocity, however, provide the

[4] Hansen, op. cit., p. 161. See also p. 163. Professor Hansen's objections (as well as those of Professor Smith, as cited in footnote 1) are primarily to the use of monetary policy *alone* to stop inflation. "In conjunction with fiscal and other policies monetary policy can play a significant role in helping to bring the economy through to more stable conditions." (p. 162.) However, Hansen's monetary recommendations (p. 166) center primarily about selective rather than general measures.

needed safety valve, tempering and graduating the impact of monetary policy and thereby enabling the central bank to apply more restraint than it might otherwise risk. The role of velocity is thus similar to that of the discount window during a period of limited reserve availability; they both moderate the build-up of undue tightness, and the crises that might otherwise ensue, by distributing pressures and providing outlets through which strains on the payments mechanism can be partially alleviated at the initiative of the market itself. Related functions are performed by the Federal funds market and by many of the financing arrangements of Government securities dealers, including repurchase agreements with the central bank. It is in part these very devices, of course, that enable velocity to increase.

While it is literally true that these changes in velocity "offset" changes in the supply of money, they are unlikely to do so completely if the liquidity function has an interest-elasticity less than infinity and the consumption or investment functions are at all responsive to changes in the cost or availability of funds. And the partial offset which velocity does provide gives the central bank a necessary margin of flexibility and safety, allowing it to restrain the growth of the money supply (within limits) without continuous fear that a sudden financial crisis will occur. It is noteworthy that the inflationary pressures of 1955–57 tapered off *gradually* despite the vigorous application of monetary policies during this period. In view of the usual uncertainty regarding the actual state of business conditions, it is doubtful whether the authorities would ever have the courage (or the foolhardiness) to impose any significant degree of monetary restraint were it not for the built-in shock absorber represented by variations in velocity. Fluctuations in velocity are thus to be expected and in a real sense are an integral part of the mechanism of monetary control, in effect being merely the other side of the squeeze on liquidity which assists in transmitting the effects of a restrictive monetary policy throughout the economy. Similarly, declines in velocity in the downward phase of the cycle allow the monetary authorities to expand the money supply more than they might otherwise think

prudent, and simultaneously provide room for velocity to rise once again when the recovery gets underway. Without these fluctuations in velocity the central bank would be forever at the brink of a precipice, fearing that the slightest wrong move would bring disaster; as a result, it would be most likely to do nothing at all.

A special application of the above considerations relates to the task of stemming inflation without simultaneously halting real economic growth. In brief, the problem is to allow GNP to rise in line with potential real economic growth, but not so much as to exceed that rate of increase and become inflationary. To permit this increase in GNP, it is obviously necessary that either M or V (or both) must increase, and if inflationary pressures are at all severe it is far less dangerous to allow the expansion in GNP to take place mainly via higher velocity rather than mainly through increasing the money supply. To allow GNP to expand through increases in velocity brings self-limiting factors into play which make it unlikely that the inflation will get out of control, while to choose the alternative path — increasing the money supply — is to materially lessen, and perhaps abandon, restraint. There is a considerable difference between both the effects and the extent of increases in velocity that represent a reaction to monetary restraint, and those that have occurred from time to time in nations that have inflated the money supply excessively despite the presence of strong inflationary forces.

As long as idle balances exist, the desired expansion in GNP can be accomplished with a constant money supply and higher turnover; at the same time, *some* expenditure is choked off, an atmosphere of restraint is maintained, and the money authorities are able to retain close contact with market developments. Charts I and II suggest that when interest rates are low and idle balances large, a small rise in rates is likely to result in a large transfer of funds from hoards to active circulation, increasing velocity substantially. In this phase there is considerable truth to the "offset" viewpoint. But as interest rates continue to rise, due to continued monetary restraint and persistent demands for funds, idle balances are likely to approach minimum levels. Correspondingly, velocity is likely to encounter an upper limit, a rough and perhaps flexible ceiling, but a ceiling nevertheless. As it becomes increasingly difficult to obtain the release of additional funds from the now depleted idle balances, velocity will be subject to new constraints, economic activity will become increasingly responsive to monetary policy, and further expansion of GNP will be inhibited. There is presumably some point where continued limitation of the money supply would entirely halt the growth of GNP, and perhaps initiate a downward movement. In practice, however, some additions to the money supply are likely to be occurring continuously, since the art of limiting the stock of money usually takes the form of allowing smaller increments than would otherwise take place, rather than imposing an absolute barrier to any increase. The problem thus reduces itself to the relative increase in the money supply as compared with velocity.

Again an analogy involving rediscounting is apt: providing for economic growth primarily through increased velocity rather than primarily by expanding the money supply is the more restrictive alternative in a way very similar to deliberately "forcing" the banks to obtain reserves from the discount window rather than by supplying funds through open market purchases. In both of the more restrictive alternatives the central bank keeps the reins taut, remaining in close contact with market conditions — which react with increasing sensitivity — while simultaneously enabling some expansion to take place.

Aggregate economic policy rarely seeks to achieve stability, but instead usually aims at "controlled" expansion. Within limits, monetary policy can make a positive contribution toward this end, in part because of — rather than in spite of — fluctuations in velocity.

40

THE ROLE OF MONEY IN KEYNESIAN THEORY*

Lawrence S. Ritter†

The previous selection argued that fluctuations in velocity do not seriously impair the effectiveness of monetary policy. Indeed, it held to some extent they are even helpful, acting as a safety-valve in tempering and graduating the impact of monetary policy.

This conclusion was in part based on the premise that increases in velocity cannot go too far or continue for too long a time — "as interest rates continue to rise, due to continued monetary restraint, idle balances are likely to approach minimum levels and, correspondingly, velocity is likely to encounter an upper limit, a rough and perhaps flexible ceiling, but a ceiling nevertheless."

That was written in 1958, and it was then estimated that the "ceiling" or "upper limit" of velocity had about been reached at the then-existing rate of turnover of the money supply of about 3⅓ times per year.

* From *Banking and Monetary Studies*, edited by Deane Carson (Irwin, 1963). Reprinted by the courtesy of the publisher.

† New York University.

The passage of time has not been kind to those ideas. If any complacency with respect to the effectiveness of monetary policy was discernible in Selection 39, the record of the years since it was written have battered it rather badly: in mid-1966, well under a decade later, income velocity had risen to slightly over 4⅓, an increase of about 30 per cent over and above its presumed "upper limit". How flexible can a ceiling be and still be a ceiling?

At the same time as V has been blithely climbing higher and higher, some other economists have been proclaiming, strangely enough, that the supply of money needs to be "rediscovered" — that M, per se, is all pervasive in spending decisions, and that its significance has been neglected by the "Keynesian Revolution" that has swept macroeconomics in the past three decades. These are the modern Quantity theorists, who appear to be untroubled by the postwar behavior of velocity. To the modern Quantity theorist, Keynesian economics downgrades the importance of the supply of money to the point where "money does not matter", and to the Quantity theorist this is a state of affairs which calls for prompt rectification.

What is the role of money in Keynesian theory? How can we explain the postwar behavior of velocity? What are its implications for monetary policy? It is to the complex of such issues that the present selection — written five years after the previous selection — is addressed.

In recent years it has frequently been asserted, primarily by Quantity theorists, that the main characteristic of Keynesian theory is that "money does not matter."[1] The view that "money matters" is held to be the exclusive province of the Quantity theory, and extensive statistical tests are thereupon conducted to demonstrate that the supply of money has had an important influence on the level of economic activity. On this basis, Keynesian theory is, *ipso facto*, declared fallacious.

The purpose of this essay is to examine carefully the role of money in Keynesian theory, in order to evaluate the thesis that in the Keynesian system "money does not matter." It turns out that the validity of this point of view depends in large part on which version of Keynesian theory one has in mind, just as the validity of many Keynesian criticisms of the Quantity theory depend on which version of the latter one has in mind.

I. KEYNES WITHOUT MONEY

The most familiar version of Keynesian economics, which we will call Model A, is the elementary simplification of Keynes in which the only determinants of the level of national income are the consumption function and a given volume of investment (including government) spending. Consumption spending is seen as depending mainly upon income, and investment spending is assumed to be given, determined autonomously. Occasionally, in order to include an accelerator effect, investment spending may also be made to depend partly upon income. Within this context, the equilibrium level of national income is found where realized income, resulting from consumption plus investment expenditures, equals anticipated income, on the basis of which spending decisions are made. Alternatively, equilibrium income is that level of income at which planned investment equals planned saving.

It is this simplified model which has been popularized by the widely known "Keynesian cross" diagram, in which either consumption and investment or saving and investment are plotted on the vertical axis, and anticipated income is plotted on the horizontal axis. Equilibrium income is determined where aggregate demand equals anticipated income or, alternatively, where planned investment equals planned

[1] See, for example, Milton Friedman's statements in *Studies in the Quantity Theory of Money* (Chicago: University of Chicago Press, 1956), p. 3; *Employment, Growth, and Price Levels*, Hearings before the Joint Economic Committee, U.S. Congress, 1959, pp. 606–7; and *A Program for Monetary Stability* (New York: Fordham University Press, 1960), p. 1.

saving.[2] This particular analytical system has also been the basis for the bulk of orthodox Keynesian multiplier theory: a sustained increase in autonomous spending is assumed to raise equilibrium income by a multiple of the initial increment in spending. The specific value of the multiplier is determined solely by the size of the marginal propensity to consume. Such an uncomplicated formula for the value of the multiplier can only be derived from an equally uncomplicated frame of reference, such as that outlined above.[3] For if the value of the multiplier depends solely on the size of the marginal propensity to consume, it must be assumed, implicitly or explicitly, that spending is insensitive to such increases in interest rates and tightening of credit availability as would normally accompany an expansion in income.

On the basis of this model, countless public policy recommendations dealing almost exclusively with the implications of alternative fiscal policies, have been advanced over the years in the name of Keynesian economics. In this scheme of things, the Quantity theory's characterization of the Keynesian system as one in which "money does not matter" is quite accurate: national income is determined without any reference whatsoever to either the supply of or the demand for money, and public policy prescriptions are confined to the area of fiscal policy. Monetary policy is completely extraneous. That this model evidently commands considerable allegiance, even today, is attested to by the great amount of attention paid in 1962 and 1963 to alternative forms of tax reduction, and to the size of the resulting budget deficit, as compared with the relative lack of interest in how such a deficit should be financed, i.e., whether by monetary creation or otherwise.

II. KEYNES WITH MONEY

Although Model A is probably the most popular version of Keynesian economics it is not the same economics to be found in Keynes' *The General Theory of Employment, Interest, and Money.* As far as Keynes himself was concerned, and as the title of his major work indicates, money plays a significant role in the determination of income and employment. Let us call the orthodox Keynesian system, as advanced in *The General Theory* and much subsequent literature, Model B.

Most important, Keynes did not assume that investment spending is exogenous, a given datum, but rather that it depends on relationships *within* the system, namely on comparisons between the expected rate of profit and the rate of interest. The rate of interest, in turn, depends on the supply of and demand for money. The demand for money, or liquidity preference, is viewed as consisting of two parts, the demand for idle money balances (with the amount demanded increasing as the rate of interest falls) and the demand for active or transaction balances (with the amount demanded increasing as the level of income rises).

In contrast to the partial Keynesian system, represented by Model A, the complete Keynesian system, Model B, requires that *two* conditions be fulfilled before income can be said to be in equilibrium. Not only must planned investment equal planned saving, as before, but in addition at any moment in time the amount of money people want to hold must equal the supply of money, the amount that is available for them to hold. If the second condition is not satisfied, the rate of interest will rise or fall, thereby altering the volume of investment and consequently changing the equilibrium level of income.[4]

---

[2] This has been a standard textbook diagram for well over a decade. See Paul A. Samuelson, *Economics* (5th ed.; New York: McGraw-Hill Book Co., Inc., 1961), chap. xiii, or Abba P. Lerner, *Economics of Employment* (New York: McGraw-Hill Book Co., Inc., 1951), chap. v.

[3] See Paul A. Samuelson, "The Simple Mathematics of Income Determination," in *Income, Employment, and Public Policy* (New York: W. W. Norton & Co., Inc., 1948), pp. 133–55; and L. S. Ritter, "Some Monetary Aspects of Multiplier Theory and Fiscal Policy," *Review of Economic Studies,* Vol. XXIII, No. 2 (1956), pp. 126–31.

[4] The diagrammatics of the complete Keynesian system thus are not contained in the "Keynesian cross," but rather in Hicks' *IS* and *LM* curves. See J. R. Hicks, "Mr. Keynes and the Classics: A Suggested Interpretation," *Econometrica,* Vol. V (1937), pp. 147–59, reprinted in *Readings in the Theory of Income Distribution* (Philadelphia: The Blakiston Co., 1946), pp. 461–76. Also see Alvin H. Hansen, *Monetary Theory and Fiscal Policy* (New York: McGraw-Hill Book Co., Inc., 1949), chap. v, and his *A Guide to Keynes* (New York: McGraw-Hill Book Co., Inc., 1953), chap. vii.

If, at a given interest rate and income, planned investment equals planned saving but the amount of money desired exceeds (falls short of) the supply, the interest rate will rise (fall), thereby reducing (increasing) investment spending and lowering (raising) the level of income. As the interest rate rises, the desired amount of idle balances contracts, and as income falls the desired amount of active balances contracts, until the amount of money demanded is reduced to the point where it is equal to the given supply. Thus, the equilibrium level of income eventually is reached, with both planned investment equal to planned saving and the demand for money equal to the supply, but the interest rate is now higher and income now lower than initially postulated.

Here there is room for monetary policy to operate: if the monetary authorities want to prevent upward pressure on the interest rate, and the consequent drop in income, they can increase the supply of money enough to satisfy the demand at the initial interest rate and income level. On the other hand, if they want to permit money income to fall, they can sit back and let nature take its course. Both of these are rather passive policies. More aggressive actions would call for increasing the money supply even more than enough to satisfy the initial demand, in order to stimulate an increase in income rather than merely prevent a decrease; or actually reducing the money supply, even though it is already less than the demand, to provide added impetus to the decline in income.

It is obvious that a policy of doing nothing is but one alternative among a spectrum of possibilities. The Federal Reserve at times seems to suggest that those changes in interest rates which occur when the central bank is passive are none of its doing. It is implied that changes in interest rates which take place when the central bank is holding the money supply constant are solely the result of "free market forces," and are in some sense preferable to changes which result from more active monetary policies. But as long as interest rates could be different if the central bank did something

rather than nothing, it follows that interest rates are what they are in part because the central bank prefers them that way.

All this does not mean that the monetary authorities are omnipotent. In the orthodox Keynesian system, monetary policy is important but not always in the same degree. As a general principle, monetary policy is likely to be *less* effective the more interest-elastic the demand for idle balances (for then a change in the money supply will not succeed in altering the interest rate) and the less interest-elastic the investment and consumption schedules (for then a change in the interest rate will not induce a change in spending). This has typically been construed by most Keynesians to mean that monetary policy is likely to be less effective in combating depression than in stopping inflation. In a severe depression, the public may prefer to hold additional amounts of money at low interest rates rather than lend it out or buy securities, so that the rate of interest may reach a floor below which it will not fall; investment prospects may appear so bleak that reductions in interest rates become of negligible importance; and job prospects may appear so dismal that consumer spending on durable goods is severely inhibited, despite such additions to the public's wealth as are brought about by expanding the stock of money.

In formal Keynesian terms, during severe depressions the interest-elasticity of liquidity preference may become so great as to prevent increases in the supply of money from reducing the interest rate, as they normally would. And investment and consumer spending may become so unresponsive to changes in interest rates and in wealth as to preclude what would be expected to be their normal reactions. In terms of the equation of exchange, $MV = PT$, increases in the money supply would be offset by proportionate reductions in the velocity of money. Under such circumstances, money again "does not matter" in the Keynesian system, in the sense that increases in the money supply beyond a certain point will not affect the volume of spending, and for all practical purposes we are back in the world of Model A above.

It is important to realize, however, that

severe depression is only a special case in the general Keynesian system. And even then, *decreases* in the money supply would not be looked upon as trivial. In other instances, the supply of money may be of crucial importance. From the beginning, for example, it has been a basic tenet of Keynesian doctrine that inflation cannot proceed very far without an increase in the supply of money. Rising incomes are seen as leading to larger demands for transactions balances, which in the absence of increases in the money supply must be drawn from formerly idle balances, inducing a rise in interest rates. This process can continue until idle balances are depleted, or perhaps somewhat further if there is some interest-elasticity in the demand for active balances at high interest rates. But, unless the money supply is increased, the expansion in spending is viewed as having to grind to a halt before too long, because rising interest rates and tightening monetary conditions in general will sooner or later choke off investment spending.[5] Indeed, so strongly has this position been held by some orthodox Keynesians that they have at times objected to the use of monetary policy to stop inflation because of the fear that it is likely to be *too* effective.[6] In brief, in the orthodox Keynesian system sometimes the supply of money is not very important, sometimes it is critically important, and most of the time it is somewhere in between, depending in each instance on the circumstances at hand.

It is rather ironic that Keynes should be the target of a blanket charge by Quantity theorists that he is responsible for propagating the view that "money does not matter." For in Keynes' own mind he was enlarging the scope of monetary theory, not narrowing it.[7] Before Keynes,

prevailing monetary theory in the form of the Quantity theory of money, had been concerned almost exclusively with the determination of the general level of prices, to the neglect of the influence of money on real output and employment. As expressed by Jean Bodin in 1569, through John Locke, David Hume, David Ricardo, John Stuart Mill, and Irving Fisher, the Quantity theory had always stressed that the supply of money determined primarily the absolute price level. The velocity of money was held to be an institutional datum and aggregate real output was assumed at the full employment level by virtue of Say's Law. In terms of the equation of exchange, $MV = PT$, V and T were assumed to be given so that changes in the money supply would result in proportionate changes in prices.[8]

The policy implications of the pre-Keynesian Quantity theory were simple and paralyzing. Increases in the supply of money, even in periods of substantial unemployment, could never achieve any permanent benefit. They could only be harmful, by raising prices proportionately — a view that is deeply imbedded in popular folklore to this day. It is this framework, rather than the Keynesian, which in a fundamental sense views money as unimportant. Here money is seen as "neutral," a veil behind which "real" forces work themselves out just about as they would in the absence of money. In the Keynesian approach, on the other hand, money also plays a role in the determination of real output. For the first time money becomes more than merely a veil, and a monetary economy is seen as behaving very differently from a barter economy.

---

[5] "A rise in prices and incomes leads to an increase in requirements for money balances in active circulation. This tends to reduce the amount available for inactive balances and so causes the rate of interest to rise, which checks investment. The rope which holds the value of money is a limitation on its supply. If the monetary authorities are compelled to increase the supply of money, the rope frays and snaps in their hands." Joan Robinson, *Essays in the Theory of Employment* (Macmillan, 1937), pp. 17–21 (spliced quotation). Also see J. R. Hicks, *op. cit.*, p. 470.

[6] See Alvin H. Hansen, *Monetary Theory and Fiscal Policy*, pp. 161–63. For a closely related view see Keynes, *op. cit.*, pp. 322–23.

[7] See *The General Theory*, Preface, chap. xvii, and

pp. 292–94. On this point see also Dudley Dillard, "The Theory of a Monetary Economy," in Kenneth Kurihara (ed.), *Post-Keynesian Economics* (New Brunswick, N.J.: Rutgers University Press, 1954), pp. 3–30.

[8] As expressed by Irving Fisher, in the most widely accepted pre-Keynesian statement of the Quantity theory: "Since a doubling in the quantity of money will not appreciably affect either the velocity of circulation or the volume of trade, it follows necessarily and mathematically that the level of prices must double. There is no possible escape from the conclusion that a change in the quantity of money must normally cause a proportional change in the price level." Irving Fisher, *The Purchasing Power of Money* (Macmillan, 1911), pp. 156–57 (spliced quotation).

III. NEW DEPARTURES

Model C is a lineal descendant of Model B, but comes to rather different conclusions. Although Model C uses most of the orthodox Keynesian apparatus, it is so unorthodox in its handling of selected parts of that apparatus as to make it debatable whether it should be classified as a version of Keynesian theory. Perhaps it should be given a category of its own and called Radcliffism, since it has been most closely associated with the work of the Radcliffe Committee and Professors Gurley and Shaw.[9] In any case, in this model changes in the money supply are seen as no more likely to be effective against inflation than they were against depression in Model B!

The analysis of Model C differs from both previous models in that it does not ignore the liquidity preference function, as A does, nor does it stress the significance of its interest-elasticity, as B does. Rather than being ignored, the liquidity preference function is an integral part of Model C, *but the demand for liquidity is no longer viewed as identical with the demand for money.* And rather than stressing the importance of the interest-elasticity of the demand schedule for money, attention is directed instead to the likelihood of *shifts* in that schedule. While the orthodox Keynesian literature has a great deal to say about shifts in the investment demand function, through the influence of changes in expectations, it tends to ignore the possibility of shifts in the demand for money, and instead concentrates almost exclusively on its interest-elasticity.

In the orthodox Keynesian system, Model B, the demand for liquidity is synonymous with the demand for money. The ready availability of interest-yielding money substitutes, however,

destroys that equation. Such near monies as time deposits, savings and loan shares, and Treasury bills are virtually as liquid as cash and in addition yield an interest return. Thus, the demand for money (demand deposits plus currency) may contract even though the demand for liquidity broadly conceived remains stable. Liquidity preference, in other words, may be satisfied partially by holdings of money substitutes in place of money itself.

There are two reasons for the demand for money in the orthodox Keynesian system. In the first place, active money balances are needed for transactions purposes. The demand for active balances is assumed to bear a more or less constant ratio to income, so that an expansion in income will lead to a proportionate increase in the amount of active balances desired. In the second place, idle cash is demanded because of uncertainties regarding the future course of interest rates. Idle cash is held primarily because of the fear that interest rates might rise (bond prices fall), imposing capital losses on bondholders. This is the main reason why Keynes believed that the amount of idle cash desired would increase as the rate of interest falls.[10] The lower the rate of interest, the more it is likely to drop below what are considered "safe" or "normal" levels, leading to the expectation that its future course is likely to be upward, with consequent losses in capital values. Under such circumstances, it is prudent to get out of bonds and into a more liquid asset. In *The General Theory* the only liquid asset available is cash.

The existence of short-term money substitutes, however, provides an alternative to holding money for both of these purposes. With respect to *active* balances, there is no reason to assume that these need be held solely in the form of money. For immediate transactions purposes, there is little alternative to possessing the medium of exchange itself. But for payments scheduled for several months in the future, there are many assets available which can serve as a substitute for holding cash without diminishing liquidity, and which at the

[9] *Report* of the Committee on the Working of the Monetary System (London, 1959), and J. G. Gurley and E. S. Shaw, *Money in a Theory of Finance* (Washington, D.C.: The Brookings Institution, 1960). See also J. G. Gurley, *Liquidity and Financial Institutions in the Postwar Economy*, Study Paper 14, Joint Economic Committee, U.S. Congress (1960); R. S. Sayers, "Monetary Thought and Monetary Policy in England," *Economic Journal*, Vol. LXX, No. 280 (December, 1960), pp. 710–24; and A. B. Cramp, "Two Views on Money," *Lloyds Bank Review*, No. 65 (July, 1962), pp. 1–15.

[10] See *General Theory*, pp. 201–2. Also see Day and Beza, *Money and Income* (New York: Oxford University Press, Inc., 1960), pp. 17–20.

same time provides an interest income. Firms with scheduled payments to make at particular dates in the future can hold Treasury bills, sales finance company paper, or repurchase agreements with government securities dealers, for example — all of which can easily be arranged to come due when the cash is needed. The very purpose of tax anticipation bills is to fill just such a need. Similarly, households can hold time deposits, paying interest from date of deposit to date of withdrawal, pending anticipated payments. For possible emergencies, lines of credit can be arranged on a standby basis in place of holding idle cash.

Many other methods exist through which both households and business firms can economize on their average holdings of transactions cash without impairing their liquidity positions. Indeed, there is ample evidence that high short-term interest rates in the postwar period have stimulated the expenditure of considerable ingenuity in the economical management of cash balances, with consequent reductions in the required ratio of active money balances to income. To the extent that this is accomplished, an expansion in income will not lead to a proportionate increase in the amount of transactions cash desired.

With respect to *idle* balances, the existence of short-term money substitutes also provides an alternative to holding cash when it is feared that long-term interest rates might rise (bond prices fall). If it is thought that long-term rates are too low (bond prices too high) for safety, investors need not increase their holdings of idle cash to get liquidity, but instead can purchase Treasury bills or other interest-bearing liquid assets. With highly liquid money substitutes, the concept of a "safe" yield level is almost meaningless and the chance of suffering a capital loss close to nil; indeed, the very definition of a liquid asset is one which can be turned into cash on short notice with little or no loss in dollar value.

The concept of a "safe" yield level is crucial in decisions as to whether or not to buy *long-term* securities, because the existence of uncertainty regarding future long rates gives rise to the fear of taking substantial capital losses (or the hope of making capital gains). But the

rationale behind buying *short-term* liquid assets is that if yields rise no loss need be suffered. The securities will mature shortly anyway, and thereby turn into cash at their face value. And, in any event, even if one has no choice but to dispose of them before maturity, the resulting capital losses (or gains) are likely to be small. Unlike long-terms, a rather large change in yields on short-term instruments involves but a small change in their price.[11]

In brief, the amount of money desired may not increase when the rate of interest falls, even though the amount of liquidity desired does increase. At least part of the accumulation of liquidity is likely to take the form of interest-bearing near monies instead of nonearning cash. In comparison with Model B, the demand for idle cash balances will have contracted throughout the range of interest rates, even though the liquidity preference function may have remained stable. Under these circumstances, with both segments of the demand for money susceptible to leftward shifts, monetary policies confined to regulating the supply of money are not likely to be as successful in stemming inflation as orthodox Keynesian theory believes. Since the significant variable is not the supply of money, per se, but rather the supply relative to the demand, the flexibility of demand makes control of the supply, alone, an unreliable in-

[11] A rise in yields from 4 per cent to 5 per cent on a $1,000 face value 30-year bond bearing a 4 per cent coupon involves a fall in price from $1,000 to $845. A similar rise in yield on a 3-month security of similar coupon involves a fall in price from $1,000 to only $997.

The point can be made even more dramatically. Assume, not too unrealistically, that at the extreme long-term yields on government securities might be expected to vary between 2 per cent and 6 per cent in the forseeable future, and short-term yields between 1 per cent and 7 per cent. The holder of a $1,000 30-year bond bearing a 4 per cent coupon might then anticipate, at the extreme, that its price might possibly vary between the limits of $723 and $1,450. For a 3-month security of similar coupon, however, the possible range of price variation would be only from $992 to $1,008. In one case possible range of price variation is $727 on a $1,000 security, and in the other case it is only $16. Safety of principal is tenuous in the former, and practically assured in the latter.

These figures can be calculated from any bond basis book. See also Burton G. Malkiel, "Expectations, Bond Prices, and the Term Structure of Interest Rates," *Quarterly Journal of Economics*, Vol. LXXVI, No. 2 (May, 1962), pp. 197–218.

strument through which to affect the level of economic activity. These results do not depend, as in orthodox Keynesian theory, on the short-run interest-elasticity of the demand for money, but rather on shifts in that demand.

In Model B, for example, if the economy is initially in equilibrium, with planned investment equal to planned saving and the demand for money equal to the supply, an exogenous increase in spending will raise money income and increase the amount of transactions cash desired proportionately. Limitation of the money supply — holding it constant — will then automatically result in an excess demand for money, which will raise interest rates, check investment, and thereby bring the expansion in income to a halt. There will probably be some slippage, as the rise in interest rates attracts some funds out of idle cash holdings into transactions balances, with the degree of slippage depending on the interest-elasticity of the demand for idle balances and the specific ratio between active cash and income. But that same rise in interest rates, and the related tightening of monetary conditions in general, will tend to discourage some expenditures. In any event, sooner or later idle balances will be depleted. If the monetary authorities want to accelerate the process, they can provide added impetus by actually reducing the money supply rather than merely holding it stable.

In the world envisaged by Model C, on the other hand, these results are not as likely to be realized. If the required ratio of transactions cash to income contracts as income rises, the expansion in income will not lead to a proportionate increase in the amount of active cash desired. It may not even lead to an absolute increase. Limitation of the money supply then may not produce very much of an excess demand for money, so that upward pressure on interest rates will be negligible, investment will not be checked, and the rise in spending will proceed unhindered. If, at the same time, the demand for idle balances has also shifted to the left, then — regardless of its interest-elasticity — formerly idle balances will become available for transactions use, again with minimal increases in interest rates. Instead of an excess demand for money, there might conceivably be

an excess supply, with consequent *downward* pressure on interest rates. Even if the monetary authorities were to actually reduce the supply of money, they might be hard put to keep pace with the contraction in demand. And although idle balances must sooner or later be depleted, this will pose no obstacle to the continued rise in spending if the desired active cash to income ratio continues to contract.

Of course, the process need not be this straightforward. Models B and C need not be mutually exclusive, but may be combined over several cycles. Interest rates may indeed rise during periods of cyclical expansion, especially if the expansion is vigorous, as spending increases more rapidly than can be accommodated by contractions in the demand schedules for money. However, rising interest rates are likely to stimulate new financial techniques for economizing on cash balances.[12] These techniques of cash management, introduced during periods of tight money, are not likely to be abandoned when rates recede in the subsequent recession. As a result, the contraction in the demand for money may not be clearly evident until the *next* upturn in business conditions. When that upturn comes, the supply of money may be more than ample to finance it, even though, by past standards, it would appear to be less than adequate. In effect, liquidity is accumulated during the recession, in the form of money substitutes instead of money, and is then released when needed to finance expenditures when economic activity revives.

Presumably, the central bank could always reduce the money supply drastically enough to counteract the decline in the demand for money, and thereby produce the results it wants. But with business prospects cloudy, as they generally are, and with past guidelines unreliable indicators of the current adequacy of the money supply, the monetary authorities are usually not sure enough of where they stand to

[12] See Hyman P. Minsky, "Central Banking and Money Market Changes," *Quarterly Journal of Economics*, Vol. LXXI, No. 2 (May, 1957), pp. 171–87; and L. S. Ritter, "The Structure of Financial Markets, Income Velocity, and the Effectiveness of Monetary Policy," *Schweizerische Zeitschrift für Volkswirtschaft und Statistik*, Vol. XCVIII, No. 3 (September, 1962), pp. 276–89.

take decisive action in *any* direction. This inaction is then rationalized by the invocation of moral principles, as ethical values are attributed to the determination of interest rates by "free market forces" and to "minimize intervention" in general.

It is for these reasons that Model C shifts attention away from the money supply narrowly defined to the significance of liquidity broadly conceived. Traditional monetary policy, which is confined to the control of the money supply, is seen as having to give way to a more broadly based liquidity policy if it is to successfully influence economic activity within the context of the present-day financial environment.[13] It is thus Radcliffe monetary theory, rather than orthodox Keynesian theory, which poses the most fundamental challenge to the modern Quantity theory of money.

IV. IMPLICATIONS FOR VELOCITY

The differences between orthodox Keynesian theory (Model B), Radcliffe theory (Model C), and the modern Quantity theory of money can be summarized most conveniently in terms of their implications for the behavior of velocity. This simultaneously affords a comparison of their respective evaluations of the effectiveness of monetary policy. For if monetary policy is to be effective — i.e., if changes in the money supply are to produce changes in aggregate spending, and thus in income — then velocity must either remain more or less stable or else move in the same direction as the money supply.

If the phrase "money matters" is to have any operational meaning, it must imply the existence of such conditions. In terms of the equation of exchange, if changes in M are to produce changes in MV and thus in PT, then V must necessarily remain rather stable or else reinforce the change in M. On the other hand, to the extent that velocity falls when the money supply is increased, or rises when the money

supply is decreased, or changes in the absence of changes in the money supply, the effectiveness of monetary policy is correspondingly reduced. If these offsetting changes in velocity are so great that the influence of monetary policy is negligible, then "money does not matter." In between these two extremes lies a continuum of possibilities.

It should be noted that the modern Quantity theory is not precisely the same as the pre-Keynesian Quantity theory. As presented by Milton Friedman, the present-day version of the Quantity theory is no longer strictly an explanation of what determines the price level. Friedman uses the Quantity theory to explain major depressions as well as inflations, so that it is now, like the Keynesian approach, essentially a theory of income determination.[14]

In addition, Friedman accepts variations in velocity as consistent with the Quantity theory. Unlike Irving Fisher, Friedman does not view velocity as an institutional datum, nor as a numerical constant, but rather as a functional relationship in which the demand for money is a function of a number of variables within the system, such as interest rates, income, wealth, and expected changes in the price level. Depending on movements in these variables, velocity may vary both cyclically and secularly. This also represents a major shift in emphasis by the Quantity theory in the direction of the Keynesian approach, wherein velocity has *always* been functionally related to such variables.

Nevertheless, the two are still rather far apart. In Friedman's view, under normal circumstances the demand-for-money function is so stable and inelastic that such changes in ve-

---

[13] In the words of the Radcliffe Report (paragraph 981, p. 337): "The factor which monetary policy should seek to influence or control is something that reaches far beyond what is known as 'the supply of money.' It is nothing less than the state of liquidity of the whole economy."

[14] In terms of the equation of exchange, T is no longer assumed as given by virtue of Say's Law, so that changes in the supply of money can affect output and employment as well as the price level. See Milton Friedman, "The Quantity Theory of Money — A Restatement," in *Studies in the Quantity Theory of Money*, and Chapter 1 in *A Program for Monetary Stability*. Friedman prefers to view the Quantity theory as a theory of the demand for money rather than a theory of income determination, with the addition of the supply of money necessary before income can be determined. However, this is a purely semantic matter. In the same sense, neither is orthodox Keynesian theory a theory of income determination until the supply of money is given.

locity as do occur will not be very bothersome. Velocity may fall somewhat when the money supply is increased, or rise somewhat when the money supply is decreased, or even change to some extent in the absence of changes in the money supply so as to produce minor fluctuations in income despite stability in the stock of money. But these changes in velocity are assumed to be small. Velocity is no longer seen as constant, but it *is* seen as fluctuating only very moderately.[15] Thus, changes in velocity are not likely to appreciably offset changes in the money supply, and major fluctuations in income are not likely to take place in the absence of major fluctuations in the stock of money. As a result, the modern Quantity theory views monetary policy as highly effective. Aside from minor short-run fluctuations in income, monetary policy is seen as both necessary *and sufficient* for the attainment of economic stability.

Radcliffe monetary theory, on the other hand, looks upon monetary policy in a rather different light: "Though we do not regard the supply of money as an unimportant quantity, we view it as only part of the wider structure of liquidity in the economy. It is the whole liquidity position that is relevant to spending decisions, and our interest in the supply of money is due to its significance in the whole liquidity picture. The fact that spending is not limited by the amount of money in existence is sometimes argued by reference to the velocity of money. It is possible, for example, to demonstrate statistically that during the last few years the volume of spending has greatly increased while the supply of money has hardly changed: the velocity of money has increased. We have not made more use of this concept because we cannot find any reason for supposing, or any experience in monetary history indicating, that there is any limit to velocity."[16]

While the Quantity theory views traditional monetary policy as both necessary and sufficient, and Radcliffe views it as too narrowly conceived to be of much use, Keynesian theory lies in between these two extremes. Sometimes changes in velocity are seen as nullifying changes in the money supply, sometimes they are seen as reinforcing,[17] and most of the time they are seen as somewhere in between. The crucial determinants of the behavior of velocity in the orthodox Keynesian system are the interest and wealth-elasticities of the spending and liquidity preference functions, and these are likely to vary depending on the particular historical, institutional, and expectational circumstances at hand. Since velocity is not something the monetary authorities can depend upon, in the sense of being able to reliably anticipate its behavior, monetary policy emerges from the Keynesian system as usually necessary but rarely sufficient for the attainment of national economic objectives.

Although it is not the purpose of this paper to evaluate the implications of the empirical evidence, a brief look, in closing, at the postwar movements in velocity would not be inappropriate. As Figure I indicates, velocity has fluctuated between an annual rate of 1.93 in the first quarter of 1946 and 3.87 in the fourth

[15] In Friedman's words: "It is, of course, true that velocity varies over short periods of time. The fact of the matter, however, is that these variations are in general relatively small." *Monetary Policy and Management of the Public Debt*, Hearings before the Joint Economic Committee, U.S. Congress, 1952, p. 720. From the same source, p. 743: "Income velocity is a reasonably stable magnitude. It has been declining over the last century . . . however, the decline appears to have been rather gradual, and income velocity is relatively stable over short periods." From *Studies in the Quantity Theory of Money* (p. 21): "There is an extraordinary empirical stability and regularity to such magnitudes as income velocity that cannot but impress anyone who works extensively with monetary data. This very stability and regularity contributed to the downfall of the Quantity theory, for it was overstated and expressed in unduly simple form. The numerical value of velocity itself, whether income or transactions, was treated as a natural 'constant.' Now this it is not; and its failure to be so, first during and after World War I and then, to a lesser extent, after the crash of 1929, helped greatly to foster the reaction against the Quantity theory. The studies in this volume are premised on a stability and regularity in monetary relations of a more sophisticated form than a numerically constant velocity."

[16] Radcliffe, *Report*, pp. 132–33.

[17] "In conditions like those of the last decade, it seems unwise to expect that induced changes in V will largely undo the effects of central bank operations; at times they could be reinforcing. The Radcliffe Report seems to me to give misleading impressions in this regard, whatever its other merits." Paul A. Samuelson, "Reflections on Monetary Policy," *Review of Economics and Statistics*, Vol. XLII, No. 3 (August, 1960), p. 268.

FIGURE I

Income Velocity, Quarterly, 1946–62 *

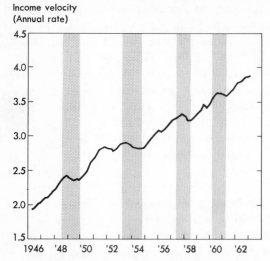

Income velocity
(Annual rate)

* Income velocity is the quotient of gross national product divided by the average money supply over the period, both seasonally adjusted. The money supply is defined as demand deposits, adjusted, plus currency outside banks. Shaded areas indicate periods of recession in general business conditions.

quarter of 1962.[18] Over the period as a whole, velocity has shown a marked upward trend, with fluctuations about that trend coinciding with cyclical fluctuations in general business conditions. Each cyclical peak in velocity has typically been accompanied by rising interest rates and other signs of monetary stringency, leading observers to believe that velocity could not rise much further, that it was close to its upper

[18] In the first quarter of 1963, the latest data available at the time of writing, velocity reached a post-1929 high of 3.88. It should be noted that with our present money supply of about $150 billion, even so small an absolute change in velocity as 0.1 would correspond to a change in gross national product of $15 billion.

limit.[19] But then, after a slight decline during recession periods, velocity has promptly resumed its upward climb as soon as business conditions have turned up again. Not only has velocity risen to successively higher peaks from cycle to cycle, but in each period of business recovery it has equaled or exceeded its prior-cycle peak *within only two quarters* after recovery has begun.

How much higher can velocity rise? Recent levels of velocity, approaching a turnover rate of 4 times per annum, are comparable to previous peaks of 4 reached in 1919 and again in 1929. This has once again revived speculation that velocity is approaching its upper limit. However, as of late 1962 and early 1963, liquidity has appeared to be ample throughout the economy, no upward pressure has been evident on interest rates, and the money and capital markets have been characterized more by ease than by tightness. There is thus less evidence today that velocity is approaching a ceiling than there was six years ago, when velocity was around 3.3. Recent increases in velocity would appear to stem from a decrease in the demand for money, rather than a scarcity of supply, indicating that there is probably considerable room for further advance still remaining.

The "extraordinary empirical stability" that Quantity theorists find in the behavior of velocity is revealed only to the disciples. But whether the Radcliffe Report is correct, that for all practical purposes velocity has no upper limit whatsoever, remains to be seen.

[19] See, for example, L. S. Ritter, "Income Velocity and Anti-Inflationary Monetary Policy," *American Economic Review*, Vol. XLIX, No. 1 (March 1959), pp. 120–29 [Selection 39].

Editorial Postscript: *By the third quarter of 1966 income velocity had risen to about 4.4. You can find what it is today by consulting a recent issue of the* Federal Reserve Bulletin. *Merely divide a recent quarter's GNP by the average seasonally adjusted money supply (demand deposits plus currency) for that quarter.*

CHAPTER TWELVE

COST-PUSH INFLATION AND THE DILEMMA OF MONETARY-FISCAL POLICY

41

INFLATIONARY DEPRESSION AND THE REGULATION OF ADMINISTERED PRICES*

Abba P. Lerner†

*Hardly have we finished with one problem before another is upon us. And this one —
cost-push inflation — may be even less amenable to treatment than the velocity problem.*

*For many years economists discussed inflation (or rising prices) entirely in terms of ex-
cessive demand; that is, inflation was due to consumer plus investment plus government
spending in excess of the value of output that the economy could produce at full employment with the existing price level. This excessive aggregate spending or demand,
with investment greater than savings at full employment, raised prices as explained
in Selection 1. But in recent years a new concept has gained recognition: inflation can
be due to cost-push factors as well as orthodox demand-pull elements. Inflation can
begin before we get to full employment.*

*Recognition of cost-push factors became widespread when consumer prices not only
failed to decline but actually continued to advance during the recessions of 1953–54 and
1957–58. The phenomenon of a rising price level during a period of substantial unemployment was inconsistent with orthodox demand-pull explanations, as in Selection 1,
which assumed that real output, rather than prices, would rise until roughly full employment was reached. Only after we reached full employment were prices supposed to rise.
But in 1957–58 spending was declining, not increasing, and employment was rather
substantial, and yet the price level continued to creep upward. As a result, alternative
explanations were sought and the phenomenon of creeping inflation and cost-push
causation gained wide attention.*

*Cost-push inflation arises when strong unions obtain wage increases in excess of in-
creases in productivity or entrepreneurs jack up profit margins to increase their share
of the national income; in other words, when costs (which are properly defined to include profits) increase and prices then rise in consequence. Usually cost inflation is
blamed on the "monopolistic" position of strong unions, but the "monopolistic" position of large corporations is also frequently mentioned (see Galbraith, Selection 42).*

* From *The Relationship of Prices to Economic
Stability and Growth,* Compendium of Papers Submitted to the Joint Economic Committee, U.S. Congress, 1958. Reprinted by the courtesy of the author.

† University of California, Berkeley.

This phenomenon of cost-push inflation creates a dilemma for monetary and fiscal policy. Prices may rise without an increase in demand, but monetary-fiscal policy exerts its impact through demand factors. If prices rise because of cost factors while there is still a fair amount of unemployment, and "tight money" is imposed by the central bank to stop the inflation, the result will be a decrease in aggregate demand. However, if aggregate demand was not excessive originally in terms of the level of employment, this will only result in insufficient aggregate spending and more unemployment. Monetary-fiscal policy is ostensibly designed to bring about full employment, not depressions.

On the other hand, with the higher price level a larger money supply is needed to support the higher level of (money) income. Money incomes must be allowed to rise if we are to maintain or reach full employment. But an expansionary monetary-fiscal policy will aid and abet the cost inflation! If monetary-fiscal policy always steps in to validate the higher price and income level, what is to prevent strong unions or powerful corporations from repeating the process to obtain still higher wages or profits? Must we deliberately create unemployment if we are to escape inflation? Are we to have inflation if we try to maintain full employment? This is the dilemma facing monetary-fiscal policy today: whether monetary-fiscal policy, which exerts its effects through aggregate demand, is able to cope with cost-push inflation.

The following article contains a lucid diagnosis of the problem. Whether the prescription is as sound as the diagnosis is lucid is a matter each reader will have to decide for himself.

I. THE DIAGNOSIS

Inflation, by which I mean a condition of rising prices, may be the result of action either by buyers or by sellers. We are much more familiar with inflation caused by buyers trying to buy more goods than are available, that is, spending more money than can buy (at current prices) the available supply of goods. When this happens, prices are bid up to the level at which the buyers are no longer trying to buy more than is available. The market is then cleared with every buyer able to buy as much as he wants to buy. If, as a result of this development, there arises a still further increase in the amount of money spent by the buyers, perhaps because they have received more money as sellers of something else, we have a continuing inflationary process.

Such a process cannot go very far unless there is an increase in the supply of money. Otherwise, with the rising prices, the public finds that the stock of money is too small for the greater volume of transactions, in monetary terms, that is going on. Many people then reduce their buying or increase their selling (so as to hold on to or to get hold of more money) and this tends to stop the inflationary process. But if

the monetary authorities increase the supply of money, or permit the supply of money to be increased, then the inflationary process can continue.

Because we are much more familiar with this particular type of inflation, we have tended to assume that it is the only kind. This has led to the habit of considering an increase in the supply of money not as merely one of the necessary conditions for an inflationary process to be able to continue, but as the cause of the inflation, which it need not be. Our overoccupation with this particular type of inflation has also led many economists, including myself, to use the word "inflation" not only to stand for the condition of rising prices, but also to stand for "excess demand," the attempt to buy more goods than are available at the current prices, which is the cause of this type of inflation.

This extension of the meaning of the word inflation would be quite harmless if it were true, as it apparently was assumed to be true, that rising prices could come about only as a result of excess demand by buyers. This usage furthermore had the advantage of permitting the condemnatory word inflation to be used for attacking a condition in which prices were prevented from rising, as by price controls, when the economy would be better served if they were permitted to rise. Such price control under conditions of excess demand could then be called a kind of inflation — repressed inflation — which can be even more harmful to the economy, and to society in general, than an open inflation with rising prices. So it seemed like a good idea to identify inflation with a condition of excess demand, whether the resulting tendency for prices to rise was permitted to express itself or not. Repressed inflation could therefore be called a certain kind of inflation and given a blacker name, and this seemed harmless even though it was something like calling an anti-Communist a certain kind of Communist.

But excess demand by buyers is not the only possible cause of a condition of rising prices. Prices may rise not because of the pressure of buyers who are finding it difficult to buy all they want to buy at the current prices. Prices may rise because of pressures by sellers who insist on raising their prices even though they may find it not especially easy to sell. We would then have not a buyer-induced inflation but a seller-induced inflation. To distinguish this from the kind of inflation we have discussed above, and which we may call a buyers' inflation (or demand inflation), we may call this kind of inflation a sellers' inflation.

If sellers' inflation is possible as well as buyers' inflation, it is not such a good idea to use the word "inflation" to stand for excess demand. That use of language tends to suggest that if there is no "inflation" in the sense of excess demand there can be no inflation in the sense of rising prices. It leaves us with no way of describing the kind of situation in which we find ourselves when prices are rising because of upward pressure by sellers, and the authorities, in endeavoring to stop the rise in prices, have taken steps which have been very effective in removing excess demand, but which have not removed the upward pressure on prices from the sellers side. Indeed such measures as budgetary restraint and tight money can be so effective in removing excess demand that they can overdo this and remove some demand that is not in excess. They would bring about a condition of deficient demand, or not enough de-

mand to enable us to make full use of our productive potential. Nevertheless, prices may keep on rising. The net result would be both inflation and depression at the same time — prices rising even though we are not fully utilizing our available labor force and productive potential.

This appears paradoxical only because of our habit of using one word, "inflation", to represent two different things, rising prices and excess demand, that do not necessarily have to go together in the actual world.

The distinction between buyers' inflation and sellers' inflation is related to but is not exactly the same as the distinction between demand inflation and cost inflation. While demand inflation seems to be synonymous with buyers' inflation, cost inflation suggests that there is a difference between costs, on the one hand, and profits, on the other, in their operation on price. This is especially true when the phrases "cost-push inflation" or "wage-cost inflation" are used as synonymous with "cost inflation." The impression is given that the whole of the blame falls on labor or on trade unions. When trade unions raise wages by more than can be absorbed by increasing productivity, costs rise. The employer then seems to be completely innocent of "profit inflation" in passing on the increase in costs as long as he does not increase his rate of markup, i.e., as long as he does not increase the prices he charges for the product in a greater proportion than his costs have increased.

There is, however, no essential asymmetry between the wage element and the profit element in the price asked for the product. A sellers' inflation could just as well be started by an increase not in the wage asked, but in the percentage of markup of price above cost. Prices would rise and wages would then be raised by workers in attempts to maintain (or restore) their original buying power. Business would then "innocently" raise their prices again only in proportion to the increase in their costs, and we would have the inflation upon us as well as boring discussions about who started it first and the famous chicken and egg.

The "who started it first" debate is a complete waste of time because there is no original situation in which there was a "just" or "normal" distribution of the product between wages and profits. Any increase can be seen either as the disturbance which bears the full responsibility for the inflation, or as nothing but the correction of an inequity perpetrated in previous history — all depending on the point of view. The term "sellers' inflation," by treating wages and profits on exactly the same footing, avoids the fruitless game of mutual recrimination. Sellers' inflation takes place whenever wage earners and profit takers together attempt to get shares that amount to more than 100 per cent of the selling price. When the sum of what they try to get comes to more than 100 per cent of the selling price it is futile to ask whether this is because the wages demanded are too high or whether it is because the profits insisted on are too great. No matter where justice may lie between the two claims, the only significant thing for our problem is that the sum of the claims is more than 100 per cent. That is what causes the inflation.

It is, of course, impossible for the two parties to succeed in getting more than 100 per cent of the proceeds between them, but it is precisely on an impossibility such as this that any continuing process depends. Buyers' inflation is similarly built on an attempt to reach the impossible. In that case, it is the attempt of buyers to buy more than 100 per cent of the goods than can be made available. Their attempt bids up prices, but since that does not (and cannot) succeed in enabling them to obtain more than 100 per cent of the goods that there are available, they continue the attempt and we have the continuing process of buyers' inflation. In our case, the impossibility that generates the process is the attempt of wage earners and profit takers between them to get more than 100 per cent of the money proceeds from the sale of the product. Each increases the part he tries to take, by increasing wages or by increasing prices. Since they cannot succeed, they keep on raising wages and prices and so we have the continuing process of sellers' inflation.

There is great resistance to recognizing the possibility of sellers' inflation. Sometimes, this takes the form of saying that there must have been some excess buyers' demand or prices could not have risen. This begs the whole question. Since it assumes, without apparently thinking it necessary to provide any support for the assumption, that the only possible cause of rising prices is excess buyers' demand, the argument assumes what it wants to prove.

A more sophisticated version of this argument points out that if output shrinks by less than the increase in prices, and this is usually the case during a sellers' inflation, there must have been an increase in the total amount spent in buying the output. The arithmetically irrefutable increase in expenditure is then triumphantly exhibited as the excess buyers' demand that is responsible for the inflation. Expenditure is the same thing as buyers' demand, but an increase in expenditure is not the same thing as excess buyers' demand. An increase is not the same thing as an excess. An excess of demand by buyers induces the price increases — it is the cause of the price increases. An increase in expenditure could be induced by — it could be the result of — the increases in prices brought about by the pressure of sellers. If there is no increase in expenditure the number of units of goods bought must fall in the same proportion as the price per unit is raised by the sellers. A 10 per cent increase in prices would thus result in a fall in output of about 10 per cent. This involves depression and unemployment that the authorities naturally seek to remedy by monetary and fiscal measures. Such remedies all involve increases in money expenditure, so that even if only a part of the unemployment is corrected (and this is usually the case because of the authorities' reluctance to undertake inflationary measures when prices are rising), we would observe an increase in total expenditure. Buyers' demand, however, instead of being excessive, could still be deficient, i.e., it could still be insufficient to enable the potential output of the economy to be sold (at the prices demanded by the sellers). An observed increase in total expenditure is therefore no proof that the price rise is due to excess buyers' demand. The increase in expenditure could have been induced by attempts by the authorities to keep down unemployment induced by price increases imposed by the sellers. In a sellers' inflation, an increase in expenditure is perfectly compatible with deficient buyers' demand.

A still more sophisticated argument along the same line goes on to claim that even if prices are being raised by the insistence of sellers rather than by the pressure of buyers, the orthodox measures of reducing total demand would still check the inflation. By reducing total expenditure, or perhaps by merely refusing to permit the increase in total expenditure needed to accommodate the increased prices, the authorities would bring about depression and unemployment. This would stop the sellers from increasing prices. The question then resolves itself into how much unemployment would be necessary to stop the sellers' inflation, and whether it is morally desirable or politically possible for the authorities to induce or permit unemployment of the required volume and duration.

It has been suggested that even if the authorities are not really prepared to bring about the degree of depression necessary to negate the pressure of sellers' inflation, they could still do the trick by solemnly announcing a policy of refusing to provide the increase in expenditure called for by a continuing sellers' inflation. The threatened unemployment would then sober the sellers into calling off their inflationary wage and price increases.

It seems pretty certain first that such declarations would not be believed and that the bluff would quickly be called. But, even if it were believed as regards the economy as a whole, that would not prevent any specific wages or prices from being raised while the local conditions still permitted this. It would perhaps even aggravate the wage and price increases as each tried to get his increase quickly, while the local going was still good.

All this brings us to the perhaps only too obvious conclusion that sellers' inflation cannot be cured or prevented by measures directed against excess demand by buyers. It can be successfully treated only by attacking the pressure on prices by sellers.

Before we can consider just how one can attack the pressure on prices by sellers, it would be desirable to get a perspective on the whole

problem by a quick look at the general theory of inflation and deflation.

II. ORTHODOX REMEDIES: MONETARY AND FISCAL POLICY IN CLASSICAL AND KEYNESIAN ECONOMICS

A somewhat schematic formulation of the development of thought on this subject shows four theoretical models of the operation of the economy.

Model A assumes perfectly flexible prices and wages, so that any excess of buyers' demands makes prices and wages rise, and any deficiency of buyers' demand (through the unemployment that results) makes prices and wages fall, until price stability and full employment are restored. Both monetary policy and fiscal policy are unimportant, or even unnecessary. As long as the volume of money is kept fairly stable by some automatic device, such as the gold standard, the price level will automatically adjust itself so as to yield full employment with price stability and without inflation.

Model B embodies the recognition that we do not have the degree of price flexibility in the downward direction to make complete laissez faire a satisfactory monetary and fiscal policy. Unemployment (caused by deficient buyers' demand) does not reduce the wage and price level quickly enough to the level needed to restore full employment. The process is rather complex. To achieve the task, unemployment must reduce the wage level, and thereby the price level, to the degree necessary to increase the value of the existing stock of money (as each dollar becomes more valuable) to the extent necessary to increase expenditure in real terms (as each dollar spent constitutes more real purchasing power) to the volume necessary to give a satisfactory level of employment. This process can last for years, during which time prices and wages are falling as different resistances to the reductions are gradually overcome. Meanwhile, there continues an expectation of price and wage reductions still to come. This expectation induces investors as well as consumers to postpone their expenditures as long as prices are still falling, so that buyers' demand is reduced still further and the depression can get very much worse before it gets better.

The recognition of the nature of such a process leads to the abandonment of laissez faire in monetary and fiscal policy. Instead of waiting for the price level to fall until it has adjusted itself to the volume of money expenditure, a policy is developed of adjusting the volume of money expenditure to the existing price level, so as to reach and maintain a satisfactory level of employment at the current prices.

This switch from laissez faire to an active monetary and fiscal policy is also applied in the opposite direction to deal with excess buyers' demand. Although there is not the same resistance to price and wage increases as there is to price and wage decreases, the necessary adjustment to excess buyers' demand by rising prices still takes time. It is no instantaneous adjustment (if only because of the existence of long-term contracts, and because of attempts to stop profiteering by preventing the necessary price increases) and so it causes disturbances that are unjust and reduce the efficiency of the economy. The policy is therefore applied in both directions, providing for increasing the volume of money expenditure whenever necessary to prevent or correct an insufficiency of buyers' demand; and for decreasing the volume of money expenditure whenever that is necessary to prevent or correct an excess of buyers' demand.

The volume of expenditure may be adjusted either by working the stock of money (by monetary policy) or by working on the velocity of circulation of money (by fiscal policy), or by some combination of the two.

Model B, which is, of course, the Keynesian general theory of employment policy, differs from model A primarily in incorporating a policy of increasing or decreasing demand, if it should become too little or too great. (It has a steering wheel to keep the car on the road.) Because of this difference, a secondary distinction arises. With policy coming into the picture, it becomes important which of two instruments of policy is to be used, monetary policy or fiscal policy. Model B makes use of both instruments. (The car can use either kerosene or gasoline.)

Model C is not really a new model. It rather consists of a series of publicity releases of model B dolled up to emphasize one or another of its qualities as if this were a new invention that made model B obsolete. One very crude pamphlet of this series emphasizes the ability of model C to cut down on demand, if it becomes excessive or threatens to become excessive, seeming to imply that model B was a depression model, which could work only in the direction of increasing demand, if it became deficient or threatened to become deficient. (Model C has a steering wheel that can be turned to the right.)

A more refined variant of model C, let us call it model C*, is concerned with the relative effectiveness of monetary policy and of fiscal policy in different circumstances. An economy may be so saturated with money so that further increases in the stock of money would not be effective in increasing expenditure, and reductions in the stock would have no significant effect in reducing total expenditure. (This is sometimes expressed, though not explained, by saying that changes in the money supply would be offset by opposing changes in the velocity of circulation.) Monetary policy is then useless and expenditure can be increased or decreased only by fiscal policy — by the Government increasing or decreasing its own expenditure, e.g. on public works, or permitting others to spend more by reducing taxes or forcing them to spend less by increasing taxes.

It is then suggested that model B works only in this case which is called the Keynesian case. It should more properly be called Keynesian special case (of the Keynesian general theory) when it is appropriate to concentrate entirely on fiscal measures to increase or decrease expenditure on consumption and investment. (Only gasoline can be used.)

In this kind of situation, even extreme price flexibility is unable to restore or maintain the desired level of real demand, because it operates after all, as nothing but a roundabout way of increasing or decreasing the real volume of money in terms of buying power. It is a kind of automatic monetary policy which is useless for the same reasons as other monetary policy is useless, when the economy is so saturated with money that changing the quantity has no appreciable effect.

When the economy is at the other extreme

from being saturated with money, and money is very tight, the situation is naturally reversed. Fiscal measures for increasing expenditure on consumption or investment are ineffective, because an increase in expenditure anywhere in the economy, say in Government expenditure on public works, results in an increase in demand for money to hold in connection with the increased volume of transactions. In the very tight money situation, this raises the rate of interest, or in some other way reduces expenditure somewhere else. Similarly, a decrease in expenditure anywhere releases holdings of money which permit an increase of expenditure somewhere else. Fiscal policy then is helpless, and what is called for is monetary policy to increase or decrease the money supply. (Only kerosene can be used.) This case is then called the Classical Case, as if it were one in which the Keynesian theory does not apply and where model B should be replaced by model C* (which can burn kerosene). This case should more properly be called the Classical Special Case (of the Keynesian general theory). The Keynesian theory (model B) covers both situations in which fiscal policy is strategic (when model B uses gasoline), and situations in which monetary policy is strategic (when model B uses kerosene), as well as the more normal situations when both policies are effective (when model B can make use of both fuels, mixing the proportions to suit the terrain).

Model D is a genuinely different model, in which unemployment not only fails to make prices and wages fall quickly enough to serve as a cure for the unemployment, but is even unable to prevent prices and wages from continuing to rise. When we have strong trade unions with the power to raise wages, strong corporations with the power to set prices administratively, and a general atmosphere in which it is considered normal, natural and only fair for wages to be increased regularly, and by amounts greater than the average increase in productivity or in the share of the product that labor can obtain, prices increase, and the economy is subject to sellers' inflation. It is now no longer a question of whether fiscal policy or monetary policy is more effective in regulating the volume of buyers' demand or expenditure, since the inflation is caused not by excess buyers' demand, but by the existence of powerful institutions and mores that enable sellers to insist on and obtain continually higher prices. The widespread and generous feeling that workers are entitled to the increases in wages that they get is made much easier by a recognition that any raise need not be taken out of profits, since it is possible, as well as proper, to "pass it along" to the ultimate purchaser in higher prices. Indeed, it is usually considered only right that profits, in dollars, should be increased so as to protect real profits from the declining value of the dollar.

We have already mentioned the argument that a really firm refusal on the part of the monetary authorities to prevent the volume of money from increasing, no matter what happened, would bring the sellers to their senses. Realizing, or discovering, that they will not be able to sell so much if they raise their prices, they will refrain from raising prices, and they will not grant, or ask for, wage increases that raise costs by more than can be squeezed out of profits.

There are several reasons why this is not practical. In the first place, the policy of firmly or obstinately holding the money supply constant does not prevent excess buyers' demand from coming about. It does not even prevent an increase in total expenditure. This is because the policy of holding the money supply constant is essentially a kind of monetary policy, and we may be in the Keynesian special case where monetary policy is not effective. That we are at the present time in such a situation is suggested by the fact that, while the supply of money has been held fairly stable in recent years, the volume of expenditure has continually increased. (Another way of expressing this, which is more common perhaps because it sounds like an explanation, is to say that the velocity of circulation has increased and that this has frustrated the restrictive monetary policy.)

There is, of course, a limit to the degree to which expenditure can increase without an accompanying increase in the money stock, and if the inflation were a buyers' inflation it would come to an end when this limit was reached (i.e., when the velocity of circulation could not increase any more). But where the inflation is a sellers' inflation, it does not stop at that point. After the increase in prices has absorbed all the increase in expenditure that is compatible with a constant money stock (i.e., that can be attributed to an increase in the velocity of circulation) it continues to increase. The increase in prices goes on further until it has reduced real expenditure and employment sufficiently to overcome the institutional forces that enable sellers to demand higher and higher prices. The question is how strong are these institutions? Or, in other words, how severe a state of depression and unemployment would have to be maintained in order to destroy these institutions or to induce sellers not to use their power to raise prices; and how able and willing the authorities would be to bring about and maintain this degree of depression and unemployment?

The continuing increase in wages and prices in the present recession would be some indication that it would require quite a severe and prolonged depression to change people's notions of what is the proper development of wage rates (and of the corresponding prices, since the right of wages to increase goes together with the right of profits at least not to fall). It would take perhaps an even more severe level of unemployment to destroy the power of labor to force the wage increases on more reluctant employers who grant wage increases only when they feel they are forced to — i.e., that they would lose more from the strikes and other weapons of the trade unions than they would lose by agreeing to the higher wages (and passing them on).

At the same time, a policy of full employment seems to have won a firm place in the country's economic policy (even though its application may be rather shaky), not only because of the general acceptance of the desirability of prosperity, for human as well as for international political reasons, but because neither political party can afford the blame for even a mild depression. With such a setup, there is no need to worry whether the cure is worse than the disease — whether the depression would be more harmful than the inflation that it would prevent. This cure is not one that any government would carry out or even seriously attempt to carry out.

None of the problems of sellers' inflation or of inflationary depression could arise in a perfectly competitive economy, because in a perfectly competitive economy we cannot have the institutions and mores that give sellers the power to push prices up. In a perfectly competitive economy, all that is needed for stability of the price level is a monetary and fiscal policy to keep buyers' demand from becoming either excessive or deficient. No one holds back any product from the market — or can establish a price which results in some of the potential product or the available labor not being taken off the market, so that unless there is excess buyers' demand, prices cannot rise, and if there is a deficient buyers' demand, prices must fall. Unless there is full utilization of resources, we cannot have inflation, and if there is a depression (or recession), we will have deflation (i.e., falling prices). In a perfectly competitive economy, we cannot have inflation and depression at the same time.

But where prices are administered by decrees of large firms, and wages are administered by joint decrees of powerful unions, together with powerful employers or employer groups, the situation is different. Sellers' inflation is a by-product of the process; and, together with sellers' inflation, we can also have depression — indeed we will have depression with our sellers' inflation, just to the degree that the authorities try to cure the inflation by reducing ("excess") demand.

In an economy where there are both administered and competitive sectors, the phenomenon of sellers' inflation can spill over from the administered to the competitive part. It can even happen that the contagion of sellers' inflation in the competitive sector is more pronounced than in the administered sector. There is then a tendency to assume that the sellers' inflation thesis has thereby been disproved. Actually, this does not prove anything either way in the debate that can rage as to whether the inflation is a sellers' inflation or a buyers' inflation.

The contagion can be explained as follows. Prices and wages being raised in the administered sector but not in the competitive sector, there will be a switch in demand from the products of the administered sector to the products of the competitive sector. There is then a deficiency of demand in the administered sector and an excess of demand in the competitive sector. With factors of production immobile, there is unemployment in the administered sector, but there it does not cause either prices or wages to fall so that the unemployment persists. Attempts to reduce total spending, so as to check the rise in the overall price level, would increase still further the unemployment in the administered sector (while removing some, or all, of the excess demand in the competitive sector). Pressure is then put on the Government to alleviate the depression; and, in doing so, it must create enough demand to maintain the higher price level in both sectors.

As the economy gets used to such a process, in which wages and prices are rising all the time, an increase in strategic or key prices or wage rates in the administered sector come to be recognized all over the economy as presaging a general rise in prices. The competitive sector then does not wait for the excess demand to appear. Its workers demand higher wages, its employers expect to be able to get the higher prices out of which to be able to pay the higher wages, and they grant the increases and raise the prices. They do not have to go into the elaborate calculations of what output and price maximize profit. They have the businessman's rough rule of thumb of a more or less traditional markup on their cost. This brings them straight away to the position that would be reached after the excess demand has materialized and has been validated and adjusted by the monetary policy undertaken by the authorities to cure or prevent the unemployment threatened by the increase in wages and prices in the administered sector.

The economist is tempted to draw diagrams showing the point of maximum profits of a firm, competitive or monopolist, and to demonstrate, in classical vein, that an increase in wages will move that point to the left, reducing the optimum output of the firm and causing the firm to restrict output and to raise the price by less than the increase in cost. This should cause unemployment, which, in the competitive sector, would restore the previous price and wage levels. The sellers' inflation has disappeared into thin air.

The answer to this, in classical vein, is that the demand will not remain the same, because the phenomenon is not happening only to an individual firm (in which case it would be proper to assume the conditions of demand to be unchanged), but that the monetary and fiscal authorities, in providing additional overall demand to cure or prevent the unemployment in the administered sector, will raise every demand curve so that the firm will be able to sell as much as before and provide the same employment as before, even though the price is sufficiently higher to enable the higher wage to be paid. Profits, or the gap between cost and price, will also be higher, of course, although in real terms, allowing for the fall in the value of the dollar, everything will be just the same as in the beginning.

The answer in the businessman's language is that he has to increase his price in proportion to the increase in costs, in applying his regular markup; and his experience is that since this is happening to everybody, including his competitors, and employment in the country is more or less being maintained, he will be able to pass it on to the consumer.

Although the infection starts with the administered sector of the economy, there is no reason why the epidemic should not hit the competitive (and nonadministered monopolistic) sectors of the economy sometimes more severely and sometimes less severely than it hits the administered sector. This is why the observation that prices rise more or less in the unadministered sector than in the administered sector proves nothing at all either way as to whether the inflation is a buyers' inflation or a sellers' inflation. But only a sellers' inflation is compatible with a depression.

III. THE PRESCRIPTION

The inflation and the inflationary depression that result from administered wages and prices have important similarities to, and are no less socially harmful than, the monopolistic exploitation that would result from the administration of excessive prices by public utilities. We have gone a long way toward eliminating the latter evil by the regulation of prices that may be set by public utilities for the services they supply. The same kind of device can be used to eliminate the former evil. Just as the public utility prices can be and are being regulated so as to prevent monopolistic exploitation, so administered prices and wages can and should be regulated, so as to prevent sellers' inflation and the depression it may bring with it.

The regulation of administered prices and wages so as to prevent sellers' inflation would have to follow somewhat different lines. It would not be directly concerned as to whether there is more than or less than a fair rate of return on investments. That would be left to the strong competitive forces that still prevail in our economy. Nor would any other regulations whatsoever be involved other than price regulation. The function of the regulation here proposed would be only to prevent restrictive prices or wages from being administered. A restrictive price is one that results in the demand for a product falling below capacity output. A restrictive wage is one that results in less than full employment in the specific labor market to which it applies. With a monetary and fiscal policy concentrating on the maintenance of adequate buyers' demand for full employment at a constant price level, while preventing buyers' inflation, it would be possible for wages per hour to rise on the average at the same rate as productivity per hour, with aggregate profits rising too at the same pace as aggregate wages and aggregate output (except that increases in the degree of competition, which might be induced, could reduce the share going to profits and increase the share going to labor).

The regulatory body would therefore have to follow a set of rules which would do the following things:

(1) They would permit an administered price increase only when production and sales are at capacity. Such price increases should not be withheld on account of profits being high.

(2) They would enforce decreases in administered prices whenever production and sales are significantly below capacity. A price decrease should not be waived on account of profits being low, or even negative on this item in the firm's output, as long as the price more than

covers current operating costs (more strictly, short period marginal costs).

(3) They would permit increases in administered wages in general at a rate equal to the average trend of increase in national productivity.

(4) They would permit increases in administered wages greater than this wherever the labor market is tight — with say less than half the national average rate of unemployment.

(5) They would permit only smaller increases in administered wages, or no increases at all, where the labor market is slack — with say more than twice the national average rate of unemployment. (The expected continuing increase in product per head makes it possible to avoid reductions in money wages although it is unavoidable, for price stability, that some prices must fall if others rise.)

This is, of course, not a fully worked out solution ready for immediate application. There remains much to be developed — such as generally acceptable criteria of capacity of different firms and industries and generally acceptable measures of slackness or tightness in particular labor markets, or measures for dealing with possible attempts by monopolistic industries to restrict the installation of capacity, if they are prevented from restricting the utilization of existing capacity. (This would bring out the existence of a specific monopoly situation that calls for treatment quite apart from the problem of inflation.) The intensification of competition which the regulation would enforce would also, in some instances, lead to the elimination of high cost competitors. While the public would benefit from the increased efficiency of the economy — in higher wages and lower prices — such elimination of competition would conflict with certain existing so-called antitrust policies that have become in effect anticompetition policies and need to be reconsidered.

There remain also important problems of organization and administration of the regulatory body, as well as the need for widespread and intensive public discussion to bring about the familiarity with, and the understanding of, the nature of the proposed regulation which is essential for its effective operation in a democracy. And in the course of such examination and debate, important developments, changes and improvements are to be expected. Nevertheless, the general lines indicated seem to be inevitable if sellers' inflation is to be attacked directly and if we are not to depend on irrelevant nostrums or pious exhortation because we do not dare to attack the problem at its roots.

4 2

ADMINISTERED PRICES AND MONETARY-FISCAL POLICY

*John K. Galbraith**

Professor Galbraith has adopted the concept of cost-push inflation in a modified form. While most economists see cost-inflation as basically due to wage increases in excess of productivity gains and place primary causation at the door of powerful unions, Professor Galbraith places a great share of the responsibility at the door of large corporations possessing substantial monopoly power and able to raise their prices without regard to potential competition.

The following selection consists of Professor Galbraith's testimony before the Subcommittee on Antitrust and Monopoly in 1957 (Part I of the selection) and in 1959 (Part II). In the first part he discusses the effects of an anti-inflationary monetary policy on small as compared with large firms; in the second part he discusses the general problem of inflation and its remedies. In both parts the concept of "administered prices" by large corporations figures prominently.

I.†

The inflation of recent years has been paralleled by the more or less equally persistent hope that it might be controlled by monetary measures — by higher interest rates and a tighter supply of loanable funds. It has been assumed, generally speaking, that this policy will operate uniformly across the economic system. Borrowing will be checked more or less equally in all industries. Within the individual industry, to be sure, the "least credit-worthy borrower" will be the first to lose his line of credit. But he is assumed to be the natural child of misfortune.

Farmers, residential builders, independent dealers, and other smaller businessmen have complained particularly about the tight money policy. This, I believe it fair to say, has been attributed not to any special effect of the policy on these groups, but to their inborn tendency to chronic complaint.

Banks and larger business enterprises have, with rare exceptions, approved of the tight money policy. This has been attributed, not to any preferential position under the policy, but to a higher order of industrial statesmanship, a more accurate perception of the needs of the situation, or a greater willingness to make the required sacrifices, or possibly to endure while others did so.

Closer examination shows, however, that discrimination in the effect of monetary policy is not only likely but almost certainly inevita-

* Harvard University.

† Statement submitted to the Subcommittee on Antitrust and Monopoly of the Committee on the Judiciary, United States Senate, on July 11, 1957. Reprinted by the courtesy of the author.

ble. The difference is between those industries in which individual firms have a greater or less degree of control over the prices that they charge and those industries in which there is no control. The Kansas wheat farmer or the Wisconsin dairyman has no control over the price of the product which he sells. His price is given to him by the market. If the wheat farmer or dairyman prices his product above the market, he simply does not sell it. If he prices at less than the market, he forgoes a return he might have had. So he must always take the market price. All of his operations are subordinate and subject to that market price. The same is true in only slightly lesser degree for the small dealer, the home builder, and the small retailer. Their prices (or margins) are also given to them by the market.

It is equally plain that in other industries prices are subject to a greater or less control by individual firms. A fortnight ago the United States Steel Corp. raised the price of steel. No one, least of all the corporation itself, doubted its ability to do so and to make the price stick. This power over prices — the plenary power to set them within a considerable range — is commonplace over the great range of industrial enterprise. Its roots are complex, but the essentials are clear and reasonably well agreed among students of the subject.

In one form or another the firms of an industry will enjoy measurable discretion over their prices whenever the number of such firms in the particular market is fairly small or where one or two firms have a large share of that market and are able to exercise a strong price leadership that other firms follow. A moment's reflection will persuade one that these conditions are normal to a great number of industries — steel, automobiles, rubber, aluminum, most chemicals, nickel, refinery products — and it will be equally obvious that these conditions are not normal in agriculture, home building, or other small-scale enterprise where firms are small and very numerous.

The analysis of the effect of this ability to administer the prices of an industry has been greatly handicapped by the conviction that it is somehow improper. Actually, such administration is not only possible but also inevitable when an industry is in the hands of a relatively small number of firms. And it is equally inevitable that a great many industries will be conducted by a comparatively small number of large firms. That is the nature of capitalism wherever it is found. A large amount of price administration by private firms is thus part of the system. Those who deplore it are wasting their breath. The problem is to understand it and to live with it.

I come now to the effect of monetary policy in industries where prices are administered as compared with those industries where prices are subject to full determination by the market. Steel may be thought of as an example of the first type of situation and most agriculture as an example of the second. (The existence of price supports for some products does not especially affect the argument. Prices are still beyond the control of the individual farmer.)

Although there is a highly developed case to the contrary, monetary policy invokes neither supernatural processes nor even black magic. To the extent that it is effective as an antidote to inflation, it cuts down on the total volume of spending. This it accomplishes by raising interest rates and cutting down on the supply of funds available for lending. As the result of the higher interest rates and the lesser availability of loans, it is hoped that business firms and consumer-borrowers will borrow less and ultimately invest, which is to say spend, less. With less business investment — spending for business plant and machinery — and less spending of borrowed funds by consumers, there will, it is hoped, be less pressure on markets and less tendency for prices to rise. This is the essential theory of monetary policy.

The first impact of this policy is the higher interest rate. Plainly the impact of this will be very different on a firm that has control over its prices and hence can pass along this higher cost as compared with the firm whose prices are given and which, accordingly, must bear the cost itself. The point need not be labored. The United States Steel Corporation justified its price increases of two weeks ago by the contention that its costs had risen. In doing so it not only conceded its ability to pass higher costs, including higher interest charges, to the consumer but based its policy on the need to do so. But no such opportunity is open to the farmer or to the smaller businessman. They cannot raise their prices, for these are market-determined. They themselves shoulder the costs of the policy.

The second impact of monetary policy is through the rationing of credit. This involves denying loans in whole or in part to some borrowers. By common agreement these are "the least creditworthy" of the clients of the bank. As I have earlier suggested, it is commonly assumed that these uncreditworthy borrowers are more or less randomly distributed about the economy and between industries. We may feel sorry for them, but they have selected themselves for trouble by their weakness, and that is the law of life.

But it will now be evident that this view is too bland. Firms in those industries that are able, by the nature of the market, to pass interest costs along will, in the nature of things, be a better credit risk than firms in those industries which bear the pinch of monetary policy. Monetary policy makes certain industries uncreditworthy while not similarly touching others. Moreover, in the administered price markets firms are likely to be larger than those in the market-controlled industries. If firms are numerous in a market, they are likely to be small. The large firm with large and predictable credit needs and with multiple bank connections will usually have a better position in the queue, when credit is being rationed, than the small borrower.

Finally, the large firm in the administered price industry has an alternative to bank credit. Should the banks have difficulty supplying its needs, it can have resort to the money market. If its price position is really strong, it can increase its current revenue and finance operations and expansion out of these. Steel firms have repeatedly used the need for investment funds as the defense of their price policy. No such course is open to the firm whose prices are controlled by the market. If it cannot control its prices, it cannot raise them to get funds it is unable to borrow.

The conclusion from the foregoing follows: Monetary policy — the effort to control infla-

tion through restriction of credit — operates with particular impact on the market-controlled or most purely competitive sector of the economy. This means agriculture, small business, residential building, and so forth. It touches far more lightly, or may even exempt, firms, usually the larger ones, in markets where numbers are small and prices are administered.

This analysis leads to conclusions on two problems of current import. It raises questions as to the efficacy of present monetary policy in preventing inflation. That things are not going well here will surely not be denied very much longer. The old-fashioned test of success of a policy is results. As monetary policy has been applied with steady rigor the companion effect, so far, has been a steady increase in prices. Price stability, if one may coin a phrase, has remained just around the corner. If monetary policy works for only a part of the economy, this is a plausible explanation of its failure. And as the figures show, the dominant industrial sector of the economy has been able to increase its investment sharply at a time when credit policy was presumed to be restricting it. One has difficulty under these circumstances only in deciding why it is expected that the policy should be succeeding.

The second conclusion concerns the broader social wisdom of a policy which functions as does this one. Capital formation is the substance of economic growth; it is the thing of which growth is made. Monetary policy restrains the economic growth, in general, of farmers and smaller business firms while not perceptibly discouraging that of larger firms with a stronger market position. The policy may even, the figures suggest, be giving to the latter what it denies to the former. Larger firms are getting the credit which is denied to the smaller firms.

II.*

During the last 2 years, if I sense matters correctly, there has been an increasing mea-

* Statement submitted to Subcommittee on Antitrust and Monopoly of the Committee on the Judiciary, United States Senate, on March 11, 1959. Reprinted by the courtesy of the author.

sure of agreement on the causes of inflation and the logic of its remedies. Evasion of the more awkward conclusions is still possible and it is still practiced, but increasingly the hard core of the problem is showing through. The visible and inescapable bones of the problem can be described briefly and, on a matter where words are so often used to obscure meaning, there is a positive advantage in brevity.

First of all, let me lay down the primary economic and political condition which controls any useful discussion of this problem. This is the overriding importance of high employment. The opportunity for a job and the income that goes with it come first in our thinking on economic policy. This is understandable. Unemployment is rarely considered desirable or healthy by those who have experienced it and for most people it remains the major misfortune, the major risk of our economic society. High employment is also related to a high rate of economic growth, and vice versa. High output is an inducement to investment. Low output and idle plant capacity reduce the incentive to investment. This is a point which I would like to emphasize and underline. The strongest possible inducement to plant expansion — to growth — is to have existing plant operating at or near capacity, and those who argue for reducing the rate of use of capacity as a measure of inflation control are inevitably arguing for some reduction in the rate of economic expansion.

It follows from what I have just said that no policy designed to promote the stabilization of prices has any chance of permanent success if it depends, either directly or indirectly, on deliberately continued unemployment. It is my own hope that sooner or later, we will do something to remove both the stigma and the economic penalties which are associated with involuntary unemployment. When this is done we shall be committed to less stringent goals of economic management and full employment may well cease to be such a social imperative as now. But it is equally clear that we haven't accomplished this reform yet — and won't for some time. Those who recommend such policies may get a certain amount of applause for

their soundness and for their courage in committing other people to misfortune. This should not be confused with popular approval.

Next, we must be clear that at high employment, prices in the American economy — or more particularly, in one important sector of it — are not stable. Structural defects exist in the design of economic systems as they exist in machines. There is such a defect in our system. We do not remove it either by pretending that it doesn't exist or by horrified denunciation of those who point it out.

In that sector of the economy where firms are large and the control over prices is substantial, there is opportunity for large discretionary increases in prices when demand is favorable. The demand that is favorable to high employment is favorable to such discretionary price action. There is a powerful motive for the use of this price discretion whenever wages are raised. So the increase in wages is covered by a price increase — usually with something more. So long as demand is at or so long as it is near full employment levels, we must expect that, in industries characterized by relatively small numbers of strong firms and strong unions, prices and wages will react on each other in a steady upward spiral.

Even with considerable idle capacity, the spiral will continue in some industries, the leading case, of course, being steel. In fact, commodity inflation, that is, nonservice inflation, since the late forties is largely accounted for by the increase in prices of steel, steel products, machinery, automobiles, pulp and paper, rubber, tobacco, and beverages. These, in general, are the concentrated industries. Prices of textiles and apparel and most importantly of food and agricultural products have contributed little to the inflation.

And, generally, when the index has been stable, this is a very important point, it has not been because of stability in the concentrated industries, but because of the offsetting effect of falling prices in the unconcentrated industries.

The remedies follow with certain obstinacy from the diagnosis. The possible courses of action are four, only four, and they are as follows:

(1) Do nothing.

(2) Rely on monetary or fiscal measures or a combination of the two.

(3) Break up the large corporations, presumably also the unions.

(4) Design some direct approach to the problem of wage and price setting in the concentrated industries which will insure that these are noninflationary.

Let us review now each of these possible courses of action.

To do nothing is, of course, to accept inflation. There are a few forthright supporters of this position. There are a great many more indirect or unconscious advocates who oppose all available courses of action or hope that the problem will yield to a combination of prayer, incantation, and admonition. To do nothing is not a tolerable choice. Let us reflect very well and carefully on the kind of inflation we are talking about. It is led by the prices of the largest and strongest firms. It is paced more or less by the wages of the larger and stronger unions. Those who suffer, it follows, are the weaker firms and weaker unions. Also the public servants, schoolteachers, and unorganized workers who usually do not have effective bargaining power. And also the retired and the aged who have no real bargaining position at all in the economy.

Those who endorse an inflation of this modern sort are therefore endorsing a policy of giving the most to the biggest and strongest and the least to the smallest and weakest. This is not the whole case against inflation. But this point must be seen with all clarity. The modern inflation is not neutral. Because of its inherent identification with economic strength, it is inequitable, regressive, and reactionary. As I have elsewhere put the matter, under inflation countervailing power ceases to regulate relations between groups. Thus public interest becomes all but certain.

Now we come to monetary and fiscal policy which do not make contact with present forms of inflation, at least in a useful or practical way. The administered price sector can advance its prices and does whenever the economy is close to full capacity and employment.

We have seen that the level of use of capacity and the level of employment depends on the level of demand for goods. Both monetary policy and fiscal policy make contact with this problem by reducing the level of demand. To be effective, they must reduce, therefore, the level of demand enough to create idle capacity and unemployment since the inflation occurs when idle capacity and unemployment are not present in substantial amount.

But a policy of creating idle capacity and unemployment collides with the higher objective of full employment and full use of capacity. We set higher store by these, as I have stressed, than we do by price stability; therefore we cannot have policies which seek price stability by increasing unemployment, by reducing demand. Let me say in this connection that monetary policy, under all circumstances, is a secondary instrument of public policy. Nothing has been more salutary than our discovery — or more properly, our rediscovery — in the last few years that there is no subtle monetary magic here by which an economy can be guided and directed. The less reliance we place on monetary policy, as a broad rule, the better off we will be.

The case of tax and expenditure policy is somewhat different. To say that fiscal policy — the purposeful use of taxes and expenditures to influence the level of economic activity — will not of itself bring stabilization at full employment, is not to say that fiscal policy is unimportant. When there is unemployment and idle capacity, an excess of Government expenditures over receipts is by far the surest way of expanding economic activity. Then we should have a deficit — let us not duck the hard words here — and when output and employment are high, the budget should be balanced. But even though a balanced budget does not insure price stability at full employment it is one of the conditions necessary for stability at full employment. Budget balancing, I think we should always add, does not necessarily mean reducing expenditures. If the services that are needed by the community exceed the revenues produced at full employment demand, then the proper course is to raise taxes.

Now, the position so far is this: At or near full employment, we shall have inflation in the concentrated industries. Monetary and fiscal policy can be a remedy only by severely cutting back output and employment, and this remedy is worse than the disease.

The third possibility is to break up the large corporations and perhaps also the large unions. Can we not enforce the antitrust laws with all vigor and extend them somehow to the unions? The antitrust laws serve a valuable purpose in our economy. They bring the conscience of the community to bear on the problem of economic power. For this reason they restrain the strong firm in its relation with its weaker competitors, or its suppliers, or its customers. It is for this reason that they have always had a strong claim on the interest of men of moral sense. The antitrust laws could be stronger and better enforced than they are.

But to suppose that the antitrust laws will work the kind of revolution which will reconcile full employment with price stability is out of the question. This would mean a wholesale revision in industrial structure — a wholesale disintegration of existing business units. Even though desirable, there is not the slightest indication from the legal history that the antitrust laws are the instrument for such a revolution. As applied to industry, the policy would be politically divisive. And, needless to say, the application to unions would provide a field day for those who would think the attack on inflation was a wonderful excuse for an attack on labor organization as such.

So I would conclude and this I would argue with considerable vigor — that there is no hope for an inflation remedy in the antitrust laws. To argue that there is may be to engender doubts about the effectiveness of the antitrust laws for the other very important purposes which they serve.

So, only one course of action remains. This is some form of public intervention in the part of the economy where full employment or an approach to full employment means inflationary price and wage increases. Such intervention, when it comes, will not be the result of advocacy by me or by any particular individual; it will be because of the absence of alternatives.

We are coming to accept the need for such intervention. A recent survey of professional economists by the Joint Economic Committee shows that between 40 and 50 per cent of those interviewed or surveyed accepted the need for wage and price regulation as at least a reserve weapon against inflation. It can be assumed that economists have not come to this conclusion very willingly.

What is perhaps more striking is the way the need for such intervention is implicit in the philosophy and economic pronouncements of the present administration. The administration has warned repeatedly that restraint is essential in wage and price making. The last Economic Report of the President says, in remarkably categoric language:

Increases in money wages and other compensation not justified by the productivity performance of the economy are *inevitably* inflationary.

It adds:

Self-discipline and restraint *are essential* if reasonable stability of prices is to be reached within the framework of free competitive institutions. . . . [Italic added.]

Apart, perhaps, from its tendency to single out wages for special attention, the only difference one need have with the administration is its belief that the problem can be solved by such warnings. This, of course, is fantastic.

As Prof. Ben W. Lewis has said in his wise and amusing testimony before this committee, these unstructured admonitions have a perfect record of accomplishing nothing. One cannot imagine that the economists serving the President believe such warnings will work, and one wonders if they really wish to stake their professional reputations on the success of such a feeble course of policy.

And I would suggest, Mr. Chairman, at some juncture some committee address a communication to Dr. Saulnier and to his colleagues on the Council of Economic Advisers and ask them if they are willing, as a professional matter, to state whether they believe that these admonitions that are issued in general terms every year, really work or are expected to work. If not, then they should stop issuing them.

I would like to say, in my view these admonitions reflect only the appalling tendency of our time for words to become not a portent of action, but a substitute for it. But I would also point out that if one asks for effective action instead of futile admonition, the economic philosophy of the Eisenhower administration brings one abruptly and inescapably to the issue of what we do, or the issue of controls.

Let me now suggest, as we enter upon discussion of such intervention, two or three of the principles that I would say should govern our policy in this area. We should recognize, first, that this should be a limited intervention. There is no need for intervention where there is nothing wrong. As we have seen, apparel prices, food prices, many other prices, are not administered and are not a source of inflationary pressure under the circumstances of which we are speaking. On occasion, declines in these series have offset increases elsewhere, to bring an illusory appearance of stability. Therefore, there is no need to intervene. The control of demand, the regulation of demand which is implicit in the notion of having a balanced budget at full employment and, therefore, not adding to the inflation, will still take care of this sector. We should beware of the man who says, "If you control anything, you must control everything." That will be to do nothing at all, and this may sometimes be his aim.

Second, the machinery should be simple and its aim should be restraint and not rigid price and wage fixing. We are seeking to remove the inflationary effect of large increases in prices that are now at the discretion of steel, machinery, automotive, and other producers in the concentrated industries. And we are seeking to prevent wage increases in excess of what can be absorbed from requiring or being the excuse for such price advances. We can fall far short of perfection in this effort and still improve vastly on the present situation. The present situation, to repeat, allows at full employment for large discretionary increases without any restraint of any kind. If we insist on perfection in this effort, we shall probably also end up doing nothing.

Third, the effort to achieve stability should, if at all possible, be carried on in a conciliatory spirit. Our problem is that the economy is not stable, its prices are not stable at or near full employment. The task is to correct a fault in the system and not to assess blame.

The actual procedures will require discussion and it is worth hoping that this will get underway promptly. Desirable procedure — and my purpose is not to be dogmatic but to give a concrete image of what I have in mind — will, I think, involve some kind of official finding each year as to the wages advances that can be afforded within a framework of stable prices. (If the recent admonitions had no other fault, the total lack of a statement of what is expected is sufficient to render them worthless.)

This finding of the advances which are generally consistent with the increase in productivity should, of course, be after full hearings and full discussion. Perhaps then, since the situation in each industry will be different, there might be tripartite committees representing labor, management, and the public to deal in decentralized fashion with the application of the standards to particular industries. If a new collective-bargaining agreement required no price increases and none occurred, there would be no action of any sort.

Were it claimed that a price increase were required in steel, machinery, automobiles, or elsewhere, this claim would come before the committee for investigation and finding of fact. Certainly in the beginning the sanctions for noncompliance should be mild and with reliance on the force of public opinion.

However, we should always have in mind that too easy acceptance of noncooperation is discrimination against the man who does cooperate. We should also remind ourselves that the constant chase of wages by prices and prices by wages, which is our present situation, or which has been our situation in much of the time since World War II, is calculated to keep labor-management negotiations in a state of turmoil. The overall objective which we are seeking here is to eliminate price inflation. To take this factor of price inflation out of industrial relations would, in turn, greatly simplify and regularize union-management negotiation.

43

HOW BAD IS INFLATION?*

Sumner H. Slichter†

Thus far we have assumed that inflation is "bad." But possibly a little bit of inflation, a slow creeping inflation of perhaps 2 or 3 per cent a year, is the price we must pay if we are to have full employment and adequate economic growth.

I.

"The recent decline in consumer spending," said a conference of distinguished Americans, "is only a lull in a continuing inflation that threatens the stability of the national economy and the security of the entire Western world." This view of inflation is typical of hundreds of statements that have been made during the past few years. It reflects the uncritical and almost hysterical fear that the thought of inflation arouses in a large part of the community. It also reflects failure to see some of the problems that confront the country and that can be solved best through a slow rise in prices.

It is, of course, true that extreme inflation is disastrous, and that many countries have experienced it during the past thirty years. The great inflation in Germany in the early twenties is the one that is best known in this country. Not only did the German inflation wipe out the savings of millions of people but it badly reduced the efficiency of the economy. When prices are doubling every few weeks or less, as they were doing in Germany, no one can afford to take time to plan his expenditures carefully. The lack of careful planning was especially wasteful in the case of outlays for machinery and buildings.

But the extreme sort of inflation experienced by Germany is not easily started, and it is not likely to occur here. To produce the German type of inflation there must be lack of faith in the capacity of the government to perform the ordinary job of governing. What is likely to happen in the United States is a *slow* rise in prices — a rise interrupted frequently by small or moderate recessions, but nevertheless a rise. Of course, even a small increase of 2 per cent or 3 per cent a year, though hardly enough to be noticed at any given moment, is sufficient to cause substantial injustice. For example, a rise of only 2 per cent a year will reduce the purchasing power of the dollar by 45 per cent in thirty years, so that the pension or life insurance that one started to buy in one's youth will have lost nearly half its purchasing power before one has reached the age of retirement.

The obvious injustices of even a slow long-term rise in prices lead many people to insist that such a rise must be prevented — that nothing but a stable price level will be satisfactory. At the risk of being called an irresponsible and dangerous thinker, let me say that in the kind of economy possessed by the United States a slowly rising price level is actually preferable to a stable price level. The reason for this conclusion is that the maintenance of a stable price level would conflict with other important interests of the country. For example, the maintenance of a stable price level in the long run would require that the country considerably relax its efforts to keep business recessions as mild as possible. Furthermore, the maintenance of a stable price level would require the acceptance of chronic unemployment or drastic intervention by the government in the relations between employers and employees. Finally, the policies necessary to keep prices stable would severely handicap the United States in its efforts to contain communism by building up the economies of the free world.

The champions of a stable price level do

* *Harper's Magazine*, August, 1952. Reprinted by the courtesy of the executors of the estate of the late Professor Slichter.
† Professor Slichter of Harvard University died in 1959.

not seem to be aware of the conflicts between the goal which they advocate and other desirable goals. Indeed, they are so impressed by the injustices caused by inflation that they fail to see that serious injustices would have to be imposed in order to keep the price level stable — injustices even greater than those which would accompany a slowly rising price level. Let us look more closely at the reasons for believing that a slowly rising price level is preferable to a stable one.

II.

Suppose that the desire of the people of the United States to raise their standard of consumption were so strong that the demand for goods slightly exceeded the supply of goods. The productive capacity of industry would be fully used. Practically every man, woman, and child who wished to work would have a job, enterprises as a whole would not lack for customers, and there would be a strong incentive for industry to enlarge its capacity. Would this be a bad state of affairs? I do not believe that most people would regard it as bad. They like demand to be large enough to strain the productive capacity of industry and to provide jobs for all job seekers. *And yet the situation that I have described would be inflationary.* The excess of demand over supply would cause prices to creep upward.

In a vigorous and dynamic economy in which consumers are eager to live better, and in which producers are good at bringing out new and improved articles and have efficient sales organizations, the situation that I have described is likely to exist for much of the time. But these periods of vigorous demand, in which the price level usually rises slowly, are interrupted from time to time by business recessions. When sales start to fall off, should the community stand aside and let the recession develop without restraint? Or should the community take vigorous steps to combat the depression and to keep it as mild as possible?

Everyone knows today that the country will not tolerate a policy of doing nothing about recessions. And in the divided world of today, in which every recession in business gives oppor-

tunities for Communist activity, it is imperative that the United States avoid severe or even moderate recessions. Since this country is such a large part of the world's economy, producing about 40 per cent of the world's goods and consuming nearly as much, even a moderate drop in business here would dangerously disrupt the economies of other free countries.

But the policy of keeping recessions as mild as possible is incompatible with the ideal of long-run stability of the price level. In order for the price level to remain stable in the long run, the fall in prices that accompanies each recession must be great enough to cancel out the rise in prices during the preceding boom. If the country halts each recession fairly promptly, prices will not fall sufficiently to wipe out the rise of the former boom. Hence each revival of business will start from a higher price level than the previous revival, and the long-term movement of prices will be slowly upward. Although a slow climb of prices would create injustice by diminishing the purchasing power of pensions, insurance, and some savings, let us not overlook the fact that recessions also create injustice. A drop in prices sufficiently severe to cancel the rise of prices in the preceding boom would be accompanied by severe unemployment. People who were eager and able to work would have to remain idle while the demand for goods was being allowed to drop until some earlier price level had been restored. Hence the cost of long-run stability of prices would be the unnecessary unemployment and loss of output that accompany recessions sufficiently severe to cancel the price rise of the previous booms.

III.

The problem of a wise price policy is complicated by the rise of powerful trade unions in recent years. The bargaining power of unions naturally varies with the demand for goods and labor. At some point short of full employment the bargaining power of most unions becomes so great that they are able to push up money wages faster than the engineers and managers can increase output per man-hour. The ability of unions to raise money wages is enhanced by stiff taxes upon corporate profits.

Since a large part of any wage advance would diminish the tax liability of the employer, and to that extent cost him nothing, his incentive to resist the wage demands of unions is weakened.

The ability of unions to raise wages faster than the engineers and managers raise output per man-hour confronts the community with two more or less unpleasant possibilities. One possibility is that the rise in labor costs might come out of profits instead of being passed on in the form of higher prices. But the number of men that employers are willing to hire depends upon their success in making money. Hence a drop in profits would mean fewer jobs and more unemployment. The increase in unemployment would weaken the bargaining power of unions. After unemployment had reached a certain level, probably around 4 or 5 per cent of the labor force, the unions would not be able to raise wages faster than the average advance in output per man-hour. Hence rising wages would no longer produce an increase in labor costs and unemployment. The community, however, would get stable labor costs only by sacrificing the output of several million men — that is, by accepting a lower standard of living.

Another possibility is that the community might attempt to protect itself against rising labor costs by placing legal restrictions on collective bargaining. Such restrictions would be most difficult to enforce, and they would, of course, involve much sacrifice of freedom on the part of both employees and employers. Most people would probably regard this remedy as worse than the disease.

Confronted with the unpleasant choice of chronic unemployment or government regulation of collective bargaining, the community is likely to decide that prices should be encouraged to rise sufficiently to offset the rise in labor costs. This policy would mean a slowly rising price level and all of the injustices that go with it. It would, however, enable the community to avoid the disadvantages of chronic unemployment or of government regulation of collective bargaining.

Cannot ways be developed of limiting the bargaining power of unions so that free collective bargaining would be preserved but so that unions would be unable to impose a cost inflation on the community? I have seen no promising proposals. The prohibition of industry-wide bargaining, which has been suggested, would probably hurt employers more than unions. The Swedish trade unions are now wrestling with the tendency for collective bargaining to inflate labor costs and thus indirectly to inflate prices. The Swedish unions are proposing tax changes which, they hope, will stiffen the resistance of employers to the unions' wage demands. Their proposals do not seem to me to be very promising, but the fact that the unions have made them is significant. It may seem startling for unions to attempt to build up the bargaining power of employers — but the union leaders are faced with a novel problem. They find that agreements among unions to practice restraint in pressing for higher wages break down after several years, and neither the leaders nor the members like the tendency for rising wages to push up prices.

IV.

A stable price level, or the conditions that accompany it, would handicap the United States in its efforts to unite the free nations of the world against communism and to make these nations prosper so that communism cannot flourish within their borders. Ever since the end of the war, the United States has been giving economic aid in large volume to the rest of the world. Everyone realizes, of course, that economic aid is a stopgap. It is not satisfactory to either giver or receiver. In the long run it strains the generosity of the giver. Even more important, it is inconsistent with the dignity and independence of the receivers. The large grants of foreign aid by the United States must be replaced within several years by something else, and it is obvious what this "something else" must be. To some extent it can be investments by this country in other lands, but in the main, it must be greatly increased imports by the United States from other countries.

The needed rise of imports into the United States is about $4 billion or $5 billion a year. This is the increase in sales to us which would enable other countries to continue to purchase from us as much as they have recently been buying. Foreign countries can supply a multitude of goods that enterprises and consumers in this country would gladly buy — iron ore, aluminum, copper, machine tools, scientific instruments, gloves, lemons, cameras, toys, fish, cheese, hams, china, fine worsteds, silverware, glassware, fine furniture, wines and spirits, motorcycles, bicycles, and many other things. And the influx of a wide variety of foreign-made goods is precisely what the American system of free enterprise needs in order to make it still more competitive, still more enterprising, and still more dynamic.

But will American businessmen, farmers, and workers tolerate a large rise in imports? Are they willing to let the rest of the world sell to us as much as it buys from us? During the last year there have been disturbing signs that they will not. Last year Congress imposed quotas on foreign-made cheese. Furthermore, the Trade Agreements Extension Act of last summer requires the Tariff Commission to investigate applications from domestic industries for relief from injury by foreign competition. Fifteen industries have applied for such relief. A member of the Senate has proposed that all imports of commodities containing materials which are controlled by allocations to industrial users in the United States shall be restricted by quota to half of the pre-Korean War level. The idea behind this proposal is to impose on foreign sellers a handicap roughly equivalent to the handicap imposed on American producers by the limited availability of certain materials. The proposed restriction, however, is so drastic that it would undo all the gains made by most countries in building up their sales to the United States in the past two years and more.

The proposals to limit imports into the United States must be good news to Russia. They come at the very time when Russia is endeavoring to tempt European countries to trade with her by offering to buy part of the output of their depressed consumer-goods industries. The United Nations' technicians estimate that the percentage increase in industrial production during the last year was consider-

ably greater in Russia than in the United States. As Russia gains in capacity to produce, she will be able to offer more attractive trade deals to the countries of Western Europe. The United States must be ready to match these Russian offers — in fact, it should anticipate them by encouraging a large increase in sales by Western Europe (and Japan and other countries as well) to the United States. One can easily envisage the enormous good will this country would gain in Britain, France, Western Germany, Belgium, Italy, the Netherlands, Japan, and other countries by enlarging its purchases from them by several billion dollars a year.

A large rise in imports by the United States from the rest of the world is not simply something that would be desirable. It must actually happen; it must be the cornerstone of American economic policy. More imports by us are necessary to replace the inevitable reduction in our aid to other countries and to offset the more and more attractive trading opportunities Russia will be able to offer to Europe, Japan, and other regions. Americans should understand plainly that without a large increase in imports the foreign policy of the United States lacks a solid economic foundation.

How can a substantial rise in imports be brought about? Several steps are needed. One of them certainly is to maintain such a strong demand for the output of domestic industry that growing imports will not seriously disturb businessmen and will not greatly arouse American protectionism. But a strong demand for goods here means at least a slowly rising level. Hence the success of American foreign policy requires the kind of market conditions that produce a slow advance in prices.

V.

Is not a slowly rising price level bound soon to become a galloping inflation? If people expect prices to rise, will they not prefer to own goods rather than cash, bank deposits, mortgages, or bonds? As more and more people attempt to shift from money and fixed dollar assets into goods, will not the price level increase faster than before, and will not this faster rise stimulate still more people to buy goods, real estate, and stocks? Hence is not even a creeping rise in prices dangerous?

It is true that all extreme inflations started out as slow and creeping ones, but it is not true that a slow advance in prices easily becomes a rapid rise. One reason is that the prospect of a general increase in prices does not mean that the price of any particular article will rise. Hence the expectation of a general advance may not be effective in getting people to buy specific goods. A second reason is that styles are constantly changing and goods are constantly being improved. Each of these conditions limits buying in advance of needs. A third reason is that the purchases by enterprises and individuals are restricted at all times by uncertainties concerning the size of their future incomes. Finally, and most important, both business concerns and individuals are limited in buying by the size of their present incomes. Enterprises and individuals may go into debt in order to spend more than their incomes, but willingness to incur debt is limited, and the increase in indebtedness can be controlled by proper credit policies. Hence, with reasonably strict credit policies, the rate at which prices rise can be controlled.

These remarks make plain that when I point out that the goal of stable prices conflicts with other desirable goals and that the country has problems which can best be solved by permitting a slow rise in prices, I am not opposing all efforts to control inflation. Indeed, the more successfully the country checks recessions, the more willing it must be to keep the rise of prices during booms to the minimum required by rising labor costs. Hence successful fights against recessions increase the need for strict credit policies during booms. Today the federal government is pursuing an inexcusably lax policy toward the danger of inflation. Just as the expanding defense program is about to raise the outlays of the government substantially above its income, the government has terminated the controls on installment credit and relaxed the controls on real-estate credit.

Although a slowly rising price level will cause substantial injustice, the magnitude of the injustice should not be exaggerated. People will be able to protect the purchasing power of most of their savings by investing in real estate and stocks, and by keeping their savings banks accounts to a minimum. Mutual funds offer the small saver a way of diversifying his investment in stocks. The cost of life insurance and pensions will, of course, be considerably increased because, if prices rise, people will need more insurance and larger pensions. More than offsetting these injustices, however, will be the avoidance of the unemployment that is necessary in order to keep prices stable. The net advantage to the country of a slowly-rising price level over a stable one is the greater amount of employment, and hence the greater amount of production and the higher standard of consumption, that are made possible by a slowly advancing price level.

44

ANALYTICAL ASPECTS OF ANTI-INFLATION POLICY*

Paul A. Samuelson† and Robert M. Solow†

This selection, by two of the most distinguished economists in the United States, summarizes the issues and the alternatives in anti-inflation policy.

I.

Just as generals are said to be always fighting the wrong war, economists have been accused of fighting the wrong inflation. Thus, at the time of the 1946–48 rise in American prices, much attention was focused on the successive rounds of wage increases resulting from collective bargaining. Yet probably most economists are now agreed that this first postwar rise in prices was primarily attributable to the pull of demand that resulted from wartime accumulations of liquid assets and deferred needs.

This emphasis on demand-pull was somewhat reinforced by the Korean war run-up of prices after mid-1950. But just by the time that cost-push was becoming discredited as a theory of inflation, we ran into the rather puzzling phenomenon of the 1955–58 upward creep of prices, which seemed to take place in the last part of the period despite growing overcapacity, slack labor markets, slow real growth, and no apparent great buoyancy in over-all demand.

It is no wonder then that economists have been debating the possible causations involved in inflation: demand-pull versus cost-push; wage-push versus more general Lerner "sellers' inflation"; and the new Charles Schultze theory of "demand-shift" inflation. We propose to give a brief survey of the issues. Rather than pronounce on the terribly difficult question as to exactly which is the best model to use in explaining the recent past and predicting the

* From *American Economic Review*, Vol. L, No. 2 (May, 1960). Reprinted by the courtesy of the publisher (the American Economic Association) and the authors.

† Massachusetts Institute of Technology.

likely future, we shall try to emphasize the types of evidence which can help decide between the conflicting theories. And we shall be concerned with some policy implications that arise from the different analytical hypotheses.

History of the Debate: The Quantity Theory and Demand-Pull. The preclassical economists grew up in an environment of secularly rising prices. And even prior to Adam Smith there had grown up the belief in at least a simplified quantity theory. But it was in the neoclassical thought of Walras, Marshall, Fisher, and others that this special version of demand determination of the absolute level of money prices and costs reached its most developed form.

We can oversimplify the doctrine as follows. The real outputs, inputs, and relative prices of goods and factors can be thought of as determined by a set of competitive equations which are independent of the absolute level of prices. As in a barter system, the absolute level of all prices is indeterminate and inessential because of the "relative homogeneity" properties of these market relations. To fix the absolute scale factor, we can if we like bring in a neutral money. Such money, unlike coffee or soap, being valued only for what it will buy and not for its intrinsic utility, will be exactly doubled in demand if there is an exact doubling of all prices. Because of this important "scale homogeneity," fixing the total of such money will, when applied to our already determined real system of outputs, factors, and relative prices, fix the absolute level of all prices; and changes in the total of such money must necessarily correspond to new equilibria of absolute prices that have moved in exact proportion, with relative prices and all real magnitudes being quite unaffected.[1]

As Patinkin and others have shown, the above doctrines are rather oversimplified, for they do not fully analyze the intricacies involved in the demand for money; instead they ignore important (and predictable) changes in such proportionality coefficients as velocity of circulation. But by World War I, this particular, narrow version of demand-pull inflation had more or less triumphed. The wartime rise in prices was usually analyzed in terms of rises in the over-all money supply. And the postwar German inflation was understood by non-German economists in similar terms.

But not all economists ever agree on anything. Just as Tooke had eclectically explained the Napoleonic rise in prices partially in terms of the war-induced increase in tax, shipping, and other costs, so did Harold G. Moulton and others choose to attribute the World War I price rises to prior rises in cost of production. And it is not without significance that the great neoclassical Wicksell expressed in the last years of his life some misgivings over the usual version of wartime price movements, placing great emphasis on movements in money's velocity induced by wartime shortages of goods.

Of course, the neoclassical writers would not have denied the necessary equality of competitive costs and prices. But they would have regarded it as superficial to take the level of money costs as a predetermined variable. Instead, they would argue, prices and factor costs are simultaneously determinable in interdependent competitive markets; and if the level of over-all money supply were kept sufficiently in check, then the price level could be stabilized, with any increases in real costs or any decreases in output being offset by enough backward pressure on factor prices so as to leave final money costs and prices on the average unchanged.

[1] But as Hume had early recognized, the periods of rising prices seemed to give rise to at least transient stimulus to the economy as active profit seekers gained an advantage at the expense of the more inert fixed-income, creditor, and wage sectors. The other side of this Hume thesis is perhaps exemplified by the fact that the post-Civil War decades of deflation were also periods of strong social unrest and of relatively weak booms and long periods of heavier-than-average depressions — as earlier National Bureau studies have suggested.

Many writers have gone erroneously beyond the above argument to untenable conclusions such as the following: A rise in defense expenditure matched by, say, excise taxes cannot raise the price level if the quantity of money is held constant; instead it must result in enough decrease in wage and other factor costs to offset exactly the rise in tax costs. Actually, however, such a fiscal policy change could be interpreted as a reduction in the combined public and private thriftiness; with M constant, it would tend to swell the volume of total spending, putting upward pressure on interest rates and inducing a rise in money velocity, and presumably resulting in a higher equilibrium level of prices. To roll back prices to their previous level would take, even within the framework of a strictly competitive neoclassical model, a determined reduction in previous money supply. (This illustrates the danger of going from the innocent hypothesis, that a balanced change in all prices might in the long run be consistent with no substantive changes in real relations, to an overly simple interpretation of a complicated change that is actually taking place in historical reality.)

While the above example of a tax-induced price rise that takes place within a strict neoclassical model might be termed a case of cost-push rather than demand-pull, it does not really represent quite the same phenomena that we shall meet in our later discussion of cost-push. This can perhaps be most easily seen from the remark that, if one insisted on holding prices steady, conventional demand reduction methods would work very well, within the neoclassical models, to offset such cost-push.

Demand-Pull à la Keynes. Aside from the neoclassical quantity theory, there is a second version of demand-pull associated with the theories of Keynes. Before and during the Great Depression, economists had become impressed with the institutional frictions and rigidities that made for downward inflexibilities in wages and prices and which made any such deflationary movements socially painful. Keynes's *General Theory* can, if we are willing to oversimplify, be thought of as a systematic model which uses downward inflexibility of wages and prices to convert any reduction in money spending into a real reduction in output and employment rather than a balanced reduction in all prices and factor costs. (This is overly simple for at least the following reasons: in the pessimistic, depression version of some Keynesians, a hyperdeflation of wages and prices would not have had substantive effects in restoring employment and output, because of infinite elasticity of liquidity preference and/or zero elasticity of investment demand; in the general form of the *General Theory*, and particularly after Pigou effects of the real value of money had been built in, if you could engineer a massive reduction in wages and costs, there would have been some stimulating effects on consumption, investment, and on real output; finally, a careful neoclassical theory, which took proper account of rigidities and which analyzed induced shifts of velocity in a sophisticated way, might also have emerged with similar valid conclusions.)

While the Keynesian theories can be said to differ from the neoclassical theories with respect to analysis of deflation, Keynes himself was willing to assume that attainment of full employment would make prices and wages flexible upward. In *How to Pay for the War* (1939), he developed a theory of inflation which was quite like the neoclassical theory in its emphasis upon the demand-pull of aggregate spending even though it differed from that theory in its emphasis on total spending flow rather than on the stock of money. His theory of "demanders' inflation" stemmed primarily from the fact that government plus investors plus consumers want, in real terms among them, more than 100 per cent of the wartime or boomtime available producible output. So prices have to rise to cheat the slow-to-spend of their desired shares. But the price rise closes the inflationary gap only temporarily, as the higher price level breeds higher incomes all around and the real gap reopens itself continually. And so the inflation goes on, at a rate determined by the degree of shifts to profit, the rapidity and extent of wage adjustments to the rising cost of living, and ultimately by the extent to which progressive tax receipts rise enough to close the gap. And, we may add, that firmness by the central bank in limiting

the money supply might ultimately so increase credit tightness and so lower real balances as to bring consumption and investment spending into equilibrium with available civilian resources at some higher plateau of prices.

Cost-Push and Demand-Shift Theories of Inflation. In its most rigid form, the neoclassical model would require that wages fall whenever there is unemployment of labor and that prices fall whenever excess capacity exists in the sense that marginal cost of the output that firms sell is less than the prices they receive. A more eclectic model of imperfect competition in the factor and commodity markets is needed to explain the fact of price and wage rises before full employment and full capacity have been reached.

Similarly, the Keynes model, which assumes stickiness of wages even in the face of underemployment equilibrium, rests on various assumptions of imperfect competition. And when we recognize that, considerably before full employment of labor and plants has been reached, modern prices and wages seem to show a tendency to drift upward irreversibly, we see that the simple Keynesian system must be modified even further in the direction of an imperfect competition model.

Now the fact that an economic model in some degree involves imperfect competition does not necessarily imply that the concepts of competitive markets give little insight into the behavior of relative prices, resources allocations, and profitabilities. To some degree of approximation, the competitive model may cast light on these important real magnitudes, and for this purpose we might be content to use the competitive model. But to explain possible cost-push inflation, it would seem more economical from the very beginning to recognize that imperfect competition is the essence of the problem and to drop the perfect competition assumptions.

Once this is done, we recognize the qualitative possibility of cost-push inflation. Just as wages and prices may be sticky in the face of unemployment and overcapacity, so may they be pushing upward beyond what can be explained in terms of levels and shifts in demand. But to what degree these elements are important in explaining price behavior of any period becomes an important quantitative question. It is by no means always to be expected that by observing an economy's behavior over a given period will we be able to make a very good separation of its price rise into demand and cost elements. We simply cannot perform the controlled experiments necessary to make such a separation; and Mother Nature may not have economically given us the scatter and variation needed as a substitute for controlled experiments if we are to make approximate identification of the casual forces at work.

Many economists have argued that cost-push was important in the prosperous 1951–53 period, but that its effects on average prices were masked by the drop in flexible raw material prices. But again in 1955–58, it showed itself despite the fact that in a good deal of this period there seemed little evidence of over-all high employment and excess demand. Some holders of this view attribute the push to wage boosts engineered unilaterally by strong unions. But others give as much or more weight to the co-operative action of all sellers — organized and unorganized labor, semimonopsonistic managements, oligopolistic sellers in imperfect commodity markets — who raise prices and costs in an attempt by each to maintain or raise his share of national income, and who, among themselves, by trying to get more than 100 per cent of the available output, create "sellers' inflation."

A variant of cost-push is provided by Charles Schultze's "demand-shift" theory of inflation. Strength of demand in certain sectors of the economy — e.g., capital goods industries in 1955–57 — raises prices and wages there. But elsewhere, even though demand is not particularly strong, downward inflexibility keeps prices from falling, and market power may even engineer a price-wage movement imitative in a degree of the sectors with strong demand. The result is an upward drift in average prices — with the suggestion that monetary and fiscal policies restrictive enough to prevent an average price rise would have to be so very restrictive as to produce a considerable level of unemployment and a significant drop in production.

II.

Truths and Consequences: The Problem of Identification. The competing (although imperfectly competing) theories of inflation appear to be genuinely different hypotheses about observable facts. In that case one ought to be able to distinguish empirically between cost and demand inflation. What are the earmarks? If I believe in cost-push, what should I expect to find in the facts that I would not expect to find were I a believer in demand-pull? The last clause is important. It will not do to point to circumstances which will accompany any inflation, however caused. A test must have what statisticians call power against the main alternative hypotheses.

Trite as these remarks may seem, they need to be made. The clichés of popular discussion fall into the trap again and again. Although they have been trampled often enough by experts, the errors revive. We will take the time to point the finger once more. We do this because we want to go one step further and argue that this problem of identification is exceedingly difficult. What appear at first to be subtle and reliable ways of distinguishing cost-induced from demand-induced inflation turn out to be far from airtight. In fact we are driven to the belief that aggregate data, recording the *ex post* details of completed transactions, may in most circumstances be quite insufficient. It may be necessary first to disaggregate.

Common Fallacies. The simplest mistake — to be found in almost any newspaper discussion of the subject — is the belief that if money wages rise faster than productivity, we have a sure sign of cost-inflation. Of course the truth is that in the purest of excess-demand inflation wages will rise faster than productivity; the only alternative is for the full increase in the value of a fixed output to be siphoned off into profits, without this spilling over into the labor market to drive wages up still further. This error is sometimes mixed with the belief that it is possible over long periods for industries with rapid productivity increase to pay higher and increasingly higher wages than those where output per man-hour grows slowly.

Such a persistent and growing differential is likely eventually to alter the skill- or quality-mix of the labor force in the different industries, which casts doubt on the original productivity comparison.

One sometimes sees statements to the effect that increases in expenditure more rapid than increases in real output necessarily spell demand inflation. It is simple arithmetic that expenditure outrunning output by itself spells only price increases and provides no evidence at all about the source or cause of the inflation. Much of the talk about "too much money chasing too few goods" is of this kind.

A more solemn version of the fallacy goes: An increase in expenditure can come about only through an increase in the stock of money or an increase in the velocity of circulation. Therefore the only possible causes of inflation are M and V and we need look no further.

Further Difficulties. It is more disconcerting to realize that even some of the empirical tests suggested in the professional literature may have little or no cutting power in distinguishing cost from demand inflation.

One thinks automatically of looking at the timing relationships. Do wage increases seem to precede price increases? Then the general rise in prices is caused by the wage-push. Do price increases seem to precede wage increases? Then more likely the inflation is of the excess-demand variety, and wages are being pulled up by a brisk demand for labor or they are responding to prior increases in the cost of living. There are at least three difficulties with this argument. The first is suggested by replacing "wage increase" by "chicken" and "price increase" by "egg." The trouble is that we have no normal initial standard from which to measure, no price level which has always existed and to which everyone has adjusted; so that a wage increase, if one occurs, must be autonomous and not a response to some prior change in the demand for labor. As an illustration of the difficulty of inference, consider average hourly earnings in the basic steel industry. They rose, relative to all manufacturing from 1950 on, including some periods when labor markets were not tight. Did this represent an autonomous

wage-push? Or was it rather a delayed adjustment to the decline in steel wages relative to all manufacturing, which took place during the war, presumably as a consequence of the differential efficiency of wage control? And why should we take 1939 or 1941 as a standard for relative wages? And so on.

A related problem is that in a closely interdependent economy, effects can precede causes. Prices may begin to ease up because wage rates are expected to. And more important, as wage and price increases ripple through the economy, aggregation may easily distort the apparent timing relations.

But even if we could find the appearance of a controlled experiment, if after a period of stability in both we were to notice a wage increase to a new plateau followed by a price increase, what could we safely conclude? It would be immensely tempting to make the obvious diagnosis of wage-push. But consider the following hypothetical chain of events: Prices in imperfect commodity markets respond only to changes in costs. Labor markets are perfectly competitive in effect, and the money wage moves rapidly in response to shifts in the demand for labor. So any burst of excess demand, government expenditure, say, would cause an increased demand for labor; wages would be pulled up; and only then would prices of commodities rise in response to the cost increase. So the obvious diagnosis might be wrong. In between, if we were clever, we might notice a temporary narrowing of margins, and with this information we might piece together the story.

Consider another sophisticated inference. In a single market, price may rise either because the demand curve shifts to the right or because the supply curve shifts to the left in consequence of cost increases. But in the first case, output should increase; in the second case, decline. Could we not reason, then, that if prices rise, sector by sector, with outputs, demand-pull must be at work? Very likely we can, but not with certainty. In the first place, as Schultze has argued, it is possible that certain sectors face excess demand, without there being aggregate pressure; those sectors will indeed show strong price increases and increases in output (or pressure on capacity). But in a real sense, the source of inflation is the failure of other sectors, in which excess capacity develops, to decrease their prices sufficiently. And this may be a consequence of "administered pricing," rigid mark-ups, rigid wages and all the paraphernalia of the "new" inflation.

To go deeper, the reasoning we are scrutinizing may fail because it is illegitimate, even in this industry-by-industry way, to use partial equilibrium reasoning. Suppose wages rise. We are led to expect a decrease in output. But in the modern world, all or most wages are increasing. Nor is this the first time they have done so. And in the past, general wage and price increases have not resulted in any decrease in aggregate real demand — perhaps the contrary. So that even in a single industry supply and demand curves may not be independent. The shift in costs is accompanied by, indeed may bring about, a compensating shift in the subjectively-viewed demand curve facing the industry. And so prices may rise with no decline and possibly an increase in output. If there is anything in this line of thought, it may be that one of the important causes of inflation is — inflation.

The Need for Detail. In these last few paragraphs we have been arguing against the attempt to diagnose the source of inflation from aggregates. We have also suggested that sometimes the tell-tale symptoms can be discovered if we look not at the totals but at the parts. This suggestion gains force when we recognize, as we must, that the same general price increase can easily be the consequence of different causes in different sectors. A monolithic theory may have its simplicity and style riddled by exceptions. Is there any reason, other than a desire for symmetry, for us to believe that the same reasoning must account for the above-average increase in the price of services and the above-average increase in the price of machinery since 1951 or since 1949? Public utility prices undoubtedly were held down during the war, by the regulatory process; and services ride along on income-elastic demand accompanied by a slower-than-average recorded productivity increase. A faster-than-average price increase amounts to the corrective relative-price change

one would expect. The main factor in the machinery case, according to a recent Joint Economic Committee study, appears to have been a burst of excess demand occasioned by the investment boom of the mid-fifties. And to give still a third variant, Eckstein and Fromm in another Joint Economic Committee study suggest that the above-average rise in the wages of steelworkers and the prices of steel products took place in the face of a somewhat less tight labor and product market than in machinery. They attribute it to a joint exercise of market power by the union and the industry. Right or wrong, it is mistaken theoretical tactics to deny this possibility on the grounds that it cannot account for the price history in other sectors.

Some Things It Would Be Good to Know. There are at least two classical questions which are relevant to our problem and on which surprisingly little work has been done: One is the behavior of real demand under inflationary conditions and the other is the behavior of money wages with respect to the level of employment. We comment briefly on these two questions because there seems to us to be some doubt that ordinary reversible behavior equations can be found, and this very difficulty points up an important question we have mentioned earlier: that a period of high demand and rising prices molds attitudes, expectations, even institutions in such a way as to bias the future in favor of further inflation. Unlike some other economists, we do not draw the firm conclusion that unless a firm stop is put, the rate of price increase must accelerate. We leave it as an open question: It may be that creeping inflation leads only to creeping inflation.

The standard way for an inflationary gap to burn itself out short of hyperinflation is for the very process of inflation to reduce real demands. The mechanisms, some dubious, some not, are well known: the shift to profit, real-balance effects, tax progression, squeeze on fixed incomes. If price and wage increases have this effect, then a cost-push inflation in the absence of excess demand inflicts unemployment and excess capacity on the system. The willingness to bear the reduced real demand is a measure of the imperfectness of markets permitting the cost-push. But suppose real demands do not behave in this way? Suppose a wage-price rise has no effect on real demand, or a negligible one, or even a slight positive one? Then not only will the infliction not materialize, but the whole distinction between cost-push and demand-pull begins to evaporate. But is this possible? The older quantity theorists would certainly have denied it; but the increase in velocity between 1955 and 1957 would have surprised an older quantity theorist.

We do not know whether real demand behaves this way or not. But we think it important to realize that the more the recent past is dominated by inflation, by high employment, and by the belief that both will continue, the more likely is it that the process of inflation will preserve or even increase real demand, or the more heavily the monetary and fiscal authorities may have to bear down on demand in the interests of price stabilization. Real-income consciousness is a powerful force. The pressure on real balances from high prices will be partly relieved by the expectation of rising prices, as long as interest rates in an imperfect capital market fail to keep pace. The same expectations will induce schoolteachers, pensioners, and others to try to devise institutions to protect their real incomes from erosion by higher prices. To the extent that they succeed, their real demands will be unimpaired. As the fear of prolonged unemployment disappears and the experience of past full employment builds up accumulated savings, wage earners may also maintain their real expenditures; and the same forces may substantially increase the marginal propensity to spend out of profits, including retained earnings. If there is anything to this line of thought, the empirical problem of verification may be very difficult, because much of the experience of the past is irrelevant to the hypothesis. But it would be good to know.

The Fundamental Phillips Schedule Relating Unemployment and Wage Changes. Consider also the question of the relation between money wage changes and the degree of unemployment. We have A. W. Phillips' interesting paper on the U. K. history since the Civil War (our Civil War, that is!). His findings are remarkable, even if one disagrees with his interpretations.

In the first place, the period 1861–1913, during which the trade-union movement was rather weak, shows a fairly close relationship between the per cent change in wage rates and the fraction of the labor force unemployed. Due allowance must be made for sharp import-price-induced changes in the cost of living, and for the normal expectation that wages will be rising faster when an unemployment rate of 5 per cent is reached on the upswing than when it is reached on the downswing. In the second place, with minor exceptions, the same relationship that fits for 1861–1913 also seems to fit about as well for 1913–48 and 1948–57. And finally Phillips concludes that the money wage level would stabilize with 5 per cent unemployment; and the rate of increase of money wages would be held down to the 2–3 per cent rate of productivity increase with about 2½ per cent of the labor force unemployed.

Strangely enough, no comparably careful study has been made for the U.S. Garbarino's 1950 note is hardly a full-scale analysis, and Schultze's treatment in his first-class Joint Committee monograph is much too casual. There is some evidence that the U.S. differs from the U.K. on at least two counts. If there is any such relationship characterizing the American labor market, it may have shifted somewhat in the last fifty to sixty years. Secondly, there is a suggestion that in this country it might take 8 to 10 per cent unemployment to stabilize money wages.

But would it take 8 to 10 per cent unemployment forever to stabilize the money wage? Is not this kind of relationship also one which depends heavily on remembered experience? We suspect that this is another way in which a past characterized by rising prices, high employment, and mild, short recessions is likely to breed an inflationary bias — by making the money wage more rigid downward, maybe even perversely inclined to rise during recessions on the grounds that things will soon be different.

There may be no such relation for this country. If there is, why does it not seem to have the same degree of long-run invariance as Phillips' curve for the U.K.? What geographical, economic, sociological facts account for the difference between the two countries? Is there a difference in labor mobility in the two countries? Do the different tolerances for unemployment reflect differences in income level, union organization, or what? What policy decisions might conceivably lead to a decrease in the critical unemployment rate at which wages begin to rise or to rise too fast? Clearly a careful study of this problem might pay handsome dividends.

III.

A Closer Look at the American Data. In spite of all its deficiencies, we think the accompanying scatter diagram in Figure I is useful. Where it does not provide answers, it at least asks interesting questions. We have plotted the yearly percentage changes of average hourly earnings in manufacturing, including supplements (Rees's data) against the annual average percentage of the labor force unemployed.

The first defect to note is the different coverages represented in the two axes. Duesenberry has argued that postwar wage increases in manufacturing on the one hand and in trade, services, etc., on the other, may have quite different explanations: union power in manufacturing and simple excess demand in the other sectors. It is probably true that if we had an

FIGURE I

Phillips Scatter Diagram for U.S.
(The circled points are for recent years.)

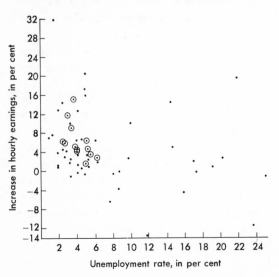

unemployment rate for manufacturing alone, it would be somewhat higher during the postwar years than the aggregate figure shown. Even if a qualitative statement like this held true over the whole period, the increasing weight of services in the total might still create a bias. Another defect is our use of annual increments and averages, when a full-scale study would have to look carefully into the nuances of timing.

A first look at the scatter is discouraging; there are points all over the place. But perhaps one can notice some systematic effects. In the first place, the years from 1933 to 1941 appear to be *sui generis*: money wages rose or failed to fall in the face of massive unemployment. One may attribute this to the workings of the New Deal (the 20 per cent wage increase of 1934 must represent the NRA codes); or alternatively one could argue that by 1933 much of the unemployment had become structural, insulated from the functioning labor market, so that in effect the vertical axis ought to be moved over to the right. This would leave something more like the normal pattern.

The early years of the first World War also behave atypically although not so much so as 1933–39. This may reflect cost-of-living increases, the rapidity of the increase in demand, a special tightness in manufacturing, or all three.

But the bulk of the observations — the period between the turn of the century and the first war, the decade between the end of that war and the Great Depression, and the most recent ten or twelve years — all show a rather consistent pattern. Wage rates do tend to rise when the labor market is tight, and the tighter the faster. What is most interesting is the strong suggestion that the relation, such as it is, has shifted upward slightly but noticeably in the forties and fifties. On the one hand, the first decade of the century and the twenties seem to fit the same pattern. Manufacturing wages seem to stabilize absolutely when 4 or 5 per cent of the labor force is unemployed; and wage increases equal to the productivity increase of 2 to 3 per cent per year is the normal pattern at about 3 per cent unemployment. This is not so terribly different from Phillips' results for the U.K., although the relation holds there with a greater consistency. We comment on this below.

On the other hand, from 1946 to the present, the pattern is fairly consistent and consistently different from the earlier period. The annual unemployment rate ranged only narrowly, from 2.5 per cent in 1953 to 6.2 per cent in 1958. Within that range, as might be expected, wages rose faster the lower the unemployment rate. But one would judge now that it would take more like 8 per cent unemployment to keep money wages from rising. And they would rise at 2 to 3 per cent per year with 5 or 6 per cent of the labor force unemployed.

It would be overhasty to conclude that the relation we have been discussing represents a reversible supply curve for labor along which an aggregate demand curve slides. If that were so, then movements along the curve might be dubbed standard demand-pull, and shifts of the curve might represent the institutional changes on which cost-push theories rest. The apparent shift in our Phillips curve might be attributed by some economists to the new market power of trade-unions. Others might be more inclined to believe that the expectation of continued full employment, or at least high employment, is enough to explain both the shift in the supply curve, if it is that, and the willingness of employers (conscious that what they get from a work force is partly dependent on its morale and its turnover) to pay wage increases in periods of temporarily slack demand.

This latter consideration, however, casts real doubt on the facile identification of the relationship as merely a supply-of-labor phenomenon. There are two parties to a wage bargain.

U.S. and U.K. Compared. A comparison of the American position with Phillips' findings for the U.K. is interesting for itself and also as a possible guide to policy. Anything which will shift the relationship downward decreases the price in unemployment that must be paid when a policy is followed of holding down the rate of wage and price increase by pressure on aggregate demand.

One possibility is that the trade-union leadership is more "responsible" in the U.K.; indeed the postwar policy of wage restraint seems visible in Phillips' data. But there are other interpretations. It is clear that the more fractionated and imperfect a labor market is, the higher the over-all excess supply of labor may have to be before the average wage rate becomes stable and the less tight the relation will be in any case. Even a touch of downward inflexibility (and trade-unionism and administered wages surely means at least this) will make this immobility effect more pronounced. It would seem plausible that the sheer geographical compactness of the English economy makes its labor market more perfect than ours in this sense. Moreover, the British have pursued a more deliberate policy of relocation of industry to mop up pockets of structural unemployment.

This suggests that any governmental policy which increases the mobility of labor (geographical and industrial) or improves the flow of information in the labor market will have anti-inflationary effects as well as being desirable for other reasons. A quicker but in the long run probably less efficient approach might be for the government to direct the regional distribution of its expenditures more deliberately in terms of the existence of local unemployment and excess capacity.

The English data show a quite clearly nonlinear (hyperbolic) relation between wage changes and unemployment, reflecting the much discussed downward inflexibility. Our American figures do not contradict this, although they do not tell as plain a story as the English. To the extent that this nonlinearity exists, as Duesenberry has remarked, a given average level of unemployment over the cycle will be compatible with a slower rate of wage increase (and presumably price increase) the less wide the cyclical swings from top to bottom.

A less obvious implication of this point of view is that a deliberate low-pressure policy to stabilize the price level may have a certain self-defeating aspect. It is clear from experience that interregional and interindustrial mobility of labor depends heavily on the pull of job opportunities elsewhere, more so than on the push of local unemployment. In effect the imperfection of the labor market is increased, with the consequences we have sketched.

IV.

We have concluded that it is not possible on the basis of a priori reasoning to reject either the demand-pull or cost-push hypothesis, or the variants of the latter such as demand-shift. We have also argued that the empirical identifications needed to distinguish between these hypotheses may be quite impossible from the experience of macrodata that is available to us; and that, while use of microdata might throw additional light on the problem, even here identification is fraught with difficulties and ambiguities.

Nevertheless, there is one area where policy interest and the desire for scientific understanding for its own sake come together. If by deliberate policy one engineered a sizable reduction of demand or refused to permit the increase in demand that would be needed to preserve high employment, one would have an experiment that could hope to distinguish between the validity of the demand-pull and the cost-push theory as we would operationally reformulate those theories. If a small relaxation of demand were followed by great moderations in the march of wages and other costs so that the social cost of a stable price index turned out to be very small in terms of sacrificed high-level employment and output, then the demand-pull hypothesis would have received its most important confirmation. On the other hand, if mild demand repression checked cost and price increases not at all or only mildly, so that considerable unemployment would have to be engineered before the price level updrift could be prevented, then the cost-push hypothesis would have received its most important confirmation. If the outcome of this experience turned out to be in between these extreme cases — as we ourselves would rather expect — then an element of validity would have to be conceded to both views; and dull as it is to have to embrace eclectic theories, scholars who wished to be realistic would have to steel themselves to doing so.

Of course, we have been talking glibly of a vast experiment. Actually such an operation would be fraught with implications for social welfare. Naturally, since they are confident that it would be a success, the believers in demand-pull ought to welcome such an experiment. But, equally naturally, the believers in cost-push would be dead set against such an engineered low-pressure economy, since they are equally convinced that it will be a dismal failure involving much needless social pain. (A third school, who believes in cost-push but think it can be cured or minimized by orthodox depressing of demand, think that our failure to make this experiment would be fraught with social evil by virtue of the fact that they expect a creep in prices to snowball into a trot and then a gallop.)

Our own view will by now have become evident. When we translate the Phillips diagram showing the American pattern of wage increase against degree of unemployment into a related diagram showing the different levels of unemployment that would be "needed" for each degree of price level change, we come out with guesses like the following:

1. In order to have wages increase at no more than the 2½ per cent per annum characteristic of our productivity growth, the American economy would seem on the basis of twentieth-century and postwar experience to have to undergo something like 5 to 6 per cent of the civilian labor force's being unemployed. That much unemployment would appear to be the cost of price stability in the years immediately ahead.

2. In order to achieve the nonperfectionist's goal of high enough output to give us no more than 3 per cent unemployment, the price index might have to rise by as much as 4 to 5 per cent per year. That much price rise would seem to be the necessary cost of high employment and production in the years immediately ahead.

All this is shown in our price-level modification of the Phillips curve, Figure II. The point A, corresponding to price stability, is seen to involve about 5½ per cent unemployment; whereas the point B, corresponding to 3 per cent unemployment, is seen to involve a price rise of about 4½ per cent per annum. We rather expect that the tug of war of politics will end us up in the next few years somewhere in between these selected points. We shall probably have some price rise and some excess unemployment.

Aside from the usual warning that these are simply our best guesses we must give another caution. All of our discussion has been phrased in short-run terms, dealing with what might happen in the next few years. It would be wrong, though, to think that our Figure II menu that relates obtainable price and unemployment behavior will maintain its same shape in the longer run. What we do in a policy way during the next few years might cause it to shift in a definite way.

Thus, it is conceivable that after they had produced a low-pressure economy, the believers in demand-pull might be disappointed in the short run; i.e., prices might continue to rise even though unemployment was considerable. Nevertheless, it might be that the low-pressure

demand would so act upon wage and other expectations as to shift the curve downward in the longer run — so that over a decade, the economy might enjoy higher employment with price stability than our present-day estimate would indicate.

But also the opposite is conceivable. A low-pressure economy might build up within itself over the years larger and larger amounts of structural unemployment (the reverse of what happened from 1941 to 1953 as a result of strong war and postwar demands). The result would be an upward shift of our menu of choice, with more and more unemployment being needed just to keep prices stable.

Since we have no conclusive or suggestive evidence on these conflicting issues, we shall not attempt to give judgment on them. Instead we venture the reminder that, in the years just ahead, the level of attained growth will be highly correlated with the degree of full employment and high-capacity output.

But what about the longer run? If the per annum rate of technical progress were about the same in a low- and high-pressure economy, then the initial loss in output in going to the low-pressure state would never be made up; however, in relative terms, the initial gap would not grow but would remain constant as time goes by. If a low-pressure economy could succeed in improving the efficiency of our productive factors, some of the loss of growth might be gradually made up and could in long enough time even be more than wiped out. On the other hand, if such an economy produced class warfare and social conflict and depressed the level of research and technical progress, the loss in growth would be compounded in the long run.

A final disclaimer is in order. We have not here entered upon the important question of what feasible institutional reforms might be introduced to lessen the degree of disharmony between full employment and price stability. These could of course involve such wide-ranging issues as direct price and wage controls, antiunion and antitrust legislation, and a host of other measures hopefully designed to move the American Phillips curves downward and to the left.

FIGURE II

Modified Phillips Curve for U.S.
This shows the menu of choice between different degrees of unemployment and price stability, as roughly estimated from last twenty-five years of American data.

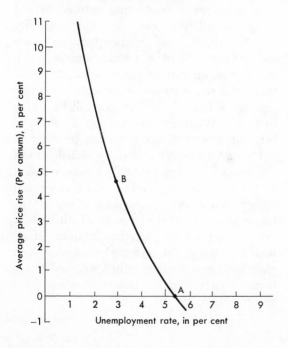

45

DOES MONEY ALWAYS DEPRECIATE?*

R. G. Lipsey†

This fascinating article discusses the future value of money, and what to do about it, in terms of the experience of the past.

It is a commonplace observation that there is a general tendency, observable throughout history, for the level of prices to rise. There have, of course, been periods when prices fell, but it is considered trite to observe that there is a strong trend, one might even call it an historical law, for prices to rise — sometimes slowly and sometimes rapidly, but generally to rise — with the passage of time.

This observation is often made the basis of advice to savers and investors. There are some people, whom I shall call savers, who are mainly concerned to have purchasing power available at some future date, possibly at the time of their old age. There are other people, whom I shall call investors, who look primarily for a good return on their investment but who, if they are prudent, must also be concerned to maintain the real value of their capital in the face of changes in the price level.

The saver will often be advised not to buy ordinary life insurance or annuities, but to place his money in real estate or other commodities whose money value will rise *pari passu* with the general level of prices. In this way, he is told, the real value of his savings will be protected in spite of the historical law of continued inflation. The investor is very often advised to invest in equities and not in bonds, even though the yield on bonds may seem attractive in relation to the yield on equities. It is pointed out to him that both the interest payments and the final redemption value of bonds are fixed in money terms so that, when the loss in real capital value due to inflation is taken into account, the actual yield on his investment may

be very much lower than the nominal interest payment. It will be pointed out, for example, that the real rate of return for most war-time investors in government bonds was negative, the average annual rate of change of prices having been greater than the money rate of interest.

Thus, not only have we encountered what seems to be a generally-accepted historical law, but we have found a number of important practical applications which translate the law into advice to savers and investors. It is important to note that these applications of the "historical law of rising prices" to decisions about savings and investment imply some definite time horizon.

The time horizon of the person buying life insurance or an annuity is unlikely to exceed forty or fifty years. He will want to know something like the following: "What are the chances of my savings being reduced in real value by inflation over, say, the next fifty years?". The investor deciding between bonds and equities will have a time horizon which will vary from two or three to twenty or so years, and ten years may be selected as a representative figure. The investor will be asking himself: "What are the chances of the real value of my capital being reduced by inflation if I accept a promise to repay a stated sum of money, say, ten years hence?". The observation that the British price level in 1960 is very much higher than it was in 1360 may be interesting, but it provides no evidence on which to base answers to these very specific questions. If we wish to consider the historical evidence which relates to these questions, then we need a very detailed picture of the course of prices from year to year.

---

* From *Lloyds Bank Review*, No. 58 (October, 1960). Reprinted by the courtesy of the publisher and the author.
† University of Essex.

PRICE MOVEMENTS OVER SEVEN CENTURIES

Economists often complain of the paucity of data in their subject compared to that available in, say, astronomy, where observations have been carefully collected over many thousands of years. This complaint is often justified. For many economic time series there are no figures before the second world war; other series extend back to the 1930's or 1920's, while in a few cases it is possible, by means of a major effort of estimation and "guesstimation", to extend a series back for, say, one hundred years. In the case of British prices, however, the situation does not conform with this generally gloomy picture. A few years ago, Professor Phelps Brown and Miss Sheila Hopkins published an index of prices in Britain which extends back to 1264.[1]

This remarkable index provides a reasonably accurate indication of variations over the last seven centuries in the cost of purchasing a constant bundle of goods. The main components

[1] "Seven Centuries of the Prices of Consumables, compared with Builders' Wage-rates", E. H. Phelps Brown and Sheila V. Hopkins, *Economica*, Vol. XXIII, No. 92.

of the bundle are: farinaceous products, meat and fish products, butter and cheese, drink, fuel and light, and textiles. It will be seen that the index by no means includes all those commodities whose price variations would be of interest to investors. Variations in the index over periods of ten and fifty years should, however, give a reasonable general indication of changes in the purchasing power of the saver's and investor's pounds.

The Phelps Brown-Sheila Hopkins series is presented from 1275 (on a logarithmic scale) in Figure I. It is obvious that any straight-line trend drawn through the series would be upward sloping, indicating that the trend of British prices is rising through time. The line actually drawn on the chart is a linear trend line fitted to the data by least squares, which is the method most commonly used in elementary statistical analysis.[2] This line indicates

[2] The equation of the line is $\log P = 1.8032 + .0022N$, where P is the price index and N the year, with $1275 =$ year 1. The graph is plotted on a logarithmic scale where *equal vertical distances* indicate *equal percentage changes* in the price level. The index runs to 1954 and, in order to bring the data up to date, the retail price index was used to extend it to 1959. For a very few years in the sixteenth century the index is not available, so that a price level comparison cannot be made for these years.

FIGURE I

Price Index of Consumables in Southern England 1275–1959
(1451–75 = 100)

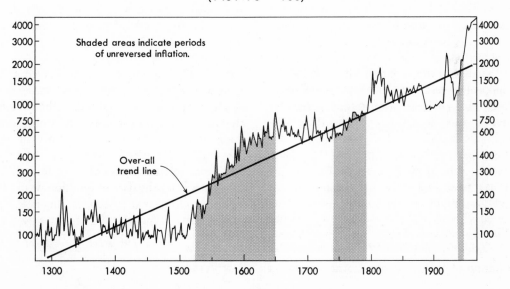

that the average trend in British prices over the seven centuries in question has been an increase of one-half of one per cent per annum. This rising trend is undoubtedly the basis for the postulated historical law of rising prices.

If we look carefully at the actual price series in Figure I, however, we see that there are very many periods in history in which the price level movements *do not* follow the trend line. There are periods in which the price level fell, and there are other long periods in which there is no discernible upward or downward trend in the level of prices. The percentage changes between the main peaks and troughs of the price level over these seven centuries are as follows: —

Period	Number of Years	Percentage change in Price Level %
1275–1525	250	+ 29
1525–1650	125	+550
1650–1744	94	— 38
1744–1813	69	+263
1813–1893	80	— 51
1893–1920	27	+183
1920–1932	12	— 59
1932–1959	27	+322

If we compare the value of the price index in each year with its value in the preceding year, we find that there were 343 years in which the price level rose from one year to the next, and 328 years in which the price level fell, while in the remaining instances the price level held constant. The short-run variability of the price index is shown by the following facts: the longest period of *uninterrupted* price rise was the thirteen years from 1940 to 1952; the next longest period was the seven years from 1912 to 1918, while there were only three periods of six successive years of price rises — 1478–83, 1762–67, and 1835–40. The longest periods of successive price decreases were the three five-year periods 1473–77, 1651–55 and 1826–30.

It is apparent that the price level fell from one year to the next almost exactly as many times as it rose, although it may be argued that *annual variations* in an index so heavily weighted with agricultural commodities are not of very great interest. The above facts do suggest, however, that before we jump from the observation of the rising trend over the period as a whole to the giving of practical advice to savers and investors, it is necessary to make a detailed examination of the price level movements.

HOW PRICES HAVE CHANGED

Let us start at the year 1275 and find out whether the price level was higher or lower *ten years* from that date, that is, in 1285. We then repeat this procedure every year from 1275 until 1949, noting each time whether the price level was higher or lower ten years after the date in question. We may then repeat the whole procedure, only this time using a time horizon of *fifty years*. Starting at 1275, we consider the price level fifty years from that date; we repeat the procedure for every year until 1909, relating the price level in that year to the price level in 1959.

Figure II summarizes the result of these experiments. It shows, for example, that when the time span is fifty years the most frequent outcome is for the price level to *fall* by an amount between zero and 9 per cent. There were eighty-two instances in which the price level fell by an amount between zero and 9 per cent over the interval of half a century. The next most frequent result is for the price level to *rise* by an amount not greater than 10 per cent. There were sixty-nine instances in which the price level rose by an amount not greater than 10 per cent over a half-century period. When the time span is changed to ten years, the frequency of price level increases of up to ten per cent (125 instances) is almost the same as the frequency of price level decreases between zero and nine per cent (124 instances).[3]

The frequency distribution for the change in the price level over a fifty-year time horizon does show a definite bias towards inflation. There are 635 years between 1275 and 1909, and a guess that the price level would be higher fifty years from the date in question would have

[3] The class intervals are such that the upper limit of each class is 10 per cent larger than the lower limit. The upper limit is included in each class. This means that the very few cases in which prices 10 or 50 years hence were unchanged have been included in the class — 9 per cent to 0.

FIGURE II

Percentage Change in the Price Level over Ten and Fifty Year Spans

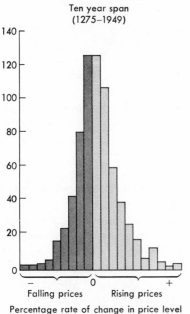

Ten year span
(1275–1949)

Falling prices   Rising prices

Percentage rate of change in price level

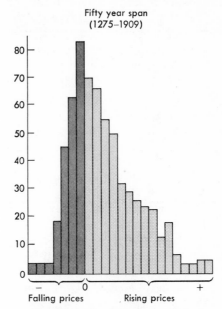

Fifty year span
(1275–1909)

Falling prices   Rising prices

Percentage rate of change in price level

Note: For key to class intervals see Diagram 2.

been correct in 66 per cent of these years and wrong in only 34 per cent. At any time during these seven centuries, in other words, a guess that the purchasing power of money would on balance decline during the ensuing fifty years was twice as likely to be correct as a guess that prices would fall or at best remain stable. Nevertheless, it is hardly a great triumph for the supposed law of historical depreciation of money that in one out of every three instances the implied assumption that prices would rise over the following half-century turns out to be quite wrong. When, moreover, we adopt a time horizon of only ten years, the tendency towards inflation becomes much less marked than it is over a fifty-year horizon. For the years between 1275 and 1949, a guess that the price level would be higher ten years after the date in question would have been right 57 per cent of the time and wrong a full 43 per cent.

As far as the general evidence of history goes, therefore, the odds are somewhat in favour of the bet that, starting from any year over the last seven hundred years, the price level could

be expected to increase over a period of ten years. But the odds are not overwhelming, and in 43 out of every 100 cases it would eventually turn out that prices had fallen instead of rising.

A casual glance at Figure I shows that the periods of price increase are not spread evenly throughout the seven hundred years. More light may be shed on the evidence of history if we consider the price movements in each century. The following table shows the results of a guess taken every year of each century as to the change in the price level over periods of ten and fifty years. The details for the ten-year time horizon are shown in Figure III.

It will be seen from this table that in most centuries it was a fairly good bet that the price level would rise over a period of fifty years. There are only two centuries, the fourteenth and the nineteenth, in which the odds favour a fall in the price level when the time horizon is fifty years. If, in every year from 1800 to 1899 one had taken a bet that the price level fifty years hence would be higher than it was in the year in question, one would have been

A guess taken in each of these years that the price level would be higher:	fifty years from each date in question	ten years from each date in question
	Percentage of Correct Guesses	
	%	%
1275–1299	60	36
1300–1399	43	48
1400–1499	60	48
1500–1599	99	81
1600–1699	57	47
1700–1799	91	75
1800–1899	45	46
1900–1909	100	80
1900–1949	—	68

wrong 55 per cent of the time. On balance, however, the evidence of history is fairly strongly in favour of inflation if one's time horizon is fifty years, although there are some quite long periods which provide exceptions to this rule. Thus, the peak level of 216 in the year 1316 was not again exceeded until 1546 — as much as 230 years later. The peak level of 1650 was not surpassed for 61 years, nor that of 1711 for 82 years. It was more than a century before prices again reached the levels seen during the Napoleonic wars.

If we now consider a time-span of ten years, the picture is markedly different. If we took a bet in each year that the price level would be higher ten years from the date in question, we would be wrong more times than we would be right in the thirteenth, fourteenth, fifteenth, seventeenth and nineteenth centuries. How is it, then, that even with a ten-year time horizon

FIGURE III

Percentage Change in the Price Level over Ten Year Span
Details for each century 1275–1949

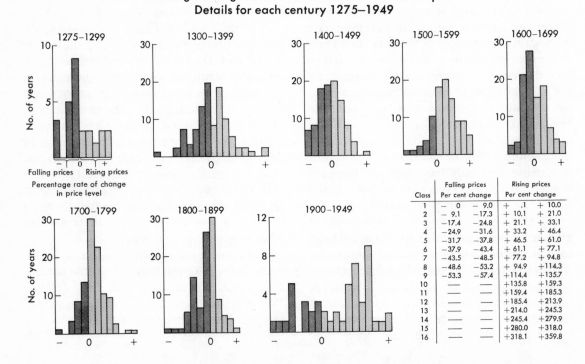

Class	Falling prices Per cent change		Rising prices Per cent change	
1	— 0	— 9.0	+ .1	+ 10.0
2	— 9.1	—17.3	+ 10.1	+ 21.0
3	—17.4	—24.8	+ 21.1	+ 33.1
4	—24.9	—31.6	+ 33.2	+ 46.4
5	—31.7	—37.8	+ 46.5	+ 61.0
6	—37.9	—43.4	+ 61.1	+ 77.1
7	—43.5	—48.5	+ 77.2	+ 94.8
8	—48.6	—53.2	+ 94.9	+114.3
9	—53.3	—57.4	+114.4	+135.7
10	—	—	+135.8	+159.3
11	—	—	+159.4	+185.3
12	—	—	+185.4	+213.9
13	—	—	+214.0	+245.3
14	—	—	+245.4	+279.9
15	—	—	+280.0	+318.0
16	—	—	+318.1	+359.8

the odds do nevertheless slightly favour inflation over the whole period? It is for the reason that in two centuries, the sixteenth and the eighteenth, the odds are very heavily weighted in favour of inflation; in all the other centuries the odds were in favour of deflation, but with a much smaller margin. Clearly, the *evidence of history* does not support the person who argues as follows: "Favourable inducements to invest in bonds (with, say, a ten-year maturity date) should be discounted severely, because bonds do not provide a necessary hedge against the almost inevitable inflation". In most of the centuries between 1275 and the present time a person following this advice would have been wrong more times than he would have been right.

FIVE MAJOR INFLATIONS

We must now take a closer look at Figure I and ask ourselves: what is the basis for the widespread belief in the historical law of rising prices? The first thing we notice is that there have been five major inflations in the seven centuries under consideration. The inflations which caused *permanent* increases in the price level have been concentrated into only three historical periods, while there have been two additional periods in which a serious inflation was followed by an almost equally serious deflation.

The first inflation covers a period of approximately 125 years from about 1525 to, say, 1650. The causes of this price rise are by no means crystal clear. The inflation of the later part of the period is probably accounted for by the influx of Spanish gold and silver from the New World. This influx increased steadily throughout the sixteenth century, reaching a maximum in 1600. It was one of the main causes of this, the longest sustained inflation in recorded British history. The total quantities of treasure which Earl Hamilton has shown to have arrived in Europe in the *first half* of this century do not, however, seem to have been sufficient to account for the price increases of that period. It appears most likely that the inflation in the early part of the period was purely domestic in origin. The cause may well have been a debasement of the coinage by the Tudor monarchs who, for the first time in British history, pro-

vided a central government of sufficient authority to create legal tender by their own fiat.

After the specie flow dried up early in the seventeenth century, the price level showed no discernible trend for the next one hundred years. The last half of the eighteenth century — from 1744 until the Napoleonic wars — was the second great period of prolonged inflation. There is no general agreement on the reasons for this inflation, but the most likely cause is a large expansion in the money supply caused by the rapid growth in the number of banks, particularly country banks, during this period.

The third period of inflation is that associated with the Napoleonic wars. The price level rose rapidly from 1793, and the pace of inflation quickened after suspension of specie payments by the Bank of England in 1797. The price level reached its peak in 1813, and from that time on prices fell rapidly. From 1825 to 1870 prices fluctuated considerably, averaging out at about the 1795–6 level. After 1874 the price level fell sharply, but even at the low point touched in 1893 it was still slightly above the 1793 figure. Thus the peace-time inflation of the last half of the eighteenth century was a permanent one whose effects were never reversed, whereas the war-time inflation associated with the Napoleonic wars was a temporary inflation whose effects were subsequently completely reversed.

The last two periods of inflation are those associated with the two world wars of the twentieth century. During the first world war the price level rose sharply, but fell again quite drastically throughout the 1920's. The price level again rose severely during the second world war but, *unlike the experience of the first war, this price level movement was not even temporarily reversed, so that a permanently higher level of prices was established.*

This brief inspection of the historical data suggests several conclusions:

(1) There have been a number of major inflationary periods in the last seven centuries. There have been three periods, 1525–1650 (debasement of the coinage plus Spanish gold and silver), 1750–1790 (rise of banking?) and 1939–1946

(second world war) which witnessed a *permanent* upward shift in the price level. The inflations in the other two periods — 1790–1813 (Napoleonic wars), and 1914–20 (first world war) — were followed by deflations of more or less equal severity, so that there was not a major permanent upward shift in the level of prices.

(2) There have been few periods of long-sustained deflations comparable in size and magnitude to the major inflationary periods. Omitting the deflations which merely reversed the price increases of the Napoleonic and the first world wars, the only major long-run deflation is the one found in the nineteenth century.

(3) There are several long periods in history during which the trend of prices was neither inflationary nor deflationary, so that the price level was approximately stable.

(4) All long-run price trends, rising, falling or stable, are interrupted by short-run price fluctuations associated with such phenomena as cyclical variations in the level of business activity, good and bad harvests, changes in the terms of trade, and many other "random shocks". These short-run variations are large and frequent enough to cause a bet on changes in the price level over so short a period as, say, ten years to be a most hazardous affair. In general, the shorter the period over which the price level variation is being considered, the more hazardous is the bet. A fifty-year period gives some margin in favour of inflation, a ten-year period gives very little, and a one-year period gives almost none.

(5) The three major inflations of British history have all been associated with large changes in the quantity of money: gold and silver associated with the discovery of America, credit money associated with the development of banking, and the monetary expansion associated with the deficit financing of the second world war. It is important to note, however, that, as it stands, this observation does not provide serious evidence in favour of the quantity theory of money. In order to provide any sort of serious test of the quantity theory, it would be necessary to show that the quantity of money did *not* increase substantially during the periods in which the price level did *not* rise, as well as to show that the quantity of money *did* increase during periods when the price level *did* rise.

The person who, starting from 1275 and moving year by year to 1949, bets on a rise in the price level is really betting that his time period will extend into one of these major periods of economic upheaval. The importance of this point can be shown if we merely remove the three historical periods of prolonged permanent inflation. We again tell our imaginary investor to make guesses about the change in the price level ten years from the date in question every year from 1275 onwards, only we now give him the added information that his guesses will not involve any of the great inflationary years, 1525–1650, 1744–92 and 1939–46.[4] If our investor still insists on betting on a rise in prices, he will in fact be wrong more times than he will be right. The odds against his being right are 52 to 48.

Thus we see how much the investor who uses historical precedent as a basis for an assumed bias towards inflation is relying on the occurrence of one of the major economic upheavals over the period of his investment. On the complete evidence of history there is a slight margin of the odds in favour of inflation, but it is hardly sufficient to justify ignoring any important differential inducement to invest in bonds rather than equities. On the other hand, if the investor has reason to believe that the period of his investment will *not* extend into a major economic upheaval, then, *if he wishes to proceed on historical evidence*, he should place the odds very slightly in favour of *deflation* rather than inflation.

[4] In other words, he starts at 1275 and guesses the price level in 1285, and runs to 1514, guessing the change from that year to 1524. He starts again in 1651, running to 1733 (relating 1733 to 1743). He starts again in 1793 and runs to 1928 (relating 1928 to 1938). He starts again at 1947 and goes to 1949 (relating the price level in 1949 to that in 1959).

IS INFLATION MORE LIKELY NOW?

Of course, the investor may still argue that, in the world as it has been since the second world war, there is a definite presumption in favour of inflation; but this view has to be based on totally different arguments from those of historical precedent. The case for such a view usually proceeds in two steps, the first arguing that inflation is now more easily achieved, and the second that the motivation to cause inflation is now much stronger than in the past.

The first step merely refers to the general abandonment of convertibility of currencies into precious metals and the consequent adoption of fiat currencies: "Never before has it been so easy to expand the money supply; today new currency can be created merely by the operation of the printing presses". This step is permissive; it argues that inflations are more easily brought about than in the past. The second step provides the central authority with the motive for availing itself of this possibility. The motive is generally provided by full-employment policy. If the State accepts the obligation of maintaining full employment, then periodic bouts of deficit financing may be necessary to prevent major slumps. These will cause a secular expansion in the (easily increased) money supply which will be accompanied by a secular upward drift in the price level.

An alternative second step to the argument merely states that periods of full employment are, and always have been, inflationary, and that steady average price levels in the past have been achieved by alternating periods of full employment with periods of heavy unemployment. If the State now succeeds in removing the periods of heavy unemployment, this will give the trend of prices an upward tilt through the operation of natural market forces, even though a balanced budget is achieved.

This is not the place to attempt to assess these arguments. We merely note that the first step depends on the belief that the expansion of bank credit will prove to be very much easier than was debasement of the metallic coinage in the past. The second step in the argument depends on the belief that governments will in the future be more inclined to resort to in-

flation to achieve their objective of full employment than they were inclined to resort to debasement in the past to achieve other objectives such as the successful prosecution of wars. This may well be so; but when so stated, the arguments do not seem to be of the sort which all reasonable men are bound to accept as conclusive without the need of further discussion and the presentation of further evidence.

The argument just considered runs as follows: "The major inflations of history are all associated with major changes in the quantity of money. In the future one can expect an increase in both the frequency and the magnitude of such inflation-inducing changes in the money supply. Therefore, inflation will be a much more common phenomenon in the future than it has been in the past. Price rises will in fact be so frequent that, *unlike the past,* a bet on a rise in the price level over a time-span of ten years will be a likely winner". The argument thus amounts to saying that, because the future will be so very unlike the past, past experience of price level variations can safely be ignored. On the other hand, the argument based on the "historical law of rising prices" amounts to saying that prices have risen in the past and, because future price level experience *will be similar to that of the past,* inflation can be expected in the future. (I hasten to add that I am in general agreement with Professor Popper's criticism of such historical laws based on pure extrapolation.) Whatever one feels about the strengths of the two types of argument just outlined, it is apparent that one cannot have it both ways. Clearly the two positions cannot be held simultaneously, for they contradict each other.

If investors are advised to expect continued inflation on the basis of the new arguments, they are being told that the future experience of changes in the money supply will be *very different* from what it was in the past. If, on the other hand, the advice is based on historical precedent, so that the investor is to expect inflation in the future *because* this has been the experience of the past, then the advice rests on a very shaky basis indeed. The evidence of simple historical precedent is at best inconclusive.

CHAPTER THIRTEEN

THE ADMINISTRATION OF MONETARY POLICY

46

RULES VERSUS AUTHORITIES IN MONETARY POLICY*

Henry C. Simons†

A dispute has raged for a number of years regarding the proper way to administer monetary policy: should human judgment and discretion determine the proper course of action in light of central bankers' views of economic conditions, or should a set of rules or formulas be established which automatically indicate the direction monetary policy should take under differing circumstances. The late Professor Henry C. Simons, of the University of Chicago, here stresses that the monetary system should be governed by rules rather than by discretion.

The monetary problem stands out today as the great intellectual challenge to the liberal faith. For generations we have been developing financial practices, financial institutions, and financial structures which are incompatible with the orderly functioning of a system based on economic freedom and political liberty. Even more disturbing, perhaps, than the institutional trend is the trend of thinking and discussion among special students of money — the fact that economists have become accustomed to deal with monetary problems in a manner which impliedly belies their professed liberalism.

The liberal creed demands the organization of our economic life largely through individual participation in a game *with definite rules*. It calls upon the state to provide a stable framework of rules within which enterprise and competition may effectively control and direct the production and distribution of goods. The essential conception is that of a genuine division of labor between competitive (market) and political controls — a division of labor within which competition has a major, or at least proximately primary, place.

A liberal system adapted to modern conditions would be, of course, exceedingly complex by comparison with an authoritarian collectivism. It would involve a large measure of political control: outright collectivism in some areas; deliberate enforcement of competition in others; prevention of extreme inequality, largely via taxation, in the distribution of property, income, and power. Moreover, such a system is attainable, through economic reconstruction, only by years of careful planning and wise legislation; and once realized, however perfectly, it would require continuous modifi-

* Abridged from "Rules versus Authorities in Monetary Policy," *The Journal of Political Economy*, Vol. XLIV, No. 1 (February, 1936), by permission of The University of Chicago Press.

† Professor Simons of the University of Chicago died in 1946.

cation, with at least minor changes in the rules, to meet new developments and new conditions.

There is thus little point in contrasting a liberal system and a planned economy — except for the coincidence that the latter phrase has been appropriated by reformers who have little sympathy with, and less understanding of, the liberal position.

There is imminent danger, however, that actual governmental policies will undermine irreparably the kind of economic and political life which most of us prefer to the possible alternatives. This danger manifests itself mainly in three ways: (1) in the displacement of price competition by political (governmental or monopoly) control in many areas where such competition, if established, preserved, and properly canalized, is peculiarly competent for promoting the general welfare; (2) in the neglect of the unquestioned positive responsibilities of governments under the free-enterprise system; and (3) in measures and policies which involve delegation of legislative powers and the setting-up of *authorities instead of rules.*

It is this danger of substituting authorities for rules which especially deserves attention among students of money. There are, of course, many special responsibilities which may wisely be delegated to administrative authorities with substantial discretionary power; health authorities, for example, cannot well be limited narrowly in their activities by legislative prescriptions. The expedient must be invoked sparingly, however, if democratic institutions are to be preserved; and it is utterly inappropriate in the money field. An enterprise system cannot function effectively in the face of extreme uncertainty as to the action of monetary authorities or, for that matter, as to monetary legislation. We must avoid a situation where every business venture becomes largely a speculation on the future of monetary policy. In the past, governments have grossly neglected their positive responsibility of controlling the currency; private initiative has been allowed too much freedom in determining the character of our financial structure and in directing changes in the quantity of money and money substitutes. On this point there is now little

disagreement. In our search for solutions of this problem, however, we seem largely to have lost sight of the essential point, namely, that definite, stable, legislative rules of the game as to money are of paramount importance to the survival of a system based on freedom of enterprise.

Indeed, it may be said that economists, as students of money and banking, have accepted and propagated the first serious heresy among liberals. Managed currency (along with protectionism) is the prototype of all current "planning" schemes — in the sense of all the illiberal connotations of planning. To be sure many economists still protest vigorously against proposals for currency management; but they and their teachers before them joined zealously in the movement for central banking — and it is precisely here that the heresy is clearly manifested.

This unwitting defection among custodians of the liberal faith is explicable, and may be apologized for, in terms of an unfortunate habit of distinguishing too sharply between currency and banking problems, and in terms of a disposition to look upon banking arrangements as merely a detail or subsidiary system within the supposedly automatic mechanism of the gold standard. Only of late is it clearly realized that the money problem has been swallowed up in the credit problem or that gold has long been reduced largely to the status of a decorative symbol within a welter of national policies as to central banking, government finance, and foreign trade.

Economist-liberals are now on the defensive. On most fronts, however, their position is, or can be made, very strong intellectually. Conspicuous weakness is to be found only with respect to the problems of money and banking. There is little agreement, and not much relevant discussion, as to how the monetary rules of the game might effectively be altered to prevent or greatly to mitigate the affliction of extreme industrial fluctuations. We cannot effectively answer radical critics of the present system, or expose the stupid schemes of plausible reformers, by saying that the problems which they find in other areas are really just problems of money (although this observation is usually correct and pointed), when we have no good solutions to propose, with some unanimity, in the money field.

Our problem is that of defining an adequate monetary system based on simple rules and of finding the way toward such a system. We cannot seek merely to return to some arrangement of the past. The monetary problem never was solved in the past. There is no adequate system of rules to be found in earlier arrangements — except in the sense that the specific form of the rules was formerly, in a more flexible economy, a matter of less importance. Moreover, we have become so habituated to the fact and to the idea of "management," especially with respect to banking, that we shall find it hard either to reject the palliatives which management offers or even to face squarely our intellectual task.

In a free-enterprise system we obviously need highly definite and stable rules of the game, especially as to money. The monetary rules must be compatible with the reasonably smooth working of the system. Once established, however, they should work mechanically, with the chips falling where they may. To put our present problem as a paradox — we need to design and establish with the greatest intelligence a monetary system good enough so that, hereafter, we may hold to it unrationally — on faith — as a religion, if you please. The utter inadequacy of the old gold standard, either as a definite system of rules or as the basis of a monetary religion, seems beyond intelligent dispute. But if that system lacks peculiarly the virtues which now seem important, they are also patently lacking in most of the systems proposed as substitutes.

The possibilities of genuine economic reconstruction, and the requirements of sound liberal strategy, may be defined in terms of three objectives: (1) restoration of a maximum of competitiveness in industry (including the labor markets); (2) transition to a less preposterous structure of private money contracts; and (3) ultimate establishment of a simple, mechanical rule of monetary policy. As regards this third objective, the writer feels that his earlier persuasion as to the merits of the rule of a fixed quantity of money was fundamentally correct, although the scheme is obviously too simple as

a prescription under anything like present conditions. Its limitations, however, have to do mainly with the unfortunate character of our financial structure — with the abundance of what we may call "near-moneys" — with the difficulty of defining money in such manner as to give practical significance to the conception of quantity.

The shortcomings of price-index stabilization, as the fundamental basis of a monetary system, are numerous and serious from either an analytical or an empirical viewpoint. It is easy to maintain that such a rule falls far short of the ideal in monetary arrangements — far too easy, indeed, when those who criticize are not obliged or inclined to define the better rules by comparison with which the one in question is so defective. The advocates of a stable price level (with all the irritating excesses of their advocacy) are proposing a solution which is genuinely consistent with traditional liberal principles — and, precisely on that account, are faring rather badly in the debate which the proposal has provoked among professional economists and journalists. The most vigorous and pungent criticism comes from specialists who themselves have no intelligible solutions to offer and who generally have been spared the suspicion that a solution in terms of definite rules is of any importance.

If price-level stabilization is a poor system, it is, still from a liberal viewpoint, infinitely better than no system at all. And it seems now highly questionable whether any better system is feasible or possible at all within the significant future. Given the present financial structure, and given the present multitude of uncoordinated monetary measures and monetary authorities, is there any other rule of policy around which some order and system might be achieved? How else may the present chaos of private financial practices, central-bank action, fiscal measures, and tariff changes be pulled together into something which resembles a monetary system? How else can we possibly escape from a situation where monetary policy is merely the composite of the uncertain daily actions of an indefinite number of agencies, governmental and private? Some ordering of this chaos is imperative. It may be achieved, either by setting up a superior, independent authority or by bringing the totality of monetary measures under the discipline of some rule; and only the advocates of price-index stabilization have offered a feasible way out along the latter lines.

This solution, if unsatisfying, is likewise not simple administratively. Question is often raised as to whether stabilization of a price level is possible. The problem is better formulated, however, when we ask by what agency it might best be undertaken and what methods would be appropriate in its execution.

The task is certainly not one to be intrusted to banking authorities, with their limited powers and restricted techniques, as should be abundantly evident from recent experience. Ultimate control over the value of money lies in fiscal practices — in the spending, taxing, and borrowing operations of the central government. Thus, in an adequate scheme for price-level stabilization, the Treasury would be the primary administrative agency; and all the fiscal powers of Congress would be placed behind (and their exercise religiously limited by) the monetary rule. The powers of the government to inject purchasing power through expenditure and to withdraw it through taxation — the powers of expanding and contracting issues of actual currency and other obligations more or less serviceable as money — are surely adequate to price-level control. At present, monetary powers are dispersed indefinitely, among governmental agencies and private institutions, not to mention Congress itself. Since the powers of the legislature are ultimate and decisive, a program looking toward coordination and concentration of responsibility must focus on fiscal policy as its mode of implementation.

The scheme clearly requires the delegation of large administrative powers. The Treasury might be given freedom within wide limits to alter the form of the public debt — to shift from long-term to short-term borrowing or vice versa, to issue and retire demand obligations in a legal-tender form. It might be granted some control over the timing of expenditures. It might be given limited power to alter tax rates by decree and to make refunds of taxes previously collected. How wide and numerous these powers should be, need not concern us here. Any legislation granting such authority, however, must also impose the duty and responsibility of exercising that authority in accordance with a sharply defined policy.

Given the suitable mandate, the grant of administrative powers should err, if at all, on the side of generosity. The more adequately implemented the rule of monetary policy, the easier will be its actual execution. The greater the powers available for its execution, the smaller will be the probable demands for their exercise. If it is clear that the administrative authority is adequately equipped to make the rule effective, then the rule will be, to some extent, self-enforcing, in so far as the actions of enterprisers and speculators come to be predicated upon its enforcement.

Not only must the price-level rule be implemented through fiscal measures; it must also serve as a control upon all governmental measures which have significant monetary effects. In other words, it must be accepted by the community, and obeyed by legislatures, as the guiding principle of government finance — as the basic criterion of sound fiscal policy. While the rule cannot wisely be written into our fundamental law, it must provide the same sort of limitation and mandate as would a constitutional provision. As things stand now, there is almost nothing which a dominant party may not do or leave undone financially, without rebuke. (There is still some moral pressure, to be sure, against outright issue of paper money; but this only invites evasion through the use of short maturities and through resort to the inelegant expedient of paying the banks to create money for the Treasury.) A federal administration can now spend far beyond its revenues, and grossly debase the currency, without even placing itself on the defensive before public opinion. On the other hand, the "principles" to which reactionaries would have us return are perhaps worse than none at all. That the old moral prohibitions have lost their force is here not altogether an occasion for regret. But we cannot get along without some such rules — without some moral sanctions and mandates which politicians must obey in matters of finance.

And there is probably nothing more promising than the idea of a stable price level as a symbol articulating deep-rooted sentiments and as a source of discipline in fiscal practice.

The following observations may now be submitted, to define the author's general position and to guard against misinterpretation:

1. A democratic, free-enterprise system implies, and requires for its effective functioning and survival, a stable framework of definite rules, laid down in legislation and subject to change only gradually and with careful regard for the vested interests of participants in the economic game. It is peculiarly essential economically that there should be a minimum of uncertainty for enterprisers and investors as to monetary conditions in the future — and, politically, that the plausible expedient of setting up "authorities" instead of rules, with respect to matters of such fundamental importance, be avoided, or accepted only as a very temporary arrangement. The most important objective of a sound liberal policy, apart from the establishment of highly competitive conditions in industry and the narrow limitation of political control over relative prices, should be that of securing a monetary system governed by definite rule.

2. To assure adequate moral pressure of public opinion against legislative (and administrative) tinkering, the monetary rules must be definite, simple (at least in principle), and expressive of strong, abiding, pervasive, and reasonable popular sentiments. They should be designed to permit the fullest and most stable employment, to facilitate adjustment to such basic changes (especially in technology) as are likely to occur, and, secondarily, to minimize inequities as between debtors and creditors; but the problems here, while of first importance, should be conceived and dealt with mainly as problems of a transition period. Once well established and generally accepted as the basis of anticipations, any one of many different rules (or sets of rules) would probably serve about as well as another.

3. The responsibility for carrying out the monetary rules should be lodged in a federal authority, endowed with large administrative powers but closely controlled in their exercise by a sharply defined policy. The powers of the monetary authority should have to do primarily or exclusively with fiscal arrangements — with the issue and retirement of paper money (open-market operations in government securities) and perhaps with the relation between government revenues and expenditures; in other words, the monetary rules should be implemented entirely by, and in turn should largely determine, fiscal policy.

4. Political control in this sphere should be confined exclusively to regulation of the quantity of money and near-money, the *direction* of investment (the allocation of investment funds) being left to the control of competition and kept as far as possible outside the influence of political agencies (or central banks).

5. A liberal program of monetary reform should seek to effect an increasingly sharp differentiation between money and private obligations and, especially, to minimize the opportunities for the creation of effective money substitutes (whether for use as circulating media or in hoards) by private corporations. The abolition of private deposit banking is clearly the appropriate first step in this direction and would bring us in sight of the goal; but such a measure, to be really effective, must be accompanied, or followed closely, by drastic limitation on the formal borrowing powers of all private corporations and especially upon borrowing at short term.

6. A monetary rule of maintaining the constancy of some price index, preferably an index of prices of competitively produced commodities, appears to afford the only promising escape from present monetary chaos and uncertainties. A rule calling for outright fixing of the total quantity of money, however, definitely merits consideration as a perhaps preferable solution in the more distant future. At least, it may provide a point of departure for fruitful academic discussion.

47

MONEY SUPPLY AND STABLE ECONOMIC GROWTH*

Edward S. Shaw†

In Selection 46 Henry Simons outlined the philosophical basis for preferring that monetary policy be executed in accordance with a fixed "rule." However, the closest he came to specifying what the particular rule should be was to advocate that the monetary authorities attempt to maintain a stable price level. In this selection, Professor Shaw, following in the Simons tradition, proposes a more specific rule: that the money supply be increased by 3 or 4 per cent each year, regardless of current economic trends.

Professor Shaw and Professor Milton Friedman of the University of Chicago are the two leading proponents today of the Simons or "Chicago School" position. (A more comprehensive statement of this view is contained in Professor Friedman's A Program for Monetary Stability, published in 1960 by the Fordham University Press.) This position is closely associated with the Quantity theory as opposed to the Keynesian method of analysis.

Our purposes are to discuss the meaning of "money" and to review American experience with money. We shall also consider a proposal for monetary policy that only a corporal's guard of economists will defend, namely, that monetary policy be added to the array of built-in economic stabilizers, taken off discretionary control, and put under automation.

DEFINITIONS OF MONEY

EVERYONE ROLLS HIS OWN

It is almost true that everyone rolls his own definition of money and has his own rules for measurement of the money supply. To confuse matters further, some people do not think that the definition matters. Others insist on attaching restrictive adjectives, so that one has to cope, for example, with "high-powered money," "fiat money," "token money," "inside money," "outside money," and "near-money." Sometimes an object is counted as money when it is held privately in the country of issue, and not-money when it is held by government or by people abroad. The Chairman of the Board of Governors of the Federal Reserve System is not optimistic that the confusion will settle: "I think all of us have to study a great deal more before we can say positively and precisely that this is what constitutes the money supply."

Following is Table I, in Federal Reserve terminology, from which is concocted now one,

MONEY OR NOT?

Item	Amount (Billions of Dollars)
Money supply	
Currency component	31.1
Demand deposit component	119.5
Related deposits	
Time	
Commercial banks	109.9
Mutual savings banks	44.0
Postal Savings System	0.5
Foreign	1.2
U.S. Government	
Treasury cash holdings	0.4
At commercial and savings banks	3.8
At Federal Reserve Banks	0.8

now another, definition of money with measurements to match. The figures apply to a date chosen at random, October 30, 1963.

* From *United States Monetary Policy*, revised edition (edited by Neil H. Jacoby and published for The American Assembly of Columbia University by Frederick A. Praeger, 1964). Reprinted by the courtesy of the publisher and the author.

† Stanford University.

"Money," as the composite of some items above, increased in amount over the preceding year at a very modest pace. "Money" comprising a different combination of these items increased more rapidly than usual. If you suspect that growth in money was under tight restraint, you can tailor a definition to your suspicion. If you prefer to think that restraint was mild, you can be right again — with a different definition.

There is authority for counting as money only the hard core of the first two items in the list above — that part balanced by the banking system's stock of gold and of claims on the federal government. There is authority, too, for extending the list to include traveler's checks issued by the American Express Company. One can find enumerations of "money" that include anything called a "deposit" in anything called a "bank" along with "shares" in savings and loan associations and credit unions.

The definition in common usage begins with the dictum "A dollar is a dollar." A unit of money bearing the price, or face value, of $1 today bears the same price tomorrow and next year. It discharges a debt for $1 any time, and it always buys something else with a price tag of $1. No one haggles over money's price.

This definition is not quite as rigorous as it may seem, because it would count in money not merely the "currency component" with legal-tender quality but the "demand-deposit component" as well. The latter does depreciate a little in price, subject as it is to service charges. It would appreciate a little, if Congress once again permitted interest credits on checking balances. This definition is flexible enough to admit nearly everything that people use as money — as a means of payment.

Modern money is a debt, differing from other forms of debt in that its price does not vary. It is a debt of the monetary system — the commercial banks, the Federal Reserve Banks, and the Treasury monetary accounts. It is issued to other sectors of the economy in payment by the monetary system for purchases principally of nonmonetary securities and monetary metals. It is an IOU even though there is nothing that it promises to pay, no interest yield to the holder, and no maturity date.

THE SUPPLY OF MONEY

At any moment the supply or quantity of money, according to our preference among definitions, is the monetary system's aggregate of fixed-price debt. It is the sum of all legal tender in pockets and tills (except bank tills) together with the sum of unused credits to checking accounts (except interbank accounts).

An observation at a moment of time does not give as accurate a "fix" as is necessary for precision in relating the supply of money to, for instance, national income for a year. Instead of a momentary measurement, one needs an average figure for money outstanding. Normally, too, this raw statistic for money should be cleansed of its very short-run or seasonal fraction and used in "seasonally adjusted" form. Then one cannot confuse a change that is quickly reversible with a change that has come to stay for a while.

An average supply or quantity of money may be outrageously inflationary if it is spread over a small community, grossly deflationary if the community is much larger. Especially in a growth context, it is often the money supply per capita that one needs for analytical purposes. This is not a datum regularly accessible in official tabulations or elsewhere, possibly because most of us are preoccupied with the behavior or misbehavior of money in the short run, too few of us with monetary phenomena in periods long enough for significant change in the population of money-users.

The money we are discussing is *nominal* money — the face value of the monetary system's debt. In the belief that money-users are not blinded by money-illusion and are concerned with money because of its value and not because of its price, economists suppose that it is *real* money, rather than nominal money, that affects patterns and levels of economic activity and economic welfare. Real money is the purchasing power of nominal money. The supply of real money is the supply of nominal money deflated by some one or other index of prices for things that money buys. These with experience in monetary analysis are ruefully aware that no price index is quite right for measurement of the real money supply and of changes in it. Perhaps this explains why the Federal Reserve does not publish the data on real money balances.

As one puts the quantity of money into one statistical disguise after another, he can get very different impressions of its behavior. The quantity of nominal money increased from the annual average of $143.4 billion in 1961 to $146.8 billion in 1962. Quantity grew, it seems, by 2.4 per cent. But did it? If we deflate the data for nominal money by a price index based on 1954, it appears that real money increased a bit less than 1 per cent. And real money per capita, for our noninstitutional population, declined by 0.7 per cent. Was there monetary expansion in 1961–62 or monetary contraction? Was the Federal Reserve "easy" or "hard"?

The "supply of money" that central banks manipulate, that people hold most of the time and spend once in a while, that economists investigate is not, then, a simple concept. It can be a figure so transformed in the statistical beauty parlor as to be hardly recognizable by its closest friends. There is more than meets the eye in any measurement of the supply or quantity of money.

ELASTICITY IN THE SUPPLY OF MONEY: TOO MUCH ELASTICITY AT THE WRONG TIME

It was a common complaint, before passage of the Federal Reserve Act in 1913, that our monetary system was inelastic. Limitations on its ability to expand the money supply or to adjust the relative amounts of currency and deposits made it vulnerable to shock in short periods and restrictive of economic growth over the long run. The Federal Reserve Act and its amendments put elasticity into the monetary structure. Administration of the act put elasticity into monetary policy.

Partly out of conviction, partly to incite controversy, we are going to argue that the monetary system now is too elastic. Moreover, its expansions and contractions have often been ill-timed. The old monetary system had its flaws, but the new monetary system too has been guilty of permitting or even promoting short-run economic stability, and it has infre-

quently hit on the right degree of elasticity for economic growth. The optimal monetary system still eludes us.

THE STATISTICAL RECORD

Table II below roughly traces our monetary experience during 1900–62. It measures growth in nominal money over the entire period and during eight subperiods. The subperiods begin with 1900–14, when the old monetary system was running out its last miles under critical inspection by a bevy of monetary commissions, public and private.

STOP AND GO IN MONETARY POLICY

Period	Change in nominal money (Billions of Dollars)	Annual rate of change (Percentage)
1900–14	5.7	5
1914–19	11.9	15
1919–29	2.9	1
1929–33	−6.6	−7
1933–41	28.4	12
1941–45	54.2	21
1945–51	20.3	3
1951–62	25.2	2
1900–62	142.0	5.5

In four of the subperiods after 1914, policies of the new monetary system were stipulated primarily by the Treasury Department. These Treasury intervals were 1914–19, 1933–41, 1941–45, 1945–51. In two of these intervals, the monetary system was conscripted for war finance. For the greater part of 1933–41, the broad objective of policy was to restore liquidity in an economic system that had been parched and seared by deflation. The Treasury's concern for the marketability of its debt distinguishes the years 1945–51.

There were three subperiods when monetary policy was stipulated by the Federal Reserve Board, alias the Board of Governors of the Federal Reserve System. These interludes of board tenure were 1919–29, 1929–33, 1951–62. The first and third of these periods opened with a palace revolution, in the federal executive, against the Treasury's excessive concern for the marketability of its debt at low and steady rates of interest. The first culminated in a shift of power within the Federal Reserve and in adoption of policies that led directly to the disaster of monetary moratorium in 1933. The third period continues, with the Federal Reserve in high repute despite the gathering, from time to time, of vigilantes into monetary commissions.

In 1900 the nominal supply of money was at the near-microscopic level of $5.9 billion. At the close of 1962, the nominal supply of money was 25 times larger, or $147.9 billion. The average annual compound rate of growth was approximately 5.5 per cent. One had no need for a microscope to see the money supply at the end of 1962.

For perspective, the growth rate of 5.5 per cent in nominal money may be compared with the more modest growth rate of about 3 per cent in real value of money. Evidently prices rose at the average annual rate of 2.5 per cent. It may come as a mild surprise that this degree of price inflation has been our method of repudiating about $105 billion in nominal money: nominal money increased by $142 billion; real money by perhaps $37 billion in 1900–62. In terms of its purchasing power, the dollar has shriveled with age.

THE MODEL-T PERIOD

Let us consider the pre-Federal Reserve years 1900–14 a little more closely. In correspondence with accelerating growth in physical production and in the nation's real income and wealth, the money stock grew at the average rate of 8 per cent in 1900–6. After 1906 the tempo of growth slackened throughout the economy, the annual rate of growth in money falling to a little less than 3 per cent. The money supply declined in one year (1907); and it rose in each year of depression, including the dismal year of 1908. From year to year during 1900–14, variation in money's growth rate was less than during four of the seven subsequent intervals.

Waving aside the seasonal stresses of the old monetary system, which were amenable to treatment on the principle of the Aldrich-Vreeland Act, one is tempted to shed a nostalgic tear for our monetary experience in the decade and one half prior to the Federal Reserve Act. The monetary system was Model-T, but it bounced along with surprising efficiency.

DRAG-RACING THE MONETARY SYSTEM

The Federal Reserve Act multiplied the horsepower and brake power in the monetary system. Since 1914, effective control of the system has alternated between Treasury and Federal Reserve Board. The Treasury takes out its aggressions on the throttle of the new machine. The Board reaches for the brakes. And the money supply lurches along a sawtoothed course of growth.

In 1914–19, the average annual rate of growth in nominal money was accelerated to 15 per cent. Then the brakes were put on. In 1920–21, money was contracted by 14 per cent. After rising 2½ per cent, as an annual average, in 1921–29, money sank again in 1933 and touched on a level previously passed in 1918. This is not a profile of monetary stability.

During two of the years in the period 1919–33, the Federal Reserve Board presided over a decline of more than 10 per cent in nominal money. In both years, 1921 and 1931, the monetary brakes were applied to an economic system that was already on the skids of deflation. In seven of the fourteen years there was not monetary contraction, and in six of these seven years monetary contraction was superimposed on other depressing circumstances. It is true that during two years of cyclic recession — 1924 and 1927 — the Board followed the precedent of the old monetary system in increasing liquidity. But these were years when such a stimulus was less urgent than in five of the six years when the Board departed from the pre-1914 tradition.

The Board's license to drive the monetary system was, in effect, suspended in 1933, when the Treasury took over the controls. Probation was granted in 1936–37, but once more the Board applied the brakes too hard in reducing the money supply by 7 per cent during the fourteen months after March, 1937. The United States economy slid into the recession of 1937–38, and again the Board's license to drive was lifted.

Over fourteen years, 1919–33, the board had

"managed" the creation and destruction of $9 billion in nominal money. Over the next eight years, apart from the interlude of 1936–37, the Treasury chauffeur reversed monetary policy and subjected the economic system to an absurdly high rate of monetary expansion. By 1941, the prestige of monetary management was, properly, very low indeed.

In reaction to the monetary experience of 1919–33, the Congress added to the monetary system's capacity for both acceleration and deceleration in the series of reforms that appeared in 1933–45. Retrospectively, it seems that the rational thing to do was to minimize chances for pilot error in managing money, even to the extent of putting the monetary system on automatic pilot and disengaging manual controls. Instead, new opportunities were approved for discretionary action by the monetary authority, whether Treasury or Board. The principle of reform was to create still more latitude for mistakes of policy.

The mistakes came quickly, first on the part of the Board in its deflationary tactics of 1936–37, then on the part of the Treasury during wartime. This is not the occasion to debate wartime economic controls. One may simply offer the opinion that the rate of growth in nominal money during 1941–45, on the order of 21 per cent annually, is a blemish on our record that no amount of rationalization can erase. We expanded the nominal money supply at a rate surpassing by a wide margin even the requirements for rapid real growth in wartime, then deputized thousands of price policemen in OPA and WPB to patrol the channels of money flow. The money accelerator was pushed to the floorboard, and policemen were deployed in droves to keep the public out of the way of the money juggernaut. The new monetary system was a high-powered vehicle for our folly.

LEANING AGAINST WINDS AND MAINTAINING EVEN KEELS — FOR SUSTAINABLE GROWTH

Until the Accord between Board and Treasury was sealed, in March, 1951, nominal money continued to grow as rapidly as was necessary to support market prices of federal securities. It was the Board that sensed the

inflationary implications of Treasury policy and insisted on resuming monetary control. The Board's chronic disposition to restraint was tempered until spring, 1953, by exigencies of the Korean War. Then the foot shackled since 1936–37 was freed and instinctively stepped on the monetary brakes again. The ensuing screech of complaint in the security markets announced the recession of 1953–54.

The foot is never far from the brake: There was contraction of nominal money by 0.7 per cent in 1957 and 0.6 per cent in 1960. The foot is never hard on the accelerator: The maximum in year-to-year rates of growth was 3.9 per cent, in 1958. Growth in money during 1953–62 averaged 1½ per cent in annual data — the lowest rate for any period of prolonged prosperity during the century.

A little probing behind annual data discloses continual adjustment by the Board in money's growth rate. Growth at 1½ per cent annually seems to have qualified as "sustainable" growth: It is the Board's way of "leaning against the winds" of inflation in prices and of deficits in the balance of payments. But holding the economic system to an "even keel" requires somewhat more instability in money's accumulation than annual data reveal. From mid-1953 to mid-1963, quarterly variations in nominal money, expressed as annual rates of change, followed this pattern:

Annual rate of change (Percentage)	Numbers of quarters
Negative	6
0–1.0	10
1.1–2.0	9
2.1–3.0	4
3.1–4.0	4
4.1–5.0	6
5.1	1

The extremes of quarterly variation in nominal money, expressed in annual rates of change, have been contraction of 3.4 per cent and expansion of 5.1 per cent. When does judgment call for acceleration? The answer is that seven of the eleven quarters in which expansion exceeded 3 per cent followed business-cycle troughs by three quarters or less: Acceleration comes when cyclical recessions are over and recoveries are setting in. When does judgment call for the brakes? The answer is that five of the six quarters in which money contracted came in the immediate vicinity of business-cycle peaks: Deceleration in money, along with other factors, terminates booms. Monetary management within years is a reflex to cyclical instability. It has cultivated booms in their youth, helped to cut them off in their maturity.

One may probe still deeper to find money management in daily, even hourly operations at the trading desk of the New York Federal Reserve Bank. The buying this morning and selling this afternoon are "defensive" tactics against the perturbations that might divert accumulation of money along tangents that do not meet the Board's specifications, in its "dynamic" policy, for cyclical reflexes and secular growth. Money-management is a full-time occupation: If there is a movement to spare from leaning against the wind, it must go to keeping an even keel.

A HALF-CENTURY OF ELASTICITY

Monetary reform in the Federal Reserve Act and its amendments did put elasticity into the monetary system, as much elasticity as the money-manager might wish, within some broad constraints. One of two money-managers, the Treasury, set one standard of elasticity that permitted average annual growth in money of $4.9 billion in twenty-three years. The second money-manager, the Board, permitted no net monetary expansion in 1919–33, reduced money in 1936–37, and during 1953–62 provided money-growth at the average rate of 1½ per cent while now and again decreasing money at short-cycle peaks. In the present regime of the Board, money grows slowly in the long run, varies cyclically within a rather narrow range, and is sheltered against passing instabilities by continual intervention.

DISCRETION OR AUTOMATION — MANAGER OR ROBOT

There are alternative designs for a monetary system. The design that this country has hit

upon builds into the system enormous capacity for both inflation and deflation. How to use this capacity depends on the judgment or discretion of the money-manager. Our experience with managed elasticity has been reviewed in recent years by critics singly, in committees, in commissions, and in assembly, the consensus being an endorsement of managed elasticity as applied by the Board of Governors.

Still, a few dissident voices are faintly heard to suggest that an alternative principle could hardly have done worse in the past half-century and might do better in the next. This is the principle of the automatic pilot, of rules rather than discretion. Starting from a money stock that is not obviously subversive of full employment at a relatively stable price level, it would expand money by formula. Various formulae have been suggested, the pure gold standard among them or a composite commodity standard. The formula we discuss below may be called the "demand standard" for monetary control.

THE DEMAND STANDARD

Feed this rule into an automatic money pilot: Increase the stock of nominal money, continuously and not by fits and starts, at the secular rate of increase in demand for real money. Perhaps the rate should be the 1½ per cent that the Board adopted in 1953–62, but probably not, since the American economy developed symptoms of chronic monetary restraint. The rate of 5½ per cent would not do, since we tried it in 1900–62 and found it inflationary. As a first approximation, split the difference at 3½ per cent.

What are the premises of the demand standard? One is that the real stock of money a community desires to hold in its asset portfolios increases secularly at about the same rate as real income, given rates of interest that affect choice between money and other assets. Another is that real income grows along a stable trend line, associated with secularly stable rates of interest. A third is that deviations in growth of nominal money from growth in desired real money induce price-level changes in the long run and output changes in the short run that may impede economic development. Satisfy stable growth in demand for real money with stable growth in supply of nominal money, and the result is to minimize money mischief.

There could be more complex rules for the money robot than the steady-rate rule. If real money demanded (when employment is full) does not rise secularly along a straight percentage path, automatic alarms might be rung to put the robot on a new course. If the community wishes a possible tonic of secular inflation, growth in nominal money could be accelerated a little to overshoot growth in full-employment demand for real money. The objection now to complex rules of growth in nominal money is that they overtax our knowledge of growth in desired balances.

The idea that demand should be the target for supply is familiar for any other good than money. In the case of money, it does raise eyebrows. "Demand for money" is not a concept in popular use. There is no mention of it in the Federal Reserve Act. One small tabulation remotely akin to it is published in the *Federal Reserve Bulletin*. What is it, and why is it a plausible target for money supply?

We know that money has a fixed price. It can always be sold, with no delay, at the fixed price: It is liquid, as nothing else is. This quality justifies holding money as an asset rather than a like amount of less liquid assets with unstable prices. And a rational calculation of the best portfolio mixture of money and other assets is made in terms not of money's nominal value but instead in terms of money's purchasing power. Demand for money is demand for liquid purchasing power in asset portfolios.

There are three ways of adapting a nominal supply of money to the desired real supply. If nominal money is short, more may be issued so that demand is satisfied. Or, the excess demand evaporates as income and wealth are depressed by the public's attempt to accumulate money through reducing purchases and increasing sales of other things. Eventually, price deflation can increase the real value of the money supply into balance with full-employment demand. The simple adjustment between

supply and demand, that does not punish the community with short-run depression and long-run deflation, is the first one of issuing more nominal money.

Similarly, there are three ways of correcting an excess supply of money. One is to issue less nominal money. The second is short-run booms in real income and wealth that culminate in the third solution, price inflation. The simple adjustment is the first one. Demand for money is a relevant standard for control of supply because excess demand or excess supply forces the public into wasteful adjustments of income, wealth, and prices.

BUT WHAT ABOUT THE SHORT RUN?

Central banks have fallen into the habit of "high-level busy work," as at the trading desk of the New York Federal Reserve Bank, poking and prodding the money supply even though no one can know, from day to day, whether money is in excess supply or excess demand and even though day-to-day adjustments of demand to supply are easy for the public to make. The demand standard would forbid continual nudges of accelerator and brake.

Seasonal patterns of change in real balances demanded can be estimated and are stable. Instructions to the robot could be written for emission of money in seasonal rhythm. Then there would be little danger that seasonal excesses of supply or demand could provoke excessive and cumulative adjustments in output, employment, and prices.

Apart from theology, few credos are immutable. Apparently one of them is that monetary management can be a delicate, pervasive, and powerful instrument for smoothing the short business cycle. What basis of dissent is there for the advocate of automatic control to stand on? Principally, that the short cycle is so short. Allowing for the ambiguity of cycle indicators, for lags in response of money management to them, and for the lag between money stimulus and cyclical effect, there just is not space in the short cycle for turnarounds of monetary policy. That is why, in our recent experience, money expands in time to accelerate a cyclical recovery and contracts at the peak or after. That is why, in making amends for previous error, monetary management adjusts nominal money by fits and starts.

Monetary control in the cycle has been romanticized. It is an illusion, one may argue, that men of refined intuition, alert to the daily flux of economic statistics, resolving their differences by majority poll can anticipate the need months hence for a change in nominal money now. They cannot compete with the automaton whose steady rate of growth in nominal money supplies more than is demanded in recession and so limits the recession, or supplies less money than is demanded in a boom and so limits the boom.

THE DEMAND STANDARD IN ACTION

By the rule of the demand standard, the nominal supply of money would be increased at a constant rate compounded, perhaps, with seasonal wavelets of issue. The rate might be adjusted only with Congressional assent, since full and free debate on the matter of long-run inflation or deflation is no less important than full and free debate on such issues as tax burdens, foreign aid, or ventures into space.

Money would continue to be the debt of the monetary system. And the monetary system as it stands would be no less efficient in supplying money at a steady rate than it is in supplying money at variable rates to the taste of Board or Treasury. The purchasing power that the monetary system commands by issuing money could be spent, as it is now, on credit instruments or gold or bank buildings of glass and aluminum. Monetary expansion could be continuous spending of money created for the purpose, the objects of this spending by the monetary system being determined by the community's choice among alternative uses of the savings that accumulate in real money balances.

The demand standard is a break from monetary tradition in the United States and not only because it would substitute rule for authority. In addition, it bans "credit needs" of the community as a criterion for monetary policy. The monetary system would have credit to dispose of in the sense that presumably it would buy securities as the technique of money

issue though it might be instructed to buy something else, possibly stockpiles of raw materials or highway construction. Its role as a credit institution would be derivative from its role as a supplier of money, and credit extended would be merely one possible application of the purchasing power represented by money issue.

The Federal Reserve Act is not the constitution of a monetary system. It is a body of rules about credit. The Board has concerned itself predominantly since 1914 with the behavior of security markets, the allocation of credit between markets, and the quality of credit. The Treasury has intervened in money management to secure high prices and low yields on its own credit instruments, with excess money supply as a by-product. A new monetary charter should contain a Section I, specifying the growth rate of money, and a Section II, specifying uses of the purchasing power that money issue confers on the monetary system. A preamble would state unambiguously that Section II is ancillary to Section I.

ANOTHER BUILT-IN STABILIZER

This country takes pride in its built-in stabilizers, the economic balance wheels that automatically limit our deviations from normal growth. Serious consideration has been given to formula flexibility in taxation. It is hardly a radical proposal that monetary control should be added to the measures that go into action, without forethought or discretion, against disturbances in the growth process. Two lines of argument favor the proposal. One is that discretionary control of money has not done well. The other is that automatic control can do better.

THE POSITIVE CASE FOR AUTOMATIC CONTROL

The case for automatic control does not rest only on disillusionment with discretionary control. There are five principal ways in which stable growth in nominal money can increase economic welfare.

1. Stable growth in money lays the foundation for a solvent and efficient payments mechanism. In inflation, bank capital is reduced

relative to bank deposits. Deflation under-mines bank capital, through deterioration in asset quality.

2. Stable growth in money removes one hazard of private and governmental economic planning. That is the uncertainty about the length of the monetary yardstick that planners use to measure prospective costs and revenues. Our yardstick, the value of the dollar, has been rubberized, stretching in each deflation and snapping back in each bout of inflation.

3. Stable growth in money and stability in the price level create a favorable environment for flexible individual prices and price rela-tionships. Each inflation and deflation spawns its own brood of price ceilings and escalators, or price floors and subsidies. Flexibility of the price level promotes rigidity of price relation-ships. Insofar as a private-enterprise society re-lies upon flexible price relationships to allocate resources and guide demands, flexible price levels reduce its productive potential.

4. Steady growth in money avoids inflations that distort the form of real capital, and it re-lieves the economic system of the interruptions in capital formation that result when deflation is applied as the remedy of inflation. Monetary restraint does not correct damage done by exces-sive monetary ease: It compounds damage. During inflation, savings are misapplied to capital projects that are made to seem worth while by advancing prices. During deflation, savings are destroyed by underemployment of men and resources. Savings misapplied or lost are never recoverable.

5. Steady growth in money and stability in the price level contribute to development of orderly financial arrangements throughout the community. Deflation creates its distinctive pattern of debt, financial assets, and financial institutions. Inflation gives rise to a different pattern. Costs and risks of allocating loanable funds are increased when the financial system is subjected alternately to the shocks of infla-tion and deflation. Stop-and-go growth in money is a nervous tic in the economic system that the financial structure amplifies, sometimes dangerously, for continuity in the saving-invest-ment process.

AN INNING FOR THE OPPOSITION

Antiautomation and prodiscretion have swept the polls of opinion among laymen and economists alike. On what grounds can man-aged money attract so devoted a following? The list below is short, and its exposition con-cise, but it may indicate why prolonged indul-gence in monetary management is habit forming.

1. Changes in the growth rate of nominal money can be the antidote for instability in-itiated outside of the monetary system. If money's growth rate were frozen, the economy would be easier prey to nonmonetary distur-bances.

Rejoinder. The antimanagement brief does not deny that monetary policy *could* perform miracles, promoting stable growth and fending off shocks to growth. But our experience con-tains no miracles. Management skills are not equal to the job of realizing the potentialities of monetary policy.

2. The first half-century of our experience with discretionary management has not been a fair test. It has been distorted by two world wars and their aftermath in crisis and disaster. The Treasury and the Board have done notably well under the circumstances. In a tranquil world the Federal Reserve Act would be a sound charter for sound money.

Rejoinder. Peace and tranquility are not on the horizon for the next half-century. It is just as well to take the pessimistic view that temp-tations to misuse the monetary system will re-cur. There will be occasions when the Treasury will insist on borrowing cheaply in disregard of monetary stability. There will be occasions when the Board will deem it wise to disappoint the inflationary expectations that Treasury policy has generated. Now is the time, while there is still relative peace and tranquility, to take precautions against mismanagement in the future.

3. Monetary management is now on an un-precedented level of sophistication. The Board, perhaps even the Treasury, understands that the monetary system's proper target of control is money. It has set for itself the goal of stable

growth in nominal money and can achieve as much automation as is safe.

Rejoinder. We are in an era of relative monetary stability. The Board and the Treasury are dedicated men applying exceptional skills to their tasks. Yet, with monetary management at its best, discontinuities occur in monetary growth that are not easy to rationalize. The cessation of growth in money for two years, in 1959–61, was a mistake. The expansion of $8 billion in nominal money during the succeeding two years may be interpreted as confession of error. Stop-go in monetary growth is an expensive school for monetary management.

4. Disarming monetary policy as a contra-cyclical weapon would put a burden on fiscal policy that it is not qualified to bear. Our experience with fiscal policy in the cycle is not reassuring. Congress moves too deliberately when there is opportunity for adjustments in rates of taxation and spending: The opportunity always slips by. In contrast, the Board can move sensitively to cyclical impulses, adjusting the monetary pedal to cyclic tempo. Fiscal policy is inflexible, monetary policy flexible.

Rejoinder. The cat-and-mouse game with the short business cycle has been lost. Monetary and fiscal policy are as likely to induce and aggravate short cycles as they are to stifle them. Built-in stabilizers have a superior record. Automatic money can be a built-in stabilizer, mechanically creating excess money supply in recession, excess money demand in booms. It has no intellect to be tricked into right responses at wrong cycle phases.

5. The economy is doomed to inflation by cost-push. As the price level is raised by nonmonetary market forces, nominal money must accommodate to it in order that production and employment can be sustained. Money is not an independent source of inflation or deflation.

Rejoinder. The monetary theory of inflation has been locked in battle with nonmonetary theories of inflation for generations. Apparently no finite number of demonstrations that cost-push starts in the wake of monetary expansion and stops in the wake of monetary

contraction will break the lineage of structuralism.

6. Demand for real money does not grow along a simple trend line. It follows that growth in nominal money along such a line would be destabilizing, tending to induce inflation when demand for real money slows down, deflation when demand for real money speeds up. The demand standard is a fickle standard.

Rejoinder. Undoubtedly there is no simple, infallible rule for growth in nominal money. Yet, historical evidence seems to be that a simple formula for monetary expansion would have averted the liquidity crisis of 1929–33, or 1936–37, or spring, 1953, or spring, 1958. The demand standard invokes a naïve rule for growth in money, but knowledge about demand for money is not yet sufficient to justify a more sophisticated rule and is even less adequate for discretionary management.

7. If growth in money is stabilized, the economy may still suffer from unstable growth in money substitutes. Perhaps the forces that now result in uneven accumulation of money will shift their impact to other financial assets so that little will be gained by automating money only.

Rejoinder. Our blackest experiences with nonmonetary financial assets have resulted from monetary instability. The collapse of nonmonetary financial institutions in the 1930's is one case in point, the monetization of federal securities in 1941–51 another. If monetary stability were to be sabotaged by financial instability from nonmonetary sources, there are or could be automatic restraints that would bring the saboteurs into line.

8. The demand standard is provincial. It would isolate the American economy behind a fluctuating foreign-exchange rate or it would induce gross instability, behind a stable foreign-exchange rate, in international balances of payments. A domestic rule for growth in nominal money is a "Fortress America" rule that violates our international responsibilities.

Rejoinder. The transition from dollar shortage on foreign-exchange markets to dollar surfeit is hardly evidence that managed money means a stable balance of payments. Damage is done in international monetary relationships by the changes in direction that typify discretionary policy. The automatic dollar standard would dispel uncertainty, among this country's trading partners, as to its monetary policy and reduce their incentive to regional monetary coalitions.

48

THE THEORETICAL BASIS OF CENTRAL BANKING*

R. S. Sayers†

Selections 48 and 49 present vigorous arguments against the Simons-Friedman-Shaw position.

The essence of central banking is discretionary control of the monetary system. The purpose of central banking has been defined in various ways: to maintain stability of the price level, to keep the economy on an even keel, and so on. These aims could be varied far more than they are in the literature: under some circumstances the purpose of central banking might be defined as the maintenance of the gold standard, the maintenance of a sterling standard, or the maintenance of a dollar standard. But these varieties are of purpose; central banking is an institutional arrangement that may be made to serve any one of a number of purposes. The choice of purpose — the object of monetary policy — is not irrelevant to the choice of method: a community might hope more reasonably in some cases than in others to attain its ends by making its monetary system work to rule. And working to rule is the antithesis of central banking. A central bank is necessary only when the community decides that a discretionary element is desirable. The central banker is the man who exercises his discretion, not the machine that works according to rule.

Most economists nowadays take it for granted that there must be a central bank, at any rate in every highly developed economy. Yet central banks are comparative novelties. Even in England central banking history falls well within the last two hundred years, while in the United States and most other countries it is practically confined to the twentieth century. The very term "central banking" is not as old as the century. Before we take such a youngster entirely for granted, perhaps we should look rather critically at the foundation on which it rests. Why has the world apparently abandoned the attempt to leave its monetary systems to work by rule?

An automatic monetary system does have certain seductive advantages. The monetary unit is, after all, of crucial importance in all contractual relationships in the economy, and a long tradition in English political economy lies behind the view that any tampering with the monetary unit is a fraud on either debtors or creditors. The Ricardian view was that the nation had decided, and decided rightly, that the value of the monetary unit should be made to depend upon the world value of gold, and

* From R. S. Sayers, *Central Banking After Bagehot* (The Clarendon Press, Oxford, 1957). Reprinted by the courtesy of the publisher and the author.

† London School of Economics.

that the supply of money should be so closely tied to conditions in the market for gold that there should be no room for human manipulation, however well intentioned. Any discretionary action would be "tinkering with the currency." Some earlier writers had admitted the possibility of circumstances in which discretionary action might improve on the blind forces of the market-place; but some of these were reluctantly converted, after the experiences of the first twenty years of the nineteenth century, to the view that the steering-wheel was safer under Adam Smith's Invisible Hand than under the hand of the Old Lady of Threadneedle Street [the Bank of England]. Experience in the eighteen-twenties and eighteen-thirties was not much better, or at least could be represented as being not much better; conscious guidance of the monetary system appeared to imply arbitrary interference with the value of money. Ricardian contempt for the "company of merchants" who directed the Bank of England lived on, to inspire the Currency School of the thirties and forties with a prejudice against any form of discretionary control. Some of these writers asserted that certain basic forms of money could be identified and their supply controlled by strict rule of law. Others acknowledged the problems imposed by the development of commercial banking and of commercial credit and wished them away. In western Europe related controversies revealed the same distrust of conscious control. Especially in France, Germany, and Austria during the third quarter of the nineteenth century, the general issue of central banking versus "free banking" was vigorously debated by economists. This debate was shaped largely by the practical question whether the issue of bank-notes should be monopolized by a "central bank," but the arguments are closely akin to those relevant to central banking in the broader sense. It was argued, for example, that a single bank of issue, obliged to the government for its privileged position, would be susceptible to the pressure of short-sighted governments, whereas a host of competing banks of issue would be more elusive, clinging more tightly to the commercial prudence that would restrain their issues. It was argued that the misbehaviour of

a central bank could bring catastrophe to the whole system, whereas the misbehaviour of one among a number of equally privileged banks would leave the remaining banks free to step into its shoes as a servant of the public. More generally, it was argued that a central bank would take risks with its reserves beyond any risk that would be taken by any one bank in a multiple reserve system. Most of these arguments boil down to an assertion that men are not to be trusted with discretionary powers, and that departures from automatism in the regulation of the monetary system sooner or later lead to trouble, and bad trouble at that. It is not difficult to support this attitude by reference to the monetary history of any country; even the most cautious have had their episodes of rapid inflation, and some have had pretty desperate deflations as well, all or most of these inflations and deflations being consequent upon avoidable human decision. Would not an automatic machine be more conducive to steady economic progress, as well as more defensible in equity.

There are some important if more subtle supports for this crude argument. The more we learn of monetary history, the more we see that people have not always blundered thoughtlessly or immorally; it is rather that there are traps in the very nature of monetary policy. There is, for instance, the inherent difficulty of taking the right decision sufficiently early. The central banker has to try to act in anticipation of events, whereas the graphs prepared by his statistical department reveal the events only weeks or months afterwards. When the central banker has to choose between two courses, one of which is politically disagreeable, he is strongly tempted to doubt the diagnosis that urges the disagreeable course. All too readily he postpones the disagreeable, pending clearer omens. On the other hand, he is apt to hasten action that relieves pressure on the credit situation, because such action ordinarily has political attractions. The difficulty of early diagnosis coupled with ordinary human weakness thus gives to central banking an inflationary bias, undermining the value of the monetary unit.

When trying to spot in the surrounding obscurity the dangerous trend that he must try to counter, the central banker is also handicapped by his human susceptibility to the views of the business men with whom it is his duty to keep touch. When optimism is in the air, the central banker breathes it and may be unable to realize that danger signals are necessary; when all around him are sensing danger ahead, the central banker must be superhuman if he is to show the green light quickly enough. The central banker may thus exaggerate the ups and downs of the economy, squeezing credit just when a boom is breaking, and encouraging an incipient boom just when restraint would have been most useful.[1]

Discretionary control of the monetary situation thus bears within itself the risks of exaggerating the ups and downs of trade and of undermining the value of the monetary unit. Yet the elimination of the trade cycle and the conservation of the value of money are among the most important aims of monetary policy. Are we therefore to say that this is a realm in which reliance on human discretion is so peculiarly dangerous that we must prefer some automatic monetary system? My own view is that these inherent weaknesses in central banking can, at any rate in most countries, be kept within manageable bounds. Economic forecasting remains and must remain a chancy business, but advances in statistical techniques, and perhaps in economic theory too, are making the task of diagnosis rather less of a sophisticated blindman's-buff. The susceptibilities of central bankers to the business atmosphere become less dangerous as they become more conscious of their responsibilities; the central bankers may indeed go further and infect the business men themselves with something of their coldness. The rise of economic commentators whose roots are in the academic rather than the business world may have helped to

[1] The reader may be tempted to find confirmation in the historical phenomena of low interest rates persisting far into a period of trade revival, to be followed by extremely high rates after the boom has cracked. These phenomena have however been associated most clearly with the absence of well-developed central banking; they have been the automatic responses of monetary systems in which central bankers have not accepted an obligation to iron out the trade cycle.

give central bankers the poise that is so desirable. Certainly the economic history of this century encourages the view that central bankers can be found to diagnose reasonably accurately, to act quickly, and to maintain for themselves the desirable half-way house between ivory towers and the hurly-burly of the marketplace. And as experience in central banking accumulates, it is reasonable to expect that the inherent weaknesses will be kept increasingly under control. The worst episodes in recent monetary history — the great inflations — have been marked by the subjection of central bankers to overriding political pressures, against which no "fixed rules" could have stood. 1929–32 remains a black mark against the central bankers of the United States, but it is already permissible to argue that the last ten years have shown that some of the lessons have been learned by the central bankers and will not be forgotten.

The strength of these arguments in support of central banking is necessarily a matter of opinion. Those who are more afraid of human weakness and less confident in man's capacity to master his economic environment may logically enough protest that the case for central banking is not strong enough. But there is another argument of totally different kind, an argument in no way depending on estimates of human nature. The root of the argument lies in the artificiality of any legal definition of money. The money-quality of assets is something imposed by the business habits of people; it is attached in varying degree to various assets; and the attachment can be and is varied over time in a completely unpredictable manner. To label something as "money," the supply of which is to behave according to rules laid down by the legal authority, is to build on shifting sand. Every textbook writer wanting to illustrate arguments about the supply of money knows how arbitrarily he has to represent a country's money. Are time-deposits to be included or excluded? Are the liabilities of savings banks to be included or excluded? Such difficulties — and they are many — spring from the fact that there is no hard and fast line between what is money and what is not money. In the ordinary business of life nature does not make a jump, and Marshall no doubt would have reiterated this doctrine in the context of monetary economics if he had reached his later volumes in good time.

When we worry ourselves about changes in the supply of money, our concern is in fact with the changing liquidity position in the economy, and any survey that is to be comprehensive must take account of the behaviour of every kind of financial institution. If there were any basic money the supply of which at all times determined according to fixed rules the behaviour of every conceivable financial institution, there would be logical point in governing the supply of that money according to fixed rules. But there is not; there is not even finality in the list of financial institutions whose behaviour is relevant. New financial institutions arise to exploit new opportunities; they may not at first be recognized as financial institutions, and indeed may not at first be such, but may imperceptibly acquire some importance in financial affairs.

The relevance of the evolution of financial institutions may be illustrated by reference to some actual situations. The question of controlling the supply of money in England was under constant debate throughout the first half of the nineteenth century; but there was no agreement as to what constituted the money — for the very good reason that any definition is necessarily arbitrary. Most participants in these debates recognized the importance of certain assets which they regarded either as money-substitutes or as part of a complex money supply, and on either basis it was relevant to consider the relationship of these assets to money itself or to the other parts of the money-supply. For example, the relation between country bank-note issues and the Bank of England issues was relevant — but there was disagreement about what the relationship was, partly because it was a changing relationship. Similarly the relation of bank deposits and bills of exchange to the supply of money, defined in some narrower sense, was much debated. In retrospect, there can be no doubt that the relationship between these various classes of assets was in fact rapidly changing: the degree to which the community was imputing the

money-quality to them was changing. Bank deposits, as we now recognize, were becoming much more important in the monetary situation, and the law was clutching at a slippery eel when it sought to apply a rule of thumb to the monetary situation by regulating the issue of bank notes alone. This was the design of the famous Bank Charter Act of 1844; men soon found how to escape its intentions, though the empty shell long remained, a memorial to those who believed that either nature or the law had drawn a sharp line of distinction between what was money and what was not money and that an automatic machine could sufficiently govern the monetary situation.

In our own time one of the most important changes in monetary institutions has been the growth of consumer credit, and of the specialist finance companies that facilitate the growth of that credit. This is merely the latest development in institutions that alter the liquidity situation of the people who make up the economy. No rule of thumb based on the structure and behaviour of financial institutions of a quarter of a century ago could have provided by anticipation for the changes in the liquidity position caused by the consumer credit operations. Yet any control of the monetary situation, if it is to have any chance of success in maintaining full employment or stabilizing the value of money, must take cognizance of these changes in financial institutions. It is idle to say that one can somewhere find an ultimate form of money and rule that off as the grand regulator of the economic situation, a regulator that can be made to behave properly by legislator's orders. Our economic systems are not like that.[2]

---

[2] Even in our own generation there are economists who base arguments for monetary reform on the supposed possibility of identifying once and for all something called 'money'. See e.g. Milton Friedman, *Essays in Positive Economics*, from which the following is taken (p. 135): 'a reform of the monetary and banking system to eliminate both the private creation or destruction of money by central-bank authority. The private creation of money can perhaps best be eliminated by adopting the 100 per cent reserve proposal, thereby separating the depositary from the lending function of the banking system.' I find all such proposals tempting, but they are based on a complete misconception of the origin of money.

So we must have central bankers to exercise a discretionary influence upon the monetary situation. And it follows that there is no code of eternal rules for them to follow. They have to adapt their ways to the shape of the community's constantly changing financial habits. By comparative study we may, of course, hope to find some generalizations about the behaviour of central banks, and the experience of some may offer guarded guidance to others; but we are doomed to disappointment if we look for rules applicable to all times and all places. We have central banks for the very reason that there are no such rules.

49

HUMAN JUDGMENT AND CENTRAL BANKING*

Walter A. Morton[†]

I agree that a fixed rule of monetary policy, or for that matter of any policy, is preferable to administrative discretion, provided, however, that a rule can be found appropriate to all circumstances to which it must be applied. If, moreover, such a rule can be discovered, then the distinction between rules and authorities will soon disappear because any sensible authority would apply the rule whether or not it was enacted into law. The issue is then whether such a rule has been discovered.

Everyone agrees that price stability is one of the aims of monetary policy; the only question is whether it shall be made the sole criterion for credit expansion and contraction without regard to other considerations, such as the volume of employment, prices of stocks, bonds, and real estate, and the solvency of the banking system. If the application of the price stability rule simply implies cheap money during a period of falling prices (and vice versa), then it may be ineffective in maintaining aggregate demand which in turn maintains prices. If, however, it implies further action such as gov-

ernment deficits, subsidized consumption, public works, etc., then the policy in practice is not likely to be different from Keynesianism and subject to the same limitations. Which of these two interpretations is intended?

The Chicago school believes the economic system to be inherently stable except insofar as unstable money creates fluctuations. In contrast, the Keynesians conceive the economic system to be inherently unstable unless aggregate demand is maintained by monetary and fiscal policy. I do not think we need to be restricted to these two views and then be forced to choose between the classical-Chicago and the Keynesian position. We can rather adopt an intermediate position incorporating the truth of both classicism and Keynesianism.

In the broader philosophical tradition these views may be compared to deism, theism, and humanism. The deists believed that the universe was so ordered from the beginning to make intervention unnecessary. The theists believed divine interference occasionally beneficial. The humanists simply accept the order of nature where it suits them and alter the course of events to serve human ends. The physiocrats and the classicists resemble the deists, believing that the price system under competition will produce full employment and

* *American Economic Review*, Vol. XLI, No. 2 (May, 1951). Reprinted by the courtesy of the publisher (the American Economic Association) and the author.

† University of Wisconsin.

the best allocation of resources. The Keynesians hold the system to be unstable because the rate of interest, an essential cog in the price system, fails to regulate savings and investment so as to maintain aggregate demand at a level sufficient to insure full employment. Keynes is the prophet, and the state and the central bank play God. The third position, which I hold, can be designated as the historical-analytical theory. It holds with the classicists that the self-equilibrating factors have worked in the past and still are working to maintain high-level employment. But it also holds with Keynes that these forces are not always adequate to this purpose, because the price mechanism is not adapted to overcome disequilibria in the system created by historical conjunctures and by institutions which affect the distribution of wealth and income, and the habits of consumption, saving, and investment. Economic stability therefore requires optimal wage-price relationships and optimal aggregative relationships. Policy at any time must therefore be based upon a judgment regarding the nature of the disequilibrium. Is it Keynesian or classical? And it is the function of policy makers to form a judgment and act accordingly. No simple Keynesian or classical faith comforts us and provides us with a cloud by day or a fire by night which leads us into the promised land. Instead, we are left with a constant human struggle to act as best we can with the knowledge at our disposal. This is what, in fact, the theorist does when he stoops to the level of practical administrative decision regarding the important affairs of economic life.

I conclude that it is better to have no fixed rule and to tolerate the blunders of discretion than to blindly accept a rule based on faith or simple deductive analysis without the test of historical experience. Discretionary policy should, however, be freed from dogmas of classicism and Keynesianism. Human judgment is not infallible but it is all we have and has gotten us as far as we have come.

PART 5

FISCAL POLICY AND
DEBT MANAGEMENT

CHAPTER FOURTEEN

FISCAL POLICY

50

FISCAL MYTHS*

President John F. Kennedy

The following address, on mythology in fiscal policy and the public debt, was President Kennedy's 1962 commencement address to the Yale graduating class. President Kennedy was awarded an honorary degree by Yale at the commencement ceremonies.

President [A. Whitney] Griswold, members of the faculty and fellows, graduates and their families, ladies and gentlemen:

Let me begin by expressing my appreciation for the very deep honor that you have conferred upon me. As General de Gaulle occasionally acknowledges America to be the daughter of Europe, so I am pleased to come to Yale, the daughter of Harvard. It might be said now that I have the best of both worlds. A Harvard education and a Yale degree.

I am particularly glad to become a Yale man because, as I think about my troubles, I find that a lot of them have come from other Yale men. Among business men I have had a minor disagreement with Roger Blough of the Law School Class of 1931, and I have had some complaints too from my friend Henry Ford, of the Class of 1940. In journalism I seem to have some differences with John Hay Whitney of the Class of 1926 — and sometimes I also displease Henry Luce of the class of 1920 — not to mention always — William F. Buckley Jr. of the Class of 1950.

* President Kennedy's commencement address at Yale University, delivered on June 11, 1962.

I even have some trouble with my Yale advisers. I get along with them, but I'm not always sure how they get along with each other. I have the warmest feelings for Chester Bowles of the Class of 1924, and for Dean Acheson of the Class of 1915, and my assistant McGeorge Bundy of the Class of 1940. But I am not 100 per cent sure that these three wise and experienced Yale men wholly agree with each other on every issue.

So this Administration, which aims at peaceful cooperation among all Americans, has been the victim of a certain natural pugnacity developed in this city among Yale men. Now, that I, too, am a Yale man it is time for peace.

Last week at West Point, in the historic tradition of that academy, I availed myself of the powers of Commander in Chief to remit all sentences of offending cadets. In that same spirit, and in the historic tradition of Yale, let me now offer to smoke the clay pipe of friendship with all of my brother Elis. And I hope that they may be friends not only with me but even with each other.

In any event I am very glad to be here, and as a new member of the club I have been checking to see what earlier links existed between the institution of the Presidency and Yale. I found that a member of the Class of 1878, William Howard Taft, served one term in the White House as preparation for becoming a member of this faculty. And a graduate of 1804, John C. Calhoun, regarded the Vice Presidency, quite naturally, as too lowly a status for a Yale alumnus and became the only man in history to ever resign that office.

ISSUES OF YESTERYEAR

Calhoun in 1804 and Taft in 1878 graduated into a world very different from our's today. They and their contemporaries spent entire careers, stretching over forty years, in grappling with a few dramatic issues on which the nation was sharply and emotionally divided — issues that occupied the attention of a generation at a time: the national bank, the disposal of the public lands, nullification or union, freedom or slavery, gold or silver.

Today these old sweeping issues have largely disappeared. The central domestic problems of our time are more subtle and less simple. They relate not to basic clashes of philosophy of ideology, but to ways and means of reaching common goals — to research for sophisticated solutions to complex and obstinate issues.

The world of Calhoun, the world of Taft, had its own hard problems and notable challenges. But its problems are not our problems. Their age is not our age. As every past generation has had to disenthrall itself from an inheritance of truisms and stereotypes, so in our time we must move on from the reassuring repetition of stale phrases to a new, difficult, but essential confrontation with reality.

For the great enemy of the truth is very often not the lie — deliberate, contrived and dishonest — but the myth — persistent, persuasive and unrealistic. Too often we hold fast to clichés of our forebears. We enjoy the comfort of opinion without the discomfort of thought.

Mythology distracts us everywhere — in government as in business, in politics as in economics, in foreign affairs as in domestic affairs.

But today I want to particularly consider the myth and reality in our national economy. In

recent months many have come to feel as I do that the dialogue between the parties — between business and government — between the Government and the public — is clogged by illusion and platitude and fails to reflect the true realities of contemporary American society.

I speak of these matters here at Yale because of the self-evident truth that a great university is always enlisted against the spread of illusion and on the side of reality.

No one has said it more clearly than your President Griswold:

"Liberal learning is both a safeguard against false ideas of freedom and a source of true ones."

Your role as university men, whatever your calling, will be to increase each new generation's grasp of its duties.

THREE ILLUSIONS SET FORTH

There are three great ideas of our domestic affairs in which, today, there is a danger that illusion may prevent effective action.

They are:

First, the question of the size and shape of government's responsibilities; secondly, the question of public fiscal policy; and third, the matter of confidence — business confidence, or public confidence — or simply confidence in America.

I want to talk about all three and I want to talk about them carefully and dispassionately — and I emphasize that I am concerned here not with political debate but with ways to separate false problems from real ones.

If a contest in angry argument were forced upon it, no Administration could shrink from response, and history does not suggest that American Presidents are totally without resources in an engagement forced upon them because of hostility in one sector of society. But in the wider national interest we need not partisan wrangling but common concentration on common problems. I came here to this distinguished university to ask you to join in this great task.

Let us take first the question of the size and the shape of government. The myth is that government is big, and bad — and steadily getting bigger and worse.

Obviously this myth has some excuse for existence. It is true that in recent history each new Administration has spent much more money than its predecessors. Thus President Roosevelt outspent President Hoover and, with allowances for the special case of the second World War, President Truman outspent President Roosevelt. Just to prove that this was not a partisan matter, President Eisenhower then outspent President Truman by the handsome figure of $182,000,000,000. It is even possible, some think, that this trend may continue.

But does it follow from this that big government is growing relatively bigger? It does not. For the fact is for the last fifteen years the Federal Government, and also the Federal debt, and also the Federal bureaucracy, have grown less rapidly than the economy as a whole.

If we leave defense and space expenditures aside, the Federal Government since the Second World War has expanded less than any other major section of our national life; less than industry; less than commerce; less than agriculture; less than higher education; and very much less than the noise about big government.

The truth about big government is the truth about any great activity: it is complex. Certainly it is true that size brings dangers, but it is also true that size can bring benefits. Here at Yale, which has contributed so much to our national progress in science and medicine, it may be proper for me to mention one great and little noticed expansion of government which has brought strength to our whole society: the new role of our Federal Government as the major patron of research in science and in medicine.

Few people realize that in 1961, in support of all university research in science and medicine $3 out of every $4 came from the Federal Government. I need hardly point out that this has taken place without undue enlargement of government control; that American scientists remain second to none in their independence and in their individualism.

I am not suggesting that Federal expenditure cannot bring on some measure of con-

trol. The whole thrust of Federal expenditures in agriculture has been related by purpose and design to control, as a means of dealing with the problems created by our farmers and our growing productivity. Each sector, my point is, of activity must be approached on its own merits and in terms of specific national needs.

Generalities in regard to Federal expenditures, therefore, can be misleading. Each case — science, urban renewal, agriculture, natural resources — each case must be determined on its merits if we are to profit from our unrivaled ability to combine the strength of public and private purposes.

Next, let us turn to the problem about fiscal myths. Here the myths are legion and the truth hard to find. But let me take as a prime example the problem of the Federal budget.

We persist in measuring our Federal fiscal integrity today by the conventional, or administrative, budget with results which would be regarded as absurd in any business firm, in any country of Europe, or in any careful assessment of the reality of our national finances.

The administrative budget has sound administrative uses. But for wider purposes it is less helpful. It omits our special trust funds and the effect they have on our economy. It neglects changes in assets or inventories. It cannot tell a loan from a straight expenditure. And worst of all it cannot distinguish between operating expenditures and long-term investments.

This budget in relation to the great problems of Federal fiscal policy, which are basic to our country in 1962, is not simply irrelevant; it can be actively misleading. And yet there is a mythology that measures all our national soundness or unsoundness on the single simple basis of this same annual administrative budget.

If our Federal budget is to serve not the debate but the country, we must find ways of clarifying this area of discourse.

Still in the area of fiscal policy, let me say a word about deficits. The myth persists that Federal deficits create inflation, and budget surpluses prevent it. Yet sizeable budget surpluses after the war did not prevent inflation, and persistent deficits for the last several years have not upset our basic price stability.

Obviously, deficits are sometimes dangerous

— and so are surpluses. But honest assessment plainly requires a more sophisticated view than the old and automatic cliché that deficits automatically bring inflation.

There are myths also about our public debt. It is widely supposed that this debt is growing at a dangerously rapid rate. In fact, both the debt per person and the debt as a proportion of our Gross National Products have declined sharply since the end of the second World War.

In absolute terms, the national debt since the end of World War II has increased only 8 per cent while private debt was increasing 305 per cent and the debt of state and local governments on whom people frequently suggest we should place additional burden — the debt of state and local government has increased 378 per cent.

Moreover, debts public and private are neither good nor bad in and of themselves. Borrowing can lead to over-extension and collapse — but it can also lead to expansion and strength. There is no single simple slogan in this field that we can trust.

Finally, I come to the problem of confidence. Confidence is a matter of myth and also a matter of truth — and this time let me take the truth of the matter first.

It is true and of high importance that the prosperity of this country depends on the assurances that all major elements within it will live up to their responsibilities.

If business were to neglect its obligations to the public; if labor were blind to all public responsibility; above all, if Government were to abandon its obvious — and statutory — duty of watchful concern for our economic health — and any of these things should happen — then confidence might well be weakened and the danger of stagnation would increase. This is the true issue of confidence.

But there is also the false issue — and in its simplest form it is the assertion that any and all unfavorable turns of the speculative wheel — however temporary and however plainly speculative in character — are the result of — and I quote — a lack of confidence in the national Administration.

This, I must tell you, while comforting, is not wholly true. Worse, it obscures the reality which is also simple. The solid ground of mutual confidence is the necessary partnership of government with all of the sectors of our society in the steady quest for economic progress.

Corporate plans are not based on a political confidence in party leaders but on an economic confidence in the nation's ability to invest and produce and consume.

Business had full confidence in the Administration in power in 1929, 1954, 1958 and 1960. But this was not enough to prevent recession when business lacked full confidence in the economy. What matters is the capacity of the nation as a whole to deal with its economic problems and its opportunities.

The stereotypes I have been discussing distract our attention and divide our efforts. These stereotypes do our nation a disservice not just because they are exhausted and irrelevant, but above all because they are misleading — because they stand in the way of the solution of hard and complicated facts.

It is not new that past debates should obscure present realities. But the damage of such a false dialogue is greater today than ever before simply because today the safety of all the world — the very future of freedom — depends as never before upon the sensible and clearheaded management of the domestic affairs of the United States.

The real issues of our time are rarely as dramatic as the issues of Calhoun's. The differences today are usually matters of degree. And we cannot understand and attack our contemporary problems in 1962 if we are bound by traditional labels and worn-out slogans of an earlier era.

But the unfortunate fact of the matter is that our rhetoric has not kept pace with the speed of social and economic change. Our political debate, our public discourse on current domestic and economic issues, too often bears little or no relation to the actual problems the United States faces.

What is at stake in our economic decisions today is not some grand warfare of rival ideologies which will sweep the country with passion, but the practical management of a modern economy. What we need are not labels and clichés but more basic discussion of the so-phisticated and technical questions involved in keeping a great economic machinery moving ahead.

The national interest lies in high employment and steady expansion of output and stable prices and a strong dollar. The declaration of such an objective is easy. The attainment in an intricate and interdependent economy and world is a little more difficult. To attain them we require not some automatic response but hard thought.

Let me end by suggesting a few of the real questions on our national agenda.

First, how can our budget and tax policies supply adequate revenues and preserve our balance-of-payments position without slowing up our economic growth?

Two, how are we to set our interest rates and regulate the flow of money in ways which will stimulate the economy at home without weakening the dollar abroad? Given the spectrum of our domestic and international responsibilities, what should be the mix between fiscal and monetary policies?

Let me give several examples from my experience with the complexity of these matters, and how politically labels and ideological approaches are irrelevant to the solutions.

Last week a distinguished graduate of this school, Senator [William] Proxmire [Democrat of Wisconsin] of the class of 1938, who is ordinarily regarded as a liberal Democrat, suggested that we should follow in meeting our economic problems a stiff fiscal policy with emphasis on budget balance and an easy monetary policy with low interest rates in order to keep our economy going.

In the same week the Bank for International Settlements in Basle, Switzerland, a conservative organization representing the central bankers of Europe, suggested that the appropriate economic policy in the United States should be the very opposite — that we should follow a flexible budget policy as in Europe, with deficits when the economy is down, and a high monetary policy on interest rates, as in Europe, in order to control inflation and protect gold.

Both may be right or wrong. It will depend on many different factors. The point is that this is basically an administrative or executive problem in which political labels or clichés do not give us a solution.

A well-known business journal this morning, as I journeyed to New Haven, raised the prospects that a further budget deficit would bring inflation and encourage the flow of gold. We have had several budget deficits beginning with $12,500,000,000 deficit in '58. And it is true that in the fall of 1960 we had a gold dollar loss running at $5,000,000,000 annually.

This would seem to prove the case that a deficit produces inflation and that we lose gold. Yet there was no inflation following the deficit of 1958 nor has there been inflation since then. Our wholesale price and index since 1958 has remained completely level in spite of several deficits, because the loss of gold has been due to other reasons — price instability, relative interest rates, relative export-import balances, national security expenditures — all the rest.

Let me give you a third and final example. At the World Bank meeting in September, a number of American bankers attending predicted to their European colleagues that because of the fiscal 1962 budget deficit there would be a strong inflationary pressure on the dollar and a loss of gold.

Their predictions of inflation were shared by many in business and helped push the market up. The recent reality of non-inflation helped bring it down.

We have had no inflation because we have had other factors in our economy that have contributed to price stability. I do not suggest that the Government is right and they are wrong. The fact of the matter is, in the Federal Reserve Board and in the Administration this fall, a similar view was held by many well-informed and disinterested men — that inflation was the major problem that we would face in the winter of 1962. But it was not.

COMPLEXITIES UNDERSCORED

What I do suggest is that these problems are endlessly complicated. And yet they go to the future of this country and its ability to prove to the world what we believe it must prove. I am suggesting that the problems of fiscal and monetary policy in the Sixties as opposed to the kinds of problems we faced in the Thirties demand subtle challenges for which technical answers — not political answers — must be provided.

These are matters upon which government and business may, and in many cases will, disagree. They are certainly matters that government and business should be discussing in the most sober, dispassionate and careful way if we are to maintain the kind of vigorous economy upon which our country depends.

How can we develop and sustain strong and stable world markets for basic commodities without unfairness to the consumer and without undue stimulus to the producer?

How can we generate the buying power which can consume what we produce on our farms and in our factories?

How can we take advantage of the miracles of automation with the great demand that it will put upon high-skilled labor and yet offer employment to the half a million of unskilled school dropouts every year who enter the labor market — 8,000,000 of them in the Nineteen Sixties?

How do we eradicate the barriers which separate substantial minorities of our citizens from access to education and employment on equal terms with the rest?

How, in sum, can we make our free economy work at full capacity, that is, provide adequate profits for enterprise and adequate wages for labor and adequate utilization of plant and opportunity for all?

These are the problems that we should be talking about, that the political parties and the various groups in our country should be discussing. They cannot be solved by incantations from the forgotten past.

But the example of Western Europe shows that they are capable of solution. That government, and many of them are conservative governments, prepared to face technical problems without ideological preconceptions, can coordinate the element of a national economy and

bring about growth and prosperity — a decade of them.

Some conversations I have heard in our country sound like old records, long-playing, left over from the middle Thirties. The debate of the Thirties had its great significance and produced great results. But it took place in a different world with different needs and different tasks. It is our responsibility today to live in our own world, and to identify the needs and discharge the tasks of the Nineteen Sixties.

If there is any current trend toward meeting present problems with old clichés, this is the moment to stop it — before it lands us all in the bog of sterile acrimony.

Discussion is essential, and I am hopeful that the debate of recent weeks, though up to now somewhat barren, may represent the start of a serious dialogue of the kind which has led in Europe to such fruitful collaboration among all the elements of economic society and to a decade of unrivaled economic progress.

But let us not engage in the wrong argument at the wrong time, between the wrong people in the wrong country, while the real problems of our time grow and multiply, fertilized by our neglect.

Nearly 150 years ago Thomas Jefferson wrote:

"The new circumstances under which we are placed call for new words, new phrases, and the transfer of old words to new objects." That is truer today than it was in the time of Jefferson, because the role of this country is so vastly more significant.

There is a show in England called "Stop the World, I Want to Get Off." You have not chosen to exercise that option. You are part of the world, and you must participate in these days of our years in the solution of the problems that pour upon us, requiring the most sophisticated and technical judgment.

And, as we work in concert to meet the authentic problems of our time, we will generate a vision and an energy which will demonstrate anew to the world the superior vitality and the strength of the free society.

51

FEDERAL EXPENDITURE AND REVENUE POLICY FOR ECONOMIC STABILITY*

National Planning Association Committee†

Fiscal policy — governmental policy regarding taxation and government spending — is, along with monetary policy, one of our main stabilization weapons. Government spending and taxation have a significant impact upon the flow of income and economic activity. The collection of taxes, per se, reduces the disposable income of the population and thus tends to reduce private spending; government spending increases total expenditure by adding to the stream of private spending.

If we initially assume a balanced budget, an expansionary fiscal policy to get out of a depression would then involve reducing tax rates and/or increasing government spending — that is, deficit financing. A contractionary fiscal policy to stem inflation would involve the reverse, raising the tax rates and/or lowering government spending — that is, a surplus budget.

The following selection is an extraordinary document. It has been said, and not without a great deal of truth, that if all the economists in the country were laid end to end they would not reach a conclusion. The reader of this volume can certainly attest to the validity of that statement. Yet here we have sixteen of the country's foremost economists, representing a wide range of opinion, unanimously agreeing on a subject as controversial as the proper fiscal policy to modify inflation and depression.

Notice the objections stated against the principle of the annually balanced budget — tax receipts equal to government expenditure over a twelve-month period — as difficult to attain in practice as well as unsound in theory. The practical difficulties arise from the fact that Congress sets tax rates; the tax receipts forthcoming then depend to a great extent upon the level of national income. Changes in income are reflected in similar changes in tax revenues. A rise (fall) in national income, with tax rates unchanged, automatically tends to increase (decrease) tax revenues, and, assuming government expenditure unchanged, thereby automatically leads in the direction of a budget surplus (deficit).

If income rises, an attempt to eliminate the resulting surplus by reducing tax rates will encourage private spending. This will tend to increase income further and, to that extent, be self-defeating by yielding more revenue than anticipated. Similarly, if income falls, an attempt to eliminate the resulting deficit by raising tax rates will further discourage private spending. This will tend to lower income further, and, to that extent, be self-defeating by yielding less receipts than anticipated.

* Reprinted by the courtesy of the National Planning Association. Statement drafted unanimously by the economists mentioned at a conference called by the National Planning Association at Princeton, New Jersey, September 16–18, 1949. The conference was called at the request of the Subcommittee on Monetary, Credit, and Fiscal Policies of the Joint Committee on the Economic Report, U.S. Congress.

† The committee was composed of Howard R. Bowen, Grinnell College; Howard S. Ellis, University of California; J. Kenneth Galbraith, Harvard University; James K. Hall, University of Washington; Albert G. Hart, Columbia University; Clarence Heer, University of North Carolina; E. A. Kincaid, University of Virginia; Simeon E. Leland, Northwestern University; Paul A. Samuelson, Massachusetts Institute of Technology; Lawrence H. Seltzer, Wayne University; Sumner H. Slichter, Harvard University; Arthur Smithies, Harvard University; Tipton R. Snavely, University of Virginia; H. Christian Sonne, National Planning Association; Jacob Viner, Princeton University; and Donald H. Wallace, Princeton University.

INTRODUCTION

Although our economic system accords a dominant role to private enterprise, government expenditures and receipts have now reached a scale that make them crucially important factors in our national welfare. This makes it more than ever desirable that every dollar of government expenditures be used as efficiently as possible. We are not rich enough to afford waste of resources by government any more than by anyone else.

It is equally important that the expenditure and revenue programs of government, in their formulation and execution, be consistent with the progress and stability of the private economy. The fiscal policy of the government must make useful positive contributions to the maintenance of high levels of employment and income — the goals declared in the Employment Act of 1946 to be a national objective.

Government affects business through both sides of its budget. Payments to government employees, bond holders, veterans, the aged, and the needy all constitute income that can be used to buy consumption goods from business; government procurement affords a direct market for business. On the other side of the budget, taxes capture funds that consumers might have spent or that business firms might have invested in improved facilities. Taken by themselves, tax collections tend to shrink the market of private business, contract employment, and lower prices; just as, taken by themselves, government expenditures tend to expand the market for business, increase employment, or raise prices.

It is not only the size of revenue and expenditure that counts; their composition must also be considered in any appraisal of the effects of government policy. The economic effects of a billion dollars collected in the form of income taxes will be different from those of a billion dollars collected in excise taxes. Spending to build roads may stimulate private investment in automobiles, trucks, and garages; there are other forms of expenditure that may have adverse effects on private investment. Rationally or irrationally, government spending and taxing may greatly affect the climate within which families and businesses make their decisions.

THE PRINCIPLE OF AN ANNUALLY BALANCED BUDGET

The traditional goal of fiscal policy was to secure a balanced budget in every single year. But that objective has now proved impracticable and, besides, has serious disadvantages in principle. There is not even a clear or unique concept of "budget" to which the requirement of balance could be applied. For instance, in *the regular budget*, bookkeeping transfers to the social security trust account are classified as expenditures. As a result of this, that budget may show a deficit at a time when *the cash budget* shows an excess of receipts over outgo. But even the cash budget may not be adequate to portray the effects of fiscal policy; taxes may have their impact when tax liabilities are incurred rather than when payment is made; purchases may have their impact when contracts are entered into rather than when disbursements are made. However, where a single budget concept is used in economic analysis bearing on stabilization policy we prefer the cash budget to any available alternative.

Compared to the full span of the business cycle, a year is a short period of time. To insist upon a balance in every single year is certainly undesirable and to attain it is probably impossible. To attempt to raise tax rates every time there is a decrease in national income will only result in discouraging private consumption and investment at a time when these are most in need of expansion; on the other hand, to try to eliminate a tax surplus by cutting tax rates or expanding government activities would serve to increase inflationary pressures at a time when they are already acute.

If the budget were balanced in good years as well as bad, there would have to be either big fluctuations in expenditure programs or severe and perverse changes in tax rates. To vary expenditures in this manner would disrupt the essential services provided by government. Applied to military expenditures, it would mean a large defense program in boom years and a small defense program in depression years. This is both ineffective and wasteful. Government would be increasing its employment of resources when they were scarce and cutting down on their use when they were abundant. This, of course, would aggravate the fluctuations in private business.

THE PROBLEM OF CONTROLLING GOVERNMENT EXPENDITURES

Annual budget balancing is, thus, both difficult in practice and unsound in principle. But one great merit it does have: it provides a yardstick by which legislators and the people can scrutinize each activity of government, testing it both for efficiency of operation and for its worthwhileness in terms of cost. Every government program undertaken has to be paid for in a clear and unequivocal sense. The Legislature and the Executive are required to justify additional taxes equal to the cost of any new program. This is a principle every citizen can understand. If dropping the principle of annual budget-balancing were to mean dropping all restraints to unwise and inefficient expenditure, grave damage would be done to our economic and political system.

Were expenditures divorced entirely from the need for taxation, political opposition to extension of the government's expenditure programs would largely disappear. The scale on which the public sector absorbs resources would grow beyond what was really desired by the people as a whole; sooner or later the country would find itself in a state of chronic inflation. Such inflation is a sign of weak government and comes from eagerness to spend without a willingness to tax. Accordingly other general principles, other habits of thought and of action must be set forward to insure the standards of judgment and the self-discipline of government's activities and to do better what the principle of annual budget policy attempted — though imperfectly — to accomplish.

Experience shows that business activity has its ups and downs. There is thus a strong case for counter-cyclical fiscal action — surpluses in good times and deficits in bad. If we do not adopt such a policy deliberately we are likely to be forced into an imperfect version of it through the pressure of events. One of the major questions for the future is how such a policy can be administered with the restraint and efficiency that is supposed to be achieved through the balanced budget rule. If a flexible policy is to win acceptance, it must not be used as an excuse to introduce expenditure or tax programs that cannot be justified on their merits. Boondoggling should have no place in a rational fiscal program.

We doubt whether it would be possible, or even desirable, to rely exclusively on fiscal action to offset fluctuations in private business. That course could easily involve changes of impractical magnitudes in taxes and expenditures; it would mean placing excessive reliance on one measure for achieving economic stability and growth; it would involve problems in forecasting beyond the reach of present knowledge and techniques.

We can, however, reasonably expect that the budget be formulated in the light of economic judgment available that takes full account of the actual course of events and should contribute to economic stability rather than aggravate instability. In view of uncertainties, part of the planning process should be preparation for quick adaptation of fiscal operation to changing circumstances. Certain automatic devices for bringing remedial forces quickly into play are in a stage where they deserve consideration.

GUIDES TO FISCAL POLICY IN NORMAL TIMES

When the economy is prosperous and stable and there is no clear-cut reason to expect a change in any particular direction, the objective of policy should be to adapt the budget to changes in the government's requirements but to leave its economic impact on total employment and purchasing power unchanged. This could be approximately achieved if newly planned increases or decreases in expenditures were to be matched with corresponding changes in planned tax receipts. The net expansionary or contractionary effect of the budget would then remain roughly the same. Thus, in conditions of continued prosperity, a modified version of the balanced budget rule could be used as a guide: taxes should grow or shrink corresponding to desired changes in expenditures. Thus proposed increases in expenditures would be exposed to the traditional test of whether they are worth their cost in terms of taxes.

However, if recent events and the outlook for the near future pointed, on balance, toward unemployment and deflation in the private sector of the economy, then budgetary changes should be made in the direction of producing a moderately expansionary effect. New government expenditure programs should still be considered on their merits, but the additional taxation that in prosperous times would accompany them should now be deferred. Taxes that are deferred in these circumstances should be put into effect as soon as that can be done without impeding recovery. There should be no delay in making the tax reductions warranted by any reductions in government expenditures; and if expenditure requirements are expected to decline in the future, anticipatory tax reductions could be enacted.

On the other hand, if the weight of the evidence appeared to be on the inflationary side, the opposite policy should be followed. The rule that increased expenditures should be accompanied by increased tax yields should be rigidly followed. Tax reductions that would normally be in order should be deferred; and tax increases should anticipate expected increases in expenditures.

GUIDING PRINCIPLES IN TIME OF
ACUTE RECESSION OR BOOM

Where there is a definite expectation, justified by events, of serious recession or inflation, more strenuous fiscal measures would be called for, and the policies described above should be supplemented by emergency fiscal action.

In the event of severe recession, it is not only politically necessary, but economically desirable, to provide additional employment projects that can be started and ended quickly. Temporary tax relief should be given in order to stimulate private spending and employment. Other incentives for private investment, such as guarantees, should be considered. There can be no social or economic justification for allowing mass unemployment to persist for extended periods at a time when there is abundant need for roads, schools, hospitals, and other useful objects of public expenditures. However, we recognize that there are difficult

questions of extent and timing connected with any such program. An over-ambitious government program may impede the course of recovery in the private sectors of the economy by dislocating resources and delaying needed price adjustments. On the other hand, a program that was over-cautious could needlessly fail to advance recovery by not stimulating the demand for the products of private industry. Much skill and judgment are required to move from depression to stable prosperity. We must not rely on the private economy, unaided by government action, to perform that task. The government must not shirk the responsibility placed on it by the Employment Act, and fiscal policy is one of the most promising instruments it possesses.

On any occasion when serious inflation is in prospect, emergency measures would be needed to curtail expenditures and increase taxation. Wartime and postwar experience provides convincing evidence that the political obstacles to a fiscal policy adequate to combat inflation are so great that there is little practical danger of going too far. The survival of a relatively free and stable price system depends heavily on our willingness to fight inflation by fiscal methods.

A policy that helps to maintain stable prosperity will be no more likely in practice to result in an upward trend in the national debt than one that does not. The course of events may in fact be such that stabilization requires steady reduction in the debt. Budgeting surpluses to fight inflation will provide for the reduction of the public debt in a helpful rather than a painful fashion. Surpluses are not feasible in times of depression. They are desirable where the private economy is strong enough for the government to tax more than it spends without causing unemployment. The private economy is not likely to possess this strength if government policies aggravate rather than offset business fluctuations.

ADDITIONAL POSSIBILITIES FOR A
FLEXIBLE FISCAL POLICY

While we consider these guides for budget policy essential to a stabilization program, the annual budget cannot, in the nature of things, be based on precise forecasts; nor can it be expected to compensate for sudden and short-run fluctuations in business that occur within the period of its operation. Even though the budget can and should be amended in the light of changing circumstances, the legislative process is necessarily too cumbersome to make delicately timed adjustments in fiscal policy. Therefore, we consider whether further flexibility can be achieved by two devices which may be called *"automatic flexibility"* and *"formula flexibility."*

"Automatic flexibility" means a tax system such that revenue under a given set of tax rates will fall sharply if unemployment develops, and rise sharply in the opposite case of inflation; and expenditure programs under which increased outlays arise from increased unemployment.

"Formula flexibility" means a system under which pre-announced tax cuts and upward revisions of spending programs will come into force if unemployment exceeds a certain figure or production falls below a certain level, and preannounced changes in the opposite direction if price indexes rise at more than a certain speed.

AUTOMATIC FLEXIBILITY

Automatic flexibility is exemplified by the unemployment compensation system. If unemployment increases, employers' contributions at once decline, while the unemployed begin almost immediately to draw more in benefits. Thus the government finds itself automatically taking less money out of the public's pockets and putting more in.

There are now many such flexible elements in federal taxes and revenues; and they have greatly increased in importance with the growth of the budget. Besides the unemployment compensation system, there is, for example, substantial automatic flexibility in personal and corporate income taxes.

Automatic flexibility can slow down and perhaps halt a decline of activity or a rise of prices; it can give time for restorative forces to come into play, but it will not, by itself, pull activity back to a full-employment level or restore prices to a pre-inflation level.

We feel strongly that the existing automatic flexibility makes an important contribution to economic stability, which should not be frittered away, as it would be, for instance, by rigid application of the annual-balanced-budget rule. But we do not believe it prudent for policy to regard automatic flexibility as more than a first line of defense; more must be done to cope with serious economic fluctuations.

FORMULA FLEXIBILITY

The enactment by Congress of rules under which tax rates, and perhaps of rules under which expenditure programs will shift in certain contingencies specified in advance is a possibility that deserves further exploration. For example, the period during which unemployed workers can draw unemployment compensation might be extended according to a flexible schedule based on the volume of unemployment. The withholding rate under the personal income tax for any calendar quarter might rise by a stated amount above a standard rate whenever, say, the index of retail prices has increased by over a certain amount in the preceding six months. The withholding rate might be lowered whenever standard indices of production and employment drop below stated levels or trends.

The question of formula flexibility shades off into the question of granting to the Executive wider discretionary authority than it now possesses to initiate changes in the timing or extent of the fiscal program. This raises difficult issues of political principle and administrative responsibility. We can here do no more than call attention to them.

CONCLUSION

In this statement, we have confined ourselves to fiscal policy of the federal government. But, while essential, that is only one element in a stabilization policy. The policies of state and local governments can make useful contributions within their more limited spheres. Monetary and credit policies including debt management must play an active role in their own right and must be properly coordinated with fiscal policy. All necessary measures must be taken to preserve and stimulate competition. Supported by such measures, federal fiscal policy offers the best prospect of achieving sustained prosperity within the framework of our existing economic system.

52

THE THEORY BEHIND THE TAX CUT*

Morgan Guaranty Survey

If when a man bites a dog it is news, then when the venerable Morgan Guaranty Trust Company — the successor to J. P. Morgan and Company — decides to explain Keynesian economics to everyman it must rate at least a front page headline. (However, lest you think that Wall Street has completely lost its head, see Selection 55.)

As Congress, which prides itself on its practicality, moves toward final consideration and probable enactment of the "Revenue Act of 1964," the legislators are fashioning a monument to a long line of theorists. For, in a sense, the real authors of the pending tax-cut bill are such academic economists as John Maurice Clark, R. F. Kahn, John R. Hicks, and — theoretician as well as man of practical affairs — John Maynard Keynes.

Names like these have not been much invoked in support of tax reduction; indeed, reference to some of them would have given the cause more hurt than help. Nevertheless, they — and others involved in the development of modern income-and-employment theory — laid the intellectual groundwork over the past four decades for the action Congress is now contemplating. Without their work, it is hardly likely the nation today would be prepared for a step so unconventional as deliberate reduction of the Federal government's revenues at a time when the budget already is in deficit and the economy is expanding.

Thus passage of tax-cut legislation, if it comes as expected, may seem to validate the spirit if not the letter of the oft-quoted Keynesian overstatement: "The ideas of economists and political philosophers, both when they are right and when they are wrong, are more powerful than is commonly understood. Indeed the world is ruled by little else."

BENEATH THE FRINGE

The reason for looking to the theoretical origins of tax reduction, however, is not merely to

* From the *Morgan Guaranty Survey*, January 1964. Reprinted by the courtesy of the Morgan Guaranty Trust Company.

nail down the genealogy of an idea. Much more important is a widespread understanding of the intended workings of this form of economic stimulus, its limitations and risks, and the need for auxiliary policies to help it in the task of promoting sound growth.

During the debate of the past year and a half, the case for cutting tax rates has accumulated a considerable fringe of half-truth and oversimplification, tacked on by advocates in their zeal to convert doubters of various kinds. Some of the liberals who have reversed traditional positions to support tax relief, for instance, clearly do so in an assumption that the fiscal boost to the economy will be reinforced by generous monetary stimulus. There are conservatives, on the other hand, who accept prolongation of the budget deficit only on the rigorous condition that it be financed entirely by the issuance of long-term Treasury securities. Both expectations may have to be disappointed if tax reduction is to do its job safely and effectively.

MULTIPLY AND ACCELERATE

The theoretical basis for tax reduction as an economic booster involves two concepts so reasonable that the layman is likely to dismiss them as obvious, yet so susceptible of elaboration that the economist has been able to build them into a specialty of his science. These are the "multiplier" and the "accelerator." Modern theory uses these two concepts to explain fluctuations in output and employment — and to suggest how an economy that is underproducing and underemploying can be prodded to better performance. The multiplier concept relates to consumption, the accelerator to investment.

When an outside force such as the government applies a stimulus to the economy — for example, by reducing taxes — a fairly direct effect on consumption can be expected. Consumers tend, with reasonable regularity, to spend between 92% and 94% of their disposable income. It can be rather confidently expected, therefore, that after a cut in individual income taxes the immediate beneficiaries will spend a substantial part of their new-found funds on goods and services.

Some part of this addition to gross business receipts flows into the hands of a second group of consumers in the form of wages, salaries, interest, dividends, and other kinds of payment. This second group is then likely to step up its own consumption outlays, providing still a third group with the wherewithal to raise its spending. Likewise on to a fourth round, and a fifth, ultimately raising the question: Why doesn't the multiplication process, once initiated with even a relatively modest starter, go on and on until there are no longer any idle resources left in the economy with which to meet the increased consumption demand?

The answer, according to multiplier theory, is that the consumption stream started by the tax cut suffers "leakages" in each round of reaction. Personal saving, drawing funds away from consumption (and, normally, transferring them to some form of investment), is one such leakage. A part of each added surge of gross business receipts flows into corporate retained earnings, another form of leakage. Expenditures on imports give rise to a third, since part of the amount spent leaves the domestic economy. Most important of all in size is the combined drain of Federal, state, and local taxes.

TWO FOR ONE

Statisticians have expended a great deal of effort trying to calculate the percentage of leakage that typically occurs at each stage of the spending process. Estimates tend to cluster near or just slightly below 50%. This suggests that, for each $1 of tax-cut money initially spent on consumer goods, another 50 cents would be spent at a second stage, 25 cents at a third, 12½ cents at a fourth, and so on. Computing the downward progression yields a total of $2 in expenditures at all stages, with virtually the entire sum accounted for by the end of the first six expenditure rounds.

Since cumulative spending for consumer goods, on this basis, is just double the amount of the initial stimulus, the multiplier is said to have a numerical value of two. With a lower estimate of leakage, the multiplier would be higher. The Council of Economic Advisers has used a multiplier valued at two in its try at judging the direct effect on consumption of the cuts that have been proposed in income taxes. If, as now appears probable, the direct gain to consumers is to be something over $9 billion annually (allowing both for the cuts in individual income tax rates and for somewhat higher dividends likely to result from the cut in corporate tax rates), a multiplier of two would raise consumer spending by more than $18 billion above what it would be in the absence of tax reduction. Since the reduction in tax liabilities would be permanent, to be enjoyed by consumers year after year, the higher level of consumption expenditures — once achieved — could also be expected to be permanent.

Of course, the full impact could not reasonably be expected to occur until well into 1965 at the earliest, since the proposed two-stage tax cut would become fully effective only at the start of that year. Actually, the multiplier probably would take even longer to work itself out fully. Past consumer behavior indicates that considerable time lags sometimes occur before consumption habits are completely adjusted to changes in disposable income. This suggests the likelihood of some rise in the personal savings rate immediately after tax reduction occurs, and consequently a somewhat slow start for the multiplier. It also affords, however, the comforting inference that the promised tax cut has not already been largely discounted by consumers, as is sometimes suggested.

FOR INVESTMENT, A "FLASH POINT"

While the multiplier is at work in the realm of consumption, a proportionally even greater reaction, according to the theoretical diagram, takes place in investment. This is attributed to a phenomenon known in the language of economic analysis as "acceleration."

Theoreticians recognize that, so long as substantial excess industrial capacity exists, businessmen will be slow to invest in new plant and equipment. However, as the multiplier process narrows the gap between capacity and output, a dramatic response in investment activity becomes likely. A sort of "flash point" is approached, in other words, at which something like an investment explosion takes place.

This interpretation of investment behavior rests on an assumption, seemingly reasonable, that the typical business firm tries to maintain a fixed relation between its capital equipment and what it regards as the normal demand for its products. Unless it judges demand to be heading for a permanently higher level, the firm is likely to confine new investment to meeting replacement needs. When the firm's managers become convinced, however, that a new and lasting element of demand for their products is emerging, they will step up their investment outlays so as to assure maintenance of the desired capital-output ratio. At this stage, incidentally, some of the income leakage that went on during the multiplier process begins to be recaptured, as firms draw on retained earnings and tap personal savings via capital issues or other borrowings.

The results that this turn of events can produce are evident from a simple hypothetical example. A firm that has been using 100 units of machinery may have been replacing ten units a year (reflecting, say, an average machine life of ten years). If it should decide at some point that a permanent increase of 5% in product demand is coming, it would then need 105 units to carry on its operations. Its total demand for new equipment in the single year in which the reassessment of prospects occurred would jump from the pattern of ten units per year to fifteen per year, an increase of 50%.

When the theoretical "flash point" is reached in any given enterprise, the percentage change in investment demand can thus be far greater than the change in underlying product demand. This difference is what gives the accelerator its name. The historical fact that plant and equipment outlays are subject to much wider swings than is business as a whole gives support to the accelerator concept, even though a part of the volatility can reasonably be ascribed to other causes, such as the overexuberance of ex-

pectations that typically occurs in the final phase of a business cycle expansion. In turn, the concept recognizes that firms make investment outlays for modernization and cost-cutting apart from the needs of replacement or expansion. The play of these forces is simply regarded as one of the environmental factors amid which the main drive of multiply-and-accelerate goes on.

FEEDBACK TO CONSUMPTION

To the extent that the accelerator actually works, it also creates a new stimulus in consumer-goods activity, wholly apart from the primary multiplier. The expansion of capital-goods production generates its own flow of consumer income, which is spent and respent in what can be thought of as a second chain reaction. This, in turn, plays back to the investment area, providing it as well with a second round of support. In fact, once the initial stimulus has begun to work, a theoretical leap-frogging is set up between the multiplier and the accelerator.

It is much more difficult — even in the realm of theory — to put a quantitative value on the combined multiplier-accelerator effect than on the primary consumption multiplier alone. Most economists have avoided predicting how far the interaction might go beyond the $18-billion rise in consumption expenditures indicated by the multiplier of two. A few have ventured to suggest that gross national product may eventually benefit by three and one-half to four times the net initial reduction in overall tax liabilities. On the total tax cut of $11 billion implied by the bill passed by the House of Representatives, this would point to an ultimate effect on GNP of something like $40 billion. This exceeds by roughly $10 billion the gap which the Council of Economic Advisers currently estimates as existing between potential and actual output.

Thus, on this basis at least, the proposed tax program is tailored generously enough to achieve the goals at which it aims, including a significant whittling down of the unemployment rate. In practice, of course, the one-two punch of the multiplier-accelerator is subject to the influence of all other forces that may be operating in the economy at any given time. At a point when business activity was about to start downhill, it might take a considerable multiplier effect merely to compensate for the basic weakness. If piled atop an already buoyant trend, the amplifying of demand could produce an unhealthy inflationary surge.

Psychologically, the present environment appears favorably disposed to effective working of a tax-cut stimulus. No large group in the populace is set against the proposed action. The impact of the intended cut would be well distributed to achieve strong consumption effect, while investment incentives would be directly enhanced by the four-point lowering of the corporate tax rate and the rollback of existing confiscatory rates on high-bracket individual incomes. With these reinforcing elements in its favor, the expected cut in taxes could well lead to a longer and stronger expansion than even the optimistic consensus of year-end economic forecasts implies.

HANDLE WITH CARE

Tax reduction, all this makes clear, is a high-powered tonic to pour into the body economic. Yet there is no certainty that it contains the specific for whatever has been retarding the body's metabolism. Fortunately, the means exist for either moderating or supplementing the effects of tax reduction as they begin to appear. The principal auxiliaries for this purpose are monetary policy and debt-management policy, and it is of crucial importance that they be kept free to move as required. Any precommitment to maintenance of a given degree of monetary ease could be disastrous if the vigor already in the economy turns out to be substantially more than is even now apparent. Inflationary tendencies could quickly be revived, with particular detriment to the country's balance of international payments.

By the same token, a fixed insistence on financing additional Federal debt out of savings — that is, by the issue of long-term bonds — could under conceivable circumstances nullify the stimulative effect of tax reduction. Rigid adherence to long-term financing — intended to assure that the deficit is not monetized — would place the Treasury in competition for private savings with all other users of capital. This might or might not be desirable, depending on the total economic situation at the time.

If business shows a tendency to respond quickly and strongly to the tax-cut stimulus, the restraining influence of Treasury long-term debt issuance would be welcome. But if, as seems unlikely but is not impossible, the underlying strength of business should falter before the tax-cut stimulus takes hold, then an enforced adherence to long-term financing by the Treasury could produce a faster and steeper run-up in interest rates than would be consistent with the objective of lifting the economy to fuller utilization of its capacity. At some point in such a run-up, a certain number of private borrowers might be dissuaded from some of their borrowing and, in turn, from some of their business undertakings, producing the ironic result of a Federal deficit "soundly" financed but accompanied by little or none of the economic benefit the expectation of which is the justification for running the deficit.

Large-scale financing of government deficits through the banking system has been a flagrant source of trouble in the past, but only when it has occurred in an already overheated economy. It is important that Treasury and Federal Reserve officials watch the temperature and pressure gauges with special care during an experiment as important as the one now envisaged. But, as they watch, their hands should be kept free to operate the policy levers as developing circumstances may indicate.

Like all experiments, tax reduction carries some risk of failure and some risk of oversuccess. Considerable boldness has been required to bring it as close to launching as it now is. Even more boldness, tempered with prudence, may have to be displayed before the experiment is finished.

53

PRINCIPLES OF BUDGET DETERMINATION*

Richard A. Musgrave†

The following selection by Professor Richard A. Musgrave puts fiscal policy to stabilize the economy in perspective as only one of the several functions which the budget is expected to perform. His classification and analysis sheds considerable light on what is usually a most confused area of thinking. Professor Musgrave's approach is developed in more detail in his book, The Theory of Public Finance (McGraw-Hill, 1959).

The people of the United States are generally agreed that the economy is to be organized on the premise of free consumer choice, that production is to be carried on by privately owned and operated firms, and that the market should be relied upon where possible to transmit the desires of the consumer to these firms. This being our basic form of organization, why is it that a substantial part of the economy's output is provided for through the budget? This question must be answered to begin with, if we wish to say something about the "proper" scope or composition of the budget.

The budgetary activity of the Government is needed because the pricing system of the market cannot deal with all the tasks that must be met in order to operate a sound economy and a healthy society. Certain tasks must be performed by government. Some may deplore this fact and dream of a setting where everyone could live in peace without any kind of governmental activity; others may feel that the necessity of social and economic policy at the governmental level enriches the challenge of social life and makes for a more balanced society. Whatever one's values in this respect, the nature of things is such that budgetary activity is needed. The question then is under what circumstances and why this need arises.

The answer to this question is too complex to permit a simple and uniform solution. In my own thinking I have found it useful to distinguish between three major functions of budget policy, including —

1. The provision for social wants, which requires the Government to impose taxes and make expenditures for goods and services, to be supplied free of direct charge to the consumer;

2. The application of certain corrections to the distribution of income as determined in the market, requiring the Government to add to the income of some by transfers while reducing the income of others by taxes; and

3. The use of budget policy for purposes of economic stabilization, rendering it necessary under some conditions to raise the level of demand by a deficit policy and under others to curtail demand by a surplus policy. I shall comment briefly on the nature of each of these three functions, and on how they are interrelated.

PROVISION FOR SOCIAL WANTS

When I say that the Government must provide for the satisfaction of social wants, it does not follow that the government itself must carry on the production of the goods and services which are needed to satisfy these wants. This may be necessary in some cases, as for instance with the provision for police protection, which can hardly be left to a private agent, but this is the exception rather than the rule. In most cases there is no such need. If new planes

* From *Federal Expenditure Policy for Economic Growth and Stability*, Compendium of Papers Submitted to the Joint Economic Committee, U.S. Congress, 1957. Reprinted by the courtesy of the author.
† Princeton University.

or government buildings are to be provided for, they may be purchased from private firms. The essence of budgetary provision for the satisfaction of social wants, therefore, is not production by government. It is payment for goods and services through budgetary finance, and supply of such services free of direct charge to the consumer.

What, then, are the social wants which must be provided for in this fashion? Some people have argued that they are wants which in a mysterious fashion are experienced by the Nation as a whole, and thus reflect the desires of the collective entity. This makes little sense in our setting. The desire for the satisfaction of social wants is experienced by individuals, no less than that for the satisfaction of private wants. This is not where the difference lies. The basic problem of social wants arises because their satisfaction, by their very nature, requires that the goods and services in question must be consumed in equal amounts by all. Social wants differ in this important respect from private wants, where each consumer may arrange his personal pattern of consumption such as to satisfy his own personal tastes. Thus, I may go to the market and purchase whatever amounts and type of clothing, housing, or food may suit my tastes and resources; but I must be satisfied with the same municipal services as are received by my neighbors, or with the same degree and type of foreign protection as is granted to all other citizens of the United States. This crucial fact, that certain services must be consumed in equal amounts by all, has important consequences.

One consequence is that you cannot apply what I like to refer to as the exclusion principle.[1] Since all people must consume the same amounts, no one can be excluded from the enjoyment of services aimed at the satisfaction of social wants. Everyone benefits, whether he contributes little or heavily to their cost. Now you might say that this is not too diffi-

[1] A second consequence, which has been pointed out by Professor Samuelson, is that there would be no single best solution to the budget problem, applying the usual criterion of economic efficiency, even if the preferences of all individuals were known. This aspect is omitted from the present discussion.

cult a problem. Let the tax collector see to it that everyone pays. Unfortunately this overlooks the real difficulty. The real difficulty is not that people are unwilling to pay unless forced to; it is that of determining just how much various people should be called upon to contribute.

This difficulty does not arise with the satisfaction of private wants in the market. Here the individual consumer is forced to bid against others in order to get what he wants. The pricing mechanism, as it were, is an auctioning device by which things go to those who value them most, as evidenced by what they are willing to pay. People must bid to get what they want, and thereby provide the producer with the necessary signal of what to produce. In the case of social wants this signal is not forthcoming. Consumers know that they cannot be excluded and that their own contribution will weigh very lightly in the total picture. Thus they will not reveal their true preferences on a voluntary basis and offer to pay accordingly. Therefore it is no easy task to determine just what social wants should be recognized and how much each should be called upon to contribute. A further difference is this: For goods supplied in the satisfaction of private wants, competition sets a uniform price in the market. Individual consumers, depending on their personal tastes, can buy different amounts at that price. For goods supplied in the satisfaction of social wants, all must consume the same amount, and those who value public services more highly must pay a higher unit price.

This much is clear, but the question is just what should be supplied and just how much each should pay. The market cannot give the solution and a political process is needed to accomplish this task. By choosing among various budget programs, including various expenditure plans and various tax plans to cover the costs, the voters can express their preferences in the matter. Since they know that the law, once decided upon, will apply to each of them, they will find it in their interest to reveal their preferences and to vote for the plan, or the approximation thereto, which is most appealing to them. Thus preferences are revealed through the political process. While the minority might be dissatisfied, and strategies might be used in voting, an acceptable approximation to the preferences of the individual members of the group is reached.

All this is somewhat of an oversimplification. Individuals do not vote personally on each issue. Rather, they elect representatives who vote for them. Thus, the function of the representatives is to crystallize public opinion with regard to such issues, budgetary and other, and to find groups of issues on which their constituents can agree. The Member of Congress is a go-between, whose function it is to work out compromises and solutions which are acceptable to the majority. By saying this I do not mean to slight the educational function of political leadership, nor do I wish to underestimate the importance of the contribution to be rendered by the executive branch and by the civil service. All these are important, but the basic process is one of transforming individual preferences into social wants.

In taking this view of social wants, I am thinking in the framework of what since Adam Smith has been referred to as the benefit principle of taxation. In other words, budget policy should provide for goods and services in response to the social wants of individuals, and to make this possible, individuals should contribute as closely as possible in response to their evaluation of these social wants. The great value of this approach, from the point of view of the economist, is that it requires us to determine public expenditures together with the revenue side of the budget. In this basic sense, there can be no theory of public expenditures without a theory of taxation, and vice versa.

What does the benefit approach mean regarding the distribution of the tax bill between people with different levels of income? I will not attempt to answer this in a categorical form, but I can point to the considerations on which the answer should depend: This is whether the goods and services supplied for the satisfaction of social wants are largely in the nature of necessities or luxuries. If they are largely in the nature of necessities, the answer leads to regression; if they are primarily in the nature of luxuries the answer points to progres-

sion. If people wish to spend the same fraction at all levels of income the answer leads to proportional taxation.[2] While a moderate degree of progression would seem the reasonable answer, this is by no means the only consideration entering into the distribution of the total tax bill.

Finally, a word about the matter of budgetary balance. Insofar as the satisfaction of social wants is concerned, the budget must be balanced, in the sense that goods provided for through the budget must be paid for over their useful life. This merely reflects the fact that resources used for the satisfaction of social wants cannot be used for other purposes, and someone must bear the cost. At the same time, we shall see that this is only one among other considerations. It does not follow that the total budget must be balanced.

I need hardly add that this brief discussion of social wants does not cover the entire picture. Not all public services are supplied in response to the individual preferences of the consumers. There may be instances when the majority decides that certain wants of individuals should be satisfied, even though these individuals would prefer to be given the cash and use it for other purposes. Free education or hospital services may be cited to illustrate this case. This type of public service requires a different explanation. However, note that the benefits derived from such services extend beyond the specific beneficiary, and thus approach what I have described as the central type of social wants.

ADJUSTMENTS IN THE DISTRIBUTION OF INCOME

I now turn to the second function of budget policy, which is to provide for adjustments in the distribution of income. We are all agreed that it is the responsibility of society to undertake certain adjustments in the distribution of income, which results from the forces of the market, the laws of inheritance, and differ-

[2] In technical terms, the tax structure will be proportional if the income elasticity of social wants is unity, progressive if it is greater than unity, and regressive if it is smaller than unity.

ences in abilities to acquire income. Babies must be assured adequate food, the sick and the aged must be given proper care, and so forth. Beyond this, some hold to an idea of the good society which requires a fairly extensive degree of income equalization, others would favor a moderate degree of equalization, while still others might oppose any such measure and favor a high degree of inequality. These are matters of social philosophy and value judgment on which we all have our own views. Moreover, consideration must be given to the interrelation between income distribution and the total income which is available for distribution.

My concern here is not with the question as to which is the best set of values. While I happen to feel that progressive taxation is fair, this is not the point. My point is that if society wishes to make distributional adjustments, it is desirable as a matter of economic policy to make them through the tax-transfer mechanism of the budget. This is preferable to distributional adjustments via manipulation of particular prices, be it of products or of factors of production. Certainly, we cannot accept the stricture that the purpose of taxation is to finance public services and nothing else, and that, therefore, they "must not" be used for distributional adjustments. There is no such law in the order of things. Indeed, where distributional adjustments are to be made, this is the logical way in which to make them.

The determination of the desired degree and type of distributional adjustment is again a matter of political process, and I will not discuss it here. Let us suppose that some degree of income equalization is to be accomplished. This calls for taxes on some people with incomes above the average and for transfer payments to some people with incomes below the average. Insofar as distributional adjustments are concerned, the budget must again be balanced. Now you may argue that such a general tax-transfer scheme does not appear in the budget, except perhaps in the social-security programs, and that our budget does not engage in distributional adjustments. This is not the case. The distributional adjustments are implicit in a distribution of the overall tax bill

in a way which is more progressive than would be justified on the basis of assigning the cost of social wants on a benefit basis. In other words, the budget as we know it and as it is enacted reflects the net result of various component policies. More about this in a moment.

Just as my discussion of allocating the cost of social wants moved in the context of a benefit approach to taxation, so does the problem of distributional adjustment belong in the sphere of ability to pay and equal sacrifice doctrines. The two approaches are wholly compatible if each is viewed in its own context. The argument that the cost of public services should be allocated in accordance with ability to pay sounds nice, but it gives us no foundation on which to decide what public services should be rendered. This can be done only in relation to individual preferences and implies the spirit of benefit taxation. I can see no other approach that leads to a sensible solution. At the same time, it is non sequitur to argue that progressive taxation is out of order because (assuming this to be the case) benefit taxation requires proportional rates. The element of progression may be called for in order to implement distributional adjustments, which is quite a different matter.

Failure to distinguish between the problem of distributional adjustment and the problem of providing for the satisfaction of social wants leads to confusion on both counts. If the degree of distributional adjustment is tied to the level of the budget, some may favor an increase in the level of public services as a means of extending distributional adjustments, even though they do not support budget expansion on the basis of benefit taxation; and others, who would favor an expansion of the budget on this basis will oppose it because in practice it is related to an extension of distributional adjustments. Moreover, these relationships change with the level of taxation and the existing tax structure. While there was a time when the marginal taxpayer was the fellow with the large income, we are now in a situation where increased levels of public services largely involve increased tax contributions from (or exclude tax reductions for) people in the middle or middle to lower income groups. Thus the politics of the fiscal problem are changed and essential public services will go begging in the process.

BUDGET POLICY AND STABILIZATION

I now turn to my third function of budget policy, which is the use of tax and expenditure measures as a means of economic stabilization. The great achievement of the fiscal-policy discussion of the last 25 years is the by now fairly general recognition that fiscal policy must play an important role in economic stabilization. The old view that the budget should be balanced is applicable only if we consider our first and second functions of budget policy, and even here some temporary exceptions may arise. Once the stabilization function is introduced, deficit finance is called for under conditions of potential depression, and surplus finance is called for under conditions of potential inflation. The point to be noted here is that the stabilization objective of budget policy can be achieved without contradicting the other requirements of budget policy, namely, efficient provision for social wants and the application of distributional adjustments.

Regarding the proper level of public services, this means that there is no excuse for make-work expenditures during a depression, just as there is no excuse for cutting essential public services during periods of high activity. Precisely the same fallacy is involved in both cases. An increase in public services during the depression is in order, only to the extent that the decline in private expenditures for some purposes (such as investment) frees resources which people may wish to allocate in part to the satisfaction of social wants; and a decrease in public services is in order during the boom only to the extent that people wish to divert resources from public use to meet an increased demand for resources for other uses. This sets the limits of the permissible adjustment: There is no justification for raising the level of public services merely to increase aggregate demand, since this can be done also by lowering taxes; and there is no justification for cutting public services merely to curtail demand since this can be done also by raising taxes.

Moreover, there is no need for permitting considerations of stabilization policy to interfere with desired distributional adjustments. Thus it was argued frequently during the thirties and forties that taxes on lower incomes should be avoided because this would undermine demand and that therefore a more progressive tax structure was needed; and vice versa for the current case of inflation where it is held that progression should be reduced to secure a shift to resources from consumption to investment, thus providing for increased capacity in order to check inflation. The argument makes sense in both cases if we assume that the total level of tax yield is given, but it breaks down if we allow for adjustments in the level of taxation. The level of taxation which is required for purposes of stabilization should depend upon the distribution of the tax bill, and not the other way round.

NET BUDGET AND SEPARATION OF ISSUES

To bring my point into focus, let me exaggerate a little and assume that there are actually 3 different budgets, pursuing respectively my 3 functions of budget policy. First, there is the budget to provide for the satisfaction of social wants, where taxes are allocated in line with a benefit principle of taxation. By its nature, this budget is balanced over the useful life of the services which are supplied. Secondly, there is the budget to provide for distributional adjustments, involving tax and transfer payments. By its nature, this budget is balanced as well. Then there is the budget designed to stabilize the level of demand. By its nature this budget involves either taxes or transfer payments, proportional to what is considered the proper state of income distribution.

We may think of these budgets as being determined in an inter-dependent system, where the manager of each of the three branches takes the action of the other branches as given.[3] Having determined the three bud-

---

[3] To illustrate, let me assume that there are two taxpayers only, X and Z. Assume further that the full employment income equals $100, and that earnings are divided such that X receives $70 while Z receives

gets, the Government may proceed to administer each budget separately. This would involve various sets of taxes and/or transfers for any one person. To simplify matters, it will be desirable to clear the tax and transfer payments against each other, and thus to administer one net budget policy only.

The actual tax and expenditure plan enacted by the Congress in any one year reflects such a net budget. This is of advantage as a matter of administrative convenience, but it blurs the issues. While it may be difficult as a matter of legislative procedure to determine independently each of the three subbudgets noted in my discussion, some lesser steps may be taken in the organization of the budget process, on both the executive and the legislative side, to move the problem into a better perspective. To say the least, an understanding of the three objectives as distinct issues is prerequisite to efficient budget planning.

The preceding discussion will suffice to show that it is exceedingly difficult to establish a simple set of principles by which to secure an efficient determination of public expenditures. This task involves the determination of the total budget plan, including the revenue as well as the expenditure side and it comprises quite distinct sets of objectives or functions of budget

policy. The issues involved are the more difficult as they cannot be solved, or be solved in part only, by the ordinary tools of economic analysis. The political process of decision-making becomes an inherent part of the problem.

At the same time, the complexity of the problem establishes no presumption that the use of resources for the satisfaction of social wants is less efficient than its use for the satisfaction of private wants. This must be kept in mind if we are to see the problem of social-want satisfaction in its proper perspective. While it is obvious that any expenditure objective, once decided upon, should be accomplished at minimum cost, the objective of efficiency in public expenditure planning must not be confused with minimizing the level of such expenditures. By the very nature of the budget as an allocation problem, the danger of inefficiency arises with insufficient as well as with excessive outlays.

	X	Z	Total
Satisfaction of social wants:			
Goods and service expenditures			22.0
Taxes	13.2	8.8	22.0
Balance			00.0
Distribution adjustment:			
Taxes	10.0	10.0	10.0
Transfers			10.0
Balance			00.0
Stabilization adjustment:			
Taxes	12.0	8.0	20.0
Transfers			
Balance			20.0
Net budget:			
Taxes	35.2	6.8	42.0
Transfers			
Goods and service expenditure			22.0
Balance			20.0

$30. Now suppose that the Distribution Branch imposes taxes of $10 on X and pays $10 of transfers to Z, the desired distribution being such that X is to receive 60 per cent and Z is to receive 40 per cent.

Next, let me suppose that with an income of $100, distributed in this fashion, private expenditure on consumption equals $60 and that expenditures on investment equals $30. Moreover, the manager of the Stabilization Branch is informed that expenditures for the satisfaction of social wants equal $22. This means that total expenditures equal $112 and are $12 above the full employment level. To simplify matters, let us hold investment constant. In order to lower consumption by $12 the Stabilization Branch will impose taxes of $20, it being assumed that the ratio of consumption to income is constant at 60 per cent. In order not to interfere with the distributional adjustment, $12 will be paid by X and $8 by Z.

The income of X now equals $70 − $10 − $12 = $48, while that of Z equals $30 + $10 − $8 = $32. Now suppose that both wish to spend 27.5 per cent of their income on the satisfaction of social wants. Thus for the satisfaction of social wants taxes equal $13.20 for X and $8.80 for Z, with total expenditures for the satisfaction of social wants equal to $22.

The three subbudgets involve the following transactions:

Instead of collecting 3 separate taxes from X it will be more convenient to collect the total of $35.20; and instead of collecting 2 taxes from Z and paying 1 transfer, it will be more convenient to collect net taxes of $6.80. We thus have net tax receipts of $42 which after allowing for goods and service expenditures of $22 leave us with a surplus of $20, equal to the surplus in the stabilization operation. A similar illustration might be given where the stabilization operation involves a deficit, in which case there appears a corresponding deficit in the net budget. Finally note that the distribution of the tax bill in the net budget is more progressive than that for carrying the cost of social wants, but less progressive than that involved in the distributional adjustment only.

54

DEFICIT, DEFICIT, WHO'S GOT THE DEFICIT?*

James Tobin†

As a background to understanding the analysis underlying this selection, it may be useful to review Selection 9 briefly. Recall that a surplus sector, with saving greater than investment, must repay debts, hoard, or lend an amount equal to its surplus. And that a deficit sector, with investment greater than saving, must borrow, dishoard, or sell financial assets in an amount equal to its deficit.

Any one sector may invest more or less than it saves, or borrow more or less than it lends. However, for the economy as a whole, saving must necessarily equal investment and borrowing must equal lending plus hoarding. Thus surplus sectors, which save more than they invest, necessarily imply the existence of other deficit sectors. This is not only because ex post the economy-wide total of saving must equal investment, but also because a surplus sector must use its surplus to lend, repay debts, or hoard. This implies the existence of deficit sectors to do the borrowing or dishoarding.

Question: *Sir, on that point, what do you think of the President's tax cut proposal and his idea that it would spur revenues even though we would have what he calls a temporary deficit? Does this make sense to you?*

Answer: *My own background is that of a small businessman who has had to scratch right hard to keep his head above water at times. The arithmetic of this thing just doesn't work out. I couldn't in my business increase my expenses and reduce my revenues and stay alive. I don't think a government can do it without an eventual change in our form of government.*
— Interview with REP. HOWARD W. SMITH
(D, Va.),
Chairman of the House Committee on Rules.

For every buyer there must be a seller, and for every lender a borrower. One man's expenditure is another's receipt. My debts are your assets, my deficits your surplus. If all of us were consistently "neither borrower nor lender," as Polonius advised, no one would ever need to violate the revered wisdom of Mr. Micawber. But if the prudent among us insist on running and lending surpluses, some of the rest of us are willy-nilly going to borrow to finance budget deficits.

In the United States today one budget which is usually left holding a deficit is that of the federal government. When no one else borrows the surpluses of the thrifty, the Treasury ends up doing so. Since the role of debtor and borrower is thought to be particularly unbecoming to the federal government, the nation feels frustrated and guilty.

Unhappily, crucial decisions of economic policy are too largely blind reactions to these feelings. The truisms that borrowing is the counterpart of lending, and deficits the counterpart of surpluses, are overlooked in popular and Congressional discussions of government budgets and taxes. Both guilt feelings and policy are based on serious misunderstanding of the origins of federal budget deficits and surpluses.

American *households* and *financial institutions* consistently run financial surpluses. They have money to lend, beyond their own needs to borrow. Chart 1 shows the growth in their combined surpluses since the war; it also shows some tendency for these surpluses to rise in periods of recession and slack business activity. Of course, many private households have financial deficits. They pay out more than their incomes for food, clothing, cars, appliances,

* From *The New Republic*, January 19, 1963. Reprinted by the courtesy of the publisher and the author.
† Yale University.

CHART 1

Financial Surpluses of Consumers, Non-profit Institutions, and Financial Institutions, 1947–61

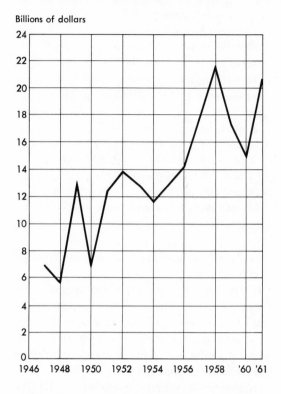

Billions of dollars

Who is to use the $20 billion of surplus funds available from households and financial institutions? *State and local governments* as a group have been averaging $3–4 billion a year of net borrowing. Pressures of the expanding populations of children, adults, houses and automobiles, plus the difficulties of increasing tax revenues, force these governments to borrow in spite of strictures against government debt. *Unincorporated business,* including farms, absorb another $3–4 billion. To the *rest of the world* we can lend perhaps $2 billion a year. We cannot lend abroad — net — more than the surplus of our exports over our imports of goods and services, and some of that surplus we give away in foreign aid. We have to earn the lendable surplus in tough international competition. Recent experience shows clearly that when we try to lend and invest too much money abroad, we either have to borrow it back or else pay in gold.

These borrowers account for $8–10 billion. The remainder — some $10–12 billion — must be used either by *non-financial corporate business* or by the *federal government.* Only if corporations as a group take $10–12 billion of external funds, by borrowing or issuing new equities, can the federal government expect to break even. This is, moreover, an understatement of what is required to keep the federal debt from rising. For the federal government itself provides annually $3 to $4 billion of new lending; and the Treasury would have to borrow to finance these federal lending programs even if the government absorbed no *net* funds from the economy. It is *gross* federal borrowing which offends the fiscal conservative, whether or not the proceeds are used to acquire other financial assets.

The moral is inescapable, if startling. If you would like the federal deficit to be smaller, the deficits of business must be bigger. And would you like the federal government to run a surplus and reduce its debt? Then business deficits must be big enough to absorb that surplus as well as the funds available from households and financial institutions.

That does not mean that business must be run at a loss — quite the contrary. Sometimes, it is true, unprofitable businesses are forced to

houses, taxes, etc. They draw on savings accounts, redeem savings bonds, sell securities, mortgage houses or incur installment debt. But deficit households are far outweighed by surplus households. As a group American *households* and *non-profit institutions* have in recent years shown a net financial surplus averaging about $15 billion a year — that is, households are ready to lend, or put into equity investments, about $15 billion a year more than they are prepared to borrow. In addition, *financial institutions* regularly generate a lendable surplus, now of the order of $5 billion a year. For the most part these institutions — banks, savings and loan associations, insurance companies, pension funds, and the like — are simply intermediaries which borrow and re-lend the public's money. Their surpluses result from the fact that they earn more from their lending operations than they distribute or credit to their depositors, shareowners and policyholders.

borrow or to spend financial reserves just to stay afloat; this was a major reason for business deficits in the depths of the Great Depression. But normally it is businesses with good profits and good prospects which borrow or sell new shares of stock, in order to finance expansion and modernization. As the President of AT&T can testify, heavy reliance on outside funds, far from being a distress symptom, is an index and instrument of growth in the profitability and worth of the corporation. Financial deficits incurred by business firms — or by households and governments — do not usually mean that they are living beyond their means and consuming their capital. Financial deficits are typically the means of accumulating non-financial assets — real property in the form of inventories, buildings and equipment.

When does business run big deficits? When do corporations draw heavily on the capital

CHART 2

Net Financial Surpluses, Deficits of the Federal Government and of Nonfinancial Corporations, 1947–61

Billions of dollars

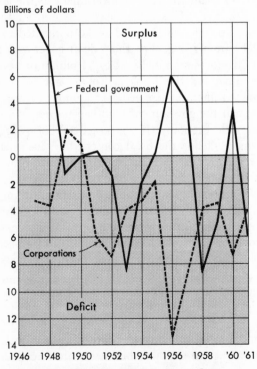

Source: Board of Governors of the Federal Reserve System.

markets? The record is clear: when business is very good, when sales are pressing hard on capacity, when businessmen see further expansion ahead. Though corporations' internal funds — depreciation allowances and plowed-back profits — are large during boom times, their investment programs are even larger.

Chart 2 shows the financial deficits or surpluses of corporate business and of the federal government since the war. Three facts stand out. First, the federal government has big deficits when corporations run surpluses or small deficits — and vice versa. Second, government surpluses and business deficits reach their peaks in periods of economic expansion, when industrial capacity is heavily utilized: 1947–48, 1951–52, 1956–57. Third, the combined deficit of corporate business and the federal government is greater now than in the early postwar years; this is the counterpart of the upward trend in available surpluses as shown in Chart 1.

Recession, idle capacity, unemployment, economic slack — these are the enemies of the balanced government budget. When the economy is faltering, households have more surpluses available to lend, and business firms are less inclined to borrow them.

The federal government will not succeed in cutting its deficit by steps which depress the economy, perpetuate excess capacity, and deter business firms from outside funds. Raising taxes and cutting expenses seem like obvious ways to balance the budget. But because of their effects on private spending, lending and borrowing, they may have exactly the contrary result. Likewise, lowering taxes and raising government expenditures may so stimulate private business activity and private borrowing that the federal deficit is in the end actually reduced.

This may seem paradoxical, and perhaps it is. Why is it that the homely analogy between family finance and government finance, on which our decisive national attitudes toward federal fiscal policy are so largely based, misleads us? If John Jones on Maple Street is spending $8,700 a year but taking in only $8,000, the remedy is clear. All Mr. Jones need do to balance the family budget is resolutely to live within his income, either spending some $700 less or working harder to increase his earnings. Jones can safely ignore the impact of either action on the incomes and expenditures of others and the possible ultimate feedback on his own job and income. The situation of John F. Kennedy on Pennsylvania Avenue, spending $87 billion a year against tax revenues of $80 billion is quite different. Suppose he spends $7 billion less, or tries through higher tax rates to boost federal revenues by $7 billion. He cannot ignore the inevitable boomerang effect on federal finances. These measures will lower the sales, payrolls and profits of business firms, whether they were selling aircraft to the government or pleasure boats to taxpayers. These business firms will in turn spend less for new machinery; their employees and stockholders will spend less on vacation trips. This chain is not endless. But before it ends, it will shrink total spending and income in the economy by a multiple of the original $7 billion. The federal tax base shrinks correspondingly. In the end the federal deficit will be reduced by much less than $7 billion; perhaps it will even be increased.

Incidentally, many of the very critics who are most vocal in chiding the government for fiscal sin advocate policies which would make fiscal

virtue even more elusive. They want to keep private borrowing in check by tight credit policies and high interest rates. They want to increase corporations' *internal* flow of funds by bigger depreciation allowances and higher profit margins, making business still less dependent on external funds to finance investment, even in boom times. When these apostles of sound finance also tell the government to shun external finance, have they done their arithmetic? If everyone is self-financing, who then will borrow the surpluses?

The nation is paying a high price for the misapplied homely wisdom which guides federal fiscal policy. The real toll is measured by unemployment, idle capacity, lost production and sluggish economic growth. But fiscal conservatism is also self-defeating. It does not even achieve its own aim, the avoidance of government deficits. Federal fiscal and monetary policies consciously and unashamedly designed to stimulate the economy would have sufficient justification in economic expansion itself. But they might well "improve" the federal budget too — by inducing business to use the private surpluses that now have no destination other than a rising federal debt.

55

A HOMELY, MISUNDERSTOOD ANALOGY*

Wall Street Journal

The Wall Street Journal disputes the conlusions reached by Professor Tobin in the previous selection.

That the Government should conduct its financial affairs like a family or a company is an idea which encounters deep disapproval among the economists who influence Washington pol-

* Editorial in *The Wall Street Journal*, February 12, 1963. Reprinted by the courtesy of *The Wall Street Journal*.

icy. It may be all right for households and businesses to balance the books, in their view, but that emphatically does not apply to the Federal Government.

How far this aversion can be carried is illustrated in a remarkable little essay by James Tobin in a recent New Republic. Mr. Tobin is a Yale professor who was a member of President Kennedy's Council of Economic Advisers until last July.

First of all, we are told that for every lender there must be a borrower. And from this seemingly simple proposition it develops that a large portion of the lendable surplus — that is, savings — generated in the private economy just about has to be used by the Federal Government — that is, go into its deficits — if untoward results are to be avoided.

"The moral," writes Mr. Tobin, "is inescapable, if startling. If you would like the Federal deficit to be smaller, the deficits of business must be bigger. And would you like the Federal Government to run a surplus and reduce its debt? Then business deficits must be big enough to absorb that surplus as well as the funds available from households and financial institutions."

This kind of analysis seems to presuppose that the pool of money and credit available to the nation is fixed; that while its incidence can be shifted among various economic segments, its total weight cannot be increased or reduced. Yet in the real world it is plain enough that a business can grow more productive and profitable without automatically deepening a Federal deficit, and that Government spending and deficits can be reduced without increasing business deficits.

If Mr. Tobin and his friends were right, the business history of the U.S. couldn't have happened. The enormous expansion of business over the generations has for the most part been accompanied by negligible Government activity. It is only in recent times that Government and its deficits have weighed so heavily on the economy — interestingly enough, a period increasingly punctuated by complaints of inadequate economic growth.

Part of the trouble lies in a certain amount of semantic confusion. Mr. Tobin discusses business "deficits" as though they were of the same structure as Federal deficits. In the same somewhat ambivalent way, Government economists sometimes try to show they are operating on business principles, even while denying the validity of the analogy in general.

What Mr. Tobin, at any rate, actually seems to be talking about are not real deficits of corporations but such business liabilities as are incurred through the exchange of bonds for working assets intended to bring about expansion or modernization or both. And the people's savings can go not only into corporate debt but into equity capital also used for productive purposes.

A Federal deficit, in contrast, is incurred to allow the Government to increase its spending on projects which are largely non-productive, like weapons and numerous less essential things. A business, moreover, cannot indefinitely run a true deficit without going bankrupt; that is, its expenses cannot forever exceed its earnings in the fashion the Federal Government thinks commendable for itself.

Finally, no business can print its own money if it wishes to avoid legal difficulties. But that is what the Federal Government does in effect when it finances its deficits through the banking system. And that inflation, past and potential, is a deterrent, to put it mildly, to sound economic growth.

So it is quite true that the Federal Government does not in practice operate the way a normal family or business does. But the failure of the Federal practice is hardly a justification for this consistent violation of all the rules of financial prudence.

What Mr. Tobin disparagingly calls "the homely analogy" between business finance and Government finance would be accurate enough — if only the economists currently in favor could understand it.

CHAPTER FIFTEEN

DEBT MANAGEMENT

56

FINANCING FEDERAL DEFICITS*

Federal Reserve Bank of Richmond

The national debt, which in mid-1966 totaled about 325 billion dollars, is essentially the net result of past and present fiscal policy, mostly past. A budget deficit requires that the Government either borrow or print money to cover the deficit, and most modern governments choose to borrow (i.e., sell government securities). As a result, we acquire a national debt. Since the debt is not likely to become much smaller in our lifetime, it is important to analyze the ways in which it might be managed to have the least harm, and even the maximum benefit, with respect to economic stability. This is done in the following three selections.

In general, the Federal Government can finance an excess of expenditures over receipts in any of four ways. It can (1) draw down its cash balances, (2) sell securities to the non-bank public, (3) sell securities to the Federal Reserve, or (4) sell securities to commercial banks. These alternatives are not mutually exclusive, of course, and in actual practice some combination of them is generally utilized. For clarity, however, it is probably desirable to describe the effects of each separately.

Drawing Down Cash Balances. To take a concrete example, suppose that Federal expenditures in a given quarter exceed revenues by $1 billion, leaving a deficit of that amount to be financed. If the Treasury were able and willing to draw down its cash balances, it obviously could finance the deficit without borrowing.

The economic and financial effects depend

to a considerable extent on whether the Treasury reduces the deposit balances it holds at the Federal Reserve or those held at commercial banks. If the Treasury finances the entire deficit by drawing down balances at the Federal Reserve, the result will be more expansionary than if balances are reduced in tax and loan accounts at commercial banks. Checks drawn on the Federal Reserve to cover the deficit wind up as an increase of $1 billion in private deposits in commercial banks. When the checks are presented for collection at the Federal Reserve, member bank reserve accounts increase by the same amount. Since only part of the additional reserves are needed to back the increased private deposits, the excess reserves provide the base for a multiple expansion of bank credit and the money supply.

In actual practice, however, financing a deficit by drawing down cash balances is less expansionary than implied above. As a matter of policy, the Treasury keeps its working balances at the Federal Reserve at a fairly constant level.

* From Federal Reserve Bank of Richmond *Monthly Review*, December 1964. Reprinted by the courtesy of the Federal Reserve Bank of Richmond.

Consequently, it would probably issue a call on its tax and loan accounts at commercial banks in order to replenish its balances at the Federal Reserve. This would have the effect of unwinding the changes described in the previous paragraph, and member bank reserves would be the same as at the beginning. The only substantive change would be the increase in the statistically measured money supply resulting from the transfer of Treasury deposits at commercial banks, which are not counted as part of the money supply, to private deposit accounts, which are included in the money supply statistics.

This method of financing would clearly not offset the stimulative "fiscal" impact of the deficit. Rather it would probably provide moderate additional stimulus, since the public's liquidity position would be improved as the result of its acquisition of new money balances formerly held by the Government.

Selling to the Nonbank Public. Should the Treasury sell $1 billion worth of certificates, notes, or bonds to the nonbank public and spend the proceeds, the public would wind up with the same amount of money (demand deposits) as before but with $1 billion more in securities. Moreover commercial banks would find their reserve positions unchanged from the initial level.

This can be illustrated with the following T-accounts. (a) If the nonbank public buys $1 billion of securities from the Treasury and pays for them with checks drawn on deposit accounts at commercial banks, clearing the checks would involve the following changes at commercial banks and Federal Reserve Banks:

COMMERCIAL BANKS
Billions of Dollars

Assets		Liabilities	
Reserves	−1	Private Demand Deposits	−1

FEDERAL RESERVE
Billions of Dollars

Assets		Liabilities	
		Member Bank Deposits	−1
		U.S. Treasury General Account	+1

(b) As the Treasury spends the $1 billion, the public deposits it in commercial banks, and the changes above are reversed.

COMMERCIAL BANKS
Billions of Dollars

Assets		Liabilities	
Reserves	+1	Private Demand Deposits	+1

FEDERAL RESERVE
Billions of Dollars

Assets		Liabilities	
		Member Bank Deposits	+1
		U.S. Treasury General Account	−1

The net effects on the balance sheets of the Fed and the commercial banks are, of course, nil, and all relevant accounts return to their pre-deficit values. There is, however, an increase of $1 billion in the Government securities holdings of the nonbank public resulting from the public's acquisition of the new bonds.

Does a Federal deficit financed in this way give the economy an expansionary boost? No definitive answer to this question is available, but most analysts would probably answer in the affirmative. Although the public as a whole ends up with the same amount of money (demand deposits) as before, a redistribution of money within the public sector has occurred. Those who bought the Government securities voluntarily adjusted their liquid asset positions, giving up money for bonds, thereby indicating they did not need the money for immediate spending. On the other hand, those who received money as a result of the Government's fiscal operation acquired something of a windfall and presumably would soon adjust their rate of spending to their new higher incomes. Thus, it can be argued that a rise in the velocity of money occurs.

On the negative side, it should be noted that the increased supply of securities on the market tends to push interest rates upward, thereby tending to restrain private spending for goods and services by making expenditures for financial assets relatively more attractive. Spending may also be reduced as rising interest rates result in capital losses on the public's fixed-income assets.

Selling to the Federal Reserve. At the other extreme, the Treasury could finance the deficit by selling securities to the Federal Reserve. The central bank would pay for the securities by crediting the Treasury's account. When the Treasury pays out the proceeds, the public's money holdings rise. Deposit of the new money in banks raises bank deposits and reserves in identical amounts and creates excess reserves which may be used for credit and monetary expansion. The result would be clearly expansionary.

In terms of T-accounts, the effects may be traced out as follows:

(a) The central bank buys $1 billion of securities from the Treasury.

FEDERAL RESERVE
Billions of Dollars

Assets		Liabilities	
Government Securities	+1	U.S. Treasury General Account	+1

(b) The Treasury spends the proceeds with the public, which deposits them in commercial banks.

COMMERCIAL BANKS
Billions of Dollars

Assets		Liabilities	
Reserves	+1	Private Demand Deposits	+1

FEDERAL RESERVE
Billions of Dollars

Assets		Liabilities	
		Member Bank Reserves	+1
		U.S. Treasury General Account	−1

Both the public's money holdings and commercial banks' reserves increase by the amount of the deficit. Additional monetary expansion would then take place as banks put their excess reserves to work.

In fact, however, substantial deficits cannot be permanently financed by selling securities directly to the Federal Reserve. The System is authorized to buy securities directly from the Treasury, subject to the restriction that the amount outstanding cannot exceed $5 billion at any time. This is regarded by the Treasury only as a source of temporary accommodation, and in practice the authority is almost never used.

Selling to Commercial Banks. The economic effect of financing a deficit through selling securities to commercial banks would vary, depending on the action taken by the Federal Reserve. If the central bank did not supply member banks with reserves with which to purchase the Treasury securities, the economic impact would be much the same as if the Treasury had sold securities to the nonbank public. If, on the other hand, the Federal Reserve supplied reserves equal to the amount of the bond issue, the effect would be the same as if the Federal Reserve had bought the securities directly. Many intermediate possibilities obviously exist between these extremes. The System, for example, might decide to supply just that amount of reserves which would enable banks to acquire the Treasury issues without liquidating other earning assets.

To elaborate the first case, assume the commercial banks were fully loaned up, having no excess reserves. The commercial banks could purchase $1 billion of Government securities only by liquidating an equivalent amount of loans and/or investments. Such liquidation would reduce the public's holdings of money by $1 billion, exactly offsetting the increase resulting from the Government's excess of expenditures over tax receipts. So far as the commercial banks are concerned, the net effect would be nothing more than a substitution in bank portfolios of Government securities for other loans and/or investments. If banks bought the new securities by liquidating other investments, the economic impact would be almost precisely the same as if the Treasury had sold the new securities to the nonbank public. The public would end up with the same amount of money as before but with $1 billion more in securities (those liquidated by the banks). Interest rates would tend to rise, and the expansionary impact of the deficit would be partially offset. If banks made room for the new Governments by letting loans run off, the result would be slightly different. Instead of ending up with more securities than before, the nonbank public would wind up with less indebtedness.

On the other hand, if the central bank provided the commercial banks with reserves equal to the amount of the deficit, banks could buy the new Governments without liquidating other loans and investments and have reserves to spare. When the Treasury disbursed the proceeds of the bond sale to meet its obligations, the Government checks would be deposited in commercial banks and private deposits would rise by $1 billion. Since bank reserves would increase by a like amount, the result would be identical to that achieved when the Federal Reserve bought the securities directly. Only a fraction of the reserves would be needed to support the new private deposits, and a multiple expansion of bank credit and the money supply would result as banks lent and invested their excess reserves.

Summary. Assuming that member banks operate with a minimum of excess reserves, as they have in recent years, the economic effect of financing a deficit through the banking system depends primarily on the action taken by the Federal Reserve. If the System supplies no additional reserves, purchases by commercial banks are virtually equivalent to purchases by the nonbank public. If the System supplies reserves equal to the amount of the new Treasury issues, purchases by banks are equivalent to direct purchases by the Federal Reserve. The critical question, therefore, is not who buys the bonds but what course of action the central bank decides to follow. This in turn depends primarily on economic conditions. If a national emergency requires a large increase in Government expenditures at a time when labor is fully employed and prices are rising, restrictive monetary policy would be in order. At the other extreme, with national income falling and unemployment rising, appropriate policy might call for aggressive reserve expansion. Between the extremes, proper monetary policy might assume an almost infinite variety of postures. The point is that no method of financing a deficit is inherently "sound." Sound financing will depend entirely on the environmental setting.

57

A NOTE ON THE RETIREMENT OF PUBLIC DEBT DURING INFLATION*

Lawrence S. Ritter†

There is a widespread impression among the general public, and among many economists also, that the public debt, which invariably rises during periods of recession, should be retired during periods of inflation; that this will in some way combat inflationary forces.

The following article, which attempts to clarify the effects of debt retirement, reaches a rather different conclusion.

* From the *Journal of Finance*, Vol. VI, No. 1 (March 1951). Reprinted by the courtesy of the publisher (the American Finance Association).
† New York University.

The effects of debt retirement depend upon both the source of the funds used for the redemption and the unit of decision from whom the obligations are redeemed. In the case where the funds used to retire debt come from a current Treasury cash surplus, three steps may be differentiated for purposes of analysis. There is involved *first* the collection of taxes by the Treasury and *then* the shifting of the funds collected to the Treasury's balance at the Federal Reserve. The collection of net taxes over and above expenditure results in the public holding tax receipts in place of spendable funds — the level of disposable income is reduced as funds are shifted from the hands of the public to the purse of the Treasury. Let us call this Step A. The deflationary aspects are then emphasized when the Treasury calls its accounts at the commercial banks, shifting the funds to its Federal Reserve balance and thereby taking reserves from the commercial banks. Let us call this Step B. Either step would be anti-inflationary; both together are heavily so.

With the funds thus acquired the Treasury can then retire debt (Step C) held by the Federal Reserve, the commercial banks, or the nonbank public. If the Treasury retires Federal Reserve held debt, checking on its account with the Federal Reserve, the only result is to cancel outstanding obligations and corresponding Treasury balances at the central bank. The net effect of the *entire process* (i.e., including Steps A and B) is to give the public tax receipts in place of purchasing power, to eliminate a corresponding amount of commercial bank reserves, and, of course, to wipe out part of the government debt.

The actual process of debt retirement per se (Step C) is in no way deflationary. It is the collection of net taxes over and above expenditure and the transfer of the funds to the Federal Reserve (i.e., Steps A and B) that exert the deflationary impact. The debt retirement per se (Step C) merely wipes out liquid assets *already out of* the hands of the public or commercial banks. It also eliminates a Treasury checking account, but this will hardly impair the Treasury's power to spend.

On the other hand, if the Treasury retires commercial bank-held debt with funds acquired through Steps A and B, it shifts reserves *back to the commercial banking system* in return for the government securities. It is clear once more that the retirement considered by itself (Step

C) could hardly be termed anti-inflationary. With the debt held by the Federal Reserve selected for redemption, the net effect was that commercial bank reserves remained cut; in the present case they are returned to the system. In fact, excess reserves increase since the total effect (including Steps A and B) is to leave reserves at the same level while decreasing the deposits of the public in the commercial banks. Far from being anti-inflationary, the actual process of retiring debt from commercial bank holdings is a factor that returns reserves to the member banks. It is thus a *negating* element that reduces the anti-inflationary effects of Steps A and B.

Similar results flow from the retirement of public-held debt. In this case the Treasury dispenses cash to the public (and reserves to the banking system) in return for government securities, a procedure which is hardly calculated to restrain private spending.

The conclusions seem clear. If a truly restrictive policy is desired during strongly inflationary periods, do *not* retire commercial bank-held or public-held debt. The only debt that should be retired during periods of inflationary pressure is that held by the Federal Reserve. It could be retired via a current surplus, through borrowing from the commercial banks, or borrowing from the public. Treasury borrowing from the public is generally recognized as anti-inflationary if it takes funds that would have been spent, assuming the Treasury would have spent the same amount in any case. Similarly, Treasury borrowing from the commercial banks can contribute to an anti-inflation program if the funds so obtained are used for purposes of retiring Federal Reserve-held debt.

An effective anti-inflation program during periods of heavy inflationary pressures which combines both fiscal policy and debt management would mean (1) the raising of a budget cash surplus as the inflation approaches, (2a) allowing the surplus to merely accumulate in Treasury accounts with the Federal Reserve, which is preferable to using it to retire debt held outside the central bank, or (2b) using it to retire Federal Reserve-held debt. If, due to political factors, a current surplus cannot be raised, debt management could still aid, with the Treasury borrowing from the public or commercial banks (preferably the former) and either shifting the funds to the Federal Reserve (to remain there idle) or using them to retire Federal Reserve-held debt. Such a policy is best thought of as a supplement rather than an alternative to the raising of a surplus.

The debt in the hands of the commercial banks and the non-bank public would, as has been suggested, best be repaid *after* the boom, or during a depression. The retirement of debt in the hands of these groups would thus be best used as an anti-deflationary device, rather than the anti-inflationary tool which it is not.

5 8

DEBT MANAGEMENT AND ECONOMIC STABILIZATION POLICY*

Henry C. Wallich†

In this selection Professor Wallich analyzes some of the practical problems of debt management and their implications for economic stabilization policy.

My topic is "Debt Management and Economic Stabilization Policy." The problems to be treated under this heading are quite as complex as the forbidding title suggest. But while not much can be done to simplify the problems, I can at least try to simplify the title. It boils down to this: How does the public debt affect the stability of the economy? In particular, what bearing does our handling of the debt have upon the threat of inflation?

THE DEBT IN STATISTICAL PERSPECTIVE

Before launching into the heart of this subject, I would like to place the public debt in a statistical setting. The total amount of the debt today is approximately $320 billion. This amounts to 46 per cent of the gross national product. In 1946, the public debt amounted

to 117 per cent of the then GNP. In other words, whereas immediately after the war the public debt was substantially larger than the GNP, it now is substantially smaller.

The interest on the public debt now runs at about $9 billion annually. This is equal to 1.3 per cent of the GNP and to less than 10 per cent of total budget expenditures. In 1939 interest on the public debt amounted to not quite $1 billion and constituted 1.1 per cent of GNP and 11 per cent of budget expenditures. In 1929 interest amounted to $700 million, which represented 1 per cent of GNP and 11 per cent of budget expenditures. In 1929 interest amounted to $700 million, which represented 1 per cent of GNP and 21 per cent of total budget expenditures, while in 1920 interest on the public debt was $1 billion which meant 1.2 per cent of GNP and 16 per cent of budget expenditures.

These figures seem to show two things: first, interest on the public debt has always represented a fairly sizable part of our budgetary expenditures. Percentagewise, it is now less than it was in 1939, 1929 or 1920. This reflects,

* From *United States Monetary Policy* (Duke University and the American Assembly of Columbia University, 1959). Reprinted by the courtesy of the publisher (Duke University) and the author. The data have been brought up to date as of the end of 1965.

† Yale University. At the time of writing Professor Wallich was on leave from Yale University to serve as Assistant to the Secretary of the Treasury.

of course, the staggering increase in the Federal Budget. Secondly, interest as a percentage of GNP has risen over the years. The increase, however, has been moderate. It is hard to argue that the interest charge by itself constitutes an unbearable burden for the Nation.

Finally, let us look at the public debt as part of our total structure of public and private debt. At the present time, total debt in the economy, including business, home owners, consumers, state and local governments, and the Federal Government and avoiding double counting, comes to approximately $1400 billion. Of this, the Federal Government represents about 25 per cent. In 1946, the total debt in the economy added up to $446 billion, of which the federal debt represented a hefty 58 per cent. Comparing this total indebtedness of the economy with GNP, we find that at present the ratio of all debt to GNP is 1.85. Going back as far as 1929, we find that the ratio of debt to GNP was 2.06. These figures again seem to show two things. First the figures demonstrate that the public debt, after its tremendous rise during the thirties and the war, is now playing a rapidly diminishing role within our total debt structure. Secondly, they show that over a long period of years, going back to 1929, the ratio of all debt to GNP has not changed materially. In other words, we have not loaded the economy down with an increasing burden of debt. Of course, this does not mean that the burden may not have increased significantly for particular groups of borrowers in the economy.

I apologize for the excessive statistical detail of this analysis. I think it is helpful, however, because it brings us down to one important conclusion. Such problems as the Treasury and the Nation today face in the handling of the public debt are in no way the result of impossible magnitudes. The amounts involved are greater than in the past, but not greater in a degree that might make the problems appear to defy solution. The problems are of an order that will yield to the proper skill — and the will — to deal with them.

Now, let us move closer to the debt and look at in more detail. Of the $320 billion, $62 billion are in federal trust accounts, and $41 billion are held by the Federal Reserve.

This takes over $100 billion out of the debt and makes the publicly held debt about $220 billion. Of this $220 billion, $50 billion represents savings bonds, Series E and H. These savings bonds do not present the same problems as the rest of the debt. They are widely distributed. They are on the whole firmly held, and they constitute a gradually expanding total. The problems they present are of a kind that can be left out of a discussion of the problem of debt management as usually thought of. This brings us down to approximately $170 billion of debt. Here, in this $170 billion are centered the principal problems of public debt management.

MECHANICS OF DEBT MANAGEMENT

To clarify what is commonly meant by debt management, let us briefly remind ourselves of the mechanics. Time does not stand still and neither does the public debt. It has been said that if one wants time to pass quickly, one need only sign a 90-day note. The Treasury can confirm the truth of this, and it applies not only to short-term obligations. All sections of the public debt are continually moving down to shorter maturity categories. Decisions then have to be made on how to deal with these maturing obligations. Most of the time they have to be refunded; i.e., the holders of the maturing obligations are offered a new issue in exchange. In addition, new securities must be offered for cash from time to time. Such cash offerings are apt to be heavy when the Government is running a deficit as has been true lately. But even with a balanced budget, cash offerings are necessary, from time to time, to meet seasonal needs, and to meet attrition on the refundings; i.e., to pay off holders of maturing obligations who want cash rather than a new security.

The amount and timing of Treasury financing is largely determined by the maturities as they arrive, and by the course of federal receipts and expenditures. Given these data, the principal decision to be made by debt management is to determine the maturity of the new issue or issues. This is based upon a careful study of the amount of funds available in different sectors of the market. The interest rate to be paid follows from this initial decision. Broadly speaking, it is the rate that prevails in the market for comparable maturities. The rate can be made slightly more or less attractive depending upon how much "sweetening" appears to be needed to make the operation a success. For cash offerings particularly, but also for refundings, some sweetening usually is necessary in order to make the issue a success. That practice is universally followed by corporate borrowers and the Treasury, although on a more modest scale, must employ it too, when it tries to sell at one time a large block of securities in a market that ordinarily can supply investable funds only rather gradually. The yield of an issue can further be adjusted by selling it at a slight premium or discount. The Treasury recently has done both, in order to attune its offerings more closely to the market. A cash issue can be given added attractiveness for commercial banks by allowing them to credit the proceeds to the Treasury's tax and loan accounts. This in effect means that the buyer can delay cash payment for some days and meanwhile receive interest on the new security. In setting the yield of the new security by means of all these devices, the Treasury of course is always trying to get the best deal at the cheapest cost for the Government, consistent with other debt management objectives.

The pricing of a new issue is an extremely delicate and difficult operation. Consequently, the market often finds itself in a state of uncertainty and nervous anticipation when the Treasury must make up its mind about the proper price for a new issue. For certain types of securities, the Treasury has found it possible to avoid the need to put a fixed price on its offerings. It can do so by offering these securities at auction. That allows the market to put its own price on the new securities. In effect, the auction method puts the burden of pricing upon the dealers and investors who participate in the bidding.

The auction method, in which a successful bidder pays the price he bids, has shown itself suited only, however, to short-term securities. Here it has proved useful by reducing the uncertainty and unsettlement in the market that tend to arise when the Treasury sells issues at a fixed price which may or may not be exactly what the market expects. For long-term issues, the auction method would present real difficulties to the dealers and investors in pricing their bids. Secretary Morgenthau tried to auction long-term bonds during the thirties but soon abandoned the attempt. The risk for the participants and the penalty to them for bidding too high and so being caught with too high a cost for a longer-term security apparently made the procedure too onerous for all but a small number of highly specialized bidders.

In many of the Treasury financings more than one security is offered in order to tap several sectors of the market. In a cash offering the Treasury decides what amounts of each individual security it wants to offer. In refundings it has been the practice to allow the holders of the maturing securities some choice as to which of the Treasury offerings they wish to acquire in exchange. Typically the shortest issue offered becomes the "anchor" of the operation which must assure its success if the longer issue or issues prove less attractive than anticipated.

THE INFLATIONARY THREAT

After this digression into the field of mechanics, let us return to the main theme: the effect of debt management on economic stability and particularly on the stability of the dollar. We noted earlier that the portion of the public debt which constitutes the core of the problem amounts to about $170 billion. We must now look more closely at the maturity structure of this debt because it is this maturity structure, the amount of debt with shorter and longer maturities, that determines the impact of the debt upon economic stability.

Of the 170 billion, close to half matures within one year, a quarter within one to five years, while the remainder falls into the category of over five years. This whole debt structure continually shortens, of course, unless new longer-term issues are put out. Without such longer issues, the short-term part, maturing within one year, eventually would predominate. If no longer-term debt were issued for five years, the under one-year category would grow to three-quarters of that debt. Here is the principal inflationary threat that the public debt presents at this time.

Growth of Near Money. This inflationary threat, if not met by debt lengthening, would make itself felt in several ways. First, the ownership of short-term securities, as contrasted with longer term, makes their holder more liquid. A 90-day bill is almost as good as cash and is treated as the virtual equivalent of cash by most holders. An increase in securities that represent "near money" therefore comes dangerously close to an increase in money itself.

There exists a perfectly legitimate need, of course, for a certain amount of short-term securities. When short-term rates are above a rock-bottom level, holders of cash balances like to invest part of them temporarily in order to get a return. It seems legitimate for the Treasury to meet this need. If the Treasury did not meet it, very likely the market itself would generate other short-term investment opportunities, through commercial paper and the like, to meet the demand.

Debt Monetization. The danger lies in an excessive supply of short-term securities. These are near money, and therefore add to total liquidity. When issued in excess of the market's need for them, moreover, they become inflationary, in a second and perhaps even more powerful way: when they exceed the amount that investors want to absorb, they are likely to be bought by banks. When the banking system acquires these additional assets, it creates additional deposits; i.e., money. In other words, part of the public debt then would be monetized by being acquired by the banking system. In lieu of an increase in near money we then face an increase in money itself.

We may trace very summarily the process by which securities are forced into the banks. When non-bank investors do not want to buy additional securities at going rates, the Federal Reserve is faced with two choices; to supply the banks the reserves sufficient to buy the securities, or to see interest rates go up until somehow all securities are taken by non-bank investors. Unless the latter alternative is chosen, which at times may be undesirable, short-term securities not wanted by non-bank

buyers will be pushed into the banks. The banks are the marginal buyers, and their buying is inflationary.

Frequency of Financings. A third inflationary result of a large short-term debt remains to be observed. A large short-term debt means that the Treasury faces a steady stream of maturities; the Treasury then is in the market almost constantly to refinance these obligations. During such financing periods, the Federal Reserve cannot use its credit controls as freely as at other times. If it did, it might jeopardize the success of the financing. Treasury financing therefore may interfere with credit restraint by the Federal Reserve and so may permit a kind of inflationary leakage to occur.

Other Possible Consequences. These three factors — the increase in near money, the increase in bank holdings of public debt, and interference with Federal Reserve operations — are the principal inflationary dangers surrounding the public debt at this time. Conceivably, the public debt can become inflationary in still other ways which may be worth mentioning although they are not relevant now. For instance, the support of the bond market by the Federal Reserve can become an inflationary practice. We engaged in this immediately after the War and until early 1951, up to the "Accord" between Treasury and Federal Reserve. During that period, the Treasury felt, rightly or wrongly, that wide fluctuations in the new and as yet undigested public debt might upset the economy. It also feared that wide fluctuations in the bond market might make Treasury financing very difficult. Hence the Federal Reserve kept the bond market from falling below pre-determined levels, by buying all bonds offered at that price. The result was to increase bank reserves and expand the money supply. Because of the inflationary implications of that process, the support of the bond market was given up in 1951.

The public debt might become inflationary also if it became very much larger than it is today and the interest burden heavier than taxpayers were willing to bear. Deficit financing might then be resorted to that in the end would lead to inflation. Some economists believe that this has been the process through which historically a high public debt has pushed governments on the path of inflation. Or perhaps the level of interest rates that would be necessary to induce non-bank investors to hold the debt might encounter resistance, because these rates set the tone for all borrowing rates in the economy. Clearly those features are not present in our situation today. So long as the total interest burden is moderate and so long as there is a willingness to accept the necessary level of interest rates as the price of economic stability, no inflationary threat need issue from that side.

A public debt is capable of exerting deflationary effects also, which are the obverse of its inflationary potential. For instance, an effort to fund short-term debt may have deflationary consequences, if the flow of long-term funds into private investment is curtailed too severely. So may an effort to compete too aggressively, if it leads to a sharp rise in interest rates that would make private borrowing difficult. At this point, however, I would like to pursue principally the problems of the inflationary potential of the debt.

PRESENT PROBLEMS

Our problems today are those which result from the shortening of the debt and from the danger that it may increasingly pass into the hands of the banks. These problems are compounded at the moment by the deficit that has had to be financed for the fiscal year 1959, of about $13 billion. While the financing of the deficit has been completed and while it was accomplished with only a modest amount of borrowing from banks, its ultimate repercussions probably have not yet materialized. A good part of this financing was done by selling short-term debt to corporations. It remains to be seen whether this can be refinanced when it matures without recourse to the banks.

What the Treasury must do under these circumstances to curb the inflationary potential of the debt is clear: We must try to lengthen the debt, or at least keep it from shortening, and we must try to place it with non-bank lenders. This, however, is more easily said than done. Since 1951, the Treasury has had to face predominantly tight money and capital markets with rising interest rates. This reflects the predominantly prosperous character of the period. Investment in plant and equipment, in homes, and in public improvements has been heavy. The demands made upon the capital market have been correspondingly strong. In periods of intense competing demands, the Treasury has found it somewhat difficult to maintain its position in the market, for reasons to be discussed presently.

About the fact that longer-term Treasuries have been difficult to market, there can be no doubt. A glance at the survey of ownership conducted regularly by the Treasury shows how in important sectors we have been losing part of our market. Over the period beginning June, 1951 — to eliminate the years immediately following the war — the holdings of insurance companies have gone from $17.1 billion to $12.1 billion in 1958. During the same period, those of mutual savings banks have dropped from $10.2 billion to $7.3 billion.

Some gains were registered, for instance, in the area of state and local pension funds, where holdings went from $3 billion to about $5.5 billion. But the basic fact that emerges from the figures is that government securities have lost ground with the big institutional investors. Progress has been made predominantly with investors who tend to buy government obligations for reasons of law or circumstances or habit. This is not a sufficiently promising basis on which to rest the prospects of debt lengthening.

Why Are Long Terms Hard to Sell? At first blush, it would seem as if the Treasury ought never to encounter any difficulties in marketing its obligations. The government's credit is better, after all, than that of any other borrower. The secondary market for Treasury securities likewise is better, because of the great size and widespread ownership of the issues. In addition, government securities have certain other attractions, such as freedom from call provisions in most instances, and the faculty in most cases of being used for payment of estate taxes. In fact, government securities appear to be sufficiently attractive to the market to command invariably a premium over other obligations. Why then are they frequently difficult to market? We seem to face a paradox; government securities are so attractive that they sell at a premium, and because they sell at a premium, they are not wanted.

What are the factors that today make some investors shy away from longer-term governments?

As far as individual investors are concerned, high taxes and fear of inflation both militate against investment in government securities. High taxes mean that there is less new money to be invested. High taxes also create a preference for tax exempts. Fear of inflation, meanwhile, creates a bias in favor of equity investment.

For most institutional investors, with the principal exception of pension funds, fear of inflation is no fundamental deterrent to the purchase of governments. This is demonstrated by the willingness of these institutional investors to buy other kinds of fixed-interest obligations, such as corporate bonds and mortgages. Nevertheless, inflation fear may impose a special risk premium that other borrowers may be willing and able to pay. This would strengthen these competing borrowers vis-a-vis the Treasury.

Competing Advantages of Various Assets. Moreover, in competition with these other fixed-interest securities, governments have lost some of the advantages that they previously enjoyed. This process is worth looking at in greater detail. The liquidity that used to be considered an important attraction of governments has been reduced, in the eyes of many investors, by the widening range of fluctuations in the market. Moreover, the big institutional investors nowadays are meeting their liquidity needs in good measure by an appropriate staggering of their portfolio maturities. Amortized mortgages contribute to this "portfolio liquidity."

The difference in credit standing between the Treasury and top-ranking corporations no longer seems to loom large enough, in the eyes of institutional investors who can afford broad diversification, to justify a significant premium. In a world in which the government is committed to avoiding major depressions, and with the memories of the Great Depression more

than twenty years old, the risk premium on seasoned corporate securities has shrunk to a very small fraction of 1 per cent.

Meanwhile, institutional investors have developed new and profitable outlets for their funds. The net return on mortgages and on private placements tailored to suit the convenience of both sides is well above anything the Treasury and even corporations with marketable obligations now offer. As an added touch of irony, in some of these assets the Treasury is competing with itself — for instance, in guaranteed and insured mortgages and in shipping loans. Furthermore, the big institutional lenders have built up quite elaborate facilities for acquiring and servicing these competing assets which they must keep functioning. Many of them also habitually make advance commitments to borrowers. As a result, they have tended to build up a kind of inner circle of customers, who are taken care of first when funds become scarcer. Treasury securities, precisely because they can be bought readily without elaborate machinery, have become residual.

Problems of Marketing. There are still further factors that make life difficult for the Treasury, which result from the nature of its financing operations. Treasury issues usually are large. Hence they are capable of having a powerful effect upon the market. The Treasury may offer what looks like an attractively priced issue — and what happens? Unless the market situation is favorable, the market may well go down on the announcement. In that case the Treasury has not only lost its advantage, but it may have so upset the market as to actually make it unreceptive. If this happens a couple of times in a gradually tightening market, investors who bought will be sorry and may well conclude that they had better sit out the next round in anticipation of still more favorable terms later on.

Another handicap to the Treasury may lie in the relative infrequency of its long-term offerings. This spacing of long issues may be necessary to allow funds to build up in the market. It may also, however, lead to the establishment of an unrealistic price level. The spread between Treasuries and corporates may become unrealistically wide when corporates are exposed to a constant stream of new offerings while Treasuries are not. If the Treasury then makes a new offering on the basis of the price relationships, established in this form, demand may turn out to be very limited.

This points to still another difficulty. A successful issue must be priced sufficiently below the market to attract buying in volume. Corporations usually follow this practice. Yet the Treasury does not like to give away too much to the market, and would be subject to criticism if it did. Since the Treasury employs no underwriting, other than what it gets through the voluntary efforts of banks and dealers, this handicap may be felt strongly at times.

These and other considerations indicate why the Treasury may encounter difficulties when it tries to sell longer-term securities. They provide a partial answer to the question frequently addressed to the Treasury — "Why don't you pay the price? Why don't you bid for the money and squeeze out other borrowers?" The fact is that since the Accord of 1951, the Treasury has been "paying the price." But the Treasury does not want to "squeeze" other borrowers unduly. It does not want to see municipalities, home owners, and small businessmen pushed out of the market. Aggressive bidding by the Treasury may work hardships. It would also provoke criticism and might generate pressure for aid to be given to the injured interests through some form of Treasury subsidy. That in turn would increase the Treasury's own financing needs. Finally, it is worth remembering that to compete aggressively by "paying the price" may prove unwise from a long-run point of view if it causes the Treasury to borrow at the peak of the market.

These are the difficulties that the Treasury faces when it tries to sell longer-term securities during a boom. They do not apply in equal measure to short-term financing. Price movements are much narrower in the short-term market and the supply of funds forthcoming in response to a good short-term yield is more elastic. As an ultimate resort, moreover, there are always the banks, who are willing to buy short-term but not long-term securities.

In consequence of the difficulties of selling long terms, which at times borders on practical impossibility, and the relative ease of selling short terms, the Treasury, in periods of high activity such as 1952–53 and 1956–57, has found itself selling predominantly short-term securities.

FINANCING IN RECESSION

In a recession period, the picture changes very drastically. As private demand for short- and long-term credit dries up, investors become eager buyers of government obligations, including long terms. The prospect for a sharp rise in the price of long terms induces additional demand on a speculative basis. The Treasury must then decide whether to seize such opportunities to put out large amounts of long-term securities.

The argument against debt lengthening in recessions is familiar. By selling long-term debt and so lengthening the average maturity of the debt, the Treasury runs the risk of keeping long-term interest rates from falling. A fall in these rates, with a consequent encouragement of investment, is one of the mechanisms on which we rely for economic recovery. In the 1954 recession, the view prevailed that the Treasury should not do anything that might keep long-term rates from falling and no long-term financing was undertaken prior to February, 1955, when the recovery was well along. In the recession of 1958, the Treasury sold $4.2 billion long-term bonds, and $12.7 billion of shorter maturity but still in excess of five years. The rapid turnabout of the recession suggests that this did not have a material effect upon the turning point.

"Anticyclical Debt Management."   What are the merits of the argument? Should the Treasury abstain from long-term financing in recessions? Or should it on the contrary seize these opportunities? If the Treasury had perfect control under all conditions with regard to the securities it wants to issue, the doctrine of anticyclical debt management would have considerable merit. This doctrine says that public debt management should be used as an instrument of economic stabilization, much as monetary policy and fiscal policy are used. To implement a stabilization policy, the debt managers would sell long-term securities in a boom to reduce the liquidity of the economy, while the monetary authorities tightened credit and while fiscal policy aimed at a budget surplus. All these policies would be pulling in one direction. In a recession, contrariwise, monetary policy would ease credit, fiscal policy would run a deficit, and debt management would aid liquidity by short-term financing. By distributing the load over three instruments of policy, the pressure against any one of them would be reduced and success attained more speedily.

This pretty picture of three co-ordinated policy instruments is misleading. In a boom, the managers of the public debt may encounter serious difficulties, under present conditions and with present techniques, in the long-term refunding that they are supposed to do. Contrary to the counter-cyclical doctrine, the Treasury is compelled in a boom to engage in substantial short-term refunding of its maturing obligations. In a recession, the Treasury has no difficulty in financing either long or short. According to the doctrine it should finance short to increase liquidity of the economy. But if it does so, the result is that in fact it never does any long-term financing. There then is never a good time for the Treasury to do long-term financing — in a boom it cannot, in a recession it must not.

The anticyclical doctrine of debt management evidently finds its limits in these realities of the Treasury's position. If long-term financing remains inadequate in a boom, it must be pushed at some other time. Perhaps it could be undertaken during some intermediate period, i.e., during a recovery, as was done in 1955. In any case, unless the Treasury finances long at some time, a large part of the debt eventually will become very short. Then a new danger appears — the danger of inflation through excess liquidity and monetization of the debt by the banks. When this danger appears, the need to forestall it becomes overriding. No permanent advantage would be gained by trying to accelerate the recovery from recession, if the result is subsequent inflation followed very likely by renewed collapse.

It is on grounds like these that a policy of lengthening the debt in recession, such as was pursued during the 1958 dip, must be justified.

One need not go so far as some, however, who argue that the Treasury should conduct its debt operations with total disregard of the needs of anticyclical policy. Those who believe this argue that by financing long in recessions and short in booms the Treasury will simply be doing what comes naturally. Moreover, they say, the Treasury will also finance in the cheapest possible way, because permanent financing would then be undertaken when interest rates are lowest. Counter-cyclical debt management, to the extent that it is possible, would be expensive. If the policy of financing cheaply and easily should have adverse effects upon the business cycle, aggravating both boom and recession, the proponents of this theory suggest that corrective action should be left to the Federal Reserve.

This it seems to me, puts too heavy a burden upon monetary policy. It also sets a dangerous precedent in suggesting that the Treasury be virtually absolved from the broad considerations of economic stability. The proper solution, it would seem, lies in the middle: The Treasury must make sure, first of all, that the debt does not get into unmanageable short-term form. But to the extent compatible with this goal, the Treasury, like every other agency of the Government, must be conscious of the impact of its policies upon the business cycle.

COURSES OF ACTION

What can the Treasury do to strengthen its position with investors and improve its access to the money and capital market? There are, of course, no miraculous cures. There is a strong prospect, however, that if we adapt our techniques to changing circumstances and if we take advantage of opportunities as they occur, we can keep the debt from getting shorter and eventually can lengthen it.

The Budget. One sector in which appropriate action would greatly help the Treasury's debt management problem is fiscal policy. The problems of debt management during the present recovery have been intensified by the large deficit. Its financing has meanwhile been completed. But the fact is that the deficit continued on a very large scale after we had already returned to a high level of economic activity, i.e., part of it came too late from a fiscal policy point of view. The deficit has meant that the Treasury not only had to refinance maturities of old debt, as it must always do, but had to raise large amounts of new money besides. Doing this in a recovery period, when interest rates have been rising, has compounded the problems of debt management.

As the budget comes into balance, the task of debt management will be greatly eased. The task will then be limited to refinancing, rather than new financing, except for seasonal needs. Even so, however, a balanced budget, though highly desirable, will not remove all the difficulties of long-term financing.

The reason for this is easy to see. As the securities in the public debt approach their maturities, they tend to move out of the hands of their original holders. The original holders are interested in long-term securities and hence tend to sell securities approaching maturity to investors who are interested in short-term instruments. When the securities finally mature and are refinanced, it is no use offering these short-term holders new long-term securities. They would not be interested. To sell new long-term securities it is necessary to go to long-term investors and to interest them from scratch in Treasury issues, in competition with all the other investment outlets available to them. This is true with a balanced budget as well as with a deficit.

The balanced budget proposed by the President would ease debt management greatly in other respects, however. Principally it would do so by reducing the threat of inflation which now hangs over the market. This would be a consummation devoutly to be wished for many other reasons, of course, besides debt management.

"Routinizing" the Short-Term Debt. A second sphere of action is the area of the short-term debt. Just as an example of what the Treasury has already done, I would like to mention some steps that have recently been taken. It had become clear that much was to be gained if the refinancing of short-term debt could be handled more smoothly, with less disturbance to the market and to the Federal Reserve. To move in this direction, the Treasury took three steps. First, it concentrated its short-term maturities as much as possible in four months of the year, February, May, August, and November. This will serve to reduce the frequency of the Treasury's trips to the market. Second, an effort was made to even up as far as possible the amounts of short-term debt coming due on each of these four dates. This will help to assure a smoother operation in rolling over the short-term maturities. Third, the Treasury developed a 26-weeks bill, a 9½-months bill, and one-year bills, in addition to the familiar 13-weeks bill. All these are sold at auction. The auctioning process for short-term securities, as mentioned earlier, is taken in stride more readily by the market than other forms of financing. These measures contribute to putting the short-term debt on a more routine basis, rolling over from maturity to maturity, not always staying in the hands of the same investors, but nevertheless functioning as a fairly stable block that has its firm place in the structure of liquid assets. These improvements in the short-term area, which still have some way to go, will be helpful also in setting the stage for longer term financing.

DEBT REPAYMENT

In this discussion of debt management, one topic so far has been missing: the repayment of public debt. In the budgetary circumstances in which we find ourselves, debt repayment is, of course, not an immediate issue. But even over the longer run, many people accord it a low priority. For some, this low priority for debt repayment seems to follow from their preference for high government expenditures; for others, it follows from a preference for a tax cut as soon as a budgetary surplus becomes available.

Both sides overlook the fact that debt repayment is not simply a gesture in the direction of fiscal soundness. It can become in effect one of the most powerful instruments for promoting economic growth that the government can employ.

The mechanism through which debt repayment can stimulate growth is very simple. It does so by making possible an increase in productive investment. The taxes which provide the means for debt repayment serve to reduce mainly consumption, although in lesser degree they may also weigh against saving. The reduction in consumption creates room in the economy, in terms of men, machines and materials, for additional investment. When debt is repaid, investors find themselves with idle funds for which they need an outlet and which enable them to finance this additional productive investment. In other words, the budgetary surplus from which debt is repaid acts as a kind of national saving, which is employed, of course, through private channels.

It is sometimes thought that debt repayment must be deflationary, because a deficit is inflationary. This view rests on the assumption, however, that the process of debt repayment must necessarily be the reverse of debt creation. That is not the case. An inflationary deficit, as commonly envisaged, is typically one financed by the banks, which involves money creation. Debt repayment, to be sure, quite likely will mean repayment of bank-held debt — though the maturing securities that are paid off might also be held by non-bank investors. But when bank-held debt is repaid, there is no reason to assume that the Federal Reserve will remove, by open market operations, the resulting excess reserves. The banks, therefore, will be under pressure to find new outlets for these funds, and will expand their loans.

A prerequisite for the proper functioning of this mechanism is that the economy should operate at a high level and that a budget surplus, though helping to restrain inflationary excesses, does not adversely affect production and employment. In a healthy economy, this may be expected to be the case most of the time. The maintenance of high-level activity can be aided, if necessary, by an appropriate Federal Reserve policy of easier credit.

The simple mechanism set forth does not, of course, work so simply in practice. The debt that the government pays off typically is held, not by long-term investors, but by banks, because it has become short-term debt.

The immediate consequence of debt repayment therefore tends to be an expansion of bank loans, not of long-term lending. But in the fluid market the effect of this spreads to all sectors and benefits all who seek to borrow.

In closing, I would like to point once more to the interest that every citizen has in the successful management of the public debt. This success is an essential condition for defeating the threat of inflation. If the problems of debt management should ever become so difficult — which I do not anticipate — that heavy short-term financing and bank borrowing must be resorted to for long periods, the danger of inflation would mount rapidly. Large scale creation of near money and large scale monetization of debt can, in the long run, mean little else.

High officials of the Treasury have pointed out that investors, therefore, are not without self interest in the success of the management of the public debt. In saying this, they have been aware, of course, that in a free market investors will always look for the highest yield compatible with standards of safety. Institutional investors, in particular, have an obligation to their depositors and policyholders to get the best return they can. No institutional investor can, in order to support the Treasury, prejudice the interests of those who have entrusted their funds. But the question may perhaps be asked how the long-run interest of these depositors and policyholders are best served. Might it not be that in the end they would benefit by sacrificing a little income in return for greater stability of purchasing power of their principal? It is perfectly true that in a free market a single investor cannot influence the course of events by making a sacrifice on his part. Yet, attitudes and standards of action could develop that, if adopted by all investors, would impose a sacrifice upon none. A habit and an attitude toward Treasury securities of this kind would ultimately work out in the interest of all.

59

"A MODEST PROPOSAL"*

Linhart Stearns†

Recently a small group of policy makers from Washington met with several respected Wall Streeters in order to discuss the problem of how to finance the Government in face of the general unpopularity of bonds without either impeding the progress of the recovery or feeding the generally expected inflation.

The professional economists and experts on banking and government finance did not come up with new ideas which met with any general enthusiasm. The meeting seemed destined to run into a dead end when a Mr. X made a startling proposal.

Mr. X attacked the problem from an entirely fresh point-of-view. He said that, as he was a partner in a large stock exchange firm, he was closer to the thinking of the public than were the rest of the group. It was only because of this more common touch that he dared to speak up among such an erudite and responsible meeting of fiscal experts. But as securities and their marketing were his business and as government bonds were securities that had to be sold just like other issues, he felt that he might be able to contribute a plan.

Mr. X pointed out that the public would not buy bonds because of the conviction that the inflation was inexorable and that the holder of bonds was bound to lose out in purchasing power. Besides, almost everybody already had suffered losses in bonds and it is well known that people are loath to buy securities in which they once lost money. Therefore, anything called a bond had become an almost unsalable item unless it contained features so favorable as to be ruinous to the issuer.

On the other hand, the public's eagerness to buy anything which was called a common

stock seemed limitless and little discretion was brought to bear in making the decisions of what to buy and how much to pay.

In the circumstances Mr. X thought that if the Government did what any intelligent underwriting house would do, namely, tailor its issues to the desires of the market, there should be good promise of a successful flotation. Obviously the Government should attune itself to the times — bonds were passé, stocks were now the thing and, therefore, the Government should bring out a common stock issue.

Calling a Government issue a stock rather than a bond would in itself assure its acceptance by the public. But Mr. X thought that the success of the issue could be further assured if it capitalized on the investing public's enthusiasms and if it were given a certain aura in the market. As regards the latter, of course, there were limits to the advertising and promotion either printed or spoken. It was important not to run afoul of the S.E.C. or the various state security commissions. However, the market itself was eager to emphasize the favorable aspects of any common stock issue and, in fact, was prone to imagine favorable factors without any unethical encouragement. Thus Mr. X pointed out, a common stock prospectus could be circumspect and straightforward in its statements and still assure the issue a good reception. In fact in several instances common stock issues had gone over with a bang merely because his firm had headed the selling group — nobody seemed to care what was in the prospectus.

Mr. X felt that the Government was in the position to issue the perfect common stock which couldn't fail to gain the ultimate in popularity. Investors looked for certain things in common stocks. These were 1) growth, 2) protection against inflation, 3) market popularity, 4) leverage. Contrary to old-fashioned opinion, investors were hardly interested in

* With apologies to Jonathan Swift. From the *Bernstein-Macaulay Newsletter*, October 1, 1958. Reprinted by the courtesy of Bernstein-Macaulay, Inc., investment counselors, and the author.

† Chairman of the Board, Bernstein-Macaulay, Inc.

cash dividends or rate of income return or book values. They even gave little heed to price because of the general conviction that any price paid for a stock today would be proved low in the future — growth, inflation and market popularity would make any cavilling about value superfluous.

Now the Government stock issue could be designed to satisfy all four investor objectives. To this end Mr. X proposed that 3% of all government *expenditures* accrue as earnings for the Government's common stock. It was too early to discuss the technical details but in general each department would have to pay 3 cents into the common stock fund for every $1 it spent. (This would not be too hard for the bureaucrats to swallow because sales taxes were already ubiquitous. Besides it might be a good thing if this 3% tax on government spending served to remind officials of the nuisances and burdens the rest of us bear.)

The prospectus of the issue could carry a table showing the course of government expenditures, say, from 1929 to date as well as the corresponding figures for 3% thereof. It would be obvious that the earnings for the common stock would have grown more than twenty-fold in the three decades. Few "Blue Chips" now outstanding could equal this growth record. The public judges growth by the record of the past and extends that record into the distant future. There is no doubt that, in view of the public's confidence in the future, it would envisage a truly startling earning prospect for the Government's common stock. It would probably be considered the premier growth stock in the country.

The stock would also be considered a perfect inflation hedge. Its earnings would be geared exactly to the one factor the public believes determines the extent of inflation — government spending. Furthermore the stock would represent ownership in a huge amount of material things both above and below ground to say nothing of things in the air and perhaps, in the near future, on other planets. The real-estate in Washington alone is a tremendous inflation hedge. Then, there are millions of acres of public lands, National Parks, military installations, etc. The public would not be backward in conjecturing that oil, uranium or any number of other riches would be found and prove to make the stock even a better inflation hedge. Mr. X reminded his audience that it was not necessary for the investing public to believe that any of these assets would ever be sold at a profit or distributed. Stocks were considered inflation hedges if the public knew or guessed that assets existed even if they were never to be realized on.

Market popularity for the issue was assured by its size and the huge operations of the venture. No other issue could possibly be kept in the public eye as much as the Government's common stock. Every day hundreds of items about some aspect of the issuer's operations would be prominently displayed in the press and reported over the air. News about an issuer keeps investors interested in the issuer's stock and the government stock would enjoy the highest amount of advertising. Mr. X said that in this connection there was only one drawback — the management of the venture might not be highly regarded and there would be some doubts about the enterprise's efficiency. Such reservations, however, would not react too badly on the stock because poor management and inefficiency would increase government expenditures and thus would increase the stock's earning power!

With respect to leverage, the stock would also appeal to the public. It might follow over $280 *billion** of debt and many billions of contingent liabilities. Mr. X felt that probably the stock would at most represent an equity of 40%. This would depend on the issue price which he discussed later.

As the stock was to be presented as a growth security it was important to keep the cash dividend extremely low but to raise it consistently by minute amounts. A generous dividend would give the stock the wrong aura for it then would be considered a good income stock suitable for widows and orphans and not a dynamic security. Everybody knows that sound, good income-bearing stocks are not too popular. Present day investors don't want income but only a capital gain. It would be a

* Ed. note: The size of the national debt at the time of writing.

great mistake to make the dividend too attractive.

Furthermore as most of the earnings would not be paid out in cash dividends the Government would keep them to reinvest in its operations. This would generally be deemed another assurance of growth. Of course, it did not matter whether the retained earnings were profitably invested; all the public cared about was that the earnings were retained and invested in more properties. This is shown by the dramatic rise in common stock prices as compared to the slow growth of profits of business enterprises as a whole. In many cases the reinvestment of retained earnings has produced little in the way of increased profits.

The stock would also have considerable glamor because the possibility that it could be split would be ever present. Furthermore there were hidden and unreported earnings (of course the public gave little heed at present to possible unconsolidated losses). Such subsidiaries as T.V.A., F.H.A., C.C.C., etc., could all be conceived as immensely profitable during the public's more optimistic periods. From time to time it would be rumored that there would be a spin-off of one unit or another — T.V.A., for instance. This would improve the quotation for the stock although, as in the case of a stock split, the stockholder would have nothing he didn't have before.

Mr. X made an estimate of the probable price at which the stock could be issued. So ideal an issue should command a price earnings ratio at least as high as those that have been applied to such stocks as IBM, M M & M, Polaroid, etc. These have at times sold at about 45 times earnings and Mr. X said that his firm would surely be willing to issue the Government's stock on this basis. Perhaps they might even be willing to exceed this figure. On the basis of government expenditures of $80 billion, the earnings applicable to the stock would be $2.4 billion. Multiplying this figure by 45 would bring the total value of the issue to $108 billion. He suggested a price of $400 a share (around the price of IBM) which means that 270 million shares would be issued — about as many shares as General Motors has outstanding.

The proposed issue of government common stock would absorb the funds so insistantly seeking refuge from inflation and so would probably keep the stock market in check. Thus the present inflationary enthusiasm in the stock market would no longer threaten an orderly recovery. Furthermore, the funds paid to the Government for the stock would be more than sufficient to pay off the entire short-term debt while no new money or credit would be created. Thus the danger of monetary inflation would be avoided. The oft-expressed desire to extend the maturity of the government debt would also be accomplished — in effect the Government would then have only long term maturities and a stock issue which need never be retired.

Finally, as only a small part of the "tax" on expenditures assigned to the stock would be paid out in dividends, the Treasury would effect a savings in its carrying charges — the dividends would be less than the interest on an equivalent amount of Treasury securities now outstanding.

Mr. X pointed out that, if it were desirable to issue more stock, increasing the percentage of expenditures reserved for the stock could offset any dilution. He mentioned, also, that warrants to buy the stock — say at 20% above issue price — could be sold to satisfy the most speculatively inclined investors and to bring additional sums into the Treasury. At a later date convertible bond issues would also be possible.

Mr. X's idea was considered so novel that none of those at the meeting were willing to support him except behind closed doors. However, it was deemed advisable to get the public reaction to the plan and that, therefore, its outlines should be "leaked off the record" as a trial balloon. That is why this was written.

PART 6

THE WORLD ECONOMY

CHAPTER SIXTEEN

INTERNATIONAL FINANCE

60

THE INTERNATIONAL MONETARY POSITION
OF THE UNITED STATES*

Robert Triffin†

International trade is, in principal, no different from trade between any two units. Certainly it cannot be distinguished by distance — for trade between Detroit and Windsor, Ontario, is hardly a stone's throw, while trade between Detroit and Los Angeles is a matter of thousands of miles. The characteristic and distinguishing features of international trade revolve about two things: the existence of independent sovereign nations, and the need to use more than one kind of money in effecting the exchange, so that some ratio of exchange between the two currencies must be established.

Much attention was devoted in the postwar period to problems of chronic deficit countries, that is, countries that persistently buy more from abroad than they sell. For years we talked of the "dollar shortage" of the rest of the world; lately the shoe has been somewhat on the other foot, as the United States itself has encountered strong competition from abroad and has met with a substantial gold drain. In the following selection Professor Triffin examines the international monetary position of the United States and relates it to the broader problem of international liquidity. Although this article was written in 1959, the problem is much the same today as it was then. He concludes with a proposal for international monetary reform that has attracted widespread interest. Professor Triffin's views are developed in more detail in his Gold and the Dollar Crisis *(Yale University Press, 1960).*

I.

I am very much afraid that the evolution of the last 10 years has now brought us to a point where we can no longer afford to ignore

* From *Employment, Growth and Price Levels*, Part 9A of *Hearings* before the Joint Economic Committee, United States Congress, October, 1959. Reprinted in Robert Triffin, *Gold and the Dollar Crisis* (New Haven: Yale University Press), 1960. Reprinted here by the courtesy of the author and Yale University Press.
† Yale University.

the impact of our domestic policies upon our balance of payments and reserve position. I must admit that this way of looking at things is still very unfamiliar to most of my colleagues in the academic world, although it has recently begun to force itself upon the attention of economists in business and Government circles.

For many years after the war, our only problem in this field was to reduce to more manageable proportions our enormous surpluses with the rest of the world, and to find adequate means to finance them. The so-called "dollar shortage" theory dominated economic thinking and inspired economic policy, both here and abroad. The authors of these theories, however, and policymakers themselves were extraordinarily slow in realizing the full extent of their own success in dealing with the problem. Only our large gold losses of last year finally woke us all to the fact that our balance of payments had shown persistent deficits on overall account ever since 1949, and that our net international reserve position had been declining continuously at a rate of about $1¼ billion over the 8 years, 1950–57. This latter figure rose abruptly to $3.3 billion in 1958, and is likely to exceed $4 billion this year. While our gold losses have been dammed up somewhat this year by sharp increases in interest rates, they have nevertheless continued, and been accompanied by a further upward spiraling of our short-term indebtedness abroad. Finally, and for the first time in many years, this country — the richest in the world, by far — is now experiencing large and growing deficits even in its current account, i.e., its purchases of goods and services abroad far exceed its sales to foreign countries, even though a substantial portion of these sales are financed and supported by extraordinary aid programs, particularly in relation to the disposal of our agricultural surpluses. More and more is being heard about our producers "having priced themselves out of the world markets."

The situation clearly calls for an "agonizing reappraisal" of our foreign economic policies, but we are in great danger of misinterpreting the evidence and of taking refuge in the kind of policies which, although extremely plausible on the surface, are not likely to be as effective as one might think in redressing our own position and are most likely, on the other hand, to trigger off a disastrous reversal in the postwar trend toward freer and expanding world trade.

II.

Two major questions emerge from any objective examination of our current balance of payments and reserve position. Does the evolution of our balance of payments on current account suggest that we may be in danger of pricing ourselves out of the world markets? Does the evolution of our international reserve position suggest that we might have difficulties in maintaining the free convertibility of the dollar at its present value in terms of gold and foreign exchange?

I do not pretend to be able to give you a definite answer to the first of these two questions, but I might point out some reasons for serious concern in this respect.

As the richest country in the world, with far-flung economic, political and military responsibilities, we should be able to finance a large and steady capital outflow toward the underdeveloped countries, to help sustain their economy and their defense establishment. With far less resources than we have, the British estimate that they should aim for such purposes, at a current account surplus averaging more than $1 billion a year. On a comparable basis, an average surplus of, let us say, $4 billion a year in our own balance of payments would not seem excessive. This is indeed just about the level around which our capital exports — public and private — have fluctuated, rather narrowly, over the last 9 or 10 years. Our current account surplus, however, has long been insufficient to cover such exports. It averaged slightly more than $2 billion over the years 1952–57, fell to $1.5 billion in 1958, and turned into an annual deficit rate of more than $1 billion in the first half of this year.

Even more disturbing as an indication of our relative competitiveness in world trade is the evolution of our current account with Western Europe. This is the area which is most directly in competition with us in the field of manufactures, while our balance with the rest of the world is more responsive to cyclical conditions and to the level of foreign aid and capital made available to these countries. Discounting some highly abnormal movements connected with the peak of the European boom and the Suez crisis, in 1956–57, our current account with Western Europe has shown a pronounced and markedly unfavorable trend ever since 1951. Our surpluses of the immediate postwar years had thinned out rapidly even before then, falling from $5 billion a year in

1947 to $1.8 billion in 1951. They averaged less than $100 million a year in 1952–57, and have now shifted to an annual deficit rate of $800 million in 1958 and more than $2 billion in the first half of this year.

The combination of a relatively stable level of capital exports — about $4 billion a year — with much smaller and fast declining surpluses on current account, turning into an actual deficit in 1959, has left us with a persistent and growing deficit on overall account, running today at the rate of about $5 billion a year. A small portion of this, however, is covered by long-term foreign capital exports to the United States and by other untraceable transactions appearing as "errors and omissions" in our balance of payments estimates. The remainder has given rise to annual gold losses and increases in our short-term indebtedness abroad totaling, on the average, more than $1 billion a year in 1952–57, $3.4 billion in 1958 and, at an annual rate, $3.7 billion in the first half of this year.

A continuation of this trend would clearly be untenable in the long run. It is not to be anticipated in any case. The incipient, but strong, recovery of economic activity in Europe and the end of the steel strike should produce some improvement over the forthcoming months. Yet, this is most unlikely to redress the situation fully and to bring about a reasonable and tenable equilibrium in our over-all balance of payments account, at satisfactory levels of trade and of net capital exports by the United States to the rest of the world.

Among the policy measures which suggest themselves, two are particularly plausible and yet likely to prove both ineffective and unwise. The first, and most obvious one, would be a sharp curtailment of our foreign-aid programs. The trouble with this is that such curtailment would be offset, in very large part, by corresponding cuts in our exports. Of a total capital flow of $5.4 billion in 1958, less than $800 million went to Western Europe, and more than $4.6 billion to the rest of the world, i.e., mostly to the underdeveloped countries. A comparison of our capital exports to this area with our current account surplus with it shows a high degree of correlation, as the ability of

these countries to run deficits with us on current account depends primarily on the financing made available to them by our own capital exports and foreign aid. A lesser flow of capital to them is thus likely to be matched, in very large part, by declining purchases of U.S. exports by them, and to bring relatively little improvement in our overall balance of payments.

We must also note that most of our aid programs and official capital exports are closely linked to political objectives which we would hardly abandon on mere balance of payments grounds.

This may yet leave some room for so-called tied loans, ensuring that the recipients of aid use it to buy in this market rather than to add to their reserves or to spend the dollars in other areas. This would be a palliative at best, the practical results of which are likely to prove disappointing as a great deal of our aid — such as the financing of our exports by agricultural surpluses — is already tied in this manner, or is, in any case, used in fact for purchases in the United States.

A second, and even more disastrous, line of action would be to reverse the liberal trading policies pursued by us for more than 20 years, and which have helped so spectacularly in the recovery and liberalization of world trade in general. This could hardly fail to trigger off similar reactions abroad, to arrest and reverse the current trend toward liberalization by foreign countries and to stifle further our own export trade.

The remedies, I feel, should be sought in a different direction. First of all, the current relaxation of world tensions may possibly enable us to reduce the terrifying and disproportionate defense burdens — internal and external — which probably accounts, more than any other single factor, for the revolutionary shift in the international dollar balance from prewar to postwar days. This is, however, only a hope yet, and one about which I feel totally incompetent to hazard any guess or suggestion.

We should, secondly, continue to press vigorously for the elimination of remaining discrimination on dollar goods and the further reduction of other obstacles to trade and payments by foreign countries, particularly in Europe. A more determined support for GATT and its efforts to outlaw unjustified discrimination and liberalize other damaging restrictions on world trade should also serve as a basis for greater efforts on the part of our own producers to prospect foreign markets and expand the level of our exports.

We should, in the third place, do everything we can to encourage European countries to assume a larger share of the burden of development financing, and to allow the recipients to spend the proceeds of such financing in the United States as well as in Europe itself. (This is another reason, by the way, for us to be chary of "tying" our own lending operations any more than they already are.) Success along these lines should probably involve some redirection of our own programs away from bilateral assistance, and toward multilateral assistance, such as is implicit in the present IDA project.

Fuller European participation in the financing of developmental needs seems to me particularly crucial at the present juncture, since I am not confident that the various measures mentioned above will be sufficient to bring about a sufficiently rapid and drastic improvement in our overall balance of payments position. Time will be needed to restore, in a politically desirable and feasible manner, full competitiveness in our external trading position. Creeping inflation here must be arrested, while our rates of growth and productivity are stepped up at the same time by appropriate investments in research and technology. We should also be aided by the inevitable adjustment of foreign wage and consumption levels to the steep increases in production and the large balance of payments surpluses achieved by foreign countries over recent years. In the meantime, we shall probably be forced to keep our interest rates high enough to retain and attract foreign funds to this market, and to slow down somewhat our own capital exports. While unavoidable in the short run, this policy would be difficult to reconcile with our longer run policy objectives, internally as well as externally. The last part of my statement will come back to this point and make concrete suggestions to help us out of this dilemma.

III.

The second major question which I raised above relates to the evolution of our international reserve position and the threat which it may raise for the future stability of the dollar.

I have already mentioned the fact that the largest portion of our persistent balance of payments deficits on overall account has been financed, year after year, for nearly a decade, by a growing deterioration in our net reserve position. At the end of 1949, our gold stock exceeded the liquid dollar claims of foreign countries by more than $18 billion. This exceedingly comfortable cushion was already down last June to less than $3 billion. At the rate of loss experienced in 1958 and early 1959, these $3 billions would be wiped out within a year, and our short-term indebtedness abroad would begin to outstrip our total gold stock.

The financial press, here and abroad, has sometimes exaggerated the significance of these figures. First of all, we are not in any danger of becoming insolvent as a Nation. Our gold losses and the increase in our short-term liabilities abroad are matched — and far more than matched — by the enormous growth of our foreign investments since the war. Most of these investments, however, are long-term investments on private account and could not be mobilized quickly to meet any demand from foreigners for conversion of their liquid dollar holdings into gold.

Secondly, however, there is nothing unusual or necessarily alarming, for a country like ours, in this rough equivalence between our gold assets and the dollar balances held abroad. Sterling was made convertible last December, and has shown considerable strength ever since — as reflected in its persistent premium over the dollar on the exchange market — in the face of a level of foreign sterling balances three to four times larger than the total gold and convertible currency reserves of the United Kingdom.

The strength, and the weaknesses, of our international position cannot be gaged from any simple formula or calculation of this sort. Account should also be taken of our short-term, and even long-term, assets abroad, but also of other assets held here by foreigners and which might, under certain circumstances, be liquidated by them for reinvestment elsewhere or for repatriation to the owners' countries. Continued mismanagement of our own affairs might even prompt a flight from the dollar by our own citizens and find us unwilling or unprepared to take effective measures against it. The future of the dollar is far less dependent on transitory fluctuations in our balance of payments than on the maintenance of people's confidence in our determination to preserve its basic and still formidable strength, in our own interest as well as in the interest of the world at large. Our capital is very high in this respect, and there is no reason to think that it is in serious danger of being jeopardized by excessive complacency, or dissipated by sheer irresponsibility, on the part of the monetary and political authorities of this country.

IV.

Even the most successful readjustment of our overall balance of payments, however, will leave in its wake two major problems. The first is the impact which such a readjustment will entail for the maintenance of an adequate degree of international liquidity in an expanding world economy. The second is the need to protect our own economy and the freedom of our internal economic policies against the dangers inevitably associated with the existence of such a huge backlog of foreign short-term funds in our financial and exchange markets. The concrete, but somewhat revolutionary suggestions presented below aim at solving rationally both of these problems together. First, however, it is necessary to state them more precisely and to replace them in their historical perspective.

The present international monetary system of the world can be sketchily described as follows. A number of countries — particularly the old industrial countries of Western Europe — are both anxious and able to maintain relatively high levels of monetary reserves and to increase them more or less pari passu with increases in production, money supply and international trade turnover. Other countries — particularly in the underdeveloped areas of the world — are

content with much lower levels of reserves and a more continuous recourse to foreign aid and short-term capital, currency devaluation or trade and exchange restrictions as alternative techniques of balance of payments adjustment. Current increases in the world monetary gold stock meet only a fraction (about one-third) of the combined demand for monetary reserves defined above. Most — although not all — countries, however, have shown themselves willing to accumulate a substantial portion of their monetary reserves in the form of foreign exchange rather than gold. In choosing a particular foreign currency for this purpose, they naturally tend to select the currency that appears safest, i.e., that of a major creditor country: primarily the United Kingdom in former days, and primarily the United States today. This accumulation of a key currency as international reserves by the rest of the world necessarily entails a large amount of "unrequited" capital imports by the key currency country. Coal is brought to Newcastle, from which it should be exported instead. The international liquidity shortage, moreover, is not thereby relieved, unless the key currency country allows its resulting short-term indebtedness to grow continually and persistently at a faster pace than its own gold assets. (It may otherwise disguise the basic gold shortage into a scarcity of the key currency itself.)

This is an exact description of what has happened in fact since the war, and a major explanation of the growing threat to our own liquidity position. We have been lending long — and even given funds away — while borrowing short and losing gold. Foreign countries' gold reserves and dollar holdings have risen by $20 billion (from $15 billion to $35 billion) between the end of 1949 and the middle of this year, but only one-fourth ($5 billion) of this increase has come from new gold production — including Russian gold sales in Western markets. The remaining three-fourths ($15 billion) were derived from our own gold losses and increasing short-term liabilities to foreigners.

The restoration of overall balance in the U.S. international transactions would put an end to this process and deprive the rest of the world of the major source, by far, from which the international liquidity requirements of an expanding world economy are being met currently in the face of a totally inadequate supply of monetary gold. This might trigger off tomorrow — as it did under very similar circumstances in the early 1930's — a new cycle of international deflation, currency devaluations, and trade exchange restrictions.

The other problem that would be left unsolved by the readjustment of our current balance of payments is that of the huge legacy of short-term foreign indebtedness inherited from the past, and the huge handicap that might be placed thereby on sound policies for economic growth and stability of our own economy. Such funds are extremely volatile and may, at any time, move out of our market in response to interest rate differentials or to foreign conditions over which we have no control.

The experience of the United Kingdom, in the late 1920's and early 1930's, is particularly eloquent in this respect. The pound had been stabilized in 1925 at an overvalued level with the help of large amounts of speculative foreign funds and refugee capital, particularly from the continent, during the period of currency depreciation that followed World War I. The dangers of this situation were well perceived and led to various exchanges of views between Montague Norman of the Bank of England and Benjamin Strong of the Federal Reserve Bank of New York. Both men agreed, in general terms, that interest rates should be kept higher in London than in New York, in order to prevent an outflow of short-term funds from the first to the latter. This soon entered into conflict with domestic policy criteria in both countries. A rise of interest rates in the United States seemed highly desirable at times to slow down excessive lending here, particularly in connection with the boom in Wall Street. Even greater pressure arose in England to ease credit conditions in order to fight the economic stagnation and mass unemployment which plagued the British economy in the late 1920's.

The enormous repatriation of French refugee capital after the Poincaré stabilization of the French franc heralded the beginning of the

end. The pound still held out for a few years, but had to be bolstered in various ways, including urgent pleas to the Bank of France and other central banks to refrain from converting, at an unpropitious time, the huge amounts of sterling absorbed by them from private traders and speculators. Some reluctant cooperation was given to the British in answer to these pleas, and substantial exchange losses were incurred as a result by several central banks when the pound finally devalued in September 1931.

A disquieting parallel could be drawn between those events and our own situation today. The extent of foreign currency devaluation since the war may have given a competitive edge to those countries after their production potential had recovered from the early postwar low. Some foreign currencies may now be undervalued in relation to the dollar, as they were in relation to the pound in the late 1920's. Refugee capital flew here in large amounts after the Second World War, as it had flown to London after the First World War. Some of it may again return home, as currency conditions become definitely stabilized in Europe. Our huge gold losses of last year were due in part to such a movement. They have been slowed down this year by an extremely sharp rise in interest rates, prompted by our domestic concern with creeping inflation in this country. In this case, external and internal interest rate policy criteria happily coincided, but they may diverge tomorrow. If and when we feel reassured about our internal price and cost trends, we are likely to turn increasingly our attention to our laggard rates of economic growth as compared not only with Russia, but also with most countries in Western Europe. We may wish to ease credit and lower interest rates to spur new investments and technological progress. At this point, however, interest rates abroad might again become more attractive to financial investors, and the gold dammed up this year by our high interest rates might flow out at a rate comparable to that of 1958, or even worse.

I cannot resist quoting here an incisive remark of Santayana, which the dynamic Managing Director of the International Monetary Fund, Per Jacobsson, has used most aptly in some of his recent speeches: "Those who do not remember the past will be condemned to repeat it." John Steinbeck wrote in the same vein: "The study of history, while it does not endow with prophecy, may indicate lines of probability."

V.

My final remarks will attempt to sketch, in very succinct form, the most logical policy answer to the two problems which I have just discussed. The keystone of my proposals lies in the true "internationalization" of the foreign exchange component of the world's monetary reserves. The use of national currencies as international reserves constitutes indeed a totally irrational "built-in destabilizer" in the present world monetary system. It is bound to weaken dangerously in time the key currencies — primarily sterling and the dollar — used as reserves by other countries under this system. These difficulties are then bound, in turn, to endanger the stability of the whole international monetary superstructure erected upon these key currencies.

The logical solution of the problem is obvious enough, and would have been adopted long ago if it were not for the enormous difficulties involved in overcoming the forces of inertia and reaching agreement among several scores of countries on the multiple facets of a rational system of international money and credit creation. This is, of course, the only explanation for the survival of gold itself as the ultimate means of international monetary settlements. Nobody could ever have conceived of a more absurd waste of human resources than to dig gold in distant corners of the earth for the sole purpose of transporting it and reburying it immediately afterward in other deep holes, especially excavated to receive it and heavily guarded to protect it. The history of human institutions, however, has a logic of its own. Gold as a commodity enjoyed undoubted advantages over other commodities that could alternatively be used as money. The substitution of debt or paper money for commodity money within each country's national borders was a slow, gradual, and still recent phenomenon in world affairs. Its extension to the in-

ternational sphere is even more recent and has also developed haphazardly under the pressure of circumstances rather than as a rational act of creation on the part of any national or international authority. This explains the present, and totally irrational, use of national currencies as international reserves. Yet, the proliferation of regional, international, and supranational agencies since the war is slowly laying the groundwork for further, and long overdue, adaptations in the international monetary system, and particularly for the internationalization of the fiduciary portion — foreign exchange — of countries' monetary reserves. This portion should be made up of international deposits rather than of national currencies.

The United States and the United Kingdom should bar the use of sterling and dollars as monetary reserves by other countries. All countries should simultaneously renounce the use of these, or other, national currencies as international reserve holdings. They would be offered instead the opportunity of keeping in the form of deposits with the International Monetary Fund any portion of their reserves which they do not wish to hold in the form of gold. Deposits with the Fund would be constituted initially by transferring to the Fund the national currencies — primarily dollars and sterling now held as reserves by the central banks of member countries, plus any amount of gold which they might also wish to exchange for such deposits.

Reserve deposits at the Fund would be as fully usable as gold itself in all international settlements. They could be drawn upon by their holders to procure any currency needed in such settlements or for stabilization interventions of central banks in the exchange market. The amounts withdrawn would be merely debited from the withdrawer's deposit account and credited to the account of the country whose currency has been brought from the Fund.

Fund deposits would carry exchange rates and convertibility guarantees which would make them a far safer medium for reserve investment than any national currency holdings, always exposed to devaluation, inconvertibility, blocking, or even default by the debtor country.

They would, moreover, earn interest at a rate to be determined, and varied from time to time, in the light of the Fund's earnings on its own loans and investments.

These various features, combining the earning incentive of foreign exchange holdings with the safety incentive of gold holdings, should insure in time a large and continuing demand for Fund deposits by central banks, once they become sufficiently familiar with the system and confident in its management. In order to take account of initial diffidence and inertia, however, and to guarantee the system against the vagaries of sudden and unpredictable shifts between gold holdings and Fund deposits, all members should undertake to hold in the form of Fund deposits a uniform and agreed proportion of their gross monetary reserves. They would be entitled, but not compelled, to convert into gold at the Fund any deposits accruing to their account in excess of this minimum requirement.

A minimum deposit ratio of 20 per cent would probably be ample to initiate the new system, and would substitute for the present, exceedingly complex and rigid, system of IMF quotas. This ratio might have to be increased in time, however, in order to provide adequate lending power to the Fund and to insure beyond any shadow of doubt the full liquidity and convertibility of Fund deposits, necessary to make them as unquestionably acceptable by all countries as gold itself in all international settlements. On the other hand, prudent management of the system would, in all likelihood, make it unnecessary to resort to compulsion for that purpose, as member countries' own interests would lead them to maintain with the Fund, rather than in gold, a much larger proportion of their total reserves than the minimum percentages imposed by the Fund.

The major objection to this proposed reform in the Fund's operations would be the same as that raised against the Keynes plan for an International Clearing Union. Such a system would endow the Fund with a lending capacity which, if improperly used, might impart a strong inflationary bias to the world economy. This is no reason, however, to fall back upon a system whose deflationary bias can only be combatted

through an ever-increasing dependence upon the haphazard constitution of reserves in the form of national currencies, and an increasing vulnerability to unfavorable developments in one or a few key countries. The threat of inflationary abuses can be guarded against far more simply and directly by limiting the Fund's annual lending authority to the amount necessary to preserve an adequate level of international liquidity.

Various alternative criteria could be retained for this purpose. The simplest one might be to limit the Fund's net lending, over any 12 months period, to a total amount which would, together with current increases in the world stock of monetary gold, increase total world reserves by, let us say, 3 to 5 per cent a year. The exact figure could not, of course, be determined scientifically and would, in any case, depend in practice upon the compromise between divergent national viewpoints which would emerge from the negotiation of the new Fund agreement. A reasonably conservative solution would be to retain a 3 per cent figure as definitely noninflationary, and to require qualified votes (two thirds, three fourths, and ultimately four fifths of the total voting power, or even unanimity) to authorize lending in excess of 3, 4, or 5 per cent a year.

Assuming, for instance, that monetary gold stocks continue to increase by $700 million or $800 million a year, the Fund's annual lending quota based on a 3 per cent rate could be roughly estimated today at about $800 million to $900 million. A 4 per cent rate would raise this to about $1.4 billion, and 5 per cent to about $2 billion a year. These estimates would rise gradually, but slowly, with further increases in world reserves. They could decrease as well as increase, on the other hand, with future fluctuations in the current additions to the world monetary gold stock.

The Fund's lending operations, moreover, should be no more automatic than they are at present, and this discretion should enable it to exercise a considerable influence upon members to restrain internal inflationary abuses. The experience acquired in the 12 years of operation of the Fund is extremely valuable in this respect. Fund advances should continue to require full agreement between the Fund and the member with relation not only to the maturity of the loan, but also to the broad economic and financial policies followed by the member to insure long run equilibrium in its international transactions without excessive recourse to trade and exchange controls. The recent standby techniques of lending might, in addition, be supplemented by overdraft agreements, to be renewed at frequent intervals and guaranteeing all members in good standing rapid and automatic Fund assistance in case of need, but for modest amounts and with short-term repayment provisions. These overdraft agreements would be primarily designed to give time for full consideration of a request for normal, medium-term, loans or standby agreements, and would be guaranteed by the country's minimum deposit obligation.

A second broad category of Fund lending would take the form of investments in the financial markets of member countries. These operations would be decided at the initiative of the Fund itself, but always of course in agreement with the monetary authorities of the countries concerned. Such agreement would be necessary in any case to attach to these investments the same guarantees against exchange and inconvertibility risks as those which protect the Fund's own deposit liabilities.

The first investments of this character would be imposed upon the Fund by its absorption of the outstanding national currency reserves transferred to it by members in exchange for Fund deposits. The bulk of these reserves would be in the form of bank deposits, acceptances and Treasury bills previously held by the central banks themselves in New York and London. The Fund would have no immediate need to modify the pattern of these investments, but should be empowered to do so, in a smooth and progressive manner, insofar as useful for the conduct of its own operations. This purpose would be served by giving the Fund an option — which it would not necessarily wish to use every year — of liquidating such investments at a maximum pace of, let us say, 5 per cent annually. The resources derived from such liquidation would normally be reemployed in other markets whose need for international cap-

ital is greater than in the United States and the United Kingdom. A portion of such investments might even be channeled into relatively long-term investments for economic development through purchases of IBRD bonds or other securities of a similar character.

The acceptance of the basic reforms proposed above should eliminate all existing balance of payments grounds for permissible discrimination under the GATT. This should constitute a powerful incentive for U.S. support of these proposals, as the United States has long been the main target of such discrimination by other countries.

The gradual liberalization of remaining trade, exchange, and tariff restrictions could also be given a new impetus by these reforms if they were allied to a continuous and world-wide negotiation of *reciprocal* liberalization commitments, similar to that successfully undertaken regionally by the OEEC on the basis of the EPU agreement. Prospective credit assistance by the Fund to countries in difficulty should help spur the acceptance and implementation of such commitments by members. Yet the OEEC experience also suggests that members will insist on retaining the right to invoke escape clauses whenever such assistance is either insufficient or inappropriate to meet their deficits. As in OEEC, a joint examination of the overall policies followed by the member should be undertaken in such cases and lead to agreed proposals for monetary rehabilitation and stabilization and for the restoration of the liberalization measures reciprocally accepted by all Fund members. Ideally, the Fund should be given the right to disallow, after 1 year, for instance, continued recourse to such escape clauses if it deems them to be no longer justified. Such a decision might entail automatically the right for the country in question to allow fluctuations in its exchange rate as long as its gross reserves remain inferior to, let us say, 30 per cent of annual imports.

Finally, some fundamental reforms in the cumbersome administrative machinery of the Fund have long been overdue. Greater efforts should be made to preserve effective contacts at all levels between the Fund and the national administrations of its members. Periodic meetings of high-level representatives currently entrusted with monetary policy in their own country should determine the broad lines of the Fund's policy and the limits within which decisions can be delegated to permanent representatives or to the Fund's management itself. The OEEC and EPU experience should serve as an invaluable guide in shaping up such reforms in more concrete terms.

These and other questions cannot be fruitfully explored here. Actual possibilities for agreement can only be discovered through the process of international negotiation itself. A number of compromises and adaptations in the broad and bold aims and techniques suggested here could undoubtedly prove necessary to reach such an agreement. A number of these adaptations should probably be directed at decentralizing the heavy responsibilities placed here upon the IMF, by transferring to some existing or prospective regional groups — such as the European Economic Community, the sterling area, or the European Economic Association — the handling of all international settlements and financial assistance involving only the use of their own members' currencies.

VI.

May I close with a few words about the advantages and disadvantages which such a reform would entail for the United States itself.

Its major advantage emerges clearly, I hope, from our previous discussion. The United States would no longer have to bear the burden and court the danger, inseparable from the use of the dollar as a reserve currency by other countries. This would, it is true, deprive us of unrequited capital imports which have, in the past 10 years, allowed us to carry a heavier burden of foreign lending and aid programs than we could have financed otherwise. We would

now have to share these responsibilities — and the political influence that might accompany them — with other countries, through processes of multilateral decision making which would, at times, be irritating and frustrating. We would, on the other hand, have consolidated in the hands of the Fund a large portion of highly volatile foreign funds, whose sudden and unpredictable outflow might otherwise unleash, at any time, an unbearable drain on our gold reserves. Most of all, we would have shed thereby the straitjacket which the need to prevent such an outflow would impose upon monetary management and interest rates in this country, whenever the success of our price stabilization efforts allows us to give primary consideration once more to the furtherance of maximum feasible rates of employment and economic growth.

A second and closely related consideration is that these reforms would put an end to an absurd situation under which we have been in practice — with only minor exceptions — the sole net lender in the IMF, in spite of our persistent deficits and of the equally persistent and huge surpluses accumulated over the last 10 years by other IMF members. We would, moreover, be able for the first time to obtain ourselves assistance from the IMF — through the more flexible procedure of IMF investments rather than loans — without triggering off the dangerous psychological reactions which would now accompany a U.S. request for such assistance. The IMF itself would need to look for safe investment outlets for its expanded resources, particularly during the initial years of the new system, and this would fit in particularly well with our own need to buy the time necessary for effecting, in as smooth a manner as possible — in the interest of other countries as well as in our own — the readjustment of our current overall balance of payments deficits.

61

SOME PERSPECTIVE ON FOREIGN EXCHANGE RATES*

Federal Reserve Bank of Cleveland

Once more we encounter our old friend — gold — which has been off stage (but never very far) since way back in Chapter Two. Now, however, it is gold in its international role.

As mentioned in the introduction to Selection 60, a distinguishing feature of international trade, as compared with domestic trade, is the need to — in some way — establish ratios of exchange (or exchange rates) between the various kinds of monies involved. Indeed, the particular way in which that is done may have significant and wide-ranging repercussions, domestically as well as internationally. And it turns out that it is none other than our old friend, gold, which plays a crucial role in the way exchange rates are set under present international monetary arrangements.

Some of the consequences of those arrangements, some alternatives to them, and whether gold should or should not continue to play the role it now plays, are the subjects of the remaining selections in this book.

In recent months, much attention has been focused on the existing international monetary system. This attention essentially involves inquiry into the adequacy of international liquidity, and the relationship of the present international payments mechanism to the role and status of the U.S. dollar and the British pound sterling.

By and large, national monetary authorities and the financial community in general have expressed confidence in the present international monetary system, which is commonly called a gold exchange system. These parties recognize imperfections in the system, but believe that a more satisfactory scheme, if one is needed, can best be built upon the existing structure. Thus, their proposals usually take the form of modifications of present arrangements. Others, including a number of academic economists and some foreign observers, believe more far-reaching changes are necessary. According to some individuals, the gold exchange standard, with its dependence on the dollar and the pound, is alleged both to be built upon an unsound foundation and to be incompatible with certain domestic goals — full employment, stable prices, and an acceptable rate of economic growth. In other words, if a different system were in effect, smoother adjustments could be made and domestic economic goals could more easily be achieved.

Though the critics of the existing international monetary mechanism are often quite outspoken, they clearly are not united in presenting an alternative scheme. Rather, their suggestions reflect a diversity of value systems and analytical frames of reference. This article discusses one proposal, which involves the establishment of an international payments system based upon freely fluctuating rates of exchange between national monetary units.[1] The

* From *Economic Review*, Federal Reserve Bank of Cleveland (September, 1965). Reprinted by the courtesy of the Federal Reserve Bank of Cleveland.

[1] Students of international finance generally distinguish between freely fluctuating exchange rates and floating exchange rates. The first, and the one discussed in this article, refers to exchange rates arrived at entirely through the market mechanism; put otherwise, government intervention in the foreign exchange market is completely absent. The second, which is not discussed in this article, is a variant of the first with the notable exception that the financial authorities intervene in the foreign exchange market, with sales or purchases to keep fluctuations in exchange rates "orderly." The system that is discussed in this article is offered only for pedagogical reasons; this is done because a system of freely fluctuating exchange rates presents some clear-cut distinctions from the existing system and is useful for illustration.

proposal is discussed in an attempt to improve understanding so that sound evaluation can be made by those interested in the area.

THE MEANING, IMPORTANCE, AND DETERMINATION OF EXCHANGE RATES

Before considering an international monetary system based upon flexible exchange rates as opposed to one based upon relatively fixed rates of exchange, it might be helpful to set the stage with a general discussion of exchange rates. What are exchange rates? Why are they important? How are they determined?

Essentially, an exchange rate is a price paid for a unit of one nation's currency in terms of the currency of another. Thus, for example, the prevailing U.S. dollar-pound sterling exchange rate may be expressed as approximately £1 = $2.80; that is, it costs $2.80 to acquire one British pound. Similarly, the prevailing dollar — *Deutsche mark* exchange rate may be expressed as DM1 = $0.25; that is, it costs $0.25 to acquire one German *mark*. Turning the explanation around, it follows that the price of a dollar in terms of pounds is just a trifle over seven shillings,[2] and four marks will exchange for one dollar.

Since exchange rates express the price of one currency unit in terms of others, they provide a direct link between the prices of goods and services in different parts of the world. Consider, for example, a men's clothing chain in the United States choosing between purchasing a line of suits from a domestic manufacturer or a similar line from a manufacturer in England. Assume, further, that the decision rests largely upon price, with delivery periods and quality being essentially the same, and tariffs nonexistent. The U.S. manufacturer obviously states his price in terms of dollars. Suppose the wholesale price of suits is set at $52.00 each. The British manufacturer sets a price for his garments in terms of pounds. Suppose he is willing to sell the suits at £18 each. Where should the U.S. clothing chain make its purchase? First the purchasing agent must determine the dollar equivalent of the price in

pounds. At approximately $2.80 per pound, he quickly calculates that the price, in dollars, of the British-made garment is $50.40 (18 × $2.80). With transportation and other charges assumed negligible and with no tariff charges, the agent would probably make his company's purchase from the British manufacturer.

Knowledge of exchange rates thus is essential to international trade by enabling traders to compare, in terms of their own country's currency, the effective prices of foreign goods and services. Because commerce between nations is a substitute for mobility of productive factors (natural, human, and physical resources) across national boundaries, it is essential to overall economic efficiency.[3] And because exchange rates are essential to trade, they therefore play an important part in promoting a dynamic and expanding world economy.

In addition to the broad function of enabling international commerce, exchange rates serve two additional specific functions. First, the value and volume of a nation's imports and exports are related to the exchange rate between its currency and the currencies of other nations. Second, the composition of trade (that is, the makeup of imports and exports) is related to the exchange rate between the home currency and those of other nations.

Consider first the relationship between exchange rates and the value and volume of imports and exports. To make matters simple (though at the cost of introducing an element — hopefully not too large — of unreality), assume that prices of goods manufactured in the U.S. (as expressed in dollars) and goods manufactured in Britain (as expressed in pounds) remain stable despite exchange rate movements.

---

[2] One pound = 20 shillings.
   At £1 = $2.80, one shilling = 14 cents.

[3] This statement is clarified by an understanding of the principle of comparative advantage. For a complete discussion of this, see any basic economics textbook. In essence, the principle states that, because of the diversity in resources and means of production between countries, the world would be economically better off if each country were to specialize in the production of those goods and services in which it is relatively more efficient, and were to trade with nations who are relatively less efficient. Even if one nation were *absolutely* more efficient in the production of every commodity than the others, it would still be beneficial for this nation to specialize in those fields in which it possesses a comparative advantage. In this way world resources may be utilized most efficiently.

Assume further that initially £1 = $2.80. At this rate of exchange between the dollar and pound, traders in the U.S. will import some dollar amount of goods and services from Britain, say $280 million worth. Also, at this rate traders in the United States will export a certain dollar amount of goods and services to Britain, say $280 million worth.

Suppose now the exchange rate becomes £1 = $5.60.[4] Everything else the same, what could happen to U.S. exports to and imports from Britain? Because the dollar price of American-made goods does not change, and because the pound can now command more dollars ($5.60 as against $2.80), the British would find American-made goods and services more attractive (in terms of price) than previously. For example, an American camera, which formerly sold in Britain at £8 ($22.40), would now sell for £4. Britain can thus acquire the same dollar volume of imports from the U.S. for one-half of what it formerly cost in terms of pounds. In terms of dollars, this country would receive the same amount as before. Almost certainly, however, the British would seek to acquire more American-made goods than before, since the absolute pound price has declined, and since the price of American goods has fallen relative to the price of alternate goods produced in Britain. Thus, the dollar value of American exports to Britain would almost certainly increase.[5]

What of imports from Britain? The dollar price in the U.S. of such imports will rise in proportion to the increase in the dollar price of the pound. Thus, for example, prior to the change, a purchase of an automobile selling for £985 in England would have cost a U.S. importer (exclusive of transportation and other charges) $2,758 (985 × $2.80). A doubling of the dollar price of the pound now doubles the import price of the automobile to $5,516 (985 × $5.60). Because the dollar price of goods imported from Britain would increase

both absolutely and in relation to prices of substitute goods produced at home, Americans would likely purchase fewer British goods. But, though possible and perhaps likely, it does not necessarily follow that the dollar value of American imports would decrease. Prior to the increase in the value of the pound, Americans were spending in total, say, £100 million on British goods. Suppose now they decided to purchase fewer British goods and to spend only £80 million on imports. In terms of dollars, however, the outlay increases to $448 million (80 million × $5.60).

The preceding paragraphs have attempted to clarify the role of exchange rates in influencing the value and volume of a nation's total imports from and exports to other nations. The following brief discussion deals with the additional role played by exchange rates in influencing the product composition of a country's exports and imports. Consider, in this connection, the hypothetical Table I.

The table provides a sample of commodities produced both in the U.S. and Great Britain. The unit of each commodity is that amount costing $1 to produce in the United States (column 1). Column 2 shows the cost in Britain, in terms of British currency units, to produce the same amount of product.[6] Though all commodities appearing in the table are produced in both countries, it is likely that the real costs[7] of some commodities are relatively less in one country than in the other. And, as explained by the law of comparative advantage, it is these commodities which will generally constitute a nation's exports.[8]

The distribution between what a nation imports and what it exports becomes explicit only when an exchange rate is introduced. From a consideration of columns 1 and 2 above, one could hardly tell what commodities each country would export and import. Columns 3 through 5 translate costs in Britain, expressed in terms of shillings and pence, into their dollar equivalents. It can be observed that, at an

---

[4] Under present arrangements this can happen in one of two ways: Britain *could revalue the pound upward*, in terms of the dollar, or the U.S. *could devalue the dollar*, in terms of the pound.

[5] The amount of increase, of course, depends on the price elasticity, or degree of responsiveness, of British demand for American-made goods.

[6] The notation 4/-, for example, reads four shillings, no pence; likewise, 4/3 reads four shillings, three pence.

[7] Real costs refer to opportunity costs — the amount of one good that must be forfeited to produce a unit of another.

[8] See footnote 3.

TABLE I

Prices and Exchange Rates

Commodity	(1) Cost in U.S. in $	(2) In Shillings and Pence	(3) @£ 1 = $5	(4) @£ 1 = $4	(5) @£ 1 = $2.80
			Cost in the United Kingdom IN DOLLARS		
Margarine	$1	4/-	$1.00	$0.80	$0.56
Wool cloth	1	4/3	1.06	0.85	0.60
Cotton cloth	1	4/8	1.16	0.93	0.65
Cigarettes	1	5/-	1.25	1.00	0.70
Linoleum	1	5/6	1.38	1.10	0.77
Paper	1	6/-	1.50	1.20	0.84
Glass bottles	1	7/-	1.75	1.40	0.98
Radio tubes	1	8/-	2.00	1.60	1.12
Pig iron	1	9/-	2.25	1.80	1.26
Tin cans	1	10/-	2.50	2.00	1.40

Source: P. T. Ellsworth, The International Economy, Revised, The Macmillan Company, New York, 1958, p. 262.

exchange rate of £1 = $5.00, the first arbitrary exchange rate level, Britain would not be able to export to the U.S. *any* of the commodities in the table. With the exception of margarine, U.S. buyers would be able to purchase American-made goods at lower prices than those of equivalent British-made goods. (The British may still produce these goods for domestic sale, however, because purchase in the United States would involve additional costs — transportation, tariffs, etc. — which could offset their production cost disadvantage.) As the pound becomes cheaper in terms of the dollar, British goods become more and more competitive with equivalent American-made products. Thus, at £1 = $4.00 the British may start exporting cotton cloth, wool cloth, and cigarettes. At £1 = $2.80 the list of exported products would extend to linoleum, paper, and glass bottles. Thus, the exchange rate markedly affects the distribution of products traded between nations.[9]

Having briefly explored the meaning of exchange rates and their importance, consideration may now be turned to how exchange rates

[9] The latter effect is closely associated with the role played by exchange rates in influencing the value and volume of a country's imports and exports. Thus, it is not simply a matter where more or less of previously traded goods are purchased or sold when exchange rates vary; such changes may introduce new export and import goods into a country's trade.

are determined. As mentioned earlier, the discussion is limited to exchange rate determination under free market conditions. In such a situation the prevailing exchange rate would reflect basic supply and demand conditions. Consider, by way of illustration, the exchange rate between the U.S. dollar and the British pound. In any period the rate of exchange between the two currencies would reflect the relationship between the supply of dollars made available to Britishers by Americans and the demand for dollars by Britishers. Alternatively, it could be said that the exchange rate between the two currencies would reflect the relationship between the supply of pounds made available by Britishers to Americans and the demand for pounds by Americans.

The matter can, perhaps, be made clearer and more precise with the aid of the accompanying chart. The vertical axis measures the price of the pound in terms of dollars. (The prices above and below $2.80 were chosen for illustrative purposes because they are multiples of the present rate of exchange.) The horizontal axis measures the amount of pounds supplied and demanded. The red line sloping downward to the right shows a hypothetical relationship between the exchange rate and the demand by Americans for pound sterling. With British prices (fixed in terms of pounds) given, it is reasonable to assume that Americans will want

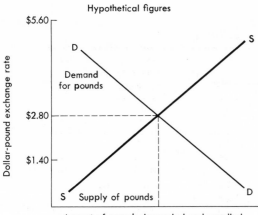

Hypothetical figures

fewer pounds as the price of the pound increases in terms of dollars. The black line sloping upward to the right shows a hypothetical relationship between the exchange rate and the supply of pounds made available by Britishers to Americans. With American prices (set in terms of dollars) given, it is hypothesized that, as the dollar becomes cheaper in terms of pounds (or put otherwise, as the pound becomes dearer in terms of dollars), the volume of pounds made available to Americans, in the course of business dealings, will increase. It should be recalled from earlier discussion that this latter result may not always occur.

Suppose now that the exchange rate were set at £1 = $5.60. Could this rate be long maintained, given the hypothesized supply-demand relationships? Probably not, for at this price the supply of pounds would exceed the demand for pounds; not all sellers of sterling will be able to find buyers. The price of the pound would therefore tend to fall. Suppose the exchange rate were set at £1 = $1.40. Could this rate be long maintained in a free market? Probably not, for at this price the demand for pounds, to purchase goods and services or investments in Britain, would exceed the supply of pounds made available. The price of the pound would therefore tend to rise. Only at £1 = $2.80 is there an exact coincidence between supply and demand. Thus, £ = $2.80 becomes an "equilibrium" rate of exchange.

This rate of exchange — £1 = $2.80 — would

be an equilibrium rate only so long as changes do not occur in the hypothesized supply and demand relationships. Shifts in these relationships would make the existing equilibrium rate unmaintainable and, hence, necessitate a new equilibrium rate.

Suppose, for some reason, Americans become more willing to spend dollars in Britain, for example, as a result of the recent popularity in this country of a British singing group known as the "Beatles." An increased willingness to acquire pounds would manifest itself in a shift of the demand curve to the right (see the accompanying chart); that is, at each dollar-pound exchange rate, Americans would seek more pounds than previously. The existing exchange rate, £1 = $2.80, would become unmaintainable; the demand for pounds would exceed the supply of pounds. Unsatisfied demanders of the pound would drive up the pound's price in terms of dollars. Only at some new figure, perhaps at £1 = $3.20, would a new equilibrium rate be found.

SOME ASPECTS OF THE EXISTING INTERNATIONAL MONETARY SYSTEM

Under present international monetary arrangements, exchange rates are allowed to vary only slightly in response to temporary changes in supply and demand factors; member countries of the International Monetary Fund (IMF) are required to maintain — through buying and selling as needed in the foreign exchange market — stable rates of exchange between their internal currency units and a spe-

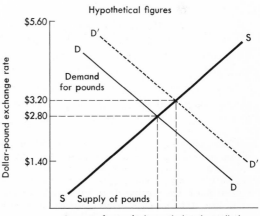

Hypothetical figures

cified weight of gold.[10] This requirement effectively establishes stable rates of exchange between a member nation's currency and the currency units of other member countries. To illustrate, the U.S. exchanges dollars for gold or gold for dollars for official foreign holders at a price of $35 an ounce; if Great Britain were to do the same, it would be at a price of £12/10s ($35 = one ounce gold — £12/10s; and $2.80 = £1). Similar relationships can be worked out for all other member countries, although not all countries buy and sell gold in the market.

Though member nations are required to maintain stable rates of exchange between their own currencies and those of other countries, this requirement does not apply in situations where "fundamental disequilibrium" exists. That is, when it becomes evident that the prevailing exchange rate no longer corresponds closely to a market-determined rate reflecting long-term supply and demand forces, the IMF will permit exchange rate adjustments. The IMF, however, has never made explicit, or given substance to, the term "fundamental disequilibrium," though what is *not* meant has been made quite apparent. According to one well-known economist closely associated with the IMF:

> No attempt has ever been made — nor perhaps could it be — to define fundamental disequilibrium precisely. But it is clearly intended to exclude merely ephemeral balance of payments disequilibria, due to temporary factors of a seasonal, speculative, or possibly even of a short cyclical type. . . . Moreover . . . it was probably implicit in the articles that exchange rates should be adjusted only at infrequent intervals.[11]

Consider what it means for a nation to guarantee to maintain a fixed rate of exchange between its own currency and a specified amount of gold or, what comes to the same thing, another country's currency, such as the U.S.

dollar. The situation facing a hypothetical country like South Morango can be used as an example. Assume that that country has declared that 60.0 units of its currency, the *morang* will exchange for one U.S. dollar, or, put otherwise, that the *morang* is equivalent to 1.667 cents. South Morango has also established fixed rates of exchange between the *morang* and the currency units of all other member countries. To maintain these exchange rates, the monetary authorities in South Morango should stand ready to buy and sell *unlimited* amounts of gold and/or dollars. For example, suppose South Morango was suffering a deficit in its international balance of payments. That is, the demand for foreign currencies to make desired purchases and investments abroad exceeds the supply of such currencies made available as a result of sales (of either goods, services, or long-term debt instruments) by South Morangoans to foreigners. In this type of situation, there would be a *natural tendency*, all things being equal, for the *morang* to fall in value. To prevent this, and thus maintain the established rate, the authorities must make either gold or dollars available at the official price.[12]

The problem, obviously, is that South Morango can neither print dollars (and for that matter any currency other than the *morang*) nor manufacture gold. Because its reserves of foreign currencies and gold — as those of any nation — are limited, there are constraints as to the magnitude and duration of balance of payments deficits that South Morango could withstand without lowering the value of the *morang* to make purchases in South Morango relatively more attractive. Sufficient monetary reserves (or adequate international liquidity) are essential to any system of fixed exchange rates.

Establishment of the IMF, in 1946, in effect

---

[10] Actual spot rates of exchange are permitted to vary by as much as one per cent in either direction from the official exchange rate. Thus, while the dollar price of the pound may fluctuate between $2.772 and $2.828, the actual limits have been somewhat narrower.

[11] See Marcus J. Fleming, *The International Monetary Fund: Its Forms and Functions*, International Monetary Fund, Washington, D.C., 1964, p. 8.

[12] As a general matter, operations to stabilize exchange rates are carried out through the use of gold and U.S. dollars. Gold, of course, is an internationally acceptable medium of exchange. The dollar, because it is fully convertible into gold at $35 an ounce, is also, therefore, a means of international payment. To a somewhat lesser extent the same applies to sterling and, in some cases, to other strong European currencies such as the *Deutsche mark*.

provided additional international liquidity; member countries could now borrow foreign exchange from the Fund to meet temporary deficits. Thus, for example, South Morango would be allowed to borrow up to a specified amount from the IMF to cover a temporary disequilibrium in her payments position. The foregoing points up the fact that international liquidity presently consists not only of gold and foreign exchange, particularly dollars and pounds sterling, but also of borrowing rights on the IMF. Insofar as a system of fixed exchange rates rests upon the existence of adequate international liquidity, the Fund has clearly made such a system more viable than it would otherwise be.

FIXED VS. FREELY FLUCTUATING EXCHANGE RATES

Defenders of fixed exchange rates — and therefore of some variant of the present international monetary system — offer a number of arguments in support of their position. Two seemingly strong economic arguments are discussed here. The first is that fixed exchange rates are an important element in promoting maximum trade between nations. The second, which is actually related to the first, is that private capital movements (especially of a long-term nature) across national frontiers — which are essential if capital is to be most efficiently utilized — require stable rates of exchange between national currency units.

Commerce between nations is a complex affair. Yet, it is necessary if the full benefits of specialization and division of labor are to be realized. Fluctuating exchange rates, which would mirror temporary changes in supply and demand conditions, would add further to the complexities of international trade. Consider, for example, the situation facing the clothing chain referred to earlier. The reader will recall that the question was whether the purchase of a particular style of men's suit should be made in this country or in Great Britain. With assured stability of exchange rates, the decision could be made quite simply; all things being equal, all the purchasing agent had to do was convert the price of the British-made garment into dollars and compare this price with that

asked by the American manufacturer. But suppose the exchange rate varies monthly, weekly, and perhaps daily. By the time payment is made to the British manufacturer the dollar price of the pound may have risen sufficiently to wipe out any price advantage originally received, that is, it would cost the purchaser more dollars than originally anticipated. To be sure, traders can hedge (cover) against adverse exchange rate fluctuations, but such protection must be paid for and thereby increases the costs of engaging in international commerce. Further, there are well-developed and efficient forward cover markets in only a few currencies. Finally, many types of transactions call for long-term financing; here hedging possibilities are almost entirely absent.

Similar problems confront individuals and enterprises considering investing money capital abroad. Such investments usually involve elements of risk not generally found at home. However, under normal circumstances, capital will usually go abroad when the expected interest return exceeds the return desired by the investor after considering domestic rates of return and his own risk expectations. Risks are compounded when exchange rates are left free to fluctuate. Suppose a U.S. investor has a choice between making an investment of $280,000 at home yielding 5 per cent and an investment of equal size in Britain yielding 10 per cent. At the end of one year the investment at home would be worth $294,000 ($280,000 × 1.05). What the investor would actually receive had he invested in Britain depends upon the prevailing exchange rate at the time the funds (investment plus interest) are repatriated. If originally the exchange rate was $2.80, the investor acquired £100,000 when converting dollars to invest in Britain. On this he would earn £10,000 as interest. With a stable rate of exchange between the dollar and pound he would bring home $308,000 (110,000 × $2.80), or a "net profit" of $14,000 over what could have been earned at home. But what if the value of the pound at the time of repatriation, in terms of dollars, has fallen to £1 = $2.00? The investor now would bring home only $220,000 (110,000 × $2.00), a net loss of $74,000 when considered against the alternative investment in the U.S. and a net loss of $88,000 when considered against what he had originally expected to earn on his British investment. Thus, the potential investor of funds abroad must speculate — sometimes far into the future — about the probable course of exchange rate movements. (This is also true under a relatively fixed-rate system, but not to the same extent.) To be sure, exchange rates can fluctuate to the investor's advantage, but insofar as investors try to avert risks of loss there is a real danger that the international flow of capital will be lessened.[13]

Opponents of fixed exchange rates also present an imposing set of arguments. Probably the major source of opposition is a belief, growing out of the theoretical developments in economic thinking during the past 30 years, that the maintenance of fixed rates of exchange may not, at all times and in all cases, be compatible with prevailing domestic goals of full-employment, price stability, and high rates of economic growth. In other words, it is argued that countries often find themselves in situations where their commitment to maintain the value of their currency in terms of gold or other currencies is at variance with internal objectives.

The argument can be more completely presented by considering a hypothetical situation in which a country, say Greece, may find itself. Suppose, in some initial period, the Greek economy can boast of having no serious unemployment problem, no significant price inflation, a socially and politically acceptable rate of economic growth, and basic balance in its balance of payments (ignoring equilibrating capital flows). Suppose for some reason — say a reduced desire on the part of foreigners for grapes produced in Greece — that exports were to decline markedly.[14] The Greek balance of

payments would therefore move into deficit position. The financial authorities must now (if Greece were under a fixed-rate system) gear themselves to the defense of the *drachma* (the currency unit of Greece). That is, the country's limited international reserves ($264 million in the first quarter of 1965) would have to be made available in support of the official international value of the *drachma*.[15] If the Greek deficit were only transitory the problem would not be serious; Greece would lose some of her international reserves, but in time these losses would probably be offset. What, however, if the disequilibrium were more long lasting? What if the Greek authorities have insufficient international liquidity to maintain the international value of the *drachma*? (It will be remembered that borrowing rights on the IMF are included in the total of Greece's international reserves.) In such a case the authorities must take remedial action or else the value of the drachma will decline by default.

What would the authorities be likely to do? First, it should be apparent that there is no simple solution. Clearly, they would attempt to stimulate exports and curtail imports.[16] As one alternative, although not always the most propitious, both objectives may be attainable by exerting a depressing influence on the domestic economy.[17] In the way of illustration, consider first the effects on the home sector. By the pursuit of restrictive monetary and fiscal policies, domestic price and income levels would most probably decline. This course would, therefore, manifest itself in growing unemployment among workers, a falling price level caus-

---

[13] The danger is particularly acute in the case of capital flows to underdeveloped nations. Most of these countries are presently limited in their exports to one or two primary products, the demand for which varies greatly in response to conditions in the industrial economies. Thus, the external value of their currencies will tend to fluctuate considerably, which they have even under existing arrangements. This has added to the already numerous risks attached to the investment of funds in these areas.

[14] It is assumed that the loss of employment and Gross National Product resulting from the decline in

exports is offset by various domestic factors — for example, a fortuitous construction spurt at home. Thus, it is also assumed that the previous import level is maintained.

[15] Thirty *drachma* = $1; 1,050 *drachma* = one ounce gold.

[16] Were Greece to have a relatively well-developed money market, the monetary authorities would also seek, by raising short-term interest rates, to attract funds from foreign money markets. At present, outside of the U.S., only several major European nations, Canada, and Japan, have even reasonably mature money markets to the extent they could conceivably rely upon short-term capital flows to offset a part of balance of payments deficits.

[17] Another alternative, which is not considered here, would be to have a once-and-for-all devaluation of the *drachma*.

ing hardship to the business and agricultural sectors, and a less than satisfactory domestic rate of growth. But, a restrictive monetary and fiscal policy may be an effective means of combatting Greece's balance of payments deficit. Thus, the authorities are confronted with the decision to trade off in part domestic objectives against international objectives. A lowering of prices in Greece relative to prices abroad makes purchases in Greece more attractive: Greeks may now find it desirable to buy at home goods that were formerly imported; similarly foreigners may now find it desirable to do more of their shopping in Greece. Thus, price effects would most likely lead to some improvement in Greece's exports and some curtailment of her imports. Further support would come about as a result of reductions in money incomes (following from declines in money wage rates and the level of employment). Reduced money incomes would likely lead to a decline in imports since individuals have less purchasing power and therefore would spend less on most goods and services, imports included.

Critics of fixed exchange rates argue that it is unnecessary for a nation to compromise — or trade off — on its domestic goals because of balance of payments considerations. To these critics, disequilibrium in a country's international payments position can and should be rectified by permitting the exchange rate to fluctuate freely in response to changing supply and demand conditions. After all, they argue, since a private enterprise economy relies upon the price mechanism to eliminate disparities between supply and demand in most domestic markets, why not let the price mechanism bring about balance in the foreign exchange market? If, at the prevailing exchange rate, Greeks wish to spend more foreign exchange abroad than is received from abroad why not, the critics of fixed exchange rates ask, let the price of foreign exchange rise in terms of the *drachma*? This would make foreign purchases more costly, thus tending to reduce imports; and because the *drachma* could be more cheaply obtained in terms of foreign currencies,

Greek exports would be stimulated. Putting the matter most simply, the critics argue that balance of payments disequilibrium should be eliminated not by reductions in domestic price (and income) levels, but by automatic reductions in the external value of the home currency. If this prescription is followed, the critics see no reason for the domestic economy having to bear the burden of deficits in a country's external transactions.

The controversy between advocates of fixed exchange rates — the existing system — and those of freely flexible exchange rates is not likely to be resolved on the basis of the arguments presented above. Both sides bring to the debate a number of additional arguments — some of a quasi-moral or ethical nature, some of a political or "practical" nature, and still others of a highly theoretical or technical nature. For example, some oppose flexible exchange rates on the grounds that governments may become "irresponsible" in their financial affairs once they can safely ignore the "discipline" imposed by the balance of payments. On the other hand, some oppose fixed exchange rates on the grounds that such a system is incompatible with a free market economy. Both of these arguments appear to have moral or ethical implications. On a totally different level, the debate focuses on such highly theoretical matters as the value of freely fluctuating exchange rates in mitigating the effects of externally generated business cycles and whether flexible rates are really able to eliminate balance of payments disequilibria.

CONCLUDING COMMENTS

A system of flexible exchange rates has not been widely advocated by government officials here and abroad. But the fact that such a system is being discussed in economic literature does suggest a growing interest in balance of payments problems throughout the world, and indicates the willingness of many analysts to consider various alternatives, even those with limitations, to handling the major economic issues that confront the world economy.

62

FLEXIBLE EXCHANGE RATES*

Milton Friedman†

Discussions of U.S. policy with respect to international payments tend to be dominated by our immediate balance-of-payments difficulties. I should like today to approach the question from a different, and I hope more constructive, direction. Let us begin by asking ourselves not merely how we can get out of our present difficulties but instead how we can fashion our international payments system so that it will best serve our needs for the long pull; how we can solve not merely this balance-of-payments problem but *the* balance-of-payments problem.

A shocking, and indeed, disgraceful feature of the present situation is the extent to which our frantic search for expedients to stave off balance-of-payments pressures has led us, on the one hand, to sacrifice major national objectives; and, on the other, to give enormous power to officials of foreign governments to affect what should be purely domestic matters. Foreign payments amount to only some 5 per cent of our total national income. Yet they have become a major factor in nearly every national policy.

I believe that a system of floating exchange rates would solve the balance-of-payments problem for the United States far more effectively than our present arrangements. Such a system would use the flexibility and efficiency of the free market to harmonize our small foreign trade sector with both the rest of our massive economy and the rest of the world; it would reduce problems of foreign payments to their proper dimensions and remove them as a major consideration in governmental policy about domestic matters and as a major preoccupation in international political negotiations; it would foster our national objectives rather than be an obstacle to their attainment.

* From *The United States Balance of Payments*, Part 3, *Hearings* before the Joint Economic Committee, U.S. Congress, November 1963. Reprinted by the courtesy of the author.

† University of Chicago.

To indicate the basis for this conclusion, let us consider the national objective with which our payments system is most directly connected: the promotion of a healthy and balanced growth of world trade, carried on, so far as possible, by private individuals and private enterprises with minimum intervention by governments. This has been a major objective of our whole postwar international economic policy, most recently expressed in the Trade Expansion Act of 1962. Success would knit the free world more closely together, and, by fostering the international division of labor, raise standards of living throughout the world, including the United States.

Suppose that we succeed in negotiating far-reaching reciprocal reductions in tariffs and other trade barriers with the Common Market and other countries. To simplify exposition I shall hereafter refer only to tariffs, letting these stand for the whole range of barriers to trade, including even the so-called voluntary limitation of exports. Such reductions will expand trade in general but clearly will have different effects on different industries. The demand for the products of some will expand, for others contract. This is a phenomenon we are familiar with from our internal development. The capacity of our free enterprise system to adapt quickly and efficiently to such shifts, whether produced by changes in technology or tastes, has been a major source of our economic growth. The only additional element introduced by international trade is the fact that different currencies are involved, and this is where the payment mechanism comes in; its function is to keep this fact from being an additional source of disturbance.

An all-around lowering of tariffs would tend to increase both our expenditures and our receipts in foreign currencies. There is no way of knowing in advance which increase would tend to be the greater and hence no way of knowing whether the initial effect would be toward a surplus or deficit in our balance of payments. What is clear is that we cannot hope to succeed in the objective of expanding world trade unless we can readily adjust to either outcome.

Many people concerned with our payments deficits hope that since we are operating further from full capacity than Europe, we could supply a substantial increase in exports whereas they could not. Implicitly, this assumes that European countries are prepared to see their surplus turned into a deficit, thereby contributing to the reduction of the deficits we have recently been experiencing in our balance of payments. Perhaps this would be the initial effect of tariff changes. But if the achievement of such a result is to be sine qua non of tariff agreement, we cannot hope for any significant reduction in barriers. We could be confident that exports would expand more than imports only if the tariff changes were one sided indeed, with our trading partners making much greater reductions in tariffs than we make. Our major means of inducing other countries to reduce tariffs is to offer corresponding reductions in our tariff. More generally, there is little hope of continued and sizable liberalization of trade if liberalization is to be viewed simply as a device for correcting balance-of-payments difficulties. That way lies only backing and filling.

Suppose then that the initial effect is to increase our expenditures on imports more than our receipts from exports. How would we adjust to this outcome?

One method of adjustment is to draw on reserves or borrow from abroad to finance the excess increase in imports. The obvious objection to this method is that it is only a temporary device, and hence can be relied on only when the disturbance is temporary. But that is not the major objection. Even if we had very large reserves or could borrow large amounts from abroad, so that we could continue this expedient for many years, it is a most undesirable one. We can see why if we look at physical rather than financial magnitudes.

The physical counterpart to the financial deficit is a reduction of employment in industries competing with imports that is larger than the concurrent expansion of employment in export industries. So long as the financial deficit continues, the assumed tariff reductions create employment problems. But it is no part of the aim of tariff reductions to create unemployment at home or to promote employment abroad. The aim is a balanced expansion of trade, with exports rising along with imports and thereby providing employment opportunities to offset any reduction in employment resulting from increased imports.

Hence, simply drawing on reserves or borrowing abroad is a most unsatisfactory method of adjustment.

Another method of adjustment is to lower U.S. prices relative to foreign prices, since this would stimulate exports and discourage imports. If foreign countries are accommodating enough to engage in inflation, such a change in relative prices might require merely that the United States keep prices stable or even, that it simply keep them from rising as fast as foreign prices. But there is no necessity for foreign countries to be so accommodating, and we could hardly count on their being so accommodating. The use of this technique therefore involves a willingness to produce a decline in U.S. prices by tight monetary policy or tight fiscal policy or both. Given time, this method of adjustment would work. But in the interim, it would exact a heavy toll. It would be difficult or impossible to force down prices appreciably without producing a recession and considerable unemployment. To eliminate in the long run the unemployment resulting from the tariff changes, we should in the short run be creating cyclical unemployment. The cure might for a time be far worse than the disease.

This second method is therefore also most unsatisfactory. Yet these two methods — drawing on reserves and forcing down prices — are the only two methods available to us under our present international payment arrangements, which involve fixed exchange rates between the U.S. dollar and other currencies. Little wonder that we have so far made such disappointing progress toward the reduction of trade barriers, that our practice has differed so much from our preaching.

There is one other way and only one other

way to adjust and that is by allowing (or forcing) the price of the U.S. dollar to fall in terms of other currencies. To a foreigner, U.S. goods can become cheaper in either of two ways — either because their prices in the United States fall in terms of dollars or because the foreigner has to give up fewer units of his own currency to acquire a dollar, which is to say, the price of the dollar falls. For example, suppose a particular U.S. car sells for $2,800 when a dollar costs 7 shillings, tuppence in British money (i.e., roughly £1 = $2.80). The price of the car is then £1,000 in British money. It is all the same to an Englishman — or even a Scotsman — whether the price of the car falls to $2,500 while the price of a dollar remains 7 shillings, tuppence, or, alternatively, the price of the car remains $2,800, while the price of a dollar falls to 6 shillings, 5 pence (i.e., roughly £1 = $3.11). In either case, the car costs the Englishman £900 rather than £1,000, which is what matters to him. Similarly, foreign goods can become more expensive to an American in either of two ways — either because the price in terms of foreign currency rises or because he has to give up more dollars to acquire a given amount of foreign currency.

Changes in exchange rates can therefore alter the relative price of U.S. and foreign goods in precisely the same way as can changes in internal prices in the United States and in foreign countries. And they can do so without requiring anything like the same internal adjustments. If the initial effect of the tariff reductions would be to create a deficit at the former exchange rate (or enlarge an existing deficit or reduce an existing surplus) and thereby increase unemployment, this effect can be entirely avoided by a change in exchange rates which will produce a balanced expansion in imports and exports without interfering with domestic employment, domestic prices, or domestic monetary and fiscal policy. The pig can be roasted without burning down the house.

The situation is, of course, entirely symmetrical if the tariff changes should initially happen to expand our exports more than our imports. Under present circumstances, we would welcome such a result, and conceivably, if the matching deficit were experienced by countries currently running a surplus, they might permit it to occur without seeking to offset it. In that case, they and we would be using the first method of adjustment — changes in reserves or borrowing. But again, if we had started off from an even keel, this would be an undesirable method of adjustment. On our side, we should be sending out useful goods and receiving only foreign currencies in return. On the side of our partners, they would be using up reserves and tolerating the creation of unemployment.

The second method of adjusting to a surplus is to permit or force domestic prices to rise — which is of course what we did in part in the early postwar years when we were running large surpluses. Again, we should be forcing maladjustments on the whole economy to solve a problem arising from a small part of it — the 5 per cent accounted for by foreign trade.

Again, these two methods are the only ones available under our present international payments arrangements, and neither is satisfactory.

The final method is to permit or force exchange rates to change — in this case, a rise in the price of the dollar in terms of foreign currencies. This solution is again specifically adapted to the specific problem of the balance of payments.

Changes in exchange rates can be produced in either of two general ways. One way is by a change in an official exchange rate; an official devaluation or appreciation from one fixed level which the Government is committed to support to another fixed level. This is the method used by Britain in its postwar devaluation and by Germany in 1961 when the mark was appreciated. This is also the main method contemplated by the IMF which permits member nations to change their exchange rates by 10 per cent without approval by the Fund and by a larger amount after approval by the Fund. But this method has serious disadvantages. It makes a change in rates a matter of major moment, and hence there is a tendency to postpone any change as long as possible. Difficulties cumulate and a larger change is finally needed than would have been required if it could have been made promptly. By the time the change is made, everyone is aware that a change is pending and is certain about the direction of change. The result is to encourage flight from a currency, if it is going to be devalued, or to a currency, if it is going to be appreciated.

There is in any event little basis for determining precisely what the new rate should be. Speculative movements increase the difficulty of judging what the new rate should be, and introduce a systematic bias, making the change needed appear larger than it actually is. The result, particularly when devaluation occurs, is generally to lead officials to "play safe" by making an even larger change than the large change needed. The country is then left after the devaluation with a maladjustment precisely the opposite of that with which it started, and is thereby encouraged to follow policies it cannot sustain in the long run.

Even if all these difficulties could be avoided, this method of changing from one fixed rate to another has the disadvantage that it is necessarily discontinuous. Even if the new exchange rates are precisely correct when first established, they will not long remain correct.

A second and much better way in which changes in exchange rates can be produced is by permitting exchange rates to float, by allowing them to be determined from day to day in the market. This is the method which the United States used from 1862 to 1879, and again, in effect, from 1917 or so to about 1925, and again from 1933 to 1934. It is the method which Britain used from 1918 to 1925 and again from 1931 to 1939, and which Canada used for most of the interwar period and again from 1950 to May 1962. Under this method, exchange rates adjust themselves continuously, and market forces determine the magnitude of each change. There is no need for any official to decide by how much the rate should rise or fall. This is the method of the free market, the method that we adopt unquestioningly in a private enterprise economy for the bulk of goods and services. It is no less available for the price of one money in terms of another.

With a floating exchange rate, it is possible for Governments to intervene and try to affect the rate by buying or selling, as the British exchange equalization fund did rather successfully in the 1930's, or by combining buying and selling with public announcements of intentions, as Canada did so disastrously in early 1962. On the whole, it seems to me undesirable to have government intervene; because there is a strong tendency for government agencies to try to peg the rate rather than to stabilize it; because they have no special advantage over private speculators in stabilizing it; because they can make far bigger mistakes than private speculators risking their own money; and because there is a tendency for them to cover up their mistakes by changing the rules — as the Canadian case so strikingly illustrates — rather than by reversing course. But this is an issue on which there is much difference of opinion among economists who agree in favoring floating rates. Clearly, it is possible to have a successful floating rate along with governmental speculation.

The great objective of tearing down trade barriers; of promoting a worldwide expansion of trade; of giving citizens of all countries, and especially the underdeveloped countries, every opportunity to sell their products in open markets under equal terms and thereby every incentive to use their resources efficiently, of giving countries an alternative through free world trade to autarchy and central planning — this great objective can, I believe, be achieved best under a regime of floating rates. All countries, and not just the United States, can proceed to liberalize boldly and confidently only if they can have reasonable assurance that the resulting trade expansion will be balanced and will not interfere with major domestic objectives. Floating exchange rates, and so far as I can see, only floating exchange rates, provide this assurance. They do so because they are an automatic mechanism for protecting the domestic economy from the possibility that liberalization will produce a serious imbalance in international payments.

Despite their advantages, floating exchange rates have a bad press. Why is this so?

One reason is because a consequence of our present system that I have been citing as a serious disadvantage is often regarded as an advantage, namely, the extent to which the small foreign trade sector dominates national policy. Those who regard this as an advantage refer to it as the discipline of the gold standard. I would have much sympathy for this view if we had a real gold standard, so the discipline was imposed by impersonal forces which in turn reflected the realities of resources, tastes, and technology. But in fact we have today only a pseudo gold standard and the so-called discipline is imposed by governmental officials of other countries who are determining their own internal monetary policies and are either being forced to dance to our tune or calling the tune for us, depending primarily on accidental political developments. This is a discipline we can well do without.

A possibly more important reason why floating exchange rates have a bad press, I believe, is a mistaken interpretation of experience with floating rates, arising out of a statistical fallacy that can be seen easily in a standard example. Arizona is clearly the worst place in the United States for a person with tuberculosis to go because the death rate from tuberculosis is higher in Arizona than in any other State. The fallacy in this case is obvious. It is less obvious in connection with exchange rates. Countries that have gotten into severe financial difficulties, for whatever reason, have had ultimately to change their exchange rates or let them change. No amount of exchange control and other restrictions on trade have enabled them to peg an exchange rate that was far out of line with economic realities. In consequence, floating rates have frequently been associated with financial and economic instability. It is easy to conclude, as many have, that floating exchange rates produce such instability.

This misreading of experience is reinforced by the general prejudice against speculation; which has led to the frequent assertion, typically on the basis of no evidence whatsoever, that speculation in exchange can be expected to be destabilizing and thereby to increase the instability in rates. Few who make this assertion even recognize that it is equivalent to asserting that speculators generally lose money.

Floating exchange rates need not be unstable exchange rates — any more than the prices of automobiles or of Government bonds, of coffee or of meals need gyrate wildly just because they are free to change from day to day. The Canadian exchange rate was free to change during more than a decade, yet it varied within narrow limits. The ultimate objective is a world in which exchange rates, while free to vary, are in fact highly stable because basic economic policies and conditions are stable. Instability of exchange rates is a symptom of instability in the underlying economic structure. Elimination of this symptom by administrative pegging of exchange rates cures none of the underlying difficulties and only makes adjustment to them more painful.

The confusion between stable exchange rates and pegged exchange rates helps to explain the frequent comment that floating exchange rates would introduce an additional element of uncertainty into foreign trade and thereby discourage its expansion. They introduce no additional element of uncertainty. If a floating rate would, for example, decline, then a pegged rate would be subject to pressure that the authorities would have to meet by internal deflation or exchange control in some form. The uncertainty about the rate would simply be replaced by uncertainty about internal prices or about the availability of exchange; and the latter uncertainties, being subject to administrative rather than market control, are likely to be the more erratic and unpredictable. Moreover, the trader can far more readily and cheaply protect himself against the danger of changes in exchange rates, through hedging operations in a forward market, than he can against the danger of changes in internal prices or exchange availability. Floating rates are therefore more favorable to private international trade than pegged rates.

Though I have discussed the problem of international payments in the context of trade liberalization, the discussion is directly applicable to the more general problem of adapting to any forces that make for balance-of-payments difficulties. Consider our present problem, of a deficit in the balance of trade plus long-term capital movements. How can we adjust to it? By one of the three methods outlined: first, drawing on reserves or borrowing; second, keeping U.S. prices from rising as rapidly as foreign prices or forcing them down; third, permitting or forcing exchange rates to alter. And, this time, by one more method: by imposing additional trade barriers or their equivalent, whether in the form of higher tariffs, or smaller import quotas, or extracting from other countries tighter "voluntary" quotas on their exports, or "tieing" foreign aid, or buying higher priced domestic goods or services to meet military needs, or imposing taxes on foreign borrowing, or imposing direct controls on investments by U.S. citizens abroad, or any one of the host of other devices for interfering with the private business of private individuals that have become so familiar to us since Hjalmar Schacht perfected the modern techniques of exchange control in 1934 to strengthen the Nazis for war and to despoil a large class of his fellow citizens.

Fortunately or unfortunately, even Congress cannot repeal the laws of arithmetic. Books must balance. We must use one of these four methods. Because we have been unwilling to select the only one that is currently fully consistent with both economic and political needs — namely, floating exchange rates — we have been driven, as if by an invisible hand, to employ all the others, and even then may not escape the need for explicit changes in exchange rates.

We affirm in loud and clear voices that we will not and must not erect trade barriers — yet is there any doubt about how far we have gone down the fourth route? After the host of measures already taken, the Secretary of the Treasury has openly stated to the Senate Finance Committee that if the so-called interest equalization tax — itself a concealed exchange control and concealed devaluation — is not passed, we shall have to resort to direct controls over foreign investment.

We affirm that we cannot drain our reserves further, yet short-term liabilities mount and our gold stock continues to decline.

We affirm that we cannot let balance-of-payments problems interfere with domestic prosperity, yet for at least some 4 years now we have followed a less expansive monetary policy than would have been healthy for our economy. Even all together, these measures may only serve to postpone but not prevent open devaluation — if the experience of other countries is any guide. Whether they do, depends not on us but on others. For our best hope of escaping our present difficulties is that foreign countries will inflate.

In the meantime, we adopt one expedient after another, borrowing here, making swap arrangements there, changing the form of loans to make the figures look good. Entirely aside from the ineffectiveness of most of these measures, they are politically degrading and demeaning. We are a great and wealthy Nation. We should be directing our own course, setting an example to the world, living up to our destiny. Instead, we send our officials hat in hand to make the rounds of foreign governments and central banks; we put foreign central banks in a position to determine whether or not we can meet our obligations and thus enable them to exert great influence on our policies; we are driven to niggling negotiations with Hong Kong and with Japan and for all I know, Monaco, to get them to limit voluntarily their exports. Is this posture suitable for the leader of the free world?

It is not the least of the virtues of floating exchange rates that we would again become masters in our own house. We could decide important issues on the proper ground. The military could concentrate on military effectiveness and not on saving foreign exchange; recipients of foreign aid could concentrate on how to get the most out of what we give them and not on how to spend it all in the United States; Congress could decide how much to spend on foreign aid on the basis of what we get for our money and what else we could use it for and not how it will affect the gold stock; the monetary authorities could concentrate on domestic prices and employment, not on how to induce foreigners to hold dollar balances in this country; the Treasury and the tax committees of Congress could devote their attention to the equity of the tax system and its effects on our efficiency, rather than on how to use tax gimmicks to discourage imports, subsidize exports, and discriminate against outflows of capital.

A system of floating exchange rates would

render the problem of making outflows equal inflows unto the market where it belongs and not leave it to the clumsy and heavy hand of Government. It would leave Government free to concentrate on its proper functions.

In conclusion, a word about gold. Our commitment to buy and sell gold for monetary use at a fixed price of $35 an ounce is, in practice, the mechanism whereby we maintain fixed rates of exchange between the dollar and other currencies — or, more precisely, whereby we leave all initiative for changes in such rates to other countries. This commitment should be terminated. The price of gold should be determined in the free market, with the U.S. Gov-

ernment committed neither to buying gold nor to selling gold at any fixed price. This is the appropriate counterpart of a policy of floating exchange rates. With respect to our existing stock of gold, we could simply keep it fixed, neither adding to it nor reducing it; alternatively, we could sell it off gradually at the market price or add to it gradually, thereby reducing or increasing our governmental stockpiles of this particular metal. In any event, we should simultaneously remove all present limitations on the ownership of gold and the trading in gold by American citizens. There is no reason why gold, like other commodities, should not be freely traded on a free market.

6 3

IN DEFENSE OF FIXED EXCHANGE RATES*

Henry C. Wallich[†]

Flexible rates have achieved a high measure of acceptance in academic circles, but very little among public officials. This raises the question whether we have a parallel to the famous case of free trade: almost all economists favor it in principle, but no major country ever has adopted it. Does the logic of economics point equally irrefutable to flexible rates, while the logic of politics points in another direction?

The nature of the case, I believe, is fundamentally different. Most countries do practice free trade within their borders, although they reject it outside. But economists do not propose flexible rates for the States of the Union, among which men, money, and goods can move freely, and which are governed by uniform

* From *United States Balance of Payments*, Part 3, *Hearings* before the Joint Economic Committee, U.S. Congress, November 1963. Reprinted by the courtesy of the author.
† Yale University.

monetary, fiscal, and other policies. Flexible rates are to apply only to relations among countries that do not permit free factor movements across their borders and that follow, or may follow, substantially different monetary and fiscal policies. It is the imperfections of the world that seem to suggest that flexible rates, which would be harmful if applied to different parts of a single country, would do more good than harm internationally.

It is quite arguable that the Appalachian area would benefit if it could issue a dollar of its own, an Appalachian dollar which in that case would sell, probably at 60 or 90 cents. Exports from that region would increase, and unemployment would diminish. A great many good things would happen, but we are also aware of what it would do to the economy of the United States — and, therefore, we do not propose that solution. The question is, Do we want to look upon the world as quite different from the United States, as hopelessly divided into self-contained units where cooperation and efforts to coordinate policies are doomed to frustration? In that case, flexible rates may be the best way to avoid a very bad situation. But should we not try to establish within the world something that begins to approximate the conditions that prevail within a country, in the way of coordination of policies, freer flow of capital and of goods and so try to achieve the benefits of one large economic area within the world? That is what we should try for.

Now to resume: The proponents of flexible rates argue, in effect, that flexible rates can help a country get out of almost any of the typical difficulties that economies experience. This is perfectly true. If the United States has a balance-of-payments deficit, a flexible exchange rate allows the dollar to decline until receipts have risen and payments fallen enough to restore balance. If the United States has unemployment, flexible rates can protect it against the balance-of-payments consequences of a policy of expansion. We would then have less unemployment. If the United States has suffered inflation and fears that it will be undersold internationally, flexible rates can remove the danger.

All of these advantages are quite clear.

Other countries have analogous advantages. If Chile experiences a decline in copper prices, flexible rates can ease the inevitable adjustment. If Germany finds that other countries have inflated while German prices have remained more nearly stable, flexible rates could help to avoid importing inflation. If Canada has a large capital inflow, a flexible rate will remove the need for price and income increases that would otherwise be needed to facilitate the transfer of real resources.

There are other adjustments, however, that must be made in all of these cases. If a country allows its exchange rate to go down, some price adjustments still remain to be made. Furthermore, each time a country makes this kind of adjustment, allowing its exchange rate to decline, other countries suffer. If the U.S. dollar depreciates, we undersell the Europeans. It could be argued that if the U.S. price levels go down instead of the exchange rate, we also

undersell the Europeans, and if because of a declining price level we have unemployment we would be buying still less from them. Nevertheless, there is a difference. A price adjustment tends to be slow and is likely to be no greater than it need be and tends to be selective for particular commodities. In contrast, an exchange rate movement is unpredictable. It can be large — we could easily have a drop of 10 or 20 per cent in an exchange rate. It comes suddenly. And it compels other countries to be on their guard.

Why, given the attractions of flexible rates, should one advise policymakers to stay away from them? Since the dollar problem is the concrete situation in which flexible rates are being urged today, it is in terms of the dollar that they must be discussed. In broadest terms, the reason why flexible rates are inadvisable is that their successful functioning would require more self-discipline and mutual forbearance than countries today are likely to muster. Exchange rates are two sided — depreciation for the dollar means appreciation for the European currencies. To work successfully, a flexible dollar, for instance, must not depreciate to the point where the Europeans would feel compelled to take counteraction. I believe that the limits of tolerance, before counteraction begins today are narrow and that a flexible dollar would invite retaliation almost immediately.

In the abstract, the European countries perhaps ought to consider that if the United States allows the dollar to go down, it is doing so in the interests of all-round equilibrium. They ought perhaps to consider that with a stable dollar rate the same adjustment might have to take place through a decline in prices here and a rise in prices there. In practice, they are likely to be alive principally to the danger of being undersold by American producers if the dollar goes down, in their own and third markets. The changing competitive pressure would fall unevenly upon particular industries, and those who are hurt would demand protection.

The most likely counteraction might take one of two forms. The Europeans could impose countervailing duties, such as the United States also has employed at times. They could alternately also depreciate European currencies along with the dollar or, what would amount to almost the same thing, prevent the dollar from depreciating. This might involve the European countries in the purchase of large amounts of dollars. If they are to peg the dollar, they could minimize their commitment by imposing a simple form of exchange control that the Swiss practiced during the last war. The Swiss purchased dollars only from their exporters, also requiring their importers to buy these dollars thereby stabilizing the trade dollar, while allowing dollars from capital movements — finance dollars — to find their own level in the market.

The large volume of not very predictable short-term capital movements in the world today makes such reactions under flexible rates particularly likely. A sudden outflow of funds from the United States, for instance (because of the fear of budget deficits or many other things that could happen), would tend to drive the dollar down. As a result, American exporters could undersell producers everywhere else in the world. It seems unlikely that foreign countries would allow a fortuitous short-term capital movement to have such far-reaching consequences. It would not even be economically appropriate to allow a transitory fluctuation in the capital account of the balance of payments to have a major influence on the current account. Such a fluctuation should not alter the pattern of trade, because the situation is likely to be reversed. Other countries therefore would probably take defensive action to make sure that no industry is destroyed and after several years may have to be rebuilt because of the ups and downs of short-term capital movements.

It can be argued that under flexible rates the effects of such a movement would be forestalled by stabilizing speculation on a future recovery of the dollar. This is possible. It is possible also, however, that speculation would seek a quick profit from the initial drop in the dollar, instead of a longer run one from its eventual recovery. Then short-run speculation would drive the dollar down farther at first. In any case there is not enough assurance that speculators will not make mistakes to permit

basing the world's monetary system upon the stabilizing effects of speculation.

In the case of countries which import much of what they consume, such as England, a temporary decline in the local currency may even be self-validating. If the cost of living rises as the currency declines, wages will rise. Thereafter, the currency may never recover to its original level.

This points up one probable consequence of flexible exchange rates: A worldwide acceleration of inflation. In some countries the indicated ratchet effect of wages will be at work. If exchange rates go down, wages will rise, and exchange rates cannot recover. In the United States the rise in the cost of imports would not be very important. But the removal of balance-of-payments restraints may well lead to policies that could lead to price increases. The American inflation of the 1950's was never defeated until the payments deficit become serious. Elsewhere, the removal of balance-of-payments disciplines might have the same effect. Rapid inflation in turn would probably compel governments to intervene drastically in foreign trade and finance.

The prospect that flexible rates would greatly increase uncertainty for foreign traders and investors has been cited many times. It should be noted that this uncertainty extends also to domestic investment decisions that might be affected by changing import competition or changing export prospects. It has been argued that uncertainties about future exchange rates can be removed by hedging in the future market. This, however, involves a cost even where cover is readily available. The history of futures markets does not suggest that it will be possible to get cover for long-term positions. To hedge domestic investment decisions that might be affected by flexible rates is in the nature of things impracticable.

The picture that emerges of the international economy under flexible rates is one of increasing disintegration. Independent national policies and unpredictable changes in each country's competitive position will compel governments to shield their producers and markets. The argument that such shielding would also automatically be accomplished by movements in the affected country's exchange rate under-rates the impact of fluctuations upon particular industries, if not upon the entire economy. That international integration and flexible rates are incompatible seems to be the view also of the European Common Market countries, who have left no doubt that they want stable rates within the EEC. The same applies if we visualize the "Kennedy round" under the Trade Expansion Act. I think if we told the Europeans that, after lowering our tariffs, we were going to cast the dollar loose and let it fluctuate, we would get very little tariff reduction. They would want to keep up their guard.

If the disintegrating effects of flexible rates are to be overcome, a great deal of policy coordination, combined with self-discipline and mutual forbearance, would be required. The desired independence of national economic policy would in fact have to be foregone — interest rates, budgets, wage and prices policies would have to be harmonized. If the world were ready for such cooperation, it would be capable also of making a fixed exchange rate system work. In that case, flexible rates would accomplish nothing that could not more cheaply and simply be done with fixed rates. It seems to follow that flexible rates have no unique capacity for good, whereas they possess great capacity to do damage.

A modified version of the flexible rates proposal has been suggested. This version would allow the dollar and other currencies to fluctuate within a given range, say 5 per cent up and down. This "widening of the gold points" is believed to reduce the danger of destabilizing speculation. It might perhaps enlist speculation on the side of stabilization, for if the dollar, say, had dropped to its lower limit, and if the public had confidence that that limit would not be broken, the only movement on which to speculate would be a rise. The spectacle of a currency falling below par may induce, according to the proponents, a strong political effort to bring it back.

This proposal likewise strikes me as unworkable. For one thing, I doubt that people would have a great deal of confidence in a limit of 5 per cent below par, if par itself has been given up. Political support for holding this second line would probably be less than the support that can be mustered to hold the first. For another, the execution of the plan would still require the maintenance of international reserves, to protect the upper and lower limits. But with fluctuating rates, dollar and sterling would cease to be desirable media for monetary reserves. International liquidity would become seriously impaired. A third objection is that under today's conditions, the complex negotiations and legislation required, in the unlikely event that the plan could be negotiated at all, could not go forward without immediate speculation against the dollar before the plan goes into effect.

It remains only to point out that, even in the absence of a high degree of international cooperativeness, a system of fixed exchange rates can be made to work. It can be made to work mainly because it imposes a discipline upon all participants, and because within this discipline there is nevertheless some room for adjustment. The principal sources of flexibility are productivity gains and the degree to which they are absorbed by wage increases. Wages cannot be expected to decline. But their rise can be slowed in relation to the rate of productivity growth, in which case prices would become more competitive relative to other countries. With annual productivity gains of 2 to 3 per cent in the United States and more abroad, it would not take many years to remove a temporary imbalance.

64

SHOULD GOLD BE SCRAPPED?*

Harry G. Johnson†

The problem of gold and its international monetary role has once more become an active issue. President de Gaulle recently re-opened the controversy with his attack on the special status of the pound and the dollar in the present international monetary system, and his invitation to join France in a return to the gold standard. Of more immediate significance, his Minister of Finance, M. Giscard d'Estaing, announced a new policy of taking settlement of French balance-of-payments surpluses only in gold. In this country, the Congress has approved a proposal to increase the supply of "free" gold by eliminating the 25 per cent cover requirement against Federal Reserve deposits, and the President has introduced a series of new measures aimed primarily at cutting the volume of U.S. private foreign investment. The President's balance-of-payments message to Congress went further than any previous official statement in endorsing the view that the present international monetary system needs to be revised and, specifically, in advocating the development of supplementary sources of reserves to relieve the strains which now result from the use of the dollar and sterling as substitutes for gold.

These recent official pronouncements and policy changes have merely brought into the open a conflict that has been building up over several years — ever since it became evident that the U.S. balance-of-payments deficit was not a transitory phenomenon, but a chronic and deep-seated malaise that would take many years to remedy through the natural processes of international economic adjustment. That conflict centers on the fact that the present international monetary system, in which the dollar plays a key role as an international reserve-asset alternative to gold, has enabled the

United States to finance its sustained deficit by relying on the willingness of foreigners to hold dollars, and increasingly on the recognition by foreign monetary authorities that they must hold dollars if they are not to precipitate a collapse of the system. At the same time, the fact that foreign monetary authorities could precipitate a collapse of the system has enabled them to exercise pressure on the U.S. to pursue policies designed to mitigate the deficit and accelerate its solution.

Essentially, the conflict derives from the system of fixed exchange-rates itself, which requires that a deficit-surplus situation be remedied by some combination of deflation in the deficity country (the U.S.) and inflation in the surplus countries (Western Europe). It has arisen because the United States has taken the position that its contribution to the adjustment should not entail a sacrifice of domestic employment, but only the prevention of increases in the domestic price level. Inflation in Europe is to be relied upon to restore adequate U.S. competitiveness in world markets. The Europeans, on the other hand, who have already endured a substantial inflation without a noticeable trend toward improvement in the U.S. balance-of-payments, and who for historical reasons intensely dislike inflation, feel that too much of the burden of adjustment is being thrust upon their shoulders, and that the United States should do a great deal more than it has. In effect, the adjustment processes required under a fixed-exchange rate system are being blocked by the refusal of each side to tolerate the policies appropriate under the logic of the system. This conflict is exasperated by the failure of each side to respect the political considerations which inhibit the adoption of policies necessary to maintain a fixed-exchange-rate system.

The conflict has been further sharpened in the past two years or so by the fact that the continuation of the U.S. deficit has been associated with a substantial increase in private capi-

* From *The National Banking Review*, June 1965. Reprinted by the courtesy of the publisher (the Comptroller of the Currency) and the author.

† University of Chicago.

tal outflows from the U.S. to Europe. I say "associated with" although many observers, especially in Europe, would say that these deficits are "caused by" the private capital outflow. Because the items in the balance of payments are economically interrelated and not simply additive, one cannot assume that an increase in the deficit can be attributed to a contemporaneous increase in any one category of payments. Instead, the increased capital outflow should be related to the continued over-valuation of the dollar relative to the European currencies, as well as to the attractive effects of the Common Market tariff. In any event, many Europeans believe that by financing the U.S. deficit they are indirectly financing U.S. private investment in Europe, which they resent. And, they cannot understand the reluctance of the U.S. authorities either to raise interest rates (which the U.S. authorities fear would create unemployment) or to impose controls on international capital movements (which the U.S. has been increasingly forced to adopt even though it goes against deep-rooted principles of free enterprise).

Since the adjustment of the balance-of-payments disequilibrium between the United States and Europe would entail the frustration of vital national policy objectives, the process is bound to be prolonged as well as politically acrimonious. This fact has major implications for the present international monetary system which few have appreciated. With long lags in the adjustment process, the international borrowing and lending required to finance the disequilibria entail international official capital movements larger in quantity and longer in duration than can be accommodated by the traditional type of reserve movements between central banks. Although the present system requires long-term international loans of the type provided under the Marshall Plan to meet the dollar-shortage problem, the monetary authorities of the leading countries have instead been elaborating the technique of short-term international credits. This technique is well adapted to overcoming speculative short-term capital movements, but is inadequate to deal with chronic balance-of-payments disequilibria.

The same point can be made in a different way. If prolonged disequilibria are to be prevented, it is necessary to devise a monetary system that will force either the deficit countries, or the surplus countries, or both, to adopt policies that will promote prompt adjustment despite their other policy objectives. The Europeans believe that the present system, in which the pound and the dollar serve as reserve currencies, enables the U.K. and the U.S. to evade the necessity of prompt adjustment; and they desire revisions of the international monetary system that will reduce or remove this possibility of evasion. General de Gaulle's recent attack on sterling and the dollar may be interpreted as an expression of that view. A return to the gold standard, which he advocated, would impose ineluctable pressures for prompt adjustment on deficit and surplus countries alike.

General de Gaulle's advocacy of a return to the gold standard has been derided as "a return to the system that broke down in 1931." But, it should be understood that the system that broke down in 1931 was not a gold standard of the classical type, but a gold-exchange standard precisely like the present international monetary standard. It broke down precisely because a few national currencies were being used on a large scale as substitutes for gold that did not exist. A return to a true gold standard, if it could be effected, would eliminate this grave deficiency in the present international monetary system, since all reserves would be hard metal and not credit-money whose use in place of gold depended on confidence. Nor is it a valid argument against a return to the gold standard that, in order to avoid a sharp deflation, the price of gold would have to be doubled or tripled, thus creating undesirable capital gains for holders and producers of gold. A change that would promote the general good cannot properly be opposed on the ground that some people will derive a windfall profit from it.

The real arguments against a return to the gold standard derive from that very characteristic of gold which, in the eyes of its proponents, gives the gold standard its virtue — the fact that the production of gold entails a real cost. This fact has two crucial implications. First, there will always be an incentive for the financial system to develop credit substitutes for gold because, on the one hand, gold yields no interest to the holder whereas credit substitutes do and, on the other hand, credit substitutes can be produced (though not maintained as efficient substitutes) at virtually zero real cost. In fact, the history of money is essentially a history of the gradual substitution of credit-money for commodity-money in response to the interaction of scarcity of the latter and ingenuity in devising the former. The economics involved ensure that a return to the gold standard would be a practical impossibility. Second, tying the international monetary system to a produced commodity, especially a mineral, as the basic money inevitably entails exposing the system to erratic changes in the stock of money resulting from the vagaries of technical change and new discoveries in the industry producing the monetary commodity. Rationality suggests that these erratic changes can and should be avoided by deliberate monetary management, and that the costs of production incurred in gold mining can be escaped by resorting to credit-money. A return to the gold standard would therefore involve a deliberate surrender of the chance to exercise rationality in monetary affairs in favor of control by erratic and unpredictable forces. It thus seems clear that the gold standard cannot be restored; fundamental forces both of economics (the principle of cost-minimization through substitution) and of social psychology (the desire to control and improve the environment) are against it.

The present gold-exchange standard, nevertheless, contains inherent and dangerous weaknesses which increasingly call for reform of the system.[1] These weaknesses all stem from the fact that, while gold is the ultimate or basic form of international reserve, it is not the only form. Since, as I have argued, it is not possible to increase the role of gold to replace this mixed system by an approximation of the gold standard, reform must move in the direction of decreasing and altering the role of gold so as to minimize the dangers that its presence imposes on the system. The logical end of this process is the eventual scrapping of gold as an

international money, and its replacement by some international monetary system based entirely on credit.

International monetary experts who have studied the contemporary international monetary system are agreed that the system poses three serious problems. One is the *long-run liquidity problem*. Under the present system, the growth of international reserves required to sustain the growth of world trade and payments depends on the vagaries of new gold production, private hoarding and Russian dishoarding of gold, and the balance-of-payments experience of the reserve currency countries. Further, if new gold supplies are inadequate, the required reserves must be supplied by continuous deficits of the reserve-currency countries. This undermines their reserve positions and the confidence on which the use of these currencies as substitutes for gold depends. A second problem is the more general one of *confidence*. Loss of confidence in one reserve currency leads to conversions into other currencies. This disturbs international monetary relationships and may prompt central banks to convert currencies into gold, which could produce an international liquidity crisis (as happened in 1931). The third is the *adjustment problem*, the lack of a clear-cut mechanism of adjustment. This lack is the result of the ability of reserve-currency countries to finance deficits by running up currency debts to others, and the ability of other countries to neutralize reserve changes. All three problems are associated with the use of national currencies as substitutes for gold, where the currencies can be converted into gold at the option or whim of the central bank holding them.

It is evident that a solution of the long-run liquidity problem requires governing the growth of whatever credit money is used as a substitute for gold in a manner that will assure an increase in the total of this money-plus-gold equal to the required growth of international reserves. A solution of the confidence problem requires restricting the convertibility of currencies into one another, and into gold, by central banks. One possible solution to both problems, towards which the central bankers have been pushed unwillingly by the prolonged

[1] On the weaknesses of the present system, see especially R. Triffin, *Gold and the Dollar Crisis*, New Haven: Yale University Press, 1960.

dollar deficit, would be to agree to a suspension of dollar conversion into gold and to trust the U.S. authorities to provide an appropriate growth of reserves by their balance-of-payments policies. Such a proposal for a dollar standard, however, would not be politically acceptable to other countries — and, given the recent U.S. balance-of-payments history, not commendable as a solution to the long-run liquidity problem. To be generally acceptable, a solution must replace the dominance of the dollar by some more-international form of credit-money arrangement, and one subject to more effective international control.

Two major alternatives have been put forward. One is the Triffin Plan, which calls for centralization of reserves in an expanded International Monetary Fund. Under this plan, countries would hold their reserves in gold and Fund deposits in some fixed ratio. The Fund would hold national-currency assets to back its deposit liabilities, and would increase international reserves, over time, by open-market operations. The other is the Bernstein Plan, or currency-reserve-unit plan, which calls for the construction of bundles of the leading national currencies, with fixed proportions between the amounts of the various currencies in the bundle (the currency-reserve unit). Under this plan, countries would be obliged to hold these bundles within a certain range of ratios to their holdings of gold; the total number of currency-reserve units outstanding and the required ratios of units-to-gold would be raised by international agreement, over time. The Triffin Plan, in short, would substitute a genuinely international credit money for national currencies in international reserves, and subject the quantity outstanding to control by an international institution. The Bernstein plan would substitute a composite bundle of national currencies for the pound and the dollar, and have the quantity-outstanding controlled by agreement among the major-currency countries.[2]

Both schemes would reduce and stabilize the

role of gold in the international monetary system. Equally, both would reduce — and the Triffin Plan would virtually eliminate — the reserve-currency role of the dollar and the pound. The major difference between these plans, apart from the more radical nature of the Triffin Plan, lies in the provision made for control of the quantity of international reserve money. This difference derives its main significance from the conflict concerning the adjustment mechanism which I have already discussed. In the International Monetary Fund, the Europeans have minority voting power and the United States has great influence; in a currency-reserve-unit scheme, the Europeans would have a majority vote if not a veto power. The Europeans would obviously prefer to have this power, given their views on the inflationary character of the present system. Consequently, the currency-reserve-unit scheme is almost inevitably the one that will emerge from current deliberations on the reform of the system. Moreover, for this same reason, the currency-reserve-unit scheme is likely to constitute more of a return to something like the discipline of the traditional gold standard than would the Triffin Plan. The mechanism of adjustment, however, would be vastly different, since indications are that it would include a variety of controls on international trade and capital movements.

In any case, it is clear that the next stage in the evolution of the international monetary system must involve a whittling down of the international monetary role of gold (as well as of the U.S. dollar). The real division between the Americans and the Europeans is no longer over that issue — the American position on it changed abruptly in mid-1963 — but over the distribution of the responsibility for adjustment of international disequilibria. Logically, the whittling down of the role of gold and the establishment of a completely credit-international-money would most likely entail the elevation of the International Monetary Fund into an independent world central bank. However, given the political jealousies between Europe and the United States and European suspicion of the IMF as a creature of the United States, that event appears to be a long way off.

---

[2] For a compendium of the many plans for international monetary reform advanced in recent years, see Herbert G. Grubel (ed.), *World Monetary Reform: Plans and Issues*, Stanford: Stanford University Press, 1963.

There is, however, some possibility that the demotion of gold from its monetary role could occur much more rapidly, and by a completely different sequence of events. The international monetary strains of the dollar-surplus epoch, as already mentioned, have been the consequence of an attempt to maintain a system of fixed exchange rates without either the deficit or the surplus countries being willing to pursue the required adjustment policies to the necessary extent. It is possible that, disenchanted with the attitudes of countries it assisted generously in the postwar reconstruction period, the U.S. will simply terminate the convertibility of dollars into gold (or of gold into dollars). In that event, gold would not be scrapped, but would become, at best, a commodity especially suitable for the conduct of intervention-operations in foreign exchange markets. Indeed, judging by the 1930's experience of floating exchange rates, the demand for gold could conceivably increase. This, however, would be a small price to pay for the establishment of a more rational international monetary system than we now have.